APPIAN

V

LCL 543

APPIAN

ROMAN HISTORY

VOLUME V

CIVIL WARS, BOOKS 3–4

EDITED AND TRANSLATED BY

BRIAN McGING

HARVARD UNIVERSITY PRESS

CAMBRIDGE, MASSACHUSETTS
LONDON, ENGLAND
2020

Library of Congress Control Number 2019940172
CIP data available from the Library of Congress

ISBN 978-0-674-99730-1

*Composed in ZephGreek and ZephText by
Technologies 'N Typography, Merrimac, Massachusetts.
Printed on acid-free paper and bound by
Maple Press, York, Pennsylvania*

CONTENTS

ΑΠΠΙΑΝΟΥ ΡΩΜΑΪΚΗ ΙΣΤΟΡΙΑ

APPIAN'S ROMAN HISTORY

XV

ΕΜΦΥΛΙΩΝ ΤΡΙΤΗ[1]

1. Οὕτω μὲν δὴ Γάιος Καῖσαρ πλείστου Ῥωμαίοις ἄξιος ἐς τὴν ἡγεμονίαν γενόμενος ὑπὸ τῶν ἐχθρῶν ἀνῄρητο καὶ ὑπὸ τοῦ δήμου τέθαπτο· ἁπάντων δὲ αὐτοῦ τῶν σφαγέων δίκην δόντων, ὅπως οἱ περιφανέστατοι μάλιστα ἔδοσαν, ἥδε ἡ βίβλος καὶ ἡ μετὰ τήνδε ἐπιδείξουσιν, ἐπιλαμβάνουσαι καὶ ὅσα ἄλλα Ῥωμαίοις ἐμφύλια ἐς ἀλλήλους ἐγίγνετο ὁμοῦ.

2. Ἀντώνιον μὲν ἡ βουλὴ δι' αἰτίας εἶχεν ἐπὶ τοῖς ἐπιταφίοις τοῦ Καίσαρος, ὑφ' ὧν δὴ μάλιστα ὁ δῆμος ἐρεθισθεὶς ὑπερεῖδε τῆς ἄρτι ἐπεψηφισμένης ἀμνηστίας καὶ ἐπὶ τὰς οἰκίας τῶν σφαγέων σὺν πυρὶ ἔδραμον· ὁ δὲ αὐτὴν χαλεπαίνουσαν ἐνὶ τοιῷδε πολιτεύματι ἐς εὔνοιαν ἑαυτοῦ μετέβαλεν. Ἀμάτιος ἦν ὁ Ψευδομάριος· Μαρίου γὰρ ὑπεκρίνετο υἱωνὸς εἶναι καὶ διὰ Μάριον ὑπερήρεσκε τῷ δήμῳ. γιγνόμενος οὖν κατὰ τήνδε τὴν ὑπόκρισιν συγγενὴς τῷ Καίσαρι, ὑπερήλγει μάλιστα αὐτοῦ τεθνεῶτος καὶ βωμὸν ἐπ-

---

[1] Ἀππιανοῦ Ῥωμαϊκῶν ἐμφυλίων γ΄ LJ; Ἀππιανοῦ ῥήτορος Ῥωμαϊκῶν ις΄ ἐμφυλίων γ΄ P

BOOK XV

CIVIL WARS, BOOK III

1. Such is the story of how Gaius Caesar, who performed exceptional service for the Romans with regard to their empire, was killed by his enemies and buried by the people. All of his murderers received their punishment, and this book and the one after it will show how this came about, particularly for the most distinguished of them. These books will also include all the other civil wars the Romans fought against each other in the same period.

2. The senate blamed Antony for his funeral oration for Caesar. The people had been particularly agitated by it, and disregarded the amnesty just passed, and ran off to set fire to the houses of the assassins. But he changed the senate from being angry with him to being well disposed toward him through the following single political stroke. There was a man called Amatius, known as the pseudo-Marius, because he pretended to be a grandson of Marius, and on Marius' account became very popular with the people. According to this pretense he was a relative of Caesar, and was extremely grief-stricken at his death.[1] He

[1] Caesar's aunt Julia (his father's sister) was married to Gaius Marius.

APPIAN

ῳκοδόμει τῇ πυρᾷ καὶ χεῖρα θρασυτέρων ἀνδρῶν εἶχε
4 καὶ φοβερὸς ἦν ἀεὶ τοῖς σφαγεῦσιν· ὧν οἱ μὲν ἄλλοι
διεπεφεύγεσαν ἐκ τῆς πόλεως καὶ ὅσοι παρ᾽ αὐτοῦ
Καίσαρος εἰλήφεσαν ἡγεμονίας ἐθνῶν, ἀπεληλύθε-
σαν ἐπὶ τὰς ἡγεμονίας, Βροῦτος μὲν ὁ Δέκμος ἐς τὴν
ὅμορον τῆς Ἰταλίας Κελτικήν, Τρεβώνιος δὲ ἐς τὴν
Ἀσίαν τὴν περὶ Ἰωνίαν, Τίλλιος δὲ Κίμβερ ἐς Βιβυ-
5 νίαν· Κάσσιος δὲ καὶ Βροῦτος ὁ Μᾶρκος, ὧν δὴ καὶ
μάλιστα τῇ βουλῇ διέφερεν, ᾕρηντο μὲν καὶ οἵδε ὑπὸ
τοῦ Καίσαρος ἐς τὸ μέλλον ἔτος ἡγεμονεύειν, Συρίας
μὲν ὁ Κάσσιος καὶ Μακεδονίας ὁ Βροῦτος, ἔτι δὲ
ὄντες ἀστικοὶ στρατηγο⟨ῦντές τε⟩[2] ὑπ᾽ ἀνάγκης καὶ
διατάγμασιν οἷα στρατηγοὶ τοὺς κληρούχους ἐθερά-
πευον, ὅσοις τε ἄλλοις ἐπενόουν, καὶ τὰ κληρουχήματα συγχωροῦντες αὐτοῖς πιπράσκειν, τοῦ νόμου
κωλύοντος ἐντὸς εἴκοσιν ἐτῶν ἀποδίδοσθαι.
6 3. Τούτοις δὲ αὐτοῖς ὁ Ἀμάτιος, ὅτε συντύχοι, καὶ
ἐνεδρεύσειν ἐλέγετο. τῷδε οὖν τῷ λόγῳ τῆς ἐνέδρας
ὁ Ἀντώνιος ἐπιβαίνων οἷα ὕπατος συλλαμβάνει καὶ
κτείνει τὸν Ἀμάτιον χωρὶς δίκης, μάλα θρασέως· καὶ
ἡ βουλὴ τὸ μὲν ἔργον ἐθαύμαζεν ὡς μέγα καὶ παρά-
νομον, τὴν δὲ χρείαν αὐτοῦ προσεποιοῦντο ἥδιστα· οὐ
γὰρ αὐτοῖς ἐδόκει ποτὲ χωρὶς τοιᾶσδε τόλμης ἀσφαλῆ
7 τὰ κατὰ Βροῦτον καὶ Κάσσιον ἔσεσθαι. οἱ δὲ τοῦ
Ἀματίου στασιῶται καὶ ὁ ἄλλος δῆμος ἐπ᾽ ἐκείνοις
πόθῳ τε τοῦ Ἀματίου καὶ ἀγανακτήσει τοῦ γεγονότος,

[2] στρατηγο⟨ῦντές τε⟩ Goukowsky; στρατηγοὶ codd.

4

built an altar on the site of Caesar's funeral pyre, and with his gang of hotheads was a constant source of fear to the assassins. Some of these had fled from the city, and those 4 who had received provincial commands from Caesar himself had left to take up their governorships, Decimus Brutus to Cisalpine Gaul, Trebonius to Asia Minor in Ionia, and Tillius Cimber to Bithynia. Cassius and Marcus Brutus, who were of particular concern to the senate, had also 5 been chosen by Caesar as governors for the following year, Cassius of Syria, and Brutus of Macedonia, but as they were still in the city and forced to continue serving as praetors,[2] in their official praetorian capacity they set about indulging the settlers with various edicts, including one that allowed them to sell their allotments, although the law prevented their transfer until twenty years had passed.

3. The word was that Amatius would actually set an 6 ambush for Brutus and Cassius when the opportunity arose. So, using this report of an ambush, and acting in his capacity as consul, Antony arrests Amatius and executes him without trial in a very precipitate manner. The senate were astonished at his action, as it was extreme and illegal, but they very happily pretended it was necessary, because they thought that Brutus' and Cassius' situation would never be secure without such determination. Amatius' 7 partisans, on the other hand, and the rest of the people as well, missed Amatius and were angry at what had hap-

---

[2] There is a small lacuna in the text at this point. Appian's assertion that Caesar had assigned Syria to Cassius and Macedonia to Brutus is usually considered a mistake.

ὅτι μάλιστα αὐτὸ ὁ Ἀντώνιος ἐπεπράχει ὑπὸ τοῦ
δήμου τιμώμενος,[3] οὐκ ἠξίουν σφῶν καταφρονεῖν· τὴν
ἀγορὰν οὖν καταλαβόντες ἐβόων καὶ τὸν Ἀντώνιον
ἐβλασφήμουν καὶ τὰς ἀρχὰς ἐκέλευον ἀντὶ Ἀματίου
τὸν βωμὸν ἐκθεοῦν καὶ θύειν ἐπ᾽ αὐτοῦ Καίσαρι
8 πρώτους. ἐξελαυνόμενοι δ᾽ ἐκ τῆς ἀγορᾶς ὑπὸ στρατιωτῶν ἐπιπεμφθέντων ὑπὸ Ἀντωνίου μᾶλλόν τε ἠγα-
νάκτουν καὶ ἐκεκράγεσαν καὶ ἕδρας ἔνιοι τῶν Καίσα-
9 ρος ἀνδριάντων ἐπεδείκνυον ἀνῃρημένων. ὡς δέ τις
αὐτοῖς ἔφη καὶ τὸ ἐργαστήριον, ἔνθα οἱ ἀνδριάντες
ἀνεσκευάζοντο, δείξειν, εὐθὺς εἵποντο καὶ ἰδόντες ἐν-
επίμπρασαν, ἕως ἑτέρων ἐπιπεμφθέντων ἐξ Ἀντωνίου
ἀμυνόμενοί τε ἀνῃρέθησαν ἔνιοι καὶ συλληφθέντες
ἕτεροι ἐκρεμάσθησαν, ὅσοι θεράποντες ἦσαν, οἱ δὲ
ἐλεύθεροι κατὰ τοῦ κρημνοῦ κατερρίφησαν.
10   4. Καὶ ὁ μὲν τάραχος ἐπέπαυτο, μῖσος δὲ ἄρρητον
ἐξ ἀρεστῆς[4] εὐνοίας τοῦ δήμου πρὸς τὸν Ἀντώνιον
ἐγήγερτο. ἡ βουλὴ δ᾽ ἔχαιρον ὡς οὐκ ἂν ἑτέρως ἐν
11 ἀδεεῖ περὶ τῶν ἀμφὶ τὸν Βροῦτον γενόμενοι. ὡς δὲ
καὶ Σέξστον Πομπήιον ὁ Ἀντώνιος, τὸν Πομπηίου
Μάγνου περιποθήτου πᾶσιν ἔτι ὄντος, εἰσηγήσατο
καλεῖν ἐξ Ἰβηρίας, πολεμούμενον ἔτι πρὸς τῶν
Καίσαρος στρατηγῶν, ἀντί τε τῆς πατρῴας οὐσίας
δεδημευμένης ἐκ τῶν κοινῶν αὐτῷ δοθῆναι μυριάδας
Ἀττικῶν δραχμῶν πεντακισχιλίας, εἶναι δὲ καὶ στρατηγὸν ἤδη τῆς θαλάσσης, καθὼς ἦν καὶ ὁ πατὴρ

---

[3] τιμώμενον LP; τιμώμενος BJ

pened, particularly because Antony had inflicted the punishment on a man honored by the people. They did not
think it was right of him to disregard them, and so they
seized the Forum, shouting at Antony and abusing him,
and demanding that the magistrates take Amatius' place
in consecrating the altar and being the first to offer sacrifice on it to Caesar. When they were driven out of the   8
Forum by soldiers sent in by Antony, they became even
angrier, and shouted even more loudly, some of them
pointing to the bases from which statues of Caesar had
been removed. One man told them that he could show   9
them the very workshop where the statues were being
broken up, and immediately following him, when they saw
it, they set fire to it. Eventually, Antony dispatched more
soldiers and some of those who resisted were killed, others
arrested; of these, the slaves were crucified and the free-
men thrown over the Tarpeian rock.

4. The disturbance was brought to an end, but from   10
what had been a certain degree of goodwill of the people
toward Antony there arose inexpressible hatred. The senate, however, were delighted, because they believed there
was no other way of relieving their anxiety about Brutus
and his followers. Antony also proposed that Sextus Pom-   11
peius (the son of Pompey the Great, who was still sorely
missed by all) should be recalled from Iberia, where Caesar's lieutenants were still campaigning against him; and
that he should be paid fifty million Attic drachmas out of
the public treasury for his father's confiscated property;
and that he now be made commander of the Mediterra-

---

4 ἀρεστῆς Goukowsky; ἀρίστης LP; ἀρρήτου BJ

αὐτοῦ, καὶ ταῖς Ῥωμαίων ναυσὶν αὐτίκα ταῖς πανταχοῦ χρῆσθαι εἰς τὰ ἐπείγοντα, θαυμάζουσα ἕκαστα ἡ
βουλὴ μετὰ προθυμίας ἐξεδέχετο καὶ τὸν Ἀντώνιον
ἐπὶ ὅλην εὐφήμουν ἡμέραν· οὐ γάρ τις αὐτοῖς ἐδόκει
Μάγνου γενέσθαι δημοκρατικώτερος, ὅθεν οὐδὲ περι-
12 ποθητότερος ἦν. ὅ τε Κάσσιος καὶ ὁ Βροῦτος, ἐκ τῆς
στάσεως ὄντε τῆς Μάγνου καὶ πᾶσι τότε τιμωτάτω,
τὴν σωτηρίαν ἐδόκουν ἕξειν ἀσφαλῆ καὶ τὴν γνώμην
ὧν ἐπεπράχεσαν ἐγκρατῆ, καὶ τὴν δημοκρατίαν ἐς
13 τέλος ἐπάξεσθαι, τῆς μοίρας σφῶν ἀνισχούσης. ἃ
καὶ Κικέρων συνεχῶς ἐπῄνει τὸν Ἀντώνιον· καὶ ἡ
βουλὴ συγγινώσκουσα αὐτῷ διὰ σφᾶς ἐπιβουλεύοντα τὸν δῆμον ἔδωκε φρουρὰν περιστήσασθαι περὶ
τὸ σῶμα, ἐκ τῶν ἐστρατευμένων καὶ ἐπιδημούντων
ἑαυτῷ καταλέγοντα.

14 5. Ὁ δέ, εἴτε εἰς τοῦτο αὐτὸ πάντα πεπραχὼς εἴτε
τὴν συντυχίαν ὡς εὔχρηστον ἀσπασάμενος τὴν
φρουρὰν κατέλεγεν, αἰεὶ προστιθεὶς μέχρι ἐς ἑξακισ-
χιλίους, οὐκ ἐκ τῶν γινομένων ὁπλιτῶν, οὓς εὐμαρῶς
ἂν ἐν ταῖς χρείαις ᾤετο ἕξειν καὶ ἑτέρωθεν, ἀλλὰ πάντας λοχαγοὺς ὡς ἡγεμονικούς τε καὶ ἐμπειροπολέμους
καὶ οἱ γνωρίμους ἐκ τῆς στρατείας τῆς ὑπὸ Καίσαρι·
ταξιάρχους δ' αὐτοῖς ἐς τὸν πρέποντα κόσμον ἐξ
αὐτῶν ἐκείνων ἐπιστήσας ἦγεν ἐν τιμῇ καὶ κοινωνοὺς
15 ἐποιεῖτο τῶν φανερῶν βουλευμάτων. ἡ δὲ βουλὴ τό τε
πλῆθος αὐτῶν καὶ τὴν ἐπίλεξιν ἐν ὑπονοίᾳ τιθέμενοι
συνεβούλευον τὴν φρουρὰν ὡς ἐπίφθονον ἐς τὸ ἀρ-
κοῦν ἐπαναγαγεῖν. ὁ δὲ ὑπισχνεῖτο ποιήσειν, ὅταν

nean, as his father had been, with Roman ships in all areas
immediately at his disposal for urgent tasks. Amazed as
they were, the senate enthusiastically accepted each of
these measures, and spent a whole day congratulating
Antony; for nobody, in their estimation, was more demo-
cratically inclined than Pompey the Great, and hence nobody was more sorely missed. Cassius and Brutus, who   12
had been members of Pompey's faction, and were at the
time very highly esteemed by everyone, thought that their
safety would be assured, that the motion about what they
had done would be validated, and that eventually, if their
fate held its course, they would restore the democracy.
Cicero praised Antony continually for this, and the senate,   13
realizing that the people were plotting against Antony because of them, granted him a bodyguard, which he chose
himself from the veterans who were staying in the city.

5. Either because he had done everything toward this   14
very end, or embracing the stroke of luck as being to his
advantage, he began to enroll his guard, continually adding to it until it numbered six thousand. These were not
common soldiers, whom he thought he could easily get
elsewhere when he needed them, but were all centurions
fit for command in his opinion, experienced fighters, and
known to him personally through service under Caesar.
He appointed tribunes for them to impose proper order,
chosen from their own number, and held them in respect,
sharing his public plans with them. The senate were suspi-   15
cious of the large number of his guards, and how he chose
them, and advised him to reduce them to an adequate
number on the grounds that they were causing hostility.
He promised to do so as soon as he had suppressed the

16 σβέσῃ τοῦ δήμου τὸ ταραχῶδες. ἐψηφισμένον δ' εἶναι
κύρια, ὅσα Καίσαρι πέπρακτό τε καὶ γενέσθαι βε-
βούλευτο, τὰ ὑπομνήματα τῶν βεβουλευμένων ὁ
Ἀντώνιος ἔχων καὶ τὸν γραμματέα τοῦ Καίσαρος Φα-
βέριον ἐς πάντα οἱ πειθόμενον, διότι καὶ ὁ Καῖσαρ τὰ
τοιάδε αἰτήματα ἐς τὸν Ἀντώνιον ἐξιὼν ἀνετίθετο,
πολλὰ ἐς πολλῶν χάριν προσετίθει καὶ ἐδωρεῖτο πόλεσι καὶ δυνάσταις καὶ τοῖσδε τοῖς ἑαυτοῦ φρουροῖς·
καὶ ἐπεγράφετο μὲν πᾶσι τὰ Καίσαρος ὑπομνήματα,
17 τὴν δὲ χάριν οἱ λαβόντες ᾔδεσαν Ἀντωνίῳ. τῷ δὲ
αὐτῷ τρόπῳ καὶ ἐς τὸ βουλευτήριον πολλοὺς κατ-
έλεγε καὶ ἄλλα τῇ βουλῇ δι' ἀρεσκείας ἔπρασσεν, ἵνα
μὴ φθονοῖεν ἔτι τῆς φρουρᾶς.

18   6. Καὶ Ἀντώνιος μὲν ἀμφὶ ταῦτα ἦν, ὁ δὲ Βροῦτος
καὶ ὁ Κάσσιος, οὔτε τινὸς παρὰ τοῦ δήμου σφίσιν ἢ
παρὰ τῶν ἐξεστρατευμένων εἰρηναίου φανέντος, οὔτε
τὴν ἐνέδραν Ἀματίου καὶ παρ' ἑτέρου ἂν αὑτοῖς ἀδύ-
νατον ἡγούμενοι γενέσθαι, οὔτε τὸ ποικίλον Ἀντωνίου
φέροντες ἀφόβως, ἤδη καὶ στρατιὰν ἔχοντος, οὔτε
τὴν δημοκρατίαν βεβαιουμένην ἔργοις ὁρῶντες, ἀλλὰ
καὶ ἐς τοῦτο ὑφορώμενοι τὸν Ἀντώνιον, Δέκμῳ μάλιστα ἐπεποίθεσαν, ἔχοντι ἐν πλευραῖς τρία τέλη στρατοῦ, καὶ πρὸς Τρεβώνιον ἐς τὴν Ἀσίαν καὶ πρὸς Τίλλιον ἐς Βιθυνίαν κρύφα ἔπεμπον χρήματα ἀγείρειν
ἀφανῶς καὶ στρατὸν περιβλέπεσθαι. αὐτοί τε ἠπεί-
γοντο τῶν δεδομένων σφίσιν ὑπὸ τοῦ Καίσαρος
19 ἐθνῶν λαβέσθαι. τοῦ χρόνου δὲ οὔπω συγχωροῦντος
αὐτοῖς, ἀπρεπὲς ἡγούμενοι, τὴν ἐν ἄστει στρατηγίαν

riotous element among the people. It had been decreed   16
that all Caesar's acts and planned projects were valid.
Since Antony held the memoranda of Caesar's plans and
also controlled Caesar's secretary, Faberius, who was completely obedient to him since Caesar himself, as he was
about to leave, had entrusted Antony with all such peti-
tions, he made many additions to secure the favor of many
people, presenting gifts to cities and dynasts, and to those
personal bodyguards of his. Although these acts all came
under the title "Caesar's memoranda," it was to Antony
that the recipients expressed their gratitude. In the same   17
way he enrolled many new members in the senate and did
other things to ingratiate himself with them, so that they
would no longer begrudge him his bodyguard.

6. While Antony busied himself with these matters, it   18
was clear to Brutus and Cassius that none of the people or
veterans were peacefully disposed toward them, and they
thought it not impossible that someone else too might
repeat Amatius' plot against them. As they were also afraid
of how unreliable Antony was, now that he had an armed
force, and could see that no actions were being taken to
strengthen the democratic government, they were suspicious of Antony for that reason also. It was Decimus Brutus, who had an army of three legions waiting in the wings,
that they trusted most; and they also sent secret instructions to Trebonius in Asia and to Tillius in Bithynia, to
collect money without attracting attention and to look
around for an army. They themselves were eager to take
up the provincial commands assigned to them by Caesar,
but the time for doing so had not yet arrived, and they   19
thought that it would be improper to leave the city prae-

προλιπόντες ἀτελῆ, δόξαν ὕποπτον φιλαρχίας ἐθνῶν
ἐνέγκασθαι, ᾑροῦντο ὅμως ὑπὸ ἀνάγκης τὸ ἐν μέσῳ
διάστημα διατρῖψαί ποι μᾶλλον ἰδιωτεύοντες ἢ ἐν
ἄστει στρατηγεῖν, οὔτε ἀφόβως ἔχοντες οὔτε τὰ
εἰκότα ἐφ' οἷς ὑπὲρ τῆς πατρίδος ἐπεπράχεσαν τιμώ-
20 μενοι. οὕτω δ' αὐτοῖς ἔχουσιν ἡ βουλὴ συνειδυῖα τὴν
γνώμην ἔδωκε σίτου τῇ πόλει φροντίσαι, ἐξ ὅσης δύναιντο γῆς, μέχρις αὐτοὺς ὁ χρόνος τῶν ἐθνῶν τῆς
21 στρατηγίας καταλάβοι. καὶ ἡ μὲν οὕτως ἔπραξεν, ἵνα
μή ποτε Βροῦτος ἢ Κάσσιος φεύγειν δοκοῖεν· τοσῆδε
αὐτῶν φροντὶς ἦν ἅμα καὶ αἰδώς, ἐπεὶ καὶ τοῖς ἄλλοις
σφαγεῦσι διὰ τούσδε μάλιστα συνελάμβανον·
22 7. Ἐξελθόντων δὲ τῆς πόλεως τῶν ἀμφὶ τὸν
Βροῦτον, ἐπὶ δυναστείας ὢν ὁ Ἀντώνιος ἤδη μοναρ-
χικῆς ἀρχὴν ἔθνους καὶ στρατιᾶς αὑτῷ περιέβλεπε·
καὶ Συρίας μὲν ἐπεθύμει μάλιστα, οὐκ ἠγνόει δὲ ὢν
δι' ὑπονοίας καὶ μᾶλλον ἐσόμενος, εἴ τι αἰτοίη· καὶ
γὰρ αὐτῷ κρύφα Δολοβέλλαν τὸν ἕτερον ὕπατον
ἐπήλειφεν εἰς ἐναντίωσιν ἡ βουλή, διάφορον αἰεὶ τῷ
23 Ἀντωνίῳ γενόμενον. αὐτὸν οὖν τὸν Δολοβέλλαν ὁ
Ἀντώνιος, νέον τε καὶ φιλότιμον εἰδώς, ἔπεισεν αἰτεῖν
Συρίαν ἀντὶ Κασσίου καὶ τὰ[5] ἐς Παρθυαίους ‹καὶ
τὸν›[6] κατειλεγμένον στρατὸν ἐπὶ τοὺς Παρθυαίους,
αἰτεῖν δὲ οὐ παρὰ τῆς βουλῆς (οὐ γὰρ ἐξῆν), ἀλλὰ

---

[5] τὸ codd.; τὰ Goukowsky
[6] ‹καὶ τὸν› add. Goukowsky

torship before their term of office was finished, and thus
incur a suspect reputation for craving provincial power.
Their preference, nevertheless, was somehow to spend
the remaining time as private citizens, rather than as praetors in Rome, where they did not believe they were safe,
nor honored appropriately for the services they had rendered on behalf of their country. The senate's opinion was   20
in sympathy with their attitude, and they assigned them
the care of the city's grain supply from all parts of the
world, until the time came for them to take command of
their provinces. They did this so that Brutus and Cassius   21
could avoid giving any impression that they were running
away. So great was the senate's anxiety and respect for
them that it was particularly on their account that they
assisted the other assassins.

7. After Brutus and his men had left the city, Antony   22
now enjoyed the sole power of a dynast, and began to look
around for a provincial command and army for himself.
He wanted Syria most of all, but he was aware that he was
under suspicion and would be more so if he made any
request; and that the senate had secretly suborned Dolabella, the other consul, to oppose him, as he had always
been at odds with him. So, knowing that Dolabella was   23
himself young and ambitious, Antony persuaded him to
ask that he should have the province of Syria rather than
Cassius, and control of Parthian affairs and the army recruited to fight the Parthians, and to ask for this not from
the senate, for that was not possible,[3] but from the people

---

[3] The senate had the power to decide provincial commands,
but in this case, Appian means, they would not think of replacing
Cassius with Dolabella, because they were so well disposed to
Cassius.

24 παρὰ τοῦ δήμου νόμῳ. καὶ ὁ μὲν ἡσθεὶς αὐτίκα προυτίθει τὸν νόμον, καὶ τῆς βουλῆς αἰτιωμένης αὐτὸν παραλύειν τὰ δόξαντα τῷ Καίσαρι τὸν μὲν ἐπὶ Παρθυαίους πόλεμον οὐδενὶ ἔφη ὑπὸ Καίσαρος ἐπιτετράφθαι, Κάσσιον δὲ τὸν Συρίας ἀξιωθέντα αὐτόν τι τῶν Καίσαρος πρότερον ἀλλάξαι, δόντα πωλεῖν τὰ κληρουχήματα τοῖς λαβοῦσι πρὸ τῶν νενομισμένων εἴκοσιν ἐτῶν· καὶ αὐτὸς δὲ αἰδεῖσθαι Συρίας οὐκ ἀξιούμε-

25 νος, Δολοβέλλας ὤν, πρὸ Κασσίου. οἱ μὲν δὴ τῶν δημάρχων τινὰ Ἀσπρήναν ἔπεισαν ἐν τῇ χειροτονίᾳ ψεύσασθαι περὶ διοσημείας, ἐλπίσαντές τι καὶ Ἀντώνιον συμπράξειν, ὕπατόν τε ὄντα καὶ τῶν σημείων ἱερέα καὶ διάφορον ἔτι νομιζόμενον εἶναι τῷ Δολοβέλλᾳ· ὁ δ' Ἀντώνιος, ἐπεὶ τῆς χειροτονίας οὔσης ὁ Ἀσπρήνας ἔφη διοσημείαν ἀπαίσιον γεγονέναι, ἔθους ὄντος ἑτέρους ἐπὶ τοῦτο πέμπεσθαι, πάνυ χαλεψάμενος τῷ Ἀσπρήνᾳ τοῦ ψεύσματος τὰς φυλὰς ἐκέλευε χειροτονεῖν περὶ τοῦ Δολοβέλλα.

26 8. Καὶ γίνεται μὲν οὕτω Συρίας ἡγεμὼν Δολοβέλλας καὶ στρατηγὸς τοῦ πολέμου τοῦ πρὸς Παρθυαίους καὶ στρατιᾶς τῆς ἐς αὐτὸν ὑπὸ Καίσαρος κατειλεγμένης, ὅση τε περὶ Μακεδονίαν προεληλύθει, καὶ ὁ Ἀντώνιος τότε πρῶτον ἔγνωστο συμπράσσων τῷ

27 Δολοβέλλᾳ. γεγενημένων δὲ τῶνδε ἐν τῷ δήμῳ τὴν βουλὴν ὁ Ἀντώνιος ᾔτει Μακεδονίαν, εὖ εἰδώς, ὅτι αἰδέσονται, μετὰ Συρίαν δοθεῖσαν Δολοβέλλᾳ, ἀντει-

by a law. Dolabella was delighted, and immediately pro-   24
posed the law. When the senate criticized him for revers-
ing Caesar's decisions, he replied that, in the first place,
Caesar had not assigned the war against the Parthians to
anybody, and, secondly, that, although Cassius had been
assigned to the command of Syria, he had himself been
the first to alter one of Caesar's decisions by authorizing
those who had received allotments to sell them before the
legally required period of twenty years was up. He added
that, as a Dolabella, he would be ashamed not to be
thought worthy of Syria, in place of Cassius.[4] The senate   25
then persuaded one of the tribunes, named Asprenas, to
lie about the heavenly signs during the voting session,
expecting Antony to be cooperative because he was consul
and augur, and was still believed to be hostile to Dolabella.
But when the voting took place, and Asprenas said that
there had been an unfavorable omen, although it was the
custom for others to be sent to deal with this, Antony was
very angry at his lie and ordered the tribes to get on with
voting about Dolabella.

8. This is how Dolabella becomes governor of Syria and   26
in command of the war against the Parthians and of the
forces enlisted for that purpose by Caesar, together with
those that had gone on ahead to Macedonia. This was the
point at which it became known for the first time that
Antony was working with Dolabella. After the transaction   27
of these matters in the people's assembly, Antony asked
the senate for Macedonia, well aware that, having given
Syria to Dolabella, they would be embarrassed to refuse

[4] On the grounds that his patrician family was more distinguished than Cassius' plebeian ancestors.

πεῖν περὶ Μακεδονίας Ἀντωνίῳ, καὶ ταῦτα γυμνῆς
28 στρατοῦ[7] γενομένης, καὶ ἔδοσαν μὲν ἄκοντες καὶ ἐν
θαύματι ἔχοντες, ὅπως τὸν ἐν αὐτῇ στρατὸν προμε-
θῆκεν ὁ Ἀντώνιος τῷ Δολοβέλλᾳ, ἠγάπων δὲ ὅμως
29 Δολοβέλλαν ἔχειν τὸν στρατὸν Ἀντωνίου μᾶλλον. ἐν
καιρῷ δὲ αὐτοὶ τὸν Ἀντώνιον τοῖς ἀμφὶ τὸν Κάσσιον
ἀντῄτουν ἕτερα ἔθνη, καὶ ἐδόθη Κυρήνη τε καὶ Κρήτη,
ὡς δ᾽ ἑτέροις δοκεῖ, τάδε μὲν ἀμφότερα Κασσίῳ, Βι-
θυνία δὲ Βρούτῳ.

30   9. Τὰ μὲν δὴ γινόμενα ἐν Ῥώμῃ τοιάδε ἦν· Ὀκτάουιος δὲ ὁ τῆς ἀδελφῆς τοῦ Καίσαρος θυγατριδοῦς
ἵππαρχος μὲν αὐτοῦ Καίσαρος γεγένητο πρὸς ἓν
ἔτος, ἐξ οὗ τήνδε τὴν τιμὴν ὁ Καῖσαρ ἐς τοὺς φίλους
περιφέρων ἐτήσιον ἔσθ᾽ ὅτε ἐποιεῖτο εἶναι, μειράκιον
δὲ ἔτι ὢν ἐς Ἀπολλωνίαν τὴν ἐπὶ τοῦ Ἰονίου παιδεύ-
εσθαί τε καὶ ἀσκεῖσθαι τὰ πολέμια ἐπέμπετο ὑπὸ τοῦ
31 Καίσαρος ὡς ἐς τοὺς πολεμίους ἑψόμενος αὐτῷ. καὶ
μετ᾽ αὐτῶν τῶν[8] ἐν τῇ Ἀπολλωνίᾳ ἱππέων ἶλαι παραλλὰξ ἐκ Μακεδονίας ἐπιοῦσαι συνεγύμναζον καὶ τῶν
ἡγεμόνων τοῦ στρατοῦ τινες ὡς συγγενεῖ Καίσαρος
θαμινὰ ἐπεφοίτων. γνῶσίς τε ἐκ τούτων αὐτῷ καὶ εὔ-
νοια παρὰ τοῦ στρατοῦ τις ἐνεγίγνετο, σὺν χάριτι
32 δεξιουμένῳ πάντας. ἕκτον δ᾽ ἔχοντι μῆνα ἐν τῇ Ἀπολλωνίᾳ ἀγγέλλεται περὶ ἑσπέραν ὁ Καῖσαρ ἀνῃρημέ-
νος ἐν τῷ βουλευτηρίῳ πρὸς τῶν φιλτάτων καὶ παρ᾽
αὐτῷ δυνατωτάτων τότε μάλιστα. τῶν δὲ λοιπῶν
οὐδενὸς ἀπαγγελθέντος πω δέος αὐτὸν ἐπεῖχε καὶ

him concerning Macedonia, especially as it had just been
stripped of an army. They gave it to him reluctantly,   28
amazed that Antony had earlier handed its army over to
Dolabella, but glad nonetheless that Dolabella rather than
Antony had the army. In return for this, they themselves   29
took the opportunity to ask Antony for other provinces for
Cassius and his supporters: they were given Cyrene and
Crete, or as others think, these both went to Cassius, while
Brutus got Bithynia.

9. Such were events at Rome. As for Octavius, the   30
grandson of Caesar's sister, he had been appointed Caesar's Master of Horse for one year, Caesar having begun
to pass this office around among his associates, sometimes
making it an annual office. As he was still in his youth, he
had been sent by Caesar to Apollonia on the Ionian gulf
to be educated and receive military training, with a view
to accompanying Caesar on campaign against the enemy.
Along with the cavalry actually stationed in Apollonia,   31
squadrons came by turns from Macedonia and trained
with him, and certain army officers visited him frequently
because he was a relative of Caesar. This got him recogni-
tion and a degree of goodwill from the army, as he received
everyone graciously. After six months in Apollonia, news   32
is brought to him one evening that Caesar had been killed
in the senate by his closest associates and those most influential with him at that particular time. As there was no
report about the rest of what had happened, Octavius was
gripped by fear, and did not know if this was a concerted
act of the senate as a whole, or was limited to the perpetra-

---

7 στρατηγοῦ codd.; στρατοῦ edd.   8 καὶ μετ᾽ αὐτῶν
τῶν Goukowsky; καὶ μετὰ τῶν P; καὶ αὐτὸν LBJ

ἄγνοια, εἴτε κοινὸν εἴη τῆς βουλῆς τὸ ἔργον εἴτε καὶ
τῶν ἐργασαμένων ἴδιον, καὶ εἰ δίκην ἤδη τοῖς πλείοσι
δεδώκοιεν ἢ καὶ κρείττους[9] τοῦδε εἶεν, ἢ καὶ τὸ πλῆθος
αὐτοῖς συνήδοιτο.

33   10. Ἐφ᾽ οἷς οἱ φίλοι ⟨οἱ⟩[10] ἐκ Ῥώμης ὑπετίθεντο
τοσαῦτα[11] ὥστε οἱ μὲν ἐς φυλακὴν τοῦ σώματος αὐτὸν
ἠξίουν ἐπὶ τὸν ἐν Μακεδονίᾳ στρατὸν καταφυγεῖν καί,
ὅτε μάθοι μὴ κοινὸν εἶναι τὸ ἔργον, ἐπιθαρρήσαντα
τοῖς ἐχθροῖς ἀμύνειν τῷ Καίσαρι· καὶ ἦσαν οἱ καὶ
34   τῶν ἡγεμόνων αὐτὸν ἐλθόντα φυλάξειν ὑπεδέχοντο· ἡ
δὲ μήτηρ καὶ Φίλιππος, ὃς εἶχεν αὐτήν, ἀπὸ Ῥώμης
ἔγραφον μήτε ἐπαίρεσθαι μήτε θαρρεῖν πω μεμνημέ-
νον, οἷα Καῖσαρ ὁ παντὸς ἐχθροῦ κρατήσας ὑπὸ τῶν
φιλτάτων μάλιστα πάθοι, τὰ δὲ ἰδιωτικώτερα ὡς ἐν
τοῖς παροῦσιν ἀκινδυνότερα αἱρεῖσθαι μᾶλλον καὶ
35   πρὸς σφᾶς ἐς Ῥώμην ἐπείγεσθαι φυλασσόμενον. οἷς
Ὀκτάουιος ἐνδοὺς διὰ τὴν ἔτι ἄγνοιαν τῶν ἐπὶ τῷ
θανάτῳ γενομένων, τοὺς ἡγεμόνας τοῦ στρατοῦ δεξι-
ωσάμενος διέπλει τὸν Ἰόνιον, οὐκ ἐς τὸ Βρεντέσιον
(οὔπω γάρ τινα τοῦ ἐκεῖθι στρατοῦ πεῖραν εἰληφὼς
πάντα ἐφυλάσσετο), ἀλλ᾽ ἐς ἑτέραν οὐ μακρὰν ἀπὸ
τοῦ Βρεντεσίου πόλιν, ἐκτὸς οὖσαν ὁδοῦ, ᾗ ὄνομα
Λουπίαι. ἐνταῦθα οὖν ἐνηυλίσατο διατρίβων.

36   11. Ὡς δέ οἱ τά τε ἀκριβέστερα περὶ τοῦ φόνου καὶ

---

[9] κρείττους P, om. LBJ; ἢ καὶ ⟨ἐν δέει⟩ τοῦδε εἶεν Schweig.
[10] οἱ add. Goukowsky   [11] τοσαῦτα Goukowsky; ταῦτα
codd.; οἱ φίλοι . . . ὥστε del. Keil ut glossema

tors; nor whether the latter had paid the penalty to the majority of the senate, or were too strong for this,[5] or whether the people too sympathized with the perpetrators.

10. In response to this, his associates in Rome advised as follows.[6] Some recommended that he protect his person by taking refuge with the army in Macedonia, and when he got information that the deed was not done collectively, take heart and avenge his enemies for Caesar. And there were some officers who undertook to protect him if he came to them. But his mother and her husband, Philippus,[7] wrote to him from Rome telling him not to be overconfident or rash, and to keep in mind the fate suffered by Caesar, after he had vanquished every enemy, a fate suffered at the hands of his closest supporters. It would be less dangerous, they said, to choose private life for the present, and hurry, cautiously, to them at Rome. Octavius went along with them because he still did not know what had happened after Caesar's death. He took leave of the army officers and crossed the Ionian gulf, not to Brundisium (for he had not yet sounded out any of the troops there, and was taking extreme care), but to another town not far from it, but off the main road, named Lupiae. There he stayed in lodgings.

11. When more accurate information about the murder

33

34

35

36

[5] The text is uncertain at this point.

[6] Most of this sentence looks superfluous and may be a scribal addition.

[7] Atia, daughter of Caesar's sister, Julia, had been married to Gaius Octavius, Octavian's father, but after his death, married the consul of 56, Lucius Marcius Philippus.

τοῦ δημοσίου πάθους τῶν τε διαθηκῶν καὶ τῶν ἐψηφισμένων ἦλθε τὰ ἀντίγραφα, οἱ μὲν ἔτι μᾶλλον
αὐτὸν ἠξίουν τοὺς ἐχθροὺς Καίσαρος δεδιέναι, υἱόν
τε αὐτοῦ καὶ κληρονόμον ὄντα, καὶ παρήνουν ἅμα τῷ
37 κλήρῳ τὴν θέσιν ἀπείπασθαι· ὁ δὲ καὶ ταῦτά οἱ καὶ
τὸ μὴ τιμωρεῖν αὐτὸν Καίσαρι αἰσχρὸν ἡγούμενος ἐς
τὸ Βρεντέσιον ᾔει, προπέμψας καὶ διερευνησάμενος,
38 μή τις ἐκ τῶν φονέων ἐγκαθέζοιτο ἐνέδρα. ὡς δὲ αὐτῷ
καὶ ὁ ἐνθάδε στρατὸς οἷα Καίσαρος υἱὸν δεξιούμενος
ἀπήντα, θαρρήσας ἔθυε καὶ εὐθὺς ὠνομάζετο Καῖσαρ. ἔθος γάρ τι Ῥωμαίοις τοὺς θετοὺς τὰ τῶν θεμένων ὀνόματα ἐπιλαμβάνειν. ὁ δὲ οὐκ ἐπέλαβεν, ἀλλὰ
καὶ τὸ αὐτοῦ καὶ τὸ πατρῷον ὅλως ἐνήλλαξεν, ἀντὶ
Ὀκταουίου παιδὸς Ὀκταουίου Καῖσαρ εἶναι καὶ Καί-
39 σαρος υἱός, καὶ διετέλεσεν οὕτω χρώμενος. εὐθύς τε
ἐς αὐτὸν ἄθρουν καὶ πανταχόθεν ὡς ἐς Καίσαρος υἱὸν
πλῆθος ἀνθρώπων συνέθεον, οἱ μὲν ἐκ φιλίας Καίσαρος, οἱ δὲ ἐξελεύθεροι καὶ θεράποντες αὐτοῦ, καὶ
ἕτεροι στρατιῶται σὺν αὐτοῖς, οἱ μὲν ἀποσκευὰς ἢ
χρήματα φέροντες ἐς τὴν Μακεδονίαν, οἱ δὲ ἕτερα
χρήματα καὶ φόρους ἐξ ἐθνῶν ἄλλων ἐς τὸ Βρεντέσιον.
40   12. Ὁ δὲ καὶ τῷ πλήθει τῶν εἰς αὐτὸν ἀφικνουμένων
καὶ τῇ Καίσαρος αὐτοῦ δόξῃ τε καὶ τῇ πάντων εἰς

---

[8] His name was originally Gaius Octavius. His father, Gaius
Octavius, had been praetor in 61 and governor of Macedonia.

and the public reaction had reached him, together with copies of Caesar's will and the decrees of the senate, his family urged him even more to beware of Caesar's enemies, as he was his son and heir, and to renounce both the will and the adoption. But believing that for him to do this, 37 and to fail to avenge Caesar, would be disgraceful, he went to Brundisium, first sending ahead to check that none of the assassins had set a trap for him. When even the army 38 there advanced to meet him, and received him as Caesar's son, he was heartened, offered sacrifice, and immediately assumed the name of Caesar, as it is customary among the Romans for adopted sons to take the name of those who have adopted them. He did not just add it to his name, but changed his own name and father's name completely, calling himself Caesar, the son of Caesar, instead of Octavius, the son of Octavius, and he continued to use these names.[8] A crowd of men in groups from everywhere immediately 39 rushed to join him, as Caesar's son, some out of friendship for Caesar, others because they were freedmen and slaves of his; and along with them others were soldiers, engaged either in conveying baggage and money to Macedonia, or different money and revenue from other provinces to Brundisium.

12. Encouraged by the numbers who were joining him, 40 by the reputation of Caesar himself, and by the goodwill

After his adoption by Caesar, his official name would have been Gaius Julius Caesar Octavianus, but ancient authors followed his own wishes and, confusingly for modern readers, usually just called him Caesar. I follow standard scholarly practice in calling him Octavian up to 27, and then Augustus, the title he took in that year.

ἐκεῖνον εὐνοίᾳ θαρρῶν ὧδευεν ἐς Ῥώμην σὺν ἀξιο-
λόγῳ πλήθει, αὐξομένῳ μᾶλλον ἑκάστης ἡμέρας οἷα
χειμάρρῳ, φανερᾶς μὲν ἐπιβουλῆς ὢν ἀμείνων διὰ τὸ
πλῆθος, ἐνέδρας δὲ δι᾽ αὐτὸ καὶ μάλιστα ὑφορώμενος,
ἀρτιγνώστων οἱ τῶν συνόντων σχεδὸν ὄντων ἁπάν-
41 των. τὰ δὲ τῶν πόλεων τῶν μὲν ἄλλων οὐ πάντῃ πρὸς
αὐτὸν ἦν ὁμαλά· οἱ δὲ τῷ Καίσαρι στρατευσάμενοί
τε καὶ ἐς κληρουχίας διῃρημένοι συνέτρεχον ἐκ τῶν
ἀποικιῶν ἐπὶ χάριτι τοῦ μειρακίου καὶ τὸν Καίσαρα
ὠλοφύροντο καὶ τὸν Ἀντώνιον ἐβλασφήμουν οὐκ ἐπ-
εξιόντα τηλικούτῳ μύσει καὶ σφᾶς ἔλεγον, εἴ τις
ἡγοῖτο, ἀμυνεῖν. οὓς ὁ Καῖσαρ ἐπαινῶν καὶ ἀνατιθέ-
42 μενος ἐν τῷ παρόντι ἀπέπεμπεν. ὄντι δ᾽ αὐτῷ περὶ
Ταρρακίνας, ἀπὸ τετρακοσίων που Ῥώμης σταδίων,
ἀγγέλλεται Κάσσιός τε καὶ Βροῦτος ἀφῃρημένοι
πρὸς τῶν ὑπάτων Συρίαν καὶ Μακεδονίαν καὶ ἐς
παρηγορίαν βραχύτερα ἕτερα Κυρήνην καὶ Κρήτην
ἀντειληφότες, φυγάδων τέ τινων κάθοδοι καὶ Πομπηίου μετάκλησις καὶ ἀπὸ τῶν Καίσαρος ὑπομνημάτων ἔς τε τὴν βουλὴν ἐγγραφαί τινων καὶ ἕτερα
πολλὰ γιγνόμενα.

43   13. Ὡς δ᾽ ἐς τὴν πόλιν ἀφίκετο, ἡ μὲν μήτηρ αὖθις
καὶ Φίλιππος ὅσοι τε ἄλλοι κηδεμόνες ἦσαν αὐτοῦ,
ἐδεδοίκεσαν τήν τε τῆς βουλῆς ἐς τὸν Καίσαρα ἀλλοτρίωσιν καὶ τὸ δόγμα, μὴ εἶναι δίκας ἐπὶ Καίσαρι
φόνου, καὶ τὴν Ἀντωνίου τότε δυναστεύοντος ἐς αὐτὸν
ὑπεροψίαν, οὔτε ἀφικομένου πρὸς τὸν Καίσαρος υἱὸν
44 ἐλθόντα οὔτε προσπέμψαντος αὐτῷ· ὁ δὲ καὶ ταῦτ᾽

of everyone toward him, he journeyed to Rome with a substantial crowd which, like a torrent, grew larger each day. Although he was safe from open attack because of the crowd, for this very reason he was particularly careful about plots, since almost all those who joined him were new acquaintances. Some of the other towns were not 41 altogether favorably disposed to him, but from the colonies those who had served with Caesar and had been distributed on allotments flocked to him, happy to see the young man, but mourning Caesar and abusing Antony for not taking action against such a terrible defilement: they said that they themselves would wreak vengeance, if someone would lead them. Octavian praised them, but put the matter off for the present and sent them away. When 42 he was at Tarracina, about four hundred stades from Rome, he receives news that Cassius and Brutus had been dispossessed of Syria and Macedonia by the consuls, and had received instead as compensation the smaller provinces of Cyrene and Crete; that certain exiles had returned; that Sextus Pompeius had been recalled; and that, on the basis of Caesar's memoranda, some new members had been added to the senate, and that many other things were going on.

13. When he arrived in the city, his mother and Philip- 43 pus and all his other relatives were again apprehensive about the estrangement of the senate from Caesar, about the decree that no punishment was to be imposed for his murder, and about the contempt shown to Octavian by Antony, who was then dominant and had not met with Caesar's son when he arrived, nor sent word to him. Octa- 44

ἐπράϋνεν, αὐτὸς ἀπαντήσειν ἐς τὸν Ἀντώνιον εἰπὼν
οἷα νεώτερος ἐς πρεσβύτερον καὶ ἰδιώτης ἐς ὕπατον
καὶ τὴν βουλὴν θεραπεύσειν τὰ εἰκότα. καὶ τὸ δόγμα
ἔφη γενέσθαι μηδενός πω τοὺς ἀνδροφόνους διώκον-
τος· ἀλλ' ὁπότε θαρρήσας τις διώκοι, καὶ τὸν δῆμον
ἐπικουρήσειν καὶ τὴν βουλὴν ὡς ἐννόμῳ καὶ τοὺς θε-
45   οὺς ὡς δικαίῳ καὶ τὸν Ἀντώνιον ἴσως. εἰ δὲ καὶ τοῦ
κλήρου καὶ τῆς θέσεως ὑπερίδοι, ἔς τε τὸν Καίσαρα
ἁμαρτήσεσθαι καὶ τὸν δῆμον ἀδικήσειν εἰς τὴν δια-
46   νομήν. ἀπερρήγνυ τε λήγων τοῦ λόγου, ὅτι μὴ κινδυνεύειν οἱ καλὸν εἴη μόνον, ἀλλὰ καὶ θνήσκειν, εἰ
προκριθεὶς ἐκ πάντων ἐς τοσαῦτα ὑπὸ τοῦ Καίσαρος
ἀντάξιος αὐτοῦ φαίνοιτο φιλοκινδυνοτάτου γεγονότος.
47   τά τε τοῦ Ἀχιλλέως, ὑπόγυά οἱ τότε ὄντα μάλιστα, ἐς
τὴν μητέρα ὥσπερ ἐς τὴν Θέτιν ἐπιστρεφόμενος
ἔλεγεν·

>   Αὐτίκα τεθναίην, ἐπεὶ οὐκ ἄρ' ἔμελλον ἑταίρῳ
>   κτεινομένῳ ἐπαμύνειν.

καὶ τόδε εἰπὼν Ἀχιλλεῖ μὲν ἔφη κόσμον ἀθάνατον ἐκ
πάντων εἶναι τοῦτο τὸ ἔπος, καὶ τὸ ἔργον αὐτοῦ μάλι-
στα· αὐτὸς δ' ἀνεκάλει τὸν Καίσαρα οὐχ ἑταῖρον,
ἀλλὰ πατέρα, οὐδὲ συστρατιώτην, ἀλλ' αὐτοκράτορα,
οὐδὲ πολέμου νόμῳ πεσόντα, ἀλλ' ἀθεμίστως ἐν βουλευτηρίῳ κατακοπέντα.

vian allayed even these fears, saying that he, the younger man and a private citizen, would call on Antony, the older man and a consul, and that he would treat the senate with due respect. As for the decree, he said that it had been passed because nobody had yet prosecuted the murderers, but that when someone summoned up the courage to do so, even the people and the senate would lend their support for a lawful measure, as well as the gods, and Antony likewise, because it was just. If he were to overlook the 45 inheritance and the adoption, he would be wronging Caesar and treating the people unfairly with respect to their share of the inheritance. As he was finishing what he had 46 to say, he blurted out a remark that it would be honorable for him not only to risk danger, but even to die, if, having been advanced ahead of everyone by Caesar to such distinction, he was to show himself worthy of a man who had been such a close companion of danger. Then turning to 47 his mother as if she were Thetis, he spoke the words of Achilles, which were at the time particularly fresh in his mind:[9]

> Would that I might die immediately, since I was not to come to the aid of my companion when he was being killed.

Having finished, he said that these words, and particularly his actions, had brought Achilles immortal glory from all men; and he called on Caesar not as a friend, but a father; not as a fellow soldier, but a commander in chief; not as one who had fallen by the law of war, but as the victim of sacrilegious murder in the senate.

[9] Homer, *Il*. 18.98.

48   14. Ἐφ᾽ οἷς αὐτὸν ἡ μήτηρ, ἐς ἡδονὴν ἐκ τοῦ δέους
ὑπαχθεῖσα, ἠσπάζετο ὡς μόνον ἄξιον Καίσαρος καὶ
λέγειν ἔτι ἐπισχοῦσα ἐπέσπερχεν ἐς τὰ ἐγνωσμένα
σὺν τῇ τύχῃ. παρῄνει γε μὴν ἔτι τέχνῃ καὶ ἀνεξικα-
49 κίᾳ μᾶλλον ἢ φανερᾷ θρασύτητί πω χρῆσθαι. καὶ ὁ
Καῖσαρ ἐπαινέσας καὶ πράξειν ὑποσχόμενος οὕτως,
αὐτίκα τῆς ἑσπέρας ἐς τοὺς φίλους περιέπεμπεν, ἐς
ἕω συγκαλῶν ἕκαστον ἐς τὴν ἀγορὰν μετὰ πλήθους.
ἔνθα Γάιον Ἀντώνιον τὸν ἀδελφὸν Ἀντωνίου, στρατηγοῦντα τῆς πόλεως, ὑπαντιάσας ἔφη δέχεσθαι τὴν
θέσιν τοῦ Καίσαρος· ἔθος γάρ τι Ῥωμαίοις τοὺς θε-
50 τοὺς ἐπὶ μάρτυσι γίγνεσθαι τοῖς στρατηγοῖς. ἀπο-
γραψαμένων δὲ τῶν δημοσίων τὸ ῥῆμα, εὐθὺς ἐκ τῆν
ἀγορᾶς ἐς τὸν Ἀντώνιον ἐχώρει. ὁ δὲ ἦν ἐς κήποις,
οὓς ὁ Καῖσαρ αὐτῷ δεδώρητο Πομπηίου γενομένους.
διατριβῆς δὲ ἀμφὶ τὰς θύρας πλείονος γενομένης ὁ
μὲν Καῖσαρ καὶ τάδε ἐς ὑποψίαν Ἀντωνίου τῆς ἀλλο-
τριώσεως ἐτίθετο, εἰσκληθέντος δέ ποτε ἦσαν προσ-
αγορεύσεις τε καὶ περὶ ἀλλήλων πύσματα εἰκότα.

51   15. Ὡς δὲ ἤδη λέγειν ἔδει περὶ ὧν ἦσαν ἐν χρείᾳ,
ὁ Καῖσαρ εἶπεν· "Ἐγώ, πάτερ Ἀντώνιε (πατέρα γὰρ
εἶναι σέ μοι δικαιοῦσιν αἵ τε Καίσαρος ἐς σὲ εὐερ-
γεσίαι καὶ ἡ σὴ πρὸς ἐκεῖνον χάρις), τῶν σοι πεπραγμένων ἐπ᾽ ἐκείνῳ τὰ μὲν ἐπαινῶ καὶ χάριν αὐτῶν
ὀφλήσω, τὰ δ᾽ ἐπιμέμφομαι, καὶ λελέξεται μετὰ παρ-
52 ρησίας, ἐς ἣν ἡ λύπη με προάγει. κτεινομένῳ μὲν οὐ
παρῆς, τῶν φονέων σε περισπασάντων περὶ θύρας,
ἐπεὶ περιέσῳζες ἂν αὐτὸν ἢ συνεκινδύνευες ὅμοια πα-

26

14. At this, his mother, transported from fear to joy, 48
hailed him as the only man worthy of Caesar, and, restraining him from saying any more, urged him to prosecute his
plans with the help of Fate. She advised him, however, to
employ ingenuity and patience rather than at this stage
open daring. Octavian applauded her and promised to act 49
in that way, and immediately sent word around to his
friends the same evening, asking them to come to the
Forum at dawn and bring a crowd with them. Here he
presented himself to Gaius Antonius, the brother of Antony, who was urban praetor, and declared that he accepted
the adoption of Caesar; for it is Roman custom that
adoptions are witnessed before the praetors. When the 50
public scribes had written down his declaration, Octavian
went straight from the Forum to Antony, who was in the
gardens formerly owned by Pompey that Caesar had given
to him. There was a long delay at the gates, which Octavian
suspected was due to Antony's aversion to him, but once
he was admitted they greeted each other and made the
proper mutual inquiries.

15. When the time came to speak of the business in 51
hand, Octavian said: "Father Antony (for Caesar's benefactions to you and your gratitude toward him justify the
claim that you are a father to me), for some of the things
that you have done in relation to him I commend you and
owe you my thanks; for others I reproach you. I will speak
with the freedom to which my grief drives me. When Cae- 52
sar was killed you were not there, as the murderers de-
tained you at the door; otherwise you would have saved
him or run the risk of suffering the same fate. And if the

27

θεῖν· ὧν εἰ θάτερον ἔμελλεν ἔσεσθαι, καλῶς, ὅτι μὴ
53 παρῇς. ψηφιζομένων δέ τινων αὐτοῖς ὡς ἐπὶ τυράννῳ
γέρα ἀντεῖπας ἐγκρατῶς· καὶ τοῦδέ σοι χάριν οἶδα
λαμπράν, εἰ καὶ τοὺς ἄνδρας ἔγνως συνανελεῖν σε
βεβουλευμένους, οὐχ, ὡς ἡμεῖς ἡγούμεθα, τιμωρὸν
ἐσόμενον Καίσαρι, ἀλλ᾽, ὡς αὐτοὶ λέγουσι, τῆς τυ-
54 ραννίδος διάδοχον. ἅμα δ᾽ οὐκ ἦσαν ἐκεῖνοι τυραν-
νοκτόνοι, εἰ μὴ καὶ φονεῖς ἦσαν· διὸ καὶ ἐς τὸ Καπιτώλιον συνέφυγον ὡς ἐς ἱερὸν ἁμαρτόντες ἱκέται ἢ ὡς
ἐς ἀκρόπολιν ἐχθροί. πόθεν οὖν αὐτοῖς ἀμνηστία καὶ
τὸ ἀνεύθυνον τοῦ φόνου, ἢ τῆς βουλῆς καὶ τοῦ δήμου
εἰ τινες ἐφθάρατο ὑπ᾽ ἐκείνων; καὶ σὲ τὸ τῶν πλεόνων
55 ὁρᾶν ἐχρῆν, ὕπατον ὄντα. ἀλλὰ καὶ θάτερα βουλομένῳ σοι ἡ ἀρχὴ συνελάμβανε, τιμωρουμένῳ τηλι-
κοῦτον ἄγος καὶ τοὺς πλανωμένους μεταδιδάσκοντι.
σὺ δὲ καὶ ὅμηρα τῆς ἀδείας, οἰκεῖα αὐτοῦ σοῦ, τοῖς
ἀνδροφόνοις ἔπεμψας ἐς τὸ Καπιτώλιον. ἀλλ᾽ ἔστων
56 καὶ ταῦτα οἱ διεφθαρμένοι σε βιάσασθαι. ὅτε μέντοι
τῶν διαθηκῶν ἀναγνωσθεισῶν καὶ αὐτοῦ σοῦ δίκαιον
ἐπιτάφιον εἰπόντος ὁ δῆμος ἐν ἀκριβεῖ Καίσαρος
μνήμῃ γενόμενοι πῦρ ἐπ᾽ αὐτοὺς ἔφερον, καὶ φεισά-
μενοι χάριν τῶν γειτόνων ἐς τὴν ἐπιοῦσαν ἥξειν ἐπὶ
ὅπλα συνέθεντο, πῶς οὐχὶ τῷ δήμῳ συνέπραξας καὶ
ἐστρατήγησας τοῦ πυρὸς ἢ τῶν ὅπλων ἢ δίκην γε
τοῖς ἀνδροφόνοις ἐπέγραψας, εἰ δίκης ἔδει κατὰ αὐτο-
φώρων, καὶ φίλος ὢν Καίσαρι καὶ ὕπατος καὶ Ἀντώνιος;

57   16. "Ἀλλὰ Μάριος μὲν ἐξ ἐπιτάγματος ἀνῃρέθη

latter was going to happen, it was just as well you were not
there. When some people proposed rewards to the mur-   53
derers for acting against a tyrant, you strongly opposed
them. For this I give you my warmest thanks, even though
you knew that these men were planning to kill you, too;
not, in my opinion, because they regarded you as a poten-
tial avenger of Caesar, but, as they themselves say, because
they thought you would succeed to his tyranny. They were   54
not tyrant slayers without being murderers at the same
time, and that is why they took refuge on the Capitol, either as guilty suppliants in a temple, or as enemies in a
citadel. How, then, did they get an amnesty and immunity
from prosecution for the murder, unless some of the senate and people had been bribed by them? You, as consul,
ought to have seen the will of the majority. Your office   55
would have enabled you to act differently, if you had
wanted, by avenging such a terrible pollution, and con-
verting the waverers. But in fact you sent hostages from
your own household to the murderers on the Capitol to
guarantee their safe conduct. But let us suppose that those
who had been bribed forced you to do this too. When   56
Caesar's will had been read, however, and you yourself had
delivered a fitting funeral oration, and the people, being
thus reminded so accurately of Caesar, had set out to burn
down the houses of the murderers, but spared them for
the sake of their neighbors, although they agreed to come
back in arms next day, why did you not cooperate with
them at that time? Why did you, as Caesar's friend, as
consul, as Antony, not take command of the torches and
weapons, or bring a case against the murderers, if a case
was needed against those caught in the act?

16. "You used the power of your office to have Marius   57

29

κατὰ τὸ τῆς ἀρχῆς μέγεθος, ἀνδροφόνους δὲ ἐκφυγεῖν
ὑπερεῖδες καὶ ἐς ἡγεμονίας ἐνίους διαδραμεῖν, ἃς
58 ἀθεμίστως ἔχουσι τὸν δόντα ἀνελόντες. Συρίαν μὲν
δὴ καὶ Μακεδονίαν εὖ ποιοῦντες οἱ ὕπατοι, σὺ καὶ
Δολοβέλλας, καθισταμένων ἄρτι τῶν πραγμάτων πε-
ριεσπάσατε ἐς ἑαυτούς. καὶ τοῦδέ σοι χάριν ᾔδειν ἄν,
εἰ μὴ αὐτίκα Κυρήνην καὶ Κρήτην αὐτοῖς ἐψηφίσασθε καὶ φυγάδας ἠξιώσατε ἡγεμονίαις αἰεὶ κατ' ἐμοῦ
δορυφορεῖσθαι· Δέκμον τε τὴν ἐγγὺς Κελτικὴν ὑπε-
ρορᾶτε ἔχοντα, καὶ τόνδε τοῖς ἄλλοις ὁμοίως αὐθέ-
59 ντην τοὐμοῦ πατρὸς γενόμενον. ἀλλὰ καὶ τάδε τὴν
βουλὴν ἐρεῖ τις ἐγνωκέναι. σὺ δ' ἐπεψήφιζες καὶ
προυκάθησο τῆς βουλῆς, ᾧ μάλιστα πάντων ἥρμοζε
διὰ σαυτὸν ἀντειπεῖν· τὸ γὰρ ἀμνηστίαν δοῦναι τὴν
σωτηρίαν ἦν ἐκείνοις χαριζομένων μόνον, τὸ δὲ ἡγεμονίας αὖθις ψηφίζεσθαι καὶ γέρα ὑβριζόντων Καί-
60 σαρα καὶ τὴν σὴν γνώμην ἀκυρούντων. ἐπὶ τάδε με
δὴ τὸ πάθος ἐξήνεγκε παρὰ τὸ ἁρμόζον ἴσως ἐμοὶ τῆς
τε ἡλικίας καὶ τῆς πρὸς σὲ αἰδοῦς. εἴρηται δ' ὅμως
ὡς ἐς ἀκριβέστερον φίλον Καίσαρι καὶ πλείστης ὑπ'
ἐκείνου τιμῆς καὶ δυνάμεως ἠξιωμένον καὶ τάχα ἂν
αὐτῷ καὶ θετὸν γενόμενον, εἰ ᾔδει σε δεξόμενον Αἰ-
νεάδην ἀντὶ Ἡρακλείδου γενέσθαι· τοῦτο γὰρ αὐτὸν
<φασὶ>[12] ἐνδοιάσαι, πολὺν τῆς διαδοχῆς λόγον ποιού-
μενον.

---

[12] φασὶ add. Steph.; οἶδα Schweig.; οἶμαι Nauck

executed by decree, but you did nothing to stop the murderers escaping and, in some cases, taking up their commands, which they hold wrongfully after killing the man who assigned them. When the situation had only just 58 settled down, you and Dolabella, the consuls, proceeded, very properly, to take Syria and Macedonia off them for yourselves. I would have thanked you for this too, if you had not immediately voted them Cyrene and Crete, and thought it right to protect fugitives against me permanently with provincial commands. You do nothing about Decimus holding Cisalpine Gaul, although he, like the rest, was one of my father's killers. Someone will say that 59 the senate made these decisions too, but you put the vote and you presided over the senate, you who more than anyone had a personal interest in opposing the measures. To grant an amnesty to the murderers was merely a favor from those wanting to assure their safety, but to vote them provinces and rewards again was an act of people insulting Caesar and subverting your judgment. Grief has, to be 60 sure, carried me this far, improperly perhaps, for one of my age and for the respect I owe you. Nevertheless, what I have said has been spoken to someone very specially dear to Caesar, thought worthy by him of the greatest honor and power, who would perhaps have been adopted by him, if he knew that you would accept descent from Aeneas rather than Heracles:[10] for ⟨they say?⟩[11] he hesitated about this when he was giving careful attention to the matter of his succession.

[10] Julius Caesar's family traced their origins to Aeneas, Antony's to Heracles.   [11] Editors have made various suggestions to fill what appears to be a small lacuna in the text.

APPIAN

61   17. "Ἐς δὲ τὸ μέλλον, ὦ Ἀντώνιε, πρὸς θεῶν τε
φιλίων καὶ πρὸς αὐτοῦ σοι Καίσαρος, εἰ μέν τι καὶ
τῶν γεγονότων μεταθέσθαι θέλεις (δύνασαι γάρ, εἰ
θέλεις)· εἰ δὲ μή, τά γε λοιπὰ τοὺς φονέας ἀμυνομένῳ
μοι μετὰ τοῦ δήμου καὶ τῶνδε τῶν ἔτι μοι πατρικῶν
φίλων συνίστασθαι καὶ συνεργεῖν· εἰ δέ σε τῶν ἀνδρῶν τις ἢ τῆς βουλῆς αἰδὼς ἔχει, μὴ ἐπιβαρεῖν. καὶ
62   τάδε μὲν ἀμφὶ τούτων· οἶσθα δ', ὅπως ἔχει μοι καὶ τὰ
οἴκοι, δαπάνης τε ἐς τὴν διανομήν, ἣν ὁ πατὴρ ἐκέλευσε τῷ δήμῳ δοθῆναι, καὶ ἐπείξεως ἐς αὐτήν, ἵνα
μὴ βραδύνων ἀχάριστος εἶναι δοκοίην μηδ' ὅσοι
καταλεχθέντες εἰς τὰς ἀποικίας ἐπιμένουσι τῇ πόλει,
63   δι' ἐμὲ τρίβοιντο. ὅσα δὴ τῶν Καίσαρος εὐθέως ἐπὶ
τῷ φόνῳ πρὸς σὲ μετενήνεκται ὡς ἐπ' ἀσφαλὲς ἐξ
ἐπικινδύνου τότε οἰκίας, τὰ μὲν κειμήλια αὐτῶν καὶ
τὸν ἄλλον ἅπαντα κόσμον ἔχειν ἀξιῶ σε καὶ ὅσα ἂν
ἐθέλῃς ἄλλα παρ' ἡμῶν ἐπιλαβεῖν, ἐς δὲ τὴν διανο-
μὴν ἀποδοῦναί μοι τὸ χρυσίον τὸ ἐπίσημον, ὃ συν-
ηθροίκει μὲν ἐς τοὺς πολέμους ἐκεῖνος, οὓς ἐπενόει,
ἀρκέσει δ' ἐμοὶ νῦν ἐς τριάκοντα μυριάδας ἀνδρῶν
64   μεριζόμενον. τὰ δὲ λοιπὰ τῆς δαπάνης, εἰ μὲν θαρρή-
σαιμί σοι, παρὰ σοῦ ἂν ἴσως ἢ διὰ σοῦ δανεισαίμην
ἐκ τῶν δημοσίων χρημάτων, ἂν διδῷς· διαπεπράσεται
δὲ αὐτίκα καὶ ἡ οὐσία."

65   18. Τοιαῦτα τοῦ Καίσαρος εἰπόντος ὁ Ἀντώνιος
κατεπλάγη, τῆς τε παρρησίας καὶ τῆς εὐτολμίας
παρὰ δόξαν οἱ πολλῆς καὶ παρ' ἡλικίαν φανείσης·
χαλεψάμενος δὲ τοῖς τε λόγοις οὐχ ὅσον ἔδει τὸ πρέ-

32

17. "As for the future, Antony, I beg you, in the name 61
of the gods who protect friends, and in the name of Caesar
himself, please repeal even what has been enacted, for you
have the power to do so, if you want. If not, at least from
now on stand beside me and help me take vengeance on
the assassins, with the help of the people and of whatever
friends of my father I still have. But if respect for the killers or for the senate holds you back, do not be hard on us.
That is enough on this topic. You know about my private 62
affairs and the cost of making the distribution to the
people that my father ordered, and the urgency of doing
it, so that I avoid appearing ungrateful by delay, so that
those who have been assigned to colonies do not stay in
the city and waste their time on my account. Of Caesar's 63
property that was transferred immediately after the murder from what was at the time a dangerous house to the
safety of yours, I ask you to keep the heirlooms and all
other trappings, and whatever else you would like from
me. But please return to me for the distribution the coined
gold that Caesar had collected for the campaigns he was
planning. That will be enough for me now to share out
among three hundred thousand men. The rest of the cost 64
perhaps I might borrow from you, if I may be so bold, or
through you from the public treasury, if you will grant it.
And my estate will be sold immediately."

18. Antony was astonished at Octavian's speech, as its 65
unexpected frankness and audacity appeared to him excessive and inappropriate for a man of his age. He was
offended by the words because they lacked the respect

πον ἐς αὐτὸν ἐσχηκόσι καὶ μάλιστα τῶν χρημάτων
66 τῇ ἀπαιτήσει, αὐστηρότερον αὐτὸν ὧδε ἠμείψατο· Εἰ
μὲν ὁ Καῖσάρ σοι μετὰ κλήρου καὶ τῆς ἐπωνυμίας, ὦ
παῖ, καὶ τὴν ἡγεμονίαν κατέλιπεν, εἰκὸς σὲ τῶν κοι-
67 νῶν τοὺς λογισμοὺς αἰτεῖν κἀμὲ ὑπέχειν. εἰ δὲ οὐδενί
πω Ῥωμαῖοι τὴν ἡγεμονίαν ἔδοσαν ἐκ διαδοχῆς, οὐδὲ
τῶν βασιλέων, οὓς ἐκβαλόντες ἐπώμοσαν μηδ᾽ ἄλλων
ἔτι ἀνέξεσθαι, (ὃ καὶ τῷ πατρί σου μάλιστα οἱ φονεῖς
ἐπιλέγοντες φασὶν ἀνελεῖν αὐτὸν βασιλιζόμενον, οὐχ
ἡγούμενον ἔτι), ἐμοὶ μὲν οὐδ᾽ ἀποκρίσεως δεῖ πρὸς σὲ
περὶ τῶν κοινῶν, τῷ δ᾽ αὐτῷ λόγῳ καὶ σὲ κουφίζω, μὴ
χάριν ὀφείλειν ἡμῖν ἐπ᾽ αὐτοῖς. ἐπράσσετο γὰρ οὐ
σοῦ χάριν, ἀλλὰ τοῦ δήμου, πλὴν ἑνὸς τοῦ μεγίστου
68 δὴ μάλιστα πάντων ἔς τε Καίσαρα καὶ σὲ ἔργου. εἰ
γὰρ τοῦ κατ᾽ ἐμαυτὸν ἕνεκα ἀδεοῦς καὶ ἀνεπιφθόνου
περιεῖδον ἐγὼ τιμὰς ψηφιζομένας τοῖς φονεῦσιν ὡς
τυραννοκτόνοις, τύραννος ὁ Καῖσαρ ἐγίγνετο, ᾧ μήτε
δόξης μήτε τιμῆς τινος ἢ τῶν ἐγνωσμένων βεβαιώ-
σεως ἔτι μετῆν. οὐ διαθήκας εἶχεν ἄν, οὐ παῖδα, οὐκ
οὐσίαν, οὐκ αὐτὸ τὸ σῶμα ταφῆς ἀξιούμενον, οὐδὲ
ἰδιώτου· ἄταφα γὰρ οἱ νόμοι τὰ σώματα τῶν τυράν-
νων ὑπερορίζουσι καὶ τὴν μνήμην ἀτιμοῦσι καὶ δη-
μεύουσι τὴν περιουσίαν.
69   19. Ὧν ἐγὼ δεδιὼς ἕκαστον ὑπερηγωνιζόμην Καίσαρος, ἀθανάτου τε δόξης καὶ δημοσίας ταφῆς, οὐκ
ἀκινδύνως οὐδ᾽ ἀνεπιφθόνως ἐμαυτῷ, τυχεῖν, πρός τε
ἄνδρας ταχυεργεῖς καὶ φόνου πλήρεις καί, ὡς ἔμαθες,
ἤδη καὶ ἐπ᾽ ἐμὲ συνομωμοσμένους πρός τε τὴν βου-

due to him, and still more by the demand for money, and he replied in these somewhat severe terms: "My boy, if 66 Caesar had left you the political leadership, along with his estate and name, it would be proper for you to ask me for an explanation of my public decisions, and for me to provide it. But since the Roman people never allowed anyone 67 to succeed to political power, not even the kings, whom they expelled and swore never to put up with any others again—this is the very charge the assassins make against your father when they say they killed him for acting like a king, no longer as a leader—I am under no obligation to give you an answer on my public decisions. For the same reason I release you too from thanking me for my actions. They were done not for your sake, but for the people's, except for one thing of the greatest importance of all both to Caesar and to yourself. For if, to ensure my own secu- 68 rity and to shield myself from hostility, I had allowed honors to be voted to the murderers as tyrant slayers, Caesar would have become a tyrant, with no further share of glory or honor or confirmation of his decisions. He would have had no will, no son, no estate, his very body would have been denied a burial, even a private one. For the laws cast out unburied the bodies of tyrants, dishonor their memory, and confiscate their property.

19. "Fearing each of these consequences, I took up the 69 struggle for Caesar, not without danger and the risk of hostility to myself, to secure his immortal glory and a public funeral. I was contending against hotheaded, murderous men, who as you know had already conspired against

70 λὴν ἀχθομένην σου τῷ πατρὶ τῆς ἀρχῆς. ἀλλὰ καὶ
ταῦτα κινδυνεύειν καὶ παθεῖν ὁτιοῦν ᾑρούμην ἑκὼν
μᾶλλον ἢ ἄταφον καὶ ἄτιμον γιγνόμενον περιιδεῖν
Καίσαρα, ἄριστον ἀνδρῶν τῶν ἐφ' ἑαυτοῦ καὶ εὐτυχέ-
στατον ἐς τὰ πλεῖστα καὶ ἀξιοτιμότατον ἐκ πάντων
71 ἐμοὶ γενόμενον. τοῖς δ' αὐτοῖς μου τοῖσδε κινδύνοις
καὶ σὺ τὰ νῦν σοι παρόντα πάντα λαμπρὰ τῶν Καίσαρος ἔχεις, γένος, ὄνομα, ἀξίωμα, περιουσίαν. ὧν σε
δικαιότερον ἦν ἐμοὶ χάριν εἰδέναι μᾶλλον ἢ τὰ ἐκλειφθέντα εἰς τὴν τῆς βουλῆς παρηγορίαν ἢ ἐς ἀντίδοσιν τῶνδε, ὧν ἔχρῃζον, ἢ κατ' ἄλλας χρείας ἢ λογι-
72 σμοὺς ἐπιμέμφεσθαι πρεσβυτέρῳ νεώτερον ὄντα. καὶ
τάδε μὲν ἀρκέσει σοι περὶ τῶνδε εἰρῆσθαι· ἐνσημαίνῃ
δὲ καὶ τῆς ἡγεμονίας με ἐπιθυμεῖν, οὐκ ἐπιθυμοῦντα
μέν, οὐκ ἀπάξιον δὲ ἡγούμενον εἶναι, καὶ ἄχθεσθαι
μὴ τυχόντα τῶν διαθηκῶν τῶν Καίσαρος, ὁμολογῶν
μοι καὶ τὸ τῶν Ἡρακλειδῶν γένος ἀρκεῖν.

73 20. "Περὶ δὲ τῶν σῶν χρειῶν, ἐθέλοντα μέν σε ἐκ
τῶν δημοσίων δανείσασθαι ἡγούμην ἂν εἰρωνείαν λέγειν, εἰ μὴ πιθανὸν ἦν ἔτι ἀγνοεῖν σε κενὰ πρὸς τοῦ
πατρὸς ἀπολελεῖφθαι τὰ κοινὰ ταμιεῖα, τῶν προσ-
όδων, ἐξ οὗ παρῆλθεν ἐπὶ τὴν ἀρχήν, ἐς αὐτὸν ἀντὶ
τοῦ ταμιείου συμφερομένων καὶ εὑρεθησομένων αὐτίκα ἐν τῇ Καίσαρος περιουσίᾳ, ὅταν αὐτὰ ζητεῖν
74 ψηφισώμεθα. ἄδικον γὰρ οὐδὲν τοῦτο ἐς τὸν Καίσαρα
ἔσται, τεθνεῶτά τε ἤδη καὶ οὐκ ἂν εἰπόντα ἄδικον
εἶναι, εἰ καὶ ζῶν ᾐτεῖτο τοὺς λογισμούς, ἐπεὶ καὶ τῶν
ἰδιωτῶν πολλοῖς ἀμφισβητοῦσί σοι καθ' ἕνα τῆς οὐ-

me; and against the senate, who were annoyed with your
father's rule. But I willingly chose to risk these dangers   70
and to suffer anything rather than allow Caesar to remain
unburied and dishonored, the best man of his time, the
most fortunate in almost every respect, and the one I honored most of all. It is because of these very dangers I   71
risked that you yourself enjoy all the present distinctions
of Caesar, his family, his name, his rank, his wealth. It
would have been more just of you, a young man, to thank
me, your senior, for these things, rather than to reproach
me for concessions made to appease the senate, or pay
them back for the things I needed, or to meet other needs
or calculations. Enough on that subject. You also hint   72
that I aspire to political dominance—it is not the case,
although I am thought to be worthy of it—and that I am
disappointed not to be included in Caesar's will, although
you agree that the family of the Heraclidae too is good
enough for me.

20. "As to your financial needs, I might have thought   73
that your wish to borrow money from the public resources
was sarcasm, had it not been a credible proposition that
you were still ignorant of the fact that the public treasuries
were left empty by your father. From the time he took up
power, the state revenues went to him, not the treasury,
and they will be found among his resources as soon as we
vote an investigation into the matter. There is nothing   74
unfair to Caesar about this, now that he is dead, and even
when alive if he had been asked for the accounts he would
not have said it was unfair. As there are many private
persons in dispute with you about individual items in the

75 σίας οὐκ ἀδήριτον αὐτὴν ἔχων γνώσῃ. τῶν δὲ μετ-
ενεχθέντων πρός με χρημάτων οὔτε τὸ πλῆθός ἐστιν,
ὅσον εἰκάζεις, οὔτε τι νῦν ἔστι παρ᾽ ἐμοί, πάντα τῶν
ἐν ἀρχαῖς καὶ δυνάμει, πλὴν Δολοβέλλα καὶ τῶν
ἐμῶν ἀδελφῶν νειμαμένων μὲν εὐθὺς ὡς τυράννου, δι᾽
ἐμὲ δὲ μετατεθέντων ἐς χάριν τῶν ὑπὲρ Καίσαρος
ἐψηφισμένων, ἐπεὶ καὶ σὺ τὰ λοιπὰ φέρων οἴσεις ἀντὶ

76 τοῦ δήμου τοῖς δυσχεραίνουσιν, ἂν σωφρονῇς. οἱ μὲν
γὰρ ἐκπέμψουσιν, ἂν σωφρονῶσι,[13] τὸν δῆμον ἐπὶ τὰς
ἀποικίας· ὁ δὲ δῆμός ἐστιν, ὥσπερ καὶ σὺ τῶν Ἑλλη-
νικῶν ἀρτιδίδακτος ὢν ἔμαθες, ἀστάθμητον ὥσπερ ἐν
θαλάσσῃ κῦμα κινούμενον· ὁ μὲν ἦλθεν, ὁ δ᾽ ἀπῆλ-
θεν. ᾧ λόγῳ καὶ τῶν ἡμετέρων αἰεὶ τοὺς δημοκόπους
ὁ δῆμος ἐπὶ πλεῖστον ἐξάρας ἐς γόνυ ἔρριψε."

77 21. Τούτων τοῖς πολλοῖς δυσχεράνας ὁ Καῖσαρ ἐς
ὕβριν εἰρημένοις ἀπεχώρει, τὸν πατέρα ἀνακαλῶν θαμινὰ ἐξ ὀνόματος, καὶ τὴν οὐσίαν ἐς πρᾶσιν αὐτίκα
προυτίθει πᾶσαν, ὅση κατὰ τὸν κλῆρον ἐγίγνετο
αὐτοῦ, προτρέπων ἐπικουρεῖν οἱ τὸν δῆμον ἐκ τῆσδε

78 τῆς σπουδῆς· φανερᾶς δὲ τῆς Ἀντωνίου πρὸς αὐτὸν
ἔχθρας γενομένης καὶ τῆς βουλῆς ζήτησιν εὐθὺς εἶναι τῶν δημοσίων χρημάτων ψηφισαμένης, οἱ πολλοὶ
ἔδεισαν ἐπὶ τῷ νέῳ Καίσαρι τῆς πατρῴας ἐς τοὺς
στρατιώτας καὶ τὸν δῆμον εὐνοίας οὕνεκα καὶ τῆς νῦν
ἐπὶ τῇ χορηγίᾳ δημοκοπίας καὶ περιουσίας, ᾗ δὴ

13 συμφρονῶσι P; σωφρονῶσι L

38

estate, you may assume that you will not have undisputed possession of it. As for the money transferred to my house, 75 it was neither as much as you suppose, nor is any of it now at my disposal. For, apart from Dolabella and my brothers, those in office and with power divided it all up immediately, on the grounds that it was the property of a tyrant, although they were brought round by me to support what we had voted concerning Caesar. If you have any sense, when you get the rest of it, you will give it to those who are disaffected instead of to the people. And, if the disaf- 76 fected have any sense, they will send the people away to their colonies. The people, as you know from your recent Greek studies, are as unstable as the waves moving on the sea: one comes, another goes.[12] In the same way, among us too, the people are forever raising the demagogues to a height, and then casting them down on their knees."

21. Furious at the many insulting things said in this 77 speech, Octavian went away calling his father repeatedly by name. He immediately offered for sale all the property which had come to him by the inheritance, trying to encourage the people to support him by moving so quickly. With Antony's hostility toward him now made clear, and 78 after the senate had voted that an investigation of the public finances should take place immediately, most people began to be apprehensive about the young Caesar because of the kindness shown by his father to the soldiers and the people, because of what was now his own popular appeal based on the distribution of the money, and because of his wealth, which had come to him in such large

[12] This is based on, rather than a direct quote from, Demosthenes (*De falsa leg.* 136).

πάνυ αὐτῷ πολλὴ προσελθοῦσα οὐκ ἐδόκει τοῖς πλεί
οσιν αὐτὸν ἐν ἰδιώτου μέτρῳ καθέξειν, ἐπὶ δὲ Ἀντωνίῳ
μάλιστα, μὴ τὸν Καίσαρα, νέον ἄνδρα καὶ ἔνδοξον
καὶ πλούσιον, ἑταιρισάμενος ὑφ᾿ ἑαυτὸν εἶναι πρότε
79 ρος ἄψαιτο τῆς Καίσαρος δυναστείας. οἱ δὲ καὶ τοῖς
τότε γιγνομένοις ἐφήδοντο, ὡς καὶ τῶν ἀνδρῶν ἀλ
λήλοις ἐμποδὼν ἐσομένων καὶ τοῦ Καίσαρος πλούτου
τῇ ζητήσει τῶν χρημάτων αὐτίκα διαλυθησομένου
καὶ σφίσι τοῦ ταμιείου περιουσίας πλήρους ἐξ αὐτῆς
ἐσομένου· τὰ γὰρ πολλὰ τῶν κοινῶν εὑρήσειν παρὰ
Καίσαρι.

80   22. Πολλοί τε αὐτῶν ἐς δίκας τὸν Καίσαρα ὑπῆγον
περὶ χωρίων, ἕτερος ἑτέρῳ ἐπιλέγοντες ἄλλα τε ἕκα
στοι καὶ τὸ κοινὸν ἐπὶ τοῖς πλείστοις, ἐκ προγραφῆς[14]
εἶναι τῶν δημευθέντων ἢ φυγόντων ἢ ἀναιρεθέντων.
ἦγόν τε τὰς δίκας ἐπὶ τὸν Ἀντώνιον αὐτὸν ἢ τὸν ἕτε
81 ρον ὕπατον Δολοβέλλαν. εἰ δέ τις καὶ ἐφ᾿ ἑτέρας ἀρ
χῆς ἐδικάζετο, πανταχοῦ τὰ πολλὰ ὁμοίως ὁ Καῖσαρ
εἰς χάριν Ἀντωνίου ἡττᾶτο, τά τε ὠνήματα τῷ πατρὶ
ἐκ τοῦ δημοσίου γενόμενα ἐπιδεικνὺς καὶ τὸ τελευ
ταῖον ψήφισμα τὸ βεβαιοῦν τὰ Καίσαρι πεπραγμένα
82 πάντα. ὕβρεις τε πολλαὶ παρὰ τὰς δίκας ἦσαν αὐτῷ,
καὶ τὸ τῆς ζημίας προύκοπτεν ἐς ἄπειρον, ἔστε Πέ
διον καὶ Πινάριον (οὗτοι γὰρ τὴν ἐκ τῶν Καίσαρος
διαθηκῶν τοῦ κλήρου μοῖραν εἶχον) μέμψασθαι τῷ
Ἀντωνίῳ περί τε σφῶν αὐτῶν καὶ περὶ τοῦ Καίσαρος
ὡς ἄδικα πασχόντων παρὰ τὸ ψήφισμα τῆς βουλῆς.

quantities that most people thought he would not retain
the status of a private citizen. But they were particularly
afraid that Antony would befriend the young, famous, and
rich Octavian, make him his subordinate and be the first
to lay hands on Caesar's fiefdom. Others were delighted   79
with what was happening at the time, believing that the
two men would get in each other's way, and that Octavian's
wealth would immediately disappear with the investigation, as a result of which they would have a treasury full of
money. For they thought they would find most of the public funds in Caesar's estate.

22. Many of them brought lawsuits against Octavian   80
concerning landed property, each making different claims,
but most having this in common, that the land belonged
to those who, as a result of being proscribed, were victims
of confiscation, exile, or execution. These suits were
brought before Antony himself or the other consul, Dolabella. If any were heard before other magistrates, in the   81
large majority of cases, because there was a desire to
please Antony, Octavian lost these too, although he
pointed out that the purchases were made by his father
from public money, and that the last decree passed by the
senate had confirmed all of Caesar's acts. Great abuses of   82
justice were inflicted on him, and his losses were continuing endlessly, until Pedius and Pinarius, who had a share
of the inheritance under Caesar's will, complained to
Antony, both on their own behalf and Octavian's, that they
were being treated unjustly in violation of the senate's

---

14 ἐκ προγραφῆς codd.; πρὸ ἐγγραφῆς Goukowsky

83 ᾤοντό τε αὐτὸν τὰ ἐς ὕβριν ἐκλύειν δεῖν μόνον, τὰ
ἄλλα δὲ πάντα κυροῦν ὅσα τῷ Καίσαρι πέπρακται. ὁ
δὲ ὡμολόγει μὲν τὰ πρασσόμενα ἴσως ἐναντίον ἔχειν
τι τοῖς συνεψηφισμένοις, καὶ τὰ ἐψηφισμένα δ' ἔφη
84 τοῖς τότε δόξασιν ἐναντίως γεγράφθαι. μόνης γὰρ
τῆς ἀμνηστίας ἐπειγούσης, τὸ μηδὲν ἀνατρέπειν τῶν
προδιῳκημένων, οὐ τοῦδ' αὐτοῦ γε χάριν οὐδὲ ἐφ'
ἅπασιν ἁπλῶς μᾶλλον ἢ ἐς εὐπρέπειαν καὶ παρηγορίαν τοῦ δήμου θορυβουμένου τούτοις, ἐπιγραφῆ-
85 ναι. εἶναι δὲ δικαιότερον τῇ γνώμῃ τοῦ ψηφίσματος
μᾶλλον ἢ τῷ ῥήματι χρωμένους μὴ παρὰ τὸ εἰκὸς
ἀντιπράττειν ἀνδράσι τοσοῖσδε ἰδίων ἢ προγονικῶν
κτήσεων κατὰ στάσιν ἐκπεσοῦσιν ὑπὲρ νεανίσκου τοσόνδε πλοῦτον ἀλλότριόν τε καὶ οὐκ ἰδιωτικὸν παρ'
ἐλπίδα λαβόντος καὶ οὐκ ἐπιδεξίως, ἀλλ' ἐς θρασύτητα τῇ τύχῃ χρωμένου. σφῶν μέντοι φείσεσθαι τὸ
86 μέρος νειμαμένων πρὸς Καίσαρα. ὧδε μὲν ὁ Ἀντώνιος
τοῖς ἀμφὶ τὸν Πινάριον ἀπεκρίνατο. καὶ εὐθὺς ἐνέμο-
ντο, ἵνα μὴ καὶ τὸ μέρος ἐν ταῖς δίκαις προσαπόλοιτο,
οὐ σφῶν ἕνεκα αὐτῶν, ἀλλὰ καὶ τόδε τοῦ Καίσαρος·
ἔμελλον γὰρ αὐτῷ μετ' οὐ πολὺ πάντα χαριεῖσθαι.

87   23. Θέας δὲ πλησιαζούσης, ἣν ἔμελλεν ὑπὲρ Βρούτου στρατηγοῦντος ἐπιδώσειν Γάιος Ἀντώνιος ὁ ἀδελφὸς Ἀντωνίου, καὶ τἆλλα τοῦ Βρούτου τῆς στρατη-

---

13 Quintus Pedius was praetor in 48 and suffect consul with
Octavian in 43. He had been a legate of Caesar in Spain in 45,

decree.[13] They thought that he should annul only Caesar's 83
abuses of power, but ratify everything else he had done.
Antony admitted that present actions were perhaps a little
inconsistent with the joint resolutions, but said that even
the resolutions had been worded differently from what
had been decided at the time. For it was only because the 84
amnesty was urgently required that the words 'not to over-
turn anything arranged beforehand' were added, not for
their own sake or to have general application to everything, but to provide plausibility and appease the people,
who were riotously supporting the measure. It would be 85
fairer, he added, to observe the spirit rather than the letter
of the decree, and not offer inappropriate opposition to so
many men who had lost their own and their ancestral
property in the civil unrest, and to do so on behalf of a
young man who had unexpectedly received such a large
fortune that did not belong to him and was not private
wealth, and who was not using his good fortune intelli-
gently, but on the most irresponsible ventures. He said he
would treat them kindly once they had separated their
share from Octavian's. This was how Antony replied to 86
Pinarius and his associates. They immediately made the
division, to make sure they did not lose their share too in
the courts. They did not do this in their own interests, but
in Octavian's, for in a little while they would be giving him
a gift of the whole amount.

23. The games were now approaching, which Antony's 87
brother, Gaius Antonius, was going to give on behalf of
Brutus, the praetor, in whose absence he was also attend-

celebrating a triumph as proconsul. He and Lucius Pinarius were
cousins of Octavian.

43

γίας ἐπιτροπεύων ἀπόντος, παρασκευή τε ἦν ἐς αὐτὴν
δαψιλὴς καὶ ἐλπὶς ἐν τῇ θέᾳ τὸν δῆμον ἐπικλασθέντα
88 καλέσειν τοὺς ἀμφὶ τὸν Βροῦτον. ὁ δὲ Καῖσαρ ἀντι-
θεραπεύων τὸ πλῆθος, ὅσον ἀργύριον ἐκ τῆς πράσεως
ἐγίγνετο, αἰεὶ κατὰ μέρος τοῖς φυλάρχοις ἀνεδίδου
νέμειν τοῖς φθάνουσι λαβεῖν· καὶ ἐς τὰ πωλητήρια
περιὼν ἀποκηρύσσειν ἔλεγεν ὅσου δύναιντο πάντα
τοὺς πιπράσκοντας ὀλιγίστου, διά τε τὰς δίκας ἀμφί-
βολα ἢ ἐπίφοβα ἔτι ὄντα καὶ διὰ τὴν Καίσαρος
σπουδήν. ἅπερ αὐτῷ πάντα τὸν δῆμον εἰς εὔνοιαν
89 ἤγειρεν καὶ ἐς ἔλεον, ὡς ἀναξίῳ τοιάδε πάσχειν. ὡς
δ᾽ ἐπὶ τῇ κληρονομίᾳ καὶ τὴν ἴδιον αὐτοῦ περιουσίαν
ὅση τε παρὰ Ὀκταουίου τοῦ πατρὸς ἢ ἑτέρωθεν ἦν
αὐτῷ, καὶ τὰ τῆς μητρὸς πάντα καὶ τὰ Φιλίππου, καὶ
τὸ μέρος τοῦ κλήρου Πινάριον καὶ Πέδιον αἰτήσας,
προύθηκεν ἐς τὴν διανέμησιν πιπράσκεσθαι, ὡς τῆς
Καίσαρος περιουσίας οὐδ᾽ ἐς τοῦτο μόνον ἀρκούσης
διὰ τὰς ἐπηρείας, ὁ δῆμος οὐκέτι παρὰ τοῦ πρώτου
Καίσαρος, ἀλλὰ παρὰ τοῦδε αὐτοῦ τὴν ἐπίδοσιν λογιζόμενος εἶναι ἐκπαθῶς αὐτὸν ἠλέει καὶ ἐπήνουν ὧδε
πάσχοντα καὶ ὧδε φιλοτιμούμενον δηλοί τε ἦσαν οὐκ
ἐς πολὺ τὴν ἐς αὐτὸν Ἀντωνίου ὕβριν ὑπεροψόμενοι.
90 24. Διέδειξαν δὲ παρὰ Βροῦτου θέας, πολυτελεστά-
τας δὴ γενομένας· ἐμμίσθων γάρ τινων ἀνακραγόν-

---

14 The *Ludi Apollinares*, instituted during the Second Punic
War, and organized by the urban praetor, were celebrated between July 6 and 13.

ing to the other praetorian duties.[14] Extensive preparations were being made, and there was a hope that the people might lose their resolve in the spectacle and recall Brutus and his associates. Octavian, on the other hand, in 88
his counterattempt to win over the crowd, continued to distribute all the money he got from his sale to the head men of the tribes by turns, to be divided by them among the first comers. He also went around the auction rooms saying that his sales' agents would set the lowest possible price on everything, given both the uncertainty of title and fear caused by the lawsuits, and the fact that he was in a hurry. All of this won him the goodwill of the people and their pity for someone who did not deserve what was happening to him. To enable the distribution, he also offered 89
for sale, in addition to his inheritance from Caesar, his own property that came to him from his father, Octavius, and whatever he had from other sources, as well as everything belonging to his mother and Philippus, and Pedius' and Pinarius' share of the inheritance, which he asked them for. He maintained that because of the abusive way he was being treated, Caesar's estate was not even sufficient for this one purpose. No longer reckoning that the benefaction was coming from the first Caesar, but from the present one, the people began to pity him deeply and praise him both for his endurance and his ambition. It was evident that they would not ignore for long Antony's abusive behavior toward him.

24. They showed their feelings clearly during Brutus' 90
games, which were certainly very extravagant. For although some, who had been hired for the purpose, shouted

των κατακαλεῖν Βροῦτόν τε καὶ Κάσσιον, ἐπεὶ τὸ λοιπὸν αὐτοῖς θέατρον συνεδημαγωγεῖτο ἐς τὸν ἔλεον,
ἐσέδραμον ἀθρόοι καὶ τὰς θέας ἐπέσχον, μέχρι τὴν
91 ἀξίωσιν αὐτῶν σβέσαι. Βροῦτος δὲ καὶ Κάσσιος, ἐπεὶ
σφῶν τὰς ἐλπίδας τὰς ἐν ταῖς θέαις ὁ Καῖσαρ δι-
έχεεν, ἔγνωσαν εἰς Συρίαν καὶ Μακεδονίαν, ὡς πρὸ
Ἀντωνίου καὶ Δολοβέλλα σφίσιν ἐψηφισμένας, χωρεῖν καὶ βιάζεσθαι. καὶ τῶνδε φανερῶν γενομένων
ἠπείγετο καὶ Δολοβέλλας εἰς τὴν Συρίαν, καὶ πρὸ
Συρίας ἐς τὴν Ἀσίαν, ὡς χρηματιούμενος ἀπ᾽ αὐτῆς.
92 ὁ δ᾽ Ἀντώνιος ἡγούμενος ἐς τὰ μέλλοντά οἱ δεήσειν
δυνάμεως, τὴν ἐν Μακεδονίᾳ στρατιάν, ἀρετῇ τε οὖσαν ἀρίστην καὶ πλήθει μεγίστην—ἓξ γὰρ ἦν τέλη
(καὶ ὅσον ἄλλο πλῆθος αὐτοῖς τοξοτῶν καὶ ψιλῶν ἢ
γυμνητῶν συνεζεύγνυτο, ἵππος τε πολλὴ καὶ παρασκευὴ κατὰ λόγον ἐντελής) δοκοῦντα προσήκειν Δολοβέλλᾳ, Συρίαν καὶ τὰ ἐς Παρθυαίους ἐπιτετραμ-
μένῳ, διότι καὶ ὁ Καῖσαρ αὐτοῖς ἐς Παρθυαίους
ἔμελλε χρῆσθαι—πρὸς ἑαυτὸν ἐπενόει μετενεγκεῖν,
ὅτι καὶ μάλιστα ἦν ἀγχοῦ, ὡς τὸν Ἰόνιον περάσαντα
εὐθὺς ἐν τῇ Ἰταλίᾳ εἶναι.

93   25. Ἄφνω δὴ φήμη κατέσκηψε, Γέτας τὸν θάνατον
τὸν Καίσαρος πυθομένους Μακεδονίαν πορθεῖν ἐπι-
τρέχοντας, καὶ ὁ Ἀντώνιος τὴν βουλὴν ᾔτει τὸν στρατὸν ὡς Γέταις ἐπιθήσων δίκην· ἔς τε γὰρ Γέτας αὐτὸν
πρὸ Παρθυαίων Καίσαρι παρεσκευάσθαι καὶ τὰ Παρ-
94 θυαίων ἠρεμεῖν ἐν τῷ παρόντι. ἡ μὲν οὖν βουλὴ τὴν
φήμην ὑπενόει καὶ τοὺς ἐπισκεψομένους ἔπεμψεν· ὁ δὲ

that Brutus and Cassius should be recalled, and the rest
of the audience were won over by the populist rhetoric to
pity them, crowds ran in and stopped the games until the
demand petered out. With the hopes they placed in the 91
games frustrated by Octavian, Brutus and Cassius decided
to go and seize by force Syria and Macedonia, which, they
argued, had been voted to them before Dolabella and
Antony. When their intentions became clear, Dolabella
also hurried to Syria, by way of Asia first, in order to collect
money there. As for Antony, in the belief that he would 92
need an army for future purposes, he conceived the idea
of transferring to himself the army in Macedonia, which
was the best in terms of courage, and very large in terms
of the number of men, for it consisted of six legions, besides all the other archers and light-armed troops stationed with them, a large force of cavalry, and a full supply
of all the corresponding equipment. Although, because
Caesar had been about to use it against the Parthians, the
Macedonian army was apparently under the command of
Dolabella, who had been entrusted with Syria and Parthian affairs, Antony planned to transfer it to himself because it was very near, and, by crossing the Ionian gulf
would immediately be in Italy.

25. Suddenly a rumor flew around that the Getae, on 93
learning of Caesar's death, had made an incursion into
Macedonia and were pillaging it. Antony asked the senate
to give him the army in order to punish them, since it had
been formed for Caesar to use against the Getae before
the Parthians, and the Parthian front was quiet at the moment. The senate were suspicious of the rumor, and sent 94

Ἀντώνιος τὸν φόβον αὐτῶν καὶ τὴν ὑπόνοιαν ἐκλύων
ἐψηφίσατο μὴ ἐξεῖναί πω κατὰ μηδεμίαν αἰτίαν περὶ
δικτάτρος ἀρχῆς μήτε εἰπεῖν μήτ᾿ ἐπιψηφίζειν μήτε
λαβεῖν διδομένην, ἢ τὸν ἐκ τῶνδέ τινος ὑπεριδόντα
95 νηποινεὶ πρὸς τῶν ἐντυχόντων ἀναιρεῖσθαι. καὶ τῷδε
μάλιστα ἑλὼν τοὺς ἀκούοντας καὶ τοῖς ὑπὲρ Δολοβέλλα πράττουσι συνθέμενος ἓν τέλος δώσειν, ᾑρέθη
τῆς ἐν Μακεδονίᾳ δυνάμεως εἶναι στρατηγὸς αὐτοκράτωρ. καὶ ὁ μὲν ἔχων, ἃ ἐβούλετο, Γάιον τὸν ἀδελφὸν αὐτίκα σὺν ἐπείξει τὸ δόγμα φέροντα τῷ στρατῷ
96 διεπέμπετο· οἱ δὲ ἐπισκέπται τῆς φήμης ἐπανελθόντες
Γέτας ἔλεγον οὐκ ἰδεῖν ἐν Μακεδονίᾳ, προσέθεσαν δέ,
εἴτε ἀληθὲς εἴτε ὑπ᾿ Ἀντωνίου διδαχθέντες, ὅτι δέος
ἦν, μὴ τῆς στρατιᾶς ποι μετελθούσης οἱ Γέται τὴν
Μακεδονίαν ἐπιδράμοιεν.

97   26. Ὧδε μὲν εἶχε τὰ ἐν Ῥώμῃ, Κάσσιος δὲ καὶ
Βροῦτος χρήματα καὶ στρατιὰν συνέλεγον, καὶ Τρεβώνιος ὁ τῆς Ἀσίας ἡγούμενος τὰς πόλεις αὐτοῖς
ἐτείχιζε καὶ Δολοβέλλαν ἐλθόντα οὐκ ἐδέχετο οὔτε
Περγάμῳ οὔτε Σμύρνῃ, ἀλλὰ μόνην ἀγορὰν ἔξω τεί-
98 χους ὡς ὑπάτῳ προυτίθει. ἐπιχειροῦντος δ᾿ ἐκείνου
σὺν ὀργῇ τοῖς τείχεσι καὶ οὐδὲν ἀννύοντος, ὁ Τρεβώνιος αὐτὸν ἔφη δέξεσθαι Ἐφέσῳ καὶ ἐς τὴν Ἔφε-
σον εὐθὺς ἀπιόντι τοὺς ἐφεψομένους ἐκ διαστήματος
ἔπεμπεν, οἳ νυκτὸς ἐπιγενομένης ἀπιόντα τὸν Δολοβέλλαν ὁρῶντες καὶ οὐδὲν ἔτι ὑπονοοῦντες, ὀλίγους
σφῶν ὑπολιπόντες ἕπεσθαι αὐτῷ, ἐς τὴν Σμύρναν
99 ἐπανῆλθον. καὶ τοὺς ὀλίγους ὁ Δολοβέλλας ἐνεδρεύ-

a mission to investigate, but Antony allayed their fear and suspicion by passing a measure that it would be illegal for any reason whatever to make a proposal about the office of dictator, or to put it to the vote, or to accept if given it. Anybody who disregarded any of these provisions could be killed with impunity by anyone who encountered him. It was this in particular that won over his audience, and 95 having agreed with Dolabella's agents that he would give him one legion, Antony was chosen supreme commander of the forces in Macedonia. Having gotten what he wanted, he immediately sent his brother Gaius on an urgent mission to communicate the decree to the army. Those inves- 96 tigating the rumor now came back and reported that they had seen no Getae in Macedonia, but they added (either truthfully or because they were instructed to do so by Antony) that there was a fear, if the army was transferred elsewhere, that the Getae would invade Macedonia.

26. While this was the situation in Rome, Cassius and 97 Brutus were collecting money and troops. Trebonius, governor of Asia, was fortifying the towns for them, and refused to receive Dolabella in either Pergamum or Smyrna when he arrived. The one thing he did allow him, however, since he was a consul, was to buy supplies outside the walls. In his anger Dolabella attacked the walls, but with- 98 out effect, and Trebonius said that he would let him into Ephesus. He immediately left for Ephesus, and Trebonius sent troops to follow him at a distance. When night came on, these men saw Dolabella heading off, and still suspecting nothing, they left a small contingent to follow him, and returned to Smyrna. Dolabella, having laid an ambush for 99

σας τε καὶ περιλαβὼν ἔκτεινε καὶ ἦλθε τῆς αὐτῆς ἔτι
νυκτὸς ἐς Σμύρναν καὶ αὐτὴν ἀφύλακτον εὑρὼν εἷλε
100 διὰ κλιμάκων. Τρεβώνιος δὲ τοῖς συλλαμβάνουσιν
αὐτὸν ἔτι εὐναζόμενον ἡγεῖσθαι πρὸς Δολοβέλλαν
ἐκέλευεν· ἔπεσθαι γὰρ αὐτοῖς ἑκών. καί τις τῶν λοχαγῶν αὐτὸν ἐπισκώπτων ἠμείψατο· "Ἴθι σύ, δεῦρο τὴν
κεφαλὴν καταλιπών· ἡμῖν γὰρ οὐ σέ, ἀλλὰ τὴν κεφαλὴν ἄγειν προστέτακται." καὶ τόδε εἰπὼν εὐθὺς
101 ἀπέτεμε τὴν κεφαλήν. ἅμα δὲ ἡμέρᾳ Δολοβέλλας μὲν
αὐτὴν προσέταξεν ἐπὶ τοῦ στρατηγικοῦ βήματος,
ἔνθα ὁ Τρεβώνιος ἐχρημάτιζε, προτεθῆναι· ἡ στρατιὰ
δὲ σὺν ὀργῇ καὶ ὁ οἰκετικὸς ἄλλος ὅμιλος αὐτῆς, ἐπεὶ
τοῦ φόνου Καίσαρος ὁ Τρεβώνιος μετεσχήκει καὶ
κτεινομένου τὸν Ἀντώνιον ἐν ὁμιλίᾳ περὶ θύρας τοῦ
βουλευτηρίου περιεσπάκει, εἴς τε τὸ ἄλλο σῶμα αὐτοῦ ποικίλως ἐνύβριζον καὶ τὴν κεφαλὴν οἷα σφαῖραν
ἐν λιθοστρώτῳ πόλει διαβάλλοντες ἐς ἀλλήλους ἐπὶ
γέλωτι συνέχεάν τε καὶ συνέτριψαν. καὶ πρῶτος ὅδε
τῶν φονέων δίκην τήνδε ἐδεδώκει.

102   27. Ὁ δ᾽ Ἀντώνιος ἐς τὴν Ἰταλίαν τὸν στρατὸν ἐκ
τῆς Μακεδονίας διενεγκεῖν ἐπενόει, καὶ προφάσεως
ἄλλης ἐς τοῦτο ἀπορῶν ἠξίου τὴν βουλὴν ἀντὶ τῆς
Μακεδονίας ἐναλλάξαι οἱ τὴν ἐντὸς Ἄλπεων Κελτικήν, ἧς ἡγεῖτο Δέκμος Βροῦτος Ἀλβῖνος, εἰδὼς μέν,
ὅτι καὶ ὁ Καῖσαρ ἐκ τῆσδε τῆς Κελτικῆς ὁρμώμενος
ἐκράτησε Πομπηίου, ὡς δὲ τὸν στρατὸν δόξων οὐκ ἐς
103 τὴν Ἰταλίαν, ἀλλ᾽ ἐς τὴν Κελτικὴν μετακαλεῖν. ἡ δὲ
βουλὴ τήνδε τὴν Κελτικὴν ἀκρόπολιν ἐπὶ σφίσιν

this small contingent, captured and killed them, and went back to Smyrna the same night while it was still dark. Finding it unguarded, he captured it by scaling the wall with ladders. Trebonius, who was still in bed, told his captors 100 to take him to Dolabella, saying that he was willing to follow them. One of the centurions answered sardonically, "You go, but leave your head here, for we were ordered to bring your head, not you." With these words he immediately cut off his head. Early in the morning Dolabella ordered it to be displayed on the governor's tribunal, where Trebonius used to transact public business. Since Trebonius had participated in the murder of Caesar by detaining Antony in conversation at the door of the senate house while the murder was taking place, the soldiers, along with the crowd of their camp followers angrily visited various abuses on the rest of his body, and on his head, which they threw to each other like a ball across the town's pavement, laughing, until they had smashed it and broken it into pieces. In this way Trebonius was the first of the assassins to meet his punishment.

27. Antony was developing plans to transport his army 102 from Macedonia to Italy, and being short of any other excuse for this step, he asked the senate to let him exchange the province of Macedonia for that of Cisalpine Gaul, of which Decimus Brutus Albinus was the governor. While he was aware that Caesar too had set out from Cisalpine Gaul when he defeated Pompey, he wanted to give the impression that he was recalling the army not to Italy, but to Gaul. The senate, who regarded this Celtic bastion 103

ἡγουμένη ἐδυσχέραινέ τε καὶ τῆς ἐνέδρας τότε πρῶτον
ᾔσθοντο καὶ τὴν Μακεδονίαν δόντες αὐτῷ μετενόουν.
ἰδίᾳ τε αὐτῶν οἱ δυνατοὶ ἐπέστελλον τῷ Δέκμῳ τῆς
ἀρχῆς ἐγκρατῶς ἔχεσθαι καὶ στρατὸν ἄλλον καὶ
χρήματα ἀγείρειν, εἰ πρὸς Ἀντωνίου βιάζοιτο· οὕτως
104 ἐδεδοίκεσάν τε καὶ ἐν ὀργῇ τὸν Ἀντώνιον εἶχον. ὁ δὲ
ἀντὶ μὲν τῆς βουλῆς ἐπενόει τὸν δῆμον αἰτῆσαι νόμῳ
τὴν Κελτικήν, ᾧ τρόπῳ καὶ ὁ Καῖσαρ αὐτὴν πρότερον
εἰλήφει καὶ Συρίαν Δολοβέλλας ὑπογύως, ἐς δὲ φόβον τῆς βουλῆς τὴν στρατιὰν ἐς τὸ Βρεντέσιον ἐκέλευε Γαΐῳ τὸν Ἰόνιον περᾶν αὐτίκα.

105 28. Καὶ ὁ μὲν ἔμελλε ποιήσειν, ὡς προσετέτακτο·
θέαι δ' ἦσαν, ἃς Κριτώνιος ἀγορανομῶν ἔμελλε τελέ-
σειν· καὶ ὁ Καῖσαρ ἐς τὰς θέας τῷ πατρὶ τόν τε χρύσεον θρόνον καὶ στέφανον παρεσκεύαζεν, ἅπερ αὐτῷ
106 κατὰ πάσας θέας ἐψηφίσαντο προτίθεσθαι. τοῦ Κρι-
τωνίου δὲ εἰπόντος οὐκ ἀνέξεσθαι τιμωμένου Καίσαρος ἐν ταῖς αὐτοῦ δαπάναις, ὁ Καῖσαρ αὐτὸν ἐς τὸν
Ἀντώνιον ἦγεν ὡς ὕπατον. Ἀντωνίου δὲ εἰπόντος ἐς
τὴν βουλὴν ἐπανοίσειν, χαλεπήνας ὁ Καῖσαρ, "Ἀνά-
φερε," εἶπεν, "Ἐγὼ δὲ τὸν θρόνον, ἕως ἂν ᾖ τὸ δόγμα,
107 προθήσω." καὶ ὁ Ἀντώνιος χαλεπήνας ἐκώλυσεν.
ἐκώλυσε δὲ καὶ ἐν ταῖς ἑξῆς θέαις ἔτι παραλογώτερον,
ἃς αὐτὸς ὁ Καῖσαρ ἐτέλει, ἀνακειμένας ἐκ τοῦ πατρὸς
Ἀφροδίτῃ Γενετείρᾳ, ὅτε περ αὐτῇ καὶ τὸν νεὼν ὁ πα-

---

15 Critonius, aedile in 44, is known only for his involvement

as falling under their own authority, were annoyed, and realizing now for the first time that they had been tricked, regretted giving Macedonia to Antony. The leading senators sent word privately to Decimus telling him to keep a firm hold on his province, and to raise another army and money in case he was faced with violence from Antony. This is a measure of how much the senate had come to fear Antony and how angry they were at him. But Antony was intending to ask the people, not the senate, to pass a law giving him Gaul, in the same way that Caesar also got it previously, and Dolabella had recently obtained Syria. In order to frighten the senate he instructed his brother, Gaius, to bring his army across the Ionian gulf immediately to Brundisium.

28. Gaius set about carrying out his orders. It was now the time of the festival that Critonius, as aedile, was due to produce.[15] Octavian was preparing his father's gold throne and crown for the occasion, as it had been decreed that these should be publicly displayed for him at all festivals. When Critonius said that he would not tolerate carrying the costs for Caesar to be honored, Octavian brought him before Antony as consul. Antony said he would refer the matter to the senate, but Octavian was annoyed and said, "Refer it, but I will display the throne as long as the decree is in force." At this Antony became angry and prohibited it, and, even more unreasonably, prohibited it at the next festival produced by Octavian himself, which had been instituted by his father in honor of Venus Genetrix when he also dedicated a temple to her in his forum, along

104

105

106

107

in this story, but it is not clear which games Appian means—perhaps the *Ludi Florales* held at the end of April.

108 τὴρ τὸν ἐν ἀγορᾷ ἅμα αὐτῇ ἀγορᾷ ἀνετίθει. τότε δὴ
καὶ μάλιστα μῖσος ἤδη σαφὲς ἐκ πάντων ἐς τὸν
Ἀντώνιον ἐγίγνετο, ὡς οὐκ ἐς τὸν νῦν Καίσαρα φιλο-
νικοῦντα μᾶλλον ἢ ἐς τὸν πρότερον ὑβρίζοντα ἀχαρί-
109 στως. αὐτός τε ὁ Καῖσαρ μετὰ πλήθους οἷα φρουρᾶς
τὸν δῆμον καὶ τοὺς εὖ τι παθόντας ὑπὸ τοῦ πατρὸς
καὶ τοὺς ἐκείνῳ στρατευσαμένους περιθέων ἐπιφθόνως
ἱκέτευεν οὗ μὲν αὐτοῦ τοιάδε καὶ τοσάδε πάσχοντος
ὑπερορᾶν καὶ ἀμελεῖν ἑκόντος, Καίσαρι δὲ τῷ σφῶν
αὐτοκράτορι καὶ εὐεργέτῃ ἀμύνειν, ἀτιμουμένῳ πρὸς
Ἀντωνίου· ἀμυνεῖν δὲ καὶ σφίσιν αὐτοῖς, οὐδὲν ἕξουσι
βέβαιον ὧν εἰλήφασι παρὰ Καίσαρος, εἰ μηδὲ αὐτῷ
110 Καίσαρι μενεῖ τὰ ἐψηφισμένα βέβαια. Ἀντωνίου τε
πανταχοῦ τῆς πόλεως ἐς τὰ ὑψηλὰ ἀναπηδῶν κατε-
βόα· "Καίσαρι μὲν δι' ἐμὲ μήτε ὀργίζεσθαι μήτε ἐνυ-
βρίζειν, εὐεργέτῃ σοῦ μάλιστα, ὦ Ἀντώνιε, ἐς τὰ
μάλιστα γεγενημένῳ· ἐμοὶ δὲ τῶν μὲν ὕβρεων, ἐς
ὅσον θέλεις, ἐμφορεῖσθαι, τὴν δὲ τῆς οὐσίας ἁρπαγὴν ἐπισχεῖν, μέχρι τοὺς πολίτας κομίσασθαι τὴν
διανέμησιν καὶ τὰ λοιπὰ πάντα ἔχειν· ἀρκέσειν γὰρ
ἐμοὶ πενομένῳ τήν τε τοῦ πατρὸς δόξαν, ἂν διαμένῃ,
καὶ τὴν τοῦ δήμου διανέμησιν, ἐὰν ἐάσῃς δοθῆναι."
111   29. Ἐφ' οἷς ἤδη παρὰ πάντων συνεχεῖς ἐγίγνοντο
καὶ φανεραὶ κατὰ τοῦ Ἀντωνίου βοαί. ἀπειλησαμένου
δὲ αὐτοῦ τῷ Καίσαρι πικρότερον καὶ τῆς ἀπειλῆς ἐξ-

with the forum itself.[16] It was at this moment particularly   108
that a general antipathy toward Antony was now becoming
clear, since it was thought that he was not so much engaging in rivalry with the present Caesar as boorishly insulting the former one. Octavian himself, accompanied by a   109
crowd that was like a bodyguard, moved about among the
people and those who had received some favor from his
father, or had served under him in the army, maliciously
begging them to overlook the many and substantial out-
rages he had suffered and not to worry about him, since
he accepted them, but to defend Caesar, their commander
and benefactor, against the affront of Antony; and they
would be defending themselves too, because they would
never be secure in what they had received from Caesar, if
the decrees passed even in honor of Caesar himself did
not remain in force. Everywhere in the city he would   110
clamber up to a high point and loudly denounce Antony,
saying, "Don't be angry with Caesar, Antony, because of
me. And don't insult the man who became your benefactor
in particular, indeed your greatest benefactor. As for me,
heap up your insults on me as much as you like, but desist
from preying on his estate until the citizens have had their
designated share; then you can take all the rest. Poor
though I may be, I will be satisfied with my father's reputation, if it lasts, and with his bequest to the people, if you
allow it to be paid."

29. As a result of this there was now a persistent and   111
open outcry from all quarters against Antony. He in turn
issued more bitter threats against Octavian, and when

---

[16] The Forum Iulium was dedicated in 46. The *Ludi Victoriae
Caesaris* were held at the end of July.

ἐνεχθείσης ἐς τὸ φανερόν, ἔτι μᾶλλον ἅπαντες ὥρ-
112 μηντο· καὶ οἱ τῆς φρουρᾶς Ἀντωνίου ταξίαρχοι,
ἐστρατευμένοι τε Καίσαρι τῷ προτέρῳ καὶ ἐς τὰ μέγιστα ὑπ' Ἀντωνίου τότε προτιμώμενοι, τὴν ὕβριν
αὐτὸν ἐπισχεῖν ἠξίουν καὶ διὰ σφᾶς καὶ δι' ἑαυτόν,
ὑπὸ Καίσαρι στρατευσάμενον καὶ τῶνδε τῶν οἱ παρ-
113 όντων ἀγαθῶν παρ' ἐκείνου τυχόντα. συγγιγνώσκων
οὖν ὁ Ἀντώνιος ἀληθέσιν οὖσιν τούτοις καὶ τοὺς προ-
φέροντας αὐτὰ αἰδούμενος, ἤδη δέ τι καὶ τοῦ Καίσαρος αὐτοῦ διὰ τὸν δῆμον ἐς τὴν ἀλλαγὴν τῆς Κελτικῆς δεόμενος, ὡμολόγει τοῖς λεγομένοις καὶ ἐπώμνυεν
αὐτὰ καὶ οἷ πάνυ ἀβούλητα εἶναι, τῆς δὲ γνώμης τοῦ
νεανίσκου ἕνεκεν μετατίθεσθαι, ἐπηρμένου τε ἐπαχθῶς ἔτι τηλικοῦδε ὄντος καὶ οὐδὲν ἔχοντος αἰδέσιμον ἢ τίμιον ἐς πρεσβυτέρους τε καὶ ἐς ἄρχοντας·
114 ἅπερ αὐτοῦ μὲν χάριν τοῦ νεανίσκου χρῄζειν ἔτι νου-
θεσίας, σφῶν δὲ τῶν ταῦτα ἀξιούντων ἕνεκα αὐτὸς
καθέξειν τῆς ὀργῆς καὶ ἐς τὴν προτέραν ἑαυτοῦ φύσιν
τε καὶ γνώμην ἐπανήξειν, ἢν κἀκεῖνος ἀπέχηται τῆς
ἀμετρίας.

115   30. Ταῦτα οἱ ταξίαρχοι ἀσπασάμενοι συνῆγον ἀμφοτέρους. οἱ δὲ ἐπεμέμφοντο ἀλλήλοις καὶ συνέβαι-
νον ἐς φιλίαν. ὅ τε νόμος ὁ περὶ τῆς Κελτικῆς πρου-
γράφετο αὐτίκα, ὀρρωδούσης πάνυ τῆς βουλῆς καὶ
ἐπινοούσης, εἰ μὲν ὁ Ἀντώνιος αὐτὸν προβουλεύοι,
κωλύειν προβουλευόμενον, εἰ δὲ ἀπροβούλευτον ἐς
τὸν δῆμον ἐσφέροι, τοὺς δημάρχους ἐς κώλυσιν ἐπι-
πέμπειν. ἦσαν δ' οἳ καὶ τὸ ἔθνος ὅλως ἐλευθεροῦν

such threats were made public, everyone responded even more aggressively against him. Even the officers of Antony's guard, who had served with the elder Caesar, and who were at the time held in the highest honor by Antony, asked him to restrain his insolence, both on their account and on his own, as he had served under Caesar and it was due to Caesar that he had met with his present good fortunes. Antony recognized the truth of these words and, out of respect for the men who spoke them, and because he now needed help from Octavian himself with the people to exchange his province for Gaul, agreed with what was being said. He swore that his actions were not what he had planned at all, but that he had changed his mind because the youngster was offensively overbearing for one who was still so young, and who had no respect or regard for his elders and for the magistrates. He maintained that for his own good the young man still needed a reprimand for this behavior, but because his officers made the request themselves, he said he would restrain his anger and revert to his previous disposition and policy, if Octavian would also refrain from his immoderate behavior.

30. The officers welcomed this reply and brought the two men together, who after some mutual recriminations agreed to form a friendship. The law concerning the province of Gaul was promulgated at once, to the utter dismay of the senators. They intended to block it in the senate, if Antony introduced it in the senate first, and, if he brought it to the people without consulting the senate first, to send in the tribunes to veto it. There were some who even recommended that the province be made free of Roman

ἡγεμονίας ἠξίουν· οὕτως ἐδεδοίκεσαν ἀγχοῦ τὴν Κελ-
116 τικὴν οὖσαν. ὁ δὲ Ἀντώνιος αὐτοῖς ἀντενεκάλει, εἰ
Δέκμῳ μὲν αὐτὴν πιστεύουσιν, ὅτι Καίσαρα ἀπέκτει-
νεν, αὐτῷ δ᾽ ἀπιστοῦσιν, ὅτι οὐκ ἀπέκτεινε τὸν κατα-
στρεψάμενον αὐτὴν καὶ κλίναντα ἐς γόνυ, ἀπορρί-
πτων ἤδη ταῦτα φανερῶς ἐς ἅπαντας ὡς ἐφηδομένους
117 τοῖς γεγονόσιν. ἐλθούσης δὲ τῆς κυρίας ἡμέρας ἡ μὲν
βουλὴ τὴν λοχῖτιν[15] ἐνόμιζεν ἐκκλησίαν συλλεγήσε-
σθαι, οἱ δὲ νυκτὸς ἔτι τὴν ἀγορὰν περισχοινισάμενοι
τὴν φυλέτιν[16] ἐκάλουν, ἀπὸ συνθήματος ἐληλυθυῖαν.
118 καὶ ὁ δημότης λεώς, ἀχθόμενος τῷ Ἀντωνίῳ, συνέπρασσεν ὅμως διὰ τὸν Καίσαρα ἐφεστῶτα τοῖς περι-
σχοινίσμασι καὶ δεόμενον. ἐδεῖτο δὲ μάλιστα μέν, ἵνα
μὴ Δέκμος ἄρχοι χώρας τε ἐπικαίρου καὶ στρατιᾶς
ἀνδροφόνος ὢν τοῦ πατρός, ἐπὶ δὲ τούτῳ καὶ ἐς χάριν
Ἀντωνίου συνηλλαγμένον. προσεδόκα δὲ ἄρα τι καὶ
119 αὐτὸς ἀντιλήψεσθαι παρὰ Ἀντωνίου. διαφθαρέντων
δὲ χρήμασι τῶν δημάρχων ὑπ᾽ Ἀντωνίου καὶ κατα-
σιωπώντων ὁ νόμος ἐκυροῦτο, καὶ ὁ στρατὸς Ἀντωνίῳ
μετ᾽ αἰτίας εὐπρεποῦς ἤδη τὸν Ἰόνιον ἐπέρα.

120   31. Τῶν δὲ δημάρχων τινὸς ἀποθανόντος, ἐς τὴν
ἀντ᾽ αὐτοῦ χειροτονίαν ὁ Καῖσαρ συνέπρασσεν Φλα-

---

[15] φυλέτιν codd.; λοχῖτιν Schweig.
[16] λοχῖτιν codd.; φυλέτιν Schweig.

[17] The reading of all the manuscripts is that Antony summoned the Centuriate Assembly, not the Tribal Assembly,

control altogether, so greatly had they come to fear the
proximity of Gaul. But Antony leveled a countercharge   116
against them, saying that they trusted Decimus with the
province because he had killed Caesar, and that they distrusted himself because he had not killed the man who had
subdued Gaul and brought it to its knees. These claims he
now hurled openly against everyone, accusing them all of
being pleased at what had happened. When the day for   117
the voting arrived the senate expected that the Centuriate
Assembly would be convened, but while it was still night
Antony's men roped off the Forum and summoned the
Tribal Assembly, who had gathered by prearranged plan.[17]
Although the common people were annoyed at Antony,   118
they nevertheless cooperated with him because Octavian
stood by the ropes and asked them to do so. He asked this
particularly to prevent Decimus, one of his father's murderers, from having command of an important territory
and army and, in addition, to oblige Antony, with whom
he was reconciled. To be sure, he also expected to get
something from Antony in return. As the tribunes had   119
been bribed by Antony and remained silent, the law was
passed and now that Antony had a plausible reason, his
army began to cross the Ionian gulf.

31. On the death of one of the tribunes of the people,   120
Octavian supported Flaminius for election as his replace-

whereas before (above, 27.104) Appian explicitly says that Antony
intended to ask the people for this law (i.e., the Tribal Assembly).
Editors since Schweighäuser have accordingly usually transposed
the two. A problem remains, in that the Centuriate Assembly met
in the Campus Martius, not the Forum.

μινίῳ· καὶ ὁ δῆμος οἰόμενος αὐτὸν ἐπιθυμοῦντα τῆς
ἀρχῆς διὰ τὸ νεώτερον τῆς ἡλικίας οὐ παραγγέλλειν,
ἐπενόουν ἐν ταῖς χειροτονίαις δήμαρχον ἀποφῆναι
121 τὸν Καίσαρα. ἡ δὲ βουλὴ τῆς αὐξήσεως ἐφθόνει καὶ
ἐδεδοίκει, μὴ δημαρχῶν τοὺς φονέας τοῦ πατρὸς ἐπὶ
τὸν δῆμον ἐς δίκην ἀπαγάγοι· Ἀντώνιός τε τῆς ἄρτι
συγκειμένης πρὸς τὸν Καίσαρα φιλίας ὑπεριδών, εἴτε
ἐς χάριν τῆς βουλῆς ἢ παρηγορίαν, ἀχθομένης τῷ
περὶ τῆς Κελτικῆς νόμῳ, εἴτε ἀπ᾽ οἰκείας γνώμης,
προύγραφεν ὡς ὕπατος μηδενὶ Καίσαρα ἐγχειρεῖν
παρανόμως, ἢ χρήσεσθαι κατ᾽ αὐτοῦ παντὶ μέτρῳ τῆς
122 ἐξουσίας. ἀχαρίστου δ᾽ ἐς τὸν Καίσαρα καὶ ὑβριστι-
κῆς ἅμα ἐς αὐτὸν καὶ τὸν δῆμον τῆς προγραφῆς γενομένης, ὁ μὲν δῆμος διώργιστο καὶ φιλονικήσειν
ἔμελλον ἐν ταῖς χειροτονίαις, ὥστε δεῖσαι τὸν Ἀντώνιον καὶ ἀνελεῖν τὴν χειροτονίαν, τοῖς ὑπολοίποις τῶν
123 δημάρχων ἀρκούμενον· ὁ δὲ Καῖσαρ, ὡς σαφῶς ἐπι-
βουλευόμενος ἤδη, πολλοὺς περιέπεμπεν ἔς τε τὰς
τοῦ πατρὸς ἀποικίδας πόλεις ἐξαγγέλλειν, ἃ πάσχοι,
καὶ τὴν ἑκάστων γνώμην καταμανθάνειν· ἔπεμπε δὲ
καὶ ἐς τὰ Ἀντωνίου στρατόπεδα ἐπιμίγνυσθαί τινας
ἀγορὰν φέροντας καὶ ἐντυγχάνειν τοῖς θαρροῦσι μάλιστα καὶ ἐς τὸ πλῆθος διαρριπτεῖν ἀφανῶς βιβλία.
124 32. Καὶ ὁ μὲν ἀμφὶ ταῦτα ἦν· οἱ ταξίαρχοι δὲ αὖθις
παρὰ Ἀντωνίου καιρὸν αἰτήσαντες ἔλεγον· "Ἡμεῖς, ὦ
Ἀντώνιε, καὶ ὅσοι ἄλλοι μετὰ σοῦ Καίσαρι στρατευ-
σάμενοι τήν τε ἡγεμονίαν αὐτῷ συνεστησάμεθα καὶ
ἐς τὰ καθ᾽ ἡμέραν αὐτῆς ὑπηρέται γιγνόμενοι διετε-

ment. The people, believing that Octavian wanted the office himself, but was not announcing his candidature because he was under age, formed a plan to vote him in as tribune at the election. The senate begrudged him this 121 promotion, and were afraid that if he were tribune he would bring his father's murderers to justice before the people. Antony, ignoring his recently agreed friendship pact with Octavian, either to oblige the senate, or to conciliate them, annoyed as they were at the law about the province of Gaul, or for his own reasons, issued an edict in his capacity as consul to the effect that Octavian should not attempt anything contrary to law; and that if he did, he would use the full measure of his authority against him. As the edict showed a lack of gratitude to Octavian, and 122 was insulting both to him and to the people, the latter became extremely angry and intended to oppose Antony vigorously in the election, with the result that he became anxious and canceled the vote, claiming that the remaining tribunes were sufficient. On the grounds that there 123 was now open conspiracy against him, Octavian sent numerous agents to his father's colonies to tell them how badly he had been treated and to find out what the feelings were in each of them. He also sent some men carrying provisions into Antony's camp to mingle with the soldiers, to establish relations with the most intrepid of them, and secretly distribute pamphlets among the ordinary soldiers.

32. This is what Octavian was doing. As for the military 124 tribunes, once again they asked for a meeting with Antony, and spoke as follows: "Antony, we and the others who served with you under Caesar together established his authority and continued to attend to its daily needs. We are

λοῦμεν, ἔχθει μὲν ἴσῳ καὶ ἐπιβουλῇ τοὺς φονέας
αὐτοῦ γιγνώσκομεν εἰς ἡμᾶς χρωμένους καὶ τὴν
βουλὴν ἐκείνοις ἐπιρρέπουσαν, τοῦ δήμου δ' ἐξελά-
σαντος αὐτοὺς ἀνεθαρρήσαμεν, οὐ πάντῃ τὰ Καίσαρος ὁρῶντες ἄφιλα οὐδὲ ἀμνήμονα οὐδὲ ἀχάριστα.
125 τὴν δ' ἐς τὸ μέλλον ἀσφάλειαν εἴχομεν ἐν σοί, φίλῳ
τε Καίσαρος ὄντι καὶ ἡγεμονικωτάτῳ μετ' ἐκεῖνον ἐκ
πάντων καὶ ἄρχοντι νῦν ἡμῶν καὶ ἐς τὰ μάλιστα ἐπι-
126 τηδείῳ. ἀναφυομένων δὲ τῶν ἐχθρῶν καὶ θρασέως ἔς
τε Συρίαν καὶ Μακεδονίαν βιαζομένων καὶ χρήματα
καὶ στρατιὰν ἐφ' ἡμᾶς συνιστάντων, καὶ τῆς βουλῆς
σοι Δέκμον ἐπαλειφούσης, καὶ σοῦ τὰς φροντίδας ἐς
τὴν Καίσαρος τοῦ νέου διαφορὰν δαπανῶντος, δέδι-
μεν εἰκότως, μὴ ἐς τὸν μέλλοντα καὶ ὅσον οὔπω παρόντα πόλεμον ἡ στάσις ὑμῶν τῷ πολέμῳ συνεπιθῆται
καὶ διαπραχθῇ τοῖς ἐχθροῖς καθ' ἡμῶν, ἃ βούλονται.
127 ὧν ἐνθυμηθέντα σε ἀξιοῦμεν, ὁσίας τε χάριν ἐς τὸν
Καίσαρα καὶ φειδοῦς ὑπὲρ ἡμῶν οὐδὲν ἐπιμέμπτων
σοι γενομένων καὶ πρὸ ἡμῶν αὐτοῦ σοῦ τῶν συμφερόντων οὕνεκα, ἕως ἔτι δύνασαι, Καίσαρι μέν, ὅπερ
ἀρκέσει, μόνον συνεπαμῦναι τοὺς φονέας τιμωρουμένῳ, σὲ δὲ αὐτίκα δυναστεύειν, ἐν ἀμερίμνῳ γενό-
μενόν τε καὶ ἡμᾶς γενέσθαι παρασκευάσαντα τοὺς
ὑπέρ τε σφῶν αὐτῶν καὶ ὑπὲρ σοῦ δεδιότας."
128   33. Τοσαῦτα τοὺς ταξιάρχους εἰπόντας ὁ Ἀντώνιος
ὧδε ἠμείψατο· "Ὅση μὲν εὐνοίᾳ καὶ σπουδῇ πρὸς
Καίσαρα περιόντα ἐχρώμην, φιλοκινδυνότατος ἐκ
πάντων ἐς τὰς ἐκείνου χρείας γενόμενος, ἴστε σαφῶς,

aware that his murderers hate and conspire against us in
equal measure, and that the senate are tending to favor
them. But when the people drove the assassins out we took
fresh courage, seeing that Caesar's cause was not altogether without friends, forgotten or unappreciated. We   125
placed our future security in your hands, as you are the
friend of Caesar, and after him the most experienced commander of all, and our current leader, and most suitable
in every way. Our enemies, however, are recovering, au-   126
daciously forcing their way into Syria and Macedonia, and
raising money and troops against us, while the senate are
setting Decimus Brutus on you. Yet you are wasting your
concerns on your disagreement with the young Caesar,
and we are quite reasonably afraid that your feud will be
an additional burden in the coming war that is all but upon
us, and that our enemies will achieve their wishes against
us. We ask you to keep all this in mind, both for the sake   127
of your piety toward Caesar, and out of consideration for
us, who in no way find fault with you, and indeed for your
own interests even more than ours: we ask you, while you
still can, simply to cooperate sufficiently with Octavian to
enable him to take vengeance on the murderers, and to
exercise dynastic power immediately yourself, thus easing
your worries and providing us with the means to ease ours,
for we fear both for ourselves and for you."

33. To this speech of the tribunes Antony made the   128
following reply: "Fellow campaigners, fellow participants
in events, you are well aware what goodwill and enthusiasm I had for Caesar when he was alive, I who was most

συστρατευσάμενοί τε καὶ τοῖς γιγνομένοις παρατυχόν-
τες· ὅση δ' αὖ κἀκεῖνος εἰς ἐμὲ χάριτι καὶ προτιμήσει
129 χρώμενος διετέλει, οὐ μαρτυρεῖν ἐμὲ δίκαιον. ἄμφω δὲ
ταῦτα καὶ οἱ φονεῖς εἰδότες συνετίθεντο κἀμὲ Καίσαρι
συνανελεῖν, ὡς ἐμοῦ περιόντος οὐ καθέξοντες ὧν ἐπενόουν. καὶ ὅστις αὐτοὺς μετέπεισε τῆς γνώμης, οὐκ
εὐνοίᾳ τῆς ἐμῆς σωτηρίας ἔπεισεν, ἀλλ' εὐπρεπείᾳ
τῆς τυραννοκτονίας, ὡς μὴ δοκῶσι πολλοὺς ὥσπερ
130 ἐχθρούς, ἀλλ' ἕνα ἀνελεῖν ὡς τύραννον. τίς ἂν οὖν
πιστεύσειεν ἐμὲ Καίσαρός τε ἀμελεῖν εὐεργέτου μοι
γεγενημένου καὶ προτιμᾶν τοὺς ἐχθροὺς ἐκείνου καὶ
τὸν φόνον ἑκόντα χαρίζεσθαι τοῖς ἐμοῖς ἐπιβούλοις,
ὡς οἴεται Καῖσαρ ὁ νέος; πόθεν οὖν αὐτοῖς ἀμνηστία
τοῦ φόνου καὶ ἡγεμονίαι; ταῦτα γὰρ ἐπικαλεῖν, ἀντὶ
τῆς βουλῆς, ἐμοὶ βούλεται. μάθετε, ὡς ἐγένετο.

131   34. "Καίσαρος ἐν τῷ βουλευτηρίῳ σφαγέντος
ἄφνω, δέος ἐπέσχεν ἐκ πάντων δὴ μάλιστα πλεῖστον
ἐμὲ φιλίᾳ τε αὐτοῦ Καίσαρος καὶ ἀγνοίᾳ τοῦ ἀκρι-
βοῦς· οὐ γάρ πω τὴν συνθήκην ἑώρων οὐδὲ ἐπὶ ὅσοις.
132 ὁ δὲ δῆμος ἐθορυβεῖτο, καὶ οἱ σφαγεῖς σὺν μονομά-
χοις τὸ Καπιτώλιον καταλαβόντες ἀπέκλειον, καὶ ἡ
βουλὴ σὺν ἐκείνοις ἦν, ᾗ καὶ νῦν ἐστι φανερώτερον,
γέρα τε τοῖς ἀνελοῦσιν ὡς τυραννοκτόνοις ἐψηφίζετο.
καὶ εἰ τύραννος ὁ Καῖσαρ ἐφάνη, ἡμῖν ὑπῆρχεν ἀπο-

prepared of all to face danger in his service. But it would
not be fair of me to bear witness to the gratitude and
special honor he in turn continually devoted to me. The   129
murderers, too, were acquainted with both these facts,
and so conspired to kill me with Caesar, because they
believed that if I were alive they would not be able to do
what they had in mind. Whoever persuaded them to
change their minds did not do so out of concern for my
safety, but to preserve the plausibility that they were tyrant slayers, and to avoid the appearance of doing away
with a number of people because they were personal enemies, as opposed to one person because he was a tyrant.
Who, then, would ever believe that I do not care about   130
Caesar, my benefactor, and that I respect his enemies
above him, and that I willingly condone his murder at the
hands of those who plotted against me also, as the young
Caesar imagines? What, then, was the source of the amnesty they received for the murder, or the provincial commands they got? For Octavian wants to lay these charges
against me rather than the senate. Let me tell you how this
happened.

34. "When Caesar was suddenly butchered in the sen-   131
ate, I more than anyone was gripped by fear, because of
my friendship with Caesar and because I lacked accurate
information, for I did not yet have an impression of the
conspiracy or how many people it was aimed against. The   132
people were creating a disturbance, the murderers and
some gladiators having seized the Capitol were keeping it
closed off, and the senate were on their side, which is even
more clearly the case now, and were in the process of voting the killers rewards for being tyrant slayers. If Caesar
had been declared a tyrant, the fact is we would all have

133 λέσθαι πᾶσιν ὡς τυράννου φίλοις. ὧδε δή με ἔχοντα
θορύβου καὶ μερίμνης καὶ δέους, ὅτε οὐκ ἦν γνώμης
παράδοξον οὐδὲ ἀπορῆσαι, σκοποῦντες εὑρήσετε,
ἔνθα μὲν ἔδει τόλμης, θρασύτατον, ἔνθα δὲ ὑποκρί-
134 σεως, εὐμήχανον. τὸ μὲν δὴ πρῶτον ἐκ πάντων καὶ τὰ
λοιπὰ συνέχον ἦν ἀναιρεθῆναι τὰ γέρα τὰ ψηφιζό-
μενα τοῖς ἀνδράσιν· ὅπερ, ἀντιτάξας ἐμαυτὸν ἐγὼ τῇ
τε βουλῇ καὶ τοῖς σφαγεῦσιν ἐγκρατῶς, ἔπραττον
σὺν θράσει παραβόλῳ καὶ ἐπικινδύνῳ, τότε μόνον
ἡγούμενος ἡμᾶς τοὺς Καίσαρος ἀσφαλῶς περιέσε-
135 σθαι, ὅταν μὴ Καῖσαρ εἶναι δόξῃ τύραννος. τῷ δ'
αὐτῷ δέει τῶν ἐχθρῶν καὶ τῆς βουλῆς αὐτῆς ἐχο-
μένων, ὅτε μὴ Καῖσαρ εἴη τύραννος, ἀνδροφονίας
αὐτοὺς ἁλώσεσθαι, καὶ διὰ τοῦτο φιλονικούντων, εἶξα
τῆς ἀμνηστίας διδομένης ἀντὶ τῶν γερῶν, ἵν' ὅσων
136 ἔχρῃζον ἀντιλάβοιμι. τὰ δὲ ἦν πόσα καὶ πηλίκα;
μήτε τὴν ἐπωνυμίαν τοῦ Καίσαρος ἀπηλεῖφθαι τὴν
ἐμοὶ μάλιστα πάντων ἡδίστην μήτε τὴν περιουσίαν
δεδημεῦσθαι μήτε τὴν θέσιν, ἐφ' ᾗ νῦν οὗτος γαυριᾷ,
διαλελύσθαι μήτε τὰς διαθήκας ἀκύρους γενέσθαι τό
τε σῶμα τεθάφθαι βασιλικῶς καὶ τιμὰς αὐτῷ τὰς
πάλαι δεδομένας ἀθανάτους διαμένειν καὶ τὰ πεπραγμένα πάντα κύρια εἶναι καὶ τὸν ἐκείνου παῖδα καὶ
τοὺς φίλους ἡμᾶς, καὶ στρατηγοὺς καὶ στρατιώτας,
ἐν ἀσφαλεῖ γενέσθαι σωτηρίᾳ καὶ ἐνδόξῳ βίῳ ἀντὶ
ἐπονειδίστου.
137   35. "Ἆρ' ὑμῖν ὀλίγα ἢ σμικρὰ τῆς ἀμνηστίας τὴν
βουλὴν ἀνταιτῆσαι δοκῶ; ἢ δοῦναι ἂν αὐτὰ ἡ βουλὴ

died as the associates of a tyrant. In the midst of the con-   133
fusion and anxiety and fear in which I found myself, at a
time when it would not have been surprising if I had been
at a loss for a plan, if you look, you will find that where
daring was needed I was the most intrepid, and where
dissimulation was required I proved very resourceful. The   134
first thing of all to be done, and the rest was dependent on
it, was to prevent the voting of rewards to the conspirators.
This I accomplished with reckless and dangerous daring,
by setting myself decisively against the senate and the assassins, because I believed at the time that we Caesarians
could be safe only if Caesar were not to be judged a tyrant.
Our enemies and the senate itself were gripped by the   135
same fear, namely that if Caesar were not to be a tyrant,
they would be convicted of murder, and for this reason
they offered stubborn resistance. So, when an amnesty
was offered instead of the honors, I yielded in order to get
what I wanted in return. How many things did I want, and   136
how important were they? That Caesar's name, to me the
sweetest of all, should not be erased; that his property
should not be confiscated by the state; that the adoption
on which this young man prides himself should not be
annulled; that the will should not be declared invalid; that
his body should receive a royal burial; that the honors
previously decreed to him should remain in force forever;
that all his acts should be confirmed; and that his son, and
we his associates, whether generals or common soldiers,
should be guaranteed safety, and a life of honor instead of
disgrace.

35. "Do you think that what I asked of the senate in   137
return for the amnesty was small or insignificant? Or that

χωρὶς τῆς ἀμνηστίας; ἦν μὲν δὴ καὶ καθαρῶς ἀντιδοῦναι τάδε τῶνδε ἄξιον καὶ φείσασθαι σὺν ἀληθεῖ
γνώμῃ φονέων ἀνδρῶν ὑπὲρ ἀθανάτου Καίσαρος δόξης καὶ ἡμῶν ἀσφαλοῦς σωτηρίας· οὐ μὴν ἐγὼ μετὰ
τῆσδε τῆς γνώμης ἐποίουν, ἀλλ᾽ ἀνατιθέμενος τὴν
138 δίκην. ἐπεί γέ τοι τῆς βουλῆς ἐς ἃ πρῶτα ἔχρῃζον
ἐκράτησα καὶ οἱ σφαγεῖς ὡς ἐν ἀμερίμνῳ μεθεῖντο,
ἀνεθάρρησα καὶ τὴν ἀμνηστίαν παρέλυον, οὐ ψηφί-
σμασιν ἢ δόγμασιν (οὐ γὰρ ἦν), ἀλλ᾽ ἀσήμῳ δη-
μοκοπίᾳ, τὸ σῶμα τοῦ Καίσαρος ἐπὶ προφάσει τῆς
ταφῆς ἐς τὴν ἀγορὰν ἐκφέρων καὶ τὰ τραύματα ἀπο-
γυμνῶν καὶ τὸ πλῆθος αὐτῶν καὶ τὴν ἐσθῆτα ἐπιδεικνὺς ᾑμαγμένην τε καὶ κατακεκομμένην καὶ τὴν ἀρετὴν καὶ τὸ φιλόδημον αὐτοῦ παλιλλογῶν, ἐκπαθῶς ἐν
μέσῳ καὶ ὀδυρόμενος μὲν ὡς ἀνῃρημένον, κατακαλῶν
139 δ᾽ ὡς θεόν. τάδε γάρ μου τὰ ἔργα καὶ ῥήματα ἠρέθισε
τὸν δῆμον, καὶ τὸ πῦρ ἧψε μετὰ τὴν ἀμνηστίαν, καὶ
ἐς τὰς οἰκίας τῶν ἐχθρῶν ἔπεμψε καὶ τοὺς ἄνδρας
140 ἐξέβαλε τῆς πόλεως. τοῦτο δ᾽ ὅπως ἀντιπραττούσης
καὶ λυπουμένης τῆς βουλῆς ἐγένετο, αὐτίκα ἔδειξαν,
ἐμὲ μὲν αἰτιώμενοι τῆς δημοκοπίας, τοὺς δὲ φονέας
ἐκπέμψαντες ἐπὶ τὰς τῶν ἐθνῶν ἡγεμονίας, ⟨Δέκμον
μὲν ἐς τὴν Κελτικήν⟩[17] Βροῦτον δὲ καὶ Κάσσιον ἐς
Συρίαν καὶ Μακεδονίαν, αἳ μεσταὶ μεγάλων στρατῶν
ἦσαν, ἐπείγεσθαι καὶ πρὸ τοῦ δεδομένου χρόνου δι-
141 δάξαντες ἐπὶ προφάσει φροντίδος σίτου. ἕτερον δή με
δέος ἔτι μεῖζον ἐπελάμβανεν, οὐκ ἔχοντά πω στρατὸν

the senate would have given them without the amnesty?
It would have been proper to make this mutual exchange
honestly, and in all sincerity spare men who were murderers for the sake of Caesar's immortal reputation and our
complete security, but in fact I did not do it with that intention, but in order to postpone punishment. So, when I   138
had prevailed on the senate for my primary needs and the
assassins were relaxing as if they were in the clear, I took
fresh courage and began to undermine the amnesty, not
with votes of the assembly or decrees of the senate (for
that was impossible), but by a subtle appeal to the people.
I brought Caesar's body into the Forum using his burial as
an excuse; I revealed his wounds, pointing out how many
there were and displaying his bloodstained and shredded
clothing; I kept talking passionately and publicly about his
courage and love for the people, weeping for him as a
murdered man, but appealing to him as god. These acts   139
and words of mine stirred up the people, kindled their
passions against the amnesty, sent them against the houses
of our enemies, and drove the murderers from the city.
That this all came about in the face of irritated opposition   140
from the members of the senate, they immediately made
clear by accusing me of rabblerousing, and sending the
assassins off to provincial commands, ⟨Decimus to Gaul,⟩
Brutus to Syria, Cassius to Macedonia, provinces filled
with a large number of troops, and instructing them to
hurry there before the appointed time, on the pretense of
looking after the corn supply. And now a new and still   141
greater fear gripped me, since I had no army of my own

---

[17] $\Delta\acute{\epsilon}\kappa\mu o\nu$ $\mu\grave{\epsilon}\nu$ $\grave{\epsilon}s$ $\tau\grave{\eta}\nu$ $K\epsilon\lambda\tau\iota\kappa\acute{\eta}\nu$ add. Goukowsky

ἴδιον οὐδένα, μὴ πρὸς ἐνόπλους τοσούσδε ἄνοπλοι
καθιστώμεθα. καὶ ὁ σύναρχος ὕποπτος ἦν, ἐμοί τε
διάφορος ὢν αἰεὶ καὶ ὑποκρινόμενος ἐπιβουλεῦσαι τῷ
Καίσαρι καὶ τὴν ἡμέραν τοῦ φόνου γενέθλιον τῇ
πόλει τιθέμενος.

142   36. "Ὧδε δὲ ἀπορῶν καὶ ἐπειγόμενος ἐξοπλίσαι
τοὺς πολεμίους καὶ ἐς ἡμᾶς ἀντ' ἐκείνων τὰ ὅπλα μετενεγκεῖν, Ἀμάτιον ἔκτεινα καὶ κατεκάλεσα Πομπήιον,
ἵνα τοῖσδε αὖθις ἁλοῦσα ἡ βουλὴ πρός με μεταθοῖτο.
143   καὶ οὐδ' ὣς αὐτῇ πιστεύων ἔπεισα Συρίαν αἰτεῖν Δολοβέλλαν, οὐ παρὰ τῆς βουλῆς, ἀλλὰ παρὰ τοῦ
δήμου νόμῳ, καὶ συνέπραξα αἰτοῦντι, ἵνα τοῖς τε
σφαγεῦσι Δολοβέλλας ἐχθρὸς ἀντὶ φίλου γένοιτο καὶ
τοῖς βουλευταῖς αἰσχρὸν ᾖ μετὰ Δολοβέλλαν ἀντει-
144   πεῖν ἐμοὶ περὶ Μακεδονίας. οὐ μέντ' ἂν οὐδ' ὥς μοι
Μακεδονίαν ἔδοσαν, οὐδ' ἐπὶ Δολοβέλλᾳ, διὰ τὴν ἐν
αὐτῇ στρατιάν, εἰ μὴ τὴν στρατιὰν προμεθῆκα τῷ
Δολοβέλλᾳ ὡς Συρίαν καὶ τὰ ἐς Πάρθους διαλαχόντι.
145   τοὺς δ' αὖ περὶ τὸν Κάσσιον οὔτε Μακεδονίαν ἀφεί-
λοντο ἂν οὔτε Συρίαν, μὴ ἕτερα αὐτοῖς ἐς ἀσφάλειαν
ἀντιλαβόντες ἔθνη. δεῆσαν οὖν ἀντιδοῦναι θεάσασθε,
οἷα ἀνθ' οἵων καὶ ὡς στρατοῦ γυμνὰ ἐδόθη, Κυρήνη
τε καὶ Κρήτῃ· ὧν καὶ οἱ ἐχθροὶ καταφρονοῦσιν οὐκ
ἀσφαλῶν σφίσιν ὄντων καὶ ἐς τὰ ἀφῃρημένα βιάζον-
146   ται. οὕτω μὲν δὴ καὶ ὁ στρατὸς ἐς Δολοβέλλαν μετ-
ενήνεκτο ἀπὸ τῶν ἐχθρῶν τέχναις καὶ μηχαναῖς καὶ
ἀντιδόσεσιν ἑτέρων· οὐ γάρ πω τῶν ὅπλων φανέντων
ὑπὸ τοῖς νόμοις ἔδει πράσσειν.

70

as yet, that we would stand defenseless against such massive armed forces. I was also suspicious of my colleague, as he was forever at odds with me, he had pretended to be involved in the plot against Caesar, and had proposed that the day of the murder should be celebrated as the birthday of the city.

36. "While I was, thus, at a loss what to do, desiring to disarm our enemies and transfer their armaments to us instead, I put Amatius to death and recalled Pompeius in order to trap the senate again by such means into changing sides to me. But even then I did not trust them, so I persuaded Dolabella to ask for Syria, not from the senate, but from the people by a law. I supported his request, to turn him from being a friend of the murderers into an enemy, and to shame the senate, after the precedent set by Dolabella, into not opposing me on Macedonia. But, as it was, they would not have given me Macedonia, even after Dolabella had been provided for, because of the army stationed there, if I had not previously transferred the army to Dolabella, on the grounds that Syria and the Parthian campaign had been allotted to him. And again, they would not have taken Macedonia away from Cassius and his party, nor Syria, unless they got other provinces for them in exchange to ensure their safety. But when an exchange was needed, look what they got instead—Cyrene and Crete, unguarded by troops. Even our enemies despise them, as they offer no security for them, and they are now trying to take by force the provinces removed from them. This, then, was how the army too was transferred from our enemies to Dolabella using craft, stratagem, and exchange; for with no sign yet of me getting armaments, I had to act using the laws.

147   37. Γεγενημένων δὲ τῶνδε καὶ τῶν ἐχθρῶν ἕτερον
στρατὸν ἀγειράντων, ἔδει μοι τοῦ περὶ τὴν Μακεδονίαν στρατοῦ καὶ προφάσεως ἠπόρουν. φήμη δὲ κατ-
148   έσκηψε Γέτας Μακεδονίαν πορθεῖν. ἀπιστουμένης δὲ
καὶ ταύτης καὶ τῶν ἐπισκεψομένων ἀπεσταλμένων,
εἰσηγησάμην ἐγὼ περὶ τῆς δικτάτορος ἀρχῆς μὴ
ἐξεῖναι μήτε εἰπεῖν μήτε ἐπιψηφίσαι μήτε λαβεῖν δι-
δομένην· ᾧ δὴ μάλιστα ὑπαχθέντες ἔδοσάν μοι τὸν
149   στρατόν. καὶ ἐγὼ τότε πρῶτον ἐμαυτὸν ἡγησάμην
ἰσόπαλον εἶναι τοῖς ἐχθροῖς, οὐ τοῖσδε τοῖς φανεροῖς,
ὡς οἴεται Καῖσαρ, ἀλλὰ τοῖς πλέοσί τε καὶ δυνατω-
150   τέροις καὶ ἀφανέσιν ἔτι εἶναι θέλουσι. ταῦτα δ᾽ ἐργα-
σαμένῳ μοι ἕτερος τῶν σφαγέων ἔλειπεν ἐν πλευραῖς,
Βροῦτος ὁ Δέκμος, ἡγούμενος καὶ ὅδε χώρας ἐπικαίρου καὶ στρατοῦ πολλοῦ· ὃν ἐγὼ καὶ θρασύτερον
εἰδὼς τὴν Κελτικὴν ἀφῃρούμην, ἐς εὐπρέπειαν ἔτι
τῆς βουλῆς Μακεδονίαν ὑπισχνούμενος ἀντιδώσειν,
151   γυμνὴν στρατοῦ γενομένην. ἀγανακτούσης δὲ τῆς
βουλῆς καὶ τὴν ἐνέδραν ἤδη καθορώσης καὶ ἴστε οἷα
καὶ ὅσα Δέκμῳ πολλῶν γραφόντων καὶ ἐπαλειφόντων
ἤδη τοὺς μετ᾽ ἐμὲ ὑπάτους, ἐγὼ θρασύτερον ἔτι τὸ μὲν
ἔθνος, ἀντὶ τῆς βουλῆς, νόμῳ παρὰ τοῦ δήμου λαβεῖν
ἐπενόησα, τὸν δὲ στρατὸν ἀπὸ τῆς Μακεδονίας ἐς τὸ
Βρεντέσιον ἐπέρων ὡς χρησόμενος δὴ ἐς τὰ ἐπείγοντα. καὶ σὺν θεοῖς, ⟨ὡς⟩[18] εἰπεῖν, χρησόμεθα, ὡς ἂν
αἱ χρεῖαι καλῶσιν.

[18] ὡς add. Goukowsky

37. "After these events, while our enemies were col- 147
lecting another army, I had need of the army in Macedonia, but was at a loss for an excuse to take it. A rumor flew
around that the Getae were pillaging Macedonia. This met 148
with disbelief, and while a commission was sent out to
investigate, I introduced a motion about the dictatorship,
that it would be illegal to propose an appointment to it, to
vote for it, or to accept it if offered. The senators were
particularly taken with this, and they gave me the army.
Then for the first time I considered myself equally 149
matched with my enemies, not merely with these openly
hostile ones, as Octavian thinks, but with the more numerous and more powerful ones who still choose to remain
unseen. With this much accomplished, there remained 150
one of the murderers on my flank, Decimus Brutus, he too
in command of a convenient province and a large army.
Knowing him to be a very daring man, I set about taking
Gaul off him by promising, as a means of preserving plausibility for the senate, to provide Macedonia in exchange,
but stripped of an army. The senate were furious, for they 151
now saw the trap, and you know what kind of letters, and
how many, they have been writing to Decimus, and how
they have been setting my successors in the consulship
against me.[18] I decided, therefore, to take a bolder course
and ask the people for this province by a law, instead of
asking the senate, and I brought the army over from Macedonia to Brundisium to use, of course, for emergencies.
And with the help of the gods, so to speak, we will use it,
as needs demand.

[18] The consuls designated by Caesar for 43 were Gaius Vibius
Pansa Caetronianus and Aulus Hirtius.

152　38. "Οὕτως ἐκ πολλοῦ δέους τοῦ πρὶν ἡμᾶς ἐπισχόν-
τος μετεβάλομεν ἔς τε ἀσφάλειαν ὑπὲρ ἡμῶν αὐτῶν
ἐγκρατῆ καὶ ἐς θάρσος ἐπὶ τοὺς ἐχθρούς· ὧν ἐκφανέν-
των ἀνεφάνη καὶ ἡ τῶν πλεόνων ἐς τοὺς πολεμίους
153　σπουδή. ὁρᾶτε γάρ, ὅση μὲν αὐτοῖς ἐστι μεταμέλεια
τῶν ἐψηφισμένων, ὅσος δὲ ἀγὼν ἀφελέσθαι με τὴν
Κελτικὴν ἤδη δεδομένην. ἴστε, ἃ γράφουσι Δέκμῳ
καὶ ὅσα τοὺς ὑπάτους τοὺς μετ᾽ ἐμὲ πείθουσι περὶ τῆς
154　Κελτικῆς μεταψηφίσασθαι. ἀλλὰ σὺν θεοῖς τε πα-
τρῴοις καὶ σὺν εὐσεβεῖ γνώμῃ καὶ σὺν ταῖς ὑμετέραις
ἀνδραγαθίαις, μεθ᾽ ὧν καὶ ὁ Καῖσαρ ἐκράτει, ἀμυνού-
μεν αὐτῷ, τῷ τε σώματι ἐπεξιόντες καὶ τῇ γνώμῃ βο-
155　ηθοῦντες. ταῦτά μοι γιγνόμενα μέν, ὦ συστρατιῶται,
ἔτι ἔχρῃζον ἀπόρρητα εἶναι, γενόμενα δὲ ἐξενήνεκται
πρὸς ὑμᾶς, οὓς ἐγὼ καὶ ἔργου καὶ λόγου κοινωνοὺς
ἐς ἅπαντα τίθεμαι. καὶ τοῖς ἄλλοις, εἴ τινες αὐτὰ οὐ
συνορῶσι, μεταφέρετε, πλὴν μόνου Καίσαρος ἀχαρίστως ἐς ἡμᾶς ἔχοντος."

156　39. Τοιαῦτα τοῦ Ἀντωνίου διεξιόντος, παρέστη τοῖς
ταξιάρχαις αὐτὸν ἅπαντα μετ᾽ ἔχθρας ἀκριβοῦς ἐς
τοὺς ἀνδροφόνους, ἐπιτεχνάζοντα τῇ βουλῇ, πεποιηκέναι. ἠξίουν δὲ καὶ ὡς τῷ Καίσαρι συναλλαγῆναι
καὶ πείσαντες αὐτοὺς συνήλλασσον αὖθις ἐν τῷ
157　Καπιτωλίῳ. οὐ πολὺ δὲ ὕστερον ὁ Ἀντώνιος τῶν σωματοφυλάκων τινὰς ἐς τοὺς φίλους παρήγαγεν ὡς
ὑπηρέτας γενομένους ἐπιβουλεύοντος αὐτῷ τοῦ Καίσαρος, εἴτε συκοφαντῶν εἴτε τῷ ὄντι νομίσας εἴτε
περὶ τῶν εἰς τὰ στρατόπεδα περιπεμφθέντων πυθόμε-

38. "In this way we have exchanged the great fear that   152
formerly gripped us for guaranteed security for ourselves
and courage against our enemies. With all this now openly
revealed, so too was the zeal of the masses against our
enemies made clear. You see how much the latter regret   153
the decrees they have passed, and what a fight they are
making to deprive me of Gaul, even though it has already
been assigned to me. You know what they are writing to
Decimus, and how hard they are trying to persuade my
successors in the consulship to repeal the decree concerning Gaul. But with the help of our paternal gods, a pious   154
policy, and your nobility, all of which helped Caesar to
conquer, we will avenge him, prosecuting our case with
the help of both body and mind. While all these things   155
were happening to me, fellow soldiers, I needed them to
remain unspoken, but now that they are in the past, I have
laid them before you, as I consider you partners in everything I do and say. If there are others who do not have the
same view of these matters, share this information with
them—but not with Octavian, who is behaving ungratefully toward me."

39. When Antony had finished setting out these details,   156
the tribunes were reassured that everything he had done
in scheming against the senate had been done out of gen-
uine hatred for the assassins. Nevertheless they asked him
to come to terms with Octavian, and, on getting his agreement, brought about a reconciliation between them again
on the Capitol. Not long after, however, Antony trans-   157
ferred some of his bodyguards to his associates, maintaining that Octavian was plotting against him and these were
his agents. He may have been making a false accusation,
or really believed it, or he had heard of the men sent into

νος καὶ τὴν ἐς τὸ ἔργον ἐπιβουλὴν μεταφέρωι ἐς τὸ
158 σῶμα. ὅ τε λόγος ἐκδραμὼν αὐτίκα θόρυβον ἤγειρε
πάνδημον, καὶ ἀγανάκτησις ἦν. ὀλίγοι μὲν γάρ, οἷς
τι λογισμοῦ βαθέος ἦν, ᾔδεσαν Καίσαρι συμφέρειν
Ἀντώνιον καὶ βλάπτοντα ὅμως περιεῖναι, ἐπίφοβον
ὄντα τοῖς φονεῦσιν· ἀποθανόντος γὰρ ἀδεέστερον
ἐκείνους ἅπασιν ἐπιτολμήσειν, βοηθουμένους μάλιστα ὑπὸ τῆς βουλῆς. ὧδε μὲν εἴκαζον οἱ συνετώτεροι·
159 τὸ δὲ πλέον, ὁρῶντες, οἷα καθ' ἑκάστην ἡμέραν ὁ Καίσαρ ὑβριζόμενός τε καὶ ζημιούμενος πάσχοι, οὐκ
ἄπιστον ἐτίθεντο τὴν διαβολὴν οὐδὲ ὅσιον ἢ ἀνεκτὸν
ἐνόμιζον Ἀντώνιον ὑπατεύοντα ἐς τὸ σῶμα ἐπιβεβου-
160 λεῦσθαι. ὁ δὲ Καῖσαρ καὶ πρὸς οὕτως ἔχοντας ἐξ-
έτρεχε σὺν ὀργῇ μανιώδει καὶ ἐβόα αὐτὸς ἐπιβου-
λεύεσθαι πρὸς Ἀντωνίου ἐς τὴν παρὰ τῷ δήμῳ φιλίαν
ἔτι οἱ μόνην οὖσαν· ἐπί τε τὰς θύρας τοῦ Ἀντωνίου
δραμὼν τὰ αὐτὰ ἐβόα καὶ θεοὺς ἐμαρτύρετο καὶ ἀρὰς
161 ἤρᾶτο πάσας καὶ ἐς δίκην ἐλθεῖν προυκαλεῖτο. οὐδενὸς δὲ προϊόντος, "Ἐν τοῖς φίλοις," ἔφη, "Δέχομαι
τοῖς σοῖς κριθῆναι," καὶ εἰπὼν ἐπέτρεχεν ἔσω. κωλυ-
θεὶς δὲ αὖθις ὤμωζε καὶ ἐλοιδορεῖτο αὐτῷ καὶ τοῖς
περὶ θύρας ἠγανάκτει κωλύουσι τὸν Ἀντώνιον ἐλεγ-
162 χθῆναι. ἀπιών τε τὸν δῆμον ἐμαρτύρετο, εἴ τι πάθοι,
πρὸς Ἀντωνίου δολοφονεῖσθαι. λεγομένων δὲ τῶνδε
σὺν πάθει πολλῷ μετέπιπτε τὸ πλῆθος, καί τις αὐτοῖς
163 τῆς πρὶν δόξης μετάνοια ἐνεγίγνετο. εἰσὶ δὲ οἳ καὶ

his encampments, and turned the plot to block his actions
into a plot against his life. But the story spread rapidly,   158
immediately causing a widespread disturbance among the
people and great indignation. For there were only a few
who had sufficient reasoning power to realize that it was
in the interests of Octavian for Antony to live, damaging
though he was, because the murderers were afraid of him.
If he were to die, they would dare anything more fear-
lessly, especially as they had the support of the senate.
While the more intelligent deduced this, the majority, see-   159
ing how much Octavian suffered every day from the indig-
nities and losses inflicted on him, regarded the accusation
as credible, and considered it sacrilegious and intolerable
that a conspiracy should be formed against Antony's life
while he was consul. Octavian hurried off, furiously angry,   160
to confront even those who held this opinion, shouting out
that he was the one being plotted against by Antony, to
alienate from him the friendship of the people, which he
alone still had. Rushing to Antony's door, he yelled the
same accusation, and called the gods to witness, swearing
all kinds of oaths, and challenging Antony to take a legal
case. When nobody came forward he said, "I agree to   161
submit myself to the judgment of your associates," and
with these words attempted to enter the house. On being
prevented from doing so, he again cried out and poured
abuse on Antony, and was indignant at the doorkeepers for
preventing Antony from being questioned. As he was leav-   162
ing, he called the people to witness that, if anything happened to him, his murder would be at the hands of Antony.
He spoke these words with such passion that the crowd
began to change their mind and regret somewhat their
previous assessment. There were doubters, even then,   163

APPIAN

τότε ἀπιστοῦντες ὤκνουν ἑκατέρῳ τὸ πιστὸν νέμειν,
καί τινες ὑπόκρισιν ἀμφοῖν τὰ γιγνόμενα διέβαλλον
εἶναι, συνθεμένων μὲν ἄρτι ἐν ἱερῷ, μηχανωμένων δὲ
ταῦτα ἐπὶ τοὺς ἐχθρούς. οἱ δὲ αὐτὰ τὸν Ἀντώνιον
ἡγοῦντο ἐπινοεῖν εἰς ἀφορμὴν φρουρᾶς πλείονος ἢ ἐς
ἀλλοτρίωσιν τῶν κληρουχιῶν Καίσαρι.

164   40. Ὡς δὲ τῷ Καίσαρι ὑπὸ τῶν κρύφα ἀπεσταλμένων ἀπηγγέλθη τὸν ἐν Βρεντεσίῳ στρατὸν καὶ τοὺς
ἀπῳκισμένους ἐν ὀργῇ τὸν Ἀντώνιον ἔχειν, ἀμελοῦν-
τα τοῦ Καίσαρος φόνου, καὶ σφᾶς ἐπικουρήσειν, ἂν
δύνωνται, ὁ μὲν Ἀντώνιος ἐς τὸ Βρεντέσιον ἐξῄει διὰ
τάδε. δείσας δὲ ὁ Καῖσαρ, μὴ μετὰ τῆς στρατιᾶς
ἐπανελθὼν ἀφρούρητον αὐτὸν λάβοι, χρήματα φέρων
εἰς Καμπανίαν ᾔει, πείσων τὰς πόλεις οἱ στρατεύ-
165 εσθαι, τὰς ὑπὸ τοῦ πατρὸς ᾠκισμένας. καὶ ἔπεισε
Καλατίαν πρώτην, ἐπὶ δ' ἐκείνῃ Κασιλῖνον, δύο τάσδε
Καπύης ἑκατέρωθεν· ἐπιδοὺς δ' ἑκάστῳ δραχμὰς πεντακοσίας ἦγεν ἐς μυρίους ἄνδρας, οὔτε ὡπλισμένους
ἐντελῶς οὔτε συντεταγμένους πω κατὰ ἴλας, ἀλλ' ὡς
166 ἐς μόνην τοῦ σώματος φυλακήν, ὑφ' ἑνὶ σημείῳ. οἱ δὲ
ἐν ἄστει τὸν Ἀντώνιον δεδιότες μετὰ στρατιᾶς ἐπαν-
ιόντα, ὡς ἐπύθοντο καὶ τὸν Καίσαρα μεθ' ἑτέρας
προσιέναι, οἱ μὲν διπλασίως ἐδεδοίκεσαν, οἱ δ' ὡς
χρησόμενοι κατ' Ἀντωνίου Καίσαρι ἠσμένιζον· οἱ δὲ
αὐτῶν τὰς ἐν τῷ Καπιτωλίῳ διαλλαγὰς ἑωρακότες
ὑπόκρισιν ἐνόμιζον εἶναι τὰ γιγνόμενα καὶ ἀντίδοσιν
Ἀντωνίῳ μὲν δυναστείας, Καίσαρι δὲ τῶν φονέων.

who were reluctant to put any trust in either of them. Some blamed events on the hypocrisy of both of them, believing that they had recently come to an agreement in a temple, and were devising all this as a stratagem against their enemies. Still others thought that it was a contrivance of Antony either as a pretext to increase his bodyguard, or to alienate the colonists from Octavian.

40. When reports came to Octavian from the agents he had sent off secretly that the army at Brundisium and those being settled in colonies would help him if they could because they were angry at Antony for neglecting Caesar's murder, Antony set off for Brundisium for this reason. Octavian was afraid that Antony would return with his army and catch him unprotected, so he went to Campania with money to persuade the towns founded by his father there to join his army. He convinced Calatia first, and then Casilinum, two towns situated on either side of Capua. By giving five hundred drachmas to each man, he collected about ten thousand men, not yet fully armed or mustered in cohorts, but serving merely as a bodyguard under one banner.[19] At Rome they were afraid of Antony coming back with an army, and when they heard that Octavian too was approaching with another army, some were doubly afraid, while others were pleased at the prospect of using Octavian against Antony. Still others, who had seen them reconciled to each other on the Capitol, thought this was all an act, designed to give Antony sole power in exchange for Octavian getting the lives of the assassins.

164

165

166

[19] Army pay in the first century BC was 225 denarii for a legionary (Appian uses drachmas for denarii). So Octavian was offering a considerable amount of money.

167   41. Ὧδε δὲ αὐτῶν θορυβουμένων, Καννούτιος ὁ
δήμαρχος, ἐχθρὸς ὢν Ἀντωνίῳ καὶ παρ᾽ αὐτὸ Καίσαρι φίλος, ὑπήντα τῷ Καίσαρι καὶ τὴν γνώμην ἐκ-
μαθὼν ἀπήγγελλε τῷ δήμῳ, μετ᾽ ἔχθρας Ἀντωνίου
σαφοῦς ἐπιέναι τὸν Καίσαρα καὶ χρῆναι δεδιότας
Ἀντώνιον ἐπὶ τυραννίδι τόνδε προσεταιρίσασθαι,
168   στρατὸν ἄλλον οὐκ ἔχοντας ἐν τῷ παρόντι. ταῦτα δ᾽
εἰπὼν ἐσῆγε τὸν Καίσαρα, αὐλισάμενον πρὸ τοῦ
ἄστεος ἀπὸ σταδίων πεντεκαίδεκα ἐν τῷ τοῦ Ἄρεως
ἱερῷ. ὡς δὲ εἰσῆλθον, ὁ μὲν εἰς τὸν νεὼν τῶν Διο-
σκούρων παρῆλθε, καὶ τὸν νεὼν περιέστησαν οἱ
στρατευόμενοι ξιφίδια ἀφανῶς περιεζωσμένοι, Καννούτιος δὲ πρότερον ἐδημηγόρει κατὰ τοῦ Ἀντωνίου[19]
καὶ τὸν Καίσαρα ἐπῄνει, στρατὸν ὑπὲρ τῆς πατρίδος
ἀγείροντα, καὶ ἀμύνειν αὐτῇ παρεκάλει κατὰ Ἀντω-
169   νίου. ὁ δὲ καὶ τοῦ πατρὸς αὐτοὺς ὑπεμίμνησκε καὶ ὧν
αὐτὸς ὑπὸ Ἀντωνίου πάθοι, δι᾽ ἃ καὶ τόνδε τὸν στρατὸν ἐς φυλακὴν εἴη συνειλεγμένος· ἔφη τε ἐς πάντα
τῆς πατρίδος ὑπηρέτης καὶ κατήκοος ἔσεσθαι καὶ ἐς
τὰ νῦν πρὸς Ἀντώνιον ἕτοιμος.
170   42. Ὧδε δ᾽ εἰπόντος αὐτοῦ καὶ τὴν ἐκκλησίαν δια-
λύσαντος ἐπὶ τῷδε, ὁ στρατὸς ἡγούμενος ἐς τὸ ἐναντίον ἐπὶ διαλλαγαῖς Ἀντωνίου τε καὶ Καίσαρος ἀφῖχθαι ἢ ἐς μόνην γε φυλακὴν τοῦ Καίσαρος καὶ τῶν
φονέων ἄμυναν, ἤχθοντο τῇ κατ᾽ Ἀντωνίου προαγο-

---

[19] Post Ἀντωνίου, om. καὶ τὸν Καίσαρα . . . κατὰ Ἀντωνίου
LBJ

41. With affairs disturbed in this way, the tribune Can- 167
nutius, an enemy of Antony, and therefore friendly to
Octavian, went to meet Octavian.[20] Having learned his
intentions, Cannutius addressed the people, saying that
Octavian was advancing in a state of open hostility against
Antony, and that those who were afraid that Antony was
aiming at tyranny should side with Octavian, as they had
no other army at present. On finishing this speech, he 168
brought Octavian, who was encamped outside Rome at
the temple of Mars, fifteen stades away, into the city.
When they arrived, Octavian proceeded to the temple of
the Dioscuri, and his soldiers surrounded it, carrying their
swords concealed. Cannutius was the first to address the
people in a speech against Antony, praising Octavian for
raising an army in defense of his country and urging him
to protect Rome against Antony. Then Octavian also re- 169
minded them of his father, and of what he himself had
suffered at the hands of Antony, which was the reason he
had recruited this army as a means of protecting himself.
And he said that he would serve and obey his country in
all things, and that he was ready to confront Antony in the
present situation.

42. After Octavian had finished this speech and subse- 170
quently dissolved the assembly, the soldiers, who thought
that they had come for the entirely opposite purpose, that
is, to support the reconciliation of Antony and Octavian,
or at least just to protect Octavian and take vengeance on
the assassins, were annoyed at the proclamation against

[20] We know of Tiberius Cannutius only during his tribunate
in 44.

ρεύσει, στρατηγοῦ τε σφῶν γεγονότος καὶ ὄντος
ὑπάτου· καὶ οἱ μὲν αὐτῶν ἐπανελθεῖν ᾔτουν εἰς τὰ
οἰκεῖα ὡς ὁπλιούμενοι· οὐ γὰρ ἄλλων ἢ τῶν ἰδίων
171 ὅπλων ἀνέξεσθαι· οἱ δὲ καὶ τὸ ἀληθὲς ὑπέφαινον. ὁ
δὲ Καῖσαρ ἠπόρητο μὲν ἐς τὸ ἐναντίον ὧν προσ-
εδόκησε μετενεχθείς, ἐλπίσας δ᾽ αὐτῶν πειθοῖ μᾶλλον
ἢ βίᾳ περιέσεσθαι, συνεχώρει ταῖς προφάσεσι καὶ
τοὺς μὲν ἐπὶ τὰ ὅπλα ἔπεμπε, τοὺς δὲ ἁπλῶς ἐς τὰ
172 οἰκεῖα. πάντας δ᾽, ἐπικρύπτων τὴν ἀχθηδόνα, ἐπῄνει
τῆς συνόδου καὶ ἐδωρεῖτο ἑτέραις δωρεαῖς καὶ δαψι-
λέστερον ἔτι ἀμείψεσθαι ἔλεγεν, αἰεὶ χρώμενος ἐς τὰ
ἐπείγοντα ὡς πατρικοῖς φίλοις μᾶλλον ἢ στρατιώταις.
173 χιλίους μὲν δὴ μόνους ἢ τρισχιλίους τάδε λέγων
ἐπέκλασεν ἐκ μυρίων οἱ παραμεῖναι (διαφέρονται γὰρ
περὶ τοῦ ἀριθμοῦ)· οἱ δὲ λοιποὶ τότε μὲν ἐξῄεσαν,
ἀνεμιμνήσκοντο δ᾽ αὐτίκα γεωργίας τε πόνων καὶ
κερδῶν στρατείας καὶ λόγων τῶν Καίσαρος καὶ εὐ-
πειθείας αὐτοῦ, πρὸς ἃ ἐβούλοντο, καὶ χαρίτων, ὧν τε
174 εἰλήφεσαν καὶ ὧν ἤλπιζον ἔτι λήψεσθαι. οἷόν τε
ὄχλος ἀνώμαλος μετενόουν καὶ τῆς προφάσεως ἐς εὐπρέπειαν ἐπιβαίνοντες ὡπλίζοντο καὶ πρὸς αὐτὸν
ἐπανήεσαν. ὁ δὲ ἤδη μετὰ χρημάτων ἄλλων τὴν Τυρρηνίαν[20] καὶ τὰ ἀγχοῦ πάντα περιῄει, στρατεύων
ἑτέρους ἐφ᾽ ἑτέροις· καὶ πάντας ἐς Ἀρρήτιον ἔπεμπεν.
175 43. Ἀντωνίῳ δ᾽ ἀφῖκτο μέσον ἐς τὸ Βρεντέσιον ἐκ
πέντε τῶν ἐν Μακεδονίᾳ τελῶν τέσσαρα· ἐπιμεμφόμε-

[20] τὴν Τυρρηνίαν Goukowsky; τήν τε Ῥάβενναν codd.

Antony, who had once been their general and was now consul. Some of them asked leave to return home in order to arm themselves, saying that they could not stand to use weapons other than their own. Others hinted at the truth. Finding himself in a situation quite the opposite of what 171 he was expecting, Octavian was at a loss for what to do, but hoping to get the better of them by persuasion rather than by force, he gave in to their excuses, and sent some of them to get their arms, and others he simply sent home. Hiding his disappointment, he praised all the assembled 172 company, presented them with new gifts, and said that he would reward them still more generously, and always employ them on urgent matters as friends of his father rather than soldiers. This speech influenced only one thousand 173 out of ten thousand to remain with him—or three thousand. (The number is disputed.) The rest then left, but soon remembered the hard work involved in farming and the profits of military service and the words of Octavian and his compliance with their wishes and the favors they had received from him and hoped to receive in the future. And so, as you would expect from a fickle mob, they 174 changed their mind, and seizing upon their excuse for the sake of appearances, they armed themselves and went back to him. Octavian was already crisscrossing Etruria and the whole surrounding area with new supplies of money, continually enlisting new forces and sending them all to Arretium.

43. Four of the five Macedonian legions had joined 175 Antony in the middle of Brundisium. Blaming him for not

νοι δ' αὐτὸν οὐκ ἐπεξελθόντα τῷ φόνῳ Καίσαρος,
χωρὶς εὐφημίας ἐς τὸ βῆμα παρέπεμπον ὡς περὶ
176 τοῦδε σφίσιν ἐκλογιούμενον πρώτου. ὁ δὲ αὐτοῖς χα-
λεπτόμενος τῆς σιωπῆς οὐ κατέσχεν, ἀλλ' ὠνείδιζεν
ἀχαριστίαν ἐκ Παρθυαίων ὑπὸ οὗ μετενεχθεῖσιν ἐς
τὴν Ἰταλίαν καὶ οὐκ ἐπιμαρτυροῦσι τοιᾶσδε χάριτος·
ἐμέμφετο δὲ καὶ ὅτι παρὰ μειρακίου προπετοῦς, ὧδε
τὸν Καίσαρα καλῶν, ἄνδρας ἐπιπεμπομένους σφίσιν
177 εἰς διαφθορὰν οὐκ αὐτοὶ προσάγουσιν αὐτῷ. ἀλλὰ
τούσδε μὲν αὐτὸς εὑρήσειν, τὸν δὲ στρατὸν ἄξειν ἐπὶ
τὴν ἐψηφισμένην οἱ χώραν εὐδαίμονα Κελτικήν, καὶ
τοῖς παροῦσιν ἑκάστῳ δοθήσεσθαι δραχμὰς ἑκατόν.
οἱ δὲ ἐγέλασαν τῆς σμικρολογίας καὶ χαλεπήναντος
αὐτοῦ μᾶλλον ἐθορύβουν καὶ διεδίδρασκον. ὁ δὲ ἐξ-
178 ανέστη τοσοῦτον εἰπών· "Μαθήσεσθε ἄρχεσθαι." αἰτήσας δὲ παρὰ τῶν χιλιάρχων τοὺς στασιώδεις (ἀνά-
γραπτος γάρ ἐστιν ἐν τοῖς Ῥωμαίων στρατοῖς αἰεὶ
καθ' ἕνα ἄνδρα ὁ τρόπος) διεκλήρωσε τῷ στρατιω-
τικῷ νόμῳ καὶ οὐ τὸ δέκατον ἅπαν, ἀλλὰ μέρος
ἔκτεινε τοῦ δεκάτου, νομίζων σφᾶς ὧδε καταπλήξειν
δι' ὀλίγου. οἱ δὲ οὐκ ἐς φόβον μᾶλλον ἢ ἐς ὀργὴν ἀπὸ
τοῦδε καὶ μῖσος ἐτρέποντο.

179   44. Ταῦτα δ' ὁρῶντες οὓς ὁ Καῖσαρ ἐπὶ διαφθορᾷ
τῶνδε προπεπόμφει, βιβλία πολλὰ τότε μάλιστα δι-
ερρίπτουν ἐς τὸ στρατόπεδον, ἀντὶ τῆς Ἀντωνίου μι-
κρολογίας τε καὶ ὠμότητος ἐς τὴν Καίσαρος μνήμην
τοῦ προτέρου καὶ βοήθειαν τοῦ νῦν καὶ χορηγίας δαψιλεῖς μετατίθεσθαι. οὓς ὁ Ἀντώνιος μηνύμασί τε με-

pursuing the matter of Caesar's murder, they conducted
him without applause to the speaker's platform, so that he
could explain this to them first. Antony was angry at their   176
silence, and did not keep his temper, but rebuked them
for their failure to thank him for transferring them from
Parthia to Italy, or to mention this favor. He also blamed
them for not personally bringing him the men sent by a
precocious youth—for that is what he called Octavian—to
subvert their cause. He would find these men himself, and   177
lead his army to the prosperous land of Gaul, which had
been voted to him, and would give one hundred drachmas
to every man present. They laughed at his tightfistedness,
and when he became angry they grew even more disor-
derly and began to scatter in all directions. Antony took
his leave, saying, "You will learn what it means to be
ruled." Then he asked the military tribunes to bring him   178
the troublemakers (for it is the practice in Roman armies
always to keep a record of each man's performance), drew
lots according to military law, and put to death not every
tenth man, but a proportion of ten percent, in the belief
that he would quickly cow them in this way. But this
turned them to anger and hate rather than fear.

44. When they saw this, the men Octavian had sent to   179
subvert the soldiers used that moment in particular to
distribute a large number of pamphlets throughout the
camp, urging them to replace Antony's meanness and cru-
elty with the memory of the elder Caesar and the assistance and generous abundance provided by the present
Caesar. Antony tried to find these men by heavy use of

γάλοις ἐζήτει, καὶ ἀπειλαῖς, εἴ τις ἐπικρύπτοι. οὐδένα
δὲ συλλαβὼν ἐχαλέπηνεν ὡς τοῦ στρατοῦ σφᾶς ἐπι-
180 κρύπτοντος. ἀπαγγελλομένων δὲ καὶ τῶν ἐν ταῖς
ἀποικίαις τε καὶ ἐν Ῥώμῃ Καίσαρι πεπραγμένων
ἐθορυβεῖτο. καὶ ἐπελθὼν αὖθις ἐπὶ τὸν στρατὸν ἔφη
χαλεπῆναι μὲν τῶν γεγονότων ὑπὸ ἀνάγκης στρατι-
ωτικῆς ὀλίγοις ἀντὶ πλεόνων ὧν ἐκόλαζεν ὁ νόμος,
αὐτοὺς δὲ εἰδέναι σαφῶς οὔτε ὠμὸν οὔτε μικρολόγον
181 Ἀντώνιον. "Ἀλλ᾽ ὁ μὲν φθόνος οἰχέσθω, κεκορεσμέ-
νος," ἔφη, "Καὶ τοῖς ἁμαρτήμασι καὶ ταῖς κολάσεσι·
τὰς δὲ ἑκατὸν δραχμὰς ὑμῖν οὐ δωρεάν (οὐ γὰρ τοῦτό
γε τῆς Ἀντωνίου τύχης), ἀλλὰ τῆς πρώτης ἐς ὑμᾶς
ἐντεύξεως προσαγορευτικὸν μᾶλλον [ἢ δωρεὰν]²¹ ἐκέ-
λευσα δοθῆναι, καὶ χρὴ νόμῳ πατρίῳ τε καὶ στρατι-
ωτικῷ καὶ ἐς τάδε καὶ ἐς πάντα εὐπειθεῖς ὑπάρχειν."
182 ὁ μὲν οὕτως εἶπεν, οὐδέν τι ἔτι προσθεὶς τῇ δωρεᾷ τοῦ
μὴ δοκεῖν ὁ στρατηγὸς ἡσσῆσθαι τοῦ στρατοῦ. οἱ δὲ
183 ἐλάμβανον, εἴτε μεταγνόντες εἴτε καὶ δεδιότες. ὁ δὲ
αὐτῶν τοὺς μὲν ταξιάρχους, εἴτε μηνίων ἔτι τῆς στάσεως εἴθ᾽ ἑτέρως ὑπονοῶν, ἐνήλλασσε, τοὺς δὲ λοιποὺς καὶ τἆλλα ἐν ταῖς χρείαις ἐδεξιοῦτο καὶ προύπεμ-
πεν ἀνὰ μέρος τὴν παραθαλάσσιον ὁδεύειν ἐπὶ
Ἀριμίνου.
184   45. Αὐτὸς δ᾽ ἐπιλεξάμενος ἐκ πάντων στρατηγίδα
σπεῖραν ἀνδρῶν ἀρίστων τά τε σώματα καὶ τὸν τρόπον ὥδευεν ἐς Ῥώμην ὡς ἐκεῖθεν ἐπὶ τὸ Ἀρίμινον ὁρ-
μήσων. ἐσήει δὲ ἐς τὴν πόλιν σοβαρῶς, τὴν μὲν ἴλην

informers and threats against anyone who hid them, but
as he caught no one he became angry, believing that the
army was sheltering them. When news arrives of what   180
Octavian had been doing in the colonies and at Rome, he
became alarmed, and appearing before the army again,
apologized for what had happened, out of military necessity, to a few men—rather than the larger number liable
by law for punishment—and said they knew very well that
Antony was neither cruel nor mean. "Let us banish ill will,"   181
he said, "having had our fill of crimes and punishments.
The one hundred drachmas which I ordered to be given
you is not a donative, for that would be unworthy of Antony's good fortune, rather a small present to mark our first
meeting; but it is necessary to remain obedient to the laws
of our country, and of the army, in this matter as in all
others." After delivering this speech, he did not yet add   182
anything to the donative, to avoid giving the impression
that the general was yielding to his army, but the troops
accepted the gift, either because they changed their mind
or they were afraid. Perhaps he was still angry about the   183
disobedience, or he had some other suspicion, but Antony
replaced their military tribunes, while he generally kept
the remainder in their jobs and sent them ahead in detachments along the seacoast toward Ariminum.

45. He himself selected a praetorian cohort comprising   184
the best men, in terms of physique and character, from the
whole army, and began to make his way to Rome, intending to set out for Ariminum from there. He entered the
city in swaggering manner, leaving his squadron of cavalry

---

[21] μᾶλλον ἢ δωρεὰν codd.; ἢ δωρεὰν secl. Mend.

APPIAN

πρὸ τοῦ ἄστεως στρατοπεδεύσας, τοὺς δ' ἀμφ' αὑτὸν
ἔχων ὑπεζωσμένους καὶ τὴν οἰκίαν νυκτοφυλακοῦντας
ἐνόπλους· συνθήματά τε αὐτοῖς ἐδίδοτο, καὶ αἱ φυλα-
185 καὶ παρὰ μέρος ἦσαν ὡς ἐν στρατοπέδῳ. συναγαγὼν
δὲ τὴν βουλὴν ὡς μεμψόμενος Καίσαρι περὶ τῶν πεπραγμένων, ἐσιὼν ἤδη μανθάνει τῶν τεσσάρων τελῶν
τὸ καλούμενον Ἄρειον κατὰ τὴν ὁδὸν ἐς Καίσαρα
μετατεθεῖσθαι. καὶ αὐτῷ τὴν εἴσοδον ἐπισχόντι τε καὶ
διαποροῦντι ἀγγέλλεται καὶ τὸ καλούμενον τέταρτον
186 ὁμοίως τοῖς Ἀρείοις ἐς Καίσαρα μετατεθεῖσθαι. δια-
ταραχθεὶς οὖν εἰσῆλθε μὲν ἐς τὸ βουλευτήριον, ὡς δ'
ἐφ' ἕτερα αὐτοὺς συναγαγὼν μικρὰ διελέχθη καὶ
εὐθὺς ἐπὶ τὰς πύλας ἐχώρει καὶ ἀπὸ τῶν πυλῶν ἐπὶ
187 Ἄλβην πόλιν ὡς μεταπείσων τοὺς ἀποστάντας. βαλ-
λόμενος δ' ἀπὸ τοῦ τείχους ἀνέστρεφε καὶ τοῖς ἄλλοις
τέλεσι προσέπεμπεν ἀνὰ πεντακοσίας δραχμὰς ἑκάστῳ, καὶ σὺν οἷς εἶχεν αὐτὸς ἐς Τίβυρον ἐξῄει, σκευὴν
ἔχων τὴν συνήθη τοῖς ἐπὶ τοὺς πολέμους ἐξιοῦσι· καὶ
γὰρ ἤδη σαφὴς ἦν ὁ πόλεμος, Δέκμου τὴν Κελτικὴν
οὐ μεθιέντος.

188 46. Δεῦρο δὲ ὄντι ἥ τε βουλὴ σχεδὸν ἅπασα καὶ
τῶν ἱππέων τὸ πλεῖστον ἀφίκετο ἐπὶ τιμῇ καὶ ἀπὸ τοῦ
δήμου τὸ ἀξιολογώτατον· οἱ καὶ καταλαβόντες αὐτὸν
ὀρκοῦντα τοὺς παρόντας οἱ στρατιῶται καὶ τοὺς ἐκ
τῶν πάλαι στρατευσαμένων συνδραμόντας (πολὺ γὰρ
καὶ τοῦτο ἦν) συνώμνυον ἑκόντες οὐκ ἐκλείψειν τὴν ἐς
Ἀντώνιον εὔνοιάν τε καὶ πίστιν, ὡς ἀπορῆσαι, τίνες
ἦσαν, οἳ πρὸ ὀλίγου παρὰ τὴν Καίσαρος ἐκκλησίαν

encamped outside, but bringing an entourage of battle-
ready troops, and armed night guards for his house. Passwords were given to these men, and the guards were
changed in rotation, just as in camp. He convened the   185
senate in order to criticize Octavian for what he had been
doing, but just as he was going in, he learns that one of his
four legions, the so-called legion of Mars, had, while on
the road, gone over to Octavian; and as he was delaying
his entry to ponder his difficulty, news is brought to him
that another legion, the Fourth, had followed the example
of the legion of Mars and gone over to Octavian's side.
Distracted as he was, he entered the senate, pretending   186
that he had convened them about other matters, said a few
words, and immediately departed to the city gates, and
from there to the town of Alba, to persuade the deserters
to change their minds. But they shot at him from the walls, 187
and he retreated. After sending five hundred drachmas a
man to the other legions, he took those he had with him
to Tibur. He was wearing the uniform of a man going to
war, for it was clear that there was already a state of war,
since Decimus Brutus had refused to give up Gaul.

46. While Antony was at Tibur nearly the whole senate,   188
and most of the equestrian order, came there to pay their
respects to him, as well as the most distinguished of the
plebeians. They found him swearing in his current soldiers
and the large number of his veterans who had flocked
to his side, and they voluntarily joined in taking the
oath that they would not abandon their goodwill and
loyalty to him: this caused people to wonder who those
men were who, a little before, had vilified Antony at

189   τὸν Ἀντώνιον ἐβλασφήμουν. ὁ μὲν δὴ λαμπρῶς οὕτως
ἐς τὸ Ἀρίμινον προεπέμπετο, ὅθεν ἐστὶν ἡ τῆς Κελτικῆς ἀρχή. καὶ ὁ στρατὸς ἦν αὐτῷ, χωρίς γε τῶν νεο-
λέκτων, τρία τέλη τὰ ἐκ Μακεδονίας μετάπεμπτα
(ἤδη γὰρ αὐτῷ καὶ τὸ λοιπὸν ἀφῖκτο), ἐξεστρατευμένων δὲ ἕν, οἳ[22] καὶ γηρῶντες ὅμως ἐδόκουν νεοσυλ-
190   λόγων ἀμείνους ἐς τὸ διπλάσιον εἶναι. οὕτω μὲν Ἀντωνίῳ τέσσαρα ἐγίγνετο τέλη γεγυμνασμένων ἀνδρῶν
καὶ ὅσον ἐξ ἔθους αὐτοῖς ἐπίκουρον ἄλλο ἕπεται, καὶ
ἡ τοῦ σώματος φρουρὰ καὶ τὰ νεόλεκτα. Λέπιδός τε
ἔχων ἐν Ἰβηρίᾳ τέσσαρα τέλη καὶ Ἀσίνιος Πολλίων
δύο καὶ Πλάγκος ἐν τῇ ἑτέρᾳ Κελτικῇ τρία ἐδόκουν
αἱρήσεσθαι τὰ Ἀντωνίου.

191   47. Καίσαρι δὲ ἦν δύο ὁμοίως ἀξιολογώτατα, τὰ
ἐς αὐτὸν ἀπὸ τοῦ Ἀντωνίου μεταστάντα, ἓν δὲ νεοσυλλόγων, δύο δὲ ἐκ τῶν πρότερον ἐστρατευμένων,
οὐκ ἐντελῆ μὲν ταῦτα τοῖς ἀριθμοῖς οὐδὲ ταῖς ὁπλίσε-
σιν, ὑπὸ δὲ τῶν νεοσυλλόγων καὶ ταῦτα ἀναπληρού-
192   μενα. συναγαγὼν δ' ἅπαντας ἐς Ἄλβην ἐπέστελλε
τῇ βουλῇ. ἡ δὲ ἐφήδετο μὲν αὖθις Καίσαρι,[23] ὡς ἀπο-
ρεῖν καὶ τότε, τίνες ἦσαν, οἳ προύπεμπον Ἀντώνιον·
ἤχθοντο δὲ τοῖς τέλεσιν οὐκ ἐς τὴν βουλήν, ἀλλ' ἐς
193   τὸν Καίσαρα μετελθοῦσιν. ἐπαινέσαντες δ' ὅμως αὐτούς τε καὶ τὸν Καίσαρα, ἔφασαν ὀλίγον ὕστερον ὅ
τι χρὴ ποιεῖν αὐτοὺς ψηφιεῖσθαι, ὅταν αὐτοῖς αἱ νέαι

---

[22] ἐξεστρατευμένων δὲ ἕν, οἳ Schweig.; ἐξεστρατευμένοι δὲ
ἔνιοι codd.   [23] Καίσαρι edd.; Ἀντωνίῳ codd.

Octavian's public meeting. Such was the brilliant sendoff   189
he received on his way to Ariminum, which is where the
province of Gaul begins. His army, apart from the new
recruits, consisted of the three legions summoned from
Macedonia (the remainder had now arrived), and one of
discharged veterans, who, even though old men, were
nevertheless thought to be twice as good as the new recruits. So Antony had four legions of well-trained troops,   190
and the usual auxiliary force accompanying them, besides
his bodyguard and the new recruits. Lepidus in Iberia
with four legions, Asinius Pollio with two, and Plancus in
Transalpine Gaul with three, were thought to be on his
side.[21]

47. Octavian had two equally impressive legions, the   191
ones that had deserted from Antony to him, also one legion of new recruits, and two of veterans, which although
under strength and not fully equipped, were filled out with
new recruits. He brought them all together at Alba and   192
then communicated with the senate. They were, once
again, delighted with him, so that on this occasion too,
people wondered who those men were who had given
Antony his sendoff. The senators were, however, annoyed
with the legions for going over to Octavian rather than to
the senate. All the same, they praised the troops and Oc-   193
tavian, and said they would vote on what they had to do as
soon as the new magistrates entered office. It was clear

[21] Caesar appointed Marcus Aemilius Lepidus (consul 46, 42)
to govern Nearer Spain and Narbonese Gaul, and Lucius Munatius Plancus (consul 42) the rest of Transalpine Gaul. Gaius Asinius Pollio (consul 40) was governor of Further Spain.

ἀρχαὶ ἐς τὰ πράγματα παρέλθωσιν. ἦν δὲ σαφές, ὅτι
χρήσονται μὲν αὐτοῖς κατὰ Ἀντωνίου· στρατὸν δὲ οὐδένα πω ἔχοντες ἴδιον οὐδὲ καταλέξαι χωρὶς ὑπάτων
δυνάμενοι ἐς τὰς νέας ἀρχὰς πάντα ἀνετίθεντο.

194   48. Τῷ Καίσαρι δ' ὁ στρατὸς πελέκεάς τε καὶ
ῥαβδοφόρους ἐσκευασμένους προσαγαγόντες, ἠξίουν
ἑαυτὸν ἀντιστράτηγον ἀποφῆναι, πολέμου τε ἡγεμονεύοντα καὶ σφῶν αἰεὶ ὑπ' ἄρχουσι ταχθέντων. ὁ δὲ
τὴν μὲν τιμὴν ἐπήνει, τὸ δὲ ἔργον ἐς τὴν βουλὴν ἀν-
ετίθετο· καὶ βουλομένους ἐπὶ τοῦτο χωρεῖν ἀθρόους
ἐκώλυε καὶ πρεσβευομένους ἐπεῖχεν, ὡς καὶ τῆς βουλῆς ψηφιουμένης ταῦτα καθ' ἑαυτήν, "Καὶ μᾶλλον, ἢν
αἴσθωνται τὴν ὑμετέραν προθυμίαν καὶ τὸν ἐμὸν
195   ὄκνον." διαλυθέντων δὲ μόλις οὕτω καὶ τῶν ἡγεμόνων
ἐς ὑπεροψίαν αὐτὸν αἰτιωμένων, ἐξελογεῖτο αὐτοῖς τὴν
βουλὴν οὐκ εὐνοίᾳ πρὸς αὐτὸν ἀποκλίνειν μᾶλλον ἢ
Ἀντωνίου δέει καὶ στρατιᾶς ἀπορίᾳ, "Μέχρι καθέλω-
μεν ἡμεῖς Ἀντώνιον καὶ οἱ σφαγεῖς φίλοι τε τῇ βουλῇ
καὶ συγγενεῖς ὄντες δύναμιν αὐτοῖς συναγάγωσιν· ὧν
196   αἰσθανόμενος ὑπηρετεῖν ὑποκρίνομαι. μὴ δὴ πρότεροι
τὴν ὑπόκρισιν ἀποκαλύπτωμεν, ὡς προλαβοῦσι μὲν
ἡμῖν τὴν ἀρχὴν ἐπικαλέσουσιν ὕβριν ἢ βίαν, αἰδε-
σθεῖσι δ' ἴσως ἐπιδώσουσιν αὐτοὶ δέει, μὴ παρ' ὑμῶν
197   λάβοιμι." τοιάδε εἰπὼν ἐθεᾶτο γυμνάσια τῶν δύο
τελῶν τῶν αὐτομολησάντων ἀπ' Ἀντωνίου, διαστάν-
των τε ἐς ἀλλήλους καὶ δρώντων ἀφειδῶς ἔργα πολέμου πάντα πλὴν ἐς μόνον θάνατον. ἡσθεὶς οὖν τῇ

that they were going to use these forces against Antony, but as they did not yet have an army of their own, and did not have the authority to enlist one without the consuls, they adjourned all business for the new magistrates.

48. The soldiers of Octavian produced *fasces* for him 194 and properly uniformed lictors, and urged him to assume the title of propraetor, since he was their leader in war and they were always marshaled under the command of magistrates. He thanked them for the honor, but referred the matter to the senate. And when the men wanted to march off en masse to secure it, he would not allow it and prevented them from sending a delegation, because, so he argued, the senate would vote these measures of its own accord, "And even more so," he said, "if they see your enthusiasm and my hesitation." In this way they were per- 195 suaded with difficulty to disperse, but when their leaders complained that he was ignoring them, he explained to them that it was not so much out of goodwill that the senate were leaning toward him, but out of fear of Antony and their own lack of an army; "And that will be the case," he continued, "until we destroy Antony, and the murderers, who are friends and relatives of the senators, and collect a military force for them. I can see this, and I am only pretending to help them. Let us not be the first to expose 196 this pretense. If we anticipate them in taking the magistracy, they will accuse us of arrogance and violence, whereas if we show respect they will perhaps give it of their own accord out of fear that I will accept it from you." After this speech he watched the training exercises of the 197 two legions that had deserted from Antony as they faced off against each other, and unsparingly did everything required in battle with the sole exception of killing. Octavian

θέᾳ καὶ τῆς προφάσεως ἐπιβαίνων ἄσμενος, ἑτέρας
αὐτῶν ἑκάστῳ πεντακοσίας δραχμὰς ἐπεδίδου καί, εἴ
τις πολέμου χρεία γένοιτο, νικήσασιν ἐπηγγέλλετο
πεντακισχιλίας. ὧδε μὲν ὁ Καῖσαρ δαψιλείᾳ δωρεῶν
τοὺς μισθοφόρους ἐκρατύνετο.

198   49. Καὶ τάδε μὲν ἦν ἀνὰ τὴν Ἰταλίαν, ἐν δὲ τῇ
Κελτικῇ τὸν Δέκμον ὁ Ἀντώνιος ἐκέλευσεν ἐς Μακεδονίαν μετιέναι, πειθόμενόν τε τῷ δήμῳ καὶ φειδόμε-
νον ἑαυτοῦ. ὁ δὲ ἀντέπεμπεν αὐτῷ τὰ παρὰ τῆς
βουλῆς οἱ κεκομισμένα γράμματα, ὡς οὐχὶ διὰ τὸν
δῆμον εἴκειν οἱ πρέπον ἢ διὰ τὴν βουλὴν Ἀντωνίῳ
199   μᾶλλον. Ἀντωνίου δ' αὐτῷ προθεσμίαν ὁρίζοντος,
μεθ' ἣν ὡς πολεμίῳ χρήσεται, μακροτέραν ὁ Δέκμος
ἐκέλευεν ὁρίζειν ἑαυτῷ, μὴ θᾶσσον γένοιτο τῇ βουλῇ
πολέμιος. καὶ ὁ Ἀντώνιος εὐμαρῶς ἂν αὐτοῦ κρατήσας ἔτι ὄντος ἐν πεδίῳ ἐπὶ τὰς πόλεις ἔκρινε προελ-
200   θεῖν. αἱ δὲ αὐτὸν ἐδέχοντο. καὶ δείσας ὁ Δέκμος, μὴ
οὐδ' ἐσελθεῖν ἔς τινα αὐτῶν ἔτι δύνηται, πλάσσεται
γράμματα τῆς βουλῆς καλούσης αὐτὸν ἐς Ῥώμην
σὺν τῷ στρατῷ· καὶ ἀναζεύξας ἐχώρει τὴν ἐπὶ τῆς
Ἰταλίας, ὑποδεχομένων αὐτὸν ὡς ἀπιόντα πάντων,
μέχρι Μουτίνην παροδεύσας, πόλιν εὐδαίμονα, τάς τε
πύλας ἀπέκλειε καὶ τὰ τῶν Μουτιναίων ἐς τὰς τροφὰς
συνέφερεν, ὑποζύγιά τε ὅσα ἦν κατέθυε καὶ ἐτάριχευε
δέει, μὴ χρόνιος ἡ πολιορκία γένοιτο, καὶ τὸν Ἀν-
201   τώνιον ὑπέμενε. στρατιὰ δ' ἦν αὐτῷ μονομάχων τε
πλῆθος καὶ ὁπλιτῶν τρία τέλη, ὧν ἓν μὲν ἦν ἀρτι-
στρατεύρων ἀνδρῶν ἔτι ἀπείρων, δύο δέ, ἃ καὶ πρότε-

was delighted with what he saw and, happy to use the excuse, gave each man an additional five hundred drachmas, and announced that if the need for real war arose, and they were victorious, he would give them five thousand drachmas. In this way, by means of lavish gifts, Octavian consolidated his hold on the mercenaries.

49. Such was the situation in Italy. In Gaul Antony ordered Decimus to withdraw to Macedonia in obedience to the Roman people, and for his own safety. In reply Decimus sent him the letter conveyed by the senate, arguing that it was inappropriate for him to yield to Antony because of what the people ordered, any more than because of what the senate ordered. When Antony fixed a deadline for him, after which he would treat him as an enemy, Decimus told him to fix a later date, and so avoid very quickly becoming an enemy of the senate. Although Antony would easily have defeated him, as he was still in open country, he decided to proceed first against the towns. When these received him, Decimus was afraid that he would not even be able to enter any of them, and forges a letter from the senate calling him to Rome with his army. Having broken camp, he set out on the road for Italy, everyone welcoming him since he was leaving the area, until he was passing through the rich town of Mutina. Here he closed the gates, collected together what the townspeople had to create a food supply, slaughtered and salted all the cattle he could find there in fear of a long siege, and waited for Antony. His army consisted of a large number of gladiators and three legions of infantry, one of which was composed of still inexperienced new recruits. The other two

198

199

200

201

ρον ὑπεστρατευμένα αὐτῷ πιστότατα ἦν. ὁ δ᾽ Ἀντώνιος ἐπελθὼν αὐτῷ σὺν ὀργῇ τὴν Μουτίνην ἀπετάφρευέ
τε καὶ ἀπετείχιζε.

202   50. Καὶ Δέκμος μὲν ἐπολιορκεῖτο, ἐν δὲ τῇ Ῥώμῃ
κατὰ τὴν ἐτήσιον νουμηνίαν ὕπατοι γενόμενοι Ἱρτιός
τε καὶ Πάνσας τὴν βουλὴν εὐθὺς ἐπὶ ταῖς θυσίαις ἐν
203 αὐτῷ τῷ ἱερῷ συνῆγον ἐπὶ Ἀντωνίῳ. Κικέρων μὲν δὴ
καὶ οἱ Κικέρωνος φίλοι πολέμιον αὐτὸν ἠξίουν ἤδη
ψηφίσασθαι, τὴν Κελτικὴν ἀκούσης τῆς βουλῆς ἐς
ἐπιτείχισμα τῆς πατρίδος βιαζόμενον ὅπλοις καὶ τὸν
ἐπὶ Θρᾷκας αὐτῷ δεδομένον στρατὸν ἐς τὴν Ἰταλίαν
204 διαγαγόντα· ἐπελέγοντο δὲ καὶ τὴν ἄλλην αὐτοῦ μετὰ
Καίσαρα προαίρεσιν, ἔν τε τῇ πόλει φανερῶς δορυ-
φορηθέντος ὑπὸ τοσῶνδε λοχαγῶν καὶ περὶ τὴν
οἰκίαν ὥσπερ ἄκραν ὅπλοις καὶ συνθήμασι κεχρημέ-
νου καὶ τἆλλα σοβαρωτέρου σφίσι φανέντος ἢ κατὰ
205 τὴν ἐτήσιον ἀρχήν. Λεύκιος δὲ Πείσων, ὁ τῷ Ἀντωνίῳ
τὴν ἀποδημίαν ἐπιτροπεύσας, ἀνὴρ ἐν τοῖς μάλιστα
Ῥωμαίων ἐπιφανής, ὅσοι τε ἄλλοι τῷ Πείσωνι δι᾽
αὐτὸν ἢ δι᾽ Ἀντώνιον ἢ κατ᾽ οἰκείαν γνώμην προσ-
ετίθεντο, καλεῖν αὐτὸν ἐς κρίσιν ἠξίουν, ὡς οὐ πάτριον
σφίσιν ἀκρίτου καταδικάζειν οὐδ᾽ εὐπρεπὲς τοῦ χθὲς
ὑπάτου τῆς ἐπιούσης ἡμέρας, οὗ γε μάλιστα συνεχεῖς
ἐπαίνους ἄλλοι τε καὶ Κικέρων αὐτὸς εἶπε πολλάκις.
206 ἡ δὲ βουλὴ τότε μὲν ἀγχώμαλοι ταῖς γνώμαις ἐς
νύκτα περιῆλθον, ἅμα δ᾽ ἔῳ περὶ τῶν αὐτῶν ἐς τὸ
βουλευτήριον συνελέγοντο· ἔνθα τῶν Κικερωνείων

had served under him before and were completely trust-worthy. Antony advanced against him angrily, and cut off Mutina with a ditch and wall.

50. While Decimus was under siege, at Rome on the 202 first day of the new year,[22] the incoming consuls, Hirtius and Pansa, offered sacrifice and then summoned a meeting of the senate in the Capitol itself to discuss Antony. Cicero and his associates recommended that Antony now 203 be voted a public enemy, since he had defied the wishes of the senate and taken Gaul by force of arms as a bastion against his country, and had brought into Italy the army given to him to use against the Thracians. They also criti- 204 cized him for the rest of his political program after the death of Caesar, for openly being protected at Rome by a large number of centurions, for guarding his house with arms and passwords as if it were a citadel, and for behaving toward them in other respects more arrogantly than befitted an annual magistrate. Lucius Piso, however, one of the 205 most distinguished men of Rome, who was representing Antony's interests in his absence, along with those who sided with Piso, either for his own sake, or because of Antony, or for some personal reason, proposed that Antony be summoned to a hearing, as it was not the custom of their fathers to condemn a man without trial, nor was it fitting to do so in the case of a man who was consul only the previous day, especially when Cicero, among others, had often lavished unstinting praise on him. The senate 206 was equally divided at that moment in their opinions, and remained in session until night. Early the next morning they reconvened in the senate house to consider the same

22 43 BC.

ἐπιβαρούντων ἐψήφιστο ἂν ὁ Ἀντώνιος πολέμιος, εἰ
μὴ τῶν δημάρχων Σάλουιος ἐς τὴν ἐπιοῦσαν ἐκέλευσεν ἀναθέσθαι. ἔστι δὲ ἐν τοῖς ἄρχουσιν ὁ κωλύων
ἀεὶ δυνατώτερος.

207   51. Οἱ μὲν δὴ Κικερώνειοι καὶ τούτῳ μάλα φορτι-
κῶς ὠνείδιζόν τε καὶ ἐνύβριζον καὶ τὸν δῆμον ἐκ-
δραμόντες ἠρέθιζον ἐπ᾽ αὐτὸν καὶ τὸν Σάλουιον ἐς
αὐτὸν ἐκάλουν. ὁ δὲ ἀκαταπλήκτως ἐξέτρεχεν, ἕως ἡ
βουλὴ κατέσχε δείσασα, μὴ μεταπείσειε τὸν δῆμον
208   ἐς μνήμην ἀγαγὼν Ἀντωνίου. οὐ γὰρ ἠγνόουν κατα-
γινώσκοντες ἀνδρὸς ἐπιφανοῦς πρὸ δίκης οὐδ᾽ ὅτι τὴν
Κελτικὴν ὁ δῆμος αὐτῷ δεδώκει· ἀλλ᾽ ὑπὲρ τῶν σφαγέων δεδιότες ὠργίζοντο πρώτῳ μετὰ τὴν ἀμνηστίαν
ἀνακινήσαντι τὰ κατ᾽ αὐτούς. διὸ καὶ τῷ Καίσαρι ἐς
αὐτὸν προκατεχρῶντο· καὶ ὁ Καῖσαρ οὐκ ἀγνοῶν
ᾑρεῖτο καὶ αὐτὸς ὅμως προκαθελεῖν τὸν Ἀντώνιον.
209   τοιάδε μὲν ἡ βουλὴ γνώμῃ τὸν Ἀντώνιον εἶχεν ἐν
ὀργῇ, ἀναθέμενοι δὲ τὴν ψῆφον, ὡς ὁ δήμαρχος ἐκέλευεν, ἐψηφίσαντο ὅμως Δέκμον τε ἐπαινέσαι οὐκ ἐκ-
στάντα Ἀντωνίῳ τῆς Κελτικῆς, καὶ τοῖς ὑπάτοις
Ἱρτίῳ καὶ Πάνσᾳ Καίσαρα συστρατηγεῖν οὐ νῦν
ἔχει στρατοῦ, ἐπίχρυσόν τε αὐτοῦ εἰκόνα τεθῆναι καὶ
γνώμην αὐτὸν ἐσφέρειν ἐν τοῖς ὑπατικοῖς ἤδη καὶ τὴν
ὑπατείαν αὐτὴν μετιέναι τοῦ νόμου θᾶσσον ἔτεσι

---

23 In senatorial debates, seniority dictated the order of speak-
ers, first current officeholders, then former consuls. This measure

question, and with the Ciceronian group now dominant, Antony would have been declared a public enemy, if Salvius, one of the tribunes, had not ordered a postponement until the next day. (For among the magistrates the one who has the veto always prevails.)

51. The Ciceronians abused Salvius too in a most vulgar manner and heaped insults on him, and hurrying out of the senate roused the people against him and summoned him to appear before them. Undaunted, Salvius was all set to rush out to them, until the senators stopped him because they were afraid that by reminding the people of Antony, he might change their mind. For the senate were not unaware of the fact that they were condemning a distinguished man before holding a trial, and that the people had granted him the province of Gaul. But since they were anxious on behalf of the assassins, they were angry with Antony for being the first to arouse hostility against them after the amnesty. This was why they were also using Octavian against him. Octavian was not unaware of this, but had nonetheless also made his own decision to eliminate Antony first. Such was the thinking that led the senate to be angry with Antony. Although they postponed the vote, as the tribune ordered, they did, however, pass a vote to praise Decimus for not abandoning Gaul to Antony; to instruct Octavian to share command of the army he had at this time with the consuls, Hirtius and Pansa; to erect a gilded statue of him; to allow him now to give his opinion among those of consular rank and to stand for the consulship itself ten years before the legal age;[23]

207

208

209

ensured the young Octavian an influential voice in the senate. The legal age for the consulship was forty-two.

δέκα, ἔκ τε τοῦ δημοσίου δοθῆναι τοῖς τέλεσι τοῖς ἐς
αὐτὸν ἀπὸ Ἀντωνίου μεταστᾶσιν, ὅσον αὐτοῖς ὁ Καῖ-
210 σαρ ἐπὶ τῇ νίκῃ δώσειν ὑπέσχετο. οἱ μὲν δὴ ταῦτα
ψηφισάμενοι διελύθησαν, ὡς τὸν Ἀντώνιον ἔργῳ διὰ
τῶνδε εἰδέναι πολέμιον ἐψηφισμένον καὶ τὸν δήμαρ-
211 χον ἐς τὴν ἐπιοῦσαν οὐδὲν ἔτι ἀντεροῦντα· Ἀντωνίου
δὲ ἡ μήτηρ καὶ ἡ γυνὴ καὶ παῖς ἔτι μειράκιον οἵ τε
ἄλλοι οἰκεῖοι καὶ φίλοι δι' ὅλης τῆς νυκτὸς ἐς τὰς τῶν
δυνατῶν οἰκίας διέθεον ἱκετεύοντες καὶ μεθ' ἡμέραν ἐς
τὸ βουλευτήριον ἰόντας ἠνώχλουν, ῥιπτούμενοί τε
πρὸ ποδῶν σὺν οἰμωγῇ καὶ ὀλολυγαῖς καὶ μελαίνῃ
212 στολῇ παρὰ θύραις ἐκβοῶντες. οἱ δὲ ὑπό τε τῆς
φωνῆς καὶ τῆς ὄψεως καὶ μεταβολῆς ἐς τοσοῦτον αἰ-
φνιδίου γενομένης ἐκάμπτοντο. δείσας δ' ὁ Κικέρων
ἐβουληγόρησεν ὧδε.

213   52. "Ἃ μὲν ἔδει γνῶναι περὶ Ἀντωνίου, ἐχθὲς ἔγνω-
μεν· οἷς γὰρ αὐτοῦ τοὺς ἐχθροὺς ἐτιμῶμεν, τούτοις
ἐψηφιζόμεθα εἶναι πολέμιον. Σάλουιον δὲ τὸν μόνον
ἐμποδὼν γινόμενον ἢ πάντων εἶναι χρὴ συνετώτερον
214 ἢ φιλίᾳ τάδε πράσσειν ἢ τῶν ἐνεστώτων ἀμαθίᾳ. ὧν
τὸ μὲν αἴσχιστόν ἐστιν ἡμῖν, εἰ δόξομεν ἀσυνετώτε-

---

24 Antony's mother was Julia, daughter of Lucius Julius Caesar
(consul 90). His wife at the time was Fulvia, the widow of Publius
Clodius Pulcher and Gaius Scribonius Curio, both prominent
populist politicians and supporters of Julius Caesar. She and Antony had a son, Antyllus, who was only about three years old at
this time. Appian's use of the Greek word *meirakion* to describe

and to arrange payment from public funds of the sum
Octavian promised to the legions that came over to him
from Antony, if they were victorious. After passing these 210
decrees the senate adjourned, so that Antony would know
that he had in fact been declared a public enemy by these
measures, and that on the following day the tribune would
have no further objection to make. Antony's mother, how- 211
ever, along with his wife, his son (who was still a young lad)
and his other relatives and friends spent the whole night
hurrying around the houses of the powerful soliciting their
help.[24] In the morning they accosted those going into the
senate, threw themselves at their feet with wailing and
weeping and, dressed in black, shouted from their position
by the doors. The senate began to waver when faced with 212
the sound and sight of this, and with such a drastic and
sudden change of fortune. Cicero was alarmed and addressed the senate as follows:[25]

52. "The decisions we needed to make about Antony 213
we made yesterday. With those honors that we granted his
enemies, we voted him a public enemy. Salvius, who alone
stood against us, must either be wiser than everyone else,
or moved to act by private friendship, or ignorance of
present circumstances. Of these alternatives, one is a dis- 214
grace to us, that is, if all of us together show ourselves to

him implies a much older boy, perhaps an unrecorded son of
Antony's previous marriage to his cousin Antonia.

[25] In composing this speech, Appian appears to make little or
no use of Cicero's famous series of attacks on Antony, the fourteen
speeches known as the *Philippics*, the fifth of which was delivered
on January 1, 43.

ροι πάντες ἑνὸς εἶναι, τὸ δὲ αὐτῷ Σαλουίῳ, εἰ φιλίαν
τῶν κοινῶν προτιμῴη· ἀμαθῶς δ' αὐτὸν ἔχοντα τῶν
παρόντων ἔδει πιστεύειν ὑπάτοις ἀνθ' ἑαυτοῦ καὶ
στρατηγοῖς καὶ δημάρχοις τοῖς συνάρχουσιν αὐτῷ
καὶ τοῖς ἄλλοις βουλευταῖς, οἳ τοσοίδε τὴν ἀξίωσίν
τε καὶ τὸν ἀριθμὸν ὄντες διά τε ἡλικίαν καὶ ἐμπειρίαν
ὑπὲρ τὸν Σάλουιον, καταγιγνώσκομεν Ἀντωνίου. ἔστι
δ' ἔν τε χειροτονίαις καὶ δίκαις αἰεὶ τὸ πλέον δικαι-
215 ότερον. εἰ δὲ καὶ νῦν ἔτι χρῄζει τὰς αἰτίας μαθεῖν,
λελέξεται διὰ βραχέος, ὡς ἐν ἀναμνήσει, τὰ μέγιστα
αὐτῶν. τὰ χρήματα ἡμῶν Καίσαρος ἀποθανόντος
ἐσφετερίσατο Ἀντώνιος. Μακεδονίας ἄρχειν παρ'
ἡμῶν ἐπιτυχὼν ἐπὶ τὴν Κελτικὴν ὥρμησε χωρὶς
ἡμῶν. τὸν στρατὸν ἐπὶ Θρᾷκας λαβὼν ἀντὶ Θρακῶν
ἐπήγαγεν ἡμῖν ἐς τὴν Ἰταλίαν. ἑκάτερα τούτων αἰτήσας ἡμᾶς ἐπ' ἐνέδρᾳ καὶ οὐ λαβὼν ἔπραξε δι' ἑαυτοῦ.
216 σπεῖραν ἐν Βρεντεσίῳ βασιλικὴν συνέταξεν ἀμφ' αὐτὸν εἶναι, καὶ φανερῶς αὐτὸν ἐν τῇ πόλει σιδηροφο-
ροῦντες ἄνδρες ἐδορυφόρουν τε καὶ ἐνυκτοφυλάκουν
ὑπὸ συνθήματι. ἦγεν ἐκ τοῦ Βρεντεσίου καὶ τὸν ἄλλον στρατὸν ἐς τὴν πόλιν ἅπαντα, συντομώτερον
217 ἐφιέμενος ὧν ἐπόθει Καῖσαρ.[24] Καίσαρος δὲ αὐτὸν τοῦ
νέου σὺν ἑτέρῳ στρατῷ φθάσαντος ἔδεισε καὶ ἐς τὴν
Κελτικὴν ἐτράπετο ὡς εὔκαιρον ἐφ' ἡμῖν ὁρμητήριον,
ὅτι καὶ ὁ Καῖσαρ ἐκεῖθεν ὁρμώμενος ἐδυνάστευσεν
ἡμῶν.

[24] ἐπόθει Καῖσαρ Goukowsky; ἐπένθει Καίσαρος codd.

be more stupid than a single individual; the other is a disgrace to Salvius himself, if he has prioritized private friendship over the common interest. If he was not well acquainted with the present circumstances he should have trusted in the consuls, rather than himself, and in the praetors, and in his colleagues who serve as tribunes with him, and in us the other senators, who are so imposing in dignity and numbers, so much his superiors because of our age and experience, and who condemn Antony. In our elections and in our jury trials justice is always on the side of the majority. But if he still needs to be told the reasons, 215 let me briefly articulate the most important of them, by way of a reminder. On Caesar's death Antony appropriated our money. He received from us the governorship of Macedonia, but made straight for Gaul without our permission. He got an army to use against the Thracians, but instead brought it to Italy to use against us. He asked us for each of these powers in order to trap us, and when they were refused he acted on his own authority. At Brundi- 216 sium he organized a royal cohort for personal protection, and men wielding swords openly formed his bodyguard in the city and stood on watch at night with a password. He set out to lead all the rest of his army from Brundisium to Rome, aiming to achieve more quickly what Caesar desired. But he was anticipated by the younger Caesar with 217 another army, became alarmed, and changed course for Gaul as a convenient base of attack against us, because Caesar too had used it as his base when he made himself our master.

218   53. Τὴν στρατιὰν ἐπὶ τοῖσδε καταπλησσόμενος,
ἵνα πρὸς μηθὲν αὐτῷ παρανομοῦντι κατοκνῇ, διεκλή-
ρωσεν ἐς θάνατον, οὐ στασιάσαντας ἢ φυλακὴν ἢ
τάξιν ἐν πολέμῳ λιπόντας, ἐφ᾽ ὧν μόνων ὁ στρατιω-
τικὸς νόμος τὴν οὕτως ὠμὴν ὥρισε τιμωρίαν, καὶ
ὅμως αὐτῇ καὶ ἐπὶ τοῖσδε ὀλίγοι μόλις ἐν τοῖς πάνυ
κινδύνοις ἐχρήσαντο ὑπ᾽ ἀνάγκης· ὁ δὲ φωνῆς ἢ
γέλωτος ἦγεν ἐς θάνατον τοὺς πολίτας καὶ θάνατον
219 οὐ τῶν ἐλεγχθέντων, ἀλλὰ τῶν διαλαχόντων. τοιγα-
ροῦν οἱ μὲν δυνηθέντες ἀπέστησαν αὐτοῦ, καὶ ὑμεῖς
αὐτοῖς ὡς εὖ πράξασι δωρεὰς χθὲς ἐψηφίσασθε· οἱ δὲ
οὐ δυνηθέντες ἀποδρᾶναι δεδιότες συναδικοῦσι καὶ
χωροῦσιν ἐπὶ χώραν ὑμετέραν πολέμιοι καὶ πολιορ-
κοῦσι στρατὸν ὑμέτερον καὶ στρατηγὸν ὑμέτερον, ᾧ
γράφετε μὲν ὑμεῖς ἐμμένειν τῇ Κελτικῇ, Ἀντώνιος δ᾽
220 ἐξιέναι κελεύει. πότερον οὖν ἡμεῖς Ἀντώνιον ψηφιζό-
μεθα εἶναι πολέμιον, ἢ Ἀντώνιος ἡμᾶς ἤδη πολεμεῖ,
καὶ ὁ δήμαρχος ἡμῶν ἔτι ἀγνοεῖ, μέχρι ἄρα Δέκμου
πεσόντος ἥ τε χώρα τοσήδε οὖσα καὶ ὅμορος ἡμῖν
καὶ ἐπὶ τῇ χώρᾳ ὁ Δέκμου στρατὸς ἐς τὰς καθ᾽ ἡμῶν
ἐλπίδας Ἀντωνίῳ προσγένηται. τότε γὰρ αὐτόν, ὡς
ἔοικεν, ὁ δήμαρχος ψηφιεῖται πολέμιον, ὅταν ἡμῶν
γένηται δυνατώτερος."

221   54. Ταῦτ᾽ ἔτι τοῦ Κικέρωνος λέγοντος οἱ φίλοι θο-
ρυβοῦντες ἀπαύστως οὐδενὶ ἀντειπεῖν ἐπέτρεπον, μέχρι Πείσωνος αὐτοῦ παρελθόντος ἥ τε ἄλλη βουλὴ
κατ᾽ αἰδὼ τοῦ ἀνδρὸς ἡσύχασε καὶ οἱ τοῦ Κικέρωνος
222 ἠνέσχοντο. καὶ ἔλεγεν ὁ Πείσων· "Ὁ μὲν νόμος, ὦ

53. "It was for this purpose that, in order to cow his   218
army so that they would not object to any of his illegal
activities, he had lots drawn to put men to death who had
not mutinied or left their watch or abandoned their post
in battle—and these are the only conditions under which
military law prescribes such a cruel punishment, a punishment which few have used, even in such situations, only
with reluctance and when forced to in the middle of extreme danger. Antony condemned citizens to death for
saying something or laughing, a death, moreover, of men
not convicted of wrongdoing but merely chosen by lot. For   219
this reason those who could do so deserted from him, and
yesterday you voted them a donative for doing the right
thing. Those who were not able to make their escape have
become his accomplices in wrongdoing under the influence of fear: they march against your territory like enemies and besiege your army and your general, to whom
you write with instructions to remain in Gaul, while Antony orders him to leave. So, is it we who are voting Antony   220
a public enemy, or is it Antony who is already making war
against us? And these are things our tribune still does
not know, and will, I suppose, not know until Decimus is
killed, and both the huge territory that borders on Italy
and Decimus' army as well contribute to boosting Antony's
hopes of success against us. It is only at that point, it seems,
when Antony has become stronger than us, that the tribune will vote him a public enemy."

54. Cicero was still speaking when his supporters pre-   221
vented anyone from replying by their constant uproar.
Eventually Piso himself came forward, and the rest of the
senate grew silent out of respect for the man, and even the
Ciceronians restrained themselves. Piso said: "Members   222

105

βουλή, δικαιοῖ τὸν εὐθυνόμενον αὐτὸν ἀκοῦσαί τε τῆς κατηγορίας καὶ ἀπολογησάμενον ὑπὲρ αὐτοῦ κρίνεσθαι· καὶ τὸν δεινότατον εἰπεῖν Κικέρωνα ἐς ταῦτα

223 προκαλοῦμαι. ἐπεὶ δὲ ὀκνεῖ μὲν παρόντος Ἀντωνίου κατηγορεῖν, ἀπόντος δ᾽ ἐγκλήματά τινα εἶπεν ὡς μέγιστα ἐκ πάντων καὶ ἀναμφίλογα ὄντα, παρῆλθον

224 ἐγὼ δείξων αὐτὰ ψευδῆ βραχυτάταις ἀποκρισεσι. τὰ ⟨γὰρ⟩²⁵ χρήματά φησιν Ἀντώνιον τὰ κοινὰ μετὰ τὴν Καίσαρος τελευτὴν σφετερίσασθαι, τοῦ μὲν νόμου τὸν κλέπτην οὐ πολέμιον ἀποφαίνοντος, ἀλλὰ ὡρισμένῃ δίκῃ ζημιοῦντος, Βρούτου δὲ τοῦ Καίσαρα κτείναντος ἐν τῷ δήμῳ καὶ τόδε κατηγορήσαντος, ὅτι ὁ Καῖσαρ τὰ χρήματα διεφόρησε καὶ κενὰ καταλέλοιπε τὰ ταμεῖα, Ἀντωνίου δὲ μετ᾽ οὐ πολὺ ζητεῖν αὐτὰ ψηφισαμένου καὶ ὑμῶν ἀποδεξαμένων τε τὴν γνώμην καὶ κεκυρωκότων καὶ γέρας τοῖς μηνύουσι δεκάτην ὑπεσχημένων, ἣν διπλασιάσομεν ἡμεῖς, εἴ τις Ἀντώνιον περὶ αὐτῶν ἔχοι τι διελέγχειν.

225 55. "Καὶ τάδε μὲν περὶ τῶν χρημάτων· τὴν δὲ Κελτικὴν ἡγεμονίαν οὐκ ἐψηφισάμεθα μὲν ἡμεῖς Ἀντωνίῳ, ἔδωκε δὲ ὁ δῆμος νόμῳ, παρόντος αὐτοῦ Κικέρωνος, ᾧ τρόπῳ καὶ ἕτερα πολλάκις ἔδωκε καὶ τήνδε τὴν ἡγε-

226 μονίαν αὐτὴν Καίσαρι πάλαι. μέρος δ᾽ ἐστὶ τοῦ νόμου τὸν Ἀντώνιον, τὴν δεδομένην οἱ μετιόντα, Δέκμῳ μὴ παραχωροῦντι πολεμεῖν καὶ τὸν στρατὸν ἀντὶ Θρᾳκῶν οὐδὲν ἔτι κινουμένων ἐς τὴν Κελτικὴν ἐπὶ τὸν ἀντιλέ-

²⁵ γὰρ add. Goukowsky

of the senate, the law requires that a man under investigation hear in person the charges against him, and that he be judged only after speaking in his own defense. And on this matter, I appeal to that most brilliant lawyer, Cicero. Since he is reluctant to accuse Antony while he is here, but in his absence brings certain charges which he considers the most serious of all, and irrefutable, I have come forward to show, in the briefest of replies, that these charges are false. For he says that Antony appropriated public monies after the death of Caesar. But, in the first place, the law does not declare the thief a public enemy, imposing instead a limited punishment; second, when Brutus killed Caesar, he made the same accusation before the people, that Caesar had plundered the money and left the treasury empty. Soon afterward Antony proposed a decree to investigate these matters, and you adopted and approved his motion and promised a reward of ten percent to informers, which we on our part will double, if anybody has anything they can prove against Antony in this matter.

55. "So much for the money. In relation to the governorship of Gaul, it was not we who voted this to Antony, but the people, who gave it to him by a law passed in the presence of Cicero himself, and in the same manner as they have often given other commissions, and indeed gave this very governorship to Caesar on an earlier occasion. One of the stipulations of the law is that Antony, on coming to his allotted province, should declare war on Decimus if he does not withdraw, and lead his army into Gaul against the man opposing him, instead of using it against the Thracians, who are no longer causing any upheaval.

APPIAN

227 γοντα μετάγειν. ἀλλὰ Κικέρων Δέκμον μὲν οὐχ ἡγεῖται πολέμιον, ἐναντία τῷ νόμῳ τιθέμενον ὅπλα, Ἀν-
228 τώνιον δὲ πολέμιον, τῷ νόμῳ συμμαχοῦντα. εἰ δὲ
αὐτὸν αἰτιᾶται τὸν νόμον, τοὺς θεμένους αἰτιᾶται· οὓς
ἔδει μεταπείθειν, οὐχὶ συνθέμενον ὑβρίζειν, οὐδὲ τὴν
χώραν Δέκμῳ μὲν πιστεύειν, ὃν ὁ δῆμος ἐδίωξεν ἐπὶ
τῷ φόνῳ, Ἀντωνίῳ δὲ ἀπιστεῖν, ὅ τι ὁ δῆμος ἔδωκεν.
229 οὐ γὰρ εὖ βουλευομένων ἐστὶ διαστασιάζεσθαι πρὸς
τὸν δῆμον ἐν καιροῖς μάλιστα ἐπικινδύνοις οὐδὲ
ἀμνημονεῖν, ὅτι καὶ τόδε αὐτὸ τοῦ δήμου πρότερον ἦν,
τὸ κρίνειν τὰ φίλια καὶ πολέμια. μόνος γὰρ ἐκ τῶν
πάλαι νόμων ὁ δῆμος αὐτοκράτωρ εἰρήνης πέρι καὶ
πολέμου σκοπεῖν. ὧν μηδὲν ὁ δῆμος ἐπιστήσειε μηδὲ
ἐπιμηνίσειεν ἡμῖν, προστάτου λαβόμενος.

230 56. "Ἀλλ' ἔκτεινέ τινας τῶν στρατιωτῶν ὁ Ἀντώνιος.
αὐτοκράτωρ γε ὢν καὶ ἐς τοῦτο ὑφ' ὑμῶν κεχειροτο-
νημένος. καὶ οὐδείς πω τῶνδε λόγον ὑπέσχεν αὐτοκράτωρ. οὐ γὰρ ἔκριναν οἱ νόμοι λυσιτελήσειν ἡμῖν
τὸν ἄρχοντα τοῖς στρατευομένοις ὑπεύθυνον εἶναι·
οὐδ' ἔστιν ἀπειθείας τι χεῖρον ἐν στρατοπέδῳ, δι' ἣν
καὶ νικῶντές τινες ἀνῃρέθησαν, καὶ οὐδεὶς εὔθυνε
231 τοὺς ἀνελόντας. οὐδὲ τῶν νῦν συγγενὴς οὐδείς, ἀλλὰ
Κικέρων ἐπιμέμφεται καὶ φόνου κατηγορῶν πολέμιον
κοινὸν ἀντὶ τῶν ὡρισμένων ἐπιτιμίων τοῖς φονεῦσι
232 τίθεται. Ἀντωνίῳ δὲ τὸ στρατόπεδον ὅπως τε ἄτακτον

But Cicero does not consider Decimus a public enemy 227
when the latter takes up arms against the law, and yet does
consider Antony a public enemy when he fights on the side
of the law. If Cicero is accusing the law itself, he is accus- 228
ing those who passed it: he should have persuaded them
to change their mind, not given his agreement and then
insulted them. And he should not have entrusted the province to Decimus, whom the people drove out of the city
after the murder, while refusing to entrust Antony with
what the people granted him. It is not fitting for good 229
counselors to argue with the people in times of especially
acute danger, or to forget that this very power of deciding
who are friends and who are enemies formerly belonged
to the people. According to the ancient laws the people
are the sole and absolute master in matters of peace and
war. Let us hope that this does not occur to the people and
that they do not get themselves a leader and vent their
anger on us.

56. "But, so another charge goes, Antony executed cer- 230
tain soldiers. Well, he was commander in chief and appointed to that position by you, and no commander in
chief has ever yet been required to account for such matters. For the laws have not judged it to our advantage that
a general should be answerable to his troops. There is
nothing worse in an army than disobedience, and even
after winning a victory some soldiers have been put to
death without anyone calling to account those who executed them. Now it is not even any of their relatives, but 231
Cicero who is complaining, accusing Antony of murder
and designating him a public enemy instead of invoking
the prescribed penalties for murderers. The desertion of 232
two of his legions shows how insubordinate and arrogant

109

ἦν καὶ ὅπως κατεφρόνει, δηλοῖ καὶ τὰ μεταστάντα
αὐτοῦ δύο τέλη, ἃ ὑμεῖς μὲν ἐψηφίσασθε Ἀντωνίῳ
στρατεύειν, αὐτομολήσαντα δὲ παρὰ τοὺς στρατιω-
τικοὺς νόμους, οὐ πρὸς ὑμᾶς, ἀλλ' ἐς Καίσαρα, ὁ
Κικέρων ὅμως ἐπήνεσε καὶ ἐκ τῶν κοινῶν ἐχθὲς ἐμι-
σθοδότησε· καὶ μή ποτε ὑμᾶς λυπήσειε τὸ παρά-
233 δειγμα. Κικέρωνα δὲ καὶ ἐς ἀνωμαλίαν ἐξέστησεν ἡ
ἔχθρα· κατηγορεῖ γὰρ Ἀντωνίου τυραννίδα καὶ κόλα-
σιν στρατιωτῶν, ἀεὶ τῶν ἐπιβουλευόντων τὰ στρατεύματα θεραπευόντων, οὐ κολαζόντων. ἐπεὶ δὲ οὐκ
ὤκνησεν οὐδὲ τὴν ἄλλην Ἀντωνίου μετὰ Καίσαρα
ἀρχὴν ὡς τυραννικὴν διαβαλεῖν, φέρε πύθωμαι καθ'
ἕκαστον ὧδε.

234   57. "Τίνα ἔκτεινεν ὡς τύραννος ἄκριτον ὁ νῦν κιν-
δυνεύων ἀκρίτως; τίνα δ' ἐξέβαλε τῆς πόλεως; τίνα δὲ
ὑμῖν διέβαλεν; ἢ καθ' ἕνα μὲν τοιόσδε ἦν, ἐπεβούλευε
235 δὲ πᾶσιν ὁμοῦ; πότε, ὦ Κικέρων; ὅτε τὴν ἀμνηστίαν
ἐκύρου τῶν γεγονότων; ἢ ὅτε μηδένα διώκεσθαι φόνου; ἢ ὅτε ζήτησιν εἶναι τῶν κοινῶν χρημάτων; ἢ ὅτε
Πομπήιον τὸν Πομπηίου τοῦ ὑμετέρου κατεκάλει καὶ
τὴν πατρῴαν ἐκ τῶν δημοσίων αὐτῷ διέλυε περιουσίαν; ἢ ὅτε τὸν Ψευδομάριον λαβὼν ἐπιβουλεύοντα
ἀπέκτεινε καὶ ἐπηνέσατε πάντες καὶ τοῦτο μόνον δι'
ὑμᾶς οὐ διέβαλε Κικέρων; ἢ ὅτε ἐψηφίζετο μὴ εἰσ-
ηγεῖσθαι περὶ δικτάτορος μηδένα μήτε ἐπιψηφίζειν, ἢ
236 νηποινεὶ πρὸς τοῦ θέλοντος ἀποθνήσκειν; ταῦτα γάρ

Antony's army was, legions which you voted should serve under Antony's command, and who deserted, in violation of military law, not to you, but to Octavian. Nevertheless Cicero praised them and yesterday had them paid out of the public treasury. I pray that you may never come to regret this precedent! Personal animosity has led Cicero 233 astray into inconsistency. For he accuses Antony of tyrannical behavior and punishing his soldiers, when it is always the case that such conspirators are lenient toward and do not punish the men serving under them. Since Cicero has not hesitated to slander as tyrannical all the rest of Antony's administration since Caesar's death, well now, let me examine his acts one by one.

57. "As someone who now stands in danger of being 234 condemned without trial, who exactly has Antony put to death without trial acting in tyrannical fashion? Who has he expelled from the city? Who has he slandered to you? Or, if he was so good toward individuals, did he plot against everyone collectively? And I ask you, Cicero, if he 235 did, when was that? Was it when he secured the amnesty for past events? When he declined to prosecute anyone for murder? When he proposed an inquiry into the public accounts? When he recalled Sextus Pompeius from exile, the son of your Pompey, and reimbursed him for his father's estate out of the public treasury? Or, was it when he caught the false Marius in the act of conspiracy, and executed him, and you all applauded, and because you did so, it was the only act of Antony that Cicero has not discredited? Was it when he brought in a decree that nobody should ever introduce a proposal to appoint a dictator, or vote for it, and that anybody disobeying the decree might be killed with impunity by anyone who wished? For these 236

ἐστιν, ἃ ἐπολιτεύσατο ἡμῖν Ἀντώνιος ἐν δύο μησίν, οἷς μόνος[26] ἐπέμεινε τῇ πόλει μετὰ Καίσαρα, ἄρτι μὲν τοῦ δήμου τοὺς φονέας διώκοντος, ἄρτι δὲ ὑμῶν δεδιότων ἐπὶ τοῖς ἐσομένοις· οὗ τίνα καιρόν, εἰ πονηρὸς

237 ἦν, ἀμείνονα εἶχεν; ἀλλ' ἐς τὰ ἐναντία· οὐκ ἦρχε. πῶς; οὐ μόνος ἦρχεν ἀποδημήσαντος ἐπὶ Συρίας Δολοβέλλα; οὐ στρατὸν εἶχεν ἕτοιμον ἐν τῇ πόλει τὸν ὑφ' ἡμῶν αὐτῷ δεδομένον; οὐκ ἐνυκτοφυλάκει τὴν πόλιν; οὐκ ἐνυκτοφυλακεῖτο διὰ τὴν τῶν ἐχθρῶν ἐπιβουλήν;

238 οὐ πρόφασιν εἶχε τὴν σφαγὴν Καίσαρος, φίλου τέ οἱ καὶ εὐεργέτου ὄντος καὶ τῷ δήμῳ μάλιστα ὑπεραρέσκοντος; οὐχ ἑτέραν εἶχεν οἰκείαν, ἐπιβεβουλευμένος ἐς τὸ σῶμα ὑπὸ τῶν ἀνδρῶν; ὧν ἔκτεινε μὲν ἢ ἐφυγάδευσεν οὐδένα, συνέγνω δέ, ὅσον εἶχε μέτρου καλῶς, καὶ διδομένας αὐτοῖς ἡγεμονίας οὐκ ἐφθόνησε δοθῆναι.

239   58. "Τὰ μὲν δὴ μέγιστα, ὦ Ῥωμαῖοι, καὶ ἀναμφίλογα Κικέρωνος ἐς τὸν Ἀντώνιον ἐγκλήματα ὁρᾶτε· ἐπεὶ δέ γε ἐπὶ τοῖς ἐγκλήμασι καὶ μαντεύματα ἐπάγουσιν, ὡς ὁ Ἀντώνιος ἔμελλε μὲν τὸν στρατὸν ἄξειν ἐπὶ τὴν πόλιν, δείσειε δὲ προλαβόντος αὐτὴν ἑτέρῳ στρατῷ Καίσαρος, πῶς οὖν, εἰ τὸ μελλῆσαι μόνον ἐστὶν ἀνδρὸς πολεμίου, τὸν ἐλθόντα καὶ παραστρατοπεδεύσαντα ἡμῖν ἀσήμαντον οὐχ ἡγεῖται πολέμιον;

26 μόνος Goukowsky; μόνοις codd.

are the public acts that Antony carried out for us during the two months in which he remained in sole control after Caesar's death, the very time when the people were pursuing the murderers, the very time you feared for the future. If he were a villain, what better opportunity could he have had? But, on the contrary, you will say, he was not in authority.[26] How can that be? Did he not exercise sole authority after Dolabella departed for Syria? Did he not keep an armed force that you gave him in readiness in the city? Did he not patrol the city by night? Was he not guarded at night because of the conspiracy of his enemies against him? Did he not have an excuse for this in the murder of Caesar, his friend and benefactor, the man on whom the people bestowed their particular affection? And did he not have another personal excuse in the fact that the murderers conspired against his life also? Yet he did not kill or exile any of them, but pardoned them, in as far as he could do so with respectability, and did not begrudge them the governorships that were granted to them.

58. "You see, then, men of Rome, the most grave and unambiguous accusations that Cicero makes against Antony. But since in addition to charges, my opponents introduce prophetic forecasts, namely that Antony was intending to lead his army against Rome, but became afraid when Octavian got there first with another army, how is it that mere intention is enough to make a man a public enemy, but when someone actually comes and pitches his camp right beside us without proper insignia, Cicero does not regard him as a public enemy?

[26] The Greek text, and Appian's precise meaning, are disputed at this point.

240 πῶς δ᾽, εἴπερ ἤθελεν ὁ Ἀντώνιος, οὐκ ἀφίκετο; ἢ τρισ-
μυρίους ἔχων συντεταγμένους ἔδεισε τρισχιλίους
τοὺς ἀμφὶ τὸν Καίσαρα ὄντας ἀνόπλους, ἀσυντά-
κτους, ἐς μόνας Καίσαρι διαλλαγὰς συνελθόντας καὶ
εὐθύς, ὡς ἔγνωσαν πολεμεῖν αἱρούμενον, καταλιπό-
241 ντας; εἰ δὲ μετὰ τρισμυρίων ἐλθεῖν ἔδεισε, πῶς ἦλθε
μετὰ μόνων χιλίων; μεθ᾽ ὧν αὐτὸν ἐς τὸ Τίβυρον ἐξ-
ιόντα πόσοι προεπέμπομεν καὶ πόσοι συνώμνυμεν
οὐχ ὁρκούμενοι; πόσους δὲ Κικέρων ἐπαίνους ἐς τὴν
242 πολιτείαν αὐτοῦ καὶ ἀρετὴν ἀνάλισκε; πῶς δ᾽ αὐτὸς
Ἀντώνιος, εἴ τι τοιοῦτον ἐγίγνωσκε, τὰ ἐνέχυρα τὰ
νῦν ὄντα πρὸ τοῦ βουλευτηρίου κατέλιπεν ἡμῖν; μητέρα καὶ γυναῖκα καὶ μειράκιον υἱόν; οἳ κλαίουσι καὶ
δεδίασι νῦν οὐ τὴν Ἀντωνίου πολιτείαν, ἀλλὰ τὴν τῶν
ἐχθρῶν δυναστείαν.

243 59. "Ταῦτα μὲν δὴ πρὸς ὑμᾶς ἐξενήνοχα δεῖγμα τῆς
Ἀντωνίου τε ἀπολογίας καὶ Κικέρωνος μεταβολῆς·
παραίνεσιν δ᾽ ἐπιθήσω τοῖς εὖ φρονοῦσι μήτε ἐς τὸν
δῆμον μήτε ἐς Ἀντώνιον ἁμαρτάνειν μηδὲ ἔχθρας καὶ
κινδύνους ἐπάγειν τοῖς κοινοῖς, νοσούσης ἔτι τῆς πολιτείας καὶ ἀπορούσης τῶν ὀξέως ἀμυνούντων, δύναμιν δ᾽ ἐν τῇ πόλει συστησαμένους, πρὶν θορυβῆσαί
τι τῶν ἔξω, τὴν ἀρκέσουσαν, τότε τοῖς ἑκάστοτε ἐπεί-
γουσιν ἐφεδρεύειν καὶ κρίνειν, οὓς ἂν ἐθέλητε, δυ-
244 ναμένους τὸ κεκριμένον τελεῖν. πῶς οὖν ἔσται ταῦτα;
ἐὰν Ἀντώνιον μὲν ἐῶμεν ἐς πρόφασιν ἢ χάριν τοῦ
δήμου τὴν Κελτικὴν ἔχειν, Δέκμον δὲ μετὰ τριῶν ὧν
ἔχει τελῶν ἐνθάδε καλῶμεν καὶ ἀφικόμενον ἐκπέμπω-

Why did Antony not come, if he had wanted to? Or, with   240
his thirty thousand regular troops are we to think that
he was afraid of Octavian's three thousand ill-equipped,
disorganized men who had joined his side only to effect a
reconciliation, and abandoned him as soon as they found
out that he had decided on war? If Antony was afraid to   241
come with thirty thousand, how is it he dared to come with
only one thousand? When he left for Tibur with them, how
many of us accompanied him on his way, and how many
of us voluntarily swore an oath of loyalty to him? What
praises Cicero lavished on his policies and virtues! If   242
Antony himself was deciding any such terrible thing, why
did he leave us the pledges that are now outside the senate
house, his mother and his wife and his young son, who
weep in fear not of Antony's policies, but of the domination of his enemies.

59. "I have brought these matters to your attention as   243
a demonstration of how to exonerate Antony, and show
how Cicero has changed his mind. I will add an exhortation to right-minded men not to wrong the people or
Antony, and not to introduce personal hostilities and dangers in public, while the state is sickly and short of resolute
defenders. Instead, put together an adequate force in the
city before causing any trouble abroad, and then keep an
eye on those who press you at any stage, and pass judgment on whoever you want to, when you have the capacity
to enforce your decision. How can this be done? By allow-   244
ing Antony to keep Gaul, using the people either as an
excuse or to oblige them, and by recalling Decimus to
Rome with his three legions and, when he arrives, sending

245 μεν ἐς Μακεδονίαν, τὰ τέλη κατασχόντες. εἰ δὲ καὶ τὰ
ἀπ᾽ Ἀντωνίου μεταστάντα δύο πρὸς ἡμᾶς μετέστη,
καθάπερ φησὶ Κικέρων, καὶ τάδε καλῶμεν ἀπὸ τοῦ
Καίσαρος ἐς τὴν πόλιν. οὕτω γὰρ πέντε τελῶν ἡμῖν
ὑπαρχόντων ψηφιζοίμεθα ἄν, ὅ τι δοκιμάζοιμεν, ἐγκρατῶς, ἐς οὐδενὸς ἀνδρὸς ἐλπίδας αἰωρούμενοι.

246 60. "Καὶ τάδε μὲν εἴρηται τοῖς ἄνευ φθόνου καὶ
φιλονικίας ἀκροωμένοις· τοῖς δὲ ἀπερισκέπτως καὶ
ἀπαρασκεύως δι᾽ οἰκείαν ἔχθραν ἢ φιλονικίαν ἐκ-
θορυβοῦσιν ὑμᾶς κριτὰς παραινῶ μὴ ταχεῖς εἶναι
μηδὲ προπετεῖς ἐς ἄνδρας μεγίστους τε καὶ στρατιᾶς
ἄρχοντας ἱκανῆς μηδὲ ἄκοντας ἐκπολεμοῦν, ἀνα-
μιμνησκομένους Μαρκίου τε τοῦ Κοριολανοῦ καὶ τὰ
ἔναγχος δὴ ταῦτα Καίσαρος, ὃν στρατιᾶς ὁμοίως
ἡγούμενον καὶ σπονδὰς ἀρίστας ἂν ἡμῖν γενομένας
προτείνοντα προπετῶς πολέμιον ψηφισάμενοι τῷ ὄντι

247 πολέμιον ἠναγκάσαμεν γενέσθαι, φείδεσθαι δὲ καὶ
τοῦ δήμου πρὸ βραχέος τοῖς φονεῦσι τοῖς Καίσαρος
ἐπιδραμόντος, μὴ ἐς ὕβριν αὐτοῦ δοκῶμεν τοῖς μὲν
ἡγεμονίας ἐθνῶν διδόναι, Δέκμον δὲ ἐπαινεῖν, ὅτι τοῦ
δήμου νόμον ἀκυροῖ, καὶ Ἀντώνιον πολέμιον κρίνειν,

248 ὅτι τὴν Κελτικὴν ἔλαβε παρὰ τοῦ δήμου. ὧν τοὺς μὲν
εὖ βουλευομένους ἐνθυμεῖσθαι χρὴ ὑπὲρ τῶν ἔτι πλα-
νωμένων, τοὺς δ᾽ ὑπάτους καὶ δημάρχους ἡγεμόνας[27]
κινδυνεύουσι τοῖς κοινοῖς γενέσθαι."

[27] ἡγεμόνας Mend.; πλείονας codd.

him off to Macedonia, but holding back the legions. And   245
if, as Cicero says, the two legions that deserted from Antony in fact deserted to us, let us summon them too to
leave Octavian and come to Rome. In this way, with five
legions at our disposal, we would be able to pass whatever
measures we approve, and do so with confidence, and without depending on the hopes of any individual.

60. "I have addressed these words to those who listen   246
without malice or aggression. Those who are thoughtlessly
and hastily agitating you out of personal hostility or rivalry
I urge not to make hurried or reckless judgments against
the most powerful men, in command of big armies, and
not to force them into war against their will. Remember
Marcius Coriolanus, and indeed, the recent case of Caesar: by recklessly voting him a public enemy when he too
was leading an army and offering a treaty that would have
been excellent for us, we forced him to become an enemy
in reality.[27] I urge you also to be considerate of the people,   247
who only recently attacked Caesar's assassins, to make sure
we do not appear to insult them by giving some of the murderers provincial governorships, and by praising Decimus
for ignoring a law of the people, while voting Antony a
public enemy because he received Gaul from the people.
It is necessary that men of good counsel take these matters   248
into account on behalf of those who are still in doubt, and
that the consuls and tribunes take on the role of leaders in
the midst of these public dangers."

[27] According to the story made famous by Shakespeare,
Gnaeus Marcius Coriolanus was forced out of Rome for his harsh
behavior, took up residence with the Volscians, and led them in
war against Rome.

249   61. Ὧδε μὲν ὁ Πείσων ἀπελογεῖτο καὶ ὠνείδιζεν ὁμοῦ καὶ ἐφόβει καὶ σαφῶς αἴτιος ἐγένετο μὴ ψηφισθῆναι πολέμιον Ἀντώνιον. οὐ μὴν ἐκράτησε τῆς Κελτικῆς αὐτὸν ἄρχειν· οἱ γὰρ τῶν σφαγέων φίλοι τε καὶ συγγενεῖς ὑπὸ δέους ἐκώλυσαν, μὴ τοῦ πολέμου λυθέντος ἐπεξέλθοι τὸν φόνον Καίσαρι συναλλαγείς· διὸ καὶ στασιάζειν αἰεὶ παρεσκεύαζον Καίσαρά τε

250 καὶ Ἀντώνιον. ἐψηφίσαντο δ᾽ Ἀντωνίῳ προαγορεῦσαι Μακεδονίαν ἀντὶ τῆς Κελτικῆς ἔχειν· τὰς δὲ ἄλλας ἐντολάς, εἴτε λαθόντες εἴτ᾽ ἐξεπίτηδες, Κικέρωνα συγγράψαι τε καὶ δοῦναι τοῖς πρεσβεύουσι προσέταξαν.

251 ὁ δὲ τὴν γνώμην παραφέρων συνέγραφεν ὧδε· "Μουτίνης Ἀντώνιον εὐθὺς ἀπανίστασθαι καὶ Δέκμῳ τὴν Κελτικὴν μεθιέναι, ἐντὸς δὲ Ῥουβίκωνος ποταμοῦ, τοῦ τὴν Ἰταλίαν ὁρίζοντος ἀπὸ τῆς Κελτικῆς, ἡμέρᾳ ῥητῇ γενόμενον ἐπιτρέψαι τὰ καθ᾽ ἑαυτὸν ἅπαντα τῇ

252 βουλῇ." οὕτω μὲν φιλονίκως τε καὶ ψευδῶς τὰς ἐντολὰς ὁ Κικέρων συνέγραφεν, οὐδεμιᾶς ἔχθρας τοσῆσδε ὑπούσης, ἀλλ᾽, ὡς ἔοικε, τοῦ δαιμονίου τὰ κοινὰ ἐς μεταβολὴν ἐνοχλοῦντος καὶ αὐτῷ Κικέρωνι κακῶς

253 ἐπινοοῦντος. ἄρτι δὲ καὶ τῶν Τρεβωνίου λειψάνων κομισθέντων καὶ τῆς ἐς αὐτὸν ὕβρεως γνωσθείσης ἀκριβέστερον, οὐ δυσχερῶς ἡ βουλὴ τὸν Δολοβέλλαν ἔκρινεν εἶναι πολέμιον.

254   62. Οἱ δ᾽ ἐς τὸν Ἀντώνιον ἀπεσταλμένοι πρέσβεις, αἰδούμενοι τῶν ἐντολῶν τὸ ἀλλόκοτον, οὐδὲν μὲν ἔφασαν, αὐτὰς δ᾽ ἐπέδοσαν αὐτῷ. καὶ ὁ Ἀντώνιος σὺν ὀργῇ πολλὰ ἔς τε τὴν βουλὴν καὶ τὸν Κικέρωνα

61. Such was Piso's defense of Antony, which criticized 249
and at the same time frightened his opponents, and which
was clearly the reason why Antony was not voted a public
enemy. He did not, however, succeed in getting control of
Gaul for Antony to govern, for the friends and relatives of
the assassins prevented this out of fear that, once the war
came to an end, he might be reconciled with Octavian and
seek to avenge the murder. That is why they continually
tried to arrange that Octavian and Antony should be at
odds with each other. They passed a motion to proclaim 250
that Antony should have Macedonia instead of Gaul, and
instructed Cicero—it is not clear whether they chose him
by accident or design—to compose a document contain-
ing the senate's other orders and give it to the envoys. But 251
Cicero falsified the decree and wrote as follows: "Antony
must immediately raise the siege of Mutina, cede Gaul to
Decimus, withdraw south of the river Rubicon (which
forms the boundary between Italy and Gaul) on a specified day, and submit all his affairs to the authority of the
senate." Such were the provocative and false instructions 252
Cicero drew up, not, so it seems, because of an underlying
personal hostility, but because some divine spirit was in-
terfering in public affairs to effect change, and was intending bad things for Cicero himself. Since it was also the case 253
that Trebonius' remains had recently been repatriated and
people had more accurate information about the violence
done to him, the senate had no difficulty in deciding to
declare Dolabella a public enemy.

62. The ambassadors who had been sent to Antony, 254
ashamed of the extraordinary character of the orders, said
nothing, but simply delivered them to him. Antony was
furious and directed fierce abuse against the senate and

ἀπερρίπτει, θαυμάζων, ὅτι Καίσαρα μὲν τὸν τὰ μέγιστα ὠφελήσαντα τὴν ἀρχὴν ἡγοῦνται τύραννον ἢ βασιλέα, Κικέρωνα δὲ οὐ νομίζουσιν, ὃν Καῖσαρ μὲν εἷλε πολέμῳ καὶ οὐκ ἀπέκτεινε, Κικέρων δὲ τοὺς ἐκείνου φονέας προτίθησι τῶν φίλων αὐτοῦ καὶ Δέκμον Καίσαρι μὲν ὄντα φίλον ἐμίσει, ἀνδροφόνον δὲ αὐτοῦ γενόμενον ἀγαπᾷ, καὶ τῷ μὲν παρ' οὐδενὸς μετὰ Καίσαρα λαβόντι τὴν Κελτικὴν προστίθεται, τῷ δὲ παρὰ
255 τοῦ δήμου λαβόντι πολεμεῖ. "Τῶν τε ἐψηφισμένων μοι τελῶν τοῖς μὲν αὐτομολήσασι γέρα δίδωσι, τοῖς δὲ παραμείνασιν οὔ, διαφθείρων οὐκ ἐμοὶ μᾶλλον ἀλλὰ
256 τῇ πόλει τὰ στρατιωτικά. καὶ τοῖς μὲν ἀνδροφόνοις ἀμνηστίαν ἔδωκεν, ᾗ κἀγὼ συνεθέμην διὰ δύο ἄνδρας αἰδεσίμους· Ἀντώνιον δὲ καὶ Δολοβέλλαν ἡγεῖται πολεμίους, ὅτι τῶν δεδομένων ἐχόμεθα. ἥδε γάρ ἐστιν ἡ ἀληθὴς αἰτία· κἂν ἀποστῶ τῆς Κελτικῆς, οὔτε πολέμιος οὔτε μόναρχός εἰμι. ταῦτα μέντοι μαρτύρομαι λύσειν τὴν οὐκ ἀγαπωμένην ἀμνηστίαν."
257 63. Τοιάδε πολλὰ εἰπὼν ὁ Ἀντώνιος ἀντέγραφε τῷ δόγματι τῇ μὲν βουλῇ πεισθῆναι ἂν ἐς ἅπαντα ὡς πατρίδι, Κικέρωνι δὲ τῷ συγγράψαντι τὰς ἐντολὰς ὧδε ἀποκρίνεσθαι· "Ὁ δῆμος ἔδωκέ μοι τὴν Κελτικὴν νόμῳ, καὶ Δέκμον ἀπειθοῦντα τῷ νόμῳ μετελεύσομαι καὶ τοῦ φόνου δίκας ἀπαιτήσω μόνον ὑπὲρ ἁπάντων, ἵνα καὶ ἡ βουλὴ καθαρεύσῃ ποτὲ τοῦ μύσους, ἐμπι-
258 πλαμένη νῦν διὰ Κικέρωνα Δέκμῳ βοηθοῦντα." τάδε μὲν ὁ Ἀντώνιος εἶπέ τε καὶ ἀντέγραψε, καὶ ἡ βουλὴ αὐτὸν αὐτίκα ἐψηφίζετο εἶναι πολέμιον καὶ τὸν ὑπ'

Cicero. He expressed astonishment that they should consider Caesar (the man who had contributed most to the Roman empire) a tyrant and a king, but not Cicero. Caesar had made him a prisoner of war, but did not kill him, while Cicero values Caesar's assassins more highly than his friends. He hated Decimus while he was a friend of Caesar, but loves him once he became his murderer. He sides with the man who received Gaul after Caesar's death from nobody, but makes war on the man who received it from the people. "He rewards those who deserted from the 255 legions voted to me, but not those who stayed, in the process subverting military discipline not so much for me as for Rome. Although he has granted an amnesty to the 256 murderers, to which I too gave my assent on account of two men who deserve respect, he regards Antony and Dolabella as public enemies because we hold on to what was given to us. That is the real reason. And if I just withdraw from Gaul, then I am no longer either public enemy or autocrat! I guarantee that this situation will bring an end to our unloved amnesty."

63. After saying a great deal along the same lines, An- 257 tony wrote in reply to the decree that he would obey the senate in all matters, as they represented his fatherland, but to Cicero who composed the instructions, this was his answer: "The people gave me Gaul by a law, and I will go after Decimus for not obeying the law. I will also exact punishment for the murder from him alone, on behalf of them all, so that the senate may at last be purged of the pollution of which it now takes its fill through Cicero's support of Decimus." In response to what Antony said, 258 and wrote in his reply, the senate immediately voted him

αὐτῷ στρατόν, εἰ μὴ ἀποσταῖεν αὐτοῦ· Μακεδονίας
δὲ καὶ τῆς Ἰλλυρίδος αὐτῆς καὶ τῶν ἐν ἀμφοτέραις
ὑπολοίπων στρατῶν Μᾶρκον Βροῦτον ἄρχειν, μέχρι
259 κατασταίη τὰ κοινά. ὁ δὲ ἴδιόν τε εἶχεν ἤδη στρατὸν
καὶ παρὰ Ἀπουληίου τινὰ προσειλήφει καὶ ναῦς εἶχε
μακράς τε καὶ ὁλκάδας καὶ χρημάτων ἐς μύρια καὶ
ἑξακισχίλια τάλαντα καὶ ὅπλα πολλά, ὅσα ἐν Δημη-
τριάδι Γαΐῳ Καίσαρι ἐκ πολλοῦ γιγνόμενα εὗρεν· οἷς
ἅπασιν αὐτὸν ἡ βουλὴ τότε ἐψηφίζετο ἐς τὰ συμ-
260 φέροντα τῆς πατρίδος χρῆσθαι. ἐψηφίσαντο δὲ καὶ
Κάσσιον ἄρχειν τε Συρίας καὶ πολεμεῖν Δολοβέλλᾳ·
τούς τε ἄλλους, ὅσοι τινὸς ἔθνους ἢ στρατοῦ Ῥωμαίων ἄρχουσιν ἀπὸ τῆς Ἰονίου θαλάσσης ἐπὶ τὴν
ἕω, πάντας ὑπακούειν ἐς ὅ τι προστάσσοι Κάσσιος ἢ
Βροῦτος.

261 64. Ὧδε μὲν ὀξέως σὺν ἀφορμῇ τοὺς ἀμφὶ τὸν
Κάσσιον ἐξελάμπρυνον, καὶ ὁ Καῖσαρ ἕκαστα μαθὼν
ἠπόρητο, τὴν μὲν ἀμνηστίαν ἡγούμενος εὐπρέπειαν
ἐσχηκέναι φιλανθρωπίας καὶ ἐλέους[28] συγγενῶν ἀνδρῶν καὶ ὁμοτίμων, καὶ τὰς βραχυτέρας ἡγεμονίας
ἀσφάλειαν· Δέκμῳ τε τὴν Κελτικὴν βεβαιοῦντας
Ἀντωνίῳ δόξαι περὶ τυραννίδος διαφέρεσθαι, ᾧ προσ-
262 ποιήματι καὶ αὐτὸν ὑπάγεσθαι κατ᾽ Ἀντωνίου· τὸ δὲ
καὶ Δολοβέλλαν πολέμιον ψηφίσασθαι δι᾽ ἕνα τῶν

[28] ἐλέους Goukowsky; ἔλεος P; ἐλέου L; ἔλεον BJ

a public enemy, and the troops under his command, if they did not detach themselves from him. As for Macedonia and Illyria itself, along with the forces still remaining in both, Marcus Brutus was to be in command, until public affairs were stabilized. Brutus already had his own army, and had received additional troops from Appuleius.[28] He also had warships and transports and about sixteen thousand talents in money, and large quantities of arms which he found in Demetrias, where they had been collected for Gaius Caesar long before. The senate now voted that he should avail of all these resources for the benefit of the fatherland. They also decided that Cassius should be governor of Syria and make war on Dolabella, and that all other provincial governors and army commanders east of the Ionian Sea should take their orders from Cassius or Brutus.

64. In this way the senate quickly took the opportunity to make things look brighter for Cassius and his associates. But on hearing all the details, Octavian did not know what to do. He regarded the amnesty as a decent display of humanity and pity for the relatives and peers of the men, and the rather minor commands as a form of protection. Confirming Decimus in Gaul seemed to Octavian to be a product of the senate's dispute with Antony about his tyranny, which was the excuse they used to employ himself against Antony. But the voting of Dolabella a public enemy because he had put one of the murderers to death,

259

260

261

262

---

[28] Marcus Appuleius (consul 20) had been quaestor in 45, and then proquaestor in Asia. On his way back from Asia in late 44, he met Brutus at Carystus in Euboea and handed over his forces and funds to him.

ἀνδροφόνων ἀναιρεθέντα καὶ Βρούτῳ καὶ Κασσίῳ
τὰς ἡγεμονίας ἐς τὰ μέγιστα ἔθνη διαλλάξαι στρα-
τόπεδά τε δοῦναι πολλὰ ἀθρόως καὶ χρήματα καὶ
ἡγεμόνας ἡγεμονῶν ἀποφῆναι πάντων, ὅσοι πέραν
εἰσὶ τῆς Ἰονίου θαλάσσης, σαφῶς εἶναι τὴν μὲν Πομπηίου μοῖραν αὐξόντων, τὴν δὲ Καίσαρος καθαιρού-
263 ντων. ἐνεθυμεῖτο δὲ καὶ τῆς ἐς αὐτὸν ὡς μειράκιον
τέχνης, εἰκόνα μὲν αὐτῷ καὶ προεδρίαν παρασχόντων
καὶ ἀντιστράτηγον ἀποφηνάντων, ἔργῳ δὲ ἴδιον αὐτοῦ τὸν στρατὸν ὄντα ἀφαιρουμένων· ὑπάτων γὰρ
264 συστρατηγούντων οὐδὲν εἶναι τὸν ἀντιστράτηγον· τά
τε γέρα τοῖς ἀπὸ Ἀντωνίου μόνοις μεταστᾶσιν ἐψηφισμένα τοὺς αὐτῷ στρατευομένους ἀτιμοῦν· καὶ τὸν
πόλεμον ὅλως αὐτῷ μὲν αἰσχύνην ἔχειν, ἔργῳ δὲ τὴν
βουλὴν ἀποχρῆσθαί οἱ κατὰ Ἀντωνίου, μέχρι καθ-
έλωσιν αὐτόν.

265   65. Ταῦτα λογιζόμενος ἐπέκρυπτε καὶ θύων ἐπὶ τῇ
δεδομένῃ ἀρχῇ πρὸς τὸν στρατὸν ἔφη· "Καὶ τάδε μοι
παρ' ὑμῶν, ὦ συστρατιῶται, γέγονεν, οὐ νῦν, ἀλλ'
ἐξ οὗ τὴν ἀρχὴν ἐδίδοτε· καὶ γὰρ ἡ βουλὴ δι' ὑμᾶς
ἔδωκεν. ὥστε ἐμὲ καὶ τούτων ἴστε τὴν χάριν ὑμῖν
ὀφλήσοντα καί, ἢν οἱ θεοὶ παρέχωσιν εὐπραγεῖν,
266 ἀποδώσοντα ἀθρόως." ὁ μὲν οὑτωσὶ τὸν στρατὸν οἰ-
κειούμενος ὑπήγετο, τῶν δὲ ὑπάτων Πάνσας μὲν ἀνὰ
τὴν Ἰταλίαν ἐξενάγει, Ἴρτιος δὲ τῷ Καίσαρι τὸν
στρατὸν ἐμερίζετο καί, ὡς αὐτῷ παρὰ τῆς βουλῆς ἐν
ἀπορρήτῳ λέλεκτο, ἐς τὸ μέρος ᾔτει τὰ δύο τέλη τὰ
παρὰ Ἀντωνίου μεταστάντα, εἰδὼς τάδε ὄντα τοῦ

the transfer of the commands of Brutus and Cassius to the largest provinces, the sudden granting of large armies and large sums of money to them, and their appointment in command of all the governors east of the Ionian Sea— these were clearly the actions of men trying to build up the party of Pompey and destroy that of Caesar. He also 263 mulled over their sly treatment of him as an adolescent, in providing him a statue and a front seat at the theater, and giving him the title of propraetor, when in fact they were taking from him the army rightfully his: for a propraetor is nothing when consuls are in joint command. And the 264 rewards voted only to those soldiers who had deserted from Antony were an insult to the men serving with himself. In short, the war brought him disgrace, for the truth was the senate were only using him against Antony until they had destroyed the latter.

65. Octavian kept these thoughts to himself, and after 265 offering sacrifice on assuming the command granted to him, he addressed the army: "These honors, too, my fellow soldiers, have come to me from you, not just right now, but from the moment that you set out to give me the command: for it was because of you that the senate granted it to me. You should know, therefore, that you will have my gratitude for this too, and that, if the gods grant us success, I will repay you in full." While he was conciliating the army 266 in this way and making it his own, one of the consuls, Pansa, was collecting recruits throughout Italy, and the other, Hirtius, was dividing the command of the army with Octavian. Following secret instructions he received from the senate, Hirtius demanded as his share the two legions that had deserted from Antony, knowing that they were the most distinguished in the army. Octavian conceded

στρατοῦ τὸ ἀξιολογώτατον. καὶ ὁ μὲν Καῖσαρ ἅπαντα
συνεχώρει, μερισάμενοι δὲ ἐχείμαζον μετ᾽ ἀλλήλων·
267 παροδεύοντος δὲ τοῦ χειμῶνος ἤδη Δέκμος μὲν
ἔκαμνεν ὑπὸ λιμοῦ, Ἵρτιος δὲ καὶ Καῖσαρ ἐς τὴν
Μουτίνην ἐχώρουν, μὴ κάμνοντα τὸν Δέκμου στρατὸν
268 ὁ Ἀντώνιος παραλάβοι. ἀκριβῶς δὲ τῆς Μουτίνης φυ-
λασσομένης ὑπὸ τοῦ Ἀντωνίου, πανσυδὶ μὲν οὐ συνεπλέκοντο αὐτῷ Πάνσαν περιμένοντες, ἱππομαχίαι δ᾽
ἦσαν πυκναί, πολὺ μὲν πλείους ἱππέας ἔχοντος Ἀν-
τωνίου· τοῦ πεδίου δὲ ἡ δυσχέρεια, διὰ χειμάρρους
ἐκτεταφρευμένου, τὴν πλεονεξίαν τὸ πλῆθος ἀπεστέ-
ρει.

269   66. Καὶ τάδε μὲν ἦν ἀμφὶ τῇ Μουτίνῃ, τὰ δ᾽ ἐν
Ῥώμῃ τῶν ὑπάτων οὐ παρόντων ὁ Κικέρων ἦγεν ὑπὸ
δημοκοπίας· καὶ συνεχεῖς ἦσαν ἐκκλησίαι, ὅπλα τε
εἰργάζετο συναγαγὼν τοὺς δημιουργοὺς ἀμισθὶ καὶ
χρήματα συνέλεγε καὶ βαρυτάτας ἐσφορὰς τοῖς
270 Ἀντωνίου φίλοις ἐπετίθει. οἱ δὲ ἑτοίμως ἐσέφερον
ἐκλυόμενοι τὴν διαβολήν, μέχρι Πούπλιος Οὐεντίδιος, ἐστρατευμένος τε Γαΐῳ Καίσαρι καὶ Ἀντωνίῳ
φίλος ὤν, οὐκ ἤνεγκε τὴν βαρύτητα τοῦ Κικέρωνος,
ἀλλ᾽ ἐς τὰς Καίσαρος ἀποικίας ἐκδραμὼν ὡς γνώριμος δύο ἐς τὸν Ἀντώνιον ἀνεστράτευσε τέλη καὶ ἐς
271 τὴν Ῥώμην συλλαβεῖν Κικέρωνα ἠπείγετο. τότε μὲν
δὴ θόρυβός τε ἦν ἄπλετος, καὶ τέκνα καὶ γυναῖκας
ὑπεξέφερον οἱ πλείους μετὰ δυσελπιστίας, καὶ ὁ
Κικέρων τῆς πόλεως ἀπεδίδρασκε. καὶ ὁ Οὐεντίδιος

everything, and once the division was made, he and Hirtius went into winter quarters together. As winter advanced Decimus now began to suffer from hunger, and Hirtius and Octavian advanced toward Mutina to prevent Antony receiving the surrender of Decimus' exhausted army. Mutina, however, was being closely guarded by Antony, and they did not join battle with him with their full force, but waited for Pansa. There were frequent cavalry engagements, but although Antony had a much larger force of cavalry, the difficult terrain of the plain, which was cut by streams, deprived him of the advantage of numbers. 267 268

66. While this was happening at Mutina, at Rome in the absence of the consuls Cicero took the lead in courting popular support. He held frequent assemblies of the people, had arms produced by uniting the workmen without paying them, collected money, and exacted heavy contributions from the partisans of Antony. These readily paid up in order to avoid slanderous accusations, until Publius Ventidius, who had served under Gaius Caesar and was an associate of Antony, was unable to endure the oppression of Cicero, and hurried off to Caesar's colonies, where he was well known, reenlisted two legions for Antony, and pressed on to Rome to arrest Cicero.[29] Boundless turmoil ensued. Most people were despondent and removed their women and children, and Cicero himself fled from the city. When Ventidius learned this he turned back to join 269 270 271

[29] Publius Ventidius Bassus was one of the tribunes of 45, and although praetor in 43, he resigned the praetorship to become one of the suffect consuls at the end of the year after the reconciliation of Octavian and Antony. No other sources mention him marching on Rome to arrest Cicero.

μαθὼν ἐς τὸν Ἀντώνιον ἀνέστρεφε. διακλειόμενος δὲ ὑπὸ Καίσαρός τε καὶ Ἱρτίου ἐς τὴν Πικηνίτιδα παρῆλθε καὶ τέλος ἄλλο συλλογίσας ἐφήδρευε τοῖς
272 ἐσομένοις. οἱ δὲ ἀμφὶ τὸν Καίσαρα, τοῦ Πάνσα μετὰ στρατιᾶς πλησιάζοντος, Καρσουλήιον αὐτῷ προσέπεμπον ἄγοντα τὴν Καίσαρος στρατηγίδα τάξιν καὶ τὸ Ἄρειον τέλος ἐς βοήθειαν τῆς διόδου τῶν στενῶν.
273 ὁ δὲ Ἀντώνιος τῶν μὲν στενῶν ὑπερεῖδεν ὡς οὐδὲν πλέον ἢ κωλύσων ἐν αὐτοῖς, ἐπιθυμίᾳ δὲ ἀγῶνος, οὐκ ἔχων τοῖς ἱππεῦσιν ἐλλαμπρύνασθαι διὰ τὸ πεδίον ἐλωδέστερον ὂν καὶ τεταφρευμένον, δύο ἐνήδρευσε τέλη τὰ ἄριστα ἐν τῷ ἕλει, τῆς ὁδοῦ, χειροποιήτου καὶ στενῆς οὔσης, ἑκατέρωθεν τῷ δόνακι κρύπτων.
274 67. Καρσουλήιου δὲ καὶ Πάνσα τὰ στενὰ νυκτὸς διαδραμόντων, ἅμα δ' ἡμέρᾳ μόνοις τοῖς Ἀρείοις καὶ πέντε ἄλλαις τάξεσιν ἐς τὴν χειροποίητον ὁδὸν ἐσβαλόντων, ἔτι καθαρεύουσαν πολεμίων, καὶ τὸ ἕλος ἑκατέρωθεν ὂν περισκεπτομένων, ὅ τε δόναξ διακινούμενος ὑπωπτεύετο, καὶ ἀσπὶς ἤδη που καὶ κράνος ἐξέλαμπε, καὶ ἡ στρατηγὶς Ἀντωνίου τάξις αὐτοῖς
275 αἰφνίδιον ἐπεφαίνετο ἐκ τοῦ μετώπου. οἱ δ' Ἄρειοι περιειλημμένοι τε πάντοθεν καὶ οὐδαμόσε διαδραμεῖν ἔχοντες ἐκέλευον ⟨τοὺς νεήλυδας⟩[29] εἰ παραγένοιντο, μὴ συνεφάπτεσθαι σφίσι τῶν πόνων, ὡς μὴ συνταράξειαν αὐτοὺς ὑπὸ ἀπειρίας, τῇ στρατηγίδι δὲ Ἀντωνίου τὴν Καίσαρος στρατηγίδα ἀντέταξαν·

[29] τοὺς νεήλυδας add. Schweig.

Antony, but his way was barred by Octavian and Hirtius, and he headed for Picenum, where he recruited another legion and waited to see what would happen. On the approach of Pansa and his army, Octavian and his staff sent Carsuleius to him with Octavian's praetorian cohort and the legion of Mars to assist him in passing through a defile.[30] Antony had ignored the defile on the grounds that he could only block Pansa's route in it, and he wanted a battle. As he had no chance to perform brilliantly with his cavalry, because the plain was marshy and cut by gullies, he placed his two best legions in ambush in the marsh, hiding them in the rushes on both sides of the road, which had been artificially constructed and was narrow.

67. After hurrying through the defile by night, at daybreak Carsuleius and Pansa, with only the legion of Mars and five other cohorts, came to the causeway, which was still free of the enemy, and reconnoitered the marsh on either side. They were suspicious of the way the rushes moved, and here and there a shield or helmet glinted in the light, and suddenly Antony's praetorian cohort appeared right in front of them. The soldiers of the legion of Mars, although surrounded on all sides and having nowhere to escape, ordered the new recruits, if they came up, not to join in their fight, so that they did not cause distraction by their inexperience. And so the praetorians of Octavian were marshaled against the praetorians of

272

273

274

275

---

[30] Decimus Carfulenus (Appian's text is corrupt) was a tribune of the people in 44 and was probably killed in the battle Appian describes here.

αὐτοὶ δὲ ἐς δύο διαιρεθέντες ἐνέβαινον ἐς ἑκάτερον
ἕλος, καὶ αὐτοῖς ἐπεστάτουν τῇ μὲν ὁ Πάνσας, τῇ δὲ
276 ὁ Καρσουλήιος. δύο δὲ τῶν ἑλῶν ὄντων δύο ἦσαν οἱ
πόλεμοι, τῇ διόδῳ εἰργόμενοι μὴ γινώσκειν τὰ ἀλ-
λήλων· καὶ κατὰ τὴν δίοδον αὐτὴν αἱ στρατηγίδες
277 πόλεμον ἄλλον ἐφ᾽ ἑαυτῶν ἐπολέμουν. γνώμη δὲ ἦν
τοῖς μὲν Ἀντωνίου τοὺς Ἀρείους ἀμύνασθαι τῆς αὐτο-
μολίας οἷα προδότας σφῶν γενομένους, τοῖς δ᾽ Ἀρείοις ἐκείνους τῆς ὑπεροψίας τῶν ἐν Βρεντεσίῳ δι-
278 εφθαρμένων. συνειδότες τε ἀλλήλοις τὸ κράτιστον ὡς
εἶεν[30] τῆς ἑκατέρου στρατιᾶς, ἤλπιζον ἐν τῷδε τῷ
ἔργῳ μόνῳ τὸν πόλεμον κρινεῖν. καὶ τοῖς μὲν αἰδὼς
ἦν τὸ δύο τέλεσιν οὖσιν δι᾽ ἑνὸς ἡσσᾶσθαι, τοῖς δὲ
φιλοτιμία μόνοις τῶν δύο κρατῆσαι.

279   68. Οὕτω μὲν ἀλλήλοις ἐπῄεσαν διωργισμένοι τε
καὶ φιλοτιμούμενοι, σφίσι μᾶλλον ἢ τοῖς στρατηγοῖς
οἰκεῖον ἡγούμενοι τόδε ἔργον· ὑπὸ δὲ ἐμπειρίας οὔτε
ἠλάλαξαν ὡς οὐκ ἐκπλήξοντες ἀλλήλους, οὔτε ἐν τῷ
πόνῳ τις αὐτῶν ἀφῆκε φωνὴν οὔτε νικῶν οὔτε ἡσσώ-
280 μενος. περιόδους δὲ οὐκ ἔχοντες οὔτε δρόμους ὡς ἐν
ἕλεσι καὶ τάφροις, ἀραρότως συνίσταντο, καὶ οὐδέτε-
ροι τοὺς ἑτέρους ὤσασθαι δυνάμενοι τοῖς ξίφεσιν ὡς
ἐν πάλῃ συνεπλέκοντο. πληγή τε οὐδεμία ἦν ἀργός,
ἀλλὰ τραύματα καὶ φόνοι καὶ στόνοι μόνον ἀντὶ
βοῆς· ὅ τε πίπτων εὐθὺς ὑπεξεφέρετο, καὶ ἄλλος ἀντι-

---

[30] εἶεν Schweig.; εἴη codd.

Antony. Pansa and Carsuleius divided their force in two
and advanced into the marsh on either side of the road,
with Pansa in command of one wing, Carsuleius of the
other. As there were two marshes, there were two battles,   276
the road running between them preventing the participants from knowing how the other was faring; and on the
road itself the praetorians were fighting another battle of
their own. The Antonians were determined to punish the   277
legion of Mars for desertion, which they regarded as a
betrayal of themselves, while the legion of Mars were
determined to punish the Antonians for condoning the
killings committed at Brundisium.[31] Recognizing in each   278
other the elite of both armies, they hoped to decide the
whole war by this single engagement. One side was moved
by the shame of two legions being beaten by one; the other
by ambition that a single legion should get the better of
two.

68. Thus spurred on by animosity and ambition they   279
attacked each other, believing that this was their battle
rather than their generals'. Being experienced soldiers
they raised no battle cry, as they knew they would not ter-
rify each other, nor in the engagement did any of them
utter a sound, either as victors or vanquished. Since there   280
was no possibility of flanking movements or charges
among the marshes and gullies, they met together in close
order, and neither side being able to push the other back,
they were locked together with their swords as in a wres-
tling match. No blow missed its mark. There were wounds
and slaughter and groaning, but no cries; and when one
fell he was immediately carried away and another took his

[31] As described above at 43.178.

281 καθίστατο. παραινέσεων δὲ ἢ ἐπικελεύσεων οὐκ ἐδέοντο, δι' ἐμπειρίαν ἕκαστος ἑαυτοῦ στρατηγῶν. ὅτε δὲ
καὶ κάμοιεν, ὥσπερ ἐν τοῖς γυμνικοῖς ἐς ἀναπνοὴν
ὀλίγον ἀλλήλων διίσταντο καὶ αὖθις συνεπλέκοντο.
θάμβος τε ἦν τοῖς νεήλυσιν ἐπελθοῦσι, τοιάδε ἔργα
σὺν εὐταξίᾳ καὶ σιωπῇ γιγνόμενα ἐφορῶσι.

282   69. Πονουμένων δὲ ὧδε πάντων ὑπὲρ φύσιν ἀνθρωπίνην, ἡ μὲν στρατηγὶς ἡ Καίσαρος ἅπασα διεφθάρη,
τῶν δὲ Ἀρείων οἱ μὲν ὑπὸ τῷ Καρσουληΐῳ μᾶλλον
ἐκράτουν τῶν κατὰ σφᾶς, οὐκ αἰσχρῶς, ἀλλὰ κατ'
ὀλίγον ἐνδιδόντων, οἱ δὲ ὑπὸ τῷ Πάνσᾳ τὸν αὐτὸν
τρόπον ἐβαροῦντο, διεκαρτέρουν δ' ὅμως ἐπ' ἴσης
ἑκάτεροι, μέχρι Πάνσας ὀβελῷ τὴν λαγόνα τρωθεὶς
ἐς Βονωνίαν ἐξεφέρετο. τότε γὰρ οἱ κατ' αὐτὸν ἀνεχώρουν, ἐπὶ πόδα πρῶτον, εἶτα μεταβαλόντες ὀξύ-
283 τερον ὡς ἐν φυγῇ. καὶ οἱ νεήλυδες ἰδόντες ἔφευγον
ἀτάκτως καὶ μετὰ βοῆς ἐς τὸ χαράκωμα, ὅπερ αὐτοῖς
ἐξείργαστο ὁ ταμίας Τορκουᾶτος συνεστώσης ἔτι τῆς
μάχης, ὑπονοήσας ἐν χρείᾳ γενήσεσθαι. οἱ μὲν δὴ
νεήλυδες ἐς αὐτὸ ἀτάκτως συνειλοῦντο, Ἰταλοὶ μὲν
ὄντες ὁμοίως τοῖς Ἀρείοις· ἡ δὲ ἄσκησις ἄρα τοῦ γέ-
284 νους ἐς τοσοῦτον ἀρετῇ διαφέρει. οἱ δὲ Ἄρειοι οὐκ
ἐσῆλθον μὲν ἐς τὸ χαράκωμα αὐτοὶ ὑπὸ ἀδοξίας,
ἀλλὰ παρ' αὐτὸ ἔστησαν· κατάκοποι δὲ ὄντες ὤργων
ὅμως, εἴ τις ἐπίοι, μέχρι τοῦ ἀναγκαίου τέλους δια-

place. They needed neither exhortation nor encourage-   281
ment, since experience made each one his own general.
When they were overcome by fatigue they drew apart
from each other for a moment to catch their breath, as in
gymnastic exercises, and then came to grips again. When
the new recruits arrived, they were amazed at the sight of
such deeds being carried out in good order and silence.

69. With everyone making superhuman efforts in this   282
way, Octavian's praetorian cohort was annihilated. The
section of the legion of Mars under Carsuleius' command
got somewhat the better of their opponents, who gave way,
not shamefully, but little by little. Those under Pansa were
struggling in the same way, but both sides persevered with
equal stubbornness until Pansa was wounded in the side
by a javelin and carried off the field to Bononia. At that
point the men under his command retired, at first step by
step, but then they changed to a more rapid movement, as
if in flight. When the new recruits saw this they fled in   283
disorder, shouting loudly, to their palisade, which the
quaestor, Torquatus, had constructed for them while the
battle was still in progress, suspecting that it would be
needed.[32] The new recruits crowded into it in disorder,
although they were no less Italian than the legion of
Mars—it is, of course, training that makes so much more
difference to courage than racial background. As for the   284
soldiers of the legion of Mars, to protect their reputation
they did not go into the palisade, but took up position
beside it. Although exhausted, they were still angry and
ready to fight to the bitter end if anybody attacked them.

[32] Manlius Torquatus, quaestor in 43, was attached to the consul Pansa.

γωνίσασθαι. Ἀντώνιος δὲ τῶν μὲν Ἀρείων ἀπέσχετο
ὡς ἐπιπόνων, τοῖς δὲ νεήλυσιν ἐπιδραμὼν πολὺν εἰργάζετο φόνον.

285   70. Ἴρτιος δὲ ἐν Μουτίνῃ τῆς μάχης πυθόμενος,
ἑξήκοντα στάδια ἀπεχούσης, ἵετο δρόμῳ μετὰ τοῦ
ἑτέρου τέλους τῶν ἀπὸ Ἀντωνίου μεταστάντων. ἤδη
τε ἦν ὀψία δείλη, καὶ οἱ νικήσαντες τῶν Ἀντωνίου
παιανίζοντες ἐπανῄεσαν· καὶ αὐτοῖς ὁ Ἴρτιος ἀσυν-
τάκτοις οὖσιν ἐπιφαίνεται συντεταγμένος ὁλοκλήρῳ
286   τέλει καὶ ἀπαθεῖ. οἱ δὲ συνετάχθησαν μὲν αὖθις ὑπ'
ἀνάγκης, καὶ πολλὰ καὶ πρὸς τούσδε ἔργα λαμπρὰ
ἐπεδείξαντο· οἷα δὲ ἀκμήτων ἡσσῶντο κεκμηκότες,
καὶ τὸ πλεῖστον αὐτῶν μάλιστα τὸ ἔργον Ἰρτίου διέφθειρε, καίπερ οὐ διώκοντος αὐτοὺς ὑπὸ φόβου τῶν
ἑλῶν, καὶ τῆς ἑσπέρας ἤδη μελαινομένης διέλυσεν
287   αὐτούς. καὶ τὸ ἕλος ἐπὶ πλεῖστον ἐπεπλήρωτο ὅπλων
τε καὶ νεκρῶν καὶ ἀνδρῶν ἡμιθνήτων καὶ τετρωμένων·
οἱ δὲ καὶ ἐρρωμένοι σφῶν ὑπὸ τοῦ κόπου κατεφρό-
288   νουν. ἱππέες δὲ αὐτοὺς ἐξ Ἀντωνίου περιθέοντες, ὅσοι
παρήσπιζον αὐτῷ, δι' ὅλης τῆς νυκτὸς ἀνελέγοντο καὶ
τοὺς μὲν ἀντὶ σφῶν αὐτῶν, τοὺς δὲ σὺν ἑαυτοῖς ἐπὶ
τοὺς ἵππους ἀνετίθεντο ἢ τῆς οὐρᾶς ἀντεχομένους
παρεκάλουν παρατροχάζειν καὶ βοηθεῖν σφίσιν ἐς
289   τὴν σωτηρίαν. ὧδε μὲν Ἀντωνίῳ καλῶς ἀγωνισαμένῳ
διέφθαρτο ἡ ἰσχὺς διὰ Ἴρτιον ἐπελθόντα. καὶ ηὐλί-
σατο ἐν κώμῃ παρὰ τὸ πεδίον ἀχαρακώτως· Ἀγορὰ
Κελτῶν ἡ κώμη καλεῖται. ἔπεσον δὲ τῶν μὲν ἄλλων

Antony steered clear of the legion of Mars as being too much trouble, but he attacked the new recruits and slaughtered many of them.

70. Hirtius learned of the battle when he was at Mutina, sixty stades away, and rushed off with the other legion that had deserted Antony. It was already late in the afternoon, and the victorious Antonians were returning, no longer in formation, singing songs of victory, when Hirtius made a sudden appearance in front of them with a whole, fresh legion, marshaled for battle. Under force of necessity Antony's men again lined up for battle, and against these enemies too performed many splendid deeds; but in their exhaustion they were overcome by the fresh troops, and the great majority of them were killed in this action of Hirtius, although he did not pursue them, as he was afraid of the marshes, and with night coming on he let them disperse. A great extent of the marsh was filled with weapons and corpses and men who were half-dead and wounded, but even the unwounded ignored their own men because of their fatigue. The cavalry of Antony's personal guard went around picking them up all night. Some they put on their horses instead of themselves, others to ride with them, still others they urged to take hold of the horses' tails, run alongside them and so help themselves to get to safety. In this way Antony's force was destroyed by Hirtius' attack, although it had fought bravely. He bivouacked for the night without building a palisade in a village called Forum Gallorum, near the plain. Besides the loss of Octavian's entire praetorian cohort, and a few

285

286

287

288

289

ἀμφὶ τοὺς ἡμίσεας ἑκατέρων, καὶ ἡ στρατηγὶς ἡ Καίσαρος ἅπασα, Ἱρτίου δὲ ὀλίγοι.

290   71. Τῆς δ' ἐπιούσης ἀνεζεύγνυον ἐς τὰ ἐν τῇ Μουτίνῃ στρατόπεδα πάντες. γνώμη δὲ ἦν Ἀντωνίῳ μὲν ἐπὶ τοσῷδε πταίσματι μὴ ἐπιχειρεῖν ἔτι τοῖς ἐχθροῖς μεγάλῃ μάχῃ μηδ' ἐπιόντων ἀμύνεσθαι, διὰ δὲ τῶν ἱππέων τὰ ἐφήμερα μόνα αὐτοὺς ἐνοχλεῖν, μέχρι παραδῴη Δέκμος αὐτὸν ἐς ἔσχατον ἤδη λιμοῦ τετρυμένος, Ἱρτίῳ δὲ καὶ Καίσαρι διὰ τοῦτο μάλιστα
291   τὰ ἐς τὴν μάχην ἐπείγεσθαι. ἐπεὶ δ' ἐκτάσσουσιν αὐτοῖς ὁ Ἀντώνιος οὐκ ἐπεξῆγεν, ἐς τὰ ἐπὶ θάτερα τῆς Μουτίνης ἀφυλακτότερα ὄντα διὰ δυσχέρειαν ἐχώρουν ὡς βιασόμενοι βαρεῖ στρατῷ παρεσελθεῖν ἐς αὐτήν. καὶ ὁ Ἀντώνιος αὐτῶν ἐξήπτετο τοῖς ἱππεῦσι καὶ τότε
292   μόνοις. ἀμυνομένων δὲ κἀκείνων αὐτὸν ἱππεῦσι μόνοις καὶ τῆς ἄλλης στρατιᾶς χωρούσης, ἐφ' ἃ ἐβούλοντο, δείσας ὁ Ἀντώνιος περὶ τῇ Μουτίνῃ ἐξῆγε δύο
293   τέλη· οἱ δὲ ἡσθέντες ἐπέστρεφον καὶ ἐμάχοντο. ἄλλα δὲ Ἀντωνίου τέλη καλοῦντος ἐκ τῶν ἄλλων στρατοπέδων, ὧν βραδέως ὡς ἐν αἰφνιδίῳ τε μετακλήσει καὶ μακρόθεν ἰόντων ἐκράτουν οἱ τοῦ Καίσαρος τῇ μάχῃ. Ἵρτιος δὲ καὶ ἐς τὸ στρατόπεδον ἐσήλατο τοῦ Ἀντωνίου καὶ περὶ τὴν στρατηγίδα σκηνὴν μαχόμενος
294   ἔπεσε. καὶ αὐτοῦ τό τε σῶμα ὁ Καῖσαρ ἐσδραμὼν ἀνείλετο καὶ τοῦ στρατοπέδου κατέσχεν, ἕως μετ' ὀλίγον ἐξεώσθη πρὸς Ἀντωνίου. διενυκτέρευσαν δὲ καὶ ἐν τοῖς ὅπλοις ἑκάτεροι.

295   72. Καὶ ὁ Ἀντώνιος δευτέρᾳ τῇδε συμπεσὼν πληγῇ

of Hirtius' men, other casualties amounted to about half of both armies.

71. The next day they all withdrew to their camps at 290 Mutina. After such a substantial reverse, Antony resolved not to confront his enemies in a great battle any more, not even in a defensive action if they attacked, but to harass them on a daily basis with his cavalry, until Decimus, now worn down by extreme famine, surrendered. On the other hand, it was precisely for this reason that Hirtius and Octavian resolved to press for battle. As Antony would not 291 come out when they offered battle, they went round to the other side of Mutina where it was less closely guarded because of the difficulty of the terrain, with the intention of forcing their way into the town by weight of numbers. Even at this point Antony hung on their rear using only his cavalry. But as the enemy, too, defended themselves 292 against him just with their cavalry, while the rest of the army advanced on its objective, Antony grew afraid for the fate of Mutina, and led out two legions. Hirtius and Octavian were delighted at this, and turning to face them started to fight. Antony ordered up other legions from his 293 other camps, but they took time to come as they had not expected the call and had a considerable distance to travel, and Octavian's forces won the battle. Hirtius even broke into Antony's camp, and was killed fighting near the general's tent. Octavian rushed in to collect his body and oc- 294 cupied the camp until he was pushed out by Antony a short time later. Both sides passed the night under arms.

72. After sustaining this second defeat, Antony con- 295

συνεβουλεύετο τοῖς φίλοις εὐθὺς ἀπὸ τοῦ πόνου. καὶ τοῖς μὲν ἐδόκει τῆς προτέρας αὐτὸν γνώμης ἔχεσθαι, πολιορκοῦντα Μουτίνην καὶ ἐς μάχην οὐκ ἐπεξιόντα· τό τε γὰρ πάθος ὅμοιον ἀμφοῖν γεγονέναι καὶ Ἵρτιον ἀνῃρῆσθαι καὶ Πάνσαν νοσεῖν καὶ σφᾶς τοῖς ἱππεῦσι πλεονεκτεῖν Μουτίνην τε ἐς ἔσχατον ἀφῖχθαι λιμοῦ

296 καὶ εὐθὺς ἐνδώσειν. ὧδε μὲν ἤρεσκε τοῖς φίλοις, καὶ ἦν τὰ ἄριστα· ὁ δὲ Ἀντώνιος, ἤδη θεοῦ βλάπτοντος, ἐδεδοίκει, μὴ ἐς τὴν Μουτίνην ὁ Καῖσαρ, ὥσπερ ἐχθὲς ἐπιχειρήσας, ἐσδράμοι ἢ αὐτὸν ἐπιχειρήσειε περιτειχίζειν, πλέον ἔχων τὸ ἐργάσιμον, "Ἐν ᾧ καὶ τῶν ἱππέων," ἔφη, "Γιγνομένων ἡμῖν ἀχρήστων, ὑπερ-

297 όψεταί με Λέπιδος καὶ Πλάγκος ἡττώμενον. εἰ δὲ Μουτίνης ἐξανασταῖμεν, Οὐεντίδιός τε ἡμῖν αὐτίκα προσέσται, τρία τέλη φέρων ἐκ τῆς Πικηνίτιδος, καὶ Λέπιδος καὶ Πλάγκος ἐρρωμένως [οἱ][31] συμμαχή- σουσι." ταῦτα ἔλεγεν, οὐκ ἄτολμος ἐν τοῖς κινδύνοις ἀνήρ, καὶ εἰπὼν εὐθὺς ἀνίστατο καὶ ὥδευεν ἐπὶ τῶν Ἄλπεων.

298 73. Δέκμῳ δὲ ἀπαλλαγέντι τῆς πολιορκίας ὁ φόβος ἐς τὸν Καίσαρα ἐνηλλάσσετο· τῶν γὰρ ὑπάτων ἐκπο- δὼν γενομένων ὡς ἐχθρὸν ἐδεδοίκει. τάς τε οὖν γε- φύρας τοῦ ποταμοῦ διέκοπτε πρὸ ἡμέρας καὶ κελητίῳ τινὰς ἐς τὸν Καίσαρα ἀποστέλλων ἐμαρτύρει μὲν ὡς αἰτίῳ τῆς σωτηρίας, ἠξίου δὲ μέσον ἔχοντα τὸν πο- ταμὸν ἐς λόγους οἱ συνελθεῖν ἐπὶ μάρτυσι τοῖς πο-

31 οἱ del. Goukowsky

sulted with his associates immediately after the battle. They thought he should persevere with his previous plan to besiege Mutina and refuse to go out to battle. For, they argued, the losses had been much the same on both sides; Hirtius had been killed and Pansa wounded; they had a bigger force of cavalry; and with the arrival of extreme famine, Mutina would very soon surrender. Such was the 296 advice of his associates, and it was the best course. But Antony, now with some divinity plaguing him, had become afraid that Octavian would break into Mutina, as he tried to do the previous day, or would put his hand to fencing him in, having greater manpower to make this workable. "In which case," he said, "even our cavalry will be of no use to us, and Lepidus and Plancus will despise me as a defeated man. But if we withdraw from Mutina, Ventidius 297 will immediately join us with three legions from Picenum, and Lepidus and Plancus will give us vigorous military assistance."[33] This is what he said—and he was not a timid man in the face of danger—and when he had finished, he immediately struck camp and set off toward the Alps.

73. Decimus may have been delivered from the siege, 298 but now Octavian provided a new source of fear. For with both consuls out of the way, he began to fear Octavian as a personal enemy. So he cut down the bridges over the river before daybreak and sent some representatives to Octavian in a boat, acknowledging him as the author of his safety and asking to enter discussions with him, with the river between them and the citizens as witnesses. For he

[33] For Lepidus and Plancus see above, 46.190 with note 21.

λίταις· πείσειν γάρ, ὅτι δαιμόνιον αὐτὸν ἔβλαψεν, ἐς
299 τὴν Καίσαρος ἐπιβουλὴν ἐπηγμένον ὑφ' ἑτέρων. Καίσαρος δὲ τοῖς ἥκουσιν ἀποκριναμένου τε πρὸς ὀργὴν
καὶ τὴν χάριν, ἣν δίδωσίν οἱ Δέκμος, διωθουμένου.
"Οὐδὲ γὰρ Δέκμον ἐγὼ πάρειμι περισώσων, ἀλλ' Ἀντωνίῳ πολεμήσων, ᾧ μοι καὶ συναλλαγῆναί ποτε
θέμις· Δέκμῳ δὲ ἡ φύσις οὐδὲ ἐς ὄψιν ἢ λόγους ἐλθεῖν
300 ἐπιτρέπει· σῳζέσθω μέντοι, μέχρι τοῖς ἐν ἄστει δοκεῖ." πυθόμενος τούτων ὁ Δέκμος ἔστη τε πρὸ τοῦ
ποταμοῦ καὶ καλῶν ὀνομαστὶ τὸν Καίσαρα, σὺν βοῇ
τὰ γράμματα τῆς βουλῆς ἀνεγίνωσκε, διδούσης οἱ
τὴν Κελτικὴν ἡγεμονίαν, ἀπηγόρευέ τε Καίσαρι χωρὶς ὑπάτων μὴ περᾶν τὸν ποταμὸν ἐς ἀλλοτρίαν ἡγεμονίαν μηδὲ ἐπὶ Ἀντώνιον ἔτι χωρεῖν· αὐτὸς γὰρ
301 αὐτὸν διώκων ἀρκέσειν. ὁ δὲ ᾔδει μὲν ὑπὸ τῆς βουλῆς
αὐτὸν ἐς τήνδε τὴν θρασύτητα αὐξανόμενον, δυνηθεὶς
δ' ἂν ἐκ προστάγματος ἑλεῖν ἐφείδετο ἔτι καὶ πρὸς
τὸν Πάνσαν ἐς Βονωνίαν τραπεὶς ἔγραφε τῇ βουλῇ
περὶ ἁπάντων. ἔγραφε δὲ καὶ Πάνσας.

302   74. Καὶ Κικέρων ἐν Ῥώμῃ τὰ μὲν ἐς τὸν δῆμον
ἀνεγίγνωσκεν ὡς ὑπάτου, τὰ δὲ τοῦ Καίσαρος τῇ
βουλῇ μόνον· θυσίας τε ἐπ' Ἀντωνίῳ πεντήκοντα
ἡμερῶν ἱκεσίους[32] ἐψηφίζετο, ὅσας οὔτε ἐπὶ Κελτοῖς
οὔτε ἐπὶ ἄλλῳ πολέμῳ ποτὲ ἐψηφίσαντο Ῥωμαῖοι, καὶ
τὸν στρατὸν τῶν ὑπάτων ἐδίδου Δέκμῳ καίπερ ἔτι
Πάνσα περιόντος (ἤδη γὰρ ἀπεγιγνώσκετο), στρατηγόν τε τὸν Δέκμον ἀπέφηνεν ἐπ' Ἀντωνίῳ μόνον εἶναι

140

said he would convince him that a divine spirit led him astray when he was brought into the plot against Caesar by others. Octavian answered the messengers angrily, rejecting Decimus' thanks, saying, "I did not come here to rescue Decimus, but to fight Antony. With him I may rightly be reconciled at some point, but nature forbids me even to look at Decimus or enter conversation with him. Let him be spared, however, as long as those in Rome approve." When Decimus heard this, he stood in front of the river bank and, calling Octavian by name, read in a loud voice the letter of the senate giving him command of Gaul. He forbade Octavian to cross the river into someone else's command without consular authority, or to continue to march against Antony; for he himself had sufficient forces to pursue him. Octavian was aware that Decimus was emboldened to behave with such impudence by the senate, and although he had the power to issue an order for his arrest, he restrained himself for the moment, and turned back to Pansa at Bononia, where he wrote a full report of events to the senate, as did Pansa.

74. In Rome Cicero read the letter of Pansa to the people, as Pansa was a consul, but only read Octavian's letter to the senate. For the victory over Antony, he carried a vote to have fifty days of thanksgiving—a longer period than the Romans had ever voted even after victory over the Celts or in any other war. He set about giving the army of the consuls to Decimus, for although Pansa was still alive, there was no hope he would survive, and he wanted to appoint Decimus the sole commander against

299

300

301

302

---

32 ἱκεσίους Schweig.; ἐτησίους codd.

καὶ εὐχὰς δημοσίας ἐποιεῖτο Δέκμον Ἀντωνίου περι-
γενέσθαι. τοσοῦτος ἦν οἶστρος αὐτῷ κατὰ Ἀντωνίου
303 καὶ ἀπειροκαλία. ἐβεβαίου τε αὖθις τοῖς δύο τέλεσι
τοῖς ἀπὸ Ἀντωνίου μεταστᾶσι τὰς ἑκάστῳ προϋπε-
σχημένας παρὰ τοῦ κοινοῦ Ῥωμαίων ἐπινικίους
δραχμὰς πεντακισχιλίας ὡς ἤδη νενικηκόσι καὶ στέφανον αὐτοὺς ἐν ταῖς ἑορταῖς αἰεὶ θαλλοῦ περιτίθε-
304 σθαι. περὶ δὲ Καίσαρος οὐδὲν ἦν ἐν τοῖς γραφομέ-
νοις, οὐδὲ τοὔνομα ὅλως· οὕτως αὐτίκα κατεφρονεῖτο
ὡς Ἀντωνίου καθῃρημένου. ἔγραφον δὲ καὶ Λεπίδῳ
καὶ Πλάγκῳ καὶ Ἀσινίῳ πολεμεῖν, ὅπως πλησιάσειαν
Ἀντωνίῳ.

305   75. Καὶ τάδε μὲν ἦν τὰ ἐν Ῥώμῃ. Πάνσας δ' ἐκ τοῦ
τραύματος ἀποθνῄσκων Καίσαρά οἱ παρεστήσατο
καὶ εἶπεν· "Ἐγὼ τῷ σῷ πατρὶ φίλος ἦν ὡς ἐμαυτῷ,
ἀναιρεθέντι δὲ οὐκ εἶχον ἐπαμύνειν οὐδὲ τοῖς πλείοσι
μὴ συνίστασθαι, οἷς γε δὴ καὶ σὺ καλῶς ποιῶν
306 ὑπήκουσας, καίτοι στρατὸν ἔχων. δείσαντες δ' ἐν
ἀρχῇ σὲ καὶ Ἀντώνιον, φιλοτιμότατον κἀκεῖνον ἐς τὴν
Καίσαρος γνώμην φανέντα, διαφερομένοις ὑμῖν ἐφή-
σθησαν ὡς ἐς ἀλλήλους συντριβησομένοις. ἐπεὶ δέ
σε καὶ στρατοῦ δεσπότην εἶδον, προσεποιοῦντο εὐ-
307 πρεπέσι καὶ ἀσθενέσι τιμαῖς οἷα μειράκιον. σοβαρωτέρου δέ σου καὶ ἐγκρατεστέρου τιμῆς τότε μάλιστα
ὀφθέντος, ὅτε τὴν ἀρχὴν ὑπὸ τοῦ στρατοῦ σοι δεδομένην οὐκ ἐδέξω, διεταράχθησαν καὶ συστρατηγεῖν
σε ἡμῖν ἀπέφηναν, ἵνα σου τὰ δύο τέλη τὰ πρακτι-

Antony. He also had public prayers offered that Decimus might prevail over Antony. Such was Cicero's frenzy and tactlessness in opposing Antony. He reconfirmed to the 303 two legions that had deserted from Antony the five thousand drachmas per man from public funds previously promised to them as the rewards of victory, on the grounds that they had already achieved victory, and gave them the permanent right to wear an olive crown at public festivals. But on the subject of Octavian there was nothing in the 304 text of the decrees, and his name was not even mentioned. He was immediately disregarded, as though Antony were already destroyed. Letters were also written to Lepidus, to Plancus, and to Asinius Pollio with instructions to close with Antony and wage war.

75. Such was the course of events at Rome. In the 305 meantime Pansa, who was dying of his wound, summoned Octavian to his side, and said, "As far as I am concerned, your father was as dear to me as my own life, but when he was killed I was unable to help him or to avoid aligning myself with the majority, to whom, I note, you too have wisely submitted, even though you had an army. In the 306 beginning, they were afraid of you and Antony, who, like you, seemed very ambitious to pursue Caesar's policies, and they were delighted when you fell out at the prospect that you would destroy each other. When they saw that you had become master of an army, they tried to win you over with plausible but paltry honors, treating you like a boy. But as soon as they could see you were a man of some 307 pride and master of your ambition, especially at that moment when you turned down the command offered by your army, they were alarmed. They appointed you to share the command with us in order that we might detach

143

κώτερα ἀποσπάσωμεν, ἐλπίσαντες ἡττηθέντος ὑμῶν
τοῦ ἑτέρου τὸν ἕτερον ἀσθενέστερόν τε καὶ μόνον ἔσεσθαι καὶ μετ’ αὐτὸν ἤδη πᾶσαν τὴν Καίσαρος ἑται-
ρείαν καθελόντες ἀνάξειν τὴν Πομπηίου· τόδε γάρ
ἐστιν αὐτοῖς τῆς γνώμης τὸ κεφάλαιον.

308   76. "Ἐγὼ δὲ καὶ Ἴρτιος τὸ προστεταγμένον ἐποιοῦ-
μεν μέχρι συστεῖλαι τὸν Ἀντώνιον ἐπιπολάζοντα
ὑπεροψίᾳ· ἡττηθέντα δὲ σοὶ συναλλάσσειν ἐπενοοῦ-
μεν, ὡς τῇ Καίσαρος φιλίᾳ τόδε χαριστήριον ἔχοντες
ἀποδοῦναι καὶ μόνον τῇ μοίρᾳ χρησιμώτατον ἐσό-
309   μενον ἐς τὰ μέλλοντα. τοῦτο δ’ οὐκ ἦν ἐκφέρειν σοι
πρότερον, ἡττημένου δὲ νῦν Ἀντωνίου καὶ Ἱρτίου
τεθνεῶτος κἀμὲ τοῦ χρεὼν ἀπάγοντος, ἐν καιρῷ λέ-
λεκται, οὐχ ἵνα μοι γινώσκῃς χάριν ἀποθανόντι, ἀλλ’
ἵνα σὺν δαιμονίᾳ μοίρᾳ γενόμενος, ὡς τὰ ἔργα ὑπο-
δείκνυσι, τά τε σαυτῷ συμφέροντα γινώσκῃς καὶ τὴν
310   ἐμὴν καὶ Ἱρτίου προαίρεσίν τε καὶ ἀνάγκην. τὸν μὲν
οὖν στρατόν, ὃν ἡμῖν αὐτὸς ἔδωκας, εὐπροφάσιστον
ἀποδοῦναί σοι, καὶ παραδίδωμι· τοὺς δὲ νεήλυδας εἰ
μὲν καθέξεις λαβών, καὶ τούσδε σοι παραδώσω, εἰ δὲ
τεθήπασι τὴν βουλὴν ἀμέτρως, ὅτι καὶ οἱ ἄρχοντες
αὐτῶν φύλακες ἡμῖν ἐπέμφθησαν εἶναι, καὶ τό τε ἔργον ἐπίφθονον ἔσται σοι καὶ πρὸ τοῦ δέοντος ἐξαν-
311   ίστησί σε, ὁ ταμίας παραλήψεται Τορκουᾶτος." ταῦτα
εἰπὼν καὶ τῷ ταμίᾳ τοὺς νεήλυδας ἐγχειρίσας ἀπέθανε. καὶ τούσδε μὲν ὁ ταμίας, καθὰ προσέτασσεν ἡ

your two more effective legions from you, hoping that when one of you was defeated, the other would be weakened and isolated, and that after getting rid of him they would destroy the whole Caesarean party and revive that of Pompey. That is the main point of their policy.

76. "Hitius and I did what we were ordered to do, 308 until we could humble Antony, who was behaving with insolent arrogance; but we intended when he was defeated to reconcile him to you, having it in our power to pay the debt of gratitude we owed to Caesar's friendship, the one thing that would be of most use to our party in the future. It was impossible to reveal this to you before, but now that 309 Antony has been defeated, and Hirtius is dead, and fate is carrying me away, the time was right for saying it—not to win your gratitude after my death, but to ensure that you, who were born to a divine destiny, as your achievements prove, recognize where your own interests lie, and understand the policy adopted by Hirtius and myself, and the necessity for it. It would, therefore, be entirely appropri- 310 ate for me to return the troops that you yourself gave us, and I do so now. If you want to have the new recruits and keep them, these too I will hand over to you. But if they are inordinately overawed by the senate, in view of the fact that their officers were sent to keep watch on us, and if the task would cause resentment against you and force your hand before it was necessary, my quaestor Torquatus will take command of them." With these words he handed the 311 new recruits to his quaestor and died. The quaestor transferred them to Decimus, as the senate instructed, and

βουλῇ, Δέκμῳ παρεδίδου, Ἵρτιον δὲ καὶ Πάνσαν ὁ
Καῖσαρ ἐπιφανῶς ἔθαπτε καὶ ἐς Ῥώμην ἔπεμπε μετὰ
τιμῆς.

312   77. Τῷ δ' αὐτῷ χρόνῳ περί τε Συρίαν καὶ Μακεδονίαν τοιάδε ἐγίγνετο. Γάιος Καῖσαρ ὅτε Συρίαν διώδευε, τέλος ἐν αὐτῇ καταλελοίπει τὰ ἐς Παρθυαίους
ἤδη διανοούμενος. τούτου τὴν μὲν ἐπιμέλειαν Και-
κίλιος Βάσσος εἶχε, τὸ δὲ ἀξίωμα Ἰούλιος Σέξστος,
μειράκιον αὐτοῦ Καίσαρος συγγενές, ὅπερ ἐκδιαιτώ-
μενον ἐς τρυφὴν τὸ τέλος ἀσχημόνως ἐπήγετο παντα-
313   χοῦ. μεμψαμένῳ δὲ τῷ Βάσσῳ ποτὲ ἐνύβρισε· καὶ
καλῶν αὐτὸν ὕστερον, ἐπεὶ βραδέως ὑπήκουσεν, ἄγειν
ἐκέλευσεν ἕλκοντας. θορύβου δὲ καὶ πληγῶν γενομένων ἡ στρατιὰ τὴν ὕβριν οὐ φέρουσα τὸν Ἰούλιον
314   κατηκόντισε. καὶ εὐθὺς ἦν μετάνοια καὶ δέος ἐκ τοῦ
Καίσαρος. συνομόσαντες οὖν, εἰ μή τις αὐτοῖς συγγνώμη καὶ πίστις γένοιτο, μέχρι θανάτου διαγωνιεῖσθαι καὶ ἐς ταὐτὸ[33] Βάσσον ἀναγκάσαντες ἄλλο
315   συνέλεξαν τέλος καὶ συνεγύμνασαν. ὧδε μέν τισι
περὶ τοῦ Βάσσου δοκεῖ, Λίβωνι δ', ὅτι τῆς Πομπηίου
στρατιᾶς γενόμενος καὶ μετὰ τὴν ἧτταν ἰδιωτεύων ἐν
Τύρῳ, διέφθειρέ τινας τοῦ τέλους, καὶ διεχρήσαντο

[33] ταὐτὸ Goukowsky; αὐτὸ codd.

Octavian organized a splendid funeral for Hirtius and
Pansa, and sent their remains to Rome with full honors.

77. In the same period, the following events took place
in Syria and Macedonia. When he was passing through
Syria, Gaius Caesar had left a legion there, as he was already thinking of an expedition against the Parthians.[34]
Caecilius Bassus had administrative charge of it, but the
title of commander was held by Sextus Julius, a young man
related to Caesar himself, who had adopted luxurious ways
and was leading the legion around in an altogether unfit-
ting manner.[35] On one occasion, when Bassus criticized
him for this, Julius insulted him, and some time later,
when he summoned Bassus and the latter was slow to
comply, he ordered his men to drag him by force before
him. A violent disturbance developed, and the men, unable to endure Julius' outrageous behavior, killed him with
their javelins. They immediately regretted this and began
to fear Caesar's reaction. So, they swore a common oath to
fight to the death if they were not pardoned and restored
to a position of trust, and they forced Bassus to take the
same oath. They also enlisted and put into training another legion. This is what some sources believe about Bassus, but according to Libo, he was a soldier in Pompey's
army, and after the latter's defeat lived as a private citizen
in Tyre, where he bribed certain legionaries, who slew

312

313

314

315

[34] The date was 47.
[35] Sextus Julius Caesar was clearly the legionary commander,
but it is not clear what job in the legion Appian means to assign
to Quintus Caecilius Bassus (who was an equestrian, not a sena-
tor).

316 τὸν Σέξστον καὶ τῷ Βάσσῳ σφᾶς ἐνεχείρισαν. ὁπο-
τέρως δ᾽ ἐγένετο, Στάιον Μοῦρκον[34] οἶδε, μετὰ τριῶν
τελῶν ἐπιπεμφθέντα σφίσιν ὑπὸ τοῦ Καίσαρος, ἐγκρατῶς ἀπεμάχοντο, ἕως ὁ Μοῦρκος ἐπεκαλεῖτο Μάρ-
κιον Κρίσπον ἡγούμενον Βιθυνίας καὶ ἀφίκετο αὐτῷ
βοηθῶν ὁ Κρίσπος τέλεσιν ἄλλοις τρισίν.

317 78. Ὡς δὲ ὑπὸ τούτων ἐπολιορκοῦντο, ὁ Κάσσιος
σὺν ἐπείξει καταλαβὼν τά τε τοῦ Βάσσου δύο τέλη
παρελάμβανεν αὐτίκα καὶ τὰ τῶν πολιορκούντων
αὐτὸν ἕξ, φιλίᾳ τε παραδόντων καὶ ὡς ἀνθυπάτῳ κατ-
ηκόων γενομένων· ἐψήφιστο γάρ, ὥς μοι προείρηται,
318 πάντας ὑπακούειν Κασσίῳ τε καὶ Βρούτῳ. ἄρτι δὲ καὶ
Ἀλλιηνός, ὑπὸ Δολοβέλλα πεμφθεὶς ἐς Αἴγυπτον,
ἐπανῆγεν ἐξ αὐτῆς τέσσαρα τέλη τῶν ἐκ τῆς ἥσσης
Πομπηίου τε καὶ Κράσσου διαρριφέντων ἢ ὑπὸ Καί-
319 σαρος Κλεοπάτρᾳ καταλελειμμένων. καὶ αὐτὸν ὁ
Κάσσιος οὐδὲν προπεπυσμένον ἐν τῇ Παλαιστίνῃ
περιέλαβέ τε καὶ ἠνάγκασεν ἑαυτῷ προσθέσθαι, δεί-
320 σαντα τοῖς τέσσαρσι μάχεσθαι πρὸς ὀκτώ. ὧδε μὲν
δὴ Κάσσιος ἐκ παραδόξου δυώδεκα τελῶν ἀθρόως
ἐκράτει καὶ Δολοβέλλαν ἐκ τῆς Ἀσίας σὺν δύο τέλεσιν ἐλθόντα τε καὶ ἐς Λαοδίκειαν ὑπὸ οἰκειότητος ἐσ-

---

[34] Στάιον Viereck; Ξέστιον codd.; Μοῦρκον Perizonius;
Μοῦλκον hic et deinceps codd.

---

[36] There was a first-century BC Roman historian by the name
of Libo (Cornell No 36), who could be Lucius Scribonius Libo

Sextus and put themselves under Bassus' command.[36]
Whichever one is right, Bassus' men stoutly resisted Staius 316
Murcus, whom Caesar sent against them with three legions, until Murcus appealed to Marcius Crispus, the governor of Bithynia, and Crispus arrived to help him with
another three legions.[37]

78. While Bassus was under siege by these forces, Cas- 317
sius suddenly arrived and immediately took over both the
two legions of Bassus and the six besieging him: these
yielded to him out of friendship and because they were
subject to his proconsular authority. For, as I have already
mentioned, a vote had been passed that everyone was to
obey Cassius and Brutus. What is more, Allienus, who had 318
been sent to Egypt by Dolabella, had recently brought
back from there four legions of soldiers dispersed as a
result of the defeats of Pompey and Crassus, or left with
Cleopatra by Caesar.[38] With no advance warning he was 319
trapped by Cassius in Palestine and forced to join his side,
as he was afraid to fight against eight legions with four. In 320
this way Cassius unexpectedly gained control of twelve
legions all at once, with which he surrounded and laid
siege to Dolabella, who had arrived from Asia with two
legions and had been admitted to Laodicea out of friend-

(consul 34, and brother-in-law of Octavian), but some analysts are
tempted to emend the text so that we have a reference to the
more famous historian, Livy.

[37] Lucius Staius Murcus (the manuscripts get his name
wrong) was given proconsular command of Syria for 44. Quintus
Marcius Crispus was governor of Bithynia in 45 and 44.

[38] Aulus Allienus (praetor 49) had served as proconsul in Sicily from 48 to 46, then as legate in Asia from 44 to 43.

δεχθέντα περικαθήμενος ἐπολιόρκει. καὶ ἡ βουλὴ μα
θοῦσα ἐφήδετο.

321   79. Μακεδονίας δὲ πέρι Γάιος Ἀντώνιος, ὁ Ἀντωνίου
Μάρκου ἀδελφός, Βρούτῳ διεφέρετο καὶ ἐπολέμει,
τέλος ἔχων ἐν ὁπλιτῶν· καὶ τὸν Βροῦτον ἡσσώμενος
322   ἐνήδρευσεν. ὁ δ' ἐκφυγὼν ἀντενήδρευσε καὶ οὐδὲν εἰρ
γάσατο ἀποληφθέντας, ἀλλὰ ἀσπάσασθαι τῷ ἰδίῳ
στρατῷ τοὺς ἐναντίους προσέταξε· τῶν δὲ οὐκ ἀντα
σπασαμένων οὐδὲ τὴν πεῖραν ἐνδεξαμένων, μεθῆκεν
323   ἀπαθεῖς ἐκ τῆς ἐνέδρας ἀπιέναι. κατὰ δὲ ἄλλας ὁδοὺς
περιελθὼν αὖθις ἐν ἀποκρήμνοις κατέστησε καὶ πά
λιν οὐκ ἐπεχείρησεν, ἀλλ' ἠσπάσατο. οἱ δέ, ὡς πολι
τῶν τε περιφειδόμενον καὶ τῆς δόξης ἄξιον ἧς εἶχεν
ἐπὶ σοφίᾳ τε καὶ πραότητι, ἠγάσαντο καὶ ἀντησπά
σαντο καὶ ἐς αὐτὸν μετεβάλοντο. ἐπέτρεψε δὲ καὶ ὁ
Γάιος ἑαυτὸν καὶ ἦν ἐν τιμῇ παρὰ Βρούτῳ, μέχρι τὸν
στρατὸν πολλάκις διαφθείρων ἐλεγχθεὶς ἀνηρέθη.
324   οὕτω μὲν δὴ καὶ Βρούτῳ μετὰ τῶν προτέρων στρατῶν
ἓξ ἐγένετο τέλη· καὶ Μακεδόνας ἐπαινῶν δύο τέλη
κατέλεξεν ἐξ αὐτῶν, καὶ ἐς τὸν Ἰταλικὸν τρόπον καὶ
τάδε ἐγυμνάζετο.

325   80. Τοιαῦτα μὲν δὴ καὶ τὰ περὶ Συρίαν καὶ Μακε
δονίαν ἦν· ἐν δὲ τῇ Ἰταλίᾳ ὁ Καῖσαρ ἐν ὕβρει θέμε
νος ἀντὶ οὗ Δέκμον ᾑρῆσθαι στρατηγὸν ἐπὶ Ἀντωνίῳ,
τὴν μὲν ὀργὴν ἐπέκρυπτε, θρίαμβον δ' ἐπὶ τοῖς εἰρ
326   γασμένοις ᾔτει. καταφρονούμενος δ' ὑπὸ τῆς βουλῆς
ὡς πρεσβύτερα τῆς ἡλικίας ἐπινοῶν, ἔδεισε, μὴ δια
φθαρέντος Ἀντωνίου μᾶλλον ἔτι καταφρονηθείη, καὶ

ship. The senate were delighted when they heard the news.

79. In Macedonia, Gaius Antonius, the brother of Marc Antony, challenged Brutus for dominance and campaigned against him with one legion of infantry. On getting the worst of it, he laid a trap for him. Brutus escaped from the ambush, and laid a counterambush, but he did no harm to those he caught in it, instead ordering his own troops to salute their adversaries. Although the latter did not return the salute and rejected the attempt, he let them out of the ambush unharmed. Circling around by other roads he stopped them again in steep terrain, and again did not attack, but saluted them. Impressed by the fact that he was sparing Roman citizens and deserved the reputation he had for wisdom and mercy, they now returned the salute and changed sides to him. Gaius also surrendered himself and was treated with honor by Brutus, until after trying to subvert the army several times he was found out and executed. In this way, Brutus too collected his forces, six legions, including his former troops; and since he had a high opinion of the Macedonians, he enlisted two legions from them. These too he trained in the Italian way.

80. Such, then, was the state of affairs in Syria and Macedonia. In Italy Octavian considered it an insult that Decimus instead of himself had been chosen for the command against Antony, but he concealed his anger and asked for a triumph for his exploits. Scorned by the senate for harboring ambitions beyond his years, he feared that if Antony were destroyed he would be despised even

τὰς ἐς αὐτὸν συμβάσεις ἐπόθει, καθὰ καὶ Πάνσας
327 αὐτῷ διεσήμαινεν ἀποθνήσκων. τούς τε οὖν ἀλωμέ-
νους ἐκ τῆς ἐκείνου στρατιᾶς ἡγεμόνας ἢ στρατιώτας
ἐφιλανθρωπεύετο, καὶ τοῖς ἰδίοις ἐγκατέλεγεν ἢ τοὺς
ἐθέλοντας αὐτῶν ἐς τὸν Ἀντώνιον ἔπεμπεν, ὡς οὐ δι᾽
328 ἔχθρας ἀνηκέστου πρὸς αὐτὸν ἰόντα· Οὐεντιδίῳ τε τῷ
Ἀντωνίου φίλῳ, μετὰ τριῶν τελῶν ὄντι, παραστρατο-
πεδεύσας καὶ δέος ἐμβαλὼν ἔπραξε μὲν οὐδὲν πολέμιον, ἐδίδου δὲ ὁμοίως συνεῖναί οἱ ἢ ἐς τὸν Ἀντώνιον
ἀδεῶς ἀπιέναι μετὰ τοῦ στρατοῦ καὶ μέμφεσθαι τῆς
ἐς τὸ κοινὸν συμφέρον ἀγνωσίας. ὧν Οὐεντίδιος συν-
329 εὶς ἐς τὸν Ἀντώνιον ἀπήει. ὁ δὲ Καῖσαρ Δέκιον, τῶν
τινα ἡγεμόνων Ἀντωνίου, περὶ Μουτίνην ληφθέντα
διὰ τιμῆς ἄγων μεθῆκεν, εἰ θέλοι, πρὸς τὸν Ἀντώνιον
ἀπιέναι· καὶ πυνθανομένῳ περὶ τῆς ἐς τὸν Ἀντώνιον
γνώμης πολλὰ ἔφη σύμβολα τοῖς εὖ φρονοῦσιν ἐξ-
ενηνοχέναι, τοῖς δ᾽ ἄφροσιν οὐδὲ τὰ πλείονα ἀρκέσειν.

330   81. Ἀντωνίῳ μὲν δὴ τάδε ὁ Καῖσαρ ἐνεσήμαινε,
Λεπίδῳ δὲ καὶ Ἀσινίῳ σαφέστερον ἔτι περὶ τῆς ἐς
αὐτὸν ὕβρεως καὶ τῆς τῶν σφαγέων ἀθρόας προαγω-
γῆς ἐπέστελλεν, ἐκφοβῶν αὐτούς, μὴ ἐς χάριν τῆς
Πομπηιανῆς ἑταιρείας καθ᾽ ἕνα τῶν Καίσαρος ἕκαστος ὅμοια Ἀντωνίῳ πάθοι, κἀκείνῳ δι᾽ ἀφροσύνην
331 καὶ ὑπεροψίαν τοῦδε τοῦ δέους τάδε παθόντι. ἠξίου τε
ἐς μὲν εὐπρέπειαν τῆς βουλῆς εἶναι κατηκόους, ἐς δὲ
τὸ σφέτερον ἀσφαλὲς συμφρονεῖν, ἕως ἔτι δύνανται,
καὶ ὀνειδίζειν ταῦτα Ἀντωνίῳ, μιμεῖσθαί τε τοὺς ὑπὸ

more, and he began to long for the reconciliation with
Antony suggested to him by Pansa when he was dying.
Accordingly, he began to show kindness to the stragglers   327
from Antony's army, both officers and soldiers, enlisting
them among his own troops, or if they wanted to return to
Antony, sending them back, in order to show that he was
not moved by implacable hatred in proceeding against
him. Octavian also camped beside Ventidius, an associate   328
of Antony, who had three legions with him. This frightened Ventidius, but Octavian took no hostile action against
him, and made the same offer as before, either to join him,
or to leave unmolested and go back to Antony and reprimand him for not recognizing their common interests.
Ventidius understood this, and went off to Antony. Octa-   329
vian also gave honorable treatment to Decius, one of
Antony's officers, who had been taken prisoner at Mutina,
and allowed him to return to Antony if he wanted to.
When Decius asked about his attitude toward Antony, Octavian replied that he had given plenty of indications to
people of good sense, and to those without it, not even
more signs would be sufficient.

81. After conveying these signals to Antony, Octavian   330
wrote still more plainly to Lepidus and Asinius concerning
the insult to himself and the rapid advancement of the
murderers. His intention was to instill in them the fear
that, in order to satisfy the Pompeian faction, all the
Caesarians would, one by one, have the same sort of
experience as Antony, who was himself suffering the consequences of his own folly and disdain for this danger. He   331
advised that, for the sake of appearances, they should obey
the senate, but also that they should confer together for
their own safety, while they still could, and reprimand

σφίσιν ὁπλίτας· οὐ διαλυομένους, οὐδ’ ὅτε παύσαιντο
τῶν στρατειῶν, ἵνα μὴ τοῖς ἐχθροῖς εἶεν εὐεπίθετοι,
ἀλλ’ ἀθρόους ἐν ἀλλοτρίᾳ συνοικίζεσθαι διὰ τὴν
ἰσχὺν μᾶλλον ἐθέλοντας ἢ καθ’ ἕνα τῶν πατρίδων

332 ἀπολαύειν. τάδε μὲν ὁ Καῖσαρ Λεπίδῳ τε ἐπέστελλε
καὶ Ἀσινίῳ· Δέκμῳ δὲ ὁ ἀρχαῖος στρατὸς ἐνόσει πιμ-
πλάμενος ἐκ λιμοῦ καὶ τὰς γαστέρας κατερρήγνυν-

333 το, ὅ τε νεοστράτευτος ἀγύμναστος ἔτι ἦν. Πλάγκος
δὲ προσεγένετο μετὰ τοῦ οἰκείου στρατοῦ, καὶ ὁ Δέκμος ἐπέστελλε τῇ βουλῇ τὸν Ἀντώνιον ἀλώμενον κυ-
νηγετήσειν αὐτίκα, ὥσπερ νενικηκότων.[35]

334 82. Οἵ τε Πομπηιανοὶ πυθόμενοι θαυμαστοὶ ὅσοι
διεφάνησαν, ἐκβοῶντες ἄρτι τὴν πάτριον ἐλευθερίαν
ἀπειληφέναι, καὶ θυσίαι καθ’ ἕνα ἦσαν καὶ χειροτο-
νίαι δέκα ἀνδρῶν ἐς εὔθυναν τῆς ἀρχῆς τῆς Ἀντωνίου.

335 πρόσχημα δὲ τοῦτο ἦν ἐς ἀκύρωσιν τῶν ὑπὸ Καίσαρος διατεταγμένων· Ἀντώνιος γὰρ οὐδὲν αὐτὸς ἢ πάνυ
σμικρά, πάντα δὲ ἐκ τῶν Καίσαρος ὑπομνημάτων
διῳκήκει, καὶ τόδε σαφῶς εἰδυῖα ἡ βουλὴ τὰ μέν τινα
αὐτῶν ἐπὶ προφάσεσι διέλυεν, ἀθρόα δὲ οὕτως ἤλπιζε

336 διαλύσειν. οἱ μὲν δὴ δέκα προύγραφον, ὅ τι τις λάβοι
παρὰ τὴν ἀρχὴν Ἀντωνίου, πάντας αὐτίκα ἀπογράφε-
σθαι καὶ διδάσκειν· ἀπειλαί τε τοῖς ἀπειθοῦσιν ἐπε-

---

[35] ναυτικῶν περ ἤδη γεγονότων. οἵ τε Πομπηιανοὶ codd.;
αὐτίκα, ὥσπερ νενικηκότων, Goukowsky; et alii alia

---

[39] The text refers here to naval actions (*nautikon*) having
taken place, which does not seem to make sense, and there is

Antony on these matters; and they should follow the example of their own soldiers, who, in order to avoid making themselves easy for their enemies to attack, did not go their separate ways, even when they retired from military service, but preferred to settle together in foreign countries because of the strength this offered, rather than for each of them individually to enjoy their home territory. This is what Octavian wrote to Lepidus and Asinius. Decimus' original army now fell sick from eating their fill after suffering from famine, and contracted dysentery, and the new soldiers were still untrained. But Plancus joined him with his own army, and Decimus wrote to the senate to say that he would immediately hunt down Antony in his wanderings, as if he and Plancus had already won the victory.[39]

82. When the Pompeians learned what had happened, an astonishing number appeared, exclaiming that they had just regained their ancestral freedom: every one of them offered sacrifices, and a ten-man commission was appointed to investigate Antony's government. This was a pretext for annulling the ordinances made by Caesar, for Antony had made no directives himself, or only very minor ones, but had conducted all his administration in accordance with Caesar's memoranda. The senate were well aware of this, but were finding excuses for revoking some of his measures, and hoped in this way to annul the whole lot of them. Accordingly, the ten commissioners gave public notice that everyone must register and account for whatever they had received during Antony's period in of-

general agreement that something must be wrong with it. Out of many editorial suggestions, I have adopted Goukowsky's reading as one example of how to extract better sense.

337 τίθεντο. καὶ τὴν ὕπατον ἀρχὴν ἐς τὸ λοιπὸν τοῦ ἔτους
οἱ Πομπηιανοὶ μετήεσαν ἀντὶ Ἱρτίου τε καὶ Πάνσα·
μετήει δὲ καὶ ὁ Καῖσαρ, οὐκ ἐς τὴν βουλὴν ἔτι πέμπων, ἀλλ' ἐς τὸν Κικέρωνα ἰδίᾳ, καὶ αὐτὸν παρεκάλει
καὶ συνάρξαι, ὡς Κικέρωνα μὲν τὴν ἀρχὴν διοική-
σοντα πρεσβύτερόν τε καὶ ἐμπειρότερον ὄντα, αὐτὸς
δὲ τὴν ἐπωνυμίαν καρπωσόμενος μόνην ἐς ἀπόθεσιν
τῶν ὅπλων εὐπρεπῆ, οὗ δὴ καὶ πρώην ἕνεκα τὸν θρί-

338 αμβον αἰτῆσαι. Κικέρων μὲν δὴ τούτοις ἐπαρθεὶς διὰ
φιλαρχίαν, ἔλεγεν αἰσθέσθαι σπονδῶν ἐν τοῖς ἔξω
στρατηγοῖς ὑπονοουμένων καὶ συνεβούλευε θεραπεῦ-
σαι τὸν ἄνδρα, ὑβρισμένον καὶ στρατοῦ ἔτι ἄρχοντα
πολλοῦ, ἀνασχέσθαι τε παρ' ἡλικίαν ἄρχοντος ἐν τῇ
πόλει μᾶλλον ἢ μηνίοντος ἐν ὅπλοις· ὡς δ' ἄν τι μὴ
πράξειε παρὰ τὸ τῇ βουλῇ συμφέρον, ἐκέλευεν αὐτῷ
συνελέσθαι τῶν τινα πρεσβυτέρων ἔμφρονα, τῆς ἐκεί-

339 νου νεότητος ἐγκρατῆ παιδαγωγόν. ἀλλὰ Κικέρωνα
μὲν ἥ τε βουλὴ τῆς φιλαρχίας ἐγέλασε, καὶ οἱ συγγενεῖς μάλιστα τῶν σφαγέων ἐνέστησαν, δεδιότες μὴ
αὐτοὺς ὁ Καῖσαρ τίσαιτο ὑπατεύων.

340 83. Ὑπερθέσεων δὲ ἐπὶ τῇ χειροτονίᾳ γιγνομένων
ἐννόμων κατὰ ποικίλας αἰτίας, ὁ Ἀντώνιος ἐν τῷ τέως
τὰς Ἄλπεις ὑπερέβαλε, Κουλλεῶνα πείσας τὸν ἐκ Λεπίδου φύλακα αὐτῶν, ἐπί τε ποταμὸν ἦλθεν, ἔνθα
ἐστρατοπεδευμένος ἦν ὁ Λέπιδος, καὶ οὔτε χάρακα

fice, and appended threats against those who disobeyed. The Pompeians sought the consulship for the rest of the 337 year in place of Hirtius and Pansa. Octavian was also going after it, although he no longer communicated directly with the senate, instead dealing privately with Cicero, whom he urged to be his colleague in office: Cicero, he said, would carry out the duties of the office, being the older and more experienced man, while he himself would merely enjoy the benefits of the title to provide a dignified way of laying aside his arms, which was why he had just recently asked for a triumph.[40] Given his ambition for office, Cicero was 338 excited by these words, and told the senate that he had learned of an agreement under consideration by the provincial commanders, and advised that they should conciliate a man who had been insulted and who still had command of a large army, and put up with an underage magistrate in Rome rather than an enraged man with an army. But in order to prevent him doing anything contrary to the interests of the senate, Cicero urged them to choose as his colleague an older man of good sense to be a firm guide for his youthfulness. But the senate laughed at Cic- 339 ero's ambition for office, and the relatives of the murderers especially opposed him, fearing that once Octavian was consul he would take vengeance on them.

83. For various reasons, there were legal delays on the 340 election. In the meantime Antony crossed the Alps, having prevailed upon Culleo who had been posted by Lepidus to guard them, and advanced to a river where Lepidus was camped. On the assumption, however, that he was making

[40] A triumphing general's victory should be so complete that he no longer needed his army.

περιεβάλετο οὔτε τάφρον ὡς δὴ φίλῳ παραστρατο-
341 πεδεύων. διαπομπαὶ δὲ ἦσαν ἐς ἀλλήλους πυκναί,
Ἀντωνίου μὲν ὑπομιμνήσκοντος φιλίας τε καὶ χαρίτων
ποικίλων, καὶ διδάσκοντος, ὅτι μεθ' αὑτὸν ὅμοια πεί-
σονται καθ' ἕνα πάντες, οἳ τῆς Καίσαρος ἐγένοντο
φιλίας, Λεπίδου δὲ τὴν μὲν βουλὴν δεδιότος πολεμεῖν
αὐτῷ κελεύουσαν, ὑπισχνουμένου δ' ὅμως οὐ πολεμή-
342 σειν ἑκόντος. ὁ δὲ στρατὸς ὁ τοῦ Λεπίδου τό τε
ἀξίωμα αἰδούμενοι τὸ Ἀντωνίου καὶ τῶν διαπομπῶν
αἰσθανόμενοι καὶ τὴν ἀφέλειαν αὐτοῦ τῆς στρατοπε-
δείας ἀγάμενοι, ἐπεμίγνυντο τοῖς Ἀντωνίου λανθάνοντες, εἶτα φανερῶς οἷα πολίταις τε καὶ συστρατιώταις
γενομένοις, τῶν τε χιλιάρχων κωλυόντων ὑπερεώρων
καὶ τὸν ποταμὸν ἐς εὐμάρειαν τῆς ἐπιμιξίας ναυσὶν
ἐγεφύρουν· τό τε καλούμενον δέκατον τέλος, ἐξεναγη-
μένον ὑπὸ Ἀντωνίου πάλαι, τὰ ἔνδον αὐτῷ παρεσκεύαζεν.

343   84. Ὧν αἰσθανόμενος Λατερήσιος, τῶν τις ἐκ τῆς
βουλῆς ἐπιφανῶν, προηγόρευε τῷ Λεπίδῳ καὶ ἀπι-
στοῦντα ἐκέλευε τὴν στρατιὰν ἐς πολλὰ διελόντα ἐκ-
πέμψαι κατὰ δή τινας χρείας, ἐς ἐπίδειξιν ἢ τῆς προ-
344 δοσίας ἢ τῆς πίστεως. καὶ ὁ Λέπιδος ἐς τρία διελών,
ἐκέλευε νυκτὸς ἐξορμᾶν ἐς φρουρὰν ταμιείων πλησιαζόντων. οἱ δὲ ἀμφὶ τὴν ἐσχάτην φυλακήν, ὡς ἐς
τὴν ἔξοδον ὁπλισάμενοι, τὰ ἐρυμνὰ τοῦ στρατοπέδου κατέλαβον καὶ τὰς πύλας ἀνεῴγνυον Ἀντωνίῳ.

camp beside a friendly force, he did not put up a palisade
or dig a ditch. Messages flew between them thick and fast.   341
Antony reminded Lepidus of their friendship and the variety of favors he had done him, pointing out that after
himself all who had been associates of Caesar would suffer
a similar fate, one by one. Lepidus was afraid of the senate,
who had ordered him to make war on Antony, but he
promised nevertheless that he would not do so of his own
accord. Lepidus' troops, having great respect for Antony's   342
reputation, noting the exchange of deputations and admir-
ing the basic nature of his camp, began to mingle with his
men, at first secretly, then openly, inasmuch as they were
citizens and fellow soldiers; and disregarding the attempts
of the tribunes to prevent this behavior, they built a pon-
toon bridge over the river to facilitate their mutual con-
tacts. The legion known as the tenth, which had originally
been recruited by Antony, got things ready for him inside
their camp.

84. Laterensis, one of the senatorial elite, saw what was   343
happening and warned Lepidus.[41] As Lepidus did not believe him, Laterensis advised him to divide his army into
several sections and send them off on various tasks, as a
means of showing whether they were loyal or disloyal.
Lepidus divided them in three, and ordered them to make   344
a sortie by night to protect some convoys that were approaching.[42] But at about the time of the last watch, the
men on duty armed themselves as if for departure, seized
the fortified parts of the camp, and opened the gates to

---

[41] Marcus Iuventius Laterensis had been praetor in 51 and
was a legate of Lepidus in 43.

[42] Or perhaps, "to protect some storehouses in the vicinity."

345 ὁ δ᾽ ἐπὶ τὴν Λεπίδου σκηνὴν ἵετο δρόμῳ, τοῦ στρατοῦ
παντὸς ἤδη τοῦ Λεπίδου παραπέμποντος αὐτὸν καὶ
τὸν Λέπιδον αἰτοῦντος εἰρήνην τε καὶ ἔλεον ἐς ἀτυ-
346 χοῦντας πολίτας. ὁ μὲν δὴ Λέπιδος, ὡς εἶχεν, ἐκ τῆς
εὐνῆς ἄζωστος ἐς αὐτοὺς ἐξέθορε καὶ ὑπισχνεῖτο ποιήσειν καὶ τὸν Ἀντώνιον ἠσπάζετο καὶ ἐξελογεῖτο τῆς
347 ἀνάγκης. οἱ δὲ αὐτὸν καὶ προσπεσεῖν Ἀντωνίῳ νομίζουσιν, ἄπρακτον μὲν ὄντα καὶ ἄτολμον, οὐ μὴν
ἅπασι τοῖς συγγραφεῦσι πιστὸν οὐδ᾽ ἐμοὶ πιθανόν·
οὐ γάρ πώ τι αὐτῷ πολέμιον ἐς τὸν Ἀντώνιον ἐπέ-
348 πρακτο, δέους ἄξιον. οὕτω μὲν ὁ Ἀντώνιος ἐς μέγα
δυνάμεως αὖθις ἐπῆρτο, καὶ τοῖς ἐχθροῖς ἦν ἐπιφο-
βώτατος· στρατὸν γὰρ εἶχεν, ὅν τε ἐξανέστησε Μουτίνης καὶ σὺν αὐτῷ λαμπρότατον ἱππικόν, τρία τε
αὐτῷ τέλη κατὰ τὴν ὁδὸν προσγεγένητο τὰ Οὐεντιδίου, καὶ Λέπιδος αὐτῷ σύμμαχος ἐγίγνετο ἑπτὰ ἔχων
ὁπλιτικὰ τέλη καὶ πολὺν ὅμιλον ἄλλον καὶ παρασκευὴν ἀξιόλογον. καὶ τοῖσδε ὁ μὲν Λέπιδος ἐπωνο-
μάζετο ἔτι, ὁ δὲ Ἀντώνιος ἅπαντα διώκει.

349   85. Ἐξαγγελθέντων δὲ τῶνδε ἐς Ῥώμην θαυμαστὴ
καὶ αἰφνίδιος ἦν αὖθις μεταβολή, τῶν μὲν ἐκ τῆς οὐ
πρὸ πολλοῦ καταφρονήσεως ἐς δέος, τῶν δὲ ἐς θάρσος ἀπὸ τοῦ δέους μεθισταμένων. αἵ τε προγραφαὶ
τῶν δέκα ἀνδρῶν κατεσπῶντο σὺν ὕβρει, καὶ αἱ χει-
350 ροτονίαι τῶν ὑπάτων ἐπείχοντο ἔτι μᾶλλον· ἥ τε
βουλὴ πάμπαν ἀποροῦσα, καὶ δεδιυῖα, μὴ συνθοῖντο
ἀλλήλοις ὅ τε Καῖσαρ καὶ ὁ Ἀντώνιος, ἔπεμπε μὲν ἐς
Βρουτόν τε καὶ Κάσσιον κρύφα ἀπὸ σφῶν Λεύκιον

Antony. He set off at a run to the tent of Lepidus, with 345
Lepidus' entire army escorting him and demanding from
Lepidus peace and compassion for his unfortunate fellow
citizens. Lepidus jumped out of bed to meet them in a 346
state of undress, just as he was, promised to do what they
asked, embraced Antony, and pleaded necessity in his own
defense. Some think that he actually fell on his knees be- 347
fore Antony, being an irresolute and timid man, but by no
means all historians trust this report, and I do not find it
credible: for he had not yet committed any hostile act
against Antony to cause him to be afraid. In this way Ant- 348
ony again rose to great power, and became an object of
extreme fear to his enemies; for he had the army with
which he had retired from Mutina, including a superb
force of cavalry, and the three legions of Ventidius that had
joined him on the road, and Lepidus had become his ally
with seven legions of heavy infantry, a large force of auxiliary troops, and splendid equipment. Lepidus retained
nominal command of these, but Antony directed everything.

85. When this news was announced at Rome, another 349
wonderful and sudden transformation took place, some
exchanging their recent contempt for Antony with fear,
and others replacing fear with daring. The public notices
of the ten commissioners were violently torn down, and
the consular elections were still further postponed. The 350
senate were completely at a loss what to do and fearful that
Octavian and Antony would join forces with each other.
They secretly sent two of their own members, Lucius and
Pansa, to Brutus and Cassius, under pretense of attending

καὶ Πάνσαν, ὡς ἐπὶ θέας εἰς Ἑλλάδα ἐξιόντας, ἀμύ-
351 νειν αὐτοῖς ἐς ὃ δύναιντο, μετεκάλει δὲ ἐκ Λιβύης ἀπὸ
τριῶν τῶν ὑπὸ Σέξτιον δύο τέλη, καὶ τὸ τρίτον ἐκέλευε
Κορνιφικίῳ παραδοθῆναι, τῆς ἑτέρας ἄρχοντι Λιβύης
καὶ τὰ τῆς βουλῆς φρονοῦντι, εἰδότες μὲν καὶ τούσδε
Γαΐῳ Καίσαρι ἐστρατευμένους καὶ τὰ ἐκείνου πάντα
352 ὑπονοοῦντες· ἡ δὲ ἀπορία σφᾶς ὧδε ἤπειγεν, ἐπεὶ καὶ
τὸν νέον Καίσαρα, δεδιότες μὴ συνθοῖτο Ἀντωνίῳ,
στρατηγὸν αὖθις ἐπὶ Ἀντωνίῳ μάλα ἀπρεπῶς ἐχειροτόνουν ἅμα Δέκμῳ.

353   86. Ὁ δὲ Καῖσαρ ἤδη τὸν στρατὸν εἰς ὀργὴν ὑπέρ
τε αὐτοῦ, ὡς συνεχῶς ὑβριζόμενος, ἀνεκίνει καὶ ὑπὲρ
σφῶν ἐκείνων, ἐπὶ δευτέραν στρατείαν πεμπομένων,
πρὶν ἐπὶ τῇ προτέρᾳ λαβεῖν τὰς πεντακισχιλίας
δραχμάς, ὅσας αὐτοῖς ὑπέσχοντο δώσειν· ἐδίδασκέ τε
πέμποντας αἰτεῖν. οἱ δ᾽ ἔπεμπον τοὺς λοχαγούς. καὶ
ἡ βουλὴ συνίει μὲν αὐτοὺς ἐς ταῦτα διδασκομένους,
ἀποκρινεῖσθαι δὲ αὐτοῖς ἔφη δι᾽ ἑτέρων πρέσβεων.
354 καὶ ἔπεμπον, οὓς ἐδίδαξαν τοῖς δύο τέλεσι τοῖς ἀπ᾽
Ἀντωνίου μεθεστηκόσιν ἐντυχεῖν ἄνευ τοῦ Καίσαρος,
καὶ διδάσκειν μὴ ἐφ᾽ ἑνὶ ποιεῖσθαι τὰς ἐλπίδας, ἀλλ᾽
ἐπὶ τῇ βουλῇ τὸ κράτος ἀθάνατον ἐχούσῃ μόνῃ, χωρεῖν δὲ πρὸς Δέκμον, ἔνθα σφίσι τὰ χρήματα ἀπαν-
355 τήσειν. ταῦτ᾽ ἐπισκήψαντες λέγειν ἐσέφερον ἤδη τὸ

---

43 It is not possible to identify Lucius and Pansa.
44 After the battle of Thapsus in 46, Julius Caesar added a new
province of Africa to the existing one. The two provinces, Africa

games in Greece, to urge them to lend all assistance possible.[43] They also recalled from Africa two of the three   351
legions under Sextius, and ordered the third to be handed
over to Cornificius, who was governor of the other province of Africa, and a senatorial supporter.[44] They knew
that these troops too had served under Gaius Caesar, and
they were suspicious of anything to do with Caesar. But   352
their difficulties drove them to this, since in spite of their
fear that the young Caesar would join forces with Antony,
they quite incongruously reappointed him to the command against Antony, along with Decimus.

86. As for Octavian, he now roused the army to anger,   353
both on account of himself for the continual insults he had
suffered, and on their own account, since they were being
sent on a second campaign before they had received the
five thousand drachmas the senate had promised to give
them for the previous campaign. He advised them to send
representatives to ask for the money, and they sent their
centurions. The senate understood that the men had been
coached to take this action, and said that they would reply
through other envoys. They instructed their representa-   354
tives to meet with the two legions that had defected from
Antony, without Octavian being present, and advise them
not to place their hopes on one man, but on the senate,
which alone had permanent power, and to go to the camp
of Decimus, where they would find their money. These   355
were the instructions they gave for what to say, and they

Vetus (Old Africa) and Africa Nova (New Africa), were reunited
by the emperor Augustus. Quintus Cornificius (Africa Vetus) and
Titus Sextius (Africa Nova) were probably praetors in 45, before
taking up their governorships in 44.

ἥμισυ τῆς δωρεᾶς καὶ δέκα ἄνδρας ἐς τὴν διανέμησιν
ἐχειροτόνουν, οἷς οὐδὲ ἑνδέκατον προσετίθεσαν εἶναι
356 τὸν Καίσαρα. οἱ μὲν δὴ πρέσβεις, οὐκ ἀνασχομένων
τῶν δύο τελῶν ἐντυχεῖν σφίσιν ἄνευ τοῦ Καίσαρος,
ὑπέστρεφον ἄπρακτοι· ὁ δὲ Καίσαρ οὐκέτι τοὺς λόγους καθίει δι᾽ ἑτέρων οὐδὲ μέλλειν ἠξίου, ἀλλ᾽ αὐτὸς
ἐς τὸν στρατὸν συνειλεγμένον ἐπελθών, τά τε ὑβρί-
σματα, ὅσα ἐς αὐτὸν ἐκ τῆς βουλῆς γεγένητο, κατ-
έλεξε, καὶ τὴν ἐς πάντας τοὺς Γαΐου Καίσαρος ἐπι-
357 βουλήν, καθ᾽ ἕνα καθαιρουμένους, δεδιέναι τε αὐτοῖς
περὶ σφῶν διεκελεύσατο, μεταφερομένοις ἔς τε πολέμιον τῆς μοίρας στρατηγὸν καὶ πολέμους ἑτέρους
ἀφ᾽ ἑτέρων, ἵν᾽ ἢ ἐκφθαρεῖεν ἢ καὶ πρὸς ἀλλήλους
στασιάσειαν· ἐπὶ γὰρ τῷδε καὶ τοῦ περὶ Μουτίνην
ἔργου κοινοῦ γεγονότος τὰ γέρα τοῖς δύο τέλεσι μόνοις δίδοσθαι, ἵν᾽ αὐτοὺς ἐς ἔριν καὶ στάσιν ἐμ-
βάλοιεν.

358   87. "Ἴστε δέ," ἔφη, "Καὶ ἐφ᾽ οἷς ὁ Ἀντώνιος ἔναγχος
ἡττήθη οἷά τε τοὺς Πομπηιανοὺς ἐπύθεσθε ἐν ἄστει
πεποιηκέναι κατὰ τῶν τινας δωρεὰς παρὰ Καίσαρος
εἰληφότων. τί δὴ πιστὸν ἢ ὑμῖν ὧν ἐλάβετε παρ᾽ ἐκείνου χωρίων τε καὶ χρημάτων ἢ ἐμοὶ τῆς σωτηρίας,
ὧδε ἐν τῇ βουλῇ δυναστευόντων τῶν οἰκείων τοῖς
359 σφαγεῦσι; κἀγὼ μὲν ἐκδέξομαι τὸ τέλος, ὅ τι ἂν ἐπι-
γίγνηταί μοι (καλὸν γάρ τι καὶ παθεῖν πατρὶ ἐπικου-
ροῦντα), ὑπὲρ δὲ ὑμῶν δέδια τοιῶνδε καὶ τοσῶνδε
360 κινδυνευόντων ἐς ἐμὴν καὶ τοῦ πατρὸς χάριν. ἴστε μὲν
δή με καθαρεύοντα φιλοτιμίας, ἐξ οὗ στρατηγεῖν μοι

then delivered half the donative and appointed ten men to distribute it, refusing to add Octavian to this group, even as an eleventh man. But the senatorial envoys re- 356 turned without accomplishing their mission, as the two legions would not agree to meet them without Octavian being present. Octavian now stopped communicating through intermediaries and thought he should delay no longer. Making a personal appearance before his assembled troops, he detailed the insults delivered to him by the senate, and the plot against all Gaius Caesar's partisans, who were being destroyed one by one. He urged them to 357 fear for their own interests if they were transferred to a general who was hostile to their party, or sent to one war after another with the purpose of either having them killed or setting them against each other. This, he said, was the reason why, although they had all conducted the campaign at Mutina together, rewards were given to only two legions, in order to cause discord and division among them.

87. "You are also aware," he said, "of the reasons why 358 Antony suffered his recent defeat, and you have heard about the actions taken by the Pompeians at Rome against those who received any benefits from Caesar. What guarantee do you have of keeping the lands and monies you got from him, what guarantee do I have of my personal safety, while the relatives of the murderers hold power in the senate as they do? For myself, I will accept my fate, 359 however it turns out for me, for it is also a noble thing to suffer in the service of a father; but I fear for you, so many and such fine men, who face danger on my behalf and my father's. You certainly know that I have am free from 360 ambition, from the occasion when you offered me the

διδόντων ὑμῶν ὑπὸ σημείοις οὐκ ἐδεχόμην· ἐν δὲ μόνον ὁρῶ νῦν ἀμφοτέροις σωτήριον, εἰ δι᾿ ὑμῶν ὕπατος
ἀποδειχθείην. τά τε γὰρ παρὰ τοῦ πατρὸς ὑμῖν δοθέ-
ντα πάντα βέβαια ἔσται, ἀποικίαι τε προσέσονται αἱ
ἔτι ὀφειλόμεναι, καὶ γέρα πάντα ἐντελῆ· ἐγώ τε τοὺς
φονέας ὑπὸ δίκην ἀγαγὼν τοὺς ἄλλους ἂν ὑμῖν κα-
ταλύσαιμι πολέμους."

361   88. Ὧν λεγομένων ἥ τε στρατιὰ προθύμως ἐπε-
βόησε, καὶ τοὺς λοχαγοὺς αὐτίκα ἔπεμπον αἰτήσο-
ντας τὴν ἀρχὴν τῷ Καίσαρι. ὑποκριναμένης δὲ τῆς
βουλῆς τὴν ἡλικίαν, ἔλεγον οἱ λοχαγοὶ ἃ ἐδιδάχθη-
σαν, ὅτι καὶ πάλαι Κορουῖνός τε ἄρξειε νεώτερος ὢν
ἔτι καὶ Σκιπίων ὕστερον, ὅ τε πρότερος καὶ ὁ δεύτερος, καὶ ἐκ τῆς νεότητος ἑκάστου πολλὰ ὄναιτο ἡ
πατρίς. τά τε ἔναγχος ταῦτά,[36] καὶ Πομπήιον Μάγνον
αὐτοῖς καὶ Δολοβέλλαν προύφερον, αὐτῷ τε Καίσαρι
ἤδη δεδόσθαι τὴν ἀρχὴν μετιέναι θᾶσσον ἐτῶν δέκα.
362   ταῦτα τῶν λοχαγῶν σὺν πλέονι παρρησίᾳ λεγόντων,
οὐκ ἀνασχόμενοί τινες τῶν βουλευτῶν λοχαγοὺς
ὄντας ὧδε παρρησιάζεσθαι, ἐπέπλησσον ὡς θρασυ-
363   νομένοις ὑπὲρ τὸ στρατιώταις πρέπον. καὶ ὁ στρατὸς
πυθόμενος ἔτι μᾶλλον ὠργίζοντο καὶ ἄγειν σφᾶς εὐθὺς ἐκέλευον ἐς τὴν πόλιν, ὡς αὐτοὶ χειροτονήσοντες

---

36 ταὐτά Goukowsky; ταῦτα codd.

45 After a law passed in 180, the minimum age for holding the
consulship was forty-two. Marcus Valerius Corvus (or Corvinus)

command with its insignia, and I refused it. But I see only one route to safety for both of us, and that is for me to be appointed consul with your help. For that way, all my father's gifts to you will be confirmed, the colonies still due will be founded, and all your rewards will be paid in full. And as for me, after bringing the murderers to justice, I would put an end to any other wars for you."

88. The army cheered this speech enthusiastically and immediately sent their centurions to ask for the consulship for Octavian. When the senate answered by referring to his youthfulness, the centurions said what they had been instructed to say, that in ancient times Corvinus had been consul when still too young, and more recently the Scipios too, both the first and the second; and that the youthfulness of each one of them had been of great benefit to the country.[45] As for recent examples, they also cited the cases of Pompey the Great and Dolabella, and noted that Octavian himself had already been granted permission to hold the consulship ten years in advance of the legal age. The centurions spoke with considerable candor, and some of the senators who could not stand such license from men who were mere centurions rebuked them for an audacity that exceeded what was fitting for soldiers. When the army heard of this, they were even more angry and urged Octavian to lead them immediately to Rome, saying that

361

362

363

held the first of the six consulships attributed to him in 348, at the unusually young age of twenty-two. Publius Cornelius Scipio Africanus, the hero of Rome's victory in the war against Hannibal, was first elected consul in 205, at the age of thirty. Publius Cornelius Scipio Aemilianus needed a suspension of the rules to take up the consulship in 147, when he was thirty-eight.

αὐτὸν ἐξαιρέτῳ χειροτονίᾳ, Καίσαρος υἱὸν ὄντα,
πολλά τε τὸν πρότερον Καίσαρα ἀπαύστως εὐφήμουν.

364 ὧδε δὲ αὐτοὺς ὁρμῆς ἔχοντας ὁ Καῖσαρ ἰδὼν ἦγεν
εὐθὺς ἀπὸ τῆς συνόδου, ὀκτὼ τέλη πεζῶν καὶ ἵππον

365 ἱκανὴν καὶ ὅσα ἄλλα τοῖς τέλεσι συνετάσσετο. περά-
σας δὲ τὸν Ῥουβίκωνα ποταμὸν ἐκ τῆς Κελτικῆς ἐς
τὴν Ἰταλίαν, ὅν τινα αὐτοῦ καὶ ὁ πατὴρ ὁμοίως ἐπὶ
τῷ πολιτικῷ πολέμῳ πρῶτον ἐπέρασεν, ἐς δύο πάντας
διῄρει· καὶ τὸ μὲν ἕπεσθαι κατὰ σχολὴν ἐκέλευσε, τὸ
δὲ ἄμεινον ἐπιλεξάμενος ἐτρόχαζεν, ἐπειγόμενος ἔτι

366 ἀπαρασκεύους καταλαβεῖν. μέρους τε τῶν χρημάτων
ὑπαντῶντος, ἃ ἐς τὰ γέρα τοῖς στρατιώταις ἡ βουλὴ
πεπόμφει, δείσας ἐπὶ τοῖς μισθοφόροις ὁ Καῖσαρ
προύπεμπε κρύφα τοὺς ἐκφοβήσοντας· καὶ οἱ μὲν
ἔφευγον μετὰ τῶν χρημάτων.

367 89. Ἐς δὲ τὸ ἄστυ τῆς ἀγγελίας ἀφικομένης θόρυβος ἦν καὶ φόβος ἄπλετος, διαθεόντων τε ἀκόσμως
καὶ γύναιά τινων ἢ παῖδας ἢ ὅσα τιμιώτατα ἄλλα ἐς
ἀγροὺς ἢ τὰ ἐρυμνὰ τῆς πόλεως μεταφερόντων· οὐ
γάρ πω σαφοῦς ὄντος, ὅτι μόνης ὀρέγοιτο ὑπατείας,
πολέμιον στρατὸν ἐπιέναι σὺν ὀργῇ πυνθανόμενοι ἐς

368 πάντα ἐδεδοίκεσαν. ἡ βουλὴ δ᾽ ἐξεπέπληκτο ἀμέτρως,
οὐδεμιᾶς αὐτοῖς οὔσης ἑτοίμου δυνάμεως, ἀλλήλους
τε, οἷον ἐν τοῖς φόβοις γίγνεται, κατεμέμφοντο, οἱ μὲν
ὅτι τὴν στρατιὰν αὐτὸν ἀφέλοιντο τὴν ἐπὶ τὸν
Ἀντώνιον ὑβριστικῶς, οἱ δὲ τῆς ἐς τὸν θρίαμβον
ὑπεροψίας, οὐκ ἄδικον ὄντα, οἱ δὲ τοῦ φθόνου τῆς
διανεμήσεως τῶν χρημάτων, οἱ δὲ οὐδὲ ἑνδέκατον ἐπι-

they would elect him themselves in a special vote, as he was Caesar's son; and they did not stop lavishly praising the first Caesar. Seeing them in such a state of eagerness, 364 Octavian led them away straight from the meeting, eight legions of infantry, a considerable force of cavalry, and the usual auxiliaries attached to the legions. Having crossed 365 the river Rubicon from Gaul into Italy—which his father had also crossed before him in the same way to set the civil war in motion—he divided his army into two. One of these groups he ordered to follow at a leisurely pace, but with the better and specially selected division he made a forced march, hurrying to catch his opponents still unprepared. On the march he came across some of the money sent by 366 the senate to pay for the soldiers' rewards, and fearing the reaction of his mercenaries, he secretly sent ahead men to frighten off the escort, who took to flight with the money.

89. When news of this reached the city, there was wide- 367 spread commotion and panic, as people rushed around in disorder and some transferred their wives and children and whatever else was most precious, to the countryside or to the strongholds of the city. For it was not yet clear that Octavian was aiming only at the consulship, and hav- ing heard that a hostile army was approaching in anger, they were completely terrified. The senate were frantic 368 beyond measure, as they had no military forces at hand, and, as happens in times of panic, they began to blame each other. Some said they had taken the command against Antony from Octavian in an overbearing manner; others blamed the contempt with which they had treated his not unjustified request for a triumph; others blamed their be- grudgery over the distribution of money; others again the fact that they had not even enrolled him as an eleventh

γράψαντες· οἱ δὲ αὐτὰ τὰ ἆθλα, οὔτε ὀξέως οὔτε
ἐντελῆ διδόμενα, τὴν στρατιὰν σφίσιν ἔλεγον ἐκπο-
369 λεμῶσαι. τῆς τε φιλονικίας τὸ ἄκαιρον μάλιστα ἐμέμ-
φοντο, Βρούτου μὲν καὶ Κασσίου πορρωτέρω τε
ὄντων καὶ συνισταμένων ἔτι, ἐν δὲ πλευραῖς Ἀντωνίου
καὶ Λεπίδου πολεμίων· οὓς ὅτε ἐνθυμηθεῖεν Καίσαρι
συναλλαγήσεσθαι, πάμπαν ἤκμαζεν ὁ φόβος. Κικέρων τε, ὃς τέως αὐτοῖς ἐπεπόλαζεν, οὐδὲ ἐφαίνετο.

370   90. Ἀθρόα δὴ πάντων ἐς πάντα ἦν μετάθεσις, ἀντὶ
μὲν δισχιλίων καὶ πεντακοσίων δραχμῶν τὰς πεντακισχιλίας, ἀντὶ δὲ τῶν δύο τελῶν τοῖς ὀκτὼ δοθῆναι,
Καίσαρά τε αὐτοῖς ἀντὶ τῶν δέκα ἀνδρῶν διανέμειν
καὶ ἐς τὴν ὕπατον ἀρχὴν παραγγέλλειν ἀπόντα. πρέσβεις τε ἐξέτρεχον, οἳ τάδε φράσειν ἔμελλον αὐτῷ
371 κατὰ σπουδήν. ὧν ἄρτι τῆς πόλεως ἐκδραμόντων μετάνοια ἐνέπιπτε τῇ βουλῇ, μὴ δεῖν οὕτως ἀνάνδρως
καταπεπλῆχθαι, μηδὲ ἑτέραν ἐνδέξασθαι τυραννίδα
ἀναιμωτί, μηδὲ ἐθίσαι τοὺς ἀρχῆς ἐφιεμένους ἐκ βίας
τυγχάνειν, μηδὲ τοὺς στρατευομένους ἐξ ἐπιτάγματος
ἄρχειν τῆς πατρίδος, ὁπλισαμένους δὲ ἐκ τῶν ἐνόν-
372 των τοὺς νόμους τοῖς ἐπιοῦσι προτείνειν· προσδοκᾶν
γὰρ οὐδὲ ἐκείνους νόμων προτεινομένων ὅπλα τῇ πατρίδι ἐποίσειν· εἰ δὲ φέροιεν, ἀνέχεσθαί τε πολιορκίας, μέχρι Δέκμος ἢ Πλάγκος ἔλθοι καὶ ἀμύνεσθαι
μέχρι θανάτου μᾶλλον ἢ ἑκόντας ἐνδέξασθαι δου-
λείαν ἄνωθεν ἀδιόρθωτον· τά τε ἀρχαῖα Ῥωμαίων ἐπὶ

commissioner; and yet others claimed that the army was
at war with them because the actual rewards had not been
given to them either in timely fashion or in full. They put   369
particular blame on their ill-timed belligerence, when
Brutus and Cassius were too far away and still organizing
themselves, while their enemies Antony and Lepidus were
on their flanks. When they contemplated the possibility
that these two would come to an agreement with Octavian,
their panic reached altogether critical levels. Cicero, who
up to this point had been their most conspicuous per-
former, did not even make an appearance.

90. There was a sudden change of position by everyone   370
on all issues. Instead of two thousand five hundred drachmas, five thousand were to be given, and to all eight legions, instead of just the two. Octavian was to make the
distribution instead of the ten commissioners, and he was
allowed to stand for the consulship in absentia. Representatives hurried from the city intending to convey this information to him urgently. But they had only just left   371
Rome when the senate began to change their mind: they
should not be browbeaten in such a cowardly manner, nor
accept another tyranny without a drop of blood being
spilled, nor accustom those seeking office to win it by violence, or serving soldiers to rule their country by ultima-
tum. They should rather arm themselves with what they
had available and confront the invaders with the laws. For   372
they did not expect even these men to bear arms against
their country when faced by the laws. But if they did, it
would be better to endure a siege until Decimus and Plancus arrived, and defend themselves to the death, than submit voluntarily to an irreversible slavery. And they cited
the noble attitude to freedom of the ancient Romans and

ἐλευθερίᾳ φρονήματα καὶ πάθη, πρὸς οὐδὲν ἐνδόντων
ὑπὲρ ἐλευθερίας, ἀνελέγοντο.

373   91. Ἐπεὶ δὲ αὐτοῖς καὶ τὰ δύο τέλη τὰ ἐκ Λιβύης
μετάπεμπτα ἐς τὸν λιμένα αὐτῆς ἡμέρας ἀφίκετο,
τοὺς θεοὺς σφᾶς ἔδοξαν ἐπὶ τὴν ἐλευθερίαν ἐποτρύ-
νειν. ἡ μὲν δὴ μετάνοια ἐκεκύρωτο, καὶ μετεψηφίζετο
374   ἄπαντα, Κικέρωνος αὖθις αὐτοῖς ἐπιφανέντος· ἥ τε
στρατεύσιμος ἡλικία προεγράφετο πᾶσα, καὶ τὰ δύο
τέλη τάδε, τὰ ἐκ Λιβύης, καὶ οἱ σὺν αὐτοῖς ἱππέες
χίλιοι καὶ τέλος ἕτερον, ὃ Πάνσας αὐτοῖς ὑπολελοί-
πει, πάντες οἵδε μερισθέντες οἱ μὲν τὸν λόφον τὸν
καλούμενον Ἰάνουκλον, ἔνθα καὶ τὰ χρήματα ἐσώρευ-
σαν, ἐφρούρουν, οἱ δὲ τὴν τοῦ ποταμοῦ γέφυραν, ἐπι-
διῃρημένων σφίσι τῶν στρατηγῶν τῶν κατὰ τὴν
πόλιν· ἄλλοι δὲ αὐτοῖς τὰ ἐν τῷ λιμένι σκάφη καὶ
ναῦς καὶ χρήματα εὐτρέπιζον, εἰ δεήσειεν ἡττωμένους
375   φυγεῖν διὰ θαλάσσης. καὶ τάδε σὺν εὐθαρσείᾳ πράσσοντες οὕτως ὀξέως ἤλπιζον ἀντικαταπλήξειν τὸν
Καίσαρα, καὶ ἢ μεταπείσειν παρὰ σφῶν ἀντὶ τοῦ
στρατεύματος αἰτεῖν τὴν ἀρχήν, ἢ ἐγκρατῶς ἀμυνεῖ-
σθαι· τούς τε τῆς ἐναντίας μοίρας νῦν γε μεταθήσε-
σθαι προσεδόκων, μέχρι περὶ τῆς ἐλευθερίας ἐστὶν ὁ
376   ἀγών. τὴν δὲ μητέρα Καίσαρος καὶ τὴν ἀδελφὴν οὔτε
φανερῶς οὔτε λάθρᾳ ζητοῦντες εὕρισκον. ἐθορυβοῦν-
το οὖν αὖθις ὁμήρων μεγάλων ἀφῃρημένοι· καὶ τῶν
Καισαριανῶν οὔπω σφίσιν ἐπικλωμένων, ὑπὸ ἐκείνων
αὐτὰς ὧδε ἀκριβῶς ἐνόμιζον ἐπικρύπτεσθαι.

377   92. Καίσαρι δὲ ἔτι τῶν πρέσβεων ἐντυγχανόντων

172

what they had suffered in refusing to give way at all in their defense of freedom.

91. When the two legions they had sent for from Africa 373 arrived in harbor the same day, it seemed to them that the gods were encouraging them to defend their freedom. Their change of mind was confirmed; they canceled all their previous decisions, and Cicero was once again to be seen in public. All men of military age were drafted into 374 the army, and those two legions from Africa, along with one thousand cavalry and another legion that Pansa had left behind for them—all were divided into units. Some guarded the hill called the Janiculum, where they also stored the money, others the bridge over the Tiber, and the city praetors were assigned command of the different units. Others made ready boats, ships, and money in the harbor, in case they were defeated and had to escape by sea. They hoped that by doing all this with confidence and 375 such speed they would alarm Octavian in return, and either persuade him to change his mind and seek the consulship from them and not the army, or resist him with determination. They also expected the members of the opposite party to change their position, inasmuch as it was now a struggle for freedom. But they were unable to find Octa- 376 vian's mother and sister, even though they looked for them openly and in secret. So they were disturbed at again being deprived of important hostages. As the Caesarians were no longer cooperating with them, they believed that it was by them that the women were being hidden so carefully.

92. While Octavian was still meeting with the senato- 377

τὰ μετεψηφισμένα ἀγγέλλεται· καὶ αὐτὸν οἱ πρέσβεις
ἀπολιπόντες ἀνέστρεφον ὑπὸ αἰδοῦς. ὁ δὲ τῷ στρατῷ
μᾶλλον ἔτι παρωξυμμένῳ κατὰ σπουδὴν ἐχώρει, σὺν
378 φόβῳ μή τι πάθοιεν αἱ γυναῖκες· ἔς τε τὸν δῆμον
τεθορυβημένον ἱππέας ἔπεμψεν ἀτρεμεῖν ἐπικελεύων,
καὶ τεθηπότων πάντων τὰ πέραν τοῦ Κυριναλίου λόφου κατέλαβεν, οὐδενὸς ἐς χεῖρας ἐλθεῖν ἢ κωλύειν
379 ὑποστάντος. ἦν τε αὖθις ἑτέρα θαυμάσιος ἄφνω μεταβολή, θεόντων ἐς αὐτὸν τῶν ἐπιφανῶν καὶ προσαγο-
ρευόντων· ἔθει δὲ καὶ ὁ δημότης λεὼς καὶ τὴν εὐτα-
380 ξίαν τῶν στρατιωτῶν ὡς εἰρηνικὴν ἀπεδέχοντο. ὁ δὲ
τὸν στρατόν, ἔνθαπερ ἦν, ἀπολιπὼν ἐχώρει τῆς ἐπιούσης πρὸς τὸ ἄστυ, φυλακὴν ἔχων ἀμφ᾽ αὑτὸν ἱκανήν.
οἱ δὲ καὶ τότε ὑπήντων δι᾽ ὅλης τῆς ὁδοῦ κατὰ μέρη
καὶ προσηγόρευον, οὐδὲν ἐνδέοντες ἢ φιλοφροσύνης
ἢ θεραπείας ἀσθενοῦς. ἡ δὲ μήτηρ αὐτοῦ καὶ ἡ
ἀδελφὴ ἐν τῷ τῆς Ἑστίας ἱερῷ μετὰ τῶν ἱερῶν παρ-
381 θένων ἠσπάσαντο. καὶ τὰ τρία τέλη, τῶν στρατηγῶν
ὑπεριδόντα, πρὸς αὐτὸν ἐπρέσβευε καὶ μετετίθετο· καὶ
τῶν στρατηγῶν οἳ ἦρχον αὐτῶν, Κορνοῦτος μὲν ἑαυτὸν ἔκτεινεν, οἱ δ᾽ ἄλλοι σπονδῶν καὶ πίστεων ἔτυχον.
382 Κικέρων τε τῶν σπονδῶν πυθόμενος ἔπραξε διὰ τῶν
Καίσαρος φίλων ἐντυχεῖν αὐτῷ, καὶ ἐντυχὼν ἀπελογεῖτο καὶ τὴν εἰσήγησιν τῆς ὑπατείας ὑπερεπῆρεν, ἣν
αὐτὸς ἐν τῇ βουλῇ πρότερον εἰσηγήσατο. ὁ δὲ τοσοῦτον ἀπεκρίνατο ἐπισκώπτων ὅτι τῶν φίλων αὐτῷ
τελευταῖος ἐντυγχάνοι.

rial envoys, news is brought to him of the rescinding of the decrees; the envoys left him and returned in embarrassment. With his army even more irritated, Octavian advanced rapidly, fearing that something bad might happen to the women of his family. The people of Rome were in 378 a state of agitation, so he sent horsemen to tell them not to be afraid, and to everyone's astonishment he seized the area north of the Quirinal hill, no one standing up to fight him or block his way. Yet again another wonderful and 379 sudden transformation took place: the nobility rushed to greet him, as did the common people too, who took the good discipline of the troops as a sign of peace. The fol- 380 lowing day, leaving his army where it was, Octavian advanced to the city, bringing with him an adequate bodyguard. On this occasion too others came in groups to meet him all along the road, and greeted him in a way that lacked nothing of friendliness or weak-willed obsequiousness. His mother and sister embraced him in the temple of Vesta in the company of the Vestal virgins. The three 381 legions, ignoring their generals, sent a deputation to him and came over to his side. Of the praetors who commanded the troops, Cornutus took his own life, while the others arranged a truce and safe passage.[46] When Cicero 382 heard of the truce he arranged through associates of Octavian to meet with him. At the meeting he defended himself and emphasized his proposal about the consulship which he himself had earlier introduced in the senate. Octavian limited himself to the ironic reply that Cicero was the last of his friends to come and meet him.

[46] Marcus Caecilius Cornutus was *praetor urbanus* in 43 and, therefore, the senior official in Rome after the death of the consuls Hirtius and Pansa.

383   93. Νυκτὸς δ᾽ ἄφνω δόξης γενομένης, ὅτι δύο τέλη
Καίσαρος, τό τε Ἄρειον καὶ τὸ τέταρτον, μεταθοῖτο ἐς
τὴν πόλιν ὡς δι᾽ ἐνέδρας ἐπὶ τὴν πατρίδα ἐπαχθέντα,
οἱ στρατηγοὶ καὶ ἡ βουλὴ πάμπαν ἀταλαιπώρως ἐπί-
384 στευσαν, καίπερ ὄντος ἐγγυτάτω τοῦ στρατοῦ· νομί-
σαντές τε ἀνθέξειν αὐτοῖς οὖσιν ἀρίστοις πρὸς τὰ
λοιπὰ τοῦ Καίσαρος, μέχρι τις ἑτέρωθεν αὐτοῖς ἰσχὺς
ἐπιγένοιτο, νυκτὸς ἔτι Μάνιον Ἀκύλιον Κράσσον ἐς
τὴν Πικηνίτιδα ἐξέπεμπον στρατὸν ἀθροίζειν, καὶ τῶν
τινα δημάρχων Ἀπουλήιον ἐς τὸν δῆμον ἐποίουν τὸ
385 εὐαγγέλιον ἐκφέρειν περιθέοντα. ἥ τε βουλὴ νυκτὸς
ἐς τὸ βουλευτήριον συνέθεον, Κικέρωνος ἐπὶ ταῖς
θύραις αὐτοὺς δεξιουμένου. ψευδοῦς δὲ τῆς δόξης φανείσης ἐν φορείῳ διέφυγεν.

386   94. Ὁ δὲ Καῖσαρ ἐπιγελάσας αὐτοῖς τὸν μὲν στρατὸν ἐγγυτέρω τῆς πόλεως προήγαγεν, ἐς τὸ πεδίον τὸ
καλούμενον Ἄρειον, τῶν δὲ στρατηγῶν τότε μὲν οὐδένα ἠμύνατο, οὐδὲ Κράσσον τὸν ἐς Πικήνην ἐκ-
δραμόντα, καίπερ οἱ προσαχθέντα ὡς εἶχε ληφθεὶς ἐν
σχήματι οἰκέτου, ἀλλὰ μεθῆκεν ἅπαντας ἐς δόξαν
φιλανθρωπίας. οὐ πολὺ δὲ ὕστερον ἐπὶ θανάτῳ πρου-
387 γράφησαν. τὰ χρήματα δέ, ὅσα τε κοινὰ ἦν ἐν τῷ
Ἰανούκλῳ ἢ ἑτέρωθι καὶ ἄλλα συνενεχθῆναι κελεύ-
σας, ὁπόσα Κικέρωνος ἐσηγουμένου πρότερον αὐτοῖς
ἐπεγέγραπτο, διένειμεν ἀνὰ δισχιλίας καὶ πεντακοσίας δραχμὰς τῷ στρατῷ, καὶ τὸ ἐπίλοιπον ἐπιδώσειν
ὑπέσχετο. καὶ τῆς πόλεως ὑπεξῆλθε, μέχρι χειροτο-

93. During the night a rumor suddenly started that two   383
of Octavian's legions, the legion of Mars and the Fourth,
had deserted to the city's side on the grounds that they had
been led against their country by deception. The praetors
and the senate put complete trust in this report without
checking it, even though the army was very near. Thinking   384
that with the help of these two elite legions they would
hold out against the rest of Octavian's army until joined by
reinforcements from somewhere else, while it was still
night they sent Manius Aquilius Crassus to Picenum to
raise troops, and ordered Apuleius, one of the tribunes, to
hurry around the city and bring the good news to the
people.[47] The senate assembled hurriedly during the   385
night, with Cicero welcoming them at the door, but when
the rumor was shown to be false, he fled in a litter.

94. Octavian laughed at them and moved his army   386
nearer to the city, to what is called the Campus Martius.
At the time he did not punish any of the praetors, not even
Crassus who had rushed off to Picenum, although he was
brought before him just as he had been captured, wearing
slave's clothes. Instead he let them all off in order to win
a reputation for clemency. Not much later, however, they
were sentenced to death on the proscription lists. He or-   387
dered that all the public funds on the Janiculum and elsewhere be collected, and he distributed to his men the
amount that had been previously assigned to them on Cicero's proposal, that is, two thousand five hundred drachmas per man, and promised that he would give them the
rest in due course. Then he left the city until the people

[47] Manius Aquillius Crassus was one of the praetors of 43. The
tribune, Publius Apuleius, was a close associate of Cicero.

388 νήσαιεν ὑπάτους αἱρετούς. αἱρεθεὶς δὲ αὐτὸς σὺν ᾧ
περ ἐβούλετο Κοΐντῳ Πεδίῳ, ὃς τὸ μέρος αὐτῷ δεδώρητο τῆς Καίσαρος κληρονομίας, ἐς τὴν πόλιν
αὖθις ὡς ὕπατος ἐσῄει, καὶ ἔθυε, δώδεκά οἱ γυπῶν
φανέντων, ὅσους φασὶ καὶ Ῥωμύλῳ τὴν πόλιν οἰκί-
389 ζοντι ὀφθῆναι. ἀπὸ δὲ τῶν θυσιῶν ἑαυτὸν εἰσεποιεῖτο
τῷ πατρὶ αὖθις κατὰ νόμον κουριάτιον. ἔστι δ' ἐπὶ τοῦ
δήμου γίγνεσθαι τὴν θέσιν· κουρίας γὰρ ἐς μέρη
τὰς φυλὰς ἢ τοὺς δήμους διαιροῦντες καλοῦσιν, ὡς
390 Ἕλληνες, εἰκάζοντι φάναι, φατρίας. ἐπινομώτατος δ'
ἐστὶ Ῥωμαίοις ὁ τρόπος οὗτος ἐπὶ τῶν ἀπατόρων· καὶ
δύνανται μάλιστα αὐτοὶ ἴσα τοῖς γνησίοις παισὶν
ἄγειν τοὺς συγγενεῖς τῶν θεμένων καὶ ἀπελευθέρους.
391 Γαΐῳ δ' ἦν τά τε ἄλλα λαμπρὰ καὶ ἐξελεύθεροι πολλοί τε καὶ πλούσιοι, καὶ διὰ τόδ' ἴσως μάλιστα ὁ
Καῖσαρ ἐπὶ τῇ προτέρᾳ θέσει, κατὰ διαθήκας οἱ γε-
νομένῃ, καὶ τῆσδε ἐδεήθη.

392   95. Νόμῳ δ' ἑτέρῳ ἀπέλυε μὴ εἶναι πολέμιον Δολοβέλλαν, καὶ εἶναι φόνου δίκας ἐπὶ Καίσαρι. καὶ εὐθὺς
ἦσαν γραφαί, τῶν φίλων τοῦ Καίσαρος γραφομένων
τοὺς μὲν αὐτόχειρας, τοὺς δὲ συνεγνωκέναι μόνον. καὶ
γὰρ τοῦτο ἐνίοις ἐπεγράφη, καί τισιν οὐδ' ἐπιδημή-
393 σασιν, ὅτε ὁ Καῖσαρ ἐκτείνετο. πᾶσι δ' ὁρισθείσης
ὑπὸ κηρύγματι μιᾶς ἡμέρας ἐς κρίσιν, ἐρήμην ἅπαντες ἑάλωσαν, ἐφορῶντος τὰ δικαστήρια τοῦ Καί-

---

48 For Quintus Pedius, see above, 22.82, 23.89.

had elected the consuls of their choice. Once he had been   388
elected himself, together with Quintus Pedius, the man he
wanted as his colleague, and who had given him his own
share of Caesar's inheritance, he entered the city again as
consul.[48] While he was offering sacrifice, twelve vultures
appeared for him, the same number, they say, seen by
Romulus when he was founding the city. After the sacri-   389
fices he had himself readopted by his father by means of
a *lex curiata*, which is what happens when the adoption
takes place before the people. (The Romans call *curiae* the
units into which they divide their tribes and local districts,
what, for comparative purposes, the Greeks call phra-
tries.) Among the Romans this is the most formal means   390
of adoption in the case of those without fathers. Such
adoptees have exactly the same rights as the natural children with respect to the relatives and freedmen of the
adopters. As well as many other magnificent advantages,   391
Caesar had a large number of wealthy freedmen, and this
was perhaps the main reason why Octavian also needed
this form of adoption in addition to his previous one,
which was a testamentary adoption.

95. With new legislation Octavian rescinded the con-   392
demnation of Dolabella as a public enemy, and authorized
legal actions for murder in the case of Caesar. Indictments
followed immediately, Caesar's associates bringing charges
against some for direct involvement in the murder and
others just for conspiracy to murder. This latter accusation
was actually brought against some who were not even in
the city when Caesar was killed. A single day was fixed by   393
public proclamation for all the accused, and all were condemned by default. Octavian presided at the tribunals,

σαρος καὶ τῶν δικαστῶν οὐδενὸς τὴν ἀπολύουσαν
φέροντος πλὴν ἑνὸς ἀνδρὸς τῶν ἐπιφανῶν, ὃς τότε
μὲν οὐδ᾽ αὐτός τι ἔπαθε, μικρὸν δ᾽ ὕστερον ἐπὶ θανάτῳ

394 μετὰ τῶν ἄλλων καὶ ὅδε προυγράφη. ἔδοξε δὲ ταῖσδε
ταῖς ἡμέραις Κόιντος Γάλλιος, ἀδελφὸς Μάρκου Γαλ-
λίου συνόντος Ἀντωνίῳ, τὴν πολιτικὴν στρατηγίαν
ἄρχων, αἰτῆσαι παρὰ Καίσαρος τὴν στρατηγίαν τῆς
Λιβύης, καὶ οὔπω³⁷ τυχὼν ἐπιβουλεῦσαι τῷ Καίσαρι·

395 καὶ αὐτοῦ τὴν μὲν στρατηγίαν περιεῖλον οἱ σύναρχοι,
τὴν δ᾽ οἰκίαν διήρπασεν ὁ δῆμος, ἡ δὲ βουλὴ κατ-
εγίνωσκε θάνατον. ὁ δὲ Καῖσαρ ἐς τὸν ἀδελφὸν
ἐκέλευσε χωρεῖν, καὶ δοκεῖ νεὼς ἐπιβὰς οὐδαμοῦ ἔτι
φανῆναι.

396   96. Τοσάδε πράξας ὁ Καῖσαρ ἐπενόει μὲν τὰς ἐς
τὸν Ἀντώνιον διαλύσεις, πυνθανόμενος ἤδη τοῖς ἀμφὶ
τὸν Βροῦτον εἴκοσι συνῆχθαι τέλη στρατοῦ, καὶ χρῄ-
ζων ἐπ᾽ αὐτὰ Ἀντωνίου, ἐξῄει δὲ τῆς πόλεως ἐπὶ τὸν
Ἰόνιον καὶ σχολαίως ἀνεζεύγνυε, τὰ παρὰ τῆς βουλῆς
ἐπιμένων· Πέδιος γὰρ αὐτὴν ἀποστάντος τοῦ Καίσαρος ἔπειθε τὰ ἐς ἀλλήλους μὴ δυσίατα ποιουμένους

397 συναλλαγῆναι Λεπίδῳ τε καὶ Ἀντωνίῳ. οἱ δὲ προ-
εώρων μὲν ὅτι μὴ σφίσι μηδ᾽ ὑπὲρ τῆς πατρίδος εἰσὶν
αἱ διαλλαγαί, ἀλλ᾽ ἐς συμμαχίαν Καίσαρι κατὰ Κασσίου τε καὶ Βρούτου, ἐπῄνουν δ᾽ ὅμως καὶ συνετίθεντο

---

³⁷ οὔπω Goukowsky; οὔτω codd.; et alii alia

and none of the judges voted for acquittal, except one nobleman, who in fact escaped trouble at the time, but a little later he too was condemned to death on the proscription lists along with the others.[49] It was in this period, so 394 it seems, that Quintus Gallius, the *praetor urbanus* and brother of Marcus Gallius who was with Antony, asked Octavian for the governorship of Africa, but even before getting it, plotted against Octavian. His colleagues stripped 395 him of his praetorship, the people looted his house, and the senate condemned him to death. Octavian ordered him to go to his brother, but although he seems to have embarked on a ship, he was never seen again.

96. With this much achieved, Octavian set his mind to 396 arranging a reconciliation with Antony, as he had learned that Brutus and his party had already collected an army of twenty legions, and he needed Antony's help against them. So he left the city and made for the coast of the Ionian gulf, withdrawing in a leisurely way, and waiting to see what the senate would do. For, once Octavian had departed, Pedius tried to persuade the senators to reconcile themselves with Lepidus and Antony, and not regard their differences as irreconcilable. Although they foresaw that 397 such a reconciliation would not be in their own or in the country's interest, but would merely provide Octavian with military assistance against Brutus and Cassius, nevertheless they gave their approval and agreed under

[49] This was Publius Silicius Corona (mentioned by Appian in *BCiv.* 4.27.118), whose career is otherwise unknown: see also Cass. Dio 46.49.5. Plutarch (*Brut.* 27.3) says that Silicius merely burst into tears at the arraignment of Brutus, and was proscribed for that.

181

ὑπ' ἀνάγκης. καὶ τὰ πολέμια δόγματα Ἀντωνίου τε
καὶ Λεπίδου καὶ τῶν ὑπ' αὐτοῖς στρατῶν κατελύετο,
398 εἰρηναῖα δὲ ἕτερα αὐτοῖς ἐπέμπετο. καὶ ὁ Καῖσαρ
αὐτοῖς συνήδετο γράφων, Ἀντωνίῳ δὲ καὶ βοηθὸς ἐπὶ
Δέκμου ὑπισχνεῖτο ἥξειν, εἰ δέοιτο. οἱ δὲ ἀντεφιλο-
φρονοῦντο μὲν αὐτὸν ἄφνω καὶ ἐπῄνουν, ὁ δ' Ἀντώνιος
ἔγραφεν αὐτὸς ἀποτίσεσθαι Δέκμον τε ὑπὲρ Καίσαρος καὶ Πλάγκον ὑπὲρ ἑαυτοῦ καὶ συμμίξειν Καίσαρι.

399 97. Τοσάδε μὲν ἀλλήλοις ἐπέστειλαν, διώκοντι δὲ
τῷ Ἀντωνίῳ Δέκμον προσγίγνεται Πολλίων Ἀσίνιος
ἄγων δύο τέλη. καὶ Πλάγκῳ μὲν Ἀσίνιος ἔπραξε
διαλλαγάς, καὶ ὁ Πλάγκος σὺν τρισὶ τέλεσι μεθ-
ίστατο ἐς τὸν Ἀντώνιον, ὥστε ἤδη βαρυτάτης δυνά-
400 μεως ἦρχεν ὁ Ἀντώνιος· Δέκμῳ δὲ ἦν τέλη δέκα, ὧν
τέσσαρα μὲν τὰ ἐμπειροπολεμώτατα ὑπὸ λιμοῦ διέφθαρτο καὶ ἐνόσει ἔτι, τὰ νεοστράτευτα δὲ ἦν ἕξ,
ἀταλαίπωρα ἔτι καὶ πόνων ἄπειρα. ἀπογνοὺς οὖν μάχεσθαι, φεύγειν ἔκρινε πρὸς Βροῦτον ἐς Μακεδονίαν.
401 ἔφευγε δ' οὐκ ἐπὶ τάδε τῶν Ἄλπεων, ἀλλ' ἐς Ῥάβενναν ἢ Ἀκυληίαν. ἐπεὶ δὲ Καῖσαρ ὥδευε ταύτῃ, ἄλλην
μακροτέραν ὁδὸν καὶ δύσπορον ἐπενόει, τόν τε Ῥῆνον
περᾶσαι καὶ τὰ ἀγριώτερα τῶν βαρβάρων ὑπερελ-
402 θεῖν· ὅθεν αὐτὸν ὑπό τε τῆς ἀπορίας καὶ τοῦ καμάτου
πρῶτοι μὲν οἱ νεοστράτευτοι καταλιπόντες ἐς Καίσαρα ἐχώρουν, ἐπὶ δὲ ἐκείνοις καὶ τὰ ἀρχαιότερα τέσσαρα ἐς Ἀντώνιον καὶ ὁ ἄλλος ὅμιλος ἤδη χωρὶς τῶν
403 σωματοφυλάκων ἱππέων Κελτῶν. ὁ δὲ καὶ τούτων τοῖς

duress. So the decrees hostile to Antony and Lepidus, and the soldiers under their command, were repealed, and new conciliatory ones sent to them. Octavian expressed 398 his delight in a letter to them, and promised to come and help Antony against Decimus Brutus, if he needed it. They instantly replied to him in a friendly spirit and complimented him. Antony wrote that he would himself punish both Decimus on Caesar's account and Plancus on his own, and would join forces with Octavian.

97. Such was the extent of their correspondence with 399 each other. While pursuing Decimus, Antony was joined by Asinius Pollio with two legions. Asinius also made an arrangement with Plancus, who came over to Antony's side with three legions, so that Antony now commanded a very powerful force. Decimus had ten legions, of which the 400 four most battle-hardened had been devastated by famine and were still unwell, while the other six were new levies, not yet used to hard work and with no experience of hardship. So, despairing of battle, he decided to flee to Marcus Brutus in Macedonia. He did not withdraw along this side 401 of the Alps, but made for Ravenna or Aquileia. However, since Octavian was on the road in this region, he devised another longer and more difficult route—to cross the Rhine and make his way over the wilder barbarian areas. At this, the new recruits, bewildered and exhausted, were 402 the first to desert him and join Octavian; they were followed by the four older legions joining Antony, along with all the rest of his force, apart from his bodyguard of Celtic cavalry. Even the men of this group who wished to do so, 403

ἐθέλουσιν ἐπιτρέψας ἐς τὰ οἰκεῖα σφῶν ἀφίστασθαι
καὶ διαδοὺς ἐκ τοῦ παρόντος ἔτι χρυσίου, μετὰ τριακοσίων τῶν παραμεινάντων μόνων ἐπὶ τὸν Ῥῆνον
ἐφέρετο. δυσπόρου δ᾽ ὄντος αὐτοῦ περᾶν σὺν ὀλίγοις,
404   ἀπελείφθη καὶ ὑπὸ τῶνδε πλὴν δέκα μόνων. ἤλλαξε
δὲ τὴν ἐσθῆτα ἐς τὸ Κελτικόν, ἐξεπιστάμενος ἅμα
καὶ τὴν φωνήν, καὶ διεδίδρασκε σὺν ἐκείνοις οἷά τις
Κελτός, οὐ τὴν μακροτέραν ἔτι περιιών, ἀλλὰ ἐπὶ
Ἀκυληίας, λήσεσθαι νομίζων διὰ τὴν ὀλιγότητα.

405   98. Ἁλοὺς δὲ ὑπὸ λῃστῶν καὶ δεθείς, ἤρετο μὲν ὅτου
Κελτῶν δυνάστου τὸ ἔθνος εἴη, μαθὼν δ᾽ ὅτι Καμίλου,
πολλὰ πεποιηκὼς εὖ τὸν Κάμιλον, ἄγειν αὐτὸν αὐτοῖς
406   ἐς τὸν Κάμιλον ἐκέλευεν. ὁ δὲ ἀχθέντα ἰδὼν ἐφιλο-
φρονεῖτο μὲν ἐς τὸ φανερὸν καὶ τοῖς δήσασιν ἐπεμέμ-
φετο ὑπ᾽ ἀγνοίας ἐνυβρίσασιν ἀνδρὶ τοσῷδε, κρύφα
407   δ᾽ ἐπέστελλεν Ἀντωνίῳ. καὶ ὁ Ἀντώνιός τι παθὼν ἐπὶ
τῇ μεταβολῇ οὐχ ὑπέστη τὸν ἄνδρα ἰδεῖν, ἀλλ᾽ ἐκέλευσε τῷ Καμίλῳ κτείναντα τὴν κεφαλὴν ἐς αὐτὸν
ἐκπέμψαι· καὶ τὴν κεφαλὴν ἰδὼν ἐκέλευσε τοῖς παρ-
408   οῦσι θάψαι. τοῦτο Δέκμῳ τέλος ἦν, ἱππάρχῃ τε Καίσαρος γενομένῳ καὶ ἄρξαντι τῆς παλαιᾶς Κελτικῆς
ὑπ᾽ ἐκείνῳ καὶ ἐς τὸ μέλλον ἔτος ὑπατεύειν ὑπ᾽ αὐτοῦ
κεχειροτονημένῳ καὶ τῆς ἑτέρας Κελτικῆς ἄρχειν. καὶ
δεύτερος τῶν σφαγέων οὗτος ἐπὶ Τρεβωνίῳ δίκην ἐδί-
409   δου μετ᾽ ἐνιαυτόν που καὶ ἥμισυ τῆς ἀναιρέσεως. τῷ
δ᾽ αὐτῷ χρόνῳ καὶ Μινούκιος Βάσιλος, σφαγεὺς καὶ
ὅδε Καίσαρος, ὑπὸ τῶν θεραπόντων ἀνῃρέθη, εὐνου-
χίζων τινὰς αὐτῶν ἐπὶ τιμωρίᾳ.

Decimus allowed to return to their own homes and, after distributing the gold he still had with him, he made his way to the Rhine with the three hundred followers who stayed. As it was difficult to cross the river with such small numbers, even these abandoned him, all but ten. He 404 changed into Celtic clothing, and, as he was already fluent in the language, he made his escape with these ten men, passing himself off as a Gaul, no longer going around by the longer route, but toward Aquileia, thinking that because his group was so small, he would escape notice.

98. But he was captured by bandits and tied up. When 405 he asked to which Celtic prince their people answered, and learned that it was Camilus, a man for whom he had done many favors, he told them to bring him to Camilus. Camilus, on seeing Decimus led to him, greeted him 406 warmly in public, and rebuked those who had tied him up for insulting so great a man through ignorance; but secretly he sent word to Antony. Antony reacted emotionally 407 to this change in fortune, and could not bear to see Decimus, but ordered Camilus to kill him and send him his head. When he saw the head he told his attendants to bury it. Such was the end of Decimus, who had been com- 408 mander of Caesar's cavalry and his governor of the older province of Gaul. He had been designated by him for the consulship of the coming year and for the governorship of the other province of Gaul. He was the second of the murderers, after Trebonius, to meet punishment, about a year and a half after the assassination. At the same time 409 Minucius Basilus, who was also one of Caesar's murderers, was killed by his slaves, because he castrated some of them as a form of punishment.

XVI

ΕΜΦΥΛΙΩΝ ΤΕΤΑΡΤΗ

1. Δύο μὲν δὴ Γαΐου Καίσαρος φονεῖς οὕτω δίκην, ἐν
ταῖς σφετέραις αὐτῶν στρατηγίαις ἐκπολεμηθέντες,
ἐδεδώκεσαν, Τρεβώνιος ἐν τῇ Ἀσίᾳ καὶ Δέκμος ἐν τῇ
Κελτικῇ· ὅπως δὲ ἔδοσαν Κάσσιός τε καὶ Βροῦτος, οἳ
καὶ μάλιστα τῆς ἐπιβουλῆς ἐπὶ τῷ Καίσαρι ἦρξαν,
καὶ γῆς ἐκράτουν ἀπὸ Συρίας ἐπὶ Μακεδονίαν ἁπάσης, καὶ στρατὸς ἦν αὐτοῖς πολύς, ἱππικός τε καὶ
ναυτικὸς καὶ ὁπλιτῶν ὑπὲρ εἴκοσι τέλη, καὶ νῆες ὁμοῦ
καὶ χρήματα, ἡ τετάρτη τῶν ἐμφυλίων ἥδε ὑποδείκνυ-
2 σιν. ἅμα δὲ τούτοις ἐγίγνοντο αἱ ἐν Ῥώμῃ τῶν ἐπὶ
θανάτῳ προγραφέντων ἔρευναί τε καὶ ἀνευρέσεις[1] καὶ
παθήματα πάμπαν ἐπαχθῆ, οἷα οὔτε ἐπὶ Ἑλλήνων ἐν
στάσεσιν ἢ πολέμοις οὔτ' ἐπὶ Ῥωμαίων αὐτῶν ἐμνη-
μονεύετο γενέσθαι, πλὴν ἐπὶ μόνου Σύλλα τοῦ πρώτου
3 τοὺς ἐχθροὺς ἐς θάνατον προγράψαντος. Μάριος μὲν
γὰρ ἐζήτει καὶ ἐκόλαζεν, οὓς εὕροι· Σύλλας δὲ ὑπὸ
μισθοῖς τε μεγάλοις καὶ κολάσεσι τῶν ἐπικρυψάντων

---

[1] αἱ εὑρέσεις codd.; ἀνευρέσεις Gaillard-Goukowsky; ἀναι-
ρέσεις Schweig.

BOOK XVI

CIVIL WARS, BOOK IV

1. So it was that two of Gaius Caesar's murderers had received their punishment, having been defeated in their own provinces, Trebonius in Asia, Decimus in Gaul. As for Brutus and Cassius, who were the main instigators of the conspiracy against Caesar, they controlled the whole region from Syria to Macedonia, commanding extensive military forces, made up of cavalry and sailors and more than twenty legions of infantry, together with ships and money. This fourth book of the *Civil Wars* sets out how they paid the price for what they did. It was during this 2 period that those in Rome proscribed to die were hunted down, found, and subjected to altogether terrible sufferings, the likes of which could not be recalled as happening either among the Greeks in their civil conflicts or wars, or among the Romans themselves, the sole exception being in the time of Sulla, who was the first to publish lists of the personal enemies he had condemned to death. For 3 Marius tracked down and punished those he could find, but Sulla proclaimed large rewards for anyone at all to kill the proscribed, and corresponding penalties for those who

ὁμοίαις τὸν ἐντυχόντα κτείνειν προέγραφεν. καὶ τὰ
μὲν ἀμφὶ Μάριόν τε καὶ Σύλλαν ἐν τοῖς περὶ ἐκείνων
προείρηται, τὰ δὲ ἑξῆς οὕτως ἐγένετο.

4   2. Καῖσαρ μὲν καὶ Ἀντώνιος ἐς φιλίαν ἀπ᾽ ἔχθρας
συνῄεσαν ἀμφὶ Μουτίνην πόλιν, ἐς νησῖδα τοῦ Λα-
βινίου ποταμοῦ βραχεῖάν τε καὶ ὑπτίαν, ἔχων ἑκάτερος ὁπλιτῶν τέλη πέντε· καὶ τάδε ἀλλήλοις ἀντικαθ-
ιστάντες ἐχώρουν σὺν τριακοσίοις ἑκάτερος ἐπὶ τὰς
5   τοῦ ποταμοῦ γεφύρας. Λέπιδος δ᾽ αὐτὸς προελθὼν
διηρεύνα τὴν νῆσον καὶ τῇ χλαμύδι κατέσειεν ἥκειν
ἑκάτερον. οἱ δὲ ἐπὶ τῶν γεφυρῶν τοὺς τριακοσίους
μετὰ τῶν φίλων ἀπολιπόντες ἐς τὸ μέσον ᾔεσαν ἐν
περιόπτῳ, καὶ συνήδρευον οἱ τρεῖς, Καίσαρος ἐν
6   μέσῳ διὰ τὴν ἀρχὴν προκαθίσαντος. δύο δὲ ἡμέραις
ἕωθεν ἐς ἑσπέραν συνιόντες τάδε ἔκριναν· ἀποθέσθαι
μὲν τὴν ὕπατον ἀρχὴν Καίσαρα καὶ Οὐεντίδιον αὐτὴν
ἐς τὸ λοιπὸν τοῦ ἔτους μεταλαβεῖν, καινὴν δὲ ἀρχὴν
ἐς διόρθωσιν τῶν ἐμφυλίων νομοθετηθῆναι Λεπίδῳ τε
καὶ Ἀντωνίῳ καὶ Καίσαρι, ἣν ἐπὶ πενταετὲς αὐτοὺς
ἄρχειν, ἴσον ἰσχύουσαν ὑπάτοις· ὧδε γὰρ ἔδοξεν ἀντὶ
δικτατόρων ὀνομάσαι, διὰ τὸ δόγμα ἴσως τὸ Ἀντωνίου
7   κωλῦον ἔτι γίγνεσθαι δικτάτορα. τοὺς δὲ ἀποφῆναι
μὲν αὐτίκα τῆς πόλεως ἄρχοντας ἐς τὰ ἐτήσια ἐπὶ τὴν
πενταετίαν, τὰς δὲ ἡγεμονίας τῶν ἐθνῶν νειμαμένους,
ἔχειν Ἀντώνιον μὲν τὴν Κελτικὴν ἅπασαν ἄνευ τῆς

---

[1] In Book 1 of the *Civil Wars*.
[2] Appian is unclear about the title. They were officially called

hid them. But events in the time of Marius and Sulla have already been narrated in the sections about them.[1] The subsequent proscriptions happened as follows.

2. Octavian and Antony met to replace their hostility 4 with friendship on a small, flat island in the river Lavinius, near the town of Mutina. Each had five legions of soldiers. These they arrayed opposite each other while they themselves advanced to the bridge over the river taking three hundred men each. Lepidus went ahead to make a per- 5 sonal inspection of the island, and signaled with his cloak to each of them to come. Leaving the escort of three hundred at the bridge with their staff, they advanced to the middle of the island in full view, and there the three sat together in council, Octavian presiding in the center because of the office he held. After meeting for two days 6 from dawn to dusk, they came to the following decisions: Octavian would resign the consulship and Ventidius take his place for the rest of the year; a new magistracy intended to bring an end to the civil wars would be created by law for Lepidus, Antony, and Octavian; they would hold this office for five years, with power equal to that of the consuls, deciding to use this terminology instead of the word "dictators," perhaps because of Antony's decree banning the future appointment of a dictator;[2] they would 7 immediately appoint the annual magistrates of the city for the next five years, dividing up the provincial governorships so that Antony would have the whole of Gaul, except

triumviri rei publicae constituendae (three-man commission for ordering the state), and Appian presumably means that they were called triumvirs rather than dictators. For Antony's abolition of the dictatorship, see *BCiv.* 3.25.94.

συναφοῦς τοῖς Πυρηναίοις ὄρεσιν, ἣν παλαιὰν ἐκάλουν Κελτικήν· ταύτης δὲ Λέπιδον ἄρχειν καὶ Ἰβηρίας ἐπὶ ταύτῃ· Καίσαρι δὲ εἶναι Λιβύην καὶ Σαρδὼ
καὶ Σικελίαν καὶ εἴ τις ἄλλη νῆσος ἐνταῦθα.

8   3. Ὧδε μὲν τὴν Ῥωμαίων ἡγεμονίαν οἱ τρεῖς ἐνεί-
ματο ⟨τὸ⟩² ἐφ' ἑαυτοῖς, τὰ πέραν ἄρα τοῦ Ἰονίου μόνα
ὑπερθέμενοι διὰ Βροῦτον καὶ Κάσσιον κρατοῦντας ἔτι
αὐτῶν, Κασσίῳ δὲ καὶ Βρούτῳ πολεμεῖν ⟨ἔκριναν⟩³

9 Ἀντώνιόν τε καὶ Καίσαρα· Λέπιδον γὰρ ὑπατεύειν ἐς
τὸ μέλλον κἂν⁴ τῇ πόλει διὰ τὰς ἐν αὐτῇ χρείας ὑπο-
μένειν, ἡγεμονεύοντα τῆς Ἰβηρίας δι' ἑτέρων· τοῦ δὲ
Λεπίδου στρατοῦ τρία μὲν αὐτὸν Λέπιδον ἔχειν ἐς τὰ
ἐπὶ Ῥώμης, ἑπτὰ δὲ τέλη νείμασθαι Καίσαρα καὶ
Ἀντώνιον, τρία μὲν Καίσαρα, τέσσαρα δὲ Ἀντώνιον,
ὡς ἂν ἐς τὸν πόλεμον αὐτῶν ἑκάτερος εἴκοσιν ἄγοι.

10 ἐπελπίσαι δὲ ἤδη τὸν στρατὸν ἐς τὰ νικητήρια τοῦ
πολέμου, ἄλλαις τε δωρεαῖς καὶ ἐς κατοικίαν δόσεσι
τῶν Ἰταλικῶν πόλεων ὀκτωκαίδεκα, αἳ καὶ περιουσίᾳ
καὶ ἐδάφεσι καὶ οἴκοις εἰς κάλλος διαφέρουσι ἔμελλον αὐτοῖς ἐδάφεσι καὶ οἴκοις αὐτῷ διανεμήσεσθαι,
ὥσπερ αὐτοῖς ἀντὶ τῆς πολεμίας δορίληπτοι γενόμε-

11 ναι. καὶ ἦσαν αἱ πόλεις ἄλλαι τε καὶ αἱ περιφανέστα-
ται μάλιστα αὐτῶν Καπύη καὶ Ῥήγιον καὶ Οὐενουσία
καὶ Βενεβεντὸς καὶ Νουκερία καὶ Ἀρίμινον καὶ Ἱπ-

12 πώνιον. οὕτω μὲν τὰ κάλλιστα τῆς Ἰταλίας τῷ
στρατῷ διέγραφον, ἔδοξε δὲ σφίσι καὶ τοὺς ἰδίους

the part bordering the Pyrenees Mountains, which was called Old Gaul; Lepidus would have this, along with Iberia; while Octavian was to have Africa, Sardinia, and Sicily, and any other islands in this region.

3. This was how the triumvirs divided up that part of 8 the Roman empire that was under their control. They postponed, of course, only the assignment of the parts beyond the Ionian gulf, since these were still under the control of Brutus and Cassius, and decided that Antony and Octavian were to wage war against Cassius and Brutus. For Lepidus was to be consul the following year and 9 remain in the city because of what needed to be done there, governing Iberia through legates. Of Lepidus' army, he himself would retain three legions to control Rome, while Octavian and Antony would divide the other seven between them, three to Octavian and four to Antony, so that each of them would take twenty legions to the war. They were now to encourage the army to win the spoils of 10 victory by granting them, along with other gifts, eighteen Italian towns to settle—towns which stood out for their wealth and the beauty of their estates and houses, and which were to be divided among them, land, buildings, and all, as a substitute for spear-won plunder from enemy territory. The most famous of these towns were Capua and 11 Rhegium and Venusia and Beneventum and Nuceria and Ariminum and Hipponium. In this way they earmarked 12 the finest parts of Italy for the soldiers. They also decided to destroy their personal enemies beforehand, so that they

---

² τὸ add. Gaillard-Goukowsky   ³ ἔκριναν add. Gaillard-Goukowsky   ⁴ καὶ codd.; κἂν Gaillard-Goukowsky

ἐχθροὺς προανελεῖν, ἵνα μὴ ἐνοχλοῖεν αὐτοῖς τάδε
καθισταμένοις καὶ πολεμοῦσι πόλεμον ἔκδημον.
13 ταῦτα μὲν ἔδοξε, καὶ ταῦτα συνεγράψαντο· καὶ αὐτῶν
ὁ Καῖσαρ ὡς ὕπατος ἀνέγνω τοῖς στρατοῖς τὰ λοιπὰ
χωρὶς τῶν ἀποθανουμένων. οἱ δ' ἀκούσαντες ἐπαιώνι-
σάν τε καὶ ἠσπάσαντο ἀλλήλους ἐπὶ διαλλαγῇ.

14   4. Γιγνομένων δὲ τούτων τέρατα καὶ σημεῖα ἐν
Ῥώμῃ πολλὰ καὶ φοβερὰ ἦν. κύνες τε γὰρ ὠρύοντο
ὁμαλῶς οἷα λύκοι, σύμβολον ἀηδές, καὶ λύκοι τὴν
ἀγορὰν διέθεον, οὐκ ἐπιχωριάζον ἐν πόλει ζῷον, βοῦς
τε φωνὴν ἀφῆκεν ἀνθρώπου, καὶ βρέφος ἀρτίτοκον
ἐφθέγξατο, καὶ τῶν ξοάνων τὰ μὲν ἵδρου, τὰ δὲ καὶ
αἷμα ἵδρου, ἀνδρῶν τε μεγάλαι βοαὶ καὶ κτύπος
ὅπλων καὶ δρόμος ἵππων οὐχ ὁρωμένων ἠκούετο.
ἀμφί τε τὸν ἥλιον ἀηδῆ σημεῖα πολλά, καὶ λιθώδεις
ἐγίγνοντο ὑετοί, καὶ κεραυνοὶ συνεχεῖς ἐς ἱερὰ καὶ
15 ἀγάλματα ἔπιπτον. ἐφ' οἷς ἡ μὲν βουλὴ θύτας καὶ
μάντεις συνῆγεν ἀπὸ Τυρρηνίας· καὶ ὁ πρεσβύτατος
αὐτῶν, τὰς πάλαι βασιλείας ἐπανήξειν εἰπών, καὶ
δουλεύσειν ἅπαντας χωρὶς ἑαυτοῦ μόνου, τὸ στόμα
κατέσχε καὶ τὸ πνεῦμα, ἕως ἀπέθανεν.

16   5. Οἱ δὲ τρεῖς ἄνδρες ἐφ' ἑαυτῶν γενόμενοι τοὺς
ἀποθανουμένους συνέγραφον, τούς τε δυνατοὺς ὑφορώμενοι καὶ τοὺς ἰδίους ἐχθροὺς καταλέγοντες, οἰ-
κείους τε σφῶν αὐτῶν ἢ φίλους ἐς τὴν ἀναίρεσιν
17 ἀντιδιδόντες ἀλλήλοις καὶ τότε καὶ ὕστερον. προσ-
κατελέγοντο γὰρ δὴ καὶ ἕτεροι μεθ' ἑτέρους, οἱ μὲν
ἀπ' ἔχθρας, οἱ δὲ μόνου προσκρούματος ἢ φιλίας

would not cause trouble while they were making these arrangements and at the same time waging war abroad. Such were the decisions they reached and consigned to 13 writing. As he was consul, Octavian read everything out to the soldiers, except the list of those who were to die, and the soldiers applauded what they heard and embraced each other to mark their reconciliation.

4. While all this was happening, there were many 14 frightening prodigies and portents at Rome. Dogs howled just like wolves—a sinister omen—and wolves, an animal not usually encountered in the city, ran through the Forum. An ox spoke in a human voice. A newborn infant spoke. Statues sweated; some even sweated blood. Men speaking in loud voices and the clash of weapons and the sound of galloping horses were heard, but nothing was seen. There were many grim signs around the sun, there were showers of stones, and lightning continuously struck the temples and statues. In response to these things, the 15 senate sent for diviners and soothsayers from Etruria. The oldest of them, having said that the monarchies of olden times would return, and that they would all be slaves except only himself, closed his mouth and held his breath until he died.

5. The triumvirs met in private to compose the list of 16 those who were to die. They put on the list not only the powerful men they distrusted, but also their personal enemies, and they traded with each other their own family and friends for execution, both at the time and later. For 17 they did, in fact, make continuous additions to the list, in some cases out of personal hostility, in others merely be-

ἐχθρῶν ἢ φίλων ἔχθρα, ἢ πλούτου διαφέροντος.
18 ἐδέοντο γὰρ ἐς τὸν πόλεμον χρημάτων πολλῶν,
Βρούτῳ μὲν καὶ Κασσίῳ τῶν ἀπὸ τῆς Ἀσίας φόρων
δεδομένων τε καὶ προσοδευομένων ἔτι καὶ βασιλέων
καὶ σατραπῶν συμφερόντων, αὐτοὶ δ' ἐπὶ τῆς Εὐρώ-
πης καὶ μάλιστα τῆς Ἰταλίας πολέμοις τε καὶ εἰσφο-
19 ραῖς τετρυμένης ἀποροῦντες· δι' ἃ καὶ τοῖς δημόταις
καὶ ταῖς γυναιξὶ λήγοντες ἐπέγραψαν εἰσφορὰς βαρυτάτας, καὶ τέλη πράσεων καὶ μισθώσεων ἐπενόη-
σαν. ἤδη δέ τις καὶ διὰ κάλλος ἐπαύλεως καὶ οἰκίας
20 προεγράφη. καὶ ἐγένοντο πάντες οἱ θανάτου τε καὶ
δημεύσεως κατεγνωσμένοι ἀπὸ μὲν τῆς βουλῆς ἀμφὶ
τοὺς τριακοσίους, ἀπὸ δὲ τῶν καλουμένων ἱππέων ἐς
δισχιλίους. καὶ ἦσαν ἐν αὐτοῖς ἀδελφοί τε καὶ θεῖοι
τῶν προγραφόντων, καὶ τῶν ὑπ' αὐτοῖς ἡγεμόνων,
ὅσοι τι τοῖς ἄρχουσιν ἢ τοῖς ἡγεμόσι προσεκεκρούκε-
σαν.

21   6. Τὸ μὲν δὴ πλῆθος αὐτῶν ἀπὸ τῆς συνόδου διελ-
θόντες ἐς Ῥώμην προγράψειν ἔμελλον, δυώδεκα δὲ
ἄνδρας, ἤ, ὡς ἕτεροι λέγουσιν, ἑπτακαίδεκα, τοὺς
μάλιστα δυνατούς, ἐν οἷς ἦν καὶ Κικέρων, ἔδοξε προ-
22 ανελεῖν ἐπιπέμψαντας ἄφνω. καὶ τῶνδε μὲν τέσσαρες
αὐτίκα ἀνῃρέθησαν ἐν ἑστιάσεσί τε καὶ ὑπαντήσεσι·
ζητουμένων δὲ τῶν ἄλλων καὶ ἐρευνωμένων νεῶν τε
καὶ οἰκιῶν, ἄφνω θόρυβος ἀνὰ τὴν νύκτα πᾶσαν ἦν
καὶ βοαὶ καὶ διαδρομαὶ μετ' οἰμωγῆς ὡς ἐν ἁλισκο-
23 μένῃ πόλει. τῷ γὰρ ἐγνῶσθαι μὲν ἀνδροληψία γίγνεσθαι, μὴ προγεγράφθαι δὲ μηδένα τῶν προκατεγνω-

cause of a grudge, or because the victims were friends of their enemies or enemies of their friends, or outstandingly wealthy. For the triumvirs needed a great deal of money 18 to carry on the war, since the taxes from Asia had been paid to Brutus and Cassius, and were still accruing to them, and kings and satraps were also contributing, while they themselves were short of money in a Europe, particularly Italy, worn out by wars and imposts. This was why 19 the triumvirs levied very heavy contributions on private citizens, and finally even on women, and devised new taxes on sales and rents. By now, too, some were proscribed because they had handsome villas or city residences. The 20 number of senators who were sentenced to death and confiscation of property was about three hundred, and of those known as equestrians about two thousand. These figures included brothers and uncles of the men writing the lists, and of the officers serving under them, anyone who had crossed the leaders or their subordinates.

6. After their meeting, they intended to go to Rome to 21 post the list of the majority of the proscribed, but they decided to send orders without warning for the prior execution of twelve, or, as some say, seventeen, of the most powerful men, among whom was Cicero. Four of these 22 were killed immediately, either at dinner or wherever they happened to be. But when the others were being hunted, and searches made in temples and houses, there was a sudden panic, which lasted all night: people were shouting and running about wailing as if in a city that was being taken by storm. For when it was known that men were 23 being arrested, but no names had been published of those

σμένων, πᾶς τις αὐτὸς ἡγεῖτο ζητεῖσθαι πρὸς τῶν
24 περιθεόντων. οὕτω δὲ ἀπογινώσκοντες αὐτῶν, οἱ μὲν
τὰ ἴδια, οἱ δὲ τὰ κοινὰ ἐμπρήσειν ἔμελλον, δρᾶσαί τι
δεινὸν ἀλόγως αἱρούμενοι πρὶν παθεῖν· καὶ τάχα ἂν
ἔδρασαν, εἰ μὴ Πέδιος αὐτοὺς ὁ ὕπατος μετὰ κηρύκων
περιθέων ἐπήλπιζε περιμείναντας ἐς ἕω τὰ ἀκριβέ-
25 στατα μαθεῖν. ἅμα δὲ ἕω παρὰ γνώμην τῶν τριῶν
ἀνδρῶν προύγραφεν ὁ Πέδιος τοὺς ἑπτακαίδεκα ὡς
μόνους τε αἰτίους δόξαντας εἶναι τῶν ἐμφυλίων κακῶν
καὶ μόνους κατεγνωσμένους, πίστεις τε τοῖς ἄλλοις
δημοσίας ἐποιεῖτο, ἀγνοῶν τὰ ἐγνωσμένα.

26 7. Καὶ Πέδιος μὲν ἐκ καμάτου τῆς νυκτὸς ἐτελεύτη-
σεν, ἐσῄεσαν δ' οἱ τρεῖς τρισὶν ἡμέραις, ἀνὰ μέρος
ἕκαστος αὐτῶν, ὁ Καῖσάρ τε καὶ ὁ Ἀντώνιος καὶ ὁ
Λέπιδος, σὺν ταῖς στρατηγίσι τάξεσι καὶ ὁπλιτῶν
27 ἕκαστος ἑνὶ τέλει. ὡς δὲ ἐσῆλθον, αὐτίκα μὲν ἡ πόλις
ἦν πλήρης ὅπλων τε καὶ σημείων διατεταγμένων ἐς
τὰ ἐπίκαιρα, αὐτίκα δὲ ἐν μέσῳ τούτων ἤγετο ἐκκλη-
σία, καὶ δήμαρχος Πούπλιος Τίτιος ἐνομοθέτει καινὴν ἀρχὴν ἐπὶ καταστάσει τῶν παρόντων ἐς πενταετὲς εἶναι τριῶν ἀνδρῶν, Λεπίδου τε καὶ Ἀντωνίου καὶ
Καίσαρος, ἴσον ἰσχύουσαν ὑπάτοις, ἣν ἄν τις Ἑλλήνων ἁρμοστὰς ὀνομάσειεν, ὃ καὶ Λακεδαιμόνιοι
τοῖς ἀρτύνειν[5] καθισταμένοις τὰ ὑπήκοα ἐτίθεντο
ὄνομα, οὔτε διαστήματος ἐς δοκιμασίαν οὔτε κυρίας

5 ἀρτύνειν Keil; ἄρτι BJ

already condemned, each person thought that he was the one being sought by those running around. Thus despair- 24 ing of their situation, some were about to set fire to their own houses, others to the public buildings, choosing without thinking to do some terrible deed before suffering one themselves. And they would perhaps have done so, if the consul Pedius had not hurried around with heralds and encouraged them to wait until daylight and get more accurate information. When morning came Pedius, contrary 25 to the intention of the triumvirs, published the list of the seventeen men deemed solely responsible for the civil disasters and the only ones condemned. To the rest he gave public guarantees, ignorant, as he was, of the decisions that had been made.

7. Pedius died from the stress of the night. The trium- 26 virs entered the city separately on three successive days, Octavian and Antony and Lepidus, each with his praetorian cohort and one legion of soldiers. With their entry, 27 the city was immediately filled with weapons and military standards positioned in strategic places. A public meeting was convened at once in the middle of all this, at which a tribune, Publius Titius, proposed a law to establish a new magistracy for settling the current situation: it was to last for five years and consist of three men, Lepidus and Antony and Octavian, with power equal to that of the consuls. A Greek would call them "harmosts," which is the name the Spartans gave to those they appointed to administer their subject territories.[3] No period was ordained for scru-

---

[3] Spartan harmosts were military governors sent into subject or conquered places, but apart from the extensive power they wielded, they are not a close analogy for the triumvirs.

ἐς τὴν χειροτονίαν ἡμέρας προτεθείσης· ἀλλ' αὐτίκα
28 ἐκυροῦτο ὁ νόμος. καὶ νυκτὸς ἄλλων, ἐπὶ τοῖς ἑπτακαίδεκα, τριάκοντα καὶ ἑκατὸν ἀνδρῶν προγραφαὶ
κατὰ πολλὰ τῆς πόλεως προυτίθετο καὶ μετ' ὀλίγον
ἄλλων πεντήκοντα καὶ ἑκατόν. καί τις προσετίθετο
τοῖς πίναξιν αἰεὶ τῶν προσκαταγινωσκομένων ἢ τῶν
προανῃρημένων ὑπ' ἀγνοίας, ἐς δόξαν τοῦ δικαίως
29 ἀνῃρῆσθαι. διετέτακτό τε πάντων τὰς κεφαλὰς ἐς
τοὺς τρεῖς ἄνδρας ἐπὶ ῥητῷ κέρδει φέρεσθαι· καὶ ἦν
τὸ κέρδος ἐλευθέρῳ μὲν ἀργύριον, θεράποντι δὲ ἐλευ-
30 θερία τε καὶ ἀργύριον. παρέχειν δὲ ἐς ἔρευναν πάντας
τὰ ἴδια. καὶ τὸν ὑποδεξάμενον ἢ κρύψαντα ἢ τὴν ἔρευναν οὐ παρασχόντα τοῖς ἴσοις ἐνέχεσθαι. μηνύειν δὲ
ἕκαστα τούτων τὸν ἐθέλοντα ἐπὶ τοῖς ἴσοις κέρδεσι.
31   8. Καὶ εἶχεν οὕτως ἡ προγραφή· "Μᾶρκος Λέπιδος,
Μᾶρκος Ἀντώνιος, Ὀκτάουιος Καῖσαρ, οἱ χειροτονη-
θέντες ἁρμόσαι καὶ διορθῶσαι τὰ κοινά, οὕτως λέγου-
32 σιν· εἰ μὴ δι' ἀπιστίαν οἱ πονηροὶ δεόμενοι μὲν ἦσαν
ἐλεεινοί, τυχόντες δὲ ἐγίγνοντο τῶν εὐεργετῶν ἐχθροί,
εἶτα ἐπίβουλοι, οὔτ' ἂν Γάιον Καίσαρα ἀνῃρήκεσαν,
οὓς ἐκεῖνος δορὶ λαβὼν ἔσωσεν ἐλέῳ καὶ φίλους θέμενος ἐπὶ ἀρχὰς καὶ τιμὰς καὶ δωρεὰς προήγαγεν
ἀθρόως, οὔτ' ἂν ἡμεῖς τοῖς ἐνυβρίσασι καὶ πολεμίους
ἀναγράψασιν ἡμᾶς ὧδε ἀθρόως ἠναγκαζόμεθα χρῆ-
33 σθαι. νῦν δέ, ἐξ ὧν ἐπιβεβουλεύμεθα καὶ ἐξ ὧν Γάιος
Καῖσαρ ἔπαθεν, ἀτιθάσευτον ὁρῶντες τὴν κακίαν ὑπὸ

tiny of the measure, nor a day fixed for voting on it, but it was passed into law straight away. That night, proscription 28 lists of a further one hundred and thirty men, in addition to the seventeen, were posted up in many parts of the city, and a little later one hundred and fifty more. Additions were constantly being made to the public notice boards of people newly condemned or previously killed by mistake, to create the impression that they had been lawfully executed. It had been decreed that the heads of all the victims 29 be brought to the triumvirs for a fixed reward, which for a free person was payable in money, and for a slave in both money and freedom. Everyone was required to make their 30 property accessible for search. Those who took in fugitives, or hid them, or refused to allow a search to be made, were liable to the same penalties as the proscribed; and anyone willing to lay information about each of these issues would get equal rewards.

8. The edict of proscription ran as follows: "Marcus 31 Lepidus, Marc Antony, and Octavius Caesar, the men elected to govern and set the republic to rights, make this declaration. If it were not for the fact that the wicked men 32 who in their treachery begged for mercy and were given it, and when they were given it became enemies of their benefactors and then conspirators against them, they would not have assassinated Gaius Caesar, men whom Caesar himself had made prisoners, but spared out of pity and admitted to his friendship, advancing their cause collectively with offices, honors, and gifts; nor would we have been compelled to treat collectively in this way those who abused us and declared us public enemies. Now that we 33 can see, however, from their plots against us and from Caesar's fate that their depravity cannot be tamed by kind-

199

φιλανθρωπίας, προλαβεῖν τοὺς ἐχθροὺς ἢ παθεῖν
34 αἱρούμεθα. μὴ δή τις τὸ ἔργον ἄδικον ἢ ὠμὸν ἢ ἄμε-
τρον ἡγείσθω, ἔς τε Γάιον καὶ ἐς ἡμᾶς οἷα πεπόνθα-
μεν ὁρῶν. Γάιον μὲν δὴ καὶ αὐτοκράτορα ὄντα καὶ
ἄρχοντα ἱερῶν, καὶ τὰ φοβερώτατα Ῥωμαίοις καθ-
ελόντα τε ἔθνη καὶ κτησάμενον, καὶ πρῶτον ἀνδρῶν
ὑπὲρ τοὺς Ἡρακλείους ὅρους ἀπλώτου θαλάσσης
ἀποπειράσαντα, καὶ Ῥωμαίοις γῆν ἄγνωστον εὑ-
ρόντα, ἐν μέσῳ τῷ ἱερῷ λεγομένῳ βουλευτηρίῳ, ὑπὸ
ὄψεσι θεῶν, κατέκανον εἴκοσι καὶ τρισὶ σφαγαῖς ἐν-
υβρίσαντες, οἱ πολέμῳ ληφθέντες ὑπ’ ἐκείνου καὶ
περισωθέντες κληρονόμοι τέ τινες αὐτοῦ τῆς οὐσίας
35 ἐγγραφέντες εἶναι· οἱ λοιποὶ δὲ ἐπὶ τῷ μύσει τῷδε
τοὺς ἐναγεῖς ἀντὶ κολάσεων ἐπὶ ἀρχὰς καὶ ἡγεμονίας
ἐξέπεμψαν, αἷς ἐκεῖνοι χρώμενοι τά τε κοινὰ τῶν χρημάτων ἥρπασαν, καὶ στρατὸν ἐξ αὐτῶν ἀγείρουσι
καθ’ ἡμῶν καὶ ἕτερον αἰτοῦσι παρὰ βαρβάρων ἀεὶ
τῆς ἀρχῆς πολεμίων, τάς τε ὑπὸ Ῥωμαίοις πόλεις τὰς
μὲν οὐ πείθοντες ἐνέπρησαν ἢ κατέσκαψαν ἢ κατήρει-
ψαν, τὰς δὲ καταπλήξαντες ἐπάγουσι τῇ πατρίδι καθ’
ἡμῶν.

36   9. "Ημεῖς δὲ αὐτῶν τοὺς μὲν ἤδη τετιμωρήμεθα,
τοὺς δὲ λοιποὺς θεοῦ συνεπιλαμβάνοντος αὐτίκα
37 δίκην διδόντας ὄψεσθε. τῶν δὲ μεγίστων ἡμῖν ἠνυ-
σμένων καὶ ὑπὸ χερσὶν ὄντων, Ἰβηρίας τε καὶ Κελτικῆς καὶ τῶνδε τῶν οἴκοι, ἕν ἐστι λοιπὸν ἔτι ἔργον,
στρατεύειν ἐπὶ τοὺς πέραν θαλάσσης αὐτόχειρας
38 Γαΐου. μέλλουσι δὴ πόλεμον ὑπὲρ ὑμῶν ἔκδημον

ness, we choose to anticipate our enemies rather than suffer at their hands. In view of what we have suffered in 34 relation to Caesar and to ourselves, let no one consider our action unjust, cruel, or excessive. Caesar was Imperator and Pontifex Maximus, he had defeated and annexed the peoples most feared by Romans, he was the first man to venture on an unsailed sea beyond the Pillars of Heracles and discover a land unknown to Rome, and yet men captured by him in war but spared, some even named in his will as heirs of his estate, attacked and murdered him by stabbing him twenty-three times in the middle of the supposedly sacrosanct senate house, in the sight of gods. The 35 rest of the senate, instead of punishing these accursed men for their vile crime, sent them off to commands and governorships, which they have used to seize public monies with which they are collecting an army against us, and are asking for another from barbarians ever hostile to our empire. Of the cities subject to Rome, some whom they could not win over they have burned, or ravaged, or destroyed; others they lead by terror against their country and against us.

9. "We have taken vengeance on some of these men 36 already, and with divine assistance you will soon see the rest punished. Although we have finished the main part of 37 this work in that we have Iberia, Gaul, and affairs here at home under control, one task still remains, and that is to campaign against Caesar's assassins overseas. As we are 38 about to fight a war on your behalf away from home, it

ἀγωνιεῖσθαι οὐκ ἀσφαλὲς οὔτε ἐς τὰ ἡμέτερα οὔτε ἐς
τὰ ὑμέτερα εἶναι δοκεῖ τοὺς ἄλλους ἐχθροὺς ὀπίσω
καταλιπεῖν, ἐπιβησομένους ταῖς ἀπουσίαις ἡμῶν καὶ
τὰ συμβαίνοντα τοῦ πολέμου καιροφυλακήσοντας,
οὐδ᾽ αὖ βραδύνειν διὰ τούσδε ἐν ἐπείξει τοσῇδε μᾶλλον ἢ ἐκποδὼν αὐτοὺς ἀθρόως ποιήσασθαι, ἄρξαντάς
γε τοῦ καθ᾽ ἡμῶν πολέμου, ὅτε πολεμίους ἡμᾶς τε καὶ
τοὺς ὑφ᾽ ἡμῖν στρατοὺς ἐψηφίζοντο εἶναι.

39   10. "Κἀκεῖνοι μὲν τοσάσδε πολιτῶν μυριάδας ἡμῖν
συναπώλλυον, οὔτε θεῶν νέμεσιν οὔτε φθόνον ἀνθρώπων ὑφορώμενοι· ἡμεῖς δὲ πλήθει μὲν οὐδενὶ χαλεπα-
νοῦμεν οὐδὲ τοὺς ἐχθροὺς ἐπιλεξόμεθα πάντας, ὅσοι
διηνέχθησαν ἡμῖν ἢ ἐπεβούλευσαν, οὐδὲ ἐκ πλούτου
πάντως ἢ περιουσίας ἢ ἀξιώσεως οὐδ᾽ ὅσους ἕτερος
πρὸ ἡμῶν αὐτοκράτωρ ἔκτεινε, τὴν πόλιν κἀκεῖνος ἐν
ἐμφυλίοις καθιστάμενος, ὃν Εὐτυχῆ προσείπατε δι᾽
εὐπραξίαν, καίπερ ἀνάγκης οὔσης τρισὶ πλέονας
40   ἐχθροὺς ἢ ἑνὶ εἶναι. ἀλλὰ μόνους δὴ τοὺς φαυλο-
τάτους τε καὶ πάντων αἰτιωτάτους ἀμυνούμεθα. καὶ
τόδε δι᾽ ὑμᾶς οὐχ ἧσσον ἡμῶν· ἀνάγκη μὲν γὰρ ἡμῶν
διαφερομένων ὑμᾶς πάντας ἐν μέσῳ δεινὰ πάσχειν,
ἀνάγκη δέ τι καὶ τῷ στρατῷ γενέσθαι παραμύθιον
ὑβρισμένῳ τε καὶ παρωξυμμένῳ καὶ πολεμίῳ πρὸς
41   τῶν κοινῶν ἐχθρῶν ἀναγεγραμμένῳ. δυνηθέντες δ᾽ ἄν,
οὓς ἔγνωμεν, ἐξ ἐφόδου συλλαβεῖν, αἱρούμεθα προγράψαι μᾶλλον ἢ ἀγνοοῦντας ἔτι συλλαβεῖν· καὶ τόδε
δι᾽ ὑμᾶς, ἵνα μὴ ἐπὶ τοῖς ὁπλίταις ἢ διωργισμένοις

seems unsafe, both for us and for you, to leave our other enemies behind to exploit our absence and keep watch on the contingencies of war for advantageous opportunities; nor on the other hand do we think we should delay in such an emergency because of these men, but rather we should remove them entirely out of our path, seeing that they began the war against us when they voted to declare us and the armies under our command public enemies.

10. "They for their part set about destroying so many 39 tens of thousands of citizens along with us, overlooking the vengeance of the gods and the hatred of men. We, however, will not vent our anger on any large group of people, nor will we identify as our enemies everyone who merely disagreed with us or plotted against us, or anyone just because of their wealth, resources, or rank; nor will we pick out as many as another Imperator before us killed, when he, too, was reestablishing order in a time of civil war, and whom you named 'Fortunate' on account of his success, although it is necessarily the case that three men have more enemies than one.[4] We will take vengeance only 40 on the worst and most guilty of all. This we will do in your interest no less than in our own. For as long as we are in dispute, it is inevitable that you will all suffer badly, caught in the middle. Necessity also requires some consolation for the army, which has been insulted, provoked, and registered as an enemy of the state by our common adversaries. Although we had the power to arrest immediately 41 those we had decided on, we prefer to publish their names rather than seize them still unawares. This, too, we do in your interests, so that it will not be possible for enraged

---

[4] A reference to the dictator Lucius Cornelius Sulla.

πλεονάζειν ἐς τοὺς ἀνευθύνους, ἀλλὰ ἀπηριθμημένους
καὶ ὡρισμένους ἔχοντες ὀνομαστὶ τῶν ἄλλων κατὰ
πρόσταγμα ἀπέχωνται.

42   11. "Ἀγαθῇ τύχῃ τοίνυν τῶν ὑπογεγραμμένων τῷδε
τῷ διαγράμματι μηδεὶς δεχέσθω μηδένα μηδὲ κρυ-
πτέτω μηδὲ ἐκπεμπέτω ποι μηδὲ πειθέσθω χρήμασι.

43 ὃς δ᾽ ἂν ἢ σώσας ἢ ἐπικουρήσας ἢ συνειδὼς φανῇ,
τοῦτον ἡμεῖς, οὐδεμίαν ὑπολογισάμενοι πρόφασιν ἢ

44 συγγνώμην, ἐν τοῖς προγεγραμμένοις τιθέμεθα. ἀνα-
φερόντων δὲ τὰς κεφαλὰς οἱ κτείναντες ἐφ᾽ ἡμᾶς, ὁ
μὲν ἐλεύθερος ἐπὶ δισμυρίαις δραχμαῖς Ἀττικαῖς καὶ
πεντακισχιλίαις ὑπὲρ ἑκάστης, ὁ δὲ δοῦλος ἐπ᾽ ἐλευθερίᾳ τοῦ σώματος καὶ μυρίαις Ἀττικαῖς καὶ τῇ τοῦ
δεσπότου πολιτείᾳ. τὰ δ᾽ αὐτὰ καὶ τοῖς μηνύουσιν
ἔσται. καὶ τῶν λαμβανόντων οὐδεὶς ἐγγεγράψεται
τοῖς ὑπομνήμασιν ἡμῶν, ἵνα μὴ κατάδηλος ᾖ." ὧδε
μὲν εἶχεν ἡ προγραφὴ τῶν τριῶν ἀνδρῶν, ὅσον ἐς
Ἑλλάδα γλῶσσαν ἀπὸ Λατίνης μεταβαλεῖν.

45   12. Πρῶτος δ᾽ ἦν ἐν τοῖς προγράφουσι Λέπιδος, καὶ
πρῶτος ἐν τοῖς προγραφομένοις ὁ ἀδελφὸς ὁ Λεπίδου
Παῦλος, καὶ δεύτερος ἦν τῶν προγραφόντων Ἀντώνιος
καὶ δεύτερος τῶν προγραφομένων ὁ θεῖος ὁ Ἀντωνίου
Λεύκιος, οἵδε μέν, ὅτι πρῶτοι πολεμίους αὐτοὺς ἐψη-

46 φίσαντο. τρίτος δὲ καὶ τέταρτος ἦν τῶν ἐν ἑτέρῳ πί-
νακι προκειμένων ἐς τὸ μέλλον ὑπάτων Πλάγκου μὲν

soldiers to take excessive action against the innocent, and to make sure that, having a set number designated by name, they will keep their hands off everyone else in accordance with their orders.

11. "So, with Fortune looking kindly on this proclamation, let no one take in, hide, send off anywhere, or be persuaded by money to do so, any of those whose names are appended below. We will place on the list of the proscribed anyone shown to have saved, abetted, or connived with them, and will accept no excuse and give no pardon. If those who kill the proscribed bring us their heads, a free man will receive twenty five thousand Attic drachmas per head, a slave his freedom and ten thousand Attic drachmas and the same citizenship as his master. Informers will receive the same rewards. No one who receives such rewards will be listed in our records, so that their identity is not made public." Such was the text of the triumviral proscription, allowing for the fact that it is a translation from Latin into Greek.

12. The first man listed of those issuing the proscriptions was Lepidus, and the first man proscribed was his brother Paullus; the second proscriber was Antony and the second man proscribed was his uncle Lucius.[5] The reason for this is that these two men had been the first to have Lepidus and Antony voted public enemies. The third and fourth victims, mentioned on another list of consuls-designate for the following year, were Plotius, the brother

___

5 Lucius Aemilius Lepidus had been consul in 50; Lucius Julius Caesar, brother of Julia, the mother of Antony, who had supported Cicero against his nephew, was consul in 64.

ὁ ἀδελφὸς Πλώτιος, Ἀσινίου δὲ ὁ πενθερὸς Κοΐντιος. καὶ οὐ κατ᾽ ἀξίωσιν ἄρα μόνην οἴδε τῶν ἄλλων προύκειντο μᾶλλον ἢ ἐς θάμβος καὶ δυσελπιστίαν, 47 μηδένα ῥύσεσθαί τινα προσδοκᾶν. ἦν δὲ καὶ Θωράνιος ἐν τοῖς προγεγραμμένοις, λεγόμενος ὑπό τινων 48 ἐπιτροπεῦσαι Καίσαρος. ἅμα δὲ ταῖς προγραφαῖς αἵ τε πύλαι κατείχοντο καὶ ὅσαι ἄλλαι τῆς πόλεως ἔξοδοί τε καὶ λιμένες ἢ ἕλη καὶ τέλματα ἢ εἴ τι ἄλλο ἐς φυγὴν ὕποπτον ἦν ἢ ἐς λαθραίους καταφυγάς· τήν τε χώραν ἐπετέτραπτο τοῖς λοχαγοῖς ἐρευνᾶν περιθέουσι, καὶ ἐγίγνετο πάντα ὁμοῦ.

49 13. Εὐθὺς οὖν ἦν ἀνά τε τὴν χώραν καὶ ἀνὰ τὴν πόλιν, ὡς ἕκαστός πη συνελαμβάνετο, ἀνδρολήψια αἰφνίδια πολλὰ καὶ τρόποι τῶν φόνων ποικίλοι τῶν τε κεφαλῶν ἀποτομαὶ τοῦ μισθοῦ χάριν ἐς ἐπίδειξιν φυγαί τε ἀπρεπεῖς καὶ σχήματα ἄτοπα ἐκ τοῦ πρὶν 50 περιφανοῦς. κατέδυνον γὰρ οἱ μὲν ἐς φρέατα, οἱ δὲ ἐς τὰς ὑπονόμους τάφρους ἐπὶ τὰ ἀκάθαρτα, οἱ δὲ ἐς καπνώδεις ὑπωροφίας ἢ τῶν τεγῶν ταῖς κεραμίσι βυ- 51 ομέναις ὑπεκάθηντο μετὰ σιγῆς βαθυτάτης. ἐδεδοίκεσαν γὰρ οὐχ ἧσσον τῶν σφαγέων οἱ μὲν γυναῖκας ἢ παῖδας οὐκ εὐμενῶς σφίσιν ἔχοντας, οἱ δὲ ἐξελευθέρους τε καὶ θεράποντας, οἱ δὲ καὶ δανεισμάτων χρήστας ἢ χωρίων γείτονας ἐπιθυμίᾳ τῶν χωρίων.

---

6 Lucius Plotius Plancus, praetor in 43, was a brother of the prominent Antonian Lucius Munatius Plancus (consul 42). Gaius

of Plancus, and Quinctius, the father-in-law of Asinius.[6] It was not just because of their rank that these were placed at the head of the list, but rather to create astonishment and despair, in that no one could expect to protect another person. Even Thoranius, said by some to have been Octavian's guardian, was on the list of the proscribed.[7] At the same time as the publication of the lists, the gates and all other exits from the city were held under guard, along with the harbors, marshes, pools, and anywhere else suspected of offering escape or a secret refuge. The centurions were given the task of patrolling and searching the countryside. All these things were happening at the same time. 47 48

13. There resulted throughout both the countryside and the city a large number of sudden arrests, wherever an individual was caught, and various forms of execution, along with decapitations to provide evidence for the reward. People fled in unseemly ways, and exchanged formerly splendid clothing for strange disguises. Some climbed down into wells, others into the filth of underground sewers; others again went up into smoky attics or sat in complete silence under close-packed roof tiles. For some were no more afraid of the assassins than they were of ill-disposed wives and children; others feared their freedmen and slaves, others their creditors, or neighboring landholders who wanted their land. In fact, all the ill 49 50 51 52

Asinius Pollio (consul 40), whose *Histories* Appian is believed to have used as a source, was also a supporter of Antony. His father-in-law, Quinctius, is a little known figure.

[7] Appian has perhaps confused Gaius Turranius (praetor 44) with the better known Gaius Toranius, who became Octavian's guardian in 59.

52 ἐπανάστασις γὰρ δὴ πάντων, ὅσα τέως ὕπουλα ἦν,
ἀθρόα τότε ἐγίγνετο καὶ ἀθέμιστος μεταβολὴ βουλευτῶν ἀνδρῶν, ὑπάτων ἢ στρατηγῶν ἢ δημάρχων,
ἔτι τάσδε τὰς ἀρχὰς μετιόντων ἢ ἐν αὐταῖς γεγονότων, ἐς πόδας ἰδίου θεράποντος ῥιπτουμένων σὺν
ὀλοφύρσεσι καὶ σωτῆρα καὶ κύριον τὸν οἰκέτην τι-
θεμένων. οἴκτιστον δὲ ἦν, ὅτε καὶ ταῦτα ὑποστάντες
οὐκ ἐλεηθεῖεν.

53 14. Ἰδέα τε πᾶσα κακῶν ἦν, οὐχ ὡς ἐν στάσεσιν
ἢ πολέμου καταλήψεσιν· οὐ γάρ, ὡς ἐν ἐκείνοις, τὸν
μὲν ἀντιστασιώτην ἢ πολέμιον ἐδεδοίκεσαν, τοῖς δ᾽
οἰκείοις σφᾶς ἐπέτρεπον, ἀλλὰ καὶ τούσδε τῶν σφαγέων μᾶλλον ἐδεδοίκεσαν, οὐδὲν μὲν αὐτοὺς ὡς ἐν
πολέμῳ καὶ στάσει δεδιότας, σφίσι δὲ αὐτίκα γιγνο-
μένους ἐξ οἰκείων πολεμίους, ἢ δι᾽ ὕπουλον ἔχθραν ἢ
ὑπὸ τῶν ἐπικεκηρυγμένων σφίσι γερῶν ἢ διὰ τὸν ἐν

54 ταῖς οἰκίαις χρυσόν τε καὶ ἄργυρον. ἄπιστος γὰρ δὴ
διὰ ταῦτα ἀθρόως ἕκαστος ἐς τὸν οἰκεῖον ἐγίγνετο καὶ
τὸ σφέτερον κέρδος τοῦ πρὸς αὐτὸν ἐλέου προυτίθει·
ὁ δὲ πιστὸς ἢ εὔνους ἐδεδίει βοηθεῖν ἢ κρύπτειν ἢ

55 συνειδέναι δι᾽ ὁμοιότητα⁶ τῶν ἐπιτιμίων. ἔς τε τὸ ἔμ-
παλιν αὐτοῖς τοῦ πρώτου τῶν ἑπτακαίδεκα ἀνδρῶν
δέους περιέστη. τότε μὲν γὰρ οὐ προγραφέντος οὐ-
δενός, ἀλλά τινων ἄφνω συλλαμβανομένων πάντες
ἐδεδοίκεσαν ὅμοια καὶ συνήσπιζον ἀλλήλοις· ἐπὶ δὲ
ταῖς προγραφαῖς οἱ μὲν αὐτίκα πᾶσιν ἔκδοτοι γεγένη-

⁶ ὁμοιότητα codd. plurimi; ὠμότητα L

feeling that had up to this point festered under the surface now broke out all at once. An improper change occurred in men of senatorial rank, whether consuls, praetors, or tribunes, both those who were about to enter these offices, or who had already held them: they were now throwing themselves sobbing at the feet of their own slaves, calling their slaves saviors and masters. Most pitiable of all was the fact that having endured this, they obtained no mercy.

14. All types of iniquity were there, but not like those 53 encountered in civil unrest, or when towns are captured in time of war. For, unlike in those situations, when people were afraid of factional rivals or the enemy, but could entrust themselves to their own households, it was precisely the latter they feared more than the assassins. They were not afraid of them as they would be of men in war or civil discord, but because they had suddenly changed from being members of their households into enemies, either from some festering hatred, or under the influence of the advertised rewards, or because of the gold and silver in their houses. It was undoubtedly for these reasons that 54 everyone became disloyal to his own kinsman, prioritizing personal gain over pity for him. Those who remained faithful and well-disposed were afraid to help or hide or abet the victims in view of their liability to the same penalties.[8] The situation was totally different for them from 55 the terror faced by the first seventeen. At that point nobody had been proscribed, and after the unexpected arrest of some people, everyone feared the same would happen to them, and they stood by each other. But after the publication of the proscription lists, some people were im-

[8] Or possibly, "in view of the ferocity of the penalties."

ντο, οἱ δὲ ἐν ἀμερίμνῳ περὶ σφῶν καὶ ἐπὶ κέρδει γενόμενοι τοὺς ἄλλους ἐπὶ μισθῷ τοῖς σφαγεῦσιν ἐκυνη-
56 γέτουν. ὁ δὲ λοιπὸς ὅμιλος, οἱ μὲν τὰς οἰκίας τῶν
ἀναιρουμένων διήρπαζον, καὶ τὸ κέρδος αὐτοὺς ἀπὸ
τῆς συνέσεως τῶν παρόντων κακῶν ἐψυχαγώγει· οἱ δὲ
ἐμφρονέστεροί τε καὶ ἐπιεικεῖς ἐτεθήπεσαν ὑπὸ ἐκ-
πλήξεως, καὶ ἦν αὐτοῖς παραλογώτερον, ὅτε μάλιστα
ἐνθυμηθεῖεν, ὅτι τὰς μὲν ἄλλας πόλεις ἐλυμήναντο
στάσεις καὶ περιέσωσαν ὁμόνοιαι, τὴν δὲ καὶ αἱ στάσεις τῶν ἀρχόντων προαπώλεσαν καὶ ἡ ὁμόνοια τοιάδε ἐργάζεται.

57   15. Ἔθνησκον δὲ οἱ μὲν ἀμυνόμενοι τοὺς ἀναιροῦν-
τας, οἱ δ᾽ οὐκ ἀμυνόμενοι ὡς οὐχ ὑπὸ τῶνδε ἀδικού-
μενοι, εἰσὶ δ᾽ οἳ καὶ σφᾶς αὐτοὺς λιμῷ τε ἑκουσίῳ
δαπανῶντες καὶ βρόχοις χρώμενοι καὶ τὰ σώματα
καταποντοῦντες ἢ ῥιπτοῦντες ἀπὸ τῶν τεγῶν ἢ ἐς
πῦρ ἐναλλόμενοι ἢ τοῖς σφαγεῦσιν ὑπίσχοντες ἢ καὶ
μεταπεμπόμενοι βραδύνοντας, ἕτεροι δὲ κρυπτόμενοι
καὶ λιπαροῦντες ἀπρεπῶς ἢ διωθούμενοι τὸ κακὸν ἢ
ὠνούμενοι. οἱ δὲ καὶ παρὰ γνώμην τῶν τριῶν ἀνδρῶν,
58 ὑπ᾽ ἀγνοίας ἢ κατ᾽ ἐπιβουλήν, ἀπώλλυντο. καὶ δῆλος
ἦν ὁ μὴ προγραφεὶς νέκυς, ὅτε οἱ προσκέοιτο ἡ κε-
φαλή· τῶν γὰρ δὴ προγεγραμμένων ἐν ἀγορᾷ πρου-
τίθεντο παρὰ τοῖς βήμασιν, ἔνθα ἔδει κομίσαντας
59 ἀντιλαβεῖν τὰ ἀγαθά. ἴση δ᾽ ἦν ἑτέρων σπουδὴ καὶ
ἀρετή, γυναικῶν τε καὶ παιδίων καὶ ἀδελφῶν καὶ
θεραπόντων, περισῳζόντων τε καὶ συμμηχανωμένων
πολλὰ καὶ συναποθνῃσκόντων, ὅτε μὴ τύχοιεν ὧν

mediately betrayed to everybody, and others, now freed of
worry about their own safety, began to join the assassins
in hunting down the rest for money. Of the general popu-   56
lation, some looted the houses of those who had been
killed, and their private gains distracted them from recognizing their present calamities. Reasonable and more intelligent people, on the other hand, were astonished and
dismayed: it seemed all the more paradoxical to them
when they took into particular consideration the fact that,
in the case of other cities, civil discord ruined them and
harmony saved them, while at Rome the disagreements
among their magistrates first ruined them, and then harmony gets to have such dreadful effects.

15. Some died defending themselves against their kill-   57
ers. Others made no resistance, as it was not their assail-
ants who were doing them wrong. There were some who
willingly starved themselves to death, or resorted to the
noose, or threw themselves into the sea, or jumped off
rooftops or into fires, or gave themselves up to their executioners, or even sent for them when they delayed. Others
hid themselves and made abject entreaties, in an attempt
to avert their miserable fate, or buy their way out of it.
Some were killed by mistake, or by design, contrary to the
intention of the triumvirs. It was clear that a corpse was   58
not that of a proscribed person if the head was still attached to it: for the heads of the proscribed were displayed
beside the rostra in the Forum, where it was necessary to
bring them in order to get the rewards. An equal degree   59
of devotion and courage was shown by others—wives and
children and brothers and slaves—who rescued the proscribed, devised schemes with them and died with them

60 ἐπενόουν· οἱ δὲ καὶ ἐπανήρουν σφᾶς ἀνῃρημένοις. τῶν
δὲ ἐκφυγόντων οἱ μὲν ὑπὸ ναυαγίων ἀπώλλυντο, ἐς
πάντα σφίσι τῆς τύχης ἐπιβαρούσης, οἱ δὲ ἐπανήχθησαν ἐκ παραλόγων ἐπί τε ἀρχὰς τῆς πόλεως καὶ
στρατηγίας πολέμων καὶ θριάμβους. οὕτως ὁ καιρὸς
ἦν ἐκεῖνος ἐπίδειξις παραδοξολογίας.

61   16. Καὶ τάδε ἐγίγνετο οὐκ ἐν ἰδιώτιδι πόλει οὐδὲ ἐν
ἀσθενεῖ καὶ σμικρῷ βασιλείῳ, ἀλλὰ τὴν δυνατωτάτην
καὶ τοσούτων ἐθνῶν καὶ γῆς καὶ θαλάσσης ἡγεμο-
νίδα διέσειεν ὁ θεός, ἐκ πολλοῦ ἄρα ἐς τὴν νῦν καθ-
62 ιστάμενος εὐταξίαν. ἐγένετο μὲν οὖν τοιάδε ἕτερα ἐν
αὐτῇ κατά τε Σύλλαν καὶ ἔτι πρὸ ἐκείνου Γάιον
Μάριον, ὧν ὁμοίως τὰ γνωριμώτατα τῶν κακῶν ἐν
τοῖς περὶ ἐκείνων ἀνελεξάμην, καὶ προσῆν ἐκείνοις
ἀταφία· ταῦτα δὲ ἀξιώσει τε τῶν τριῶν ἀνδρῶν καὶ
τοῦ ἑνὸς αὐτῶν μάλιστα ἀρετῇ καὶ τύχῃ, τὴν ἀρχὴν
συστησαμένου τε ἐς ἕδραν ἀσφαλῆ καὶ γένος καὶ
ὄνομα τὸ νῦν ἄρχον ἀφ' ἑαυτοῦ καταλιπόντος, ἐπι-
63 φανέστερα. ὧν τὰ λαμπρὰ καὶ τὰ χείρω γενόμενα ἐν
μνήμῃ τε μᾶλλον ὄντα, ὅτι καὶ τελευταῖα γέγονεν,
ἐπελεύσομαι νῦν, οὐ πάντα (οὐ γὰρ ἀξιαφήγητον
ἀναίρεσις ἁπλῆ καὶ φυγὴ ἢ τῶν τριῶν ἀνδρῶν τισι
συγγνόντων ὕστερον ἐπάνοδος ἢ ἐπανελθόντων ἀφα-
νὴς καταβίωσις), ἀλλ' ὅσα παραλογώτατα ὄντα μάλιστα ἂν ἐκπλήξειε καὶ πιστεύειν ποιήσειε τοῖς προ-
64 λεγομένοις. πολλὰ δέ ἐστι, καὶ πολλοὶ Ῥωμαίων ἐν
πολλαῖς βίβλοις αὐτὰ συνέγραψαν ἐφ' ἑαυτῶν· ὀλίγα

when their plans did not work out. Some even killed themselves over the bodies of the dead. Of those who escaped,   60
some died in shipwrecks, fate weighing heavily on them
without respite, while others were restored unexpectedly
to magistracies at Rome, to military commands, and tri-
umphs. Such was the display of extraordinary events that
this period put on.

16. These things took place in no ordinary city, nor in   61
a weak and small kingdom, but the deity shook to its foundations the most powerful of cities, mistress of so many
peoples and of land and sea, with the longstanding intention, no doubt, of establishing her present well ordered
condition. To be sure, other similar events, with the addi-   62
tion of the refusal to allow burial of the dead, had taken
place in the time of Sulla and even before him, in the time
of Gaius Marius, the most notable of which calamities I
have likewise narrated in the books concerning those men.
The present situation, however, is made more noteworthy
by the rank of the triumvirs and especially by the character
and good fortune of one of them, who established the
government on a firm foundation, and left behind him his
family and name still holding power to this day. I will now   63
describe the most brilliant and the worst of these events,
which have remained particularly memorable because
they were the last. I will not be dealing with everything—
for it is not worth recording mere killing, or exile, or the
later return to Rome of some pardoned by the triumvirs,
or their unexceptional life after returning—but only the
most extraordinary things which would cause particular
astonishment and give credibility to what I have said before. The subject is large, and many Romans have written   64
about it for themselves in many books. Because it is a long

APPIAN

δὲ ἐγὼ καθ' ἑκάστην ἰδέαν, ἐς πίστιν ἑκάστης καὶ ἐς
εὐδαιμόνισμα τῶν νῦν παρόντων, ἐπὶ κεφαλαίου διὰ
τὸ μῆκος ἀναγράψω.

65   17. Ἤρξατο μὲν δὴ τὸ κακὸν ἐκ συντυχίας ἀπὸ τῶν
ἐν ἀρχαῖς ἔτι ὄντων, καὶ πρῶτος ἀνῃρέθη δημαρχῶν
Σάλουιος. ἱερὰ δέ ἐστιν ἡ ἀρχὴ καὶ ἄσυλος ἐκ τῶν
νόμων καὶ τὰ μέγιστα ἴσχυεν, ὡς καὶ τῶν ὑπάτων
66 τινὰς ἐς τὰς φυλακὰς ἐμβαλεῖν. καὶ ἦν ὅδε ὁ δήμαρχος ὁ τὸν Ἀντώνιον ἐν μὲν ἀρχῇ κεκωλυκὼς εἶναι
πολέμιον, ὕστερον δὲ συμπεπραχὼς ἐς πάντα Κικέρωνι. πυθόμενος δὲ τῶν τριῶν ἀνδρῶν τῆς τε συμ-
φρονήσεως καὶ τῆς ἐς τὴν πόλιν ἐπείξεως τοὺς οἰ-
κείους εἱστία ὡς οὐ πολλάκις αὐτοῖς ἔτι συνεσόμενος·
67 ἐσδραμόντων δὲ ἐς τὸ συμπόσιον τῶν ὁπλιτῶν οἱ μὲν
ἐξανίσταντο σὺν θορύβῳ καὶ δέει, ὁ δὲ τῶν ὁπλιτῶν
λοχαγὸς ἐκέλευεν ἠρεμεῖν κατακλιθέντας, τὸν δὲ Σάλουιον, ὡς εἶχε, τῆς κόμης ἐπισπάσας ὑπὲρ τὴν τρά-
πεζαν, ἐς ὅσον ἔχρῃζε, τὴν κεφαλὴν ἀπέτεμε καὶ τοῖς
ἔνδον αὖθις ἐκέλευεν ἀτρεμεῖν, ὡς ἔχουσι, μὴ θορύβου γενομένου πάθοιεν ὅμοια. οἱ μὲν δὴ καὶ οἰχομένου τοῦ λοχαγοῦ τεθηπότες ἄναυδοι μέχρι βαθυτάτης
νυκτός, τῷ λοιπῷ τοῦ δημάρχου σώματι συγκατέ-
68 κειντο. δεύτερος δ' ἀνὴρ ἔθνησκε στρατηγὸς Μινούκιος, ἀρχαιρεσιάζων μὲν ἐν ἀγορᾷ· πυθόμενος δὲ

story, I will write up, in summary, just a few instances of each kind, to give credit to each, and to show the prosperity of our present situation.

17. The horror began, as it happened, with those still in office, and the first one killed was the tribune Salvius. The tribunate is, according to the laws, sacred and inviolable, and had very considerable powers, so that tribunes have even imprisoned consuls. Salvius was the tribune who at the beginning had vetoed the proposal to declare Antony a public enemy, but later he had cooperated with Cicero in everything. When he heard about the agreement of the triumvirs, and that they were hurrying to the city, he gave a banquet for his close friends, in the expectation that he would not have their company again on many occasions. When the soldiers burst in on the party, some of the guests sprang to their feet in fear and confusion, but the centurion in command ordered them to resume their places and remain quiet. Seizing Salvius by the hair, the centurion dragged him across the table as far as was necessary, and cut off his head on the spot, again ordering those in the room to stay still, just as they were, and threatening that if there was a fuss, they would suffer the same fate. And to be sure, even after the centurion left, they continued to recline in dazed silence with the remains of the tribune's body far into the night. The second person to die was the praetor Minucius, while he was presiding over an electoral meeting in the Forum.[9] When he heard that the soldiers were after him, he leaped up from his seat, and

65

66

67

68

---

[9] Perhaps the Minucius Rufus who commanded eighteen ships for Pompey at Orricum in 48 (App. *BCiv.* 2.54.225; Caes. *B Civ.* 3.7.1).

ἐπιέναι τοὺς ὁπλίτας ἀνεπήδησε καὶ περιθέων ἔτι καὶ
ἐννοούμενος, ὅποι διαλάθοι, τὴν ἐσθῆτα ἐνήλλασσεν
ἔς τι τῶν ἐργαστηρίων ἐσδραμών, τοὺς ὑπηρέτας καὶ
τὰ σημεῖα ἀποπέμψας. οἱ δὲ αἰδοῖ καὶ ἐλέῳ παραμέ-
νοντες εὐμαρέστερον ἄκοντες ἐποίησαν τοῖς σφαγεῦσι τὸν στρατηγὸν εὑρεῖν.

69   18. Ἀννᾶλιν ἕτερον στρατηγόν, τῷ παιδὶ μετιόντι
ταμιείαν συμπεριθέοντα καὶ τοὺς ψηφιουμένους παρακαλοῦντα, οἵ τε συνόντες φίλοι καὶ οἱ τὰ σημεῖα τῆς
ἀρχῆς φέροντες ἀπεδίδρασκον, πυθόμενοι προσγε-
70   γράφθαι τοῖς πίναξι τὸν Ἀννᾶλιν. ὁ δὲ ἐς πελάτην
ἑαυτοῦ τινα φυγών, ᾧ βραχὺ καὶ εὐτελὲς ἦν τέγος ἐν
προαστείῳ καὶ διὰ πάντα εὐκαταφρόνητον, ἐκρύπτετο
ἀσφαλῶς, μέχρι τοὺς σφαγέας ὁ υἱὸς αὐτοῦ, τὴν φυγὴν ἐς τὸν πελάτην ὑποτοπήσας, ὡδήγησεν ὑπὸ τὸ
τέγος, καὶ παρὰ τῶν τριῶν ἀνδρῶν τήν τε οὐσίαν
ἔλαβε τοῦ πατρὸς καὶ ἐς ἀγορανομίαν ᾑρέθη. ἀναλύ-
οντα δὲ αὐτὸν ἐκ μέθης στρατιῶταί τι προσκρούσα-
71   ντες ἔκτειναν, οἳ καὶ τὸν πατέρα ἀνῃρήκεσαν. Θου-
ράνιος δὲ οὐ στρατηγῶν μὲν ἔτι, ἀλλ' ἐστρατηγηκώς,
πατὴρ δὲ νεανίου τὰ μὲν ἄλλα ἀκολάστου, δυναστεύοντος δὲ παρ' Ἀντωνίῳ, τοὺς λοχαγοὺς ἠξίου τὴν
σφαγὴν ἐπισχεῖν οἱ πρὸς ὀλίγον, ἔστε αὐτὸν ὁ υἱὸς
αἰτήσαιτο παρ' Ἀντωνίου. οἱ δ' ἐπιγελάσαντες "Ἤτη-
72   σεν," εἶπον, "Ἀλλ' ἐπὶ θάτερα." καὶ συνεὶς ὁ πρε-

---

10 There was a Lucius Villius Annalis, who had probably been
praetor some time before 57 (Cic. *Fam.* 8.8.5–6). Appian may
have gotten the date wrong or be referring to someone else.

devising a way to escape them even as he was still tearing around, he ran into one of the workshops, changed his clothes, and dismissed his attendants along with his insignia of office. But the attendants stayed nearby out of respect and pity, thus unintentionally making it easier for the murderers to find the praetor.

18. Annalis, another praetor, while escorting his son, 69 who as a candidate for the quaestorship was canvassing the voters, was abandoned by the associates with him and by the men carrying his insignia of office when they learned that Annalis' name had been added to the proscription lists.[10] Annalis took refuge with one of his clients, who had 70 a small, mean, and thoroughly contemptible apartment in the suburbs, where he remained safely hidden until his son, suspecting that he had fled to this client, guided the murderers to the apartment. He was given his father's estate by the triumvirs and appointed to the aedileship. But when he was returning home after a drinking session, some soldiers, the very ones who had done away with his father, took offense at something and killed him. Thora- 71 nius, who was no longer praetor, but had held the office, and was the father of a generally intemperate young man who had nonetheless some influence with Antony, asked the centurions to postpone his execution for a short time, until his son could appeal to Antony for him.[11] They laughed at him, and said, "He already has, but against you, not for you." Understanding the situation, the elder Tur- 72

---

[11] As above (12.47), Appian is perhaps referring to Gaius Turranius (praetor 44) rather than Gaius Toranius, the former guardian of Octavian.

σβύτης ἕτερον αὐτίκα βραχύτατον ᾔτει διάστημα,
μέχρις οὗ τὴν θυγατέρα ἴδοι· ἰδὼν δὲ ἐκέλευε μὴ
μετασχεῖν τῶν πατρῴων, μὴ κἀκείνην ὁ ἀδελφὸς
αἰτήσαιτο παρὰ Ἀντωνίου. συνέβη δὲ καὶ τῷδε τὴν
οὐσίαν ἐς αἰσχρὰ δαπανῆσαι καὶ κλοπῆς ἁλόντι φυγεῖν ἐκ καταδίκης.

73   19. Κικέρων δέ, ὃς μετὰ Γάιον Καίσαρα ἴσχυσεν,
ὅση γένοιτο ἂν δημαγωγοῦ μοναρχία, κατέγνωστο
μὲν ἅμα τῷ παιδὶ καὶ τῷ ἀδελφῷ καὶ τῷ παιδὶ τοῦ
ἀδελφοῦ καὶ πᾶσιν οἰκείοις τε καὶ στασιώταις καὶ
φίλοις· φυγὼν δὲ ἐπὶ σκάφους οὐκ ἔφερε τὴν ἀηδίαν
τοῦ κλύδωνος, ἀλλὰ εἰς ἴδιον χωρίον, ὃ καθ᾽ ἱστορίαν
τοῦδε τοῦ πάθους εἶδον, ἀμφὶ Καιήτην πόλιν τῆς Ἰτα-
74 λίας, καταχθεὶς ἠρέμει. πλησιαζόντων δὲ τῶν ἐρευνωμένων (τοῦτον γὰρ δὴ φιλοτιμότατα πάντων Ἀντώνιός
τε ἐζήτει καὶ Ἀντωνίῳ πάντες ὑπούργουν[7]) ἐς τὸ δω-
μάτιον αὐτοῦ κόρακες ἐσπτάντες ἔκλαζον, ἐπεγείρον-
τες ἀπὸ τοῦ ὕπνου, καὶ τὸ ἱμάτιον ἀπέσυρον ἀπὸ τοῦ
σώματος, ἕως οἱ θεράποντες, σημηνάμενοι τὸ γιγνόμενον εἶναι σύμβολον ἔκ του θεῶν, ἐς φορεῖον ἐσθέ-
μενοι τὸν Κικέρωνα αὖθις ἐπὶ τὴν θάλασσαν ἦγον
75 διὰ λόχμης βαθείας λανθάνοντες. πολλῶν δὲ ἀνὰ
μέρη διαθεόντων τε καὶ πυνθανομένων, εἴ που Κικέρων ὁραθείη, οἱ μὲν ἄλλοι ἐπ᾽ εὐνοίᾳ καὶ ἐλέῳ πλεῖν
αὐτὸν ἐξαναχθέντα ἔλεγον ἤδη, σκυτοτόμος δὲ πελά-
της Κλωδίου, πικροτάτου τῷ Κικέρωνι ἐχθροῦ γεγονότος, Λαίνᾳ τῷ λοχαγῷ σὺν ὀλίγοις ὄντι τὴν ἀτρα-
76 πὸν ἔδειξεν. ὁ δὲ ἐπέδραμέ τε καὶ θεράποντας ἰδὼν

ranius asked for another very short delay until he could
see his daughter, and when he did, he told her not to claim
her share of the paternal inheritance in case her brother
asked Antony for her death too. As it turned out, this
young man also squandered his estate disgracefully, and
having been convicted of theft, went into exile to avoid his
fine.

19. Cicero, who was the dominant figure after the   73
death of Gaius Caesar, exercising as much sole control as
a popular leader could, was proscribed, along with his son
and his brother and his brother's son and all his household
and his partisans and associates. Having escaped in a small
boat, he could not endure the nausea caused by the swell,
and landed near the Italian town of Caieta at a country
place of his own, which I saw when I was researching this
incident; here he lay low. When those looking for him   74
came near (and it was him most of all that Antony was
tracking down with such determination, and everyone assisted Antony in this), some crows flew into his bedroom
cawing and waking him from sleep, and pulling his bedclothes off his body, until his attendants interpreted this
as a sign from one of the gods, put him in a litter, and again
carried him toward the sea, escaping notice by going
through a dense thicket. There were many ranging through   75
the area in groups asking if Cicero had been seen anywhere. All the others, moved by goodwill and pity, said
that he had already put to sea and was under way; but a
cobbler, a client of Clodius, who had been Cicero's most
bitter enemy, pointed out the path to Laenas, the centurion, who had a few soldiers with him. He hurried after   76

---

7 ὑπούργουν Gaillard-Goukowsky; ὑπούργον P; om. codd.
rell.

πολὺ πλείους τῶν ἀμφ᾽ αὑτὸν ὁρμῶντας ἐς ἄμυναν,
στρατηγικῶς μάλα ἀνεβόησεν· "Ἐσελθέτωσαν ἐς τὸ
χωρίον οἱ περὶ οὐρὰν λοχαγοί."

77   20. Τότε γὰρ οἱ μὲν θεράποντες ὡς ἐλευσομένων
πλεόνων κατεπλάγησαν, ὁ δὲ Λαίνας, καὶ δίκην τινὰ
διὰ τοῦ Κικέρωνός ποτε κατωρθωκώς, ἐκ τοῦ φορείου
τὴν κεφαλὴν ἐπισπάσας ἀπέτεμνεν, ἐς τρὶς ἐπιπλήσ-
σων καὶ ἐκδιαπρίζων ὑπὸ ἀπειρίας· ἀπέτεμε δὲ καὶ
τὴν χεῖρα, ᾗ τοὺς κατὰ Ἀντωνίου λόγους οἷα τυράννου συγγράφων, ἐς μίμημα τῶν Δημοσθένους, Φιλιπ-
78   πικοὺς ἐπέγραφεν. ἔθεον δὲ οἱ μὲν ἐπὶ ἵππων, οἱ δὲ
ἐπὶ νεῶν, αὐτίκα τὸ εὐαγγέλιον Ἀντωνίῳ διαφέροντες·
καὶ ὁ Λαίνας ἐν ἀγορᾷ προκαθημένῳ τὴν κεφαλὴν καὶ
79   τὴν χεῖρα μακρόθεν ἀνέσειεν ἐπιδεικνύς. ὁ δὲ ἥσθη
μάλιστα καὶ τὸν λοχαγὸν ἐστεφάνωσε καὶ πλέοσι
τῶν ἄθλων ἐδωρήσατο πέντε καὶ εἴκοσι μυριάσιν Ἀττικῶν δραχμῶν ὡς μέγιστον δὴ τόνδε πάντων ἐχθρὸν
80   καὶ πολεμιώτατον οἱ γενόμενον ἀνελόντα. ἡ κεφαλὴ
δὲ τοῦ Κικέρωνος καὶ ἡ χεὶρ ἐν ἀγορᾷ τοῦ βήματος
ἀπεκρέμαντο ἐπὶ πλεῖστον, ἔνθα πρότερον ὁ Κικέρων
ἐδημηγόρει· καὶ πλείους ὀψόμενοι συνέθεον ἢ ἀκροώ-
81   μενοι. λέγεται δὲ καὶ ἐπὶ τῆς διαίτης ὁ Ἀντώνιος τὴν
κεφαλὴν τοῦ Κικέρωνος θέσθαι πρὸ τῆς τραπέζης,
82   μέχρι κόρον ἔσχε τῆς θέας τοῦ κακοῦ. ὧδε μὲν δὴ

---

12 In his four *Philippics*, delivered between 351 and 340, Demosthenes urged the Athenians to resist Philip II of Macedon.

him, but seeing that Cicero's attendants far outnumbered his own escort and were rushing to his defense, being a very experienced commander, he called out, "Those centurions in the rear, come forward to my position!"

20. At this the attendants were terrified, thinking that   77
more soldiers were coming, and Laenas, although he had once won a case in court through Cicero, pulled his head out of the litter and cut it off, striking it three times, and sawing it off because of his inexperience. He also cut off the hand with which Cicero had written the speeches against Antony accusing him of being a tyrant, to which he had given the title *Philippics*, in imitation of the speeches of Demosthenes.[12] There was a rush to bring the good   78
news to Antony immediately, some going by horse, others by ship. Antony was sitting in the Forum when Laenas pointed out Cicero's head and hand, while still a long way off, by waving them at him. Antony was particularly de-   79
lighted, and garlanded the centurion and gave him two hundred and fifty thousand Attic drachmas over and above the stated rewards, as this man he had killed had been his greatest personal and public enemy. The head and hand   80
of Cicero were suspended for a long time from the rostra in the Forum, where previously he used to make public speeches; and more people came to see this than had come to listen to him. It is said that even while eating his meals   81
Antony placed Cicero's head in front of the table, until he had his fill of such a dreadful sight. So it was, then, that   82

Cicero's fourteen speeches against Antony were delivered between September 44 and April 43 (with the exception of the second, which circulated in written form).

Κικέρων, ἐπί τε λόγοις ἀοίδιμος ἐς ἔτι νῦν ἀνήρ, καὶ
ὅτε ἦρχε τὴν ὕπατον ἀρχήν, ἐς τὰ μέγιστα τῇ πατρίδι
γεγονὼς χρήσιμος, ἀνήρητο καὶ ἀνηρημένος ἐνυβρί-
ζετο· ὁ δὲ παῖς ἐς τὴν Ἑλλάδα προαπέσταλτο ἐς
83 Βροῦτον. Κόιντος δέ, ὁ τοῦ Κικέρωνος ἀδελφός, ἅμα
τῷ παιδὶ καταληφθεὶς ἐδεῖτο τῶν σφαγέων πρὸ τοῦ
παιδὸς αὐτὸν ἀνελεῖν· τὰ δὲ ἐναντία καὶ τοῦ παιδὸς
ἱκετεύοντος, οἱ σφαγεῖς ἔφασαν ἀμφοτέροις διαιτή-
σειν καὶ διαλαβόντες ἕτερον ἕτεροι κατὰ σύνθημα
φονεῖς ἀνεῖλον ὁμοῦ.

84   21. Ἐγνάτιοι δέ, πατὴρ καὶ υἱός, συμφυέντες ἀλλήλοις διὰ μιᾶς πληγῆς ἀπέθανον· καὶ αὐτῶν αἱ κεφαλαὶ μὲν ἀπετέτμηντο, τὰ δὲ λοιπὰ σώματα ἔτι συν-
85 επέπλεκτο. Βάλβος τὸν υἱόν, ἵνα μὴ βαδίζοντες ὁμοῦ
φανεροὶ γένοιντο, προύπεμψεν ἐς φυγὴν ἐπὶ θάλασσαν καὶ μετ᾽ ὀλίγον εἵπετο ἐκ διαστήματος. ἐξαγ-
γείλαντος δέ τινος, εἴτε ἐξ ἐπιβουλῆς εἴθ᾽ ὑπ᾽ ἀγνοίας,
τὸν υἱὸν συνειλῆφθαι, ἐπανῆλθε καὶ τοὺς σφαγέας
μετεπέμψατο. συνέβη δὲ καὶ τὸν παῖδα ἀπολέσθαι
ναυαγίῳ· οὕτω ταῖς τότε συμφοραῖς καὶ τὸ δαιμόνιον
86 ἐπέκειτο. Ἀρρούντιος τὸν υἱόν, οὐχ ὑφιστάμενον φεύγειν χωρὶς αὐτοῦ, μόλις ἔπεισεν ὡς νέον περισῴζειν
ἑαυτόν. καὶ τόνδε μὲν ἡ μήτηρ ἐπὶ τὰς πύλας πρού-
πεμψε καὶ ὑπέστρεψεν, ἵνα ἀνηρημένον τὸν ἄνδρα

---

[13] As with many of the proscribed people and their families
mentioned by Appian in the following chapters, it is not known
who these Egnatii were.

Cicero was killed and abused after his death, a man famed
for his eloquence even today, and one who had rendered
the greatest service to his country when he held the office
of consul. His son had been sent beforehand to Brutus in
Greece. But Cicero's brother, Quintus, was captured, to- 83
gether with his son. As he asked the executioners to kill
him before his son, and his son begged for the opposite,
the executioners said that they would reconcile both re-
quests, and, dividing themselves into two groups, each
group of killers took one, and at an agreed signal, put them
to death at the same time.

21. The Egnatii, father and son, died with one blow 84
while in the arms of each other, and although their heads
had been cut off, the rest of their bodies remained inter-
twined.[13] Balbus sent his son on ahead to the sea to escape, 85
so that they would not stand out traveling together, and he
followed a short distance behind.[14] When somebody told
him, either to trick him or by mistake, that his son had
been captured, he went back and sent for the executioners. As it happened, his son did die, in a shipwreck. In this
way even the divinity added its weight to the disasters of
the time. Arruntius with difficulty persuaded his son, who 86
would not agree to flee without him, to save himself as he
was a young man. His mother accompanied him to the city
gates and returned home to bury her murdered husband.

[14] Valerius Maximus (5.7.3) calls this man Octavius Balbus,
and Plutarch (*Caes.* 67.5) mentions a Gaius Octavius joining the
conspiracy against Caesar after the assassination. So this is probably Gaius Octavius Balbus.

θάψειε· πυθομένη δὲ καὶ τὸν υἱὸν ὑπὸ τῆς θαλάσσης διεφθάρθαι λιμῷ διεχρήσατο ἑαυτήν.

87   22. Αἵδε μὲν δὴ παίδων ἀγαθῶν καὶ κακῶν ἔστων εἰκόνες· ἀδελφοὶ δὲ δύο ὁμοῦ προγραφέντες, οἷς ὄνομα ἦν Λιγάριοι, ἐκρύπτοντο ὑπὸ ἱπνῷ, μέχρι τῶν θεραπόντων αὐτοὺς ἀνευρόντων ὁ μὲν αὐτίκα ἀνηρέθη, ὁ δὲ ἐκφυγών, ἐπεὶ τὸν ἀδελφὸν ἔγνω διεφθαρμένον, ἔρριψεν αὑτὸν ἀπὸ τοῦ ποταμοῦ τῆς γεφύρας ἐς τὸ

88 ῥεῦμα. καὶ αὐτὸν ἁλιέων περισχόντων ὡς οὐκ ἐναλάμενον, ἀλλὰ πεπτωκότα, ἐς πολὺ μὲν ἐφιλονίκει καὶ ἑαυτὸν ἐς τὸ ῥεῦμα ἐώθει, ἡσσώμενος δὲ τῶν ἁλιέων περιεγίγνετο "Καὶ οὐκ ἐμέ," ἔφη, "Περισῴζετε, ἀλλ᾽

89 ἑαυτοὺς ἐμοὶ προγεγραμμένῳ συναπόλλυτε." οἱ δὲ καὶ ὣς αὐτὸν οἰκτείραντες περιέσῳζον, μέχρι τινὲς τῶν στρατιωτῶν, οἳ τὴν γέφυραν ἐτήρουν, ἰδόντες ἐπέδρα-

90 μόν τε καὶ τὴν κεφαλὴν ἀπέτεμον. ἑτέρων δὲ ἀδελφῶν ὁ μὲν αὐτὸν ἔρριψε κατὰ τοῦ ῥεύματος, καὶ θεράπων αὐτοῦ τὸ σῶμα ἀνεζήτει μέχρι πέμπτης ἡμέρας, εὑρὼν δὲ ἔτι γνωρίζεσθαι δυναμένου, τὴν κεφαλὴν διὰ

91 τὸ ἆθλον ἀπέκοψε· τὸν δὲ ἕτερον ἐν κοπρῶνι κρυπτόμενον ἕτερος ἐμήνυσε θεράπων, καὶ οἱ σφαγεῖς εἰσελθεῖν μὲν ἀπηξίωσαν, δόρασι δὲ περικεντοῦντες ἐξήγαγον καί, ὡς εἶχε, τὴν κεφαλὴν οὐδὲ ἀπονίψαντες

92 ἀπέκοψαν. ἕτερος δέ, τοῦ ἀδελφοῦ συλλαμβανομένου,

When she learned that her son too had died at sea she starved herself to death.

22. Let these serve as examples of sons good and bad. As for brothers, two, by the name of Ligarius, having been proscribed together, hid themselves in an oven until their slaves found them.[15] One of them was killed immediately, and although the other escaped, when he learned that his brother had been killed, he threw himself into the current from the bridge over the Tiber. Thinking that he had fallen rather then jumped in, some fishermen held on to him. He struggled with them for a long time, trying to push himself into the current, but was overpowered by the fishermen, and survived. "You are not saving me," he said, "but destroying yourselves by helping me, as I have been proscribed." Nevertheless they had pity on him and tried to keep him safe, until some soldiers who were guarding the bridge saw him, ran up and cut off his head. There were two other brothers, one of whom threw himself into the river. A slave of his searched for his body for five days, and when he found it, it was still possible to recognize, so he cut off the head to get the reward. The other brother hid in a dung heap, but another slave informed on him. The executioners refused to go onto the dung heap, but got him out by poking him with their spears, and cut his head off just as it was, without even washing it. Another man, when his brother was arrested, ran up, not knowing that

87

88

89

90

91

92

[15] Cicero successfully defended Quintus Ligarius, a partisan of Pompey, before Caesar in 46 (the speech survives), but Ligarius joined the conspiracy against Caesar (see *BCiv.* 2.113.474). He had two brothers, one of whom is probably the Ligarius mentioned below at 23.93.

προσδραμὼν ἀγνοίᾳ τοῦ καὶ αὐτὸς ἅμα ἐκείνῳ προγεγράφθαι, "Ἐμέ," ἔφη, "Κτείνατε πρὸ τούτου." καὶ ὁ
λοχαγὸς ἔχων τὸ ἀκριβὲς ἀνάγραπτον, "Εἰκότα ἀξι-
οῖς," ἔφη· "Σὺ γὰρ πρὸ τούτου γέγραψαι," καὶ εἰπὼν
κατὰ τὴν τάξιν ἔκτεινεν ἄμφω.

93   23. Ταῦτα μὲν δὴ καὶ ἀδελφῶν δείγματα· Λιγάριον
δὲ ἡ γυνὴ κρύπτουσα μίαν ἐς τὸ ἀπόρρητον ἐπηγά-
γετο θεράπαιναν, προδοθεῖσα δὲ ὑπ' αὐτῆς εἵπετο τῇ
κεφαλῇ τοῦ ἀνδρὸς φερομένη βοῶσα· "Ἐγὼ τοῦτον
ὑπεδεξάμην, τὰ δ' ὅμοια τοῖς ὑποδεξαμένοις ἐστὶν
94   ἐπιτίμια." καὶ οὐδενὸς αὐτὴν οὔτε ἀναιροῦντος οὔτε
μηνύοντος αὐτάγγελος ἐς τοὺς ἄρχοντας ἦλθε καθ'
ἑαυτῆς, κἀκείνων αὐτὴν διὰ τὴν φιλανδρίαν ὑπεριδόν-
95   των, ἑαυτὴν ἀπέκτεινε λιμῷ. καὶ τῆσδε μὲν ἐνθάδε
ἐπεμνήσθην, ὅτι τὸν ἄνδρα περισῴζουσα ἀπετύγχανέ
τε καὶ συνεξήγαγεν ἑαυτήν· ὅσαι δὲ ἐπέτυχον τῆς φι-
λανδρίας, ἐν τοῖς περισωθεῖσι τῶν ἀνδρῶν ἀναγράψω.
96   ἕτεραι δὲ ἀθεμίστως ἐπεβούλευσαν τοῖς ἀνδράσιν.
καὶ αὐτῶν ἐστιν, ἡ Σεπτιμίῳ μὲν ἐγεγάμητο, ὑπὸ δέ
τινος Ἀντωνίῳ φίλου διεφθείρετο· ἐπειγομένη δὲ ἐκ
μοιχείας ἐς γάμον ἐδεήθη διὰ τοῦ μοιχεύοντος αὐτὴν
Ἀντωνίου, καὶ ὁ Σεπτίμιος αὐτίκα τοῖς πίναξι προσ-
97   ετέθη. καὶ μαθὼν ἐς τῆς γυναικὸς ὑπ' ἀγνοίας τῶν
οἴκοι κακῶν ἔφευγεν. ἡ δὲ ὡς φιλοφρονουμένη τὰς
θύρας ἐπέκλεισε καὶ ἐτήρει τὸν ἄνδρα, ἕως οἱ σφαγεῖς

he too had been proscribed with him, and said, "Kill me before him." The centurion, having the written details to hand, replied, "That's a reasonable request, since your name is on the list before his."[16] And so saying, he killed both of them in the right order.

23. These, then, are examples concerning brothers. 93 Ligarius was hidden by his wife, who let one maidservant into the secret. Betrayed by her, she followed her husband's head as it was being taken away, shouting, "I took this man in; those who do so are liable to the same penalties as the proscribed." As nobody killed her or informed 94 against her, she came to the magistrates and laid an accusation against herself. But when they too ignored her, because of her love for her husband, she starved herself to death. I have mentioned this woman here, because she 95 failed to save her husband and did away with herself to be with him. The women whose love for their husband was successful, I will treat when I write about the husbands who were saved. Other women plotted in criminal fashion 96 against their husbands. Among these was a woman who had married Septimius, but who had been seduced by an associate of Antony.[17] Eager to move from adultery to marriage, she submitted a request to Antony through her lover, and Septimius was immediately added to the list of the proscribed. When he learned this, he fled to his wife's 97 house, since he was unaware of his domestic woes. Pretending to take care of him, she locked the doors and kept

---

[16] The Greek can mean "kill me instead of him," or, "kill me before him." The brother means the former, the centurion takes up the latter meaning.   [17] This is perhaps the Gaius Septimius who had been praetor in 57.

παρεγένοντο· καὶ τῆς αὐτῆς ἡμέρας οἱ μὲν ἐκεῖνον
ἀνῄρουν, ἡ δὲ ἔθνε γάμους.

98   24. Σάλασσος δὲ ἐκφυγών τε καὶ ἀπορούμενος ἧκε
μὲν ἐς πόλιν νυκτός, ὅτε μάλιστα ἔδοξεν ἀμβλύνε-
σθαι τὸ δεινόν, πεπραμένης δὲ τῆς οἰκίας μόνος αὐτὸν
ὁ θυρωρὸς τῇ οἰκίᾳ συμπεπραμένος ἐπέγνω καὶ ἐς τὸ
ἑαυτοῦ οἴκημα ὑπεδέχετο καὶ κρύψειν ἐπηγγέλλετο
99   καὶ θρέψειν, ἐξ ὧν ἐδύνατο. ὁ δὲ τὴν γυναῖκά οἱ καλέ-
σαι προσέταξεν ἐκ τῆς ἐκείνης οἰκίας. ἡ δ' ὑποκρι-
ναμένη μὲν ἐλθεῖν ἐπείγεσθαι, δεδιέναι δ' ὡς ἐν νυκτὶ
καὶ θεραπαίναις τὸ ὕποπτον, μεθ' ἡμέραν ἥξειν ἔφη.
καὶ γενομένης ἡμέρας ἡ μὲν τοὺς σφαγέας μετῄει, καὶ
ὁ θυρωρὸς αὐτὴν ὡς βραδύνουσαν ἐς τὴν οἰκίαν ἀπ-
100   έτρεχεν ἐπείξων· ὁ δὲ Σάλασσος, οἰχομένου τοῦ θυ-
ρωροῦ δείσας ὡς ἐς ἐνέδραν ἀπιόντος, ἐς τὸ τέγος
ἀναδραμὼν ἐκαραδόκει τὸ γιγνόμενον, ἰδὼν δὲ οὐ τὸν
θυρωρόν, ἀλλὰ τὴν γυναῖκα τοῖς σφαγεῦσιν ἡγουμέ-
101   νην ἔρριψεν ἑαυτὸν ἀπὸ τοῦ τέγους. Φούλβιον δὲ ἐς
θεραπαίνης φυγόντα παλλακευθείσης τε αὐτῷ καὶ
ἀπηλευθερωμένης καὶ προῖκα ἐς γάμον ἐπιλαβούσης,
ἡ τοσάδε εὖ παθοῦσα προύδωκε ζηλοτυπίᾳ τῆς μεθ'
ἑαυτὴν τῷ Φουλβίῳ γεγαμημένης.

102   25. Τοσάδε μὲν δὴ καὶ γυναικῶν πονηρῶν ὑποδείγ-
ματα γεγράφθω· Στάτιος δὲ ὁ Σαννίτης, πολλὰ Σαυ-
νίταις ἐν τῷ συμμαχικῷ πολέμῳ κατειργασμένος, διὰ
δὲ περιφάνειαν ἔργων καὶ διὰ πλοῦτον καὶ γένος ἐς
τὸ Ῥωμαίων βουλευτήριον ἀνακεκλημένος, ὀγδοηκον-
τούτης ὢν ἤδη καὶ διὰ πλοῦτον προγεγραμμένος, ἀνε-

watch on her husband until the executioners arrived; and on the same day they killed him, she celebrated her marriage.

24. Being a fugitive and not knowing what to do, Salassus entered Rome at night, when he thought the danger would be markedly lessened. His house had been sold, and the only person to recognize him was the porter who had been sold along with the house, and who took him into his room and promised to hide him, and feed him as best he could. Salassus told the porter to send for his wife from her own house. She pretended to be very keen to come, but said that she was afraid of causing suspicion even to her maidservants by doing so at night, and said that she would come at dawn. At daybreak she went to collect the executioners, while the porter ran off to her house to hurry her up, in the belief that she was dawdling. With the departure of the porter, Salassus was afraid that he had gone off to set a trap, and rushed up to the roof to observe what was happening, but when he saw, not the porter, but his wife showing the executioners the way, he threw himself off the roof. Fulvius took refuge with a maidservant who had been his mistress, and to whom he had given freedom and a dowry on her marriage. Although she had been so well treated by him, she betrayed him out of jealousy of the woman who had married Fulvius after his affair with her.

25. Let the above suffice as examples of wicked women. Statius, the Samnite, who achieved much for the Samnites during the Social War, and who had been enrolled in the Roman senate on account of his famous exploits, his wealth, and his family, was now eighty years old when he was proscribed because of his wealth. He threw open his

98

99

100

101

102

πέτασε τὴν οἰκίαν τῷ τε δήμῳ καὶ τοῖς θεράπουσιν
ἐκφορεῖν, ὅσα θέλοιεν, τὰ δὲ καὶ αὐτὸς διερρίπτει, μέχρι κεκενωμένης ἐπικλείσας ἐνέπρησε καὶ ἀπώλετο,
καὶ τὸ πῦρ πολλὰ τῆς πόλεως ἄλλα ἐπενείματο.

103 Καπίτων δὲ ἐς πολὺ τὰς θύρας ὑπανοίγων τοὺς ἐσβια-
ζομένους καθ᾽ ἕνα ἀνῄρει, ὑπὸ δὲ πολλῶν ἐπιβρισάν-

104 των εἷς ἀπέθανε πολλοὺς ἀποκτείνας. Οὐετουλῖνος δὲ
χεῖρα ἤθροισε πολλὴν ἀμφὶ τὸ Ῥήγιον αὐτῶν τε τῶν
προγεγραμμένων ἀνδρῶν καὶ ὅσοι συνέφευγον αὐτοῖς,
καὶ ἀπὸ τῶν ὀκτωκαίδεκα πόλεων, αἳ τοῖς στρατοῖς

105 ἐπινίκια ἐπηγγελμέναι πάνυ ἐδυσχέραινον. τούσδε
οὖν ἔχων ὁ Οὐετουλῖνος ἀνῄρει τῶν λοχαγῶν τοὺς
διαθέοντας, μέχρι πεμφθέντος ἐπ᾽ αὐτὸν στρατοῦ
πλέονος οὐδ᾽ ὡς ἔληξεν, ἀλλ᾽ ἐς Σικελίαν πρὸς Πομπήιον, κρατοῦντά τε αὐτῆς καὶ τοὺς φεύγοντας ὑπο-

106 δεχόμενον, ἐπέρασεν. εἶτα ἐπολέμει καρτερῶς, μέχρι
πολλαῖς μάχαις ἡσσώμενος τὸν μὲν υἱὸν καὶ ὅσοι
τῶν προγεγραμμένων ἄλλοι συνῆσαν, ἐπὶ Μεσσήνης
ἔπεμψεν, αὐτὸς δέ, ὡς εἶδε πορθμευόμενον ἤδη τὸ
σκάφος, ἐμπεσὼν τοῖς πολεμίοις κατεκόπη.

107 26. Νάσων δὲ ὑπὸ ἐξελευθέρου, παιδικῶν οἱ γενομένου, προδοθεὶς ἥρπασε παρά του τῶν στρατιωτῶν
ξίφος καὶ τὸν προδότην μόνον ἀποκτείνας ἑαυτὸν τοῖς

108 σφαγεῦσιν ὑπέσχε. φιλοδέσποτος δὲ οἰκέτης τὸν κε-
κτημένον ἐπὶ λόφου ἐκάθισε καὶ αὐτὸς ἐπὶ θάλασσαν

---

[18] See above, 3.10.

house to the people and to his slaves to take away whatever they wanted, and other things he himself gave away indiscriminately. Finally, when the house had been emptied, he locked the doors, set fire to it, and died, and the fire spread to many other parts of the city. Capito, having 103 partly opened his door, for a long time continued to kill those who were trying to force their way in one by one, until he died under the weight of numbers, having single-handedly killed many of them. At Rhegium Vetulinus col- 104 lected a large band of proscribed men and those who had fled with them, as well as members of the eighteen towns which were extremely angry at being promised to the troops as the rewards of victory.[18] With these men Vetuli- 105 nus killed some of the centurions who were roaming the area, until a larger force was sent against him, and even then he did not stop, but crossed over to Sicily to join Pompeius, who controlled the island and was taking in fugitives.[19] Thereafter he continued to fight bravely, until, 106 defeated in several engagements, he sent his son and the rest of the proscribed who were with him to Messena. As for himself, when he saw that the boat was already on its way across the straits, he fell on the enemy and was cut down.

26. Naso, having been betrayed by a freedman who had 107 been a favorite of his, snatched a sword from one of the soldiers, and, having killed only the man who betrayed him, surrendered himself to the executioners. A slave who 108 was devoted to his master sat him down on a hill while he

---

[19] Sextus Pompeius, younger son of Pompey the Great, who continued his father's struggle against Julius Caesar, and subsequently resisted Octavian, until defeated and executed in 35.

ἤει μισθωσόμενος αὐτῷ σκάφος. ἐπανιὼν δὲ κτεινό-
μενόν τε εἶδε τὸν δεσπότην καὶ ἀποψύχοντος ἤδη
μέγα βοῶν "Ἐπίμεινον ἐς βραχύ, ὦ δέσποτα," εἶπε
καὶ κτείνει τὸν λοχαγὸν ἐμπεσὼν ἄφνω. μετὰ δὲ ἐκεῖνον ἑαυτὸν ἐπαναιρῶν εἶπε τῷ δεσπότῃ· "Παραμύθιον
109 ἔχεις." Λεύκιος δὲ δύο πιστοτάτοις ἀπελευθέροις χρυσίον δοὺς ἐπὶ θάλασσαν ἤει, διαδράντων δὲ ἐκείνων
ὑπέστρεψε καταγινώσκων τοῦ βίου καὶ ἑαυτὸν ἐμή-
110 νυσε τοῖς σφαγεῦσι. Λαβιηνὸς δὲ ἐν ταῖς Σύλλα προγραφαῖς πολλοὺς τῶν τότε συλλαβών τε καὶ κτείνας
ἠδόξησεν ἄρα, εἰ μὴ τὰ ὅμοια γενναίως ἐνέγκοι, καὶ
προελθὼν τῆς οἰκίας ἐκαθέζετο ἐπὶ θρόνου τοὺς σφα-
111 γέας περιμένων. Κέστιος δὲ ἐν χωρίοις παρὰ εὐνόοις
θεράπουσιν ἐκρύπτετο, λοχαγῶν δ' αἰεὶ σὺν ὅπλοις ἢ
κεφαλαῖς διαθεόντων οὐκ ἔφερε τὸ μῆκος τοῦ φόβου,
ἀλλ' ἔπεισε τοὺς θεράποντας ἅψαι πυράν, ἵνα ἔχοιεν
λέγειν, ὅτι Κέστιον ἀποθανόντα θάπτοιεν. καὶ οἱ μὲν
112 ἐνεδρευθέντες ᾖσαν, ὁ δὲ ἐσήλατο ἐς αὐτήν. Ἀπώνιος
δὲ ἀσφαλῶς ἑαυτὸν ἐπικρύψας οὐκ ἤνεγκε τὴν πονη-
ρίαν τῆς διαίτης, ἀλλὰ προήγαγεν ἑαυτὸν ἐπὶ τὴν
113 σφαγήν. ἄλλος ἐν φανερῷ καθῆστο ἑκὼν καὶ βραδυ-
νόντων τῶν σφαγέων ἀπήγξατο ἐν μέσῳ.

114   27. Λεύκιος δὲ ὁ Ἀσινίου τοῦ ὑπατεύοντος τότε
πενθερός, φεύγων διὰ θαλάσσης, οὐ φέρων τοῦ χειμῶνος τὴν ἀηδίαν ἔρριψεν ἑαυτὸν εἰς τὸ πέλαγος.

---

[20] Gaius Asinius Pollio, the well known historian and loyal

himself went down to the sea to hire a boat for him. As he was returning, he saw his master being killed, and when he was breathing his last, the slave shouted out loudly, "Wait a moment, master," and suddenly attacked the centurion and kills him. Then he killed himself, saying to his master, "There's something to console you." Lucius gave money to two of his most faithful freedmen, and was heading toward the sea when they ran off. Despairing of life, he turned around, and presented himself to the executioners. Labienus, who had arrested and killed many contemporaries in the time of the Sullan proscriptions, thought it distinctly unworthy not to suffer the same fate with fortitude, and going out in front of his house, he sat in a chair to await the executioners. Cestius was hiding in the country among slaves who were well disposed toward him, but with centurions roaming the area all the time carrying weapons, or heads, he could not stand the constant fear, and persuaded the slaves to light a pyre so they could say that Cestius had died and they were conducting his funeral. They fell for his trick and lit the pyre, and he jumped onto it. Aponius hid himself in a safe place, but he could not put up with the miserable lifestyle, and presented himself for execution. Someone else sat down of their own accord in full view, and when the executioners were slow in coming, hanged himself in public.

27. Lucius, father-in-law of Asinius, who was consul in that period, while fleeing by sea could not stand the nausea caused by the weather, and threw himself in the ocean.[20]

supporter of Caesar and then Antony, was consul only in 40. Appian uses adverbs like "then" (τότε) loosely, and probably only intends to refer to the general period.

115 Καισέννιον δὲ οἱ διώκοντες, ὑποφεύγοντά τε καὶ βο-
ῶντα οὐ προγεγράφθαι, ἀλλὰ διὰ τὰ χρήματα ἐπι-
βουλεύεσθαι πρὸς αὐτῶν, ἐπὶ τὸν πίνακα ἀγαγόντες
ἀναγινώσκειν ἑαυτοῦ τὸ ὄνομα ἐκέλευον καὶ ἀναγινώ-
116 σκοντα ἔκτειναν. Αἰμίλιος δὲ ἀγνοῶν, ὅτι προγέγρα-
πται, διωκόμενον ἄλλον ἰδὼν ἤρετο τὸν λοχαγὸν τὸν
διώκοντα, τίς ὁ προγεγραμμένος εἴη· καὶ ὁ λοχαγὸς
τὸν Αἰμίλιον γνωρίσας "Σὺ κἀκεῖνος" εἶπε καὶ τοὺς
117 δύο ἀπέκτεινε. Κίλλων δὲ ἐκ τοῦ βουλευτηρίου προϊὼν
καὶ Δέκιος, ἐπεὶ τοῖς πίναξιν ἐπύθοντο σφῶν τὰ ὀνόματα προσγεγράφθαι, οὔπω τινὸς ἐπιόντος αὐτοῖς,
ἔφευγον ἀκόσμως διὰ πυλῶν, καὶ αὐτοὺς τοῖς ἀπαν-
118 τῶσι τῶν λοχαγῶν αὐτὸς ὁ δρόμος ἐμήνυσεν. Σιλίκιος[8] δέ, ὃς ἐπὶ Βρούτῳ τε καὶ Κασσίῳ δικάζων, Καίσαρος τοῖς δικαστηρίοις μετὰ στρατιᾶς ἐφεστῶτος
καὶ τῶν ἄλλων δικαστῶν κρύφα τὴν καταδικάζουσαν
φερόντων, μόνος τὴν ἀπολύουσαν ἤνεγκε φανερῶς,
ἐκλαθόμενος τῆς μεγαλόφρονος ἐλευθεριότητος, νε-
κρὸν σῶμα ἐκκομιζόμενον ὑποστὰς τοῖς φέρουσι συν-
119 εβάσταζε τὸ λέχος. ἰδόντων δὲ τῶν φρουρούντων τὰς
πύλας, ὅτι πλεονάζουσιν οἱ νεκροφόροι παρὰ τὸ
σύνηθες ἑνὶ ἀνδρί, καὶ τοὺς μὲν φέροντας οὐχ ὑπονοούντων, τὸ δὲ λέχος ἐρευνωμένων, μὴ νεκρόν τις ὑπο-
κρίνοιτο, οἱ νεκροφόροι τὸν Σιλίκιον ἤλεγχον οὐχ

---

[8] Ἰκελίος codd.; Σιλίκιος edd.

While trying to evade his pursuers, Caesennius shouted 115
out that he had not been proscribed, but was being perse-
cuted by them for his money. They took him to the notice
board, however, and ordered him to read out his own
name, and while he was doing so killed him. Aemilius, not 116
knowing that he had been proscribed and seeing another
man being pursued, asked the centurion chasing him who
the proscribed man was. The centurion recognized Aemilius and replied, "You and that man there," and killed
them both. As Cillo and Decius were leaving the senate 117
house they found out that their own names had been
added to the proscription lists, and fled in disarray through
the city gates, although no one was going after them yet.
It was the very fact they were running that betrayed them
to the centurions who bumped into them. Silicius, who 118
was one of the judges in the trial of Brutus and Cassius
when Octavian was supervising the courts with his army,
and who was the only one openly to vote for acquittal,
when the other judges were secretly voting for conviction,
now forgetful of his principled display of independence,
took up position under the body of a dead man being carried away for burial, and joined those lifting the bier.[21]
Although the guards at the city gates noticed that there 119
was one more corpse-bearer than usual, they were not
suspicious of the bearers, but examined the bier to make
sure that no one was pretending to be dead. Silicius was
recognized, however, and killed by the executioners when

[21] The name of this man in the manuscripts is Icelius, but we
know it was Publius Silicius Corona from Dio (46.49.5), who tells
the story of him openly voting for the acquittal of Brutus and
Cassius and later being proscribed.

ὁμότεχνον σφίσιν ὄντα, ἐπιγνωσθέντα τε οἱ σφαγεῖς
ἀπέκτειναν.

120   28. Οὐᾶρος δ' ἀπελευθέρου προδιδόντος αὐτὸν ἀπέ-
δρα, καὶ ὄρος ἐξ ὄρους ἀμείβων ἐς τὸ Μιντουρναίων
ἕλος ἐνέπεσεν, ἔνθα ἑαυτὸν διαναπαύων ἡσύχαζε. τῶν
δὲ Μιντουρναίων ἐπὶ ζητήσει ληστηρίου τὸ ἕλος περιθεόντων, ἥ τε κόμη τοῦ δόνακος σαλευθεῖσα ἐνέφηνε
τὸν Οὐᾶρον, καὶ ληφθεὶς ἔλεγεν εἶναι λῃστὴς καὶ ἐπὶ
121   τῷδε θανάτῳ καταδικαζόμενος ἠνείχετο. ὡς δὲ αὐτὸν
ἔμελλον καὶ βασανιεῖν ἐς τοὺς συνεγνωκότας, οὐκ
ἐνεγκὼν ἤδη τοῦτο ὡς ἀπρεπέστερον, "Ἀπαγορεύω,"
φησίν, "Ὑμῖν, ὦ Μιντουρναῖοι, ὕπατόν με γεγενημέ-
νον, καί, ὃ τοῖς νῦν ἄρχουσι τιμιώτερόν ἐστι, προγεγραμμένον μήτε βασανίζειν μήτε ἀναιρεῖν ἔτι· εἰ γὰρ
οὐκ ἔνι μοι διαφυγεῖν, ἄμεινον ὑπὸ τῶν ὁμοτίμων πα-
122   θεῖν." ἀπιστούντων δὲ τῶν Μιντουρναίων καὶ τὸν λόγον ὑπονοούντων λοχαγὸς ἐπέγνω διαθέων καὶ τὴν
κεφαλὴν ἀπέτεμε, τὸ δὲ λοιπὸν σῶμα τοῖς Μιντουρ-
123   ναίοις κατέλιπε. Λάργον ἕτεροι συνελάμβανον ἐν χωρίοις, οὐ Λάργον, ἀλλ' ἕτερον διώκοντες· οἰκτείραντες
δ', ὅτι μὴ ζητούμενος ἁλοίη, φεύγειν μεθῆκαν ἀνὰ
τὴν ὕλην. ὁ δὲ ὑφ' ἑτέρων διωκόμενος δρόμῳ τοὺς
προτέρους κατέλαβε καί· "Ὑμεῖς," ἔφη, "Με κτείνατε
μᾶλλον, οἱ ἐλεήσαντες, ἵνα τὸν μισθὸν ἀντὶ τούτων
ὑμεῖς φέρησθε."

124   29. Ὁ μὲν δὴ ταύτην ἔδωκεν ἀμοιβὴν ἀποθνήσκων
φιλανθρωπίας, Ῥοῦφος δὲ ἔχων συνοικίαν περικαλλῆ,

the bearers accused him of not being a member of their corporation.

28. Varus ran away when he was betrayed by a freed- 120
man, and after moving from one mountain to another, chanced upon the marsh at Minturnae, where he stopped and rested quietly. The people of Minturnae were scouring this marsh looking for a bandit group, and the way the tops of the reeds were moving gave Varus' position away. When captured, he said he was a bandit, and accepted being sentenced to death. But they were also intending to 121
torture him for information on his accomplices, and this was now something he would not accept, as being beneath his dignity. "I forbid you, citizens of Minturnae," he said, "to persevere with the torture or execution of a man who has been a consul and—what is more valuable to our present rulers—a man who has been proscribed![22] If it is not possible for me to escape, it is better to suffer my fate at the hands of my equals." The people of Minturnae were 122
skeptical, and suspicious of his story, but a centurion scouring the area recognized Varus and cut off his head, leaving the rest of the body to the townspeople. Largus 123
was arrested in the countryside by men who were pursuing someone else. They took pity on him because he had been captured when he was not being hunted and let him escape into the forest. But when chased by another group he ran back and caught up with his previous captors, saying, "I would rather you killed me, so that you who took pity on me get the reward instead of those men."

29. This was how Largus repaid their kindness by his 124
death. Rufus, on the other hand, who owned a very hand-

---

[22] There was no consul at this time with the name Varus.

APPIAN

γείτονα Φουλβίας τῆς γυναικὸς Ἀντωνίου, πάλαι μὲν
ἀξιούσῃ τῇ Φουλβίᾳ πρίασθαι τὴν οἰκίαν οὐ συνεχώρει, τότε δὲ καὶ δωρούμενος προεγράφη. καὶ τὴν
κεφαλὴν ὁ μὲν Ἀντώνιός οἱ προσφερομένην οὐχ
ἑαυτῷ προσήκειν εἰπὼν ἔπεμψεν ἐς τὴν γυναῖκα, ἡ δὲ
ἀντὶ τῆς ἀγορᾶς ἐκέλευσεν ἐπὶ τῆς συνοικίας προτε-
125 θῆναι. ἔπαυλιν ἕτερος εἶχε περικαλλῆ καὶ σύσκιον,
ἄντρον τε καλὸν ἦν ἐν αὐτῇ καὶ βαθύ, καὶ τάχα διὰ
ταῦτα καὶ προυγράφη. ἔτυχε δὲ ἀναψύχων κατὰ τὸ
ἄντρον, καὶ αὐτῷ τῶν σφαγέων ἔτι μακρόθεν ἐπιθεόντων θεράπων αὐτὸν ἐς τὸν μυχὸν τοῦ ἄντρου προπέμψας ἐνέδυ τὸν τοῦ δεσπότου χιτωνίσκον καὶ ὑπεκρίνετο ἐκεῖνος εἶναι καὶ δεδιέναι· καὶ τάχα ἂν ἐπέτυχεν
ἀναιρεθείς, εἰ μὴ τῶν ὁμοδούλων τις ἐνέφηνε τὴν ἐν-
126 έδραν. ἀναιρεθέντος δὲ ὧδε τοῦ δεσπότου, ὁ δῆμος
ἀγανακτῶν παρὰ τοῖς ἄρχουσιν οὐκ ἐπαύετο, μέχρι
τὸν μὲν ἐνδείξαντα κρεμασθῆναι, τὸν δὲ περισώσαντα
127 ἐλευθερῶσαι ἐποίησεν. Ἀτέριον δὲ κρυπτόμενον θεράπων ἐμήνυσέ τε καὶ ἐλεύθερος αὐτίκα γενόμενος ἀν-
τωνεῖτο τοῖς παισὶν αὐτοῦ τὴν οὐσίαν καὶ ἐνύβριζεν
ἐπαχθῶς. οἱ δὲ αὐτῷ πανταχῇ μετὰ σιγῆς εἵποντο
κλαίοντες, ἕως ὁ δῆμος ἠγανάκτησε, καὶ οἱ τρεῖς
αὐτόν, ὡς πλεονάσαντα τῆς χρείας, ἀνεδούλωσαν τοῖς
παισὶ τοῦ προγεγραμμένου.
128   30. Περὶ μὲν δὴ τοὺς ἄνδρας τοιάδε ἐγίγνετο, ἥψατο
δὲ καὶ ὀρφανῶν διὰ πλοῦτον ἡ τότε τύχη. καὶ ὁ μὲν
ἐς διδασκάλου φοιτῶν αὐτῷ παιδαγωγῷ συνανῃρέθη,

238

some apartment block beside the property of Fulvia, the
wife of Antony, whose offer to buy the building in the past
he had turned down, although he now gave it to her as a
gift, was proscribed.[23] His head was brought to Antony,
but he said it was nothing to do with him and sent it to his
wife, who ordered that it be displayed on the apartment
block rather than in the Forum. Another man owned a   125
very handsome and well-shaded villa which had a beautiful, deep grotto. It was perhaps for this reason that he was
proscribed. He happened to be relaxing in this grotto
when the executioners came after him. While they were
still some distance away, a slave sent him off into the deepest part of the grotto, put on his master's cloak and pretended to be him and to be afraid. He might have succeeded in getting killed if one of his fellow slaves had not
revealed the trick. This was how the master came to be   126
killed, but the people would not stop expressing their anger to the magistrates, until they got the informer hanged,
and the slave who tried to save his master freed. While   127
Haterius was in hiding, a slave informed against him, and
was immediately given his freedom, but bid against Haterius' children for his estate, and insulted them intoler-
ably. They followed him everywhere weeping and in silence. Eventually the people became indignant, and the
triumvirs again made him a slave, of the proscribed man's
children, because he had overstepped himself.

30. This was the sort of thing that happened to grown   128
men, but the adversity of the times also affected orphans
because of their wealth. One of these, who was on his way

[23] This seems to be the Publius Caesetius Rufus known by
Valerius Maximus (9.5.4).

129 τὸν παῖδα περισχομένῳ τε καὶ οὐ μεθιέντι· Ἀτίλιος δὲ
ἄρτι τὴν τῶν τελείων περιθέμενος στολὴν ᾔει μέν, ὡς
ἔθος ἐστί, σὺν πομπῇ φίλων ἐπὶ θυσίας ἐς τὰ ἱερά,
ἄφνω δὲ ἐγγραφέντος αὐτοῦ τοῖς πίναξιν οἱ φίλοι καὶ
130 οἱ θεράποντες διεδίδρασκον. ὁ δὲ μόνος καὶ ἔρημος ἐκ
δαψιλοῦς παραπομπῆς ἐς τὴν μητέρα ἐχώρει· οὐ δε-
ξαμένης δὲ αὐτὸν οὐδὲ ἐκείνης ὑπὸ δέους, οὐκ ἀξιώ-
σας ἔτι ἐς πεῖραν ἐλθεῖν ἑτέρου μετὰ μητέρα, ἐς ὄρος
ἔφυγεν· ὅθεν ὑπὸ λιμοῦ ἐς τὰ πεδινὰ κατελθὼν ἐλή-
φθη πρὸς ἀνδρὸς λῃστεύειν τοὺς παροδεύοντας καὶ
131 ἐπὶ ἔργῳ καταδεῖν εἰθισμένου. οἷα δὲ παῖς ἐκ τρυφῆς
τὸν πόνον οὐκ ἐνεγκὼν ἐς τὴν ἁμαξιτὸν αὐταῖς χοινι-
κίσι διέδρα καὶ παροδεύουσι λοχαγοῖς ἑαυτὸν ἐμήνυσέ τε καὶ ἀνῃρέθη.

132   31. Γιγνομένων δὲ τούτων Λέπιδος ἐπὶ Ἴβηρσιν
ἐθριάμβευε, καὶ προυτέθη διάγραμμα οὕτως ἔχον·
"Ἀγαθῇ τύχῃ προειρήσθω πᾶσι καὶ πάσαις θύειν καὶ
εὐωχεῖσθαι τὴν ἡμέραν τὴν παροῦσαν· ὃς δ' ἂν μὴ
φαίνηται ταῦτα ποιῶν, ἐν τοῖς προγεγραμμένοις
ἔσται." ὁ μὲν δὴ τὸν θρίαμβον ἐς τὰ ἱερὰ ἀνῆγε,
παραπεμπόντων αὐτὸν ἁπάντων μετὰ σχήματος ἱλα-
133 ροῦ καὶ γνώμης δυσμενοῦς· τῶν δὲ προγεγραμμένων
τὰ μὲν ἐν ταῖς οἰκίαις διεφορεῖτο, καὶ οὐ πολὺς ἦν ὁ
τὰ χωρία ὠνούμενος, οἱ μὲν ἐπιβαρεῖν τοῖς ἠτυχηκό-
σιν αἰδούμενοι καὶ οὐκ ἐν αἰσίῳ σφίσι τὰ ἐκείνων
ἔσεσθαι νομίζοντες οὐδὲ ἀσφαλὲς ὅλως χρυσίον ἢ
ἀργύριον ἔχοντας ὁρᾶσθαι οὐδὲ τὰς ἐπικτήσεις νῦν
ἀκινδύνους, πολὺ δὲ μᾶλλον τὰ ὄντα ἐπικίνδυνα.

to his schoolmaster, was killed together with his tutor, who threw his arms around the boy and would not let go. Atilius, who had just assumed the toga of adulthood, was 129 going, as was the custom, with a band of friends to sacrifice in the temples, when his name was suddenly written up on the proscription lists, and his friends and attendants ran off. All alone and deserted by his large escort, he went to 130 his mother. As even she was too afraid to take him in, he did not think it was worth trying anyone else after his mother, and fled to the mountains. From here he came down to the plain because he was starving, and was seized by a man who was used to robbing passersby, and putting them in chains to work for him. As a boy accustomed to 131 luxury, he was unable to stand the work and made his escape to the main road still in his fetters, identified himself to some passing centurions, and was killed.

31. While these events were taking place, Lepidus cel- 132 ebrated a triumph over the Iberians, and an edict was published in the following terms: "To good fortune! Let it be proclaimed to all men and women that they celebrate this day with sacrifices and feasting. Anyone seen not doing this will be put on the list of the proscribed." Lepidus himself led the triumphal procession to the sacred precincts, accompanied by the whole population, who put on an appearance of joy, but were hostile at heart. The houses 133 of the proscribed were looted of their contents, but not many bought their estates, since people were ashamed to add to the burden of the unfortunate. They thought that their property would not bring them luck, that it was not at all safe to be seen in possession of gold and silver, and that additional acquisitions were not without danger at this time, while what they currently owned would be put

134 μόνοι δὲ οἱ διὰ θρασύτητα προσιόντες, ἅτε μόνοι,
βραχυτάτου πάμπαν ὠνοῦντο. ὅθεν τοῖς ἄρχουσιν,
ἐλπίσασιν ἐς τὰς τοῦ πολέμου παρασκευὰς τάδε ἀρκέσειν, ἐνέδει μυριάδων ἔτι δισμυρίων.

135   32. Καὶ τοῦτο ἐς τὸν δῆμον εἰπόντες προύγραφον
χιλίας καὶ τετρακοσίας γυναῖκας, αἳ μάλιστα πλούτῳ
διέφερον· καὶ αὐτὰς ἔδει, τὰ ὄντα τιμωμένας, ἐσφέρειν
ἐς τὰς τοῦ πολέμου χρείας, ὅσον ἑκάστην οἱ τρεῖς
δοκιμάσειαν. ἐπέκειτό τε ταῖς ἀποκρυψαμέναις τι τῶν
ὄντων, ἢ τιμησαμέναις κακῶς ἐπιτίμια καὶ τοῖς ταῦτα
136 μηνύουσιν ἐλευθέροις τε καὶ δούλοις μήνυτρα. αἱ δὲ
γυναῖκες ἔκριναν τῶν προσηκουσῶν τοῖς ἄρχουσι γυναικῶν δεηθῆναι. τῆς μὲν δὴ Καίσαρος ἀδελφῆς οὐκ
ἀπετύγχανον, οὐδὲ τῆς μητρὸς Ἀντωνίου· Φουλβίας
δέ, τῆς γυναικὸς Ἀντωνίου, τῶν θυρῶν ἀπωθούμεναι
χαλεπῶς τὴν ὕβριν ἤνεγκαν, καὶ ἐς τὴν ἀγορὰν ἐπὶ
τὸ βῆμα τῶν ἀρχόντων ὠσάμεναι, διισταμένων τοῦ τε
δήμου καὶ τῶν δορυφόρων, ἔλεγον, Ὁρτησίας ἐς
137 τοῦτο προκεχειρισμένης· "Ὁ μὲν ἥρμοζε δεομέναις
ὑμῶν γυναιξὶ τοιαῖσδε, ἐπὶ τὰς γυναῖκας ὑμῶν κατ-
εφύγομεν· ὃ δὲ οὐχ ἥρμοζεν, ὑπὸ Φουλβίας παθοῦ-
138 σαι, ἐς τὴν ἀγορὰν συνεώσμεθα ὑπ' αὐτῆς. ὑμεῖς δ'
ἡμᾶς ἀφείλεσθε μὲν ἤδη γονέας τε καὶ παῖδας καὶ
ἄνδρας καὶ ἀδελφοὺς ἐπικαλοῦντες, ὅτι πρὸς αὐτῶν
ἠδίκησθε· εἰ δὲ καὶ τὰ χρήματα προσαφέλοισθε,

---

24 This was the daughter of Quintus Hortensius Hortalus
(consul 69), one of the greatest orators of the Republic and a rival

at much greater risk. The only ones to come forward did   134
so out of recklessness, and bought at very low prices, because they were the only buyers. So it was that, although
the triumvirs hoped that these measures would provide
enough for their war preparations, they were still short by
two hundred million drachmas.

32. They told the people of this and published a list of   135
one thousand four hundred women who were particularly
conspicuous for their wealth. These were required to have
their property assessed and contribute to the expenses of
the war the sum approved by the triumvirs for each individual. Penalties were imposed for women hiding any of
their belongings or for making a false return, and rewards
were set for informers, both free men and slaves. The   136
women decided to make an appeal to the female relatives
of the triumvirs, and were successful with Octavian's sister
and Antony's mother. When turned away, however, from
the doors of Fulvia, Antony's wife, they were offended by
her insulting behavior, and pushing their way to the magistrates' tribunal in the Forum, where the people and the
bodyguards stood aside to let them through, they delivered a speech, having chosen Hortensia for the task:[24] "As   137
was fitting for women of our rank addressing a petition to
you, we had recourse to your womenfolk; but what was not
fitting was the treatment we received at the hands of Fulvia, and we have been driven by her to come to the Forum.
You have already taken away our fathers and sons and   138
husbands and brothers, on a charge that you were wronged
at their hands; if you also take away our money, you will

of Cicero: see Val. Max. 8.3.3. Her speech remained famous a
century later (Quint. *Inst.* 1.1.7).

περιστήσετε ἐς ἀπρέπειαν ἀναξίαν γένους καὶ τρόπων
139 καὶ φύσεως γυναικείας. εἰ μὲν δή τι καὶ πρὸς ἡμῶν,
οἷον ὑπὸ τῶν ἀνδρῶν, ἠδικῆσθαί φατε, προγράψατε
καὶ ἡμᾶς ὡς ἐκείνους. εἰ δὲ οὐδένα ὑμῶν αἱ γυναῖκες
οὔτε πολέμιον ἐψηφισάμεθα οὔτε καθείλομεν οἰκίαν ἢ
στρατὸν διεφθείραμεν ἢ ἐπηγάγομεν ἕτερον ἢ ἀρχῆς
ἢ τιμῆς τυχεῖν ἐκωλύσαμεν, τί κοινωνοῦμεν τῶν κολάσεων αἱ τῶν ἀδικημάτων οὐ μετασχοῦσαι;
140   33. "Τί δὲ ἐσφέρωμεν αἱ μήτε ἀρχῆς μήτε τιμῆς
μήτε στρατηγίας μήτε τῆς πολιτείας ὅλως, τῆς ὑμῖν
ἐς τοσοῦτον ἤδη κακοῦ περιμαχήτου, μετέχουσαι; ὅτι
φατὲ πόλεμον εἶναι; καὶ πότε οὐ γεγόνασι πόλεμοι;
141 καὶ πότε γυναῖκες συνεισήνεγκαν; ἃς ἡ μὲν φύσις
ἀπολύει παρὰ ἅπασιν ἀνθρώποις, αἱ δὲ μητέρες ἡμῶν
ὑπὲρ τὴν φύσιν ἐσήνεγκάν ποτε ἅπαξ, ὅτε ἐκινδυ-
νεύετε περὶ τῇ ἀρχῇ πάσῃ καὶ περὶ αὐτῇ τῇ πόλει,
142 Καρχηδονίων ἐνοχλούντων. καὶ τότε δὲ ἐσήνεγκαν
ἑκοῦσαι, καὶ οὐκ ἀπὸ γῆς ἢ χωρίων ἢ προικὸς ἢ
οἰκιῶν, ὧν χωρὶς ἀβίωτόν ἐστιν ἐλευθέραις, ἀλλὰ ἀπὸ
μόνων τῶν οἴκοι κόσμων, οὐδὲ τούτων τιμωμένων
οὐδὲ ὑπὸ μηνυταῖς ἢ κατηγόροις οὐδὲ πρὸς ἀνάγκην
143 ἢ βίαν, ἀλλ’ ὅσον ἐβούλοντο αὐταί. τίς οὖν καὶ νῦν
ἐστιν ὑμῖν περὶ τῆς ἀρχῆς ἢ περὶ τῆς πατρίδος φόβος; ἴτω τοίνυν ἢ Κελτῶν πόλεμος ἢ Παρθυαίων, καὶ
οὐ χείρους ἐς σωτηρίαν ἐσόμεθα τῶν μητέρων. ἐς δὲ
ἐμφυλίους πολέμους μήτε ἐσενέγκαιμέν ποτε μήτε
144 συμπράξαιμεν ὑμῖν κατ’ ἀλλήλων. οὐδὲ γὰρ ἐπὶ Καί-

reduce us to a wretched condition unbecoming our birth, our character, and our female nature. If you maintain that 139 you have been wronged at our hands too, as you say you were by our husbands, then proscribe us as you did them. But if we women have not voted any of you public enemies, have not torn down your houses, destroyed your army, or led another one against you; if we have not hindered you in obtaining offices and honors, why do we share the penalties when we had no part in the wrongdoing?

33. "Why should we pay taxes when we have no access 140 to the offices or the honors or the military commands or the entire political process, which you have now brought to such a sorry state by your rivalries? Because, according to you, there is a war on? When have there not been wars, and when have women ever paid taxes? Our nature exempts us in all societies, even though our mothers did on 141 one single occasion transcend their nature and make a contribution, when the Carthaginians were causing trouble and you were in danger of losing the whole empire and the city of Rome itself. But on that occasion they contrib- 142 uted voluntarily, not from their land, their country properties, their dowry, or their houses, without which free women have nothing to live on, but only from the jewelry they had at home, and even then not on the basis of an assessment of these items or under threat of informers and accusers, and subject to force and violence, but what they themselves were willing to give. So what is it you are afraid 143 of now for our empire and country? Let war with the Celts or the Parthians come, and we will not prove inferior to our mothers in ensuring safety; but for civil wars may we never pay a contribution, nor ever help you against each

245

σαρος ἢ Πομπηίου συνεφέρομεν, οὐδὲ Μάριος ἡμᾶς
οὐδὲ Κίννας ἠνάγκασεν οὐδὲ Σύλλας, ὁ τυραννήσας
τῆς πατρίδος· ὑμεῖς δέ φατε καὶ καθίστασθαι τὴν πολιτείαν."

145   34. Τοιαῦτα τῆς Ὁρτησίας λεγούσης, οἱ τρεῖς ἠγα-
νάκτουν, εἰ γυναῖκες ἀνδρῶν ἡσυχαζόντων θρασυνοῦν-
ταί τε καὶ ἐκκλησιάσουσι, καὶ τὰ δρώμενα τοῖς ἄρχουσιν ἐξετάσουσι, καὶ τῶν ἀνδρῶν στρατευομένων
αὐταὶ οὐδὲ χρήματα ἐσοίσουσιν· ἐκέλευόν τε τοῖς
ὑπηρέταις ἐξωθεῖν αὐτὰς ἀπὸ τοῦ βήματος, μέχρι
βοῆς ἔξωθεν ἐκ τοῦ πλήθους γενομένης οἵ τε ὑπηρέται τὸ ἔργον ἐπέσχον καὶ οἱ ἄρχοντες ἔφασαν ἐς
146   τὴν ὑστεραίαν ἀνατίθεσθαι. τῇ δ' ὑστεραίᾳ τετρακοσίας μὲν ἀντὶ χιλίων καὶ τετρακοσίων προύγραφον
ἀποτιμᾶσθαι τὰ ὄντα, τῶν δὲ ἀνδρῶν πάντα τὸν
ἔχοντα πλείους δέκα μυριάδων, ἀστὸν ὁμοῦ καὶ ξένον
καὶ ἀπελεύθερον καὶ ἱερέα καὶ πανταεθνῆ,[9] μηδενὸς
ἀφιεμένου, καὶ τούσδε μεθ' ὁμοίου φόβου τῶν ἐπιτιμίων καὶ ὑπὸ μηνύμασιν ὁμοίοις, ἵνα πεντηκοστὴν
μὲν τῶν ὄντων αὐτίκα δανείσαιεν αὐτοῖς, ἐνιαυτοῦ δὲ
φόρον ἐς τὸν πόλεμον ἐσενέγκαιεν.

147   35. Ἐκ μὲν δὴ τῶν προσταγμάτων τοιαῦτα Ῥωμαίους ἐπεῖχεν, ὁ δὲ στρατὸς σὺν καταφρονήσει χεί-
ρονα ἐποίουν. ὡς γὰρ τῶν ἀρχόντων ἐπὶ τοιοῦσδε ἔργοις ἐν σφίσι μόνον τὸ ἀσφαλὲς ἐχόντων, οἱ μὲν
αὐτοὺς ᾐτοῦντο τῶν δεδημευμένων οἰκίαν ἢ ἀγρὸν ἢ

---

[9] πανταεθνῆ codd.; ἀλλοεθνῆ Gaillard-Goukowsky

other. We did not pay tax in the time of Caesar or Pompey,   144
and neither Marius nor Cinna forced us to, nor even Sulla,
and he governed the country as a tyrant. You, on the other
hand, maintain that you are restoring ordered government."

34. While Hortensia was delivering this speech, the   145
triumvirs were angry that, at a time when men were being
quietly compliant, women were being boldly assertive, attending public meetings, scrutinizing the actions of the
magistrates, and refusing even to pay money themselves
when the men were serving in the army. They ordered the
attendants to push the women away from the tribunal, but
eventually there was booing from the crowd outside and
the attendants stopped what they were doing; the triumvirs said they were postponing the matter till the next day.
On the following day they published a list of four hundred   146
women, instead of one thousand four hundred, required
to have their property assessed, and of any men in possession of more than one hundred thousand drachmas. This
included citizen and resident alien, freedman and priest
and men of all nations, without exception. They too were
under the same threat of penalties and of the same rewards for informers, to force them immediately to lend
the triumvirs two per cent of their wealth, and to pay a
year's tax toward the war.

35. Such were the calamities that befell the Romans as   147
a result of the triumvirs' decrees, but the army contemptuously made things even worse. On the grounds that the
triumvirs' security for conducting their actions lay solely
with them, some of the soldiers demanded a house, or

ἔπαυλιν ἢ ὅλον κλῆρον, οἱ δ' αὖ παῖδας ἀνδράσι
⟨τισὶ⟩[10] θετοὺς γενέσθαι· οἱ δὲ ἀφ' ἑαυτῶν ἕτερα
ἔδρων, κτιννύντες τε τοὺς οὐ προγεγραμμένους καὶ
148   οἰκίας οὐδὲν ὑπαιτίων διαφοροῦντες. ὥστε καὶ τοὺς
ἄρχοντας προγράψαι τῶν ὑπάτων τὸν ἕτερον ἐπιστρο-
φήν τινα ποιήσασθαι τῶν ὑπὲρ τὸ πρόσταγμα γιγνομένων. ὁ δὲ τῶν μὲν ὁπλιτῶν ἔδεισεν ἅψασθαι, μὴ
σφᾶς ἐφ' ἑαυτὸν παροξύνῃ, τῶν δὲ θεραπόντων τινάς,
οἳ σχήματι στρατιωτῶν συνεξημάρτανον ἐκείνοις,
λαβὼν ἐκρέμασε.

149   36. Καὶ τὰ μὲν ἐς τέλος τῶν συμφορῶν τοῖς προγεγραμμένοις ἀπαντῶντα τοιάδε μάλιστα ἦν· ὅσα δὲ
ἐκ παραλόγου τισὶν ἐγίγνετο ἔς τε τὴν σωτηρίαν
αὐτίκα καὶ ἐς ἀξίωσιν ὕστερον, ἐμοί τε ἥδιον εἰπεῖν
καὶ τοῖς ἀκούουσιν ὠφελιμώτερον ἐς μηδ' ἐναπο-
150   κάμνοντας ⟨ἀπ⟩ελπίζειν[11] περιέσεσθαι. αἱ μὲν οὖν
φυγαὶ τοῖς δυναμένοις ἦσαν ἐς Κάσσιον ἢ Βροῦτον
ἢ ἐς Λιβύην ἐπὶ Κορνιφίκιον, καὶ τόνδε τῆς δημοκρατίας μεταποιούμενον· ὁ δὲ πολὺς ἐς Σικελίαν ᾔει, γει-
τονεύουσαν τῆς Ἰταλίας, καὶ Πομπηίου σφᾶς προθύ-
151   μως ὑποδεχομένου. λαμπροτάτην γὰρ δὴ σπουδὴν ἐς
τοὺς ἀτυχοῦντας ὁ Πομπήιος ἐν καιρῷ τότε ἔδειξε,
κήρυκάς τε περιπέμπων, οἳ πάντας ἐς αὐτὸν ἐκάλουν,
καὶ τοῖς περισῴζουσιν αὐτοὺς ἐλευθέροις τε καὶ θερά-

---

[10] τισὶ add. Gaillard-Goukowsky   [11] ἐς μηδ' ἐναπο-
κάμνοντας ⟨ἀπ⟩ελπίζειν Gaillard-Goukowsky; ἐς μηδὲν ἀπο-
κάμνοντας ἐλπίζειν codd.

field, or villa, or whole inheritance belonging to the dispossessed, others that they should be adopted by certain men as their sons. Others again behaved differently by taking matters into their own hands and killing men who had not been proscribed, or plundering the houses of those who were accused of nothing. The result was that 148 the triumvirs even had to publish an edict that one of the consuls should reverse acts that went beyond the proscription order. The consul did not dare to deal with the legionaries, for fear of arousing their anger against him, but he did arrest and hang certain slaves who were masquerading as soldiers and taking part in their crimes.

36. These are particular examples of the extreme disas- 149 ters that befell the proscribed. It is more pleasant for me to recount examples of cases where some men unexpectedly reached immediate safety and subsequent distinction, and more useful to my audience, as showing that even when despondent they should never stop hoping to survive. Some, who were able to do so, fled to Cassius, or 150 to Brutus, or to Cornificius in Africa, who was also defending the democratic cause.[25] Most went to Sicily, however, because it was close to Italy, and Pompeius received them enthusiastically. Indeed he displayed a most intense con- 151 cern for these unfortunate people at that time, sending out heralds to invite everyone to come to him, and offering to those who saved them, whether slave or free man, double

[25] Quintus Cornificius was probably appointed governor of Africa Vetus by Julius Caesar in 44. In 43 he was proscribed and eventually defeated and killed by Titus Sextius, the governor of Africa Nova, in 42.

πουσι προλέγων διπλάσια τῶν διδομένων τοῖς αἱ-
ροῦσι· λέμβοι τε αὐτοῦ καὶ στρογγύλα ὑπήντα τοῖς
πλέουσι, καὶ τριήρεις τοὺς αἰγιαλοὺς ἐπέπλεον, σημεῖά τε ἀνίσχουσαι τοῖς ἀλωμένοις, καὶ τὸν ἐντυγχά-
152 νοντα περισῴζουσαι. αὐτός τε τοῖς ἀφικνουμένοις
ἀπήντα καὶ ἐσθῆτος αὐτίκα καὶ κατασκευῆς ἐμερί-
ζετο· τοῖς δὲ ἀξίοις καὶ ἐς στρατηγίας ἢ ναυαρχίας
ἐχρῆτο. σπονδῶν τέ οἱ πρὸς τοὺς τρεῖς γιγνομένων
ὕστερον, οὐ συνέθετο, πρὶν καὶ τούσδε τοὺς εἰς αὐτὸν
153 διαφυγόντας ἐς ταύτας περιλαβεῖν. ὁ μὲν δὴ χρησι-
μώτατος οὕτως ἀτυχούσῃ τῇ πατρίδι ἐγίγνετο, καὶ
δόξαν ἐκ τοῦδε ἀγαθήν, ἴδιον ἐπὶ τῇ πατρῴᾳ καὶ οὐχ
154 ἥσσονα τήνδε ἐκείνης, προσελάμβανεν· ἕτεροι δὲ
ἑτέρως φυγόντες ἢ κρυπτόμενοι μέχρι τῶν σπονδῶν,
οἱ μὲν ἐν χωρίοις ἢ τάφοις, οἱ δὲ ἐν αὐτῷ τῷ ἄστει,
σὺν ἐπινοίαις οἰκτραῖς διεγένοντο. φιλανδρίαι τε
παράδοξοι γυναικῶν ὤφθησαν καὶ παίδων ἐς πατέρας
εὔνοιαι καὶ θεραπόντων ὑπὲρ φύσιν ἐς δεσπότας. καὶ
τῶνδε ὅσα παραδοξότατα, ἀναγράψω.

155   37. Παῦλος, ὁ ἀδελφὸς Λεπίδου, τῶν λοχαγῶν
αὐτὸν ὡς ἀδελφὸν αὐτοκράτορος αἰδουμένων, ἐπὶ
ἀδείας ἐξέπλευσεν ἐς Βροῦτον καὶ ἐς Μίλητον μετὰ
Βροῦτον· ὅθεν οὐδὲ εἰρήνης ὕστερον γενομένης κα-
156 λούμενος ἐπανελθεῖν ἠξίωσε. Λεύκιον δέ, τὸν Ἀντωνίου
θεῖον, ἡ Ἀντωνίου μήτηρ ἀδελφὸν ὄντα εἶχεν οὐδ᾽ ἐπι-
κρύπτουσα, αἰδουμένων ἐς πολὺ καὶ τήνδε τῶν λοχα-
157 γῶν ὡς μητέρα αὐτοκράτορος. βιαζομένων δ᾽ ὕστερον
ἐξέθορεν ἐς τὴν ἀγορὰν καὶ προκαθημένῳ τῷ Ἀντωνίῳ

the rewards being given for capturing them. His small
boats and merchant vessels met those who were at sea,
while his warships sailed along the shore and made signals
to the outcasts, and saved any they found. Pompeius him-   152
self went to meet the newcomers and provided them immediately with clothing and equipment. To those capable,
he assigned military and naval commands. Later, when
negotiating peace with the triumvirs, he would make no
agreement until it also included these men who had taken
refuge with him. In this way he proved of great service   153
to his unfortunate country, and from this won a high reputation of his own in addition to, and no less significant
than, that of his father. Others made their escape in dif-   154
ferent ways, or remained in hiding until the treaty, and
survived by means of pitiable devices, some in the fields
or in tombs, others in Rome itself. Examples were to be
seen of the extraordinary love of wives for their husbands,
of devotion of sons to their fathers, and of goodwill of
slaves toward their masters that went beyond the natural
order. The most remarkable of these I will now relate.

37. Paullus, the brother of Lepidus,[26] safely made his   155
way by sea to Brutus, because the centurions deferred to
him as the brother of their commander. After the death of
Brutus he went to Miletus, from where he decided not to
return to Rome, even when invited later after peace was
restored. Antony's mother sheltered his uncle Lucius, her   156
brother, without even hiding him, and the centurions also
deferred to her for a long time as the mother of their commander. When, later, they used force, she rushed out into   157
the Forum where Antony was presiding with his fellow

26 See above, 12.45.

APPIAN

μετὰ τῶν συνάρχων ἔφη· "Ἐμαυτήν, ὦ αὐτοκράτορ,
μηνύω σοι Λεύκιον ὑποδεδέχθαι τε καὶ ἔχειν ἔτι καὶ
ἕξειν, ἕως ἂν ἡμᾶς ὁμοῦ κατακάνῃς· τὰ γὰρ ὅμοια καὶ
158   τοῖς ὑποδεδεγμένοις ἐπικεκήρυκται." ὁ δὲ αὐτὴν ἐπιμεμψάμενος ὡς ἀδελφὴν μὲν ἀγαθήν, μητέρα δὲ οὐκ
εὐγνώμονα—"Οὐ γὰρ νῦν χρῆναι περισῴζειν Λεύκιον,
ἀλλὰ κωλύειν ὅτε σου τὸν υἱὸν εἶναι πολέμιον ἐψηφίζετο"—παρεσκεύασεν ὅμως Πλάγκον ὑπατεύοντα κάθοδον τῷ Λευκίῳ ψηφίσασθαι.

159   38. Μεσσάλας δὲ ἐπιφανὴς καὶ νέος ἐς Βροῦτον
ἔφυγε, καὶ αὐτοῦ δείσαντες οἱ τρεῖς τὸ φρόνημα
προύγραψαν οὕτως· "Ἐπεὶ Μεσσάλαν ἀπέφηναν ἡμῖν
οἱ προσήκοντες αὐτῷ μηδὲ ἐπιδημεῖν, ὅτε Γάιος
Καῖσαρ ἀνῃρεῖτο, ἐξῃρήσθω τῶν προγραφέντων ὁ
160   Μεσσάλας." ὁ δὲ τὴν μὲν συγγνώμην οὐκ ἐδέξατο,
Βρούτου δὲ καὶ Κασσίου περὶ Θρᾴκην πεσόντων καὶ
τοῦ στρατοῦ πολλοῦ τε ἔτι ὄντος καὶ ναῦς καὶ χρήματα καὶ ἐλπίδας ἔχοντος οὐκ ἀσθενεῖς, ἄρχειν σφῶν
τὸν Μεσσάλαν αἱρουμένων οὐκ ἀνασχόμενος, ἔπεισεν
αὐτοὺς ἐνδόντας ἐπιβαρούσῃ τῇ τύχῃ μεταστρατεύ-
161   σασθαι τοῖς ἀμφὶ τὸν Ἀντώνιον. οἰκειότερος δὲ ὢν
Ἀντωνίῳ συνῆν, μέχρι κρατούσης Ἀντωνίου Κλεοπάτρας ἐπιμεμψάμενος ἐς Καίσαρα μετῆλθεν. ὁ δὲ
αὐτὸν ὕπατόν τε ἀπέφηνεν ἀντὶ αὐτοῦ Ἀντωνίου, ἀπο-
χειροτονηθέντος, ὅτε αὖθις ἐψηφίζετο εἶναι πολέμιος,

magistrates, and said, "I denounce myself to you, commander, for taking Lucius into my house, where I am keeping him and will continue to keep him until you kill us together. For the same penalties have been decreed for the proscribed and those who take them in." Antony, although admitting she was a good sister, reproached her for being an irrational mother, saying, "You should not be trying to save Lucius now, but should have stopped him when he was voting your son a public enemy." Nevertheless, he got Plancus, who was consul, to pass a vote restoring his rights to Lucius. 158

38. When Messalla, a young man of distinction, fled to Brutus, the triumvirs, fearing his high spirit, published the following edict: "Since the relatives of Messalla have made it clear to us that he was not even in the city when Gaius Caesar was assassinated, Messalla is to be removed from the list of the proscribed."[27] Although he did not accept the pardon, after Brutus and Cassius had fallen in Thrace, and their army, still numerous and in possession of ships and money and robust hopes, chose Messalla to take command of them, he refused and persuaded them to yield to the weight of fate and join forces with Antony. He joined Antony's entourage and was quite close to him until Cleopatra gained power over Antony, and Messalla denounced him and went over to Octavian's side. Octavian appointed him consul in place of Antony himself, when the latter was deposed after again being voted a public enemy. He held a naval command at the battle of Actium 159 160 161

[27] As Appian outlines, Marcus Valerius Messalla Corvinus (consul 31) had a long and distinguished career, eventually dying in AD 8.

καὶ περὶ Ἄκτιον ναυαρχήσαντα κατὰ τοῦ Ἀντωνίου
στρατηγὸν ἔπεμψεν ἐπὶ Κελτοὺς ἀφισταμένους καὶ
162 νικήσαντι ἔδωκε θριαμβεῦσαι. Βύβλος δὲ ἐσπείσατο
ἅμα τῷ Μεσσάλᾳ καὶ ἐναυάρχησεν Ἀντωνίῳ διαλλαγάς τε πολλάκις Ἀντωνίῳ καὶ Καίσαρι ἐς ἀλλήλους
ἐπόρθμευσε καὶ στρατηγὸς ἀπεδείχθη Συρίας ὑπὸ
Ἀντωνίου καὶ στρατηγῶν ἔτι αὐτῆς ἀπέθανεν.

163   39. Ἀκίλιος δὲ ἔφευγε μὲν τῆς πόλεως λαθών,
οἰκέτου δ' αὐτὸν ἐμφήναντος ὁπλίταις, τοὺς ὁπλίτας
ἔπεισεν ἐλπίδι χρημάτων πλεόνων πέμψαι τινὰς ἀπὸ
σφῶν πρὸς τὴν γυναῖκα μετὰ συμβόλων ὧν αὐτὸς
ἐδίδου. ἡ δὲ τοῖς ἐλθοῦσιν τὸν κόσμον αὐτῆς ἅπαντα
προθεῖσα ἔφη διδόναι μὲν ὡς ἀντιδώσουσιν, ἃ ὑπέσχοντο, οὐκ εἰδέναι δέ, εἰ ἀντιδώσουσιν. οὐ μὴν
ἐψεύσθη τῆς φιλανδρίας· οἱ γὰρ ὁπλῖται καὶ ναῦν
ἐμίσθωσαν τῷ Ἀκιλίῳ καὶ προύπεμψαν ἐς Σικελίαν.
164 Λέντλος δέ, ἀξιούσης αὐτῷ συμφεύγειν τῆς γυναικὸς
καὶ ἐς τοῦτο αὐτὸν ἐπιτηρούσης, οὐκ ἐθέλων αὐτὴν
συγκινδυνεύειν ἑαυτῷ, λαθὼν ἔφυγεν ἐς Σικελίαν,
στρατηγὸς δὲ ἀποδειχθεὶς ὑπὸ Πομπηίου ἐσήμηνεν,
165 ὅτι σῴζοιτο καὶ στρατηγοίη. ἡ δ', ὅποι γῆς ἐστιν ὁ
ἀνήρ, ἐπιγνοῦσα τὴν μητέρα φυλάσσουσαν ἐξέφυγε
καὶ ἥδε σὺν θεράπουσι δύο· μεθ' ὧν ὥδευεν ἐπιμόχθως καὶ εὐτελῶς οἷα θεράπαινα, μέχρι διέπλευσεν

---

28 Lucius Calpurnius Bibulus was the son of the Marcus Bibulus who had been Julius Caesar's colleague in the consulship of

against Antony, and then Octavian sent him as a general against the Celts who were in revolt, and awarded him a triumph for his victory over them. Bibulus made his peace   162 at the same time as Messalla, was given a naval command by Antony, and often served as an intermediary in the negotiations between Octavian and Antony. He was appointed governor of Syria by Antony and died while still in office.[28]

39. Acilius escaped from the city without being seen,   163 but a slave pointed him out to the soldiers. He persuaded them, however, by the hope of a larger reward, to send some of their group to his wife with proofs of identity that he gave them. When they arrived she offered them all of her jewelry, saying that she was giving it to them on the understanding that they would fulfill what they promised in return, although, so she said, she was not sure they would. But she was not disappointed in her love of her husband, for the soldiers hired a ship for Acilius and sent him off to Sicily. When his wife asked to accompany him   164 in flight and was keeping a close eye on him to that end, Lentulus was not prepared for her to share the danger with him, and so fled to Sicily without letting her know. After Pompeius appointed him a general, Lentulus sent her a message to say that he was safe and holding a command. On learning what part of the world he had gone   165 to, and avoiding her mother's surveillance, she too made her escape with two servants. Together with them she went on the road, living rough and cheaply like a slave

59. Having sided with Brutus, he was proscribed, but he surrendered to Antony after the battle of Philippi in 42.

ἐς Μεσσήνην ἀπὸ Ῥηγίου περὶ ἑσπέραν. καὶ οὐ δυσχερῶς τὴν στρατηγίδα σκηνὴν μαθοῦσα, εὗρε τὸν
Λέντλον οὐχ οἷα στρατηγόν, ἀλλ᾽ ἐν χαμευνίῳ καὶ
κόμῃ καὶ διαίτῃ πονηρᾷ πόθῳ τῆς γυναικός.

166   40. Ἀπουλήιῳ δὲ ἠπείλησεν ἡ γυνὴ καταμηνύσειν
αὐτόν, εἰ μόνος φεύγοι· καὶ ὁ μὲν ἄκων αὐτὴν ἐπήγετο, συνήνεγκε δὲ ἐς τὴν φυγὴν αὐτῷ τὸ ἀνύποπτον,
ἅμα γυναικὶ καὶ θεράπουσι καὶ θεραπαίναις ὁδεύοντι
167 φανερῶς. Ἄντιον δὲ ἡ γυνὴ στρωματοδέσμῳ κατ-
είλησε καὶ ἐπέθηκε τοῖς μισθοῦ φέρουσι καὶ διή-
νεγκεν ἀπὸ τῆς οἰκίας ἐπὶ θάλασσαν, ὅθεν ἔφυγεν ἐς
168 Σικελίαν. Ῥηγῖνον δὲ ἡ γυνὴ νυκτὸς ἐς ὑπόνομον
λυμάτων καθῆκεν, ἐς ὃν ἡμέρας οὐχ ὑποστάντων ἐμ-
βῆναι τῶν ὁπλιτῶν διὰ δυσοδμίαν, νυκτὸς ἄλλης εἰς
ἀνθρακέα ἐσκεύασε καὶ ὄνον ἄνθρακας φέροντα ἐλαύ-
νειν ἔδωκεν· αὐτὴ δὲ ἐκ βραχέος διαστήματος ἡγεῖτο
169 φορείῳ φερομένη. τῶν δὲ ἀμφὶ τὰς πύλας ὁπλιτῶν
τινος τὸ φορεῖον ὑπονοήσαντός τε καὶ ἐρευνωμένου,
δείσας ὁ Ῥηγῖνος ἐπέδραμε καὶ ὡς ὁδῷ χρώμενος
ἠξίου τὸν ὁπλίτην φείδεσθαι γυναικῶν. ὁ δὲ αὐτὸν ὡς
ἀνθρακέα μετ᾽ ὀργῆς ἀμειβόμενος ἐγνώρισεν (ἐστρά-
τευτο γὰρ ὑπ᾽ αὐτῷ ποτε ἐν Συρίᾳ) καὶ "Ἄπιθι
χαίρων," εἶπεν, "Αὐτοκράτορ· τοῦτο γάρ μοι προσήκει
170 καὶ νῦν καλεῖν σε." Κοπώνιον δὲ τὸ γύναιον ᾔτησε

woman, until she made the crossing from Rhegium to Messena one evening. She had no difficulty locating the commander's tent, and there she found Lentulus, not looking like an officer, but lying on a camp bed with dirty hair and living a wretched existence, pining for his wife.

40. In the case of Apuleius, his wife threatened to in- 166 form on him if he fled without her. Although he took her with him unwillingly, the fact that he was traveling openly with his wife, and male and female attendants, proved advantageous to his flight. Antius' wife bundled him up in 167 a bag of bedclothes and paid some porters to carry him from the house to the coast, from where he escaped to Sicily. Reginus' wife sent him down into underground 168 sewers one night, which the soldiers could not stand to enter during the day because of the foul smell.[29] Another night she disguised him as a charcoal dealer, and gave him a donkey to drive and carry the charcoal. She herself led the way, carried in a litter a short distance in front. One of 169 the soldiers at the city gates was suspicious of her litter and searched it. Frightened by this, Reginus hurried forward and, as if he were an ordinary traveler, urged the soldier to leave women alone. The soldier, who took him for a charcoal dealer, was replying angrily when he recognized him (for he had once served under him in Syria), and said, "Go on your way without fear, general, for it is proper that I address you as such even now." Coponius' 170 wife, although previously chaste, begged a deal with An-

---

[29] This can hardly be anyone other than Gaius Antistius Reginus, one of Caesar's legates in Gaul from 53 to 50, who is perhaps the same Antistius who later supported Sextus Pompeius (see App. *BCiv.* 5.139.579).

παρὰ Ἀντωνίου, σώφρων μὲν οὖσα τέως, ἀτυχήματι
δὲ τὸ ἀτύχημα ἰωμένη.

171 41. Γέταν δὲ ὁ υἱὸς ἐν εὐρυχώρῳ τῆς οἰκίας ἔδοξε
καίειν ὡς ἀπαγξάμενον καὶ λαθὼν ἐν ἀγρῷ νεωνήτῳ
κατέλιπεν, ἔνθα ὁ πρεσβύτης μεταμορφῶν ἑαυτὸν
ἐπεδήσατο διφθέραν ἐς τὸν ἕτερον ὀφθαλμόν. καὶ
τῶν σπονδῶν γενομένων ἔλυσε τὴν διφθέραν, καὶ ὁ
172 ὀφθαλμὸς ὑπὸ τῆς ἀργίας δεδαπάνητο. Ὄππιον δὲ ὁ
υἱός, ὑπὸ γήρως ἀσθενεστάτου μένειν ἐθέλοντα, ἔφε-
ρεν ἐπὶ τοῦ σώματος, ἕως ἐξήγαγέ τε διὰ τῶν πυλῶν
καὶ τὸ λοιπὸν μέχρι Σικελίας ἄγων ἢ φέρων ἐκόμισεν,
οὐδενὸς ἄρα τὸ σχῆμα ὑπονοήσαντος ἢ ἐνυβρίσαν-
τος, οἷόν που καὶ τὸν Αἰνείαν γράφουσιν αἰδέσιμον
173 τοῖς πολεμίοις γενέσθαι φέροντα τὸν πατέρα. καὶ τὸν
νεανίαν ὁ δῆμος ἐπαινῶν ὕστερον ἀπέφηνεν ἀγορα-
νόμον· δεδημευμένης δ' αὐτῷ τῆς οὐσίας οὐκ ἔχοντι
τῆς ἀρχῆς τὸ δαπάνημα οἵ τε χειροτέχναι τὰ ἐς τὴν
ἀρχὴν ἀμισθὶ συνειργάσαντο, καὶ τῶν θεωμένων ἕκαστος ἐπὶ τὴν ὀρχήστραν ὅσον ἐβούλετο νόμισμα ἐρ-
174 ρίπτει, ἕως τὸν ἄνδρα κατεπλούτισαν. Ἀρριανοῦ δὲ
καὶ ἐν τῇ στήλῃ κεκόλαπτο ἐκ διαθηκῶν· "Τὸν ἐνθάδε
κείμενον υἱὸς οὐ προγραφεὶς προγραφέντα ἔκρυψέ τε
καὶ συνέφυγε καὶ περιέσωσε."

175 42. Μετέλλω δὲ ἤστην υἱός τε καὶ πατήρ· καὶ αὐτοῖν
ὁ μὲν πατὴρ στρατηγῶν Ἀντωνίῳ περὶ Ἄκτιον αἰχμ-

tony for her husband's life, thus curing one misfortune with another.[30]

41. Geta's son pretended to cremate the body of his father in the courtyard of their house, claiming that he had hanged himself, but took him secretly to a newly bought farm, where the old man changed his appearance by putting a bandage over one of his eyes. After the amnesty, he took off the bandage, but he had lost sight in that eye through lack of use. Oppius, being very weak because of old age, wanted to stay at Rome, but his son carried him on his back until he had brought him outside the gates, and took him the rest of the way to Sicily by guiding or carrying him. I suppose no one was suspicious of their appearance, or offered them violence, in the same way perhaps as written accounts say that Aeneas gained the respect of his enemies when he carried his father. In admiration of the young man, the people later elected him aedile, and when he could not meet the expenses of the office, as his property had been confiscated, the workmen built what he needed for his magistracy without charge, and all the spectators threw such coins as they were willing to give into the orchestra, until they made him a rich man.[31] Arrianus even left instructions in his will for the following inscription on his gravestone: "Here lies a man who was proscribed. His son, who was not proscribed, hid him, fled with him and saved his life."

42. There were two men named Metellus, father and son. The father held a command under Antony at the

171

172

173

174

175

---

[30] Gaius Coponius, praetor in 49, had commanded part of Pompey's fleet.   [31] The story of Quintus Oppius (the son), aedile in 37, is also recounted in Cass. Dio 48.53.4–6.

ἄλωτος ἑάλω καὶ ἠγνοεῖτο, ὁ δὲ υἱὸς τῷ Καίσαρι συν-
εστρατεύετο καὶ ἐστρατηγήκει καὶ ὅδε περὶ τὸ Ἄκτιον.
176 ἐν δὲ Σάμῳ διακρίνοντι τῷ Καίσαρι τοὺς αἰχμαλώτους
ὁ μὲν παῖς συνήδρευεν, ὁ δὲ πρεσβύτης ἤγετο κόμης
τε ἔμπλεως καὶ δύης καὶ ῥύπου καὶ τῆς ἐκ τῶνδε
μεταμορφώσεως. ὡς δὲ ἐν τῇ τάξει τῶν αἰχμαλώτων
ὑπὸ τοῦ κήρυκος ἀνεκλήθη, ἀνέθορεν ὁ υἱὸς ἐκ τοῦ
συνεδρίου καὶ μόλις ἐπιγνοὺς τὸν πατέρα ἠσπάζετο
177 σὺν οἰμωγῇ· ἐπισχὼν δέ ποτε τοῦ θρήνου πρὸς τὸν
Καίσαρα ἔφη· "Οὗτος μέν σοι πολέμιος γέγονεν, ὦ
Καῖσαρ, ἐγὼ δὲ σύμμαχος· καὶ χρὴ τοῦτον μέν σοι
δοῦναι δίκην, ἐμὲ δὲ γέρας εὑρέσθαι. αἰτῶ δή σε τὸν
πατέρα σῴζειν δι' ἐμὲ ἢ δι' ἐκεῖνον ἐμὲ συγκατακα-
178 νεῖν." οἴκτου δὲ ἐξ ἁπάντων γενομένου μεθῆκε σῴζεσθαι τὸν Μέτελλον ὁ Καῖσαρ, καίτοι πολεμιώτατον
αὐτῷ γενόμενον καὶ δωρεῶν πολλῶν, εἰ μεταθοῖτο
πρὸς αὐτὸν ἀπ' Ἀντωνίου, πολλάκις ὑπεριδόντα.

179   43. Μᾶρκον δὲ οἱ θεράποντες σὺν εὐνοίᾳ καὶ τύχῃ
πάντα τὸν τῆς προγραφῆς χρόνον διεφύλαξαν ἔνδον
ἐπὶ τῆς οἰκίας, μέχρι τῆς ἀδείας δοθείσης ὁ Μᾶρκος
180 ἐξῄει τῆς οἰκίας ὡς ἀπὸ φυγῆς. Ἵρτιος δὲ σὺν τοῖς
οἰκέταις ἐκφυγὼν τῆς πόλεως διώδευε τὴν Ἰταλίαν,
ἐκλύων τε δεσμώτας καὶ συνάγων τοὺς ἀποδιδράσκον-
τας καὶ πολίχνια δῃῶν, ὀλίγα πρῶτον, εἶτα καὶ μείζω,

---

32 This story is misplaced in Appian's account, having nothing
to do with the triumviral proscriptions, but is presumably included at this point because it concerns the relationship of fathers
and sons. The Caecilii Metelli were a famous Republican family,

battle of Actium and was taken prisoner, but not recognized; the son was serving with Octavian and he too held a command at Actium. At Samos Octavian was passing   176
judgment on the prisoners, and the son was sitting in counsel with him, when the senior Metellus was led forward unshaven, miserable and dirty and with his appearance completely changed as a result. When he was summoned by the herald in his rank of the prisoners, his son sprang from the dais, and, recognizing his father with difficulty, embraced him with a cry of anguish. Eventually   177
restraining his grief, he said to Octavian, "This man was your enemy, Caesar, I was your fellow soldier. It is required that you punish him and that I should be rewarded. I ask you either to spare my father on my account, or to kill me too on his account." There was an expression of   178
compassion from everyone, and Octavian spared Metellus' life, even though he had been bitterly hostile to him, and had often turned down the many gifts Octavian had offered if he would desert Antony and come over to his side.[32]

43. As for Marcus, his slaves protected him with good-   179
will and luck inside his own house for the whole period of the proscriptions, until the amnesty was declared and Marcus left the house as if he was returning from exile.[33]
Hirtius escaped from the city with his slaves and traveled   180
through Italy releasing prisoners, collecting runaways, and attacking townships, small ones at first and then larger ones. Eventually he commanded a sufficient force to sub-

but it is not possible to identify those involved in the story (which is not recorded elsewhere).

[33] As Marcus is only a praenomen, this is more likely to be a Marcius, probably the son of Quintus Marcius Rex (consul 68).

μέχρι χειρὸς ἱκανῆς ἐκράτησε καὶ τὸ Βρεττίων ἔθνος
ἐχειρώσατο καί, στρατοῦ πεμφθέντος ἐπ᾽ αὐτόν, ἐς
181 Πομπήιον μεθ᾽ ὅσων εἶχε διέπλευσε. Ῥεστίωνι δὲ οἰο-
μένῳ μόνῳ φεύγειν οἰκέτης εἵπετο λανθάνων, ἀνάθρε-
πτος μὲν αὐτοῦ Ῥεστίωνος καὶ πολλὰ πρότερον εὖ
182 παθών, διὰ δὲ μοχθηρίαν ὕστερον ἐστιγμένος. ἀνα-
παυομένῳ δὲ ἐν ἕλει τῷ Ῥεστίωνι ἐπιστὰς ὁ θεράπων
ἐξέπληξε μὲν αὐτίκα ὀφθείς, δεδοικότι δὲ ἔφη οὐ τῶν
παρόντων στιγμάτων αἰσθάνεσθαι μᾶλλον ἢ μνημο-
νεύειν τῶν πρότερον εὐεργετημάτων. καὶ αὐτὸν εἴς τι
σπήλαιον ἀναπαύσας εἰργάζετο καὶ τροφὰς αὐτῷ
183 συνέλεγεν, ὡς ἐδύνατο. ὑπονοίας δέ τινος ἀμφὶ τὸ
σπήλαιον τοῖς ἐγγὺς ὁπλίταις περὶ τοῦ Ῥεστίωνος
γενομένης καὶ χωρούντων ἐπ᾽ αὐτόν, ὁ οἰκέτης εἵπετο
συνεὶς καί τινα πρεσβύτην προοδεύοντα προδραμὼν
184 ἀπέκτεινε καὶ τὴν κεφαλὴν ἀπέτεμεν. ἐκπλαγέντων δὲ
τῶν ὁπλιτῶν καὶ ὡς ἀνδροφόνον ὁδοιπόρου περισχόντων, "Ῥεστίωνα," ἔφη, "Ἔκτεινα, τὸν ἐμαυτοῦ δεσπότην, τάδε μοι τὰ στίγματα ἐγχαράξαντα." οἱ μὲν
δὴ τὴν κεφαλὴν αὐτὸν ἀφελόμενοι διὰ τὸ γέρας, ἠπεί-
γοντο μάτην ἐς τὸ ἄστυ, ὁ δὲ τὸν δεσπότην ἀναστή-
σας διέπλευσεν ἐς Σικελίαν.
185   44. Ἄππιον δὲ ἀναπαυόμενον ἐν ἐπαύλει, τῶν ὁπλιτῶν ἐπιθεόντων, οἰκέτης τὴν ἑαυτοῦ ἐσθῆτα ἐνέδυσε,
καὶ αὐτὸς εἰς τὴν εὐνὴν οἷα δεσπότης ἀνακλιθεὶς ἑκὼν
ἀπέθανεν ἀντὶ τοῦ δεσπότου, παρεστῶτος ὡς οἰκέτου.
186 Μενηνίου δὲ τὴν οἰκίαν καταλαβόντων ὁπλιτῶν, θερά-

due the people of Bruttium. When an army was sent against him he sailed across with all his resources to join Pompeius. Restio believed that he was alone in his flight, 181 but without his knowledge he was followed by a slave who had been brought up in Restio's own house, and who although previously very well treated had later been branded for misbehavior. While Restio was taking a break in a 182 marsh the slave came up to him and startled him by his sudden appearance, but said to the terrified Restio that he was more mindful of the former kindnesses shown to him than he was aware of the present marks branded on him. He found a resting place for his master in a cave, and took work to collect food for him as best he could. The soldiers 183 in the neighborhood became suspicious of the cave with regard to Restio, and made their way there to get him. Understanding this, the slave followed them and rushed up and killed an old man who was walking along the road in front of them, and cut off his head. The soldiers were 184 astonished, and arrested him for killing a traveler, but he said, "I have killed Restio, my master, the man who branded me with these marks." The soldiers took the head from him to get the reward, and hurried off, in vain, to the city. The slave moved his master away and sailed across to Sicily.

44. When Appius was resting in a farmhouse and the 185 soldiers burst in, a slave put on his master's clothes lay down on the bed as if he was the master and voluntarily died instead of his master, who was standing beside him like a slave.[34] When soldiers seized the house of Mene- 186

---

[34] Valerius Maximus (6.8.6) and Macrobius (*Sat.* 1.11.60) tell a very similar story about a man named Panapio, which is close enough to Appius to explain a mistake by Appian.

πων ἐς τὸ τοῦ δεσπότου φορεῖον ἐνέβη καὶ ὑπὸ τῶν
ὁμοδούλων συνεργούντων ἐξεφέρετο, ἕως ὅδε μὲν ὡς
Μενήνιος ἑκὼν ἀνήρητο, Μενήνιος δὲ ἐς Σικελίαν δι-
187 έφυγεν. Οὐίνιον δὲ ἀπελεύθερος αὐτοῦ Οὐινίου, Φιλή-
μων, οἰκίαν κεκτημένος λαμπράν, ἐν τῷ μεσαιτάτῳ
τῆς οἰκίας ἔκρυψεν ἐν λάρνακι, ἃς ἀπὸ σιδήρου ἐς
χρημάτων ἢ βιβλίων ἔχουσι φυλακήν· καὶ νυκτὸς
188 ἔτρεφε μέχρι τῶν σπονδῶν. ἕτερος δὲ ἀπελεύθερος,
τάφον δεσπότου φυλάσσων, τὸν δεσπόσυνον προγραφέντα ἐφύλασσεν ἐν τῷ τάφῳ μετὰ τοῦ πατρός.
189 Λουκρήτιος ἀλώμενος σὺν δυσὶ θεράπουσιν ἀγαθοῖς
ὑπὸ ἀπορίας τῶν τροφῶν ᾔει πρὸς τὴν γυναῖκα, φορείῳ φερόμενος ὑπὸ τῶν οἰκετῶν οἷά τις ἄρρωστος, ἐς
τὴν πόλιν. ἑνὸς δὲ τῶν φερόντων τὸ σκέλος συντρί-
190 βεντος τῷ ἑτέρῳ τὴν χεῖρα ἐπιθεὶς ᾔει. παρὰ δὲ ταῖς
πύλαις γενόμενος, ἔνθα αὐτοῦ καὶ ὁ πατὴρ ὑπὸ Σύλλα
προγραφεὶς ἑαλώκει, εἶδε λόχον ὁπλιτῶν ἐκτρέχοντα
καὶ πρὸς τὸ συγκύρημα τοῦ τόπου καταπλαγεὶς συν-
191 εκρύφθη μετὰ τοῦ θεράποντος ἐν τάφῳ. τυμβωρύχων
δὲ τοὺς τάφους ἐρευνωμένων, ὁ θεράπων ἑαυτὸν τοῖς
τυμβωρύχοις παρέσχε περιδύειν, μέχρι Λουκρήτιον
192 ἐπὶ τὰς πύλας διαφυγεῖν. ἐκεῖ δὲ αὐτὸν ὁ Λουκρήτιος
περιμείνας τε καὶ τῆς ἑαυτοῦ μερισάμενος ἐσθῆτος,
ᾖκε πρὸς τὴν γυναῖκα καὶ ὑπ' αὐτῆς ἐκρύπτετο ἐπὶ
διπλῆς ὀροφῆς μεταξύ, μέχρι τινὲς αὐτὸν ἐρρύσαντο

nius, a slave got into his master's litter and was taken away by his fellow slaves, who were complicit in the affair, until he was executed, willingly standing in for Menenius, while Menenius escaped to Sicily. In the case of Vinius, Phile- 187 mon, a freedman of his who owned a splendid house hid him in the innermost part of the house, in a chest, one of those made of iron which people use for keeping money or books, and he would give him food at night until the dec- laration of the amnesty. Another freedman, who was the 188 caretaker of his master's tomb, protected his master's son, who had been proscribed, by keeping him in the tomb alongside his father. Lucretius, who had been wandering 189 around as an outcast with two faithful slaves, was forced by lack of supplies to go to his wife, and was carried to Rome by the two slaves in a litter as he was a sick man.[35] One of the bearers broke his leg, so Lucretius went on by foot, leaning on the other slave. When they reached the gates 190 where his father had been arrested—he too had been pro- scribed, by Sulla—Lucretius saw a cohort of soldiers com- ing out of the city on the double. Unnerved by the coinci- dence of being in the same place, he hid with the slave in a tomb. When tomb robbers came to investigate the tombs, 191 the slave allowed himself to be stripped by them until Lu- cretius could escape to the gates. There Lucretius waited 192 for him, shared his clothing with him, and having made his way to his wife, was hidden by her in the space between a double ceiling, until some friends got him pardoned by the

---

[35] This is almost certainly the Lucretius Vespillo mentioned by Caesar (*B Civ.* 3.7.1) as the commander of Pompeian ships in the Adriatic in 48. He was made consul by Augustus in 19.

παρὰ τῶν προγραψάντων. καὶ ὕστερον ἐπὶ εἰρήνης
ὑπάτευσεν.

193   45. Σέργιος δὲ ἐκρύφθη παρ' αὐτῷ Ἀντωνίῳ, μέχρι
Πλάγκον ὑπατεύοντα ὁ Ἀντώνιος ἔπεισε κάθοδον
αὐτῷ ψηφίσασθαι. καὶ ἐπὶ τῷδε ὁ Σέργιος ὕστερον,
ἐν τῇ Καίσαρος καὶ Ἀντωνίου στάσει, τῆς βουλῆς
ψηφιζομένης εἶναι πολέμιον τὸν Ἀντώνιον, μόνος τὴν
194   ἀπολύουσαν ἔφερε φανερῶς. καὶ οἵδε μὲν οὕτως ἐσώ-
ζοντο, Πομπώνιος δὲ εἰς στρατηγοῦ σχῆμα κοσμή-
σας ἑαυτὸν καὶ τοὺς θεράποντας ἐς ὑπηρέτας σκευ-
άσας τὴν πόλιν ὡς στρατηγὸς ὑπὸ ῥαβδούχοις
διῆλθεν, ἐπιθλιβόντων αὐτὸν τῶν ὑπηρετῶν, ἵνα μὴ
γνωσθείη πρὸς ἑτέρου, καὶ παρὰ ταῖς πύλαις ὀχη-
μάτων τε δημοσίων ἐπέβη καὶ τὴν Ἰταλίαν διώδευεν,
ἀποδεχομένων αὐτὸν καὶ παραπεμπόντων ἁπάντων
οἷα στρατηγὸν ὑπὸ τῶν τριῶν ἀνδρῶν ἐπὶ σπονδὰς ἐς
Πομπήιον ἀπεσταλμένον, μέχρι καὶ δημοσίᾳ τριήρει
διέπλευσε πρὸς ἐκεῖνον.

195   46. Ἀπουλήιος δὲ καὶ Ἀρρούντιος ὑποκριθέντες εἶναι λοχαγοὶ καὶ τοὺς θεράποντας ἐς στρατιώτας
σκευάσαντες, τὰς μὲν πύλας διέδραμον ὡς λοχαγοὶ
διώκοντες ἑτέρους, τὴν δὲ λοιπὴν ὁδὸν διελόμενοι
τοὺς δεσμώτας ἐξέλυον καὶ τοὺς ἀποδράντας συνέλεγον, μέχρι χειρὸς ἱκανῆς ἑκατέρῳ γενομένης σημεῖά
196   τε ἦν ἤδη καὶ ὅπλα καὶ ὄψις στρατοῦ. χωρῶν δὲ
ἑκάτερος αὐτῶν ἐπὶ θάλασσαν, ἀμφί τινι λόφῳ σταθ-
μεύουσι, μεγάλῳ δέει καθορῶντες ἀλλήλους. ἅμα δὲ
ἕω περινεύοντες ἐκ τοῦ λόφου ἔδοξαν ἀλλήλους ἑκάτε-

proscribers. Later, with the return of peace, he held the consulship.

45. Sergius was hidden in the house of Antony himself 193 until Antony persuaded the consul Plancus to pass a vote for his return. As a result, later on, during the civil discord between Octavian and Antony when the senate was voting to declare Antony a public enemy, Sergius was the only one to vote openly against the proposal. Such was the way 194 in which the men I have mentioned were saved. As for Pomponius, he disguised himself as a praetor and having dressed his slaves up as attendants crossed the city like a praetor escorted by lictors, his servants crowding around him so that he would not be recognized by anyone else. At the city gates he commandeered official vehicles and journeyed through Italy, with everyone welcoming him and escorting him on his way, on the assumption that he was a praetor sent by the triumvirs to Pompeius to negotiate a treaty. Eventually he sailed across to Pompeius on an official warship.[36]

46. Appuleius and Arruntius, on the other hand, pre- 195 tended to be centurions, disguised their slaves as soldiers, and rushed out through the city gates like centurions in pursuit of others. For the rest of their journey they took separate routes, releasing prisoners and collecting fugitives until each had a substantial force which now had standards and arms and looked like an army. They both 196 made their way to the coast, where they set up camp on either side of a hill, viewing each other with great apprehension. At daybreak, peering around the hill, each

---

[36] Valerius Maximus (7.3.9) recounts the same story but identifies the proscribed man as Sentius Saturninus Vetulo.

ρος στρατὸν ἐπὶ σφᾶς ἐπιπεμφθέντα εἶναι καὶ συμ-
πλακέντες ἐμάχοντο, μέχρι ποτὲ ἔγνωσαν καὶ τὰ
ὅπλα ἀπερρίπτουν καὶ ὠλοφύροντο καὶ τὴν τύχην ὡς
197 ἐπιβαροῦσάν σφισιν ἐς ἅπαντα ἐπεμέμφοντο. δια-
πλεύσαντες δὲ ὁ μὲν ἐς Βροῦτον, ὁ δ᾽ ἐς Πομπήιον, ὁ
μὲν τῷ Πομπηίῳ συγκατῆλθεν, ὁ δὲ ἐστρατήγησε
τῷ Βρούτῳ Βιθυνίας καὶ Βρούτου πεσόντος Ἀντωνίῳ
198 παραδοὺς Βιθυνίαν κατήχθη. Οὐεντίδιον δὲ ἀπελεύθερος εὐθὺς μὲν προγραφέντα κατέδησεν ὡς παραδώ-
σων τοῖς σφαγεῦσι, νυκτὸς δὲ τοὺς θεράποντας ἔπεισε
καὶ ἐσκεύασεν ὡς ὁπλίτας καὶ τὸν δεσπότην ὡς λοχαγὸν ἐξήγαγε· τήν τε ἄλλην Ἰταλίαν μέχρι Σικελίας
διώδευσαν καὶ συγκατέλυσαν πολλάκις ἑτέροις λοχαγοῖς ζητοῦσιν Οὐεντίδιον.

199   47. Ἕτερον ἐν τάφῳ κρύπτων ἀπελεύθερος, οὐ φέροντα φαντασίαν τάφου, μετήγαγεν ἐς φαῦλον οἴκημα
μισθωτόν. στρατιώτου δ᾽ αὐτῷ παρακατοικισθέντος,
οὐδὲ τοῦτον φέρων τὸν φόβον ἐς θαυμαστὴν τόλμαν
ἐκ δειλίας μετέβαλε καὶ κειράμενος ἡγεῖτο ἐν αὐτῇ
200 Ῥώμῃ διδασκαλείου μέχρι τῶν σπονδῶν. Οὐολούσιος
δὲ ἀγορανομῶν προεγράφη καὶ φίλον ὀργιαστὴν τῆς
Ἴσιδος ἔχων ᾔτησε τὴν στολὴν καὶ τὰς ὀθόνας ἐνέδυ
τὰς ποδήρεις καὶ τὴν τοῦ κυνὸς κεφαλὴν ἐπέθετο καὶ
διῆλθεν οὕτως ὀργιάζων αὐτῷ σχήματι ἐς Πομπήιον.

---

37 This is presumably the Marcus Appuleius (consul 20) mentioned in Book 3 (63.259; see n. 28). Lucius Arruntius commanded the center of Octavian's fleet at Actium (Plut. *Ant.* 66.3).

thought the other was an army sent against them, and coming to close quarters they began to fight a battle. Eventually at some point they realized what was happening, threw down their weapons and in their grief blamed fate for weighing heavily on them in all matters. Then they took ship, Appuleius to join Brutus and Arruntius to Pompeius. The latter returned from exile with Pompeius, the former took command of Bithynia for Brutus, and when Brutus fell, surrendered Bithynia to Antony and was recalled from exile.[37] As soon as Ventidius was proscribed, a freedman tied him up as if he was going to hand him over to the executioners. During the night, however, he prevailed on the slaves, disguised them as soldiers, and took his master away as if he were a centurion. On their journey through the rest of Italy to Sicily, they often stopped for the night in the company of other centurions looking for Ventidius.

47. A freedman hid another proscribed man in a tomb, but as the latter could not bear the mental image of the place, the freedman rented a miserable dwelling and moved him there. When a soldier moved in beside him, this fear was also too much for him to take, but instead of cowardice he adopted an amazing daring, and having cut his hair ran a school in Rome until the amnesty. Volusius was proscribed while holding the office of aedile. He had a friend who was an initiate of the cult of Isis, and asked him for his costume: having put on the ankle-length linen robe and the dog's head, he traveled to Pompeius celebrat-

197

198

199

200

He was made consul in 22. Seneca (*Epist.* 114.17) reports that he wrote a *History of the Punic War*.

201   Σίττιον δὲ Καληνοί, πολίτην σφῶν ὄντα καὶ πολλὰ ἐς
αὐτοὺς ἐκ περιουσίας δαψιλοῦς ἀναλώσαντα, ἐφύλασ-
σον, σιδηροφοροῦντές τε ὑπὲρ αὐτοῦ καὶ τοῖς οἰκέταις
ἀπειλοῦντες καὶ τοὺς στρατιώτας ἀπερύκοντες ἀπὸ
τῶν τειχῶν, μέχρι μαραινομένου τοῦ κακοῦ καὶ ἐς
τοὺς τρεῖς ἐπρέσβευσαν ὑπὲρ αὐτοῦ καὶ ἔτυχον Σίττιον τῆς ἄλλης Ἰταλίας εἰργόμενον ἐν τῇ πατρίδι μέ-
202 νειν. Σίττιος μὲν δὴ πρῶτος ἢ μόνος ἀνδρῶν ὅδε τῆς
ξένης ‹εἰργόμενος›[12] ἐφυγαδεύετο ἐν τῇ πατρίδι, Οὐ-
άρρων δὲ ἦν φιλόσοφός τε καὶ ἱστορίας συγγραφεύς,
ἐστρατευμένος τε καλῶς καὶ ἐστρατηγηκώς, καὶ ἴσως
203 διὰ ταῦτα ὡς ἐχθρὸς μοναρχίας προυγράφη. φιλοτι-
μουμένων δὲ αὐτὸν ὑποδέξασθαι τῶν γνωρίμων καὶ
διεριζόντων ἐς ἀλλήλους, Καληνὸς ἐξενίκησε καὶ εἶχεν ἐν ἐπαύλει, ἔνθα Ἀντώνιος, ὅτε διοδεύοι, κατ-
ήγετο· καὶ τὸν Οὐάρρωνα οὐδεὶς ἔνδον ὄντα ἐνέφηνε
θεράπων, οὔτε αὐτοῦ Οὐάρρωνος οὔτε Καληνοῦ.

204   48. Οὐεργίνιος δέ, ἀνὴρ ἡδὺς εἰπεῖν, τοὺς οἰκέτας
ἐδίδασκεν, ὅτι κτείναντες μὲν αὐτὸν δι᾽ ὀλίγα χρήματα
οὐκ ἀσφαλῆ μύσους τε πίμπλανται καὶ φόβων ἐς
ὕστερον μεγάλων, περισώσαντες δὲ δόξης τε εὐσε-
βοῦς καὶ ἐλπίδων ἀγαθῶν καὶ χρημάτων ὕστερον
205 πολὺ πλεόνων τε καὶ ἀσφαλεστέρων. οἱ μὲν δὴ συν-

---

[12] εἰργόμενος add. Gaillard-Goukowsky

---

38 As Appian himself notes (*BCiv.* 2.9.33), Marcus Terentius
Varro had written an attack on the First Triumvirate called the
Three-headed Monster. His allegiance to Pompey the Great may

ing the rites in this disguise. The people of Cales protected   201
Sittius, one of their own citizens who had spent a great
deal of money on them from his abundant resources. Taking up weapons on his behalf, they threatened his slaves
and kept the soldiers outside the walls until the troubles
began to subside, when they sent a delegation to the triumvirs for him, and succeeded in getting permission for
Sittius to remain in his hometown, while being excluded
from the rest of Italy. This Sittius was thus the first or only   202
man to be excluded from foreign territory and spend his
exile in his own town. Varro was a philosopher and a historian, a distinguished soldier and former praetor, and it
was perhaps for these reasons that he was proscribed, as
somebody hostile to autocratic rule.[38] His close friends   203
regarded it as a matter of pride to give him shelter, and
competed with each other to do so. Calenus was the successful one and kept him in his country house, where
Antony used to stop when traveling. Yet not a single slave
belonging to either Varro himself or Calenus revealed the
presence of Varro in the house.[39]

48. Verginius, who was a smooth talker, explained to his   204
slaves that if they killed him for a small and uncertain
amount of money, they would incur heavy pollution and
be filled with great fears for the future; while, should they
save him, they would enjoy a reputation for piety, excellent
prospects, and, later, a much larger and more secure sum
of money. So they went on the run with him as a fellow   205

also explain the fact that he was among the proscribed. Valerius
Maximus (8.7.3) says he lived to the age of one hundred.
[39] Quintus Fufius Calenus (consul 47) was a staunch Caesarean and trusted by Antony (see *BCiv.* 5.3.14).

271

ἔφευγον ὡς ὁμοδούλῳ καὶ γνωρισθέντος αὐτοῦ παρὰ
τὴν ὁδὸν πρὸς τοὺς ὁπλίτας ἀπεμάχοντο· ὁ δὲ ληφθεὶς ὑπὸ τῶν ὁπλιτῶν ἐδίδασκε κἀκείνους, ὅτι κατὰ
μὲν ἔχθραν αὐτὸν οὐκ ἀνελοῦσιν, ἀλλὰ χρημάτων
οὕνεκα μόνων, χρήματα δὲ αὐτοῖς εἴη δικαιότερα καὶ
πλέονα λαβεῖν ἐπὶ θάλασσαν ἐλθοῦσιν, "Ἔνθα μοι
τὸ γύναιον," ἔφη, "Ναῦν φέρουσα χρημάτων συνετά-
206 ξατο." καὶ αὐτῷ καὶ οἵδε πεισθέντες κατήεσαν ἐπὶ τὴν
θάλασσαν· ἡ γυνὴ δὲ ἀφῖκτο μὲν ἐπὶ τὴν ἠιόνα κατὰ
τὸ συγκείμενον, βραδύνοντος δὲ τοῦ Οὐεργινίου, νο-
μίσασα αὐτὸν ἐς Πομπήιον προπεπλευκέναι ἀνήγετο,
θεράποντα ὅμως ἐπὶ τῆς ἠιόνος ἐξαγγέλλειν ὑπολι-
207 ποῦσα. καὶ ὁ θεράπων τὸν Οὐεργίνιον ἰδὼν ἀνέθορέ
τε ὡς ἐς δεσπότην καὶ τὴν ναῦν ἐδείκνυεν ὡς ὁρω-
μένην καὶ τὴν γυναῖκα ἔφραζε καὶ τὰ χρήματα καὶ
208 αὐτὸς ἐφ' ὅτῳ κατελείφθη. οἱ δὲ ἐπίστευον ἅπασιν
ἤδη, καὶ τὸν Οὐεργίνιον ἀξιοῦντα σφᾶς περιμένειν,
ἔστε μετακληθείη τὸ γύναιον, ἢ συνελθεῖν οἱ πρὸς
αὐτὴν ἐπὶ τὰ χρήματα, ἐσβάντες ἐς σκάφος παρέπεμπον ἐς Σικελίαν, ἐρέσσοντες φιλοπόνως· ἐκεῖ δὲ ἔτυ-
χόν τε τῶν ἐπαγγελιῶν καὶ οὐκ ἀπέστησαν ἔτι θερα-
209 πεύοντες αὐτὸν μέχρι τῶν σπονδῶν. Ῥέβιλον δὲ
ναύκληρος ἐς τὴν ναῦν ὑποδεξάμενος ὡς διοίσων ἐς
Σικελίαν ᾔτει χρήματα, μηνύσειν ἀπειλῶν, εἰ μὴ λάβοι. ὁ δέ, οἷόν τι καὶ Θεμιστοκλῆς φεύγων ἐποίησεν,

slave, and when he was recognized on the road they tried to fight off the soldiers, but he was captured by them. He explained to the soldiers too, however, that they were not trying to kill him out of hatred, but solely for money, and that they would get more and more honorably earned money if they accompanied him to the coast. "Here," he said, "my wife has arranged with me to bring a ship full of money." They too were similarly persuaded by him and 206 went down to the coast. His wife had come to the beach as arranged, but because Verginius was delayed, she thought that he had already sailed to Pompeius. So she had put out to sea, although she did leave a slave behind on the beach to give the news. When the slave saw Ver- 207 ginius he ran up to him as he would to his master, and pointed out the ship as it was setting sail and told him about his wife and the money and reason why he himself had been left behind. The soldiers now believed the whole 208 story, and when Verginius asked them to wait until his wife could be called back, or to go with him to her to get the money, they embarked in a small boat and rowed hard to bring him to Sicily. There they received what they had been promised, and did not leave Verginius, but remained in his service until the amnesty. A ship captain took Rebi- 209 lus on board his vessel in order to bring him to Sicily, and then demanded money, threatening to inform on him if he did not get it. Rebilus followed the example of Themistocles when he was going into exile, and threatened in turn to lay information against him for receiving money to take

ἀντηπείλει μηνύσειν, ὅτι αὐτὸν ἐπὶ χρήμασιν ἄγοι,
μέχρι δείσας ὁ ναύκληρος διέσωσεν ἐς Πομπήιον.

210 49. Μᾶρκος δὲ Βρούτῳ στρατηγῶν προεγέγραπτο
μὲν καὶ ὅδε διὰ τόδε, ἡττωμένου δὲ τοῦ Βρούτου συλ-
λαμβανόμενος ὑπεκρίνατο εἶναι θεράπων, καὶ αὐτὸν
211 ὠνήσατο Βαρβούλας. δεξιὸν δὲ ὁρῶν ἐπέστησε τοῖς
ὁμοδούλοις καὶ χρήματα διοικεῖν ἔδωκεν· δεινὸν δὲ ἐν
ἅπασι καὶ συνετὸν ὄντα ὑπὲρ θεράποντος φύσιν
ὑπενόει καὶ ἐπήλπιζεν, εἰ τῶν προγεγραμμένων τις
212 εἴη, περισώσειν ὁμολογήσαντα. ἀπομαχόμενον δὲ
ἰσχυρῶς καὶ γένος ἀναπλάσσοντα καὶ ὄνομα καὶ
προτέρους δεσπότας ἐς Ῥώμην ἐπήγετο, ἐλπίσας
213 ὀκνήσειν ἐς Ῥώμην ἀφικέσθαι προγεγραμμένον. ὁ δὲ
εἵπετο καὶ ὥς. περὶ δὲ τὰς πύλας τῶν ὑπαντώντων τις
φίλων Βαρβούλα, θεασάμενος τὸν Μᾶρκον ὡς οἰκέτην
αὐτῷ παρεστῶτα, κρύφα ἐμήνυσε τῷ Βαρβούλᾳ. ὁ δὲ
ἐδεήθη Καίσαρος δι᾽ Ἀγρίππα, καὶ ἀφείθη τῆς προγραφῆς ὁ Μᾶρκος, καὶ φίλος ἐγίγνετο Καίσαρι καὶ
μετ᾽ οὐ πολὺ καὶ στρατηγὸς ἦν ἐπὶ Ἀντωνίῳ περὶ
214 Ἄκτιον. ἐστρατήγει δὲ καὶ Ἀντωνίῳ Βαρβούλας, καὶ
ἡ τύχη περιῆλθεν ἐς τὸ ὅμοιον ἀμφοτέροις· Βαρβούλας τε γὰρ ἡττηθέντος Ἀντωνίου λαμβανόμενος

---

40 Thucydides (1.137) and Plutarch (*Vit. Them.* 25) tell the
story of how Themistocles, when traveling incognito to Asia after
being ostracized at Athens, was blown by a storm to Naxos, which
the Athenians were besieging. He revealed himself to the ship's

him on his ship.[40] Eventually the captain became afraid, and delivered Rebilus safely to Pompeius.

49. Marcus was serving under Brutus' command and was another who had been proscribed for this reason. On Brutus' defeat he was arrested, but pretended to be a slave and was bought by Barbula.[41] Barbula could see that he was clever, put him in charge of his fellow slaves and entrusted him with managing his financial affairs. But as he was good at everything and more naturally intelligent than a slave, Barbula began to be suspicious and encouraged him to believe that if he admitted to being one of the proscribed he would save his life. Since Marcus strenuously defended himself and invented a family, a name, and former masters, Barbula set about bringing him to Rome, expecting that a proscribed man would be reluctant to go there. But he went with him all the same. One of Barbula's associates who went to meet him at the gates, saw Marcus standing at his side like a slave, and privately told Barbula who he was. The latter then petitioned Octavian through Agrippa and Marcus' name was removed from the proscription list. He became a close associate of Octavian, and not long after served under his command against Antony at Actium. Barbula too held a command, in his case for Antony, and fortune came round full circle for both of them. For when Antony was defeated, Barbula was cap-

210

211

212

213

214

captain, but to avoid betrayal to the Athenian forces, he had to threaten he would say he had bribed the captain to carry him.

[41] It is usually thought that Appian's story here involves the future consuls of 21, Marcus Lollius and Quintus Aemilius Lepidus (assumed also to have had the additional name Barbula).

ὑπεκρίνατο οἰκέτης εἶναι, καὶ ὁ Μᾶρκος αὐτὸν ὡς
ἀγνοῶν ὠνήσατο, ἐκθέμενος δὲ ἅπαντα τῷ Καίσαρι
ᾔτησέ τε καὶ ἔτυχε τοῖς ὁμοίοις τὸν Βαρβοῦλαν ἀμεί-
215 ψασθαι. τοῖσδε μὲν οὖν ἡ συντυχία τῶν ὁμοίων καὶ
ἐς τὸ ἔπειτα παρέμεινεν· ἦρξαν γὰρ τὴν ἐπώνυμον
ἀρχὴν ἐν ἄστει οἱ δύο ὁμοῦ.

50. Βαλβίνῳ δέ, ἐκφυγόντι καὶ κατελθόντι σὺν
Πομπηίῳ καὶ ὑπατεύοντι οὐ πολὺ ὕστερον, Λέπιδος
ἰδιώτης ὑπὸ Καίσαρος ἐκ δυνάστου γενόμενος ὑπὸ
216 τοιᾶσδε ἀνάγκης παρέστη. Μαικήνας ἐδίωκε τὸν Λεπίδου παῖδα βουλεύσεως ἐπὶ Καίσαρι, ἐδίωκε δὲ καὶ
τὴν μητέρα τῷ παιδὶ συνεγνωκέναι· Λεπίδου γὰρ
217 αὐτοῦ ἄρα ὡς ἀσθενοῦς ὑπερεώρα. τὸν μὲν δὴ παῖδα
ὁ Μαικήνας ἐς Ἄκτιον ἔπεμπε τῷ Καίσαρι, τὴν δὲ
μητέρα, ἵνα μὴ ἄγοιτο οὖσα γυνή, ἐγγύην ᾔτει παρὰ
218 τῷ ὑπάτῳ πρὸς Καίσαρα ἀφίξεσθαι. οὐδενὸς δὲ τὴν
ἐγγύην ὑφισταμένου, ὁ Λέπιδος ἀμφὶ τὰς Βαλβίνου
θύρας ἐτρίβετο πολλάκις καὶ δικάζοντι παρίστατο
καὶ διωθουμένων αὐτὸν ἐς πολὺ τῶν ὑπηρετῶν μόλις
εἶπεν· "Ἐμοὶ μὲν καὶ οἱ κατήγοροι μαρτυροῦσιν ἐπι-
είκειαν, οὐδὲ γυναικί με ἢ παιδὶ συγγνῶναι λέγοντες·
σὲ δὲ οὐκ ἐγὼ μὲν προέγραψα, κάτω δέ εἰμι τῶν προ-
219 γραψάντων.[13] ἀλλ' ἐς τὴν ἀνθρώπειον τύχην ἀφορῶν
καὶ ἐς ἐμὲ σοὶ παρεστῶτα, χάρισαί μοι τὴν γυναῖκα
ἀπαντήσειν ἐς Καίσαρα ἐγγυωμένῳ ἢ μετ' ἐκείνης

_____
[13] προγραφέντων E; προγραψάντων ceteri

tured, pretended to be a slave, and was bought by Marcus, feigning ignorance of his identity. But he laid the whole matter before Octavian and asked that he might repay Barbula with like for like; and his request was granted. This similarity of good fortune attended these men in later   215 times too, for the two of them held the consulship together at Rome.

50. Balbinus, on the other hand, an exile who had returned from exile with Pompeius and held the consulship shortly after, was solicited by Lepidus, who had been demoted from political dynast to private citizen by Octavian. Lepidus was acting under compulsion of the following circumstances. Maecenas was prosecuting Lepidus' son   216 for conspiracy against Octavian, and also the young man's mother for complicity in the crime. Lepidus himself he ignored, no doubt regarding him as powerless. Maecenas   217 sent the son to Octavian at Actium, but in order to avoid having a woman brought there under arrest, he required the mother to provide a bond in the presence of the consul to guarantee her appearance before Octavian. As nobody   218 offered the security, Lepidus loitered repeatedly at the door of Balbinus, and also approached him when he was giving judgment, and although the attendants pushed him away and kept him at a distance, he did manage with difficulty to say to him: "Even the prosecution testify to my virtue, since they do not say that I was complicit with my wife or my son. I was not the one to have you proscribed, yet I am now inferior to those who did proscribe you. But   219 keeping sight of the mutability of human affairs and of me standing before you, allow me to guarantee my wife's appearance before Octavian, or to go there with her under

ἀπελθεῖν δεδεμένῳ."[14] ταῦτα ἔτι τοῦ Λεπίδου λέγοντος,
οὐκ ἐνεγκὼν τὴν μεταβολὴν ὁ Βαλβῖνος ἀπέλυσε τῆς
ἐγγύης τὴν γυναῖκα.

220   51. Κικέρων δὲ ὁ Κικέρωνος προαπέσταλτο μὲν ὑπὸ
τοῦ πατρὸς ἐς τὴν Ἑλλάδα, τοιάδε ἔσεσθαι προσδο-
κῶντος· ἀπὸ δὲ τῆς Ἑλλάδος ἐς Βροῦτον καὶ μετὰ
Βροῦτον ἀποθανόντα ἐς Πομπήιον ἐλθὼν τιμῆς παρ'
221 ἑκατέρῳ καὶ στρατηγίας ἠξιοῦτο. ἐπὶ δὲ ἐκείνοις
αὐτὸν ὁ Καῖσαρ ἐς ἀπολογίαν τῆς Κικέρωνος ἐκδό-
σεως ἱερέα τε εὐθὺς ἀπέφηνε καὶ ὕπατον οὐ πολὺ
ὕστερον καὶ Συρίας στρατηγόν· καὶ τὴν Ἀντωνίου
περὶ Ἄκτιον συμφορὰν ἐπισταλεῖσαν ὑπὸ τοῦ Καίσαρος ὁ Κικέρων ὅδε ὑπατεύων ἀνέγνω τε τῷ δήμῳ καὶ
προύθηκεν ἐπὶ τοῦ βήματος, ἔνθα πρότερον ἡ τοῦ πα-
222 τρὸς αὐτοῦ προύκειτο κεφαλή. Ἄππιος δὲ διένειμε
τοῖς θεράπουσιν τὰ ὄντα καὶ μετ' αὐτῶν ἐς Σικελίαν
ἔπλει. χειμῶνος δὲ ἐπιλαβόντος ἐπιβουλεύοντες οἱ
θεράποντες τοῖς χρήμασιν ἐς σκάφος ἐνέθεντο τὸν
Ἄππιον, ὡς ἐς ἀσφαλεστέραν ἐλπίδα μεταφέροντες.
καὶ συνέβη τῷ μὲν ἐκ παραλόγου διαπλεῦσαι, τοῖς δὲ
223 ἀπολέσθαι τῆς νεὼς διαλυθείσης. Πούπλιος δὲ ὁ ταμίας Βρούτου, τῶν ἀμφὶ τὸν Ἀντώνιον αὐτὸν πειθόν-
των προδοῦναι Βροῦτον οὐκ ἀνασχόμενος, διὰ τόδε
καὶ προεγράφη. καὶ κατήχθη καὶ Καίσαρι φίλος ἐγί-

---

[14] δεομένῳ E; δεδεμένῳ ceteri

arrest." While Lepidus was still speaking, Balbinus could not endure this change of fortune, and released his wife from the bond.

51. Cicero, the son of Cicero, had earlier been sent 220 away to Greece by his father, who expected that something like this would happen. From Greece he made his way to Brutus, and after Brutus' death to Pompeius, both of whom honored him and thought him worthy of military command. Subsequently Octavian, by way of apology for 221 his betrayal of Cicero, immediately appointed him to a priesthood, and shortly after made him consul and governor of Syria. When Octavian dispatched a report with news of Antony's defeat at Actium, it was this Cicero, as consul, who read it out to the people and posted it on the rostra where earlier his own father's head had been displayed.[42] Appius distributed his goods among his slaves 222 and then sailed with them to Sicily. When a storm overtook them, the slaves plotted to get his money, and put Appius in a small boat, pretending that they were transferring him to give him a better hope of survival; but, as it turned out, while he unexpectedly completed the crossing, their ship was wrecked and they all died. When Publius, Brutus' 223 quaestor, held out against the attempts of Antony's supporters to persuade him to betray Brutus, he was proscribed for this, but was restored and became an associate of Octavian. On one occasion, when Octavian came to visit

---

[42] Cass. Dio 51.19.4 indicates that it was the news of Antony's death that came when the younger Cicero was suffect consul in the second half of 30. He had not entered office at the time of Actium.

γνετο καὶ ἐπιόντι ποτὲ τῷ Καίσαρι προύθηκεν εἰκόνας
Βρούτου καὶ ἐπῃνέθη καὶ ἐπὶ τῷδε ὑπὸ τοῦ Καίσαρος.

224   52. Τὰ μὲν δὴ παρὰ δόξαν τισὶ τῶν προγραφέντων
εἴς τε κίνδυνον καὶ σωτηρίαν γενόμενα, πολλὰ καὶ
ἄλλα παραλιπόντι τοιάδε μάλιστα ἦν· γιγνομένων δὲ
τούτων ἐν Ῥώμῃ, καὶ τὰ ὑπερόρια πάντα πολέμοις διὰ
τήνδε τὴν στάσιν ἐδονεῖτο· καὶ τῶν πολέμων οἱ μείζους ἦσαν ἀμφί τε Λιβύην Κορνιφικίου πρὸς Σέξ-
στιον καὶ ἐν Συρίᾳ Κασσίου πρὸς Δολοβέλλαν καὶ

225 περὶ Σικελίαν Πομπήιον. πάθη τε πολλὰ συνηνέχθη
πόλεσιν ἐκ δοριαλωσίας, ὑπεριδόντι δὲ τῶν ἐλασσό-
νων τὰ μέγιστα δὴ καὶ δι' ἀξίωσιν τῶν ἄλλων περι-
φανέστατα Λαοδικεῦσι καὶ Ταρσεῦσι καὶ Ῥοδίοις καὶ
Παταρεῦσι καὶ Ξανθίοις. καὶ αὐτῶν ἕκαστα, ὡς ἐν
κεφαλαίῳ συναγαγόντι φράσαι, τοιάδε ἦν.

226   53. Λιβύης Ῥωμαῖοι τὴν μὲν ἔτι καλοῦσι παλαιάν,
ὅσην Καρχηδονίους ἀφείλοντο· ἦν δὲ Ἰόβας εἶχεν,
ὕστερόν τε ἔλαβον ἐπὶ Γαΐου Καίσαρος καὶ διὰ τοῦτο
νέαν προσαγορεύουσι Λιβύην· εἴη δ' ἂν τῆς Νομαδι-

227 κῆς. Σέξστιος οὖν ὑπὸ Καίσαρι τῆς νέας ἡγούμενος
ᾔτει Κορνιφίκιον ἐκστῆναί οἱ τῆς παλαιᾶς, ὡς Λιβύης ἁπάσης ἐν τῇ λήξει τῶν τριῶν ἀνδρῶν Καίσαρι
νενεμημένης. ὁ δὲ οὔτε τὴν λῆξιν ἔφη γιγνώσκειν τῶν

---

43 Appian is referring to Lucius (not Publius) Sestius Quirina-
lis, suffect consul in 23 (see Cass. Dio 53.32.4).

44 That is, Julius Caesar.   45 Titus Sextius had served under
Julius Caesar in Gaul. It is not clear whether Appian means he

him, Publius put on display some images of Brutus, and even for this he was praised by Octavian.[43]

52. These have been examples of the particularly un- 224
expected things that happened to some of the proscribed leading them into peril or safety; many others I have left out. While they were taking place at Rome, wars resulting from this civil disorder were also disrupting everywhere abroad. The more important of these wars were in Africa between Cornificius and Sextius, in Syria between Cassius and Dolabella, and in Sicily against Pompeius. Towns suf- 225
fered many disasters as a result of being taken by storm. Ignoring the lesser cases, the most important, and because of their reputation the most notorious of the others oc-curred at Laodicea and Tarsus and Rhodes and Patara and Xanthus. The following is a brief summary of the sort of thing that happened at each of them.

53. The Romans still call that part of Africa they took 226
from the Carthaginians Africa Vetus; and for this reason, the land held by Juba, which they got later in the time of Gaius Caesar,[44] they call Africa Nova, although it could be regarded as Numidian Africa. Accordingly Sextius, gover- 227
nor of Africa Nova under Octavian's authority, asked Cor-nificius to cede Africa Vetus to him, because in the trium-viral allocations the whole of Africa had been assigned to Octavian.[45] Cornificius replied that he did not recognize

was appointed governor of Africa Nova by Caesar or by Octavian. As a supporter of Antony, he played a major role in the civil war in Africa until 40. Quintus Cornificius was an orator and poet, a friend of Cicero and Catullus, and a supporter of Caesar. Ap-pointed governor of Africa Vetus in 44, he was proscribed by the triumvirs in 43 and defeated and killed by Sextius in 42.

τριῶν ἐφ᾽ ἑαυτῶν πεποιημένων, οὔτε τὴν ἀρχὴν παρὰ
228 τῆς βουλῆς λαβὼν ἄλλῳ μεθήσειν χωρὶς αὐτῆς· ἐκ
μὲν δὴ τούτων ἀλλήλοις ἐπολέμουν, στρατὸν δὲ εἶχεν
ὁ μὲν βαρύν τε καὶ πλείονα, ὁ δὲ Σέξστιος κουφότερόν
τε καὶ ὀλιγώτερον, ᾧ δὴ καὶ τὰ μεσόγαια τοῦ Κορνιφικίου περιὼν ἀφίστη καὶ Οὐεντίδιον, στρατηγὸν
τοῦ Κορνιφικίου, μετὰ πλειόνων ἐπελθόντα ἀπεμά-
229 χετο πολιορκούμενος. ἐδῄου δὲ καὶ Λαίλιος, ἕτερος
τοῦ Κορνιφικίου στρατηγός, τὴν Σεξστίου Λιβύην
καὶ Κίρταν περικαθήμενος ἐπολιόρκει.

230   54. Καὶ πάντες ἐπρέσβευον περὶ συμμαχίας ἔς τε
Ἀραβίωνα βασιλέα καὶ τοὺς καλουμένους Σιττιανούς,
231 οἳ ἀπὸ τοιᾶσδε συντυχίας οὕτως ὠνομάζοντο. Σίττιος
ἐν Ῥώμῃ δίκην ἰδίαν οὐχ ὑποστὰς ἔφυγε καὶ στρατὸν
ἀγείρας ἔκ τε αὐτῆς Ἰταλίας καὶ Ἰβηρίας ἐς Λιβύην
διέπλευσε καὶ τοῖς Λιβύων βασιλεῦσι πολεμοῦσιν
ἀλλήλοις ἀνὰ μέρος συνεμάχει. ἀεὶ δὲ οἷς προσθοῖτο
νικώντων, ὁ Σίττιος ἐπὶ ὀνόματος ἐγίγνετο, καὶ ὁ
232 στρατὸς αὐτῷ γεγύμναστο λαμπρῶς. Γαΐῳ τε Καίσαρι διώκοντι τοὺς Πομπηιανοὺς ἐν Λιβύῃ συνεμά-
χησε, καὶ Σαβόρραν, Ἰόβα στρατηγὸν διώνυμον,
ἀνεῖλε καὶ γέρας τούτων ἔλαβε παρὰ Καίσαρος τὴν
Μασανάσσου γῆν, οὐχ ἅπασαν, ἀλλὰ τὸ κράτιστον
233 αὐτῆς. Μασανάσσης δ᾽ ἦν Ἀραβίωνος τοῦδε πατήρ,
Ἰόβα σύμμαχος, καὶ αὐτοῦ τὴν χώραν ὁ Καῖσαρ

the allocation made by the triumvirs on their own authority, and that since he had received his command from the senate he would not yield it to anybody else without their instruction. As a result, they went to war with each other. 228 Cornificius had a heavily armed and more numerous army, Sextius a lighter and smaller force, with which all the same he managed to traverse and cause the central parts of Cornificius' province to defect, as well as fight off Ventidius, one of Cornificius' generals, who attacked him with a larger force and put him under siege. Laelius, another 229 of Cornificius' generals, ravaged Sextius' part of Africa, invested Cirta, and laid siege to it.

54. They all sent envoys to seek the military assistance 230 of King Arabio, and the so-called Sittians, who got their name from the following circumstances. Sittius refused to 231 face a private action taken against him at Rome and went into exile.[46] Collecting an armed force from Italy itself and Iberia, he sailed over to Africa, where he allied himself in turn with various warring African kings. As those to whom he allied himself were always victorious, Sittius got a name for himself and his army had become exceptionally well trained. He fought for Gaius Caesar when he was pursuing 232 the Pompeians in Africa, and killed Juba's famous general, Saburra. As a reward for these services he received from Caesar the territory of Massinissa, not all of it, but the best part. Massinissa was the father of this Arabio and ally of 233 Juba, and Caesar had given his territory to our Sittius, and

[46] Publius Sittius, an equestrian from the town of Nuceria in Campania, was a friend of Sulla and Cicero. He enjoyed a successful career as a mercenary general in Africa, until he was assassinated in 44.

τῷδε τῷ Σιττίῳ καὶ Βόκχῳ, Μαυρουσίων βασιλεῖ, δε-
δώρητο· καὶ τὸ μέρος ὁ Σίττιος τοῖς ὑπ' αὐτὸν ἀνδρά-
234 σιν ἐπιδιεῖλεν. Ἀραβίων δὲ τότε μὲν ἐς Ἰβηρίαν ἐξέφυγε πρὸς τοὺς παῖδας τοὺς Πομπηίου, Γαΐου δὲ
Καίσαρος ἀναιρεθέντος ἐς Λιβύην ἐπανῆλθε, καὶ
Λιβύων τινὰς ἀεὶ τῷ νεωτέρῳ Πομπηίῳ πέμπων ἐς
Ἰβηρίαν καὶ γεγυμνασμένους ἀπολαμβάνων Βόκχον
235 ἀφῄρητο τὴν χώραν καὶ Σίττιον ἀνῃρήκει δόλῳ. εὔνους δὲ ὢν τοῖς Πομπηιανοῖς διὰ τάδε, κατεγίνωσκεν
ἀεὶ τῆς μοίρας ὡς ἀτυχούσης ἀμειλίκτως καὶ Σεξστίῳ
προσέθετο, εὐμενιζόμενος δι' αὐτοῦ Καίσαρα. προσ-
έθεντο δὲ καὶ οἱ Σιττιανοί, κατ' εὔνοιαν οἵδε πατρῴαν
τοῦ Καίσαρος.

236   55. Θαρρήσας οὖν ὁ Σέξστιος ἐξῄει τῆς πολιορκίας
ἐς μάχην καὶ πεσόντος τοῦ Οὐεντιδίου καὶ τοῦ στρατοῦ φεύγοντος ὑπ' ἀναρχίας, εἵπετο κτείνων τε καὶ
ζωγρῶν. καὶ τάδε μαθὼν ὁ Λαίλιος διέλυε τὴν τῆς
Κίρτης πολιορκίαν καὶ ἐχώρει πρὸς τὸν Κορνιφίκιον.
237 ὁ δὲ Σέξστιος ἐπαιρόμενος τοῖς γεγονόσιν ἐπ' αὐτὸν
ἤδη τὸν Κορνιφίκιον ἐς Ἰτύκην ᾔει καὶ ἀντεστρατο-
238 πέδευε μετὰ πλειόνων ὄντι. Λαίλιον δὲ τοῦ Κορνιφικίου μετὰ τῶν ἱππέων πέμψαντος ἔς τινα κατάσκεψιν,
ὁ Σέξστιος Ἀραβίωνα ἔπεμψεν ἱππομαχεῖν τῷ Λαιλίῳ
κατὰ μέτωπον καὶ αὐτὸς ᾔει μετὰ τῶν εὐζώνων ἐς τὰ
πλάγια τῆς ἱππομαχίας καὶ ἐμβαλὼν ἐθορύβει, μέχρι
τὸν Λαίλιον οὐχ ἡσσημένον πω δεῖσαι περὶ τῆς
ἀναχωρήσεως, μὴ ἀποκλεισθείη, καὶ λόφον ἐν μέσῳ
καταλαβεῖν, Ἀραβίωνα δὲ ἀρτώμενον αὐτοῦ κτεῖναί

to Bocchus, king of Mauretania. Sittius divided up his section among the men under his command. At the time, 234 Arabio fled to Iberia to join the sons of Pompey, but when Gaius Caesar was assassinated he returned to Africa. By continually sending some men to the younger Pompeius in Iberia, and getting them back properly trained, he had taken his territory back from Bocchus, and using a subterfuge had had Sittius killed. Although he was well disposed 235 toward the Pompeians because of this, he was always critical of their destiny as fate was pitilessly unfavorable to them, and joined Sextius, through whom he won the favor of Octavian. Sittius' partisans also attached themselves to Sextius, their reason being the goodwill they felt for Octavian's father.

55. Encouraged by this, Sextius made a sortie from the 236 besieged city to give battle, in which Ventidius was killed, his army fled in disorder, and Sextius followed, killing and taking prisoners. When Laelius heard the news, he raised 237 the siege of Cirta and made his way to Cornificius. Roused by these events, Sextius began to move against Cornificius himself at Utica and, even though Cornificus had more 238 men, he made camp opposite him. When Cornificius sent Laelius with his cavalry on a reconnaissance mission, Sextius dispatched Arabio to fight a cavalry engagement in a frontal assault, while Sextius himself with his light troops attacked on the flanks of the cavalry battle. He caused such confusion that eventually Laelius, although not yet beaten, was afraid that his route of withdrawal had been cut off, and occupied a hill in the middle. Arabio stayed

239 τε πολλοὺς καὶ τὸν λόφον περικυκλῶσαι. ὁρῶν δὲ
ταῦτα ὁ Κορνιφίκιος ἐξῄει τῷ πλέονι στρατῷ, βοηθή-
σων τῷ Λαιλίῳ· καὶ τοῦδε μὲν ὁ Σέξτιος ὄπισθεν
γενόμενος ἐξῆπτετο συντρέχων, καὶ αὐτὸν ἐπιστρεφόμενος ὁ Κορνιφίκιος ἀπεμάχετο μάλα κακοπαθῶς.

240   56. Ὁ δὲ Ἀραβίων ἐν τούτῳ πετροβάταις ἀνδράσιν
ἀνέρπουσι διὰ κρημνῶν ἐς τὸ στρατόπεδον τοῦ Κορνιφικίου παρέδυ λαθών. καὶ Ῥώσκιος μὲν ὁ φύλαξ,
τοῦ χάρακος ἁλισκομένου, τῶν ὑπασπιστῶν τινι τὴν
σφαγὴν ὑπέσχε καὶ ἀνῃρέθη, ὁ δὲ Κορνιφίκιος τῇ
μάχῃ κάμνων μετεπήδα πρὸς Λαίλιον ἐς τὸν κολωνόν,
οὐκ εἰδώς πω περὶ τοῦ στρατοπέδου· μεταπηδῶντα δ᾽
αὐτὸν οἱ τοῦ Ἀραβίωνος ἱππέες ἐπιδραμόντες ἔκτει-

241 ναν. καὶ γιγνόμενα ταῦτα ὁ Λαίλιος ἀπὸ τοῦ λόφου
καθορῶν ἑαυτὸν διεχρήσατο. τῶν δ᾽ ἀρχόντων πεσόντων ὁ στρατὸς κατὰ μέρη διέφυγεν· καὶ ὅσοι τῶν
προγεγραμμένων ἦσαν παρὰ τῷ Κορνιφικίῳ, οἱ μὲν

242 ἐς Σικελίαν διέπλεον, οἱ δ᾽ ὅπῃ δύναιντο ἕκαστος. ὁ
δὲ Σέξτιος Ἀραβίωνα μὲν καὶ τοὺς Σιττιανοὺς ἐδωρεῖτο πολλοῖς λαφύροις, τὰς δὲ πόλεις τῷ Καίσαρι
καθίστατο, συγγινώσκων ἁπάσαις.

243   57. Τοῦτο μὲν δὴ τέλος ἦν τῷ περὶ Λιβύην Σεξτίου
καὶ Κορνιφικίου πολέμῳ, βραχεῖ διὰ ταχυεργίαν δό-
ξαντι εἶναι· τὰ δ᾽ ἀμφὶ Κάσσιόν τε καὶ Βροῦτον, μικρὰ καὶ τῶν εἰρημένων ἀναλαβόντι ἐς ὑπόμνημα, ἦν

244 τοιάδε. ἐπειδὴ Γάιος Καῖσαρ ἀνήρητο, οἱ μὲν σφαγεῖς αὐτοῦ τὸ Καπιτώλιον κατέλαβον καὶ ψηφισθεί-
σης αὐτοῖς ἀμνηστίας κατέβησαν. ὁ δὲ δῆμος ἐπὶ τῇ

close to him, killing many and surrounding the hill. When 239
Cornificius saw this, he came out with the greater part of
his army in order to assist Laelius, but Sextius managed to
get behind him too, closed rapidly with him, and stuck to
his rear, until Cornificius turned to face him and took
heavy casualties in fighting him off.

56. Meanwhile Arabio stole into Cornificius' camp un- 240
observed with a group of specialist rock climbers who
crept up the cliffs. When the palisade was taken, Roscius,
who was in charge of its defense, offered his throat to one
of his shield bearers, and was killed. Cornificius, exhausted
by the fighting, began to hurry across to Laelius on the hill,
not yet knowing what had happened to his camp, but while
he was making the transfer, Arabio's cavalry attacked and
killed him. Looking down on these events from his posi- 241
tion on the hill, Laelius committed suicide. With their
leaders dead, the soldiers fled in scattered groups. Of the
proscribed who were with Cornificius, some sailed across
to Sicily, others wherever they could. Sextius rewarded 242
Arabio and the Sittians with a great quantity of booty, but
he brought the towns over to Octavian's side by pardoning
them all.

57. This was the end of the war in Africa between 243
Sextius and Cornificius, which people regarded as insignificant because it was over so quickly. In relation to Cassius and Brutus, the following recapitulates by way of reminder a little of what has already been said. When Gaius 244
Caesar was assassinated his murderers took possession of
the Capitol, but came down from there when they were
voted an amnesty. The people, however, were stirred to

ἐκκομιδῇ τοῦ σώματος ἐν οἴκτῳ Καίσαρος γενόμενος
245 ἐζήτει τοὺς φονέας περιθέων. οἱ δὲ τότε μὲν ἠμύνοντο
αὐτοὺς ἀπὸ τῶν τεγῶν, εὐθὺς δὲ ἐξῄεσαν αὐτῶν, ὅσοι
στρατηγεῖν ἐθνῶν ὑπὸ Καίσαρος αὐτοῦ κεχειροτό-
νηντο. Κάσσιος δὲ καὶ Βροῦτος ἐστρατήγουν μὲν ἔτι
τῆς πόλεως, ᾕρηντο δὲ ἐπὶ τῇ στρατηγίᾳ καὶ οἵδε ὑπὸ
Γαίου Καίσαρος ἡγεῖσθαι Συρίας μὲν ὁ Κάσσιος,
246 Μακεδονίας δὲ ὁ Βροῦτος. οὔτε δὲ ἄρχειν πω τῶν
ἐθνῶν πρὸ τοῦ χρόνου δυνάμενοι οὔτε τὸν ἐν ἄστει
φόβον ὑπομένοντες ἐξῄεσαν ἔτι στρατηγοῦντες· καὶ
αὐτοῖς ἐς εὐπρέπειαν ἡ βουλὴ σίτου φροντίσαι προσέταξεν, ἵνα μὴ τὸ ἐν μέσῳ διάστημα φεύγειν νομίζοι-
247 ντο. οἰχομένων δὲ αὐτῶν Συρία μὲν καὶ Μακεδονία εἰς
τοὺς ὑπάτους Ἀντώνιόν τε καὶ Δολοβέλλαν μετεψηφίζετο, τῆς βουλῆς πάνυ δυσχεραινούσης, ἀντεδόθη δὲ
ὅμως τοῖς ἀμφὶ τὸν Κάσσιον Κυρήνη τε καὶ Κρήτη·
ὧν ὑπεριδόντες ὡς βραχυτέρων ἐκεῖνοι στρατὸν καὶ
χρήματα ἤγειρον ὡς ἐς Συρίαν καὶ Μακεδονίαν ἐσβα-
λοῦντες.

248   58. Καὶ οἱ μὲν ἦσαν ἐν τούτοις, Τρεβώνιον δὲ ἐν
Ἀσίᾳ κτείναντος Δολοβέλλα καὶ Δέκμον Ἀντωνίου
πολιορκοῦντος ἐν Κελτοῖς, χαλεπαίνουσα ἡ βουλὴ
Δολοβέλλαν μὲν καὶ Ἀντώνιον ἐψηφίσαντο εἶναι πολεμίους, Βροῦτον δὲ καὶ Κάσσιον ἐς τὰς προτέρας
ἡγεμονίας ἐπανήγαγον καὶ Βρούτῳ τὴν Ἰλλυρίδα
προσέθεσαν τοῖς τε ἄλλοις πᾶσιν ἐκέλευσαν, ὅσοι
Ῥωμαίοις ἡγεμονεύουσιν ἐθνῶν ἢ στρατοπέδων ἀπὸ
τοῦ Ἰονίου μέχρι Συρίας, ὑπακούειν, ἐς ὅ τι κελεύοι

pity for Caesar at the removal of his body for burial, and
began to rush around in pursuit of his murderers. At the   245
time, the latter defended themselves from the roofs of
their houses, and all those who had been appointed by
Caesar himself as provincial governors immediately left
the city. Although Cassius and Brutus were still serving as
urban praetors, they too had been chosen by Gaius Caesar
to hold governorships at the end of their praetorship, Cas-   246
sius of Syria, Brutus of Macedonia. As they could not yet
assume their provincial commands before the appointed
date, nor put up with the fear they felt in the city, they set
out to leave while still praetors, and the senate, for the
sake of propriety, commissioned them as grain supervi-
sors, so that people would not think they had taken to flight
in the meantime. On their departure, the provinces of   247
Syria and Macedonia were transferred by popular vote to
the consuls Antony and Dolabella, totally against the will
of the senate. Nevertheless, in exchange Cyrene and Crete
were given to Cassius' party. They rejected them, however,
as being too insignificant, and Brutus and Cassius began
to collect an army and money in order to invade Syria and
Macedonia.

58. While they were doing this, Dolabella killed Trebo-   248
nius in Asia and Antony besieged Decimus in Cisalpine
Gaul. The senate in their anger voted Dolabella and Antony public enemies, and restored Brutus and Cassius to
their former commands, adding Illyria to that of Brutus.
They also ordered every other Roman provincial or army
commander, between the Ionian gulf and Syria, to obey

249 Κάσσιος ἢ Βροῦτος. ἐπὶ δὲ τούτοις Κάσσιος φθάνει
Δολοβέλλαν ἐς τὴν Συρίαν ἐμβαλὼν καὶ σημεῖα τῆς
ἡγεμονίας ἀνέσχε καὶ δυώδεκα τέλη στρατοῦ Γαΐῳ
Καίσαρι ἐκ πολλοῦ στρατευόμενα καὶ γεγυμνασμένα

250 προσέλαβεν ἀθρόως· οὗ τὸ μὲν ἓν αὐτῶν ὁ Καῖσαρ ἐν
Συρίᾳ καταλελοίπει, τὰ ἐς Παρθυαίους ἤδη διανοούμενος, τὴν δὲ ἐπιμέλειαν αὐτοῦ ἐπιτέτραπτο μὲν Και-
κίλιος Βάσσος, τὸ δὲ ἀξίωμα εἶχε νεανίας αὐτοῦ Καί-

251 σαρος συγγενής, Σέξτος Ἰούλιος. ἐκδιαιτώμενος δὲ
ὁ Ἰούλιος τὸ τέλος ἐς τρυφὴν ἐπήγετο ἀσχημόνως
καὶ ἐπιμεμφομένῳ τῷ Βάσσῳ ποτὲ ἐνύβρισε· καὶ καλῶν ὕστερον, ἐπειδὴ βραδέως ὑπήκουεν, ἄγειν αὐτὸν
ἐκέλευεν ἕλκοντας. θορύβου δὲ ἀσχήμονος καὶ πληγῶν ἐς τὸν Βάσσον γενομένων οὐκ ἐνεγκοῦσα τὴν

252 ὄψιν ἡ στρατιὰ τὸν Ἰούλιον συνηκόντισε. καὶ εὐθὺς
ἦν μετάνοια καὶ δέος ἐκ τοῦ Καίσαρος. συνομόσαντες
οὖν ἀλλήλοις, εἰ μή τις αὐτοῖς συγγνώμη καὶ πίστις
γένοιτο, διαγωνιεῖσθαι μέχρι θανάτου, τὸν Βάσσον ἐς

253 ταὐτὰ[15] συνηνάγκασαν. τέλος δὲ στρατεύσαντες ἕτερον, συνεγύμναζον ἄμφω καὶ Στάιον[16] Μοῦρκον, ὑπὸ
Καίσαρος αὐτοῖς σὺν τρισὶ τέλεσιν ἐπιπεμφθέντα,

254 γενναίως ἀπεμάχοντο. Μούρκῳ δ᾽ ἦκεν ἐπίκουρος
Μάρκιος[17] Κρίσπος ἐκ Βιθυνίας μετὰ τριῶν τελῶν ἄλλων, καὶ τὸν Βάσσον ἐπολιόρκουν ὁμοῦ πάντες ἓξ
τέλεσιν ἤδη.

---

15 ἐς ταὐτὰ Gaillard-Goukowsky; ἐς ταῦτα PBJ; ἐνταῦθα L
16 Σέξτιον codd.; Στάιον edd.
17 Μινούκιος codd.; Μάρκιος edd.

all orders issued by Cassius and Brutus. At this, Cassius 249
anticipated Dolabella's invasion of Syria, assumed the insignia of his governorship and at one stroke took over an
army of twelve legions that had been enlisted and trained
by Gaius Caesar long before. One of these Caesar had left 250
in Syria, as he was already thinking about attacking the
Parthians, and had placed it under the supervision of Caecilius Bassus, although a young relation of Caesar himself,
Sextus Julius, held the actual command. Julius, however, 251
had gone astray, and shamefully led the legion into luxurious ways. On one occasion, when Bassus criticized him for
this, he insulted him, and at a later point, when he was
slow to obey his summons, he ordered his men to drag
Bassus before him by force. A scandalous disturbance
arose, Bassus was hit a number of times, and then the
troops, unable to tolerate what they were seeing, killed
Julius with their javelins. In fear of Caesar, they immedi- 252
ately regretted what they had done, and so swore an oath
to each other that, unless they were granted pardon and
assurances, they would fight to the death; and they forced
Bassus to adopt the same position. Having enrolled an- 253
other legion, the two trained together and bravely resisted
Staius Murcus, whom Caesar had sent against them with
three legions. To assist Murcus, Marcius Crispus arrived 254
from Bithynia with another three legions, and all six legions now began to besiege Bassus together.[47]

[47] Cass. Dio 47.27 also covers these events. Lucius Staius
Murcus had served with Caesar in Gaul, and although not involved in the conspiracy to assassinate him, immediately after was
one of those to claim credit (App. *BCiv.* 2.119.500). Quintus Marcius Crispus was appointed governor of Bithynia by Caesar in 45.

255   59. Κάσσιος οὖν τήνδε τὴν πολιορκίαν σπουδῇ
καταλαβὼν τόν τε τοῦ Βάσσου στρατὸν αὐτίκα παρελάμβανεν ἑκόντα καὶ ἐπ᾽ ἐκείνῳ τὰ Μούρκου τέλη
καὶ Μαρκίου,[18] κατά τε φιλίαν αὐτῷ παραδιδόντων
καὶ κατὰ τὸ δόγμα τῆς βουλῆς ἐς πάντα ὑπακουό-
256   ντων. ἄρτι δὲ καὶ Ἀλλιηνός, ὑπὸ Δολοβέλλα πεμφθεὶς
ἐς Αἴγυπτον, ἐπανῆγεν ἐξ αὐτῆς τέσσαρα τέλη τῶν
ἀπὸ τῆς ἥσσης Πομπηίου τε καὶ Κράσσου διαρριφέντων ἢ ὑπὸ Καίσαρος Κλεοπάτρᾳ καταλελειμμένων·
καὶ αὐτὸν ὁ Κάσσιος ἐν τῇ Παλαιστίνῃ, τῶν ὄντων
οὐ προπεπυσμένον, ἄφνω περιέλαβέ τε καὶ ἠνάγκασε
προσθέσθαι οἱ καὶ παραδοῦναι τὸν στρατόν, δεί-
257   σαντα τέσσαρσι τέλεσι μάχεσθαι πρὸς ὀκτώ. οὕτω
μὲν ὁ Κάσσιος ἐκ παραδόξου δυώδεκα τελῶν ἀρίστων
ἀθρόως ἐκράτει. καὶ αὐτῷ τινες καὶ Παρθυαίων ἱπποτοξόται συνεμάχουν, δόξαν ἔχοντι παρὰ τοῖς Παρθυαίοις, ἐξ οὗ Κράσσῳ ταμιεύων ἐμφρονέστερος ἔδοξε
τοῦ Κράσσου γενέσθαι.

258   60. Δολοβέλλας δὲ διέτριψε μὲν περὶ τὴν Ἰωνίαν,
κτείνων Τρεβώνιον καὶ ταῖς πόλεσιν ἐπιβάλλων
ἐσφορὰς καὶ ναυτικὸν ἀγείρων ἐπὶ μισθῷ διὰ Λευκίου
Φίγλου παρά τε Ῥοδίων καὶ Λυκίων καὶ Παμφύλων
καὶ ἐκ Κιλικίας· ὡς δέ οἱ τάδε ἕτοιμα ἦν, ἐπῄει τῇ
Συρίᾳ, κατὰ μὲν τὴν γῆν αὐτὸς μετὰ δύο τελῶν, διὰ
259   δὲ τῆς θαλάσσης ὁ Φίγλος. πυθόμενος δὲ τῆς Κασσίου στρατιᾶς ἐς Λαοδίκειαν οἰκείως ἔχουσάν οἱ

18 Μινουκίου codd.; Μαρκίου edd.

59. Cassius therefore quickly intervened in this siege. 255
He immediately took command of the army of Bassus,
with his consent, and then of the legions of Murcus and
Marcius, who handed them over to him both out of friendship and because according to the decree of the senate
they were subordinate to him in all matters. It was just at 256
this time that Allienus, who had been sent to Egypt by
Dolabella, was bringing back four legions composed of
men who had been dispersed after the defeats of Pompey
and Crassus, or who had been left with Cleopatra by Caesar.[48] Cassius intercepted him in Palestine unexpectedly,
while he was not yet informed about what had been happening, and forced him to join Cassius and hand over his
army, as he was afraid to fight with four legions against
eight. In this unexpected manner Cassius won control of, 257
in total, twelve of the best legions. Even some Parthian
mounted archers also allied themselves with him, as he
had a reputation among the Parthians, since the time
when he was Crassus' quaestor, for being more prudent
than Crassus himself.

60. Dolabella was operating in Ionia, where he killed 258
Trebonius, levied tribute on the towns, and, using Lucius
Figulus, assembled a mercenary fleet from Rhodes and
Lycia and Pamphylia and Cilicia. When everything was
ready he invaded Syria, commanding two legions himself
by land, while Figulus proceeded by sea. On learning of 259
Cassius' army he made his way to Laodicea, which was

[48] Aulus Allienus had been a legate of Cicero's brother, Quintus Cicero, in Asia in 60, then praetor in 49. He was proconsul in
Sicily (48–46) and then served under Trebonius, and after the
latter's death, under Dolabella.

παρῆλθεν, ἐπί τε χερρονήσου συνῳκισμένην καὶ τὰ
ἐκ τῆς γῆς ὠχυρωμένην καὶ ἐς τὸ πέλαγος ἔχουσαν
ὅρμον, ὅθεν ἔμελλεν εὐπορήσειν τε ἀγορᾶς ἀπὸ
θαλάσσης καὶ ἀδεῶς, ὅτε βούλοιτο, ἀποπλευσεῖσθαι.
260 ὧν αἰσθανόμενος ὁ Κάσσιος καὶ δεδιώς, μὴ αὐτὸν ὁ
Δολοβέλλας διαφύγοι, τόν τε ἰσθμὸν ἔχου δισταδίου
ὄντα, λίθους καὶ πᾶσαν ὕλην ἐξ ἐπαύλεων καὶ προ-
αστείων καὶ τάφων συμφέρων, καὶ ἐπὶ ναῦς περιέπεμπεν ἔς τε Φοινίκην καὶ Λυκίαν καὶ Ῥόδον.
261   61. Ὑπερορώμενος δὲ ὑπὸ τῶν ἄλλων πλὴν Σι-
δωνίων ἐπανήχθη τῷ Δολοβέλλᾳ, καὶ κατέδυσαν μὲν
ἑκατέρου νῆες ἱκαναί, πέντε δὲ αὐτοῖς ἀνδράσιν εἷλεν
262 Δολοβέλλας. καὶ ὁ Κάσσιος αὖθις ἔπεμπεν ἐς τοὺς
ὑπεριδόντας αὐτοῦ καὶ ἐς Κλεοπάτραν, τὴν Αἰγύπτου
βασιλίδα, καὶ ἐς Σεραπίωνα, τὸν ἐν Κύπρῳ τῇ Κλεοπάτρᾳ στρατηγοῦντα. Τύριοι μὲν δὴ καὶ Ἀράδιοι καὶ
Σεραπίων, οὐδὲν τῆς Κλεοπάτρας προμαθών, ἔπεμψαν
αὐτῷ ναῦς, ὅσας εἶχον· ἡ βασιλὶς δὲ Κασσίῳ μὲν
προύφερε λιμὸν ὁμοῦ καὶ λοιμὸν ἐνοχλοῦντα τότε
Αἰγύπτῳ, διὰ δὲ οἰκειότητα τοῦ προτέρου Καίσαρος
263 συνέπρασσε τῷ Δολοβέλλᾳ. καὶ ἀπὸ τῆσδε τῆς
γνώμης αὐτῷ καὶ τὰ τέσσαρα τέλη προπεπόμφει δι'
Ἀλλιηνοῦ καὶ στόλον ἄλλον ἕτοιμον εἶχεν ἐπαμύνειν,
264 ἄνεμοι δὲ ἐπεῖχον. Ῥόδιοι δὲ καὶ Λύκιοι οὔτε Κασσίῳ
οὔτε Βρούτῳ συμμαχήσειν ἔφασκον ἐς ἐμφύλια, ἐπεὶ
καὶ Δολοβέλλᾳ δοῦναι ναῦς προπομπούς, καὶ οὐκ εἰδέναι συμμαχούσας.
265   62. Ἑτοιμασάμενος οὖν ὁ Κάσσιος αὖθις ἐκ τῶν

well disposed to him. It had been founded on a peninsula, was fortified on the landward side and had an anchorage on the sea side, from where he thought he would be able to bring in abundant supplies by sea, and sail away in safety whenever he wanted. Cassius realized this, and 260 fearing that Dolabella would escape him, collected stones and material of all sorts from farmyards, suburban houses and tombs, and blocked off the isthmus, which was two stades long. He also sent around for ships from Phoenicia, Lycia, and Rhodes.

61. Although ignored by everyone except the Sido- 261 nians, he put out to sea to fight Dolabella. A substantial number of ships were sunk on both sides, and Dolabella captured five, including their crews. Then Cassius again 262 sent a message to those who had ignored him, and also to Cleopatra, queen of Egypt, and to Serapio, her governor in Cyprus. The Tyrians, the Aradians, and Serapio (who did not consult Cleopatra first), sent what ships they had. The queen excused herself to Cassius on the grounds that Egypt was at the time suffering from famine along with plague, but she began to cooperate with Dolabella because of her relationship with the elder Caesar. It was in 263 line with this policy that she had previously sent him the four legions through Allienus, and had another fleet ready to assist him, which was being held by adverse winds. The 264 Rhodians and the Lycians, on the other hand, said that they would provide military assistance neither to Cassius nor Brutus in a civil war, and that when they gave Dolabella escort vessels they did not know that they would be involved in fighting.

62. So, having again made preparations with the means 265

παρόντων ἐπανήγετο δὶς τῷ Δολοβέλλᾳ· καὶ τὸ μὲν
πρῶτον ἀγχώμαλοι διεκρίθησαν ἀπ' ἀλλήλων, τῇ δὲ
ἑξῆς ναυμαχίᾳ ἡσσᾶτο ὁ Δολοβέλλας, καὶ ὁ Κάσσιος αἱρομένου τοῦ χώματος ἔκοπτεν αὐτοῦ τὸ τεῖχος
266 ἤδη καὶ ἐσάλευεν. τόν τε νυκτοφύλακα αὐτοῦ Μάρσον
οὐ δυνηθεὶς διαφθεῖραι· διέφθειρε τοὺς ἡμεροφυλα-
κοῦντας αὐτῷ λοχαγοὺς καὶ ἀναπαυομένου τοῦ Μάρ-
σου μεθ' ἡμέραν ἐσῆλθεν, ὑπανοιχθεισῶν αὐτῷ πυλί-
267 δων κατὰ μέρη πολλῶν. ἁλούσης δὲ τῆς πόλεως ὁ μὲν
Δολοβέλλας προύτεινε τὴν κεφαλὴν τῷ σωματο-
φύλακι αὐτοῦ καὶ τεμόντα προσέταξε φέρειν Κασσίῳ
σῶστρον ἴδιον· ὁ δὲ τεμὼν ἐπικατέσφαξεν ἑαυτόν,
268 διεχρήσατο δὲ καὶ Μάρσος ἑαυτόν. ὁ δὲ Κάσσιος τὴν
μὲν τοῦ Δολοβέλλα στρατιὰν ἐς ἑαυτὸν μεθώρκου,
Λαοδικέων δὲ τά τε ἱερὰ καὶ τὰ κοινὰ ἐσύλα καὶ τοὺς
ἐπιφανεῖς ἐκόλαζε καὶ τοὺς λοιποὺς ἐσφοραῖς βαρυ-
τάταις ἐξέτρυχε, μέχρι τὴν πόλιν περιήνεγκεν ἐς
ἔσχατον κακοῦ.

269   63. Μετὰ δὲ Λαοδίκειαν ἐπ' Αἴγυπτον ὥρμα, πυνθανόμενος μὲν Κλεοπάτραν βαρεῖ στόλῳ διαπλευσεῖ-
σθαι πρός τε Καίσαρα καὶ πρὸς Ἀντώνιον, ἐπινοῶν
δὲ κωλῦσαί τε τὸν πλοῦν καὶ τίσασθαι τῆς γνώμης
τὴν βασιλίδα καὶ πρὸ τῶνδε αὐτὴν Αἴγυπτον ἐνθυμι-
ζόμενος μάλιστα ἐν καιρῷ, τετρυμένην τε ὑπὸ λιμοῦ
καὶ ξενικὸν στρατὸν οὐ πολὺν ἔχουσαν, ἄρτι τῶν Ἀλ-
270 λιηνοῦ στρατιωτῶν ἀποστάντων. οὕτω δὲ αὐτὸν ὁρμῆς καὶ ἐλπίδος ἔχοντα καὶ καιροῦ ὁ Βροῦτος ἐκάλει
κατὰ σπουδήν, ὡς ἤδη Καίσαρος καὶ Ἀντωνίου τὸν

at his disposal, Cassius put out to sea twice against Dolabella. The first time, they separated after an inconclusive engagement, but in the following battle Dolabella was defeated; Cassius now raised his siege rampart and began to pound Dolabella's wall and weaken it. He tried without 266 success to bribe Marsus, the captain of the night watch, but he did bribe the centurions guarding the wall for him during the day, and, when Marsus was taking his rest, entered the town by daylight through a number of small gates that were secretly opened to him in different places. When the town was taken, Dolabella offered his head to 267 his bodyguard and told him to cut it off and take it to Cassius to guarantee his own safety. The guard did cut it off, but then killed himself; Marsus also took his own life. Cassius made Dolabella's troops swear a new oath of loy- 268 alty to himself, plundered the temples and public treasury of Laodicea, punished the chief citizens, and ground down the rest with the most oppressive taxes, eventually bringing extreme distress on the town.

63. After Laodicea, Cassius began to move against 269 Egypt, since he had found out that Cleopatra was sailing to join Octavian and Antony with a strong fleet, and intended to prevent its sailing, and to punish the queen for her policy. Even before this he had thought that it was a particularly good time to have designs on Egypt itself, because it was devastated by famine and had only a small mercenary army, now that the forces of Allienus had recently left. Although in this way he had the impetus, the 270 hope, and the opportunity, he was summoned urgently by Brutus because Octavian and Antony were already cross-

271 Ἰόνιον περώντων. ἄκων μὲν δὴ Κάσσιος Αἴγυπτον ἐκ
τῶν ἐλπίδων μεθίει καὶ τοὺς Παρθυαίων ἱπποτοξότας
ἀπέπεμπε τιμήσας καὶ πρέσβεις πρὸς τὸν βασιλέα
αὐτῶν ἔστελλε περὶ μείζονος συμμαχίας, ἣ μετὰ τὸ
ἔργον ἀφικνουμένη Συρίαν τε καὶ πολλὰ τῶν ἐγγὺς
272 ἐθνῶν μέχρι Ἰωνίας ἐπέδραμε καὶ ἀνεχώρησεν. αὐτὸς
δὲ ὁ Κάσσιος τὸν μὲν ἀδελφιδοῦν ἐν Συρίᾳ μεθ᾽ ἑνὸς
τέλους ἀπέλιπε, τοὺς δὲ ἱππέας προύπεμψεν ἐς Καπ-
παδοκίαν, οἳ Ἀριοβαρζάνην τε ἄφνω κατέκανον ὡς
ἐπιβουλεύοντα Κασσίῳ καὶ χρήματα πολλὰ τὰ ἐκείνου καὶ τὴν ἄλλην κατασκευὴν ἐς τὸν Κάσσιον ἐπανήγαγον.

273 64. Ταρσέων δ᾽ ἐς στάσιν διῃρημένων οἱ μὲν τὸν
Κάσσιον ἐστεφανώκεσαν ἐλθόντα πρότερον, οἱ δὲ τὸν
Δολοβέλλαν ἐπελθόντα· ἀμφότεροι δὲ τῷ τῆς πόλεως
σχήματι ταῦτα ἔπρασσον. καὶ παραλλὰξ αὐτῶν προτιμώντων ἑκάτερον, ὡς εὐμεταβόλῳ πόλει χαλεπῶς
ἐχρῶντο ἑκάτεροι· Κάσσιος δὲ νικήσας Δολοβέλλαν
καὶ ἐσφορὰν ἐπέθηκεν αὐτοῖς χίλια καὶ πεντακόσια
274 τάλαντα. οἱ δὲ ἀποροῦντές τε καὶ ὑπὸ στρατιωτῶν
ἐπειγόντων ἀπαιτούμενοι σὺν ὕβρει, τά τε κοινὰ ἀπ-
εδίδοντο πάντα καὶ τὰ ἱερὰ ἐπὶ τοῖς κοινοῖς, ὅσα εἶ-
275 χον ἐς πομπὰς ἢ ἀναθήματα, ἔκοπτον. οὐδ᾽ ἑνὸς[19] δὲ
μέρους οὐδ᾽ ὡς ἀνυομένου, ἐπώλουν αἱ ἀρχαὶ τὰ
ἐλεύθερα· καὶ πρῶτα μὲν ἦν παρθένοι τε καὶ παῖδες,
ἐπὶ δὲ γυναῖκές τε καὶ γέροντες ἐλεεινοί, βραχυτάτου

[19] οὐδενὸς codd.; οὐδ᾽ ἑνὸς Gaillard-Goukowsky

ing the Ionian gulf. Cassius reluctantly abandoned his   271
hopes for Egypt, rewarded and sent back his mounted
Parthian archers, along with an embassy to their king asking for more substantial military assistance. This force arrived after the decisive battle,[49] overran Syria and many of
the neighboring peoples as far as Ionia, and then returned
home. Cassius left his nephew in Syria with one legion and   272
sent his cavalry ahead into Cappadocia, where they immediately killed Ariobarzanes on a charge of plotting
against Cassius, and brought back to Cassius large quantities of his money and other assets.

64. At Tarsus, civil disorder had divided the people.   273
One group had awarded a crown to Cassius, who was the
first to arrive, and the other had done the same for Dolabella, who came later. Both groups had claimed to be acting on behalf of the town. As they had given preference to
each in turn, both Cassius and Dolabella treated it harshly
as being a town of changeable loyalties. After his victory
over Dolabella, Cassius levied a contribution on it of one
thousand five hundred talents. The people lacked the   274
means to pay, and when the soldiers pressed them with
violent demands, they sold all their public property and,
after that, turned into coins all the sacred objects used in
religious processions, and the temple offerings. Even so,   275
since this was not sufficient to raise even a part of the sum,
the magistrates began to sell free persons into slavery, first
girls and boys, afterward women and pitiable old men,

[49] The battle of Philippi in 42.

πάμπαν ὤνιοι, μετὰ δὲ οἱ νέοι. καὶ διεχρῶντο οἱ πλέονες ἑαυτούς, ἕως ὧδε ἔχοντας ὁ Κάσσιος ἐκ Συρίας ἐπανιὼν ᾤκτειρέ τε καὶ τοῦ λοιποῦ τῶν ἐσφορῶν ἀπέλυσε.

276   65. Τάρσος μὲν δὴ καὶ Λαοδίκεια τοιάδε ἐπεπόνθεσαν, Κάσσιος δὲ καὶ Βροῦτος συμβολήσαντες ἀλλήλοιν, Βρούτῳ μὲν ἐδόκει τὴν στρατιὰν ἁλίσαντε χωρεῖν ἐπὶ τὸ μεῖζον ἔργον ἐς Μακεδονίαν· τέλη τε γὰρ ἤδη τοῖς πολεμίοις ἐς τεσσαράκοντα εἶναι στρα
277 τοῦ καὶ αὐτῶν διεληλυθέναι τὸν Ἰόνιον ὀκτώ· Κασσίῳ δὲ ἐδόκει τῶν μὲν πολεμίων ἔτι περιορᾶν ὡς τριφθησομένων ἐν σφίσιν ἐξ ἀπορίας διὰ τὸ πλῆθος, Ῥοδίους δὲ καὶ Λυκίους ἐξελεῖν, εὔνους τε ὄντας ἐκείνοις καὶ ναυτικὸν ἔχοντας, ἵνα μὴ κατὰ νώτου σφίσι γί
278 γνωνται παρὰ τὸ ἔργον. ἐπεὶ δὲ ἔδοξεν ὧδε, ἐχώρουν Βροῦτος μὲν ἐπὶ Λυκίους, Κάσσιος δὲ ἐπὶ Ῥοδίους, τεθραμμένος τε ἐν αὐτῇ καὶ πεπαιδευμένος τὰ Ἑλληνικά. ὡς δὲ κρατίστοις τὰ ναυτικὰ ἀνδράσι συνοισόμενος ἐς μάχην, τὰς ἰδίας ναῦς ἐπεσκεύαζε καὶ ἀνεπλήρου καὶ ἐγύμναζεν ἐν Μύνδῳ.

279   66. Ῥοδίων δὲ οἱ μὲν ἐν λόγῳ μᾶλλον ὄντες ἐδεδοίκεσαν Ῥωμαίοις μέλλοντες ἐς χεῖρας ἰέναι, ὁ δὲ λεὼς ἐμεγαλοφρονεῖτο, ἐπεί οἱ καὶ παλαιῶν ἔργων πρὸς οὐχ ὁμοίους ἄνδρας ἐμνημόνευον. ναῦς τε καθ
280 εῖλκον τὰς ἀρίστας σφῶν τρεῖς καὶ τριάκοντα. καὶ

---

50 Specified below (66.282) as the Macedonian king, Deme-

who sold for a very low price, and finally the young men. Most of these committed suicide. Finally Cassius, on his return from Syria, took pity on them in their plight and released them from the rest of their indemnity.

65. Such were the sufferings of Laodicea and Tarsus. 276 As for Brutus and Cassius, they held a meeting at which Brutus was of the opinion that they should unite their forces and make for Macedonia and the more important confrontation there. For their enemies, he argued, already had an army of some forty legions, of which eight had crossed the Ionian gulf. Cassius, on the other hand, 277 thought they should continue to ignore the enemy, who would, he believed, because of their huge numbers, bring their own downfall through lack of supplies. His policy was to destroy Rhodes and Lycia, who were well disposed to Octavian and Antony, and had fleets: he wanted to make sure that they were not in their rear when it came to the decisive battle. It was this latter course they decided to 278 adopt, and Brutus set out against Lycia, and Cassius against Rhodes, where he had been brought up and given a Greek education. As he was about to engage in battle with extremely powerful naval forces, he refitted his own ships, manned them fully and conducted training exercises at Myndus.

66. The more respectable Rhodians were alarmed at 279 the prospect of a conflict with Rome, but the ordinary people were overconfident, because they remembered former battles against very different opponents.[50] And so 280

trius Poliorcetes, who besieged Rhodes unsuccessfully in 305/4, and Mithridates VI Eupator of Pontus, who failed to capture the city in 88.

τάδε πράσσοντες ἔπεμπόν τινας ἐς Μύνδον ὅμως, οἳ
τὸν Κάσσιον ἠξίουν μήτε Ῥόδου καταφρονεῖν, πόλεως
ἀμυναμένης ἀεὶ τοὺς καταφρονήσαντας, μήτε συνθηκῶν, αἳ Ῥοδίοις εἰσὶ καὶ Ῥωμαίοις, ὅπλα μὴ φέρειν
ἐπὶ ἀλλήλους· εἰ δέ τι περὶ συμμαχίας ἐπιμέμφοιτο,
ἐθέλειν παρὰ τῆς Ῥωμαίων βουλῆς πυθέσθαι, καὶ κε-
281 λευούσης ἔφασαν συμμαχήσειν. οἱ μὲν δὴ τοιάδε
μάλιστα ἔλεγον, ὁ δὲ τὰ μὲν ἄλλα τὸν πόλεμον ἀντὶ
λόγων ἔφη κρινεῖν, τὰς δὲ συνθήκας κελεύειν ὅπλα
μὴ φέρειν ἐπ' ἀλλήλους, καὶ ἐπενηνοχέναι Ῥοδίους
Κασσίῳ, Δολοβέλλᾳ συμμαχοῦντας, κελεύειν δὲ ἀλλήλοις συμμαχεῖν, Κασσίῳ δὲ δεομένῳ εἰρωνεύεσθαι
τὰ περὶ τῆς Ῥωμαίων βουλῆς, φευγούσης καὶ ἀλω-
μένης ἐν τῷ παρόντι διὰ τοὺς ἐν ἄστει τυράννους, οἳ
δώσουσι μὲν αὐτοὶ δίκας, δώσουσι δὲ καὶ Ῥόδιοι τὰ
ἐκείνων προτιμῶντες, ἢν μὴ θᾶσσον ἀνέχωνται τῶν
282 κελευομένων. ὧδε μὲν ὁ Κάσσιος αὐτοὺς ἠμείψατο,
καὶ οἱ εὖ φρονοῦντες Ῥοδίων μᾶλλον ἐδεδοίκεσαν· τὸ
δὲ πλῆθος ἐδημαγώγουν Ἀλέξανδρός τε καὶ Μνασέας
ἀναμιμνήσκοντες, ὅτι καὶ Μιθριδάτης πλέοσι ναυσὶν
ἐπιπλεύσειε τῇ Ῥόδῳ καὶ Δημήτριος ἔτι πρὸ τοῦ Μι-
θριδάτου.

283   67. Οἱ μὲν δὴ τὸν Ἀλέξανδρον ἐκ τούτων εἵλοντο
σφίσι πρυτανεύειν, ἥπερ ἐστὶν ἀρχὴ παρ' αὐτοῖς
μάλιστα αὐτοκράτωρ, καὶ ναυαρχεῖν Μνασέαν, ἔπεμπον δ' ὅμως ἐς τὸν Κάσσιον ἔτι πρεσβευτὴν Ἀρχέλαον, ὃς ἐν Ῥόδῳ τὰ Ἑλληνικὰ διδάσκαλος γεγένητο

they launched their best ships, thirty-three in number. But while doing this, they also sent some representatives to Myndus, to urge Cassius not to underestimate Rhodes, a city that had always protected itself against those who underrated her, and not to disregard the existing treaty between the Rhodians and the Romans, which bound them not to bear arms against each other. If there was a complaint about rendering military assistance, they wanted to hear it from the Roman senate, and if the senate so ordered, they would provide the assistance. This, then, was   281
the case the Rhodians made. Cassius on his part said that war, not words, would decide the other matters, but that the treaty required them not to bear arms against each other, and the Rhodians had borne arms against Cassius, when they fought alongside Dolabella; the treaty also required them to assist each other in war, but when Cassius asked for help, they prevaricated by referring to the Roman senate, whose members were at the moment wandering aimlessly in exile because of the tyrants in Rome. Those tyrants would be punished, as would the Rhodians too for preferring to side with them, unless they very quickly obeyed his commands. Such was the answer Cas-   282
sius gave them. The right-thinking Rhodians were even more alarmed, but the crowd were led on by the populist speeches of Alexander and Mnaseas, who reminded them that Mithridates had invaded Rhodes with a larger fleet, as had Demetrius before Mithridates.

67. As a result of this, they elected Alexander as their   283
prytanis, which at Rhodes is the magistracy conferring supreme power, and Mnaseas as their fleet commander. Nevertheless, they still sent an envoy to Cassius in the person of Archelaus, who had been his Greek teacher at

τῷ Κασσίῳ, δεησόμενον ἤδη τόνδε τοῦ Κασσίου λι-
παρέστερον· καὶ ἐδεῖτο, τῆς δεξιᾶς λαβόμενος, ὡς
284 γνωρίμου. "Μὴ πόλιν ἀναστήσῃς Ἑλληνίδα φιλέλ-
λην ἀνήρ, μὴ Ῥόδον φιλελεύθερος ἀνήρ· μηδὲ αἰ-
σχύνῃς ἀξίωμα Δώριον, οὐχ ἡσσημένον, ἐξ οὗ γεγό-
ναμεν, μηδὲ ἐκλάθῃ καλῆς ἱστορίας ἧς ἔμαθες ἐν
285 Ῥόδῳ τε καὶ ἐν Ῥώμῃ, ἐν Ῥόδῳ μέν, ὅσα Ῥόδιοι κατὰ
πόλεις καὶ πρὸς βασιλέας, ἄλλους τε καὶ τοὺς μάλιστα ἀμάχους δόξαντας εἶναι, Δημήτριον καὶ Μιθρι-
δάτην, ὑπὲρ ἐλευθερίας ἔπραξαν, ὑπὲρ ἧς δὴ καὶ σὺ
286 φῂς τάδε κάμνειν· ἐν Ῥώμῃ δέ, ὅσα ὑμῖν αὐτοῖς καθ'
ἑτέρων καὶ κατ' Ἀντιόχου τοῦ μεγάλου συνεμαχήσα-
μεν, ὧν εἰσιν ὑπὲρ ἡμῶν ἀνάγραπτοι στῆλαι παρ'
ὑμῖν. τάδε μὲν δὴ καὶ γένους ἕνεκα καὶ ἀξιώσεως
ἡμῶν καὶ τύχης ἐς τὸ νῦν ἀδουλώτου καὶ συμμαχίας
καὶ προαιρέσεως ἐς ὑμᾶς, ὦ Ῥωμαῖοι, λελέχθω·
287 68. "Πρὸς σὲ δέ, ὦ Κάσσιε, καὶ αἰδώς τις ἔστιν
ἐξαίρετος ἔς τε τὴν πόλιν καὶ τὴν ἐν αὐτῇ τροφήν τέ
σου καὶ παίδευσιν καὶ διατριβὴν[20] καὶ ἑστίαν, ἣν
ᾤκησας, καὶ τοὐμὸν διδασκαλεῖον αὐτὸ καὶ ἐμέ, ἐλπί-
σαντα μὲν ἐς ἕτερα τούτοις ποτὲ ἐναβρυνεῖσθαι, νῦν
δὲ ὑπὲρ τῆς πατρίδος αὐτὰ δαπανῶντα, ἵνα μηδ' αὐτή
σοι πολεμεῖν ἀναγκάζηται πεπαιδευμένῳ τε ὑφ' αὑτῆς
καὶ τεθραμμένῳ μηδὲ γένηται δυοῖν ὑπ' ἀνάγκης
θάτερον, ἢ Ῥοδίους ἀποθανεῖν πάντως ἢ Κάσσιον
288 ἡσσᾶσθαι. συμβουλεύω δὲ ἐπὶ τῇ παρακλήσει,

---

[20] ἰατρικὴν codd.; διατρτιβὴν edd.

Rhodes, in order to present a more urbane petition to Cassius. And he made his plea, taking him by the right hand in a familiar manner. "You are a man who loves Greek 284 culture—do not destroy a Greek city; you are a lover of freedom—do not destroy Rhodes. Do not shame the reputation of us Dorians, undefeated as we are since our beginning. Do not forget the glorious history you learned both at Rhodes and at Rome. At Rhodes, you learned of 285 the great achievements of the Rhodians against cities and kings, and especially against Demetrius and Mithridates, who were thought to be invincible, and how they were acting on behalf of freedom, that very freedom for which you too say you are enduring these labors. And at Rome, 286 you learned of the substantial military assistance we rendered you against, among others, Antiochus the Great, deeds you have recorded at home on inscribed columns in our honor. That is surely enough, men of Rome, about our descent and reputation, about our hitherto unenslaved fate, and about our policy of military alliance with you.

68. "As for you, Cassius, you owe a peculiar reverence 287 to this city and to the upbringing and education and life and home you had in it, as well as to my school itself and to me. I had hoped that one day I would be able to pride myself on these matters for a different purpose, but I now deploy them in the service of my country, to prevent it from being forced to go to war with you, who were educated and nourished by it, and to prevent one of two things inevitably happening: either the complete destruction of the Rhodians or the defeat of Cassius. As well as appealing 288 to you, I have advice for you, when undertaking such great

305

τοιῶνδέ σε ὑπὲρ τῆς Ῥωμαίων πολιτείας ἁπτόμενον
ἔργων θεοὺς ἡγεμόνας αἰεὶ ποιεῖσθαι παντὸς ἔργου.
289 θεοὺς δ' ὠμόσατε, ὅτε ἡμῖν ἔναγχος διὰ Γαΐου Καίσαρος συνετίθεσθε καὶ σπονδὰς ἐπὶ τοῖς ὅρκοις
ἐσπένδετε καὶ δεξιὰς ἐτίθεσθε, αἳ καὶ παρὰ πολεμίοις
290 ἰσχύουσιν, οὐ παρὰ φίλοις καὶ τροφεῦσιν; φείδου δὲ
ἐπὶ τοῖς θεοῖς καὶ δόξης τῆς κατὰ ἀνθρώπους· ὡς οὐδέν ἐστι συνθηκῶν παραβάσεως μᾶλλον, ὃ τοὺς
ἁμαρτάνοντας ἀπίστους ἐς ἅπαντα ποιεῖ καὶ φίλοις
καὶ πολεμίοις."

291   69. Ταῦτ' εἰπὼν ὁ πρεσβύτης οὐ μεθίετο τῆς χειρός,
ἀλλ' ἐπεδάκρυεν αὐτῇ, ὡς ἐρυθριᾶσαι μὲν ἐπὶ τῷ
σχήματι τὸν Κάσσιον καὶ παθεῖν τι ὑπὸ αἰδοῦς,
ὑφελόντα δὲ ὅμως εἰπεῖν· "Εἰ μὲν οὐ συνεβούλευσας
Ῥοδίοις μὴ ἀδικεῖν με, σύ με ἠδίκεις· εἰ δὲ διδάσκων
292 οὐκ ἔπεισας, ἀμυνῶ σοι. ἠδικούμην δὲ δή που σαφῶς
τὸ μὲν πρῶτον ἀδίκημα συμμαχίαν αἰτῶν καὶ παρ-
ορώμενος ὑπὸ τῶν παιδευσάντων καὶ θρεψάντων, τὸ
δὲ ἑξῆς προτιμώντων μου Δολοβέλλαν, ὃν οὐκ ἐπαί-
δευσαν οὐδὲ ἀνέθρεψαν, τὸ δὲ ἀνιαρότερον, ἐμοῦ μὲν
καὶ Βρούτου καὶ ὅσων ὁρᾶτε ἀπὸ τῆς βουλῆς ἀρίστων ἀνδρῶν φευγόντων τυραννίδα καὶ τὴν πατρίδα
ἐλευθερούντων, ὦ Ῥόδιοι φιλελεύθεροι, Δολοβέλλα δὲ
αὐτὴν καταδουλοῦντος ἑτέροις, οἷς δὴ καὶ ὑμεῖς εὔνως
ἔχοντες ὑποκρίνεσθε ἐξίστασθαι τοῖς ἐμφυλίοις ἡμῶν.
293 ἔστι δὲ ἐμφύλια μέν, εἰ καὶ ἡμεῖς δυναστείας ὠρε-
γόμεθα, πόλεμος δὲ σαφὴς τὸ γιγνόμενόν ἐστι δη-

tasks on behalf of the Roman state, always to make the gods your guide in every action. You Romans swore by the   289
gods when you recently concluded a treaty with us through Gaius Caesar, and in addition to the oaths you poured libations and offered your right hand: are assurances, valid even among enemies, not to count among friends and tutors? As well as regarding the gods, think of your reputa-   290
tion among men: for there is nothing more sure than the violation of a treaty to identify those who commit such an offense as totally untrustworthy in the eyes of friends and enemies."

69. Having finished his speech, the old man did not   291
let go of Cassius' hand, but shed tears on it, so that Cassius was embarrassed at the spectacle and felt a little ashamed, but he withdrew his hand all the same, and spoke. "If you did not advise the Rhodians to do me no wrong, then it was you who did me wrong. But if you explained the situation to them, and failed to persuade them, I will defend you. It is certainly very clear that I   292
have been wronged, in the first place because when I asked for military assistance I was ignored by the very people who educated and brought me up. And second, they preferred Dolabella to me—and they did not educate or bring him up. Even more annoying, freedom-loving men of Rhodes, is the fact that Brutus and I and all the noblest senators you see are in exile from a tyranny and trying to free their country, while Dolabella is enslaving it to others, to whom you are also well disposed, although you pretend to be avoiding involvement in our civil war. This would indeed be a civil war, if we too   293
were aiming at supreme power, but in the present case it

294 μοκρατίας πρὸς μοναρχίαν. καὶ δημοκρατίαν ἀβοήθη-
τον καταλείπετε οἱ παρακαλοῦντες ὑπὲρ αὐτονομίας·
φιλίαν τε Ῥωμαίοις προφέροντες οὐκ ἐλεεῖτε ἀκρίτους
ἐπὶ θανάτῳ καὶ δημεύσει προγραφομένους, ἀλλ' ὑποκρίνεσθε πεύσεσθαι τῆς βουλῆς τῆς ταῦτα πασχού-
σης καὶ οὐδὲ ἀμύνειν ἑαυτῇ πω δυναμένης. ἡ δ' ὑμῖν
ἤδη προαπεκρίνατο, ἐν οἷς ἐψηφίσατο τοὺς ἀμφὶ τὴν
ἕω πάντας ἀμύνειν ἐμοί τε καὶ Βρούτῳ.

295 70. "Σὺ δέ, εἰ μέν ποτε ἡμῖν περικτωμένοις τι συν-
επράξατε, ὧν εὐεργεσίας καὶ μισθοὺς ἀντικεκόμισθέ
που, καταλογίζῃ, ὅτι δὲ ἡμῖν ἐς τὴν ἐλευθερίαν καὶ
σωτηρίαν ἀδικουμένοις οὐ συμμαχεῖτε, ἐπιλανθάνῃ·
οὓς εἰκὸς ἦν, εἰ καὶ μηδὲν ἡμῖν ἐς ἀλλήλους ὑπῆρχεν,
ἀλλὰ νῦν ἄρχειν ἐθελοντὰς ὑπερμαχῆσαι τῆς Ῥω-

296 μαίων δημοκρατίας, Δωριέας ὄντας. οἱ δ' ἀντὶ τοιού-
των ἔργων καὶ λογισμῶν συνθήκας ἡμῖν προφέρετε,
γενομένας μὲν ὑμῖν καὶ τάσδε πρὸς Γάιον Καίσαρα,
τῆσδε τῆς μοναρχίας ἡγεμόνα· λέγουσι δ' ὅμως αἱ
συνθῆκαι Ῥωμαίους καὶ Ῥοδίους ἐν ταῖς χρείαις ἀλ-

297 λήλοις ἀμύνειν. ἀμύνατε οὖν ἐς τὰ μέγιστα κινδυνεύουσι Ῥωμαίοις. Κάσσιος ὑμῖν ἐστιν ὁ τὰς συνθήκας τάσδε προφέρων καὶ ἐπὶ συμμαχίαν καλῶν,
Ῥωμαῖος ἀνὴρ καὶ Ῥωμαίων στρατηγός, ὥς φησι τὸ
ψήφισμα τῆς βουλῆς, ἐν ᾧ πάντας ὑπακούειν ἡμῖν

298 ἔταξε τοὺς τοῦ Ἰονίου πέραν. τὰ δ' αὐτὰ καὶ Βροῦτος

is clearly a war between democracy and autocracy.[51] And   294
you appeal to me on behalf of your own autonomy, but you
leave a democracy helpless. You cite friendship for the
Romans, but you have no pity for those on the list of proscribed who are sentenced to death without trial and confiscation of their property. You pretend that you want to
hear from the senate, which is the victim of this situation,
and no longer able to defend itself, but the senate has already answered you before, when it decreed that all the
people in the east should protect Brutus and myself.

70. "You list all the times you have rendered us some   295
service when we were adding to our possessions, for which
you certainly received benefactions and rewards, but you
fail to mention that you offer no military assistance when
our freedom and safety are wrongly threatened. Even if
we had had no relations with each other before, it would
be fitting for you, as Dorians, now at least to begin to fight
of your own free will on behalf of Roman democracy. But   296
instead of acting or thinking like this, you cite a treaty to
us, a treaty moreover struck between you and Gaius Caesar, the leader of this autocracy. Nonetheless the treaty
states that in times of need the Romans and Rhodians are
to protect each other. Well then, in this moment of ex-   297
treme danger, protect the Romans! It is Cassius who
quotes this treaty to you and calls on you to fight alongside
him—Cassius, a Roman citizen and a Roman general, as
stated in the decree of the senate, in which everyone east
of the Ionian gulf is ordered to obey us. It is the same   298

[51] It should be remembered that for Appian the word "democracy" covers more or less any form of government that is not
monarchy.

ὑμῖν προτείνει ψηφίσματα καὶ Πομπήιος, τὴν θάλασσαν ὑπὸ τῆς βουλῆς ἐπιτετραμμένος, τὰς δ᾽ ἱκετείας
ἐπὶ τοῖς ψηφίσμασι καὶ οἶδε πάντες, ὅσοι φεύγουσιν
ἀπὸ τῆς βουλῆς, οἱ μὲν ἐς ἐμὲ καὶ Βροῦτον, οἱ δ᾽ ἐς
299 Πομπήιον. ἔστι δὲ δή που τὸ συγκείμενον, Ῥωμαίοις
Ῥοδίους βοηθεῖν, κἂν καθ᾽ ἕνα χρήζωσιν. εἰ δὲ οὔτε
στρατηγοὺς ἡμᾶς οὔτε Ῥωμαίους ἔτι, ἀλλὰ φυγάδας
ἢ ξένους ἢ κατακρίτους, ὡς οἱ προγράψαντες λέγουσιν, ἡγεῖσθε, οὐ πρὸς ἡμᾶς ἐστιν ὑμῖν ἔτι, ἀλλὰ πρὸς
Ῥωμαίους, ὦ Ῥόδιοι, τὰ συγκείμενα· ἡμεῖς δὲ ξένοι
καὶ ἀλλότριοι τῶν συνθηκῶν ὄντες πολεμήσομεν
ὑμῖν, ἢν μὴ ἐς πάντα κατακούητε."

300 71. Τοιαῦτα μὲν ὁ Κάσσιος ἐπειρωνευσάμενος τὸν
Ἀρχέλαον ἀπέλυεν, Ἀλέξανδρος δὲ καὶ Μνασέας, οἱ
Ῥοδίων ἡγούμενοι, ταῖς τριάκοντα καὶ τρισὶ ναυσὶν
ἀνήγοντο ἐπὶ Κάσσιον ἐς Μύνδον ὡς προκαταπλήξον-
τες τῷ ἐπίπλῳ· καί τί που καὶ κούφως εἶχον ἐλπίδος,
ὅτι καὶ Μιθριδάτῃ ἐς Μύνδον ἐπιπλεύσαντες ἐδόκουν
301 ἐς τὸ τοῦ πολέμου τέλος εὐτυχῆσαι. εἰρεσίᾳ δὲ ἐς ἐπίδειξιν χρώμενοι τήν τε πρώτην ἡμέραν ηὐλίσαντο ἐν
Κνίδῳ καὶ τῆς ἐπιούσης ἐπεφαίνοντο τοῖς ἀμφὶ τὸν
302 Κάσσιον ἐκ τοῦ πελάγους. οἱ δὲ θαυμάσαντες ἀντανή-
γοντο, καὶ τὸ ἔργον ἦν ἑκατέρωθεν ἰσχύος τε καὶ δυ-
νάμεως· Ῥόδιοι μὲν γὰρ ναυσὶ κούφαις διεξέπλεόν τε
τοὺς πολεμίους ὀξέως καὶ περιέπλεον καὶ ἐπανόδοις
ἐχρῶντο, Ῥωμαῖοι δὲ ἐπὶ νεῶν βαρυτέρων, ὅτε συμ-
πλακεῖεν, ἀπὸ βαρυτέρας ῥύμης ἐπεβάρουν ὥσπερ ἐν

decrees that Brutus presents for your attention, and Pompeius too, who was appointed by the senate to the command of the sea. Added to these decrees are the prayers of all these senators who are taking refuge, some with myself and Brutus, and others with Pompeius. The treaty 299 does, of course, provide for the Rhodians to assist the Romans even in cases where the application is made by a single individual. But if you do not consider us as generals or Romans, but as exiles or strangers or condemned men, as those who have proscribed us claim, then, men of Rhodes, it is not with us that you have a treaty, but with Romans. And, as we are strangers and foreigners in relation to the treaty, we will make war on you, unless you obey us in everything."

71. Having delivered this ironical speech, Cassius sent 300 Archelaus away. Alexander and Mnaseas, the Rhodian leaders, put to sea with their thirty-three ships against Cassius at Myndus, intending to strike fear into him with their surprise attack. Their hopes were probably somewhat illusory, because they thought that it was also by launching a naval attack on Mithridates at Myndus, that they had successfully brought that war to an end. Having 301 put on a demonstration by proceeding under oar, the first day they bivouacked at Cnidus. The next day they made their appearance to the forces of Cassius from the seaward side. The latter in astonishment put to sea against them, 302 and the battle on both sides was a matter of strength and power. For the Rhodians with their light ships sailed swiftly through the enemy line, turned around, and returned to the attack, while the Romans had heavier ships, and when they came to close quarters, would use their greater momentum to press hard on the enemy, like in a

303 πεζομαχίᾳ. τοῦ δὲ Κασσίου πλήθει νεῶν τὰς πολεμίας περιλαβόντος, οἱ μὲν Ῥόδιοι περιπλεῖν ἔτι καὶ
διεκπλεῖν οὐκ ἐδύναντο, ἐμβάλλουσι δ᾽ αὐτοῖς μόνον
ἐκ τοῦ μετώπου καὶ ἀναχωροῦσιν ἡ μὲν ἐμπειρία διέφθαρτο ὑπὸ τῆς στενοχωρίας κεκυκλευμένοις, αἱ δὲ
ἐμβολαὶ καὶ ἀποσιμώσεις ἐς βαρυτέρας τὰς Ῥωμαίων ναῦς ἀσθενεῖς ἐγίγνοντο, Ῥωμαίοις δ᾽ ἦσαν ἐς
304 κουφοτέρας εὔτονοι, μέχρι Ῥόδιαι μὲν τρεῖς αὐτοῖς
ἀνδράσιν ἐλήφθησαν καὶ δύο ἀνερράγησάν τε καὶ
κατέδυσαν καὶ αἱ λοιπαὶ βεβλαμμέναι διέφυγον ἐς
τὴν Ῥόδον, αἱ δὲ Ῥωμαίων ἅπασαι μὲν ἐπανῆλθον ἐς
Μύνδον, ἐπεσκευάζοντο δὲ καὶ τούτων αἱ πλέονες
βλαβεῖσαι.

305   72. Τοῦτο μὲν δὴ τῆς ἐν Μύνδῳ Ῥωμαίων τε καὶ
Ῥοδίων ναυμαχίας τέλος ἦν, καὶ αὐτὴν γιγνομένην ὁ
Κάσσιος ἀπὸ ὄρους καθεώρα· ὡς δὲ ἐπεσκεύασε τὰ
σκάφη, διέπλευσεν ἐς Λώρυμα, Ῥοδίων τι φρούριον
ἐν τῇ περαίᾳ, καὶ τὸ πεζὸν ἐς τὴν Ῥόδον διεβίβαζεν
306 ἐπὶ ὁλκάδων ὑπὸ Φαννίῳ τε καὶ Λέντλῳ. αὐτὸς δὲ
ἐπέπλει ταῖς ὀγδοήκοντα ναυσὶν ἐσκευασμέναις ἐς τὸ
φοβερώτατον καὶ περιστήσας τῇ Ῥόδῳ τὸ πεζὸν
ὁμοῦ καὶ τὸ ναυτικὸν ἡσύχαζεν ὡς ἐνδωσόντων τι τῶν
307 πολεμίων. οἱ δὲ ἐπανήχθησαν μὲν αὖθις εὐθαρσῶς,
δύο δὲ καὶ τότε ναῦς ἀποβαλόντες συνεκλείσθησαν.
καὶ ἀναδραμόντες ἐπὶ τὰ τείχη πάντα τε ὅπλων

---

[52] It is not clear who this Fannius is (perhaps the praetor of
54), but presumably it is the same man who appears below at

312

battle on land. But when Cassius with his superior number 303
of ships surrounded the enemy fleet, the Rhodians could
no longer sail round and through his line. Since they could
only attack from the front and then back off, their experience was neutralized by the narrow space where they had
been confined. Head-on ramming and broadside movements against the heavier Roman ships were ineffective,
while those of the Romans against lighter vessels had force
in them. Finally, three Rhodian ships were captured with 304
their crews, two were broken up and sank, and the rest
made their escape to Rhodes in a damaged condition. All
of the Roman ships returned to Myndus, where they were
repaired, most of them also having suffered damage.

72. Such was the result of the naval engagement be- 305
tween the Romans and the Rhodians at Myndus. Cassius
watched it unfold from a mountain. When he had repaired
his ships he sailed across to Loryma, a Rhodian fort on the
mainland opposite the island, and transported his infantry
to Rhodes in merchantmen under the command of Fannius and Lentulus.[52] He himself launched an attack with 306
his eighty ships equipped in a manner designed to produce the maximum terror, surrounded Rhodes with his
land and naval forces combined, and then made no further
moves, expecting that the enemy would weaken somewhat. In fact, they sailed out again confidently, but on this 307
occasion too they lost another two ships, and were shut in.
Then they hurried up onto the walls, manned them fully

84.354, and at 5.139.579, where he abandons Sextus Pompeius
and joins Marc Antony. Publius Cornelius Lentulus Spinther,
quaestor in 44, served under Trebonius in Asia, and after the latter's death joined Brutus and Cassius.

ἐπλήρουν καὶ ἀπεμάχοντο ὁμοῦ τοὺς περὶ τὸν Φάν-
νιον ἀπὸ τῆς γῆς ἐνοχλοῦντας καὶ τὸν Κάσσιον τοῖς
πρὸς θαλάσσῃ τείχεσι τὸ ναυτικὸν οὐκ ἀνέτοιμον ἐς
τειχομαχίαν ἐπαγαγόντα· ἐλπίζων γάρ τι τοιοῦτον
ἐπεφέρετο πύργους ἐπτυγμένους, οἳ τότε ἀνίσταντο.

308 Ῥόδος μὲν δὴ δύο πείραις καμοῦσα ἔκ τε γῆς καὶ
θαλάσσης ἐπολιορκεῖτο· καὶ οὐδέν, ὡς ἐν ἔργῳ ταχεῖ
καὶ ἀδοκήτῳ, παρεσκεύαστο αὐτοῖς ἐς πολιορκίαν.
ὅθεν ἦν εὔδηλον ἁλώσεσθαι τάχιστα τὴν πόλιν ἢ
χερσὶν ἢ λιμῷ· καὶ τάδε Ῥοδίων οἱ συνετώτεροι καθεώρων, καὶ Φάννιος αὐτοῖς καὶ Λέντλος διελέγοντο.

309   73. Γιγνομένων δ᾽ ἔτι τούτων ἄφνω Κάσσιος ἦν ἐν
μέσῃ τῇ πόλει μετ᾽ ἐπιλέκτου στρατοῦ, βίας μὲν οὐδεμιᾶς φανείσης οὐδὲ κλιμάκων ἔργου. εἴκαζον δὲ οἱ
πολλοί, καὶ δοκεῖ γενέσθαι, τοὺς χαρίεντας αὐτῷ τῶν
πολιτῶν ὑπανοῖξαι πυλίδας ἐλέῳ τῆς πόλεως καὶ προ-

310 μηθείᾳ τροφῶν. ὧδε μὲν ἑαλώκει Ῥόδος, καὶ Κάσσιος
ἐν αὐτῇ προυκάθητο ἐπὶ βήματος καὶ δόρυ τῷ βήματι
παρεστήσατο ὡς ἐπὶ δοριαλώτῳ. ἀτρεμεῖν τε κελεύ-
σας τὸν στρατὸν ἀκριβῶς καὶ θάνατον ἐπικηρύξας, εἴ
τις ἁρπάσειεν ἢ βιάσαιτό τι, αὐτὸς ἐξ ὀνόματος ἐκάλει Ῥοδίων ἐς πεντήκοντα ἄνδρας καὶ ἀχθέντας ἐκόλαζε θανάτῳ· ἑτέροις δέ, ἀμφὶ τοὺς πέντε καὶ εἴκοσιν,

311 οὐχ εὑρεθεῖσι φυγὴν ἐπέταττεν. χρήματα δὲ ὅσα ἦν
ἢ χρυσὸς ἢ ἄργυρος ἐν ἱεροῖς τε καὶ δημοσίοις,
πάντα συλήσας ἐκέλευσε καὶ τὸν ἰδιωτικὸν ἐκφέρειν
τοὺς κεκτημένους εἰς ἡμέραν ῥητήν· καὶ ἐπεκήρυξε
τοῖς μὲν ἐπικρύψασι θάνατον, τοῖς δὲ μηνύσασι

with armed soldiers, and simultaneously fought off both
Fannius, who was harassing them from the landward side,
and Cassius, who led his fleet, which was well prepared for
assaulting walls, against the walls facing the sea. For having expected this sort of situation, he was bringing up
collapsible towers, which were now erected. So Rhodes,   308
afflicted by twin attacks, was besieged by both land and
sea. And, as happens in a sudden and unexpected emergency, nothing had been done by them to prepare for a
siege. For this reason, it was clear that the city would be
captured very quickly, either by force or by famine. The
more intelligent of the Rhodians saw this, and Fannius and
Lentulus entered talks with them.

73. While these were in progress, Cassius suddenly   309
appeared in the middle of the city with an elite force,
without any sign of violence or use of ladders. Most people
assumed, and it seems to be what happened, that those
citizens who favored him opened the postern gates out of
compassion for the city and consideration of supplies.
Such was the way Rhodes was captured. Cassius took his   310
seat on a tribunal in the city and planted a spear beside it
to indicate that the city had been taken by force of arms.
Having given strict orders for the troops to remain calm,
and proclaimed the death penalty for anyone who resorted
to looting or violence, he himself summoned by name
about fifty Rhodian men, and when they were brought in,
punished them with death; another twenty-five or so who
could not be found, he condemned to exile. All the money,   311
gold, or silver that was in the temples or public treasuries
he seized, and ordered the private citizens to bring out
their personal wealth on a fixed day. He announced that
he would execute any who hid it, and set a reward of ten

312 δεκάτην, δούλοις δὲ καὶ ἐλευθερίαν. οἱ δ᾽ ἐν μὲν ἀρχῇ
πολλοὶ συνέκρυψαν, οὐκ ἐς τέλος ἐλπίζοντες ἀφίξεσθαι τὴν ἀπειλήν· διδομένων δὲ τῶν γερῶν καὶ ‹κολαζομένων›[21] τῶν μηνυομένων ἔδεισάν τε καὶ προθεσμίαν ἑτέραν λαβόντες οἱ μὲν ἐκ γῆς ἀνώρυσσον, οἱ
δὲ ἐκ φρεάτων ἀνίμων, οἱ δὲ ἐξέφερον ἐκ τάφων πολὺ
πλέονα τῶν προτέρων.

313 74. Αἱ μὲν δὴ Ῥοδίων συμφοραὶ τοιαίδε ἦσαν, καὶ
Λεύκιος Οὐᾶρος αὐτοῖς μετὰ φρουρᾶς ὑπελέλειπτο· ὁ
δὲ Κάσσιος ἡδόμενος τῇ ταχυεργίᾳ τῆς ἁλώσεως καὶ
τῷ πλήθει τῶν χρημάτων ἐπέταττεν ὅμως καὶ τοῖς
ἄλλοις ἔθνεσι τῆς Ἀσίας ἅπασι φόρους ἐτῶν δέκα

314 συμφέρειν. καὶ οἱ μὲν ἐπράσσοντο συντόνως, ἐξαγ-
γέλλεται δὲ αὐτῷ Κλεοπάτρα μέλλουσα διαπλεῖν μεγάλῳ στόλῳ καὶ παρασκευῇ βαρυτάτῃ πρὸς Καίσαρά τε καὶ Ἀντώνιον· τὰ γὰρ ἐκείνων αἱρουμένη καὶ
τέως διὰ τὸν πρότερον Καίσαρα, τότε μᾶλλον ᾑρεῖτο

315 διὰ τὸν ἐκ Κασσίου φόβον. ὁ δὲ Μοῦρκον μετά τε
ὁπλιτῶν ἀρίστου τέλους καὶ τοξοτῶν τινων ἐπὶ νεῶν
ἑξήκοντα καταφράκτων ἐς Πελοπόννησον ἔπεμπε
ναυλοχεῖν περὶ Ταίναρον, ‹. . .› περισυράμενος ἐκ
τῆς Πελοποννήσου λείαν, ὅσην ἔφθασε.

316 75. Τὰ δ᾽ ἀμφὶ Λυκίαν καὶ Βροῦτον, μικρὰ καὶ τῶν
ἀμφὶ τοῦτον ἐς ὑπόμνησιν ἀναλαβόντι ἄνωθεν, ἦν
τοιάδε. ἐπειδὴ παρὰ Ἀπουληίου στρατιάν τέ τινα
εἰλήφει, ὅσην Ἀπουλήιος εἶχεν, καὶ χρήματα ἐς ἐξα-

---

[21] κολαζομένων add. Schweig.

percent for informers, and for slaves their freedom as well. To start with, many did conceal their wealth, hoping that in the end the threat would not be carried out, but when the rewards were paid and those who had been informed against punished, they became alarmed, and having obtained another deadline, some dug their money out of the ground, others drew it out of wells, and others brought it out of tombs, in much larger amounts than before. 312

74. Such were the disasters suffered by the Rhodians. Lucius Varus was left in charge of them with a garrison. Cassius, although delighted with how quickly the city had been captured and the large quantity of money taken, nevertheless ordered all the other peoples of Asia to pay ten years' tribute. But while they began to do this diligently, news is brought to him that Cleopatra was about to sail with a large and very heavily equipped fleet to join Octavian and Antony. For she had favored their side before because of the first Caesar, but she was now an even keener supporter because of her fear of Cassius. He now sent Murcus, with one of his best legions of troops and some archers, on sixty decked ships, to the Peloponnese, to lie in wait at Taenarum, <and this he did?> collecting as much booty as time allowed from the Peloponnese.[53] 313 314 315

75. What happened to Brutus in Lycia, to summarize a little of what has been said before as a reminder of his affairs too, was as follows. When he had received from Appuleius all the troops he had under his command, to- 316

[53] It is not clear how long the lacuna in this sentence is.

κισχίλια καὶ μύρια τάλαντα, ὅσα ἐκ τῶν φόρων τῆς
317 Ἀσίας συνείλεκτο, παρῆλθεν ἐς Βοιωτίαν. ψηφισαμένης δὲ αὐτῷ τῆς βουλῆς τοῖς τε χρήμασιν ἐς τὰ
παρόντα χρῆσθαι καὶ Μακεδονίας ἄρχειν καὶ τῆς
Ἰλλυρίδος ἐπὶ τῇ Μακεδονίᾳ, τὰ μὲν ἐν τοῖς Ἰλλυ-
ριοῖς τρία τέλη τοῦ στρατοῦ παραλαμβάνει, Οὐατι-
νίου τοῦ πρότερον ἄρχοντος Ἰλλυριῶν παραδόντος, ἐν
δὲ ἐκ Μακεδονίας ἀφείλετο Γάιον, τὸν ἀδελφὸν
Ἀντωνίου. τέσσαρα δὲ ἐπὶ τούτοις ἄλλα συναγαγὼν
ὀκτὼ τὰ πάντα εἶχε, Γαΐῳ Καίσαρι τὰ πολλὰ αὐτῶν
318 ἐστρατευμένα. εἶχε δὲ καὶ ἱππέων πλῆθος καὶ ψιλοὺς
καὶ τοξότας, καὶ τοὺς Μακεδόνας ἐπαινῶν ἐς τὸν Ἰταλικὸν ἤσκει τρόπον. ἀγείροντι δὲ αὐτῷ στρατὸν ἔτι
319 καὶ χρήματα συντυχία Θρᾴκιος τοιάδε γίγνεται. Πο-
λεμοκρατία, γυνή τινος τῶν βασιλίσκων, ἀναιρεθέντος αὐτῇ τοῦ ἀνδρὸς ὑπὸ ἐχθρῶν δείσασα περὶ τῷ
παιδὶ ἔτι ὄντι μειρακίῳ, ἧκεν αὐτὸν φέρουσα καὶ ἐνεχείρισε Βρούτῳ, ἐνεχείρισε δὲ καὶ τοὺς τοῦ ἀνδρὸς
320 θησαυρούς. ὁ δὲ τὸν μὲν παῖδα Κυζικηνοῖς ἀνατρέ-
φειν παρέδωκε, μέχρι σχολάσειεν ἐπὶ τὴν βασιλείαν
καταγαγεῖν, ἐν δὲ τοῖς θησαυροῖς εὗρε παράδοξον
χρυσίου τι πλῆθος καὶ ἀργύρου. καὶ τοῦτο μὲν ἔκοπτε
καὶ νόμισμα ἐποίει.
321   76. Ὡς δὲ ἦλθέ τε ὁ Κάσσιος καὶ ἔδοξε Λυκίους
καὶ Ῥοδίους προεξαιρεῖν, ἐτράπετο Λυκίων ἐπὶ Ξαν-

---

54 Appian refers back to BCiv. 3.63.259.

gether with sixteen thousand talents in money that had
been collected from the revenues of Asia, he arrived in
Boeotia.[54] As the senate decreed that he could use this   317
money for his present needs, and that he was to be governor of Macedonia, and Illyria in addition, he takes over the
three legions of the army in Illyria, which Vatinius, the
previous governor, delivered to him, and he captured another Macedonian legion from Gaius, the brother of Marc
Antony.[55] He recruited four more in addition to these, so
that he had eight legions in all, most of whom had served
under Gaius Caesar. He also had a large force of cavalry,   318
along with light-armed troops, and archers, and the Macedonians, whom he rated highly, he trained in the Roman
manner. While he was still assembling an army and collecting money, he has the following good luck in Thrace.
Polemocratia, wife of one of the minor princes, because   319
her husband had been killed by his enemies and she was
afraid for her son, who was still a boy, arrived with her son
and entrusted him to Brutus, but also handed her husband's treasuries to him. Brutus delivered the boy to the   320
inhabitants of Cyzicus to look after, until he had the time
to restore him to his kingdom, and found in the treasuries
a prodigious quantity of gold and silver. This he struck and
converted into coinage.

76. When Cassius arrived, and they decided to begin   321
by reducing Lycia and Rhodes, the first of the Lycians

[55] Publius Vatinius had been tribune in 59 and later served
with Caesar in Gaul. He was consul (briefly) in 47 and governed
Illyria from 45 to 43. In 42 he celebrated a triumph for a victory
in Illyria. Gaius Antonius (praetor 44) was later captured by Brutus and was executed in 42.

θίους πρώτους. οἱ δὲ τά τε προάστεια σφῶν καθεῖλον,
ἵνα μὴ ἐς κατάλυσιν αὐτοῖς ὁ Βροῦτος μηδ' ἐς ὕλην
ἔχῃ χρῆσθαι, καὶ τὴν πόλιν περιταφρεύσαντες ἀπεμάχοντο ἀπὸ τῆς τάφρου, τὸ μὲν βάθος οὔσης πεντήκοντα ποδῶν βαθυτέρας, τὸ δὲ πλάτος κατὰ λόγον
τοῦ βάθους, ὥστε παρ' αὐτὴν ἑστῶτες ἠκόντιζόν τε
καὶ ἐτόξευον ὥσπερ ἐν μέσῳ ποταμὸν ἔχοντες ἀπέρα-
322 τον. ὁ δὲ Βροῦτος αὐτὴν ἔχου βιαζόμενος καὶ σκεπα-
στήρια τῶν ἐργαζομένων προυτίθει καὶ τὸν στρατὸν
ἐς ἡμέραν καὶ νύκτα ἐμέριζε, καὶ τὴν ὕλην μακρόθεν,
ὥσπερ ἐν τοῖς ἀγῶσι, σὺν δρόμῳ καὶ βοῇ μετέφερεν,
323 οὐδὲν ἐκλείπων σπουδῆς καὶ πόνου. ὅθεν αὐτῷ τὸ ἔργον ἐλπισθὲν ἢ οὐκ ἔσεσθαι κωλυόντων τῶν πολεμίων
ἢ πολλοῖς μησὶ μόλις ἔσεσθαι, ὀλίγαις ἡμέραις ἐξείργαστο, καὶ οἱ Ξάνθιοι κατακλεισθέντες ἐπολιορκοῦντο.

324   77. Καὶ αὐτοῖς ὁ Βροῦτος τοὺς μὲν ἐκ μηχανημάτων
εἰς τὰ τείχη, τοὺς δὲ ἐκ ποδὸς ἐπῆγεν ἐπὶ τὰς πύλας
καὶ πάντας ἐνήλλασσε συνεχῶς. οἱ δὲ ἀκμῆσιν αἰεὶ
κεκμηκότες συμφερόμενοι καὶ τετρωμένοι πάντες,
325 ὅμως ὑπέμενον, ἕως σφίσιν αἱ ἐπάλξεις διέμενον. ὡς
δὲ καὶ αὗται κατεσύρησαν καὶ οἱ πύργοι διερρώγε-
σαν, ὑποτοπήσας τὸ ἐσόμενον ὁ Βροῦτος ἐκέλευσε
τὰς ἐφέδρους τῶν πυλῶν τάξεις ἀποστῆναι· καὶ οἱ
Ξάνθιοι νομίσαντες ἀφυλαξίαν καὶ ἀμέλειαν εἶναι νυκτὸς ἐξέδραμον μετὰ λαμπάδων ἐπὶ τὰ μηχανήματα.
326 ταχὺ δὲ ἐκ συνθήματος αὐτοῖς τῶν Ῥωμαίων ἐπι-
δραμόντων, συνέφευγον αὖθις ἐς τὰς πύλας· καὶ τῶν

against whom Brutus turned his attention was the town of
Xanthus. The Xanthians destroyed their suburbs to prevent Brutus using them as quarters for his troops or as a
supply of wood, and dug a ditch around the town from
which they defended themselves. The ditch was more
than fifty feet deep and as wide as it was deep, so that while
standing along it they threw their missiles and shot their
arrows as if they had an uncrossable river separating them
from the enemy. Brutus set about filling it in while under   322
attack, placing cover in front of his men as they worked,
and dividing his forces into day and night teams. He
brought up material from far away, running and cheering
with his men as if in a competition, and sparing no enthusiasm or effort. The result was that the task which, because   323
of the enemy's efforts to stop it, would, it was expected,
either not be completed at all or only with difficulty after
several months, he finished in a few days, and the Xanthians were cut off and besieged.

77. Brutus led his men against them, some on siege   324
engines against the walls, others on foot against the gates,
and he continually rested his troops in relays. Although the
defenders were exhausted and always fighting against
fresh opponents, and were all wounded, nevertheless they
held out as long as their parapets remained. But when   325
these were knocked down and the towers shattered, Brutus suspected what would happen, and ordered the ranks
positioned at the gates to withdraw. The Xanthians, thinking that this was a careless failure to keep guard, made a
sortie by night against the siege engines with torches. But   326
at an agreed signal, the Romans quickly attacked, and the
Xanthians again fled to the gates, which the guards closed

φυλάκων αὐτὰς προαποκλεισάντων ὑπὸ δέους, μὴ
συνεσπέσοιεν οἱ πολέμιοι, φθόρος ἦν Ξανθίων πολὺς
ἀμφὶ ταῖς πύλαις ἀποκεκλεισμένων.

327   78. Οὐ πολὺ δὲ ὕστερον ἐξέδραμον αὖθις οἱ λοιποὶ
περὶ μεσημβρίαν, ἀναχωρούσης πάλιν τῆς τάξεως,
καὶ ἐνέπρησαν τὰ μηχανήματα ἅπαντα ἀθρόως. πε-
πετασμένων δ᾽ αὐτοῖς τῶν πυλῶν διὰ τὸ πρότερον
πάθος, συνεισέπεσον ἀμφὶ δισχιλίους μάλιστα Ῥω-
328   μαίων. καὶ ἑτέροις δὲ εἰσωθιζομένοις ἀμφὶ τὴν εἴσοδον ἐπέπεσον αἰφνίδιον αἱ πύλαι, εἴθ᾽ ὑπό του
Ξανθίων εἴτε καὶ αὐτομάτως τῶν χαλαστηρίων διαρ-
ραγέντων, ὥστε τῶν ἐσβιασαμένων Ῥωμαίων τοὺς
μὲν ἀπολέσθαι, τοὺς δὲ ἔνδον ἀποληφθῆναι, τὰς
πύλας οὐ δυναμένους ἔτι ἀνασπάσαι, χωρὶς ἀνασπα-
329   στηρίων γενομένας. βαλλόμενοι δ᾽ ἐν τοῖς στενωποῖς
ἄνωθεν ὑπὸ τῶν Ξανθίων, βιασάμενοί ποτε μόλις ἐς
τὴν ἀγορὰν ἐγγὺς οὖσαν διέδραμον· κἀνταῦθα τῶν
μὲν συμπλεκομένων σφίσι κρατοῦντες, τοξευόμενοι δὲ
χαλεπῶς καὶ οὐδὲν ἔχοντες αὐτοὶ τόξον ἢ ἀκόντιον,
παρὰ τὸ Σαρπηδόνειον, ἵνα μὴ κυκλωθεῖεν, διέδρα-
330   μον. οἱ δ᾽ ἔξω τείχους Ῥωμαῖοι περὶ τῶν ἔνδον ἀγα-
νακτοῦντές τε καὶ δεδιότες, Βρούτου περιθέοντος αὐτούς, ἐς πᾶσαν ἐμερίζοντο πεῖραν, οὔτε τὰς πύλας
δυνάμενοι ῥῆξαι σιδήρῳ περιβεβλημένας, οὔτε κλιμάκων ἢ πύργων ἐμπεπρησμένων εὐποροῦντες. ἀλλ᾽
331   οἱ μὲν ἐσχεδίαζον κλίμακας, οἱ δὲ κεραίας τοῖς τείχεσι προστιθέντες ὡς διὰ κλιμάκων ἐπεχείρουν, οἱ δὲ
καὶ σιδήρια ὀξέα καλῳδίοις περιτιθέντες ἐσφενδόνων

before they could get in, afraid that the enemy would rush in with them. There took place at the gates a large-scale slaughter of the Xanthians who had been shut out.

78. A little later the remaining Xanthians made another sortie around midday, the Roman line again withdrawing, and they set fire to all the siege engines together. But the gates were left open for them because of the previous disaster, and some two thousand Romans broke in with them. While others were pushing their way in at the entrance, the gates suddenly fell on them—either one of the Xanthians did this intentionally, or the ropes snapped of their own accord—with the result that some of the Romans who had forced their way in were killed and the others were cut off inside, as they were no longer able to raise the gates which were now without their lifting mechanism. Bombarded in the narrow streets by missiles thrown from above by the Xanthians, with difficulty they just about managed to force their way through to the forum, which was nearby. Here, although they got the better of those who engaged with them at close quarters, they came under heavy fire from archers, and not having bows or javelins themselves, they hurried through to the shrine of Sarpedon in order to avoid being surrounded. The Romans outside the walls were both annoyed and anxious for those inside, and with Brutus rushing from one to another, they tried every expedient, but were unable to break the gates, which were covered with iron, and they lacked ladders or towers, because these had been burned. Some improvised ladders, however, some placed yardarms against the walls and attacked as if they were using ladders, and others attached sharp iron hooks to ropes and

327

328

329

330

331

[τὰ σιδήρια]²² ἐς τὸ τεῖχος ἄνω καί, ὅτε καταπαγείη
τινὰ αὐτῶν, ἑαυτοὺς ἀνίμων.

332   79. Οἰνοανδεῖς δὲ γείτονες, διὰ τὴν ἐς τοὺς Ξαν-
θίους ἔχθραν τῷ Βρούτῳ συμμαχοῦντες, διὰ τῶν κρημνῶν ἐπετροβάτουν ἄνω· καὶ αὐτοὺς ἰδόντες οἱ Ῥω-
333   μαῖοι ἐμιμοῦντο ἐπιμόχθως. καὶ πολλοὶ μὲν ἐξέπιπτον,
εἰσὶ δ᾽ οἳ τὸ τεῖχος ὑπερβάντες καὶ πυλίδα ἀνέῳξαν,
ἢ προεσταύρωτο πυκνοτάτοις σταυροῖς, καὶ τοὺς
εὐτολμοτάτους αἰωρουμένους ὑπὲρ τὰ σταυρώματα
ἐσεδέχοντο. καὶ πλείους γενόμενοι τὰς πύλας ἔκοπτον, οὐ περιβεβλημένας ἔτι τῷ σιδήρῳ τὰ ἐντός,
ἀντικοπτόντων αὐτοῖς ἅμα ἔξωθεν ἑτέρων ἐς τὸ αὐτὸ
334   καὶ συνεργούντων. Ξανθίων δὲ σὺν μεγάλῃ πάνυ βοῇ
τοῖς ἀμφὶ τὸ Σαρπηδόνειον οὖσι Ῥωμαίοις ἐπιθεόντων, δείσαντες ὑπὲρ αὐτῶν, ὅσοι περὶ τὰς πύλας ἔν-
δοθέν τε καὶ ἔξωθεν αὐτὰς ἔκοπτον, ὑπὸ μανιώδους
ὁρμῆς ἐβιάζοντο καὶ διαρρήξαντες ἐσέδραμον ἀθρόοι,
δύνοντος ἄρτι τοῦ θεοῦ, μετὰ ἀλαλαγῆς, ἵνα σύμβολον εἴη τοῖς ἐντὸς οὖσιν.

335   80. Ἁλούσης δὲ τῆς πόλεως οἱ Ξάνθιοι ἐς τὰς οἰκίας
συνέτρεχον καὶ τὰ φίλτατα σφῶν κατέκαινον, ἑκόντα
τὴν σφαγὴν ὑπέχοντα. οἰμωγῆς δὲ γιγνομένης ὁ
Βροῦτος νομίσας ἁρπαγὴν εἶναι τὸν στρατὸν ἀνεῖργε
336   διὰ κηρύκων· ὡς δὲ ἔγνω τὸ γιγνόμενον, ᾤκτειρεν ἀνδρῶν φρόνημα φιλελεύθερον καὶ σπονδὰς περιέπεμπεν. οἱ δὲ καὶ τοὺς φέροντας ἔβαλλον καὶ τὰ σφέτερα

²² τὰ σιδήρια del. Mend.

threw them onto the walls above, and whenever one of them caught fast, they pulled themselves up.

79. The neighboring Oenoandans, who were assisting 332 Brutus because of their hostility toward Xanthus, now began to climb their way up the cliffs, and when the Romans saw them they copied them with considerable difficulty. Many fell off, but some got over the wall and opened a 333 small gate, which had been fenced with a dense array of stakes, and let in the most daring of the attackers, who swung themselves over the stockade. With the increase in their numbers, they now began to batter the gates, which were not faced in iron on the inside, at the same time as others on the outside helped them by battering the gates from the opposite direction for the same purpose. While 334 the Xanthians were attacking the Romans at the shrine of Sarpedon with an enormous clamor, the Romans at the gates, in anxiety for their comrades, continued to batter the gates both from inside and outside, and tried to force their way through with frantic zeal. Just after the sun god had gone down, they broke through and rushed in en masse, with a shout intended as a signal to those inside the town.

80. When the city was taken, the Xanthians ran to their 335 homes and killed those dearest to them, who willingly accepted their deaths. A wailing cry began, and thinking that plundering was taking place, Brutus ordered heralds to restrain the army. On learning what was really happening, 336 he took pity on the freedom-loving spirit of the people and sent envoys to offer a truce. But the Xanthians threw missiles at those bringing the offer, and, after killing all their

πάντα ἀνελόντες ἐς πυρὰς προνενησμένας ἐν ταῖς
οἰκίαις ἐπέθεσαν καὶ τὸ πῦρ ἅψαντες ἑαυτοὺς ἐπι-
337 κατέσφαξαν. Βροῦτος δὲ τῶν ἱερῶν περισώσας ὅσα
ἐδύνατο, μόνους θεράποντας εἷλε Ξανθίων καὶ ἐκ τῶν
ἀνδρῶν γύναια ὀλίγα ἐλεύθερα καὶ ἄνδρας οὐδὲ ἐς
338 ἑκατὸν καὶ πεντήκοντα πάντας. Ξάνθιοι μὲν δὴ τρίτον
ὑπὸ σφῶν αὐτῶν ἀπώλλυντο ἐλευθερίας οὕνεκα. καὶ
γὰρ ἐπὶ Ἁρπάγου τοῦ Μήδου, Κύρῳ τῷ μεγάλῳ
στρατηγοῦντος, ὧδε σφᾶς ἀντὶ δουλοσύνης διέφθει-
ραν, καὶ τάφος Ξανθίοις ἡ πόλις ἀποκλεισθεῖσα[23] ὑπὸ
Ἁρπάγου τότε ἐγένετο· καὶ ἐπὶ Ἀλεξάνδρου τοῦ Φιλίππου φασὶν ὅμοια παθεῖν, οὐχ ὑποστάντας οὐδὲ
Ἀλεξάνδρῳ μετὰ τοσῆσδε γῆς ἀρχὴν ὑπακοῦσαι.

339   81. Βροῦτος δὲ ἐς Πάταρα ἀπὸ Ξάνθου κατῄει,
πόλιν ἐοικυῖαν ἐπινείῳ Ξανθίων, καὶ περιστήσας αὐτοῖς τὸν στρατὸν ἐκέλευσεν ἐς πάντα ὑπακούειν ἢ τὰς
Ξανθίων συμφορὰς προσδέχεσθαι· προσήγοντό τε
αὐτοῖς οἱ Ξάνθιοι ὀδυρόμενοι τὰ σφέτερα καὶ παραι-
340 νοῦντες ἀμείνονα βουλεύσασθαι. Ξανθίοις δὲ οὐδὲν
ἀποκριναμένων πω τῶν Παταρέων, ἐδίδου τὸ λοιπὸν
αὐτοῖς τῆς ἡμέρας ἐς σκέψιν καὶ ἀνεχώρει. ἅμα δὲ
ἡμέρᾳ προσῆγεν. οἱ δὲ ἀπό τε τῶν τειχῶν ἐβόων ὑπακούειν, ἐς ὅ τι βούλοιτο, καὶ τὰς πύλας ἀνεῴγνυον.
341 ὁ δ' ἐσελθὼν ἔκτεινε μὲν οὐδένα οὐδ' ἐξήλασε, χρυσὸν
δὲ καὶ ἄργυρον, ὅσον ἡ πόλις εἶχε, συνενεγκὼν

___

[23] ἀμεληθεῖσα codd.; ἀποκλεισθεῖσα Mend.; ἀμερθεῖσα
Gaillard-Goukowsky

own families, placed the bodies on funeral pyres, which had previously been piled up in their houses, set fire to them, and took their own lives over them. Brutus saved as 337 many of the sanctuaries as he could, but he captured only slaves of the Xanthians; and of the citizens a few free women and not even one hundred and fifty men. This was 338 the third time the Xanthians perished by their own hand in the defense of freedom. For in the time of Harpagus the Mede, one of Cyrus the Great's generals, they killed themselves in this way, rather than be enslaved: shut off[56] by Harpagus, the town became for the Xanthians their tomb. In the time of Alexander, son of Philip, it is said that they suffered the same fate when they could not bear to obey even Alexander with his enormous empire.

81. From Xanthus Brutus went down to Patara, a town 339 which functions as seaport for the Xanthians. He surrounded it with his army and ordered the inhabitants to obey him in everything, or else face the disasters suffered by Xanthus. And the Xanthians were brought forward to them, lamenting their own misfortunes and advising them to adopt wiser counsels. When the inhabitants of Patara 340 still had not answered the Xanthians, Brutus gave them the rest of the day to consider the matter, and withdrew. The next morning he advanced, and the Patarans shouted from the walls that they would comply with all his wishes, and opened their gates. When he entered the town, he did 341 not execute or banish anyone, but having collected all the gold and silver held publicly by the town, he ordered all

[56] The text is corrupt at this point, and it is not clear what the verb is. The story is recounted in Herodotus (1.173–76).

ἐκέλευε καὶ τὸν ἰδιωτικὸν ἑκάστους ἐσφέρειν ὑπὸ ζημίαις καὶ μηνύμασιν, οἵοις καὶ Κάσσιος ἐκήρυξεν ἐν
342 Ῥόδῳ. καὶ οἱ μὲν ἐσέφερον, θεράπων δὲ τὸν δεσπότην
ἐμήνυσε χρυσίον κρύψαι καὶ πεμφθέντι λοχαγῷ τὸ
χρυσίον ἔδειξεν. ἀγομένων δὲ ἁπάντων ὁ μὲν δεσπότης ἐσιώπα, ἡ δὲ ἐκείνου μήτηρ περισῴζουσα τὸν
υἱὸν εἵπετο, βοῶσα αὐτὴ τὸ χρυσίον κρύψαι. ὁ δὲ
οἰκέτης, οὐδὲ ἀνερωτώμενος, τὴν μὲν ἤλεγχε ψευδο-
343 μένην, τὸν δὲ κρύψαντα. καὶ ὁ Βροῦτος τὸν μὲν νεανίαν ἀπεδέξατο τῆς σιωπῆς καὶ τὴν μητέρα τοῦ
πάθους καὶ μεθῆκεν ἀμφοτέρους ἀπαθεῖς ἀπιέναι τὸ
χρυσίον φερομένους, τὸν δὲ οἰκέτην ὡς πέρα τοῦ
προστάγματος ἐπιβουλεύσαντα τοῖς δεσπόταις ἐκρέμασε.

344   82. Τῷ δ᾿ αὐτῷ χρόνῳ καὶ Λέντλος ἐπιπεμφθεὶς
Ἀνδριάκῃ Μυρέων ἐπινείῳ τήν τε ἅλυσιν ἔρρηξε τοῦ
λιμένος καὶ ἐς Μύρα ἀνήει. Μυρέων δέ, ἃ προσέτασσε,
δεχομένων χρηματισάμενος ὁμοίως ἐς Βροῦτον ἐπ-
345 ανήει. καὶ τὸ κοινὸν τὸ Λυκίων ἐς Βροῦτον ἐπρέσβευε,
συμμαχήσειν τε ὑπισχνούμενοι καὶ ἐσοίσειν, ὅσα δύναιντο. ὁ δὲ αὐτοῖς ἐσφορὰς τε ἐπέβαλε καὶ Ξανθίων
τοὺς ἐλευθέρους ἀπεδίδου τῇ πόλει καὶ τὸ ναυτικὸν τὸ
Λυκίων ἅμα ταῖς ἄλλαις ναυσὶν ἐκέλευε περιπλεῖν ἐς
Ἄβυδον, ἔνθα καὶ τὸ πεζὸν αὐτὸς ἦγε καὶ Κάσσιον
ἐξ Ἰωνίας ἀνέμενεν, ὡς ἐς Σηστὸν ὁμοῦ διαβαλοῦν-
346 τες. Μοῦρκος δὲ ἐν Πελοποννήσῳ ναυλοχῶν Κλεοπάτραν, ἐπειδὴ ἔμαθεν αὐτὴν ὑπὸ χειμῶνος ἀμφὶ τῇ
Λιβύῃ βλαβεῖσαν καὶ τὰ ναυάγια εἶδε μέχρι τῆς Λα-

individuals to bring him their private wealth, under threat
of the same sort of penalties and rewards for informers
as Cassius proclaimed at Rhodes. The citizens handed in   342
their money, but one slave informed on his master for hiding his gold, and showed it to the centurion sent to get it.
When all involved were led away under arrest, the master
remained silent, but his mother, who had followed in order
to save her son, shouted out that she was the one who had
hidden the gold. Without being asked, the slave accused
her of lying, and said that the son had hidden it. Brutus   343
approved of the young man's silence and sympathized with
his mother's suffering. He allowed them both to leave unharmed and take the gold with them, but he crucified
the slave for going beyond the proclamation by plotting
against his masters.

82. At the same time Lentulus, who had been sent   344
against Andriace, the seaport of the Myreans, broke the
chain across the harbor and went up to Myra. The inhabitants agreed to carry out his orders, and having collected
money in the same way as at Patara he returned to Brutus.
The Lycian League also sent a mission to Brutus promis-   345
ing to give him military assistance and to contribute what
resources they could. He imposed financial contributions
on them, restored the free Xanthians to their town and
ordered the Lycian fleet together with his other ships to
sail around to Abydus, where he himself was bringing his
land forces to wait for Cassius' arrival from Ionia, so that
they might cross over to Sestus together. When Murcus,   346
who was lying in wait for Cleopatra in the Peloponnese,
learned that her fleet had been damaged by a storm off
Africa—he saw the wreckage carried on the current as far

κωνικῆς ἐκφερόμενα καὶ σὺν ἀρρωστίᾳ μόλις αὐτὴν
ἐς τὰ ἑαυτῆς ἐπανιοῦσαν, ἵνα μὴ δι' ἀπραξίας εἴη
μετὰ τοσοῦδε στόλου, διέπλευσεν ἐπὶ Βρεντεσίου καὶ
ἐς τὴν ἐπικειμένην τῷ λιμένι νῆσον ὁρμισάμενος ἐκώλυε τὴν ὑπόλοιπον τῶν πολεμίων στρατιὰν ἢ ἀγορὰν
347 ἐς Μακεδονίαν περαιοῦσθαι. καὶ αὐτὸν ὁ Ἀντώνιος
ἀπεμάχετο ναυσὶ μακραῖς, ὅσαις εἶχεν, ὀλίγαις· ἀπεμάχετο δὲ καὶ πύργοις, οὓς ἐπῆγεν ἐπὶ σχεδιῶν, ὅτε
τὸν στρατὸν ὁλκάσιν ἐκπέμποι κατὰ μέρη, πνεῦμα
ἀπὸ τῆς γῆς πολὺ φυλάσσων, ἵνα μὴ καταλαμβά-
νοιντο ὑπὸ τοῦ Μούρκου. κακοπαθῶν δὲ ἐκάλει Καίσαρα, Πομπηίῳ Σέξστῳ κατὰ Σικελίαν περὶ αὐτῆς
Σικελίας ναυμαχοῦντα.

348   83. Ὧδε δὲ εἶχε καὶ τὰ περὶ Πομπήιον. νεώτερος ὢν
ὅδε τῶν Μάγνου Πομπηίου παίδων ὑπερώφθη μὲν τὰ
πρῶτα ὑπὸ Γαΐου Καίσαρος περὶ Ἰβηρίαν, ὡς οὐδὲν
μέγα διὰ νεότητα καὶ ἀπειρίαν ἐργασόμενος, καὶ
ἠλᾶτο περὶ τὸν ὠκεανὸν λῃστεύων σὺν ὀλίγοις καὶ
349 λανθάνων, ὅτι εἴη Πομπήιος. πλεόνων δὲ ἐς τὸ λῃστεύειν αὐτῷ συνιόντων χείρ τε ἦν ἤδη καρτερὰ καὶ
ἐξεφαίνετο Πομπήιος ὤν. καὶ αὐτίκα, ὅσοι τοῦ πατρὸς
ἢ τοῦ ἀδελφοῦ στρατιῶται γεγονότες ἡλῶντο, ὡς ἐς
οἰκεῖον ἡγεμόνα συνέτρεχον, καὶ Ἀραβίων ἐκ Λιβύης
ἀφίκετ' αὐτῷ, ἀφῃρημένος τὰ πατρῷα, ὥς μοι προ-
350 είρηται. ὧδε δὲ αὐτῷ πλήθους γενομένου, ἔργα τε ἦν
ἤδη λῃστηρίου δυνατώτερα καὶ ὄνομα τοῦ Πομπηίου

as Laconia—and knew that she was returning demoralized and with difficulty to her own country, he sailed for Brundisium so that he would not remain inactive with such a large fleet. He anchored off the island lying opposite the harbor, and prevented the rest of the enemy's army and supplies from getting over to Macedonia. Antony 347 fought him off with the few warships he had, and also with towers mounted on barges, whenever he sent out detachments of his army in merchantmen, waiting for a strong breeze off the land, so that they would not be captured by Murcus. But finding himself in difficulty, he appealed to Octavian, who was conducting a naval campaign around Sicily against Sextus Pompeius, for possession of Sicily itself.

83. With regard to Pompeius the situation was as follows. Although the younger son of Pompey the Great, he 348 was at first ignored by Gaius Caesar in Iberia on the grounds that he was unlikely to accomplish anything of importance, because of his youth and inexperience. He roamed the seas with a few men committing acts of piracy, but kept hidden the fact that he was a Pompeius. When 349 more joined him to engage in piracy, his band now became powerful, and he revealed that he was a Pompeius. Immediately, all those outcasts who had served under his father or his brother made their way to him as their natural leader, and Arabio arrived to join him from Africa, where he had lost his ancestral kingdom, as I have described above.[57] In this way he acquired a very large 350 group, and with his exploits now carrying more force than a band of brigands, the name of Pompeius spread to the

[57] Above, 54.230.

ἀνὰ ὅλην τὴν Ἰβηρίαν, εὐρυτάτην ἐθνῶν οὖσαν, πε-
ριθέοντός τε καὶ μεθιπταμένου καὶ ἐς χεῖρας οὐχ ὑπο-
μένοντος ἐλθεῖν τοῖς ἡγουμένοις αὐτῆς ὑπὸ Γαΐῳ Καί-
351 σαρι. ὧν ὁ Γάιος πυνθανόμενος ἔπεμπε σὺν στρατῷ
πλέονι Καρρίναν ἐκπολεμήσοντα Πομπήιον. ὁ δὲ καὶ
τούτῳ, κουφότερος ὤν, ἐπεφαίνετο ἄφνω καὶ ἀφιπτά-
μενος ἠνώχλει καὶ πόλεις ἤδη τινὰς ᾕρει βραχυτέρας
τε καὶ μείζους.

352   84. Καὶ ὁ Γάιος ἔπεμψε τῷ Καρρίνᾳ διάδοχον Ἀσί-
νιον Πολλίωνα πολεμεῖν Πομπηίῳ. ὅν τινα πόλεμον
αὐτῶν ὁμοίως διαφερόντων, ὅ τε Γάιος Καῖσαρ
353 ἀνῃρέθη καὶ ἡ βουλὴ κατεκάλει Πομπήιον. ὁ δὲ ἐν
Μασσαλίᾳ γενόμενος περιεσκόπει ἔτι τὰ ἐν Ῥώμῃ.
αἱρεθεὶς δὲ καὶ τῆς θαλάσσης ἄρχειν, καθὰ ἦρχεν
αὐτοῦ καὶ ὁ πατήρ, ἐς μὲν τὴν πόλιν οὐδ' ὡς ἀνῆλθεν,
ὅσαι δὲ νῆες ἐν τοῖς λιμέσιν ἦσαν, λαβὼν ἐξέπλευσε
354 σὺν αἷς εἶχεν ἀπὸ τῆς Ἰβηρίας. ἐπιγενομένης δὲ τῆς
τῶν τριῶν ἀρχῆς ἐς Σικελίαν διέπλευσε καὶ Βιθυνικὸν
ἄρχοντα αὐτῆς, οὐ παριέντα οἱ τὴν νῆσον, ἐπολιόρκει, μέχρι προγραφέντες ἐπὶ θανάτῳ καὶ φυγόντες ἐκ
Ῥώμης Ἱρτιός τε καὶ Φάννιος ἔπεισαν ἐκστῆναι
Πομπηίῳ Βιθυνικὸν Σικελίας.

355   85. Ὧδε μὲν ὁ Πομπήιος Σικελίας ἐκράτησε, καὶ
ναῦς ἔχων καὶ νῆσον ἐπικειμένην τῇ Ἰταλίᾳ καὶ
στρατὸν ἤδη πολύν, ὅσον τε πρότερον εἶχε καὶ ὅσον
οἱ φεύγοντες ἐκ Ῥώμης ἐλεύθερον ἢ δοῦλον ἦγον ἢ

whole of Iberia, the most extensive of the provinces. By hurrying around and flying from one place to another, however, he avoided engaging with the governors of the province sent by Gaius Caesar. When Caesar learned of 351 this, he sent Carrinas with a large army to fight him.[58] But Pompeius had a more mobile force than Carrinas, and by suddenly making an appearance and then moving elsewhere, he harassed him and began to capture some towns, large and small.

84. Caesar then sent Asinius Pollio as successor to Car- 352 rinas to prosecute the war against Pompeius. They conducted this war with indecisive results until Gaius Caesar was assassinated and the senate recalled Pompeius. Hav- 353 ing arrived in Massilia, he continued to keep a watch on events in Rome. Appointed to the command of the sea, as his father had been too, he still did not return to Rome, but taking all the ships in the harbors, along with the ones he brought from Iberia, he set sail. On the establishment 354 of the triumvirate, he sailed to Sicily, and blockaded Bithynicus, the governor, as he would not yield the island to him.[59] Eventually, Hirtius and Fannius, both sentenced to death on the proscription lists and in exile from Rome, persuaded Bithynicus to abandon Sicily to Pompeius.

85. This was how Pompeius took control of Sicily. He 355 thus had ships, an island lying off the coast of Italy, and an army, now of considerable size, made up of the troops he had before and those brought by the exiles from Rome,

[58] Gaius Carrinas was one of the suffect consuls in 43.
[59] Aulus Pompeius Bithynicus was praetor probably in 45, then governed Sicily until he was executed by Sextus Pompeius in 42.

αἱ πόλεις ἐξ Ἰταλίας ἔπεμπον αὐτῷ, αἱ ἐς ἐπινίκια
356   τοῖς στρατοῖς ἐπηγγελμέναι. ταῖς γὰρ δὴ γνώμαις
αἵδε μάλιστα τὴν νίκην τῶν τριῶν ἀνδρῶν ἀπεύχοντο
καί, ὅσα δύναιντο, κρύφα ἀντέπρασσον· ἀποδιδρά-
σκοντές τε τῶν πατρίδων ὡς οὐκέτι πατρίδων οἱ δυνάμενοι συνέφευγον ἐς Πομπήιον, ἀγχοτάτω τε ὄντα
357   καὶ περιφίλητον ἅπασιν ἐν τῷ τότε. παρῆσαν δ᾽ αὐτῷ
καὶ ναυτικοὶ ἄνδρες ἐκ Λιβύης καὶ Ἰβηρίας, ἔμπειροι
θαλάσσης, ὥστε καὶ ἡγεμόσι καὶ ναυσὶ καὶ πεζῷ καὶ
358   χρήμασιν ὁ Πομπήιος ἐπῆρτο. καὶ τούτων ὁ Καῖσαρ
ἐπήκοος ὢν ἔπεμπε Σαλουιδιηνὸν ἐπὶ νεῶν στόλου,
Πομπήιον ὡς εὐχερὲς ἔργον ἐξελεῖν παραπλέοντα· καὶ
αὐτὸς ᾔει διὰ τῆς Ἰταλίας ὡς αὐτῷ Σαλουιδιηνῷ συμ-
359   βολήσων περὶ Ῥήγιον. Σαλουιδιηνῷ δ᾽ ὁ Πομπήιος
ἀπαντᾷ μεγάλῳ στόλῳ, καὶ πρὸ τοῦ πορθμοῦ ναυμαχίας ἀμφὶ τὸ Σκύλλαιον αὐτοῖς γενομένης αἱ μὲν τοῦ
Πομπηίου νῆες, κουφότεραί τε οὖσαι καὶ ναυτικω-
τέρων ἀνδρῶν, ταχυτῆτι καὶ ἐμπειρίᾳ προὖχον, αἱ δὲ
360   Ῥωμαίων ἅτε βαρύτεραι καὶ μείζους ἐμόχθουν. ὡς δ᾽
ὁ συνήθης τοῦ πορθμοῦ κλύδων ἐπεγίγνετο καὶ δι-
εσπᾶτο ἡ θάλασσα ἐφ᾽ ἑκάτερα ὑπὸ τοῦ ῥοῦ, οἱ μὲν
ἧσσον ἐμόχθουν ὑπὸ ἔθους τοῦ κλύδωνος, οἱ δ᾽ ἀμφὶ
τὸν Σαλουιδιηνόν, οὔτε ἑστῶτες βεβαίως ὑπὸ ἀηθείας

---

60 Quintus Salvidienus Rufus Salvius was one of Octavian's
close allies in 44 and made governor of Gaul by him in 40. Although not even a member of the senate (according to Cass. Dio

both free men and slaves, or those sent to him by the Italian towns that had been promised to the soldiers as the rewards of victory. Of course, in their heart of hearts, these 356 towns in particular prayed that the triumvirs would not win, and they did everything they could to oppose them secretly. Those with influence fled from their hometowns as no longer being their hometowns, and took refuge with Pompeius, who was very close at hand and greatly admired by everyone at that time. There also were present with 357 him seafaring men from Africa and Iberia, experienced in marine matters, with the result that Pompeius had great confidence in his commanders and his ships and his land forces and his finances. Listening to news of these events, 358 Octavian sent Salvidienus in command of a naval force to sail along the coast and destroy Pompeius, assuming that it would be an easy task.[60] He himself made his way across Italy with the intention of joining Salvidienus at Rhegium. Pompeius met Salvidienus with a large fleet, and a naval 359 engagement took place between them at the entrance of the straits near the promontory of Scyllaeum. The ships of Pompeius, being lighter and manned by better sailors, had the advantage of speed and skill, while those of the Romans were heavier and bigger, and found themselves in difficulty for that reason. When the usual swell built up in 360 the straits and the sea was churned up in different directions by the current, the crews of Pompeius suffered less, as they were used to the heavy sea. Salvidienus' men, on the other hand, were unsteady on their feet, as they were

48.33), he was designated consul for 39, but Octavian had him killed for plotting with Antony.

οὔτε τὰς κώπας ἔτι ἀναφέρειν δυνάμενοι οὔτε τὰ πη-
δάλια ἔχοντες εὐπειθῆ, συνεταράσσοντο, ὥστε κλίνον-
τος ἐς δείλην ἑσπέραν ἤδη τοῦ θεοῦ πρότερος ὁ Σαλουιδιηνὸς ἀνεκάλει. ὑπεχώρει δὲ καὶ ὁ Πομπήιος.

361 νῆες δὲ ἑκατέρων ἴσαι διεφθάρατο, καὶ τὰς λοιπὰς
λελωβημένας τε καὶ πεπονημένας ὁ Σαλουιδιηνὸς
ἐπεσκεύαζεν, ὑποχωρήσας ἐς λιμένα πρὸ τοῦ πορθμοῦ Βαλαρόν.

362   86. Ὁ δὲ Καῖσαρ ἐπελθὼν Ῥηγίνοις μὲν καὶ Ἱπ-
πωνεῦσι μεγάλας πίστεις αὐτὸς ἔδωκεν ἀναλύσειν
αὐτοὺς ἐκ τῶν ἐπινικίων (ἐδεδίει γὰρ ὄντας ἐπὶ τοῦ
πορθμοῦ μάλιστα), καλοῦντος δ' αὐτὸν Ἀντωνίου
κατὰ σπουδὴν διέπλει πρὸς αὐτὸν ἐς τὸ Βρεντέσιον,
ἐν ἀριστερᾷ ἔχων Σικελίαν καὶ Πομπήιον καὶ Σι-

363 κελίαν ὑπερθέμενος ἐν τῷ τότε. Μοῦρκος δὲ ἐπιόντος
τοῦ Καίσαρος, ἵνα μὴ ἐν μέσῳ γένηται Ἀντωνίου τε
καὶ Καίσαρος, μικρὸν ἀναχωρήσας τοῦ Βρεντεσίου,
τὰς ὁλκάδας ἐφύλασσεν ἐν τῷ πόρῳ τὸν στρατὸν ἐς

364 Μακεδονίαν ἐκ τοῦ Βρεντεσίου διαφερούσας. αἱ δὲ
προεπέμποντο μὲν ὑπὸ τριήρων, πνεύματος δὲ πολλοῦ
κατὰ θεὸν οἰκείου γενομένου διέπτησαν ἀδεῶς, οὐδὲν

365 τῶν προπομπῶν δεηθεῖσαι. καὶ ὁ Μοῦρκος ἀχθόμενος
ὅμως ἐφήδρευεν ἐπανιούσαις κεναῖς. αἱ δὲ καὶ τότε,
καὶ αὖθις ἕτερον στρατὸν ἄγουσαι, διέπλεον ἱστίοις
στρογγύλοις, μέχρι πᾶς ὁ στρατὸς καὶ ἐπ' αὐτῷ Καῖ-

not used to it, and being unable to lift their oars any more, or steer reliably with their rudders, they were thrown into confusion. The result was that with the sun god going down toward late evening, Salvidienus was the first to give the signal for retreat. Pompeius also withdrew. Both sides 361 lost an equal number of ships, and Salvidienus retired to the port of Balarus, at the entrance to the straits, where he repaired his remaining ships, damaged and in bad shape as they were.

86. On his arrival, Octavian gave his solemn assurances 362 in person to the people of Rhegium and Hipponium that he would take them off the list of victory prizes (for he was particularly apprehensive about their location right on the straits), but when Antony appealed to him as a matter of urgency, he sailed over to him at Brundisium, keeping Sicily on the left;[61] and for the time being he postponed the matter of Pompeius and Sicily. At the approach of 363 Octavian, Murcus withdrew a short distance from Brundisium to avoid finding himself between Antony and Octavian, and kept watch in the channel for the transport ships carrying the army across from Brundisium to Macedonia. These were escorted by triremes, but, with the help of a 364 god, a strong wind sprang up in their favor, and they flew across the sea in no danger and having no need of their escorts. Murcus was annoyed, but lay in wait for the ships 365 when they returned empty. Yet on that occasion too they made the crossing under full sail, and again when carrying other troops, until the whole army, and with it both Octa-

[61] This looks like a mistake: unless he sailed the long way around the western end of Sicily, the island cannot have been on his left.

366 σάρ τε καὶ Ἀντώνιος διέπλευσαν. καὶ ὁ Μοῦρκος ὑπό
του δαιμόνων βεβλάφθαι νομίζων, ὑπέμενεν ὅμως τὰς
ἐκ τῆς Ἰταλίας αὐτοῖς διαπλεούσας παρασκευὰς ἢ
τροφὰς ἢ τὸν ἐπισυλλεγόμενον στρατὸν βλάπτων,
367 ὅσα δύναιτο. καὶ αὐτῷ Δομίτιος Ἀηνόβαρβος ὑπὸ
τῶν ἀμφὶ τὸν Κάσσιον ἐς τὸ αὐτὸ ἔργον, ὡς χρησιμώτατον δή, μετὰ νεῶν ἄλλων πεντήκοντα καὶ τέλους
ἑτέρου καὶ τοξοτῶν ἐπέμφθη· ὡς γὰρ οὐκ ἔχουσι τοῖς
ἀμφὶ τὸν Καίσαρα τροφὰς δαψιλεῖς ἑτέρωθεν ἐδόκει
τὰ ἐκ τῆς Ἰταλίας διακλείσειν.

368   87. Οἱ μὲν δὴ ναυσί τε μακραῖς ἑκατὸν καὶ τριάκοντα καὶ ὑπηρετικαῖς πλέοσι καὶ στρατῷ πολλῷ διαπλέοντες ἠνώχλουν, Δεκίδιος[24] δὲ καὶ Νωρβανός οὓς
ὁ Καῖσαρ καὶ Ἀντώνιος μετὰ ὀκτὼ τελῶν ἐς Μακεδονίαν προεπεπόμφεσαν, ἐκ Μακεδονίας ἐχώρουν ἐπὶ
Θρᾴκης τῆς ὀρείου χιλίους καὶ πεντακοσίους σταδίους, μέχρι πόλιν ὑπερβάντες Φιλίππους τὰ στενὰ
Κορπίλων[25] καὶ Σαπαίων, τῆς Ῥασκουπόλιδος ὄντα
ἀρχῆς, κατέλαβον, ᾗ μόνῃ διελθεῖν ἔστιν ἐς τὴν
Εὐρώπην ἐκ τῆς Ἀσίας τὴν γνώριμον ὁδόν. καὶ τοῦτο

[24] Κεδίκιος codd.; Δεκίδιος edd. hic et deinceps
[25] Τορπιδῶν codd.; Κορπίλων edd. hic et deinceps

---

[62] Gnaeus Domitius Ahenobarbus (consul 32) was the son of
Caesar's enemy Lucius Domitius Ahenobarbus, who was killed at
the battle of Pharsalus in 48. Gnaeus first opposed the triumvirs,
but he then went over to Antony, and just before the battle of
Actium, joined Octavian.

vian and Antony, had crossed the sea. Murcus believed   366
that he had been obstructed by some divine force, but
held his position nevertheless, in order to inflict what damage he could on the equipment, supplies, or further levies
being shipped over to the enemy from Italy. Domitius   367
Ahenobarbus was sent to him by Cassius to help in the
same task, since it was obviously of vital service, together
with fifty additional ships, another legion, and a contingent of archers;[62] for as Octavian's forces had no plentiful
source of supplies from elsewhere, it seemed sensible to
cut off the route from Italy.

87. And so Murcus and Domitius, with their one hun-   368
dred and thirty warships, an even larger number of support vessels, and a big army, sailed across the sea to harass
the enemy. As for Decidius and Norbanus, whom Octavian and Antony had sent with eight legions to Macedonia
beforehand, they advanced one thousand five hundred
stades from Macedonia toward the mountainous part of
Thrace and, moving beyond the town of Philippi, they
eventually seized the passes of the Corpilans and the Sa-
paeans in the kingdom of Rhascupolis.[63] This is the only
route known to be possible for traveling from Asia to Europe, and seizing it was also the first obstacle put in the

[63] Lucius Decidius Saxa served under Julius Caesar from 49
and after Caesar's death was loyal to Antony. He fought at the
battle of Philippi and was made governor of Syria, but he was
captured and killed by the Parthians in 40 (see App. *Syr.* 51.259).
Gaius Norbanus Flaccus (consul 38) was proconsul in Spain from
36 to 32.

τοῖς ἀμφὶ τὸν Κάσσιον, ἐς Σηστὸν ἐξ Ἀβύδου περά-
369 σασι, πρῶτον ἀντεκεκρούκει. Ῥασκούπολις δὲ καὶ
Ῥάσκος ἤστην ἀδελφὼ Θρακίω βασιλίσκω, μιᾶς ἄρ-
χοντε χώρας, οἳ τότε τῇ γνώμῃ περὶ τῆς συμμαχίας
διεφέροντο. καὶ Ῥάσκος μὲν τοῖς ἀμφὶ τὸν Ἀντώνιον
συνεμάχει, Ῥασκούπολις δὲ τοῖς ἀμφὶ τὸν Κάσσιον,
370 τρισχιλίους ἱππέας ἔχων ἑκάτερος. πυνθανομένοις δὲ
τοῖς ἀμφὶ τὸν Κάσσιον περὶ τῶν ὁδῶν ὁ Ῥασκούπολις ἔφη τὴν μὲν δι' Αἴνου καὶ Μαρωνείας ἐπίτομόν
τε καὶ συνήθη καὶ λεωφόρον οὖσαν ἐπὶ τὰ Σαπαίων
στενὰ ἄγειν, κατεχόντων δὲ αὐτὰ τῶν πολεμίων ἀμή-
χανα ἐς δίοδον εἶναι, τὴν δὲ περίοδον τριπλασίονά τε
καὶ χαλεπήν.

371   88. Οἱ δὲ τοὺς πολεμίους ὑπολαβόντες οὐκ ἐς κώλυσιν μὲν ὁδῶν αὐτοῖς ἀπαντᾶν, τροφῶν δὲ ἀπορίᾳ ἐς
Θρᾴκην ἀντὶ Μακεδονίας ὑπερβῆναι, ἐβάδιζον ⟨τὴν⟩
ἐπὶ Αἴνου καὶ Μαρωνείας ὁδὸν ἀπὸ[26] Λυσιμαχείας τε
καὶ Καρδίας, αἳ τὸν ἰσθμὸν τῆς Θρᾳκίου χερρονήσου
διαλαμβάνουσιν ὥσπερ πύλαι, μετὰ δὲ ἄλλην ἡμέραν
372 ἐς τὸν Μέλανα κόλπον ἀφίκοντο. καὶ τὸν στρατὸν
ἐξετάζουσιν αὐτοῖς ἐγένοντο πάντες ὁπλιτῶν ἐννεακαίδεκα τέλη, Βρούτου μὲν ὀκτώ, Κασσίου δὲ ἐννέα,
ἐντελὲς οὐδέν, ἄλλα τε δύο[27] που τέλη μάλιστα ἀνα-

---

[26] ⟨τὴν⟩ ἐπὶ Αἴνου καὶ Μαρωνείας ὁδὸν ἀπὸ Schweig.; ὅθεν
ἐπὶ codd.; lacunam post Μαρωνείας indic. Gaillard-Goukowsky
[27] ἄλλα τε δύο Ihne; ἀλλ' ἐς δύο codd.; ἀλλ' ἐς ⟨τὰ⟩ δύο
που μέρη Gaillard-Goukowsky

way of Cassius and his men since they had crossed from
Sestus to Abydus. Rhascupolis and Rhascus were brothers 369
of the royal family of Thrace, two men ruling one country,
who had different opinions at the time about the correct
alliance to make. Rhascus had taken up arms for Antony
and Rhascupolis for Cassius, and each of them had three
thousand cavalry. When Cassius inquired about the roads, 370
Rhascupolis told them that while the one through Aenus
and Maronea was the main road normally used, and it was
short, it led to the Sapaean pass, which was occupied by
the enemy and impossible to get through; the way around,
however, was three times as long and a difficult route.

88. Brutus and Cassius, supposing that the enemy had 371
crossed into Thrace from Macedonia not to block the
roads and confront them, but because they were short of
supplies, took the Aenus and Maronea road from Lysimachea and Cardia,[64] which close off the isthmus of the Thracian Chersonesus like gates. Another day's journey brought
them to the gulf of Melas. A review of their army found a 372
total of nineteen legions, eight of Brutus, nine of Cassius,
none of them at full strength, with another two legions,
more or less, being filled,[65] so that there were about eighty

---

[64] The text is corrupt at this point. I have adopted Schweig-
haüser's emendation to make sure that, starting presumably from
Sestus, Brutus and Cassius make their way up the Thracian Cher-
sonese to Lysimachea and Cardia and then westward to Aenus
and Maronea.

[65] The text is again corrupt, with various solutions suggested.

πληρούμενα, ὡς γίνεσθαι μυριάδας ὁπλιτῶν ἀμφὶ τὰς
373 ὀκτώ. ἱππέες δὲ ἦσαν Βρούτῳ μὲν Κελτοὶ καὶ Λυσι-
τανοὶ τετρακισχίλιοι καὶ Θρᾷκες καὶ Ἰλλυριοὶ Παρ-
θηνοὶ καὶ Θεσσαλοὶ δισχίλιοι, Κασσίῳ δὲ Ἴβηρές τε
καὶ Κελτοὶ δισχίλιοι καὶ ἱπποτοξόται Ἄραβές τε καὶ
Μῆδοι καὶ Παρθυαῖοι τετρακισχίλιοι. σύμμαχοι δὲ
εἵποντο βασιλέες καὶ τετράρχαι Γαλατῶν τῶν ἐν
Ἀσίᾳ, πεζόν τε ἄγοντες πολὺν ἄλλον καὶ ἱππέας ὑπὲρ
πεντακισχιλίους.

374   89. Τοσήδε μὲν στρατιὰ τοῖς ἀμφὶ τὸν Κάσσιον
ἐπὶ τοῦ Μέλανος κόλπου διεκρίθη, καὶ τοσήδε ἐχώρουν
ἐπὶ τὸ ἔργον, τὴν λοιπὴν ἔχοντες ἐπὶ τῶν ἀλλαχόθι
χρειῶν. καθήραντες δὲ αὐτὴν τοῖς νομιζομένοις ἀν-
επλήρουν τὰς ἐκ τῶν ἐπηγγελμένων τισὶν ὀφειλομέ-
νας ἔτι δωρεάς, πολλῆς μὲν περιουσίας χρημάτων
πεφροντικότες, οἰκειούμενοι δὲ ταῖς δόσεσιν αὑτούς,
Γαΐῳ μάλιστα Καίσαρι τοὺς πλέονας ἐστρατευμένους, μή τις ἐς τὴν ὄψιν ἢ ὁμωνυμίαν τοῦ νέου Καί-
375 σαρος νεωτερίσειεν ἐλθόντος. καὶ αὖθις ἔδοξε τούτου
χάριν καὶ δημηγορῆσαι. βῆμά τε οὖν ἐπήχθη μέγα,
καὶ οἱ στρατηγοὶ μετὰ τῶν ἀπὸ τῆς βουλῆς μόνων ἐς
αὐτὸ ἀναβάντες, ὁ δὲ στρατὸς αὐτῶν, ὅ τε ἴδιος καὶ
συμμαχικός, κάτω περιστάντες, ἥδοντο εὐθὺς ἐπὶ τῇ
ὄψει τοῦ πλήθους ἀλλήλων ἑκάτεροι, ἰσχυροτάτη
σφίσι φανείη· καὶ θάρσος ἦν ἀμφοτέροις αὐτίκα καὶ
376 ἐλπὶς ἰσχυρά, τοσῶνδε στρατηγοῦσιν. αὐτά τε πρῶτα
πάντων τάδε τοῖς στρατηγοῖς τὸν στρατὸν ἐς πίστιν
συνῆγε· τίκτουσι γὰρ εὔνοιαν ἐλπίδες κοιναί. θροῦ δὲ

thousand infantry in all. For cavalry, Brutus had four thou-   373
sand Gauls and Lusitanians, and two thousand Thracians
and Illyrian Partheni and Thessalians. Cassius had two
thousand Iberians and Gauls, and four thousand mounted
archers, Arabs and Medes and Parthians. Following as
allies were kings and tetrarchs of the Galatians in Asia,
who brought another large infantry force and more than
five thousand cavalry.

89. Such was the size of the army reviewed by Cassius   374
and his staff at the gulf of Melas, and it was with this large
army that they advanced to battle, leaving the remainder
of their forces for needs elsewhere. After purifying the
army in the customary manner, they completed the payment of the promised donatives still owing to some of the
men. They had taken care to have plenty of money available in order to keep them loyal with gifts, especially
those, the majority, who had served under Gaius Caesar,
and prevent them mutinying at the sight or same name of
the young Caesar when he arrived. And once again, it was   375
decided, for the same purpose, to address the soldiers
publicly. So a large platform was erected, which the commanders mounted along with just the senators, while their
army, their own troops and the allies, stood around below
it, both groups immediately taking delight in their respec-
tive numbers, which appeared extremely powerful. And
both the generals were also immediately filled with confidence and resolute hope at commanding so many men.
This more than anything led the troops to believe in their   376
generals, for shared hopes generate a positive attitude. As
was to be expected in such a large crowd, a din arose,

ὡς ἐν τοσούτοις ὄντος οἵ τε κήρυκες καὶ οἱ σαλ-
πιγκταὶ σιωπὴν ἐποίουν, καὶ γενομένης ποτὲ ὁ Κάσσιος (προῦχε γὰρ ἡλικίᾳ) προελθὼν μικρὸν ἐκ τῆς
τάξεως ἐς τὸ μέσον ἔλεξεν ὧδε·

377   90. "Ὁ μὲν ἀγὼν πρῶτον ἡμᾶς, ὦ συστρατιῶται,
κοινὸς ὢν ἐς πίστιν ἀλλήλοις συνάγει· συνάπτει δὲ
καὶ ὅσα ὑμῖν ὑποσχόμενοι πάντα ἔδομεν, ὃ μεγίστη
πίστις ἐστὶ καὶ περὶ ὧν ἐς τὸ μέλλον ὑπισχνούμεθα.
378   αἱ δὲ ἐλπίδες εἰσὶν ἐν τῇ ἀρετῇ, ὑμῶν τε τῶν στρατευομένων καὶ ἡμῶν, οὓς ἐπὶ τοῦ βήματος τοῦδε ὁρᾶτε
379   τοσούσδε καὶ τοιούσδε ἄνδρας ἀπὸ τῆς βουλῆς. ἔστι
δὲ καὶ πλῆθος παρασκευῆς, ὅσον ἴστε, σίτου τε καὶ
ὅπλων καὶ χρημάτων καὶ νεῶν καὶ συμμάχων κατά
τε ἔθνη καὶ βασιλέας. ὥστε τί χρὴ τῷ λόγῳ παρακα-
λεῖν ἐς προθυμίαν τε καὶ ὁμόνοιαν, οὓς ἥ τε παρα-
380   σκευὴ καὶ τὰ ἔργα κοινὰ ὄντα συνάγει; περὶ δὲ ὧν
διαβάλλουσιν ἡμᾶς δύο ἄνδρες ἐχθροί, ἴστε μὲν αὐτὰ
ἀκριβέστατα, καὶ δι' αὐτὸ συστρατεύεσθε ἡμῖν ἑτοίμως, δοκεῖ δὲ καὶ νῦν ἐπεξελθεῖν ἔτι τὴν αἰτίαν, ἣ
μάλιστα ἐπιδείκνυσι τοῦ πολέμου καλλίστην τε οὖσαν ἡμῖν καὶ δικαιοτάτην τὴν πρόφασιν.

381   91. "Ἡμεῖς γὰρ Καίσαρα ἐν μὲν τοῖς πολέμοις
συστρατευόμενοί τε αὐτῷ μεθ' ὑμῶν καὶ στρατηγοῦντες ἐπὶ μέγα ἤρομεν καὶ φίλοι διετελοῦμεν ὄντες, ὡς
μὴ δοκεῖν αὐτὸν δι' ἔχθραν ὑφ' ἡμῶν ἐπιβεβουλεῦ-
382   σθαι. τὰ δὲ ἐς τὴν εἰρήνην ἐπίμεμπτος ἦν, οὐχ ἡμῖν
τοῖς φίλοις, ἐπεὶ κἂν τούτοις προετιμώμεθα, ἀλλὰ
τοῖς νόμοις καὶ τῷ κόσμῳ τῆς πολιτείας, ὧν οὐδεὶς

which the heralds and trumpeters set about silencing. When at last there was quiet, Cassius, for he was the elder of the two, moved forward a little from his place into the middle and spoke as follows:

90. "My fellow soldiers, it is the shared nature of our   377
struggle that leads us in the first place to believe in each other. Second is the fact that we have given you everything we promised, which is also the most important guarantee of what we are promising for the future. Our hopes rest in   378
the excellence, both of you, the enlisted men, and of us, the senators whose number and quality you see standing on this platform. You also know how extensively we have   379
prepared an abundance of grain and arms and money and ships and allies both from the provinces and from kings. Is there any need of words, then, to exhort you to demonstrate enthusiasm and solidarity of purpose, when our preparations and common task unite us? As to the slanders   380
that two men, personal enemies, bring against us, you know exactly what they are, and it is for that reason that you are ready to take up arms with us. Yet it still seems sensible, even now, to examine their accusation, which very clearly demonstrates that our reason for going to war is most honorable and just.

91. "By serving with Caesar in his wars, like you, and   381
exercising command, we raised him to a high position and continued to be his close associates, so that it cannot be thought that we plotted against him out of personal hatred. It was his conduct in time of peace that was objec-   382
tionable, not to us his associates, who continued to receive preferential treatment even then, but to the laws and con-

νόμος οὔτε ἀριστοκρατικὸς κύριος οὔτε δημοτικὸς ἔτι
ἦν· ἅπερ ἅπαντα οἱ πατέρες ἡμῶν ἥρμοσαν, ὅτε τοὺς
βασιλέας ἐκβαλόντες ἐπώμοσαν καὶ ἐπηράσαντο οὐκ

383 ἀνέξεσθαι βασιλέων ἐς τὸ μέλλον ἑτέρων. ᾧ τινι ὅρκῳ
βοηθοῦντες οἱ τῶν ὀμωμοκότων ἔκγονοι καὶ τὰς ἀρὰς
ἀπερύκοντες ἀφ᾽ ἑαυτῶν οὐχ ὑπεμείναμεν ἐς πολὺ
περιδεῖν ἕνα ἄνδρα, εἰ καὶ φίλος ἦν ἡμῖν καὶ χρήσιμος, τά τε κοινὰ χρήματα καὶ στρατόπεδα καὶ χειροτονίας ἀρχῶν ἀπὸ τοῦ δήμου καὶ ἡγεμονίας ἐθνῶν
ἀπὸ τῆς βουλῆς ἐς ἑαυτὸν περιφέροντα καὶ νόμον
ἀντὶ τῶν νόμων καὶ κύριον ἀντὶ τοῦ δήμου καὶ αὐτοκράτορα ἀντὶ τῆς βουλῆς γιγνόμενον ἐς ἅπαντα.

384 92. Ὧν ἴσως ὑμεῖς οὐκ ἀκριβῶς ᾐσθάνεσθε, ἀλλὰ
μόνην αὐτοῦ τὴν ἐν τοῖς πολέμοις ἀρετὴν ἑωρᾶτε. νῦν
δὲ ῥᾳδίως τε ἂν καὶ ἐκ μόνου τοῦ περὶ ὑμᾶς μέρους

385 καταμάθοιτε. ὁ γὰρ δῆμος ὑμεῖς ἐν μὲν τοῖς πολέμοις
ὑπακούετε ἐς πάντα ὡς κυρίοις τοῖς στρατηγοῖς, τὸ δὲ
κῦρος τόδε ἐν τοῖς εἰρηνικοῖς ἐφ᾽ ἡμῖν ἀντιλαμβάνετε
αὐτοί, προβουλευούσης μὲν τῆς βουλῆς, ἵνα μὴ σφα-
λεῖητε, κρίνοντες δὲ αὐτοὶ καὶ ψηφιζόμενοι κατὰ φυλὰς ἢ λόχους καὶ ἀποφαίνοντες ὑπάτους τε καὶ δη-

386 μάρχους καὶ στρατηγούς. ἐπὶ δὲ ταῖς χειροτονίαις καὶ
τὰ μέγιστα δικάζετε, κολάζοντες ἢ τιμῶντες, ὅτε κο-

387 λάσεως ἢ τιμῆς ἀξίως ἄρξαιμεν ὑμῶν. ἡ δὲ ἀντίδοσις
ἥδε τήν τε ἡγεμονίαν, ὦ πολῖται, ἐς εὐδαιμονίαν
ἄκραν ὑπερήγαγε καὶ τοὺς ἀξίους ἐτίμησε, καὶ οἱ τε-
τιμημένοι χάριν εἶχον ὑμῖν. ἀπὸ ταύτης τῆς ἐξουσίας

stitution of the state, in which not a single law, whether aristocratic or popular, remained in force. Our ancestors regulated all this, when after expelling the kings they swore an oath, supported by curses, never to tolerate other kings in the future. We, the descendants of the men who 383 swore the oath, defended it and sought to divert the curses from ourselves by refusing to endure for long the sight of one man, even if he was a friend who served our interests, vesting in himself and taking from the people control of the public finances, the military, the election of magistrates, and from the senate the right to appoint provincial governors; we refused to see him becoming in all matters the law in place of the laws, sovereign in place of the people, and sole ruler in place of the senate.

92. "Perhaps you did not fully understand this, but saw 384 only his excellence in war. Now, however, you can easily grasp it by observing simply the role that concerns you. For in times of war you, the people, obey your command- 385 ers in all respects since we hold authority, whereas in peacetime it is you who resume this authority over us. The senate deliberates first, in order to prevent you from making a mistake, but it is you who decide for yourselves, voting in tribes or centuries to appoint consuls, tribunes, and praetors. In addition to the elections, you act as jurors 386 in the most important cases, punishing and rewarding us whenever we govern you in a manner that deserves punishment or reward. This reciprocal exchange, fellow citi- 387 zens, has raised the empire to the summit of good fortune and conferred honors upon those worthy of them, and the men so honored have shown their gratitude to you. It was

ὕπατον ἐποιήσασθε Σκιπίωνα, ὅτε αὐτῷ ⟨περὶ τῶν⟩[28]
περὶ Λιβύην ἐμαρτυρήσατε· καὶ δημάρχους ἐποιεῖσθε
ἀνὰ ἔτος ἕκαστον, οὓς ἐβούλεσθε, διοισομένους ἡμῖν
ὑπὲρ ὑμῶν, εἰ δέοι. καὶ τί μοι καταλέγειν τὰ πολλά,
ὅσα ἴστε;

388   93. Ἀλλ᾽ οὐκ, ἀφ᾽ οὗ Καῖσαρ ἐδυνάστευσεν, οὐκ
ἀρχήν τινα, οὐ στρατηγόν, οὐχ ὕπατον, οὐ δήμαρχον
ἐχειροτονήσατε ἔτι, οὐκ ἐμαρτυρήσατε οὐδενί, οὐκ
ἀμοιβὴν εἴχετε δοῦναι μαρτυροῦντες. ἐν κεφαλαίῳ δὲ
εἰπεῖν, οὐδὲ εἷς ὑμῖν χάριν ὤφειλεν, οὐκ ἀρχῆς, οὐχ
389 ἡγεμονίας, οὐκ εὐθυνῶν, οὐ δίκης. ὃ δὲ οἴκτιστον
ἁπάντων ἐγένετο, οὐδ᾽ αὐτοῖς ἐδυνήθητε ἐπικουρῆσαι
τοῖς δημάρχοις ὑμῶν ὑβριζομένοις, ἥν τινα ἀΐδιον
ὑμῶν αὐτῶν ἀρχὴν ἐστήσασθε εἶναι καὶ ἱερὰν καὶ
ἄσυλον ἀπεφήνατε, ἀλλὰ καὶ τοὺς ἀσύλους εἴδετε τὴν
ἀρχὴν τὴν ἄσυλον καὶ τὴν ἐσθῆτα τὴν ἱερὰν ἐς ὕβριν
ἀφαιρουμένους ἀκρίτους, ἀπὸ μόνου προστάγματος,
ὅτι ἔδοξαν ὑπὲρ ὑμῶν χαλεπῆναι τοῖς καὶ βασιλέα
390 αὐτὸν ἐθέλουσι προσαγορεῦσαι. ὃ καὶ μάλιστα ἐπαχθῶς ἤνεγκεν ἡ βουλὴ δι᾽ ὑμᾶς· ὑμετέρα γὰρ καὶ οὐ
τῆς βουλῆς ἐστιν ἡ τῶν δημάρχων ἀρχή. ἐπιμέμψα-
σθαι δὲ σαφῶς οὐ δυναμένη τὸν ἄνδρα οὐδ᾽ ἐς κρίσιν
ἐπαγαγεῖν διὰ ἰσχὺν στρατοπέδων, ἃ καὶ αὐτά, τέως
ὄντα τῆς πόλεως, ἑαυτοῦ πεποίητο ἴδια, τὸν ἔτι λοιπὸν
τρόπον ἀμύνασθαι τὴν τυραννίδα ἐπενόησεν, ἐς τὸ
σῶμα ἐπιβουλεύσασα.

---

[28] περὶ τῶν add. Gaillard-Goukowsky

by virtue of this power that you made Scipio consul when you bore testimony to his deeds in Africa, and elected the tribunes of your choice every year, to oppose us in your interest if necessary.[66] But what is the point of listing the many things that you already know?

93. "But from the time when Caesar took over power, 388 you no longer elected a single magistrate, neither praetor, consul, nor tribune. You did not bestow your approval on anyone, and even if you did, you had nothing to give them in return. To put it briefly, nobody owed you any thanks, whether for a magistracy or a governorship, for approving accounts or securing a judgment. Most deplorable of all, 389 you were not even able to protect your own tribunes when they were abused, when this was an office you established to be permanently yours and declared sacrosanct and inviolable. On the contrary, you saw these inviolable men being brutally dispossessed of their inviolable office and sacred dress without trial, on the basis of a mere decree, because they were thought to have been angry on your behalf at those who wanted to address Caesar as king. The 390 senate took this particularly badly, because of you: for the office of tribune belongs to you, not to the senate. But they were not able to reprimand Caesar openly or bring him to trial, because of the strength of the armies, which he had also appropriated for himself, although they had been controlled by the state up to that point. So they devised the only way still remaining to protect themselves against the tyranny, by conspiring against his life.

[66] Scipio Aemilianus was elected consul in 147, although technically too young, to take command of the war against Carthage.

391   94. "Ἔδει δὲ τὴν μὲν γνώμην γενέσθαι τῶν ἀρίστων, τὸ δὲ ἔργον ὀλίγων. ἐπεὶ δὲ ἐγένετο, αὐτίκα ἡ
βουλὴ τὴν κοινὴν γνώμην ἐξέφηνε, σαφῶς μὲν ὅτε
392 καὶ γέρα τυραννοκτονικὰ ἐψηφίζοντο εἶναι· ἐπισχόν-
τος δὲ αὐτοὺς Ἀντωνίου καθ᾽ ὑπόκρισιν ἀταξίας καὶ
οὐδ᾽ ἡμῶν ἀξιούντων διὰ γέρα τῇ πόλει μᾶλλον ἢ δι᾽
αὐτὴν τὴν πατρίδα βοηθεῖν, τοῦδε μὲν ἀπέσχοντο,
οὐκ ἐθέλοντες ἐφυβρίζειν τῷ Καίσαρι, ἀλλὰ μόνης
τῆς τυραννίδος ἀπηλλάχθαι, ἀμνηστίαν δὲ ἁπάντων
ἐψηφίσαντο εἶναι καὶ σαφέστερον ἔτι, φόνου μὴ εἶναι
393 δίκας. καὶ μετὰ μικρόν, Ἀντωνίου τὸ πλῆθος ἐφ᾽ ἡμῖν
δημοκοπήσαντος, ἡ βουλὴ καὶ ἀρχὰς ἐθνῶν τῶν μεγίστων καὶ ἡγεμονίας ἔδοσαν ἡμῖν καὶ γῆς ἀπέφηναν
ἡγεῖσθαι πάσης ἀπὸ τοῦ Ἰονίου μέχρι Συρίας, πότερον ὡς ἐναγεῖς κολάζοντες ἢ ὡς ἀνδροφόνους πορ-
φύρᾳ τε ἱερᾷ καὶ ῥάβδοις καὶ πελέκεσι περικοσμοῦν-
394 τες; ᾧ λόγῳ καὶ Πομπήιον τὸν νέον, οὐδὲν μὲν ἐς
ταῦτα συνειργασμένον, ὅτι δὲ μόνον Πομπηίου Μάγνου τοῦ πρώτου περὶ τῆς δημοκρατίας ἀγωνισαμέ-
νου παῖς καὶ ὅτι μικρὰ τὴν τυραννίδα ἠνώχλει λανθάνων περὶ Ἰβηρίαν, κατεκάλεσέ τε ἐκ τῆς φυγῆς καὶ
τὸ τίμημα αὐτῷ τῶν πατρῴων ἐκ τῶν κοινῶν ἔκριναν
ἀποδοῦναι χρημάτων καὶ θαλασσοκράτορα ἀπέφηναν, ἵνα κἀκεῖνος ἀρχήν τινα ἔχοι δημοκρατικὸς ὤν.
395 τί δὴ πλέον ἔργον ἔτι τῆς βουλῆς ἢ σύμβολον ἐπιζη-
τεῖτε τοῦ κατὰ γνώμην αὐτῆς πάντα πεπρᾶχθαι, πλὴν
ἢ λόγῳ μόνον ὑμῖν ἔτι ὁμολογῆσαι; ὃ καὶ αὐτὸ πρά-

94. "While the decision had to be made by the nobles, 391
the deed itself had to be carried out by a few individuals.
But when it was done, the senate immediately made clear
that it was a shared decision by openly voting rewards for
the killing of a tyrant. Since Antony held them back, how- 392
ever, on the pretext that it would lead to disorder, and
since not even we resolved to rescue Rome for rewards
rather than for the fatherland itself, the senators refrained
from taking the decision. Because they did not want to
insult Caesar, but only to get rid of the tyranny, they voted
a general amnesty, and, to make the situation even clearer,
they decreed that there should be no persecutions for
murder. Soon after, Antony having turned the mob against 393
us with his populist agitation, the senate gave us charge of
the largest provinces and appointed us to military commands, declaring us to have authority over the whole region from the Ionian gulf to Syria. In doing this, were they
punishing us for being accursed, or were they decorating
us with sacred purple, rods, and axes for being murderers?
Using the same logic, they recalled from exile the younger 394
Pompeius (who had no role in these events), solely because he was the son of Pompey the Great who had been
the first to fight for the democracy, and because while in
hiding in Iberia he was causing a certain amount of trouble
to the tyranny. They also decided to repay him from public funds the value of his paternal inheritance, and appointed him supreme naval commander, so that he too,
being a democrat, might hold some office. What more do 395
you seek from the senate by way of gesture or sign to show
that everything has been done in accordance with their
decisions, apart only from actually admitting it to you in
words? But even this they will do and will say, and in say-

ξουσι καὶ ἐροῦσι καὶ λέγοντες ἅμα ὑμᾶς ἀμείψονται μεγάλαις δωρεαῖς, ὅταν εἰπεῖν καὶ ἀμείψασθαι δύνωνται.

396   95. "Νῦν μὲν γὰρ ὡς ἔχουσιν, ἴστε. προγράφονται χωρὶς δίκης, καὶ τὰ ὄντα αὐτοῖς δημεύεται, καὶ κτείνονται χωρὶς καταδίκης ἐν οἰκίαις, ἐν στενωποῖς, ἐν ἱεροῖς, ὑπὸ στρατιωτῶν, ὑπὸ θεραπόντων, ὑπὸ ἐχθρῶν, ἐκ μυχῶν ἀνασπώμενοι καὶ διωκόμενοι πανταχῇ, τῶν

397   νόμων τὸν ἐθέλοντα φεύγειν ἐώντων. ἐς δὲ τὴν ἀγοράν, ἐς ἣν οὐδενὸς πολεμίου κεφαλήν, ἀλλὰ ὅπλα μόνα καὶ ἔμβολα νεῶν ἐφέρομεν, ὑπάτων ἄρτι καὶ στρατηγῶν καὶ δημάρχων καὶ ἀγορανόμων καὶ ἱππέων κεφαλαὶ πρόκεινται· καὶ γέρα τούτων ἐστὶ τῶν κακῶν ὡρι-

398   σμένα. τοῦτο γὰρ ἐπανάστασίς τίς ἐστι πάντων, ὅσα τέως ἦν ὕπουλα, καὶ ἀνδροληψία αἰφνίδια καὶ μύση ποικίλα γυναικῶν τε καὶ υἱῶν καὶ ἀπελευθέρων καὶ οἰκετῶν. ἐς τοσοῦτον ἤδη καὶ τοὺς τρόπους ἡ πόλις

399   ἐπιτέτριπται. καὶ τῶνδε τοῖς πονηροῖς ἡγεμόνες εἰσὶν οἱ τρεῖς ἄνδρες, αὐτοὶ πρὸ τῶν ἄλλων ἀδελφοὺς καὶ

400   θείους καὶ ἐπιτρόπους προγράψαντες. λέγεταί ποτε πρὸς τῶν ἀγριωτάτων βαρβάρων ἡ πόλις ἁλῶναι· καὶ οὐδενὸς ἀπέτεμνον οἱ Κελτοὶ κεφαλὰς οὐδὲ ἐνύβριζον ἀνῃρημένοις οὐδὲ πολεμοῦσιν ἔτι λαθεῖν ἢ φυγεῖν

401   ἐφθόνουν. οὐδ᾿ αὐτοί πω πόλιν οὐδεμίαν ὧν δορὶ ἐλάβομεν, τοιαῦτα διεθήκαμεν οὐδὲ ἑτέρους ἐπυθόμεθα διαθεῖναι, οἷα νῦν οὐκ ἰδιῶτις πόλις, ἀλλ᾿ ἡγεμονὶς ἀδικεῖται πρὸς τῶν αὐτὴν ἁρμόσαι καὶ διορθῶσαι τὰ

402   κοινὰ κεχειροτονημένων. τί τοιοῦτον εἰργάσατο Ταρ-

ing it will reward you with generous gifts—that is, when
they have the power to speak out and repay you.

95. "For you are aware of their present situation. They 396
are proscribed without trial, and their property confiscated; without having been convicted, they are put to
death in houses, in alleys, in sanctuaries, by soldiers, by
slaves, by personal enemies; they are dragged out of hiding
places and pursued everywhere, even though the laws allow anybody to go into voluntary exile. In the Forum, 397
where we never used to bring the head of even a single
enemy, but only their weapons and ship rams, there are
now displayed the heads of men who have recently been
consuls and praetors and tribunes and aediles and members of the equestrian order—and rewards have been
fixed for such horrors. This is an outbreak of everything 398
that has for some time been festering under the surface—
the summary arrest of men, and all kinds of infamy per-
petrated against wives and sons, freedmen and slaves.
Such is the degree of moral decay too now affecting the
city. Wicked men have as their leaders in these matters the 399
triumvirs, the very people who put on the proscription
lists their own brothers and uncles and guardians ahead of
everyone else. It is said that Rome was once captured by 400
the most savage of barbarians, but the Gauls did not cut
anyone's head off, they did not abuse the dead, they did
not begrudge those with whom they were still at war the
opportunity to hide or flee. And we ourselves have never 401
yet treated any of the towns we captured in war like this,
nor have we heard of others inflicting such wrongs as now
being suffered, not by some ordinary town, but by the
leading city of the empire, at the hands of men chosen to
govern it and restore its public affairs. Did Tarquin ever 402

353

κύνιος; ὃν διὰ μιᾶς γυναικὸς ὕβριν, ἐξ ἔρωτος γενομένην, βασιλέα τε ὄντα ἐξέβαλον καὶ βασιλεύεσθαι
διὰ ἓν ἔργον οὐκέτι ὑπέστησαν.

403   96. "Καὶ τάδε, ὦ πολῖται, πράσσοντες οἱ τρεῖς ἡμᾶς
ἐναγεῖς λέγουσι, καί φασι μὲν ἀμύνειν Καίσαρι, προγράφουσι δὲ τοὺς οὐδ' ἐπιδημοῦντας, ὅτε ἀνῃρεῖτο.
ὧν καὶ οἵδε εἰσὶν οἱ πλέονες, οὓς ὁρᾶτε, διὰ πλοῦτον
ἢ γένος ἢ γνώμην δημοκρατικῆς διανοίας προγε-
404   γραμμένοι. ᾧ λόγῳ καὶ Πομπήιος μεθ' ἡμῶν προεγράφη, πόρρω μὲν ὢν περὶ Ἰβηρίαν, ὅτε ἡμεῖς ἐδρῶ-
μεν· ὅτι δέ ἐστι δημοκρατικοῦ πατρός, διὰ τὴν αὐτὴν
αἰτίαν ὑπὸ μὲν τῆς βουλῆς κατεκλήθη τε καὶ θαλασ-
405   σοκράτωρ ἐγένετο, ὑπὸ δὲ τῶν τριῶν προεγράφη. τί
δὲ γυναῖκες ἐπὶ Καίσαρι συνέγνωσαν αἱ ἐς ἐσφορὰς
προγεγραμμέναι; τί δὲ ὁ δῆμος ὁ μέχρι δέκα μυριάδων τιμᾶσθαι τὰ ὄντα κεκελευσμένος ὑπὸ μηνύμασι
καὶ ζημίαις, ᾧ τέλη καινὰ καὶ ἐσφορὰς ἐπιγράφουσι;
406   καὶ τάδε πράσσοντες οὐδ' ὡς ἀνεπλήρωσαν τοῖς
στρατευομένοις σφίσι τὰς δωρεάς. ἡμεῖς δέ, οἷς ἀσε-
βὲς οὐδὲν εἴργασται, καὶ τὰ ἐπηγγελμένα δεδώκαμεν
καὶ ἕτερα ἕτοιμα ἔχομεν ἐς ἀμοιβὰς μείζονας. οὕτως
ἡμῖν καὶ τὸ δαιμόνιον, ὡς δίκαια πράσσουσι, συνεπι-
λαμβάνει.

407   97. "Ἐπὶ δέ γε τῷ δαιμονίῳ καὶ τὰ πρὸς ἀνθρώπων
ὁρᾶν ἔχετε, ἐς τοὺς ὑμῶν πολίτας ἀποβλέποντες, οὓς
εἴδετε μὲν στρατηγοῦντας ὑμῶν πολλάκις καὶ ὑπα-
τεύοντας καὶ ἐπαινουμένους, ὁρᾶτε δὲ πρὸς ἡμᾶς ὡς

do anything like this, Tarquin, whom the Romans expelled, even though he was king, for violating one woman in an act of passion, and then undertook, because of this one act, never more to be ruled by kings?

96. "While the triumvirs are committing these out-   403
rages, fellow citizens, they call us accursed and say that they are avenging Caesar. But they proscribe people who were not even in Rome when he was killed. Most of those are the men you see here, proscribed because of their wealth or family or their views of a democratic disposition. This was the rationale why Pompeius was proscribed along   404
with us, although he was far away in Iberia when we carried out the deed: the fact that he was both recalled by the senate to be made supreme commander and proscribed by the triumvirs, has the same cause, namely that he was the son of a democratic father. What part in the conspiracy   405
against Caesar was played by those women who have been listed to pay war taxes? What part was played by those ordinary people who were ordered to submit an estimation of their property up to a value of one hundred thousand drachmas, under threat of informers and fines, and on whom new taxes and payments have been imposed? And in spite of these exactions the triumvirs still have not   406
fully paid the donatives promised to their troops. We, on the other hand, who have committed no impiety, have given what we promised, and have other funds ready to pay still larger rewards. So it is that the divinity favors us because our actions are just.

97. "In addition to the divine favor that is ours, you can   407
also see that of men, when you look at your fellow citizens. You have often seen them in command of your armies or holding the consulship and winning your approval, and

355

εὐαγεῖς καὶ δημοκρατικοὺς καταπεφευγότας καὶ τὰ
ἡμέτερα ᾑρημένους καὶ συνευχομένους ἡμῖν ἐς τὰ
408 λοιπὰ καὶ συναιρομένους. πολὺ γὰρ δικαιότερα ἡμεῖς
γέρα τοῖς περισώσασιν αὐτοὺς ἐκηρύξαμεν ὧν ἐκεῖνοι
τοῖς ἀναιροῦσιν· οὐδὲ ὁρῶσιν ἡμᾶς Γάιον μέν, ὅτι
ἠξίου μόνος ἄρχειν, ἀνῃρηκότας, τοὺς δὲ τὴν ἐκείνου
περιποιουμένους ἀρχὴν ὑπερορᾶν μέλλοντας καὶ μὴ
ἐς ἑαυτούς, ἀλλ᾽ ἐς τὸ μέσον τῷ δήμῳ προτιθέντας
409 τὴν πολιτείαν κατὰ τὰ πάτρια. ὡς οὖν οὐκ ἀπὸ τῆς
αὐτῆς γνώμης αἱρουμένων πολεμεῖν ἑκατέρων, ἀλλὰ
τῶν μὲν ὑπὲρ δυναστείας καὶ τυραννίδος, ἣν ἐν ταῖς
προγραφαῖς ἐπέδειξαν ἤδη, ἡμῶν δὲ οὐδέν, ἀλλ᾽ ἢ
μόνον ἵνα τῆς πατρίδος ἐλευθερωθείσης ἰδιωτεύοιμεν
ὑπὸ τοῖς νόμοις, εἰκότως οἵδε τε οἱ ἄνδρες καὶ πρὸ
τούτων οἱ θεοὶ τὰ ἡμέτερα κρίνουσι. μεγίστη δὲ ἐλπὶς
ἐν πολέμοις ἐστὶ τὸ δίκαιον.

410 98. "Μηδέ τῳ, εἰ Καίσαρος ἐγένετο στρατιώτης, ἐπὶ
νοῦν ἔτι ἴτω· οὐ γὰρ ἐκείνου γε ἦμεν οὐδὲ τότε, ἀλλὰ
τῆς πατρίδος, οὐδ᾽ οἱ διδόμενοι μισθοὶ καὶ δωρεαὶ
Καίσαρος ἦσαν, ἀλλὰ τοῦ κοινοῦ, ἐπεὶ οὐδὲ νῦν ἐστε
Κασσίου στρατὸς οὐδὲ Βρούτου μᾶλλον ἢ Ῥωμαίων·
ἡμεῖς δ᾽ ἐσμὲν ὑμῖν συστρατιῶται, Ῥωμαίων στρατη-
411 γοί. καὶ εἰ τόδε καὶ οἱ πολεμοῦντες ἡμῖν ἐφρόνουν,
ἐνῆν ἀκινδύνως ἅπασι τὰ ὅπλα καταθέσθαι καὶ τοὺς
στρατοὺς πάντας ἀποδοῦναι τῇ πόλει, κἀκείνην ἑλέ-
σθαι τὰ συνοίσοντα· καὶ εἰ δέχονται ταῦτα, προκα-
412 λούμεθα. ἐπεὶ δὲ οὐ δέχονται, οὐδ᾽ ἂν δέξαιντο ἔτι διὰ
τὰς προγραφὰς καὶ ὅσα ἄλλα ἔδρασαν, ἴωμεν, ὦ συ-

you now see that they have taken refuge with us, and have joined our side and are sharing our prayers and actions for the future, because they believe we are undefiled democrats. For the rewards we proclaimed for preserving the   408 lives of these men are far more just than those proclaimed by the triumvirs for killing them. Nor do they see in us the sort of people who, when they had killed Gaius Caesar because he decided to exercise sole power, were intending to overlook those laying claim to his rule, but they see people who are not appropriating the state for ourselves, but are placing it publicly at the disposal of the people according to our ancestral ways. Since, then, the two sides   409 have different reasons for choosing to go to war—our enemies for the sake of personal domination and tyranny, which they have already shown with their proscriptions, we for nothing more than to free our country and live as private citizens under the laws—it is only reasonable that these men, and before them the gods, make their decision to support our side. In war the greatest hope lies in the justice of one's cause.

98. "Let it give no one any concern that he was one of   410 Caesar's soldiers. For we were not his soldiers even then, but our country's. The pay and donatives were not given by Caesar, but by the state, just as you are not now the army of Cassius or Brutus, but of Rome, and we, Roman generals, are your fellow soldiers. If our enemies held the   411 same opinion as us, we could all lay down our arms without danger, give back all the armies to the state, and let it choose what would be in its interests. We challenge them to accept this. But since they do not accept it—and indeed   412 they could not do so, given the proscriptions and every-

στρατιῶται, μετά τε πίστεως ὑγιοῦς καὶ προθυμίας
ἀδόλου στρατευσόμενοι Ῥωμαίων τῇ τε βουλῇ καὶ τῷ
δήμῳ μόνοις ὑπὲρ ἐλευθερίας."

413   99. Ἀναβοησάντων δὲ πάντων "Ἴωμεν" καὶ εὐθὺς
ἄγειν ἀξιούντων, ἡσθεὶς ὁ Κάσσιος τῇ προθυμίᾳ κατ-
εκήρυξεν αὖθις σιωπὴν καὶ αὖθις ἔλεγε· "Θεοὶ μέν,
ὅσοι πολέμων δικαίων δεσπόται, τῆς πίστεως ὑμᾶς,
ὦ συστρατιῶται, καὶ προθυμίας ἀμείβοιντο· τὰ δ' ἐς
ἀνθρωπίνην [στρατηγῶν]²⁹ πρόνοιαν ὅτι καὶ πλέονα
καὶ ἀμείνονά ἐστιν ἡμῖν ἢ τοῖς πολεμίοις, μάθετε
414   οὕτως. τέλη μὲν ὁπλιτῶν ἴσα αὐτοῖς ἀντεπάγομεν,
πολλὰ καὶ ἐπὶ τῶν χρειῶν ἄλλα πολλαχοῦ καταλιπόν-
τες· ἱππεῦσι δὲ καὶ ναυσὶ πολὺ προύχομεν καὶ συμ-
μάχοις βασιλεῦσί τε καὶ ἔθνεσι τοῖς μέχρι Μήδων
415   καὶ Παρθυαίων. καὶ ἡμῖν μὲν ἐκ μετώπου μόνον εἰσὶ
πολέμιοι, ἡμεῖς δ' αὐτῶν καὶ κατὰ νώτου Πομπήιόν τε
ὁμογνώμονα ἡμῖν ἔχομεν ἐν Σικελίᾳ, καὶ Μοῦρκος ἐν
τῷ Ἰονίῳ καὶ Ἀηνόβαρβος στόλῳ πολλῷ καὶ ὑπηρε-
σίᾳ δαψιλεῖ καὶ δύο τέλεσι στρατοῦ καὶ τοξόταις αἰεὶ
διαπλέοντες ἐνοχλοῦσι πολλά, καθαρευούσης πο-
416   λεμίων ἡμῖν τῆς ὄπισθεν γῆς καὶ θαλάσσης. χρήματά
γε μήν, ἅ τινες καλοῦσι νεῦρα πολέμου, τοῖς μὲν οὐκ
ἔστιν, οὐδ' ἀπέδωκάν πω τὰ ὑπεσχημένα τῷ στρατῷ,
οὐδὲ κατὰ δόξαν ἀπήντησε τὰ τῶν προγραφῶν, οὐδενὸς τῶν ἐπιεικῶν ὠνουμένου χωρία ἐπίφθονα· οὐδ'
ἑτέρωθεν εὐποροῦσι, τετρυμένης στάσεσι καὶ ἐσφο-

²⁹ στρατηγῶν del. Nauck et Mend.

thing else they have done—let us go forward, fellow soldiers, with wholesome confidence and undisguised enthusiasm, to fight solely for the freedom of the senate and people of Rome."

99. They all shouted out, "Let us march!" and urged 413 Cassius to lead them forward immediately. He was delighted with their spirit, and once again proclaiming silence, resumed his address: "My fellow soldiers, may all those gods who govern just wars reward your good faith and enthusiasm. How far superior we are to the enemy in everything that human foresight can provide, let me tell you. We are leading against our enemy the same number 414 of legions as they have, although we have also left behind many others in many locations to meet our needs. In cavalry and ships we are greatly superior to them, just as we are in allied kings and nations as far away as the Medes and Parthians. And while we only have enemies in front of 415 us, we also have Pompeius on our side in Sicily to their rear, and in the Ionian gulf Murcus and Ahenobarbus are patrolling the whole time and causing considerable trouble with their large fleet, numerous crews, two legions of soldiers, and archers. Behind us, on the other hand, land and sea are clear of the enemy. As regards money, which 416 some call the sinews of war, they don't have any.[67] They have not yet paid what they promised their army, and the proceeds of the proscriptions have not met their expectation, because no good men are buying properties that will bring them hatred. Nor can they get resources elsewhere,

[67] Cicero (*Phil.* 5.5) calls an infinite supply of money the sinews of war (*nervos belli pecuniam infinitam*).

417 ραῖς καὶ προγραφαῖς τῆς Ἰταλίας. ἡμῖν δὲ ἐκ πολλῆς
φροντίδος καὶ τὰ παρόντα ἐστὶ δαψιλῆ, ὡς αὐτίκα
ὑμῖν ἄλλα χαρίσασθαι, καὶ ἕτερα πολλὰ ἐπὶ τούτοις
ἀπὸ τῶν ὄπισθεν ἐθνῶν προσοδεύεται συμφερόμενα.

418 100. "Τροφαὶ δέ, ὃ δυσπορώτατόν ἐστι στρατοῖς
μεγάλοις, ἐκείνοις μὲν οὐκ εἰσί, πλὴν ἐκ μόνης Μακεδονίας, ἔθνους ὀρείου, καὶ Θεσσαλίας, χώρας βρα-
χείας· καὶ τάδε χρὴ κατὰ γῆν αὐτοῖς φέρεσθαι κακο-
παθοῦσιν. εἰ δ᾽ ἐκ Λιβύης ἐπάγοιντο ἢ Λευκανίας ἢ
Ἰαπυγίας, διακλείσουσι πάντα Πομπήιός τε καὶ
419 Μοῦρκος καὶ Δομίτιος. ἡμῖν δὲ καὶ εἰσὶ καὶ φέρονται
καθ᾽ ἑκάστην ἡμέραν ἀπόνως διὰ θαλάττης ἔκ τε νή-
σων καὶ ἠπείρων ἀπασῶν, ὅσαι ἀπὸ Θράκης ἐπὶ ποταμὸν Εὐφράτην, καὶ τάδε ἀκωλύτως, οὐδενὸς ἡμῖν
ὄντος ὄπισθεν ἐχθροῦ· ὥστ᾽ ἐφ᾽ ἡμῖν ἔσται καὶ ταχύ-
νειν τὸ ἔργον καὶ ἐπὶ σχολῆς ἐκτρύχειν τοὺς πο-
420 λεμίους λιμῷ. τοσάδε μὲν ὑμῖν καὶ τοιάδε ἐστίν, ὦ
συστρατιῶται, παρ᾽ ἀνθρωπίνης φροντίδος ἕτοιμα· τὰ
δὲ λοιπὰ αὐτοῖς ἀνὰ λόγον ἀπαντήσειε παρά τε ὑμῶν
421 καὶ παρὰ τῶν θεῶν. ἡμεῖς δ᾽ ὑμῖν ἐπὶ τοῖς προτέροις
ἀποδόντες ἅπαντα, ὅσα ὑπεσχήμεθα, καὶ τὴν πίστιν
ὑμῶν ἀμειψάμενοι πλήθει δωρεῶν, ἀμειψόμεθα καὶ τὸ
422 μεῖζον ἔργον ἀξίως αὐτοῦ κατὰ γνώμην θεῶν. καὶ νῦν
δέ, ὅσον ἐς προθυμίαν, ἰοῦσιν ἐπὶ τὸ ἔργον ἤδη,
συνόδου τῆσδε καὶ λόγων τῶνδε ἕνεκα, ἐπιδώσομεν
εὐθὺς ἀπὸ τοῦδε τοῦ βήματος στρατιώτῃ μὲν χιλίας
καὶ πεντακοσίας δραχμὰς Ἰταλικάς, λοχαγῷ δὲ
πενταπλάσιον καὶ χιλιάρχῃ δὲ τὸ ἀνάλογον."

since Italy is exhausted by civil strife, exactions, and proscriptions. Thanks to ample foresight, we, in contrast, have   417
plenty for the present, so that we can give you more right
now, while over and above this other large sums are accruing from what is being collected in the provinces to our
rear.

100. "As for provisions, the most difficult thing to sup-   418
ply for large armies, our enemies can't get any except from
Macedonia, which is a mountainous province, and Thessaly, which is a small area; and they have to carry them
overland with great difficulty. And Pompeius, Murcus, and
Domitius will intercept everything they might try to bring
from Africa, or Lucania, or Iapygia. We, on the other hand,   419
have provisions, transported daily by sea without great
effort from all the islands and countries between Thrace
and the river Euphrates, and without interference, since
we have no enemy in our rear. The result is that it will be
up to us whether we precipitate the decisive engagement,
or wear down the enemy by hunger at our leisure. Such is   420
the extent and nature, fellow soldiers, of the preparations
made for you by human planning. With your help and that
of the gods, may the future we face match those preparations. We have paid you everything we promised for your   421
former efforts, and have rewarded your loyalty with generous gifts; we will repay you too for the greater encounter
in a manner worthy of it, and in accordance with the decision of the gods. And now, to promote the enthusiasm with   422
which you are already advancing to the battle, and to mark
this assembly and these words, we will make an additional
gift from this platform of one thousand five hundred Italic
drachmas to each soldier, five times that sum to each
centurion, and a proportional amount to each military
tribune."

423   101. Ταῦτα εἰπὼν καὶ παρασκευάσας τὸν στρατὸν ἔργῳ καὶ λόγῳ καὶ δωρεαῖς διέλυε τὴν ἐκκλησίαν. οἱ δὲ ἐπιμένοντες ἐπῄνουν ἐπὶ πλεῖστον αὐτόν τε καὶ Βροῦτον καὶ περὶ σφῶν, ὅσα εἰκὸς ἦν, ὑπισχνοῦντο.

424   οἱ δὲ αὐτοῖς τὴν δωρεὰν αὐτίκα διηρίθμουν καὶ ἕτερα ὑπὲρ αὐτὴν κατὰ προφάσεις πολλὰς τοῖς ἀρίστοις. τοὺς δὲ λαμβάνοντας ἀεὶ κατὰ μέρη προαπέλυον, ἐς

425   Δορίσκον, καὶ αὐτοὶ μετ᾽ ὀλίγον ἐφείποντο. δύο δὲ ἀετοὶ καταπτάντες ἐς τῶν σημείων δύο αἰετοὺς ἀπ᾽ ἀργύρου πεποιημένους, ἐκόλαπτον αὐτοὺς ἤ, ὡς ἑτέροις δοκεῖ, περιέσκεπον· καὶ παρέμενον δημοσίας τε τροφῆς ὑπὸ τῶν στρατηγῶν ἠξιοῦντο, μέχρι πρὸ μιᾶς τῆς μάχης ἡμέρας ἀπέπτησαν. δύο δ᾽ ἡμέραις τὸν Μέλανα κόλπον περιοδεύσαντες ἐς Αἶνον ἀφίκοντο καὶ ἐπὶ Αἴνῳ Δορίσκον τε καὶ ὅσα ἄλλα μέχρι Σερρείου ὄρους παράλια.

426   102. Τοῦ δὲ Σερρείου προύχοντος ἐς τὸ πέλαγος, αὐτοὶ μὲν ἐς τὰ μεσόγαια ἀνεχώρουν, Τίλλιον δὲ Κίμβρον μετὰ τοῦ ναυτικοῦ καὶ τέλους ὁπλιτῶν ἑνὸς καὶ

427   τοξοτῶν τινων τὴν ἀκτὴν περιπλεῖν ἔπεμπον, ἣ πάλαι μὲν ἦν ἐρημοτάτη, καίπερ εὔγεως οὖσα, τῶν Θρᾳκῶν οὔτε θαλάσσῃ χρωμένων οὔτε ἐς τὰ παράλια κατιόν-

428   των ὑπὸ δέους τῶν ἐπιπλεόντων· Ἑλλήνων δ᾽ αὐτὴν ἑτέρων τε καὶ Χαλκιδέων καταλαβόντων καὶ θαλάσσῃ χρωμένων, ἤνθει ταῖς ἐμπορίαις καὶ γεωργίαις, χαιρόντων σφίσι καὶ τῶν Θρᾳκῶν διὰ τὴν τῶν ὡραίων ἄμειψιν, μέχρι Φίλιππος ὁ Ἀμύντου τούς τε ἄλλους

101. After finishing his speech and preparing the army   423
by actions and words and gifts, Cassius dismissed the
meeting. The soldiers, however, stayed where they were,
promising on their own part to do their duty, and heaping
praise on Cassius and Brutus, who immediately distrib-   424
uted the money to them, using a variety of excuses to add
bonuses for the best men. They continuously sent the men
on ahead to Doriscus as they were being paid, unit by unit,
and followed soon after themselves. Two eagles now   425
landed on two of the silver eagles which surmounted the
standards, pecking at them, or, as others think, shielding
them with their wings, and there they remained, the generals considering them worthy of being fed from public
supplies, until the day before the battle, when they flew
away. The army marched for two days around the gulf of
Melas and came to Aenus, and after Aenus to Doriscus
and the rest of that coast as far as Mount Serrium.

102. As Mount Serrium projected into the sea, Cassius   426
and Brutus withdrew inland, but they sent Tillius Cimber
with the fleet, one legion, and some archers to sail around
the promontory.[68] Although fertile, it was in the past com-   427
pletely deserted, because the Thracians were not a maritime people, and did not come down to the coast for fear
of attack from the sea. So the Chalcideans and other   428
Greeks took possession of it, and as they were a maritime
people, it flourished in its commerce and agriculture, and
even the Thracians were delighted because of the opportunity to trade their seasonal produce. In the end, Philip,

[68] Lucius Tillius Cimber had been the one to initiate the murder of Caesar, by asking for his brother's pardon: see App. *BCiv.*
2.117.491.

καὶ Χαλκιδέας ἀνέστησεν, ὡς μηδὲν ἔτι πλὴν οἰκό-
429 πεδα μόνον ἱερῶν ὁρᾶσθαι. τήνδε οὖν τὴν ἀκτὴν
αὖθις ἔρημον οὖσαν ὁ Τίλλιος παραπλέων, ὡς οἱ
πρὸς τῶν ἀμφὶ τὸν Βροῦτον εἴρητο, στρατοπέδοις ἐπι-
τήδεια χωρία ἀνεμέτρει καὶ διέγραφε καὶ ταῖς ναυσὶ
κατὰ μέρη πρόσπλουν, ἵν᾽ οἱ περὶ τὸν Νωρβανόν, ὡς
430 ἀχρεῖον ἔτι τὸ τηρεῖν, τὰ στενὰ ἐκλίποιεν. καὶ ἐγένετο
μὲν ὡς προσεδόκησαν· ὑπὸ γὰρ τῆς φαντασίας τῶν
νεῶν Νωρβανὸς ἐπὶ τῶν Σαπαίων στενῶν ἐθορυβήθη
καὶ ἐκάλει Δεκίδιον[30] ἐκ τῶν Κορπίλων κατὰ σπουδὴν
ἐπικουρεῖν οἱ. καὶ ἐπεκούρει, τὰ δὲ τῶν Κορπίλων
στενὰ ἐκλειφθέντα οἱ περὶ τὸν Βροῦτον διώδευον.

431   103. Ἐκφανείσης δὲ τῆς ἐνέδρας ὁ Νωρβανὸς καὶ
ὁ Δεκίδιος τὰ Σαπαίων κατεῖχον ἰσχυρῶς. καὶ πάλιν
ἦν ἄπορα τοῖς ἀμφὶ τὸν Βροῦτον, ἀθυμία τε ἐνέπιπτε,
μὴ δέοι σφᾶς ἧς ὑπερεωράκεσαν περιόδου νῦν ἄρχεσθαι καὶ ἀνακυκλεύειν τὰ ἠνυσμένα, ὀψὲ καὶ τοῦ χρό-
432 νου καὶ τῆς ὥρας γεγονότων. ὧδε δὲ αὐτοῖς ἔχουσιν
ὁ Ῥασκούπολις ἔφη περίοδον εἶναι παρ᾽ αὐτὸ τὸ τῶν
Σαπαίων ὄρος ἡμερῶν τριῶν, ἄβατον μὲν ἀνθρώποις
ἐς τὸ νῦν ὑπό τε κρημνῶν καὶ ἀνυδρίας καὶ ὕλης πυ-
κνῆς· ἢν δὲ ἐθέλωσιν ὕδωρ τε ἐπάγεσθαι καὶ ὁδοποιεῖν στενὴν καὶ αὐτάρκη δίοδον, οὐ γνωσθήσεσθαι μὲν
διὰ τὴν συνηρέφειαν οὐδὲ οἰωνοῖς, τῇ τετάρτῃ δὲ ἐπὶ
Ἀρπησσὸν ποταμὸν ἥξειν, ἐκπίπτοντα ἐς τὸν Ἕρμον,

[30] Κεδίκιον LPB; Κικίλιον J; Δεκίδιον edd.

the son of Amyntas, transplanted the Chalcideans and other Greeks with the result that no trace of them remains to be seen any more, except the sites of their temples.[69] So, as ordered by Brutus, Tillius sailed along this promontory, now once again deserted, surveying places suitable for camps and marking out the sea approaches for squadrons of ships, with the purpose of making Norbanus abandon the pass, in the belief that there was no point in continuing to guard it. And it turned out as they anticipated. For, on the appearance of the ships, Norbanus became alarmed for his position at the Sapaean pass and called on Decidius to hurry from the Corpilian pass to help him.[70] He did so, and Brutus immediately marched through the now abandoned Corpilian pass.

103. Once the trick had been revealed, Norbanus and Decidius held the Sapaean pass tenaciously, and Brutus' men were again facing an impasse. They became depressed at the prospect of now having to set out on that detour they had dismissed and retrace the route they had completed, when they were pressed for time and it was late in the season. Such was their situation when Rhascupolis told them that there was a way round, a journey of three days, along Mount Sapaeum itself: up to that time it had not been used by people because of the cliffs, the lack of water, and the thick forest. But if they were willing to carry water and cut a narrow but sufficient path through, the canopy would prevent them from being seen even by birds. They would reach the river Harpessus, which flows

429

430

431

432

---

[69] Philip, son of Amyntas, was Philip II of Macedonia, father of Alexander the Great. [70] The account picks up from events described above in App. *BCiv.* 4.87.368–70.

ὅθεν ἡμέρας ἔτι μιᾶς ἐν Φιλίπποις ἔσεσθαι, τοὺς πολεμίους περιλαβόντας, ὡς ἀπειλῆφθαι τέλεον αὐτοὺς
433 καὶ οὐδὲ ἀναχώρησιν ἕξειν. τοῖς δὲ ἐδόκει τὰ λεγό-
μενα τῆς τε ἄλλης ἀπορίας οὕνεκα καὶ ἐλπίδι μάλιστα τοῦ περιλήψεσθαι τοσόνδε στρατὸν πολεμίων.

434 104. Προπέμπουσιν οὖν μέρος, Λευκίῳ Βύβλῳ πα-
ραδόντες, ὁδοποιεῖν μετὰ τοῦ Ῥασκουπόλιδος. οἱ δ᾽
ἐπιμόχθως μέν, ὅμως δὲ ἔπραττον αὐτὸ μετὰ ὁρμῆς
καὶ προθυμίας, καὶ μᾶλλον, ἐπεί τινες αὐτοῖς προπεμ-
φθέντες ἐπανῆλθον, ἰδεῖν τὸν ποταμὸν ἐξ ἀπόπτου
435 λέγοντες. τῇ δὲ τετάρτῃ κάμνοντες ὑπό τε κόπου καὶ
δίψους, ἐπιλιπόντος ἤδη τι καὶ τοῦ ὕδατος, ὃ ἐπήγοντο, ἀνέφερον, ὅτι τριήμερόν σφισι τὸ ἄνυδρον
ἐλέγετο εἶναι, καὶ ἐν φόβῳ πανικῷ περὶ ἐνέδρας ἐγίγνοντο, οὐκ ἀπιστοῦντες μὲν τοῖς προπεμφθεῖσι τὸν
ποταμὸν ἰδεῖν, ἡγούμενοι δὲ ἑτέραν ἄγεσθαι. καὶ
ἀθύμουν καὶ ἐβόων καὶ τὸν Ῥασκούπολιν, ὅτε ἴδοιεν
περιθέοντα καὶ παρακαλοῦντα, ἐλοιδόρουν καὶ ἔβαλ-
436 λον. Βύβλου δὲ αὐτοὺς ἱκετεύοντος ἐκπονῆσαι τὰ
λοιπὰ μετ᾽ εὐφημίας, ὁ ποταμὸς περὶ ἑσπέραν ἑωρᾶτο
τοῖς πρώτοις· καὶ βοῆς, ὡς εἰκός, ἱλαρᾶς[31] ἐπὶ τῇ
χαρᾷ γενομένης, ἡ βοή, μεταλαμβανόντων αὐτὴν τῶν
κατόπιν ἑξῆς, ἐπὶ τοὺς ὑστάτους περιήει. Βροῦτος δὲ
καὶ Κάσσιος ἐπεὶ ἔμαθον, ἵεντο αὐτίκα δρόμῳ, διὰ

---

[31] ἱλαρᾶς LPBJ; λαμπρᾶς L

into the Hermus, on the fourth day, and would need one
further day to reach Philippi, thus surrounding the enemy
and cutting them off completely, so that they would not
even have a route to withdraw. Brutus and Cassius decided   433
to adopt this advice because they did not know what else
to do, and particularly because they hoped to surround
such a large enemy army.

104. So they send a detachment in advance under the   434
command of Lucius Bibulus, to clear the route with Rhascupolis. They found it a very laborious task, but set about
getting it done with spirit and enthusiasm, all the more so
when some who had been sent ahead came back and said
that they had seen the river in the distance. On the fourth   435
day, when they were exhausted by the labor and thirst, and
the water that they were carrying with them was already
running somewhat short, they remembered being told
that the waterless part of the route lasted three days, and
began to panic in fear that they had been tricked. They did
not disbelieve those sent ahead who said they had seen the
river, but thought that they themselves were being led in
a different direction. So they were losing heart and shouting, and when they saw Rhascupolis rushing around encouraging them, they insulted him and threw things at
him. But while Bibulus was begging them to finish off   436
what remained to be done without using inauspicious language, toward evening the river was seen by those at the
front. As was to be expected, their joy gave rise to a happy
cheer, which was taken up by those behind in succession
until it reached the rear. When Brutus and Cassius were
informed, they immediately rushed forward, leading the

437 τῆς τετμημένης τὸν ἄλλον στρατὸν ἄγοντες. οὐ μὴν
ἔλαθόν γε τοὺς πολεμίους ἐς τέλος οὐδὲ περιέλαβον
αὐτούς· ὁ γάρ τοι Ῥάσκος, ὁ ἀδελφὸς τοῦ Ῥασκουπόλιδος, ἐκ τῆς βοῆς ὑπονοήσας ἐσκέψατο καὶ τὸ
γιγνόμενον ἰδὼν ἐθαύμασε μὲν ὁδὸν ἄνυδρον ἐλθόντος στρατοῦ τοσοῦδε, ἣν οὐδὲ θηρίον ᾤετο ὁδεύσειν
διὰ τοιᾶσδε ὕλης, καὶ ἀνήγγειλε τοῖς ἀμφὶ τὸν Νωρ-
βανόν· οἱ δὲ νυκτὸς ἔφευγον ἐκ τῶν Σαπαίων ἐπ' Ἀμφιπόλεως. καὶ οἱ Θρᾷκες ἄμφω διὰ στόματος ἦσαν ἐν
τοῖς στρατοῖς, ὁ μὲν ἀγνοουμένην ἀγαγών, ὁ δ' οὐκ
ἀγνοήσας.

438   105. Οἱ δ' ἀμφὶ τὸν Βροῦτον ἐκ παραλόγου τόλμης
ἐς Φιλίππους παρῆλθον, ἔνθα αὐτοῖς καὶ ὁ Τίλλιος
439 ἐπικατήχθη καὶ πᾶς ὁ στρατὸς συνεληλύθει. οἱ δὲ
Φίλιπποι πόλις ἐστίν, ἣ Δάτος ὠνομάζετο πάλαι καὶ
Κρηνίδες ἔτι πρὸ Δάτου· κρῆναι γάρ εἰσι περὶ τῷ
λόφῳ ναμάτων πολλαί. Φίλιππος δὲ ὡς εὐφυὲς ἐπὶ
Θρᾴκης χωρίον ὠχύρωσέ τε καὶ ἀφ' ἑαυτοῦ Φιλίπ-
440 πους προσεῖπεν. ἔστι δὲ ἡ πόλις ἐπὶ λόφου περικρή-
μνου, τοσαύτη τὸ μέγεθος, ὅσον ἐστὶ τοῦ λόφου τὸ
εὖρος. ἔχει δὲ πρὸς μὲν ἄρκτῳ δρυμούς, δι' ὧν ὁ Ῥασκούπολις ἤγαγε τοὺς ἀμφὶ τὸν Βροῦτον· πρὸς δὲ τῇ
μεσημβρίᾳ ἕλος ἔστι καὶ θάλασσα μετ' αὐτό, κατὰ
δὲ τὴν ἕω τὰ στενὰ τὰ Σαπαίων τε καὶ Κορπίλων, ἐκ

---

71 The scene owes its origins, directly or indirectly, to Xeno-
phon's famous description of the Greek expeditionary force when

rest of the army along the route that had been cut out.[71]
In the end, however, they did not escape the attention of   437
the enemy or surround them. For Rhascus, the brother of
Rhascupolis, grew suspicious because of the cheering and
investigated it. On seeing what was happening, he was
amazed at such a large army making its way through waterless terrain, which he did not believe even a wild animal
could get through because of such dense forestation, and
he immediately had the news conveyed to Norbanus; his
troops retreated during the night from the Sapaean pass
to Amphipolis. Both the Thracians were the talk of their
armies, Rhascupolis because he had led his through an
unknown route, Rhascus because he had not failed to notice this.

105. And so by an extraordinary act of daring Brutus'   438
force reached Philippi, where Tillius also disembarked to
join them, and the whole army had assembled. Philippi is   439
a town that was formerly called Datus, and before that
Crenides, because there are many springs of running water around the hill.[72] Philip fortified it because he considered it a well positioned stronghold against the Thracians,
and named it Philippi after himself. The town is situated   440
on the crest of a hill with cliffs all around and its size is
exactly that of the area of the hilltop. To the north there
are thick woods through which Rhascupolis led Brutus'
men. To the south is a marsh and then the sea. To the east
lie the Sapaean and Corpilian passes, and westward is a

---

it first caught sight of the Black Sea ("The sea! The sea!") after its
march out of present-day central Iraq in 401: see Xen. *An.* 4.7.

[72] Κρήνη (*krene*) or κρηνίς (*krenis*) is the Greek word for a
spring.

δὲ τῆς δύσεως πεδίον μέχρι Μυρκίνου τε καὶ Δραβή-
σκου καὶ ποταμοῦ Στρυμόνος, τριακοσίων που καὶ
441 πεντήκοντα σταδίων, εὔφορον πάνυ καὶ καλόν, ἔνθα
καὶ τὸ πάθος τῇ Κόρῃ φασὶν ἀνθιζομένῃ γενέσθαι,
καὶ ποταμὸς ἔστι Ζυγάκτης, ἐν ᾧ τοῦ θεοῦ περῶντος
τὸ ἅρμα τὸν ζυγὸν ἄξαι λέγουσι καὶ τῷ ποταμῷ γενέ-
442 σθαι τὸ ὄνομα. κατωφερὲς δ' ἐστὶ τὸ πεδίον, ὡς ἐπι-
δέξιον μὲν εἶναι τοῖς ἄνωθεν ὁρμῶσιν ἐκ τῶν Φιλίππων, ἄναντες δὲ τοῖς ἐξ Ἀμφιπόλεως βιαζομένοις.

443   106. Φιλίππων μὲν οὖν ἐστιν ἕτερος λόφος οὐ μα-
κράν, ὃν Διονύσου λέγουσιν, ἐν ᾧ καὶ τὰ χρυσεῖα
ἔστι τὰ Ἄσυλα καλούμενα. ἀπὸ δὲ τούτου δέκα σταδίους προελθόντι δύο εἰσὶν ἄλλοι λόφοι, Φιλίππων
μὲν αὐτῶν ὅσον ὀκτωκαίδεκα σταδίους ἀφεστῶτες,
ἀλλήλων δὲ ὅσον ὀκτώ, ἐν οἷς ἐστρατοπέδευσαν,
Κάσσιος μὲν ἐπὶ τοῦ πρὸς μεσημβρίαν, Βροῦτος δὲ
444 ἐπὶ τοῦ βορείου. καὶ τῶν ἀμφὶ τὸν Νωρβανὸν ὑποχω-
ρούντων οὐκέτι προῄεσαν· Ἀντώνιόν τε γὰρ ἐπυνθά-
νοντο πλησιάζειν, Καίσαρος ὑπολελειμμένου διὰ νόσον ἐν Ἐπιδάμνῳ, καὶ τὸ πεδίον ἦν ἐναγωνίσασθαι
445 καλὸν καὶ οἱ κρημνοὶ στρατοπεδεῦσαι. τὰ γὰρ ἑκατέρωθεν αὐτῶν, τῇ μὲν ἦν ἕλη καὶ λίμναι μέχρι τοῦ
Στρυμόνος, τῇ δὲ τὰ στενὰ καὶ ἀτριβῆ καὶ ἀνόδευτα·
τὸ δὲ μέσον τῶν λόφων, τὰ ὀκτὼ στάδια, δίοδος ἦν
ἐς τὴν Ἀσίαν τε καὶ Εὐρώπην καθάπερ πύλαι, καὶ
αὐτὰ διετείχισαν ἀπὸ χάρακος ἐς χάρακα καὶ πύλας

very fertile and beautiful plain extending some three hundred and fifty stades to the towns of Murcinus and Drabiscus and the river Strymon. It is here, so the story goes, 441 that the Maiden suffered her fate while she was picking flowers; here too is the river Zygactes in which they say that while the god was crossing it the yoke of his chariot broke, thus giving the river its name.[73] The plain slopes 442 down to the sea, an easy journey for those going downhill from Philippi, but an uphill struggle for those leaving from Amphipolis.

106. At any rate, there is another hill not far away 443 known as the Hill of Dionysus where there are goldmines called the Asyla. Ten stades further on, there are another two hills, eighteen stades away from Philippi itself and eight from each other. Cassius and Brutus made camp on these hills, Cassius on the southern and Brutus on the northern of the two. They made no further advance, even 444 though Norbanus' force was in retreat, because they heard that Antony was approaching—he had left Octavian behind at Epidamnus due to illness—and the plain was admirably situated for fighting and the hilltops for camping. For in relation to their flanks, on one side were marshes 445 and lakes all the way to the Strymon, on the other the passes and impenetrable, trackless terrain. The eight stades between the hills acted like a gate to form the main crossing from Europe to Asia, and they built a defensive wall across this space from one palisade to the other, but

[73] The Maiden is Demeter's daughter, Persephone, carried off to the underworld by her uncle, Hades, while she was picking flowers. "Zygactes" is made up of the Greek words for "yoke" and "break."

ἐν μέσῳ κατέλιπον, ὡς ἓν εἶναι τὰ δύο στρατόπεδα.
446 ἦν δὲ καὶ παρ' αὐτὸ ποταμός, ὃν Γάγγαν τινές, οἳ δὲ
Γαγγίτην λέγουσι, καὶ θάλασσα ὄπισθεν, ἐν ᾗ καὶ τὰ
ταμιεῖα καὶ ἐνορμίσματα ἔμελλον ἕξειν. Θάσον μὲν
δὴ ταμιεῖον, ἀπὸ ἑκατὸν σταδίων οὖσαν, ἐτίθεντο,
ἐνόρμισμα δὲ ταῖς τριήρεσι Νέαν πόλιν, ἀπὸ ἑβδο-
μήκοντα σταδίων.

447 107. Οἱ μὲν δὴ χαίροντες τῷ χωρίῳ τὰ στρατόπεδα
ὠχύρουν, Ἀντώνιος δὲ ὧδευε μὲν σὺν τῷ στρατῷ μετ'
ἐπείξεως, τὴν Ἀμφίπολιν ἐθέλων ἐς τὴν ὑπηρεσίαν
τῆς μάχης προλαβεῖν, ὡς δὲ αὐτὴν εὗρεν ὠχυρωμένην οἱ πρὸς τῶν ἀμφὶ τὸν Νωρβανόν, ἥσθη καὶ τὴν
παρασκευὴν ἐν αὐτῇ κατέλιπε μεθ' ἑνὸς τέλους, οὗ
Πινάριος ἡγεῖτο, αὐτὸς δὲ μάλα θρασέως πολὺ προελθὼν ἐστρατοπέδευεν ἐν τῷ πεδίῳ, σταδίους ὀκτὼ
448 μόνους ἀποσχὼν ἀπὸ τῶν πολεμίων. καὶ εὐθὺς ἦν
κατάδηλος ἡ τῶν στρατοπέδων ἐλάττωσίς τε καὶ πλε-
ονεξία. οἱ μὲν γὰρ ἦσαν ἐπὶ κολωνῷ, οἱ δὲ ἐν πεδίῳ,
καὶ οἱ μὲν ἐξυλεύοντο ἀπὸ τῶν ὀρῶν, οἱ δ' ἀπὸ τοῦ
ἕλους· καὶ ὑδρεύοντο οἱ μὲν ἐκ ποταμοῦ, οἱ δὲ ἐκ
φρεάτων ὧν αὐτίκα ὠρωρύχεισαν· τήν τε ἀγορὰν οἱ
μὲν ἀπ' ὀλίγων σταδίων ἐπήγοντο ἐκ Θάσου, οἱ δὲ
449 ἀπὸ πεντήκοντα καὶ τριακοσίων ἐξ Ἀμφιπόλεως. ἐδόκει γε μὴν ἐξ ἀνάγκης ὁ Ἀντώνιος ὧδε πρᾶξαι, κολω-
νοῦ μὲν οὐδενὸς ὄντος ἑτέρου, τὸ δ' ἄλλο πεδίον οἷα
κοιλότερον ἐκλιμνάζοντος ἐνίοτε τοῦ ποταμοῦ· παρ' ὃ
καὶ τὰς πηγὰς τῶν ὀρυσσομένων φρεάτων γλυκείας

left a gate in the middle, so that the two camps were actually one. Alongside the encampment was a river, which 446 some call the Ganga, others the Gangites, and behind it was the sea, where they intended to locate their storage depots and anchorages. So they made Thasos, which was one hundred stades away, their depot, and Neapolis, seventy stades off, the anchorage for their warships.

107. Contented with their position, they continued 447 to consolidate their camps. Antony, meanwhile, made a forced march with his army, as he wanted to occupy Amphipolis before the enemy as his base for the battle. He was delighted to find it already fortified for him by Norbanus' men, and leaving his ordnance there with one legion under the command of Pinarius, he himself advanced very daringly a great distance, and camped in the plain, only eight stades away from the enemy.[74] The relative ad- 448 vantage or disadvantage of the camps immediately became clear. For one army was encamped on a rise, the other in the plain; one got their wood from the mountains, the other from the marsh; one provided themselves with water from a river, the other from newly dug wells; one brought their supplies from Thasos a few stades away, the other from Amphipolis, a distance of three hundred and fifty stades. It appears, however, that Antony acted out of 449 necessity, as there was no other high ground and the rest of the plain was sometimes flooded by the river, as it was more low-lying; for the same reason, he discovered that the springs feeding the newly dug wells provided sweet

---

[74] Lucius Pinarius Scarpus, along with Quintus Pedius, was one of Octavian's co-heirs in Julius Caesar's will: see App. *BCiv.* 3.22.82.

450 τε καὶ δαψιλοῦς ὕδατος εὕρισκε. τό γε μὴν τόλμημα,
εἰ καὶ ἐξ ἀπορίας ἐγένετο, κατέπλησσε τοὺς πολεμίους, ἐγγὺς οὕτω καὶ εὐθὺς ἐξ ἐφόδου σὺν καταφρονήσει παραστρατοπεδεύσαντος. φρούριά τε ἤγειρε
πολλὰ καὶ πάντα κατὰ σπουδὴν ὠχύρου τάφροις καὶ
τείχεσι καὶ χαρακώμασιν. ὠχύρουν δὲ καὶ οἱ πο-
451 λέμιοι, ὅσα αὐτοῖς ἐνέλειπεν. ὁ δὲ Κάσσιος τὴν ὁρμὴν
τοῦ Ἀντωνίου μανιώδη οὖσαν ὁρῶν διετείχιζεν, ὃ ἔτι
μόνον αὐτοῖς ἔλειπεν ἐς τὸ ἕλος ἀπὸ τοῦ στρατοπέδου,
διὰ στενότητα ὑπεροφθέν, ὡς μηδὲν ἔτι ἀτείχιστον
εἶναι πλὴν κατὰ πλευρὰς Βρούτῳ μὲν τὰ ἀπόκρημνα,
Κασσίῳ δὲ τὸ ἕλος καὶ τὴν θάλασσαν ἐπὶ τῷ ἕλει· τὰ
δὲ ἐν μέσῳ πάντα διείληπτο τάφρῳ καὶ χάρακι καὶ
τείχει καὶ πύλαις.

452   108. Οὕτω μὲν ὠχυροῦντο αὐτῶν ἑκάτεροι καὶ ἐν
τοσούτῳ μόνοις ἱππεῦσι καὶ ἀκροβολισμοῖς ἐπει-
453 ρῶντο ἀλλήλων. ὡς δὲ ἐξείργαστο πάντα, ὅσα ἐπενόουν, καὶ ὁ Καῖσαρ ἀφῖκτο, οὔπω μὲν ἐρρωμένος ἐς
μάχην, φορείῳ δὲ ἐπὶ τὰς συντάξεις τοῦ στρατοῦ κο-
μιζόμενος, οἱ μὲν ἀμφὶ τὸν Καῖσαρα εὐθὺς ἐξέτασσον
ἐς μάχην, οἱ δ᾽ ἀμφὶ τὸν Βροῦτον ἀντεξέτασσον μὲν
ἐπὶ τῶν ὑψηλοτέρων, οὐ κατῄεσαν δέ· οὐ γὰρ ἐγνώκε-
σαν ἐς τὴν μάχην ἐπείγεσθαι, ταῖς ἀγοραῖς ἐλπίζον-
454 τες ἐκτρύσειν τοὺς πολεμίους. ἦν δὲ τὰ μὲν πεζὰ ἑκατέροις ἐννεακαίδεκα ὁπλιτῶν τέλη, τοῖς μὲν ἀμφὶ τὸν
Βροῦτον ἐνδέοντα τοῖς ἀριθμοῖς, τοῖς δ᾽ ἀμφὶ τὸν
Καῖσαρα καὶ ἐπλεόναζον·[32] ἱππέες δὲ ἅμα τοῖς ἑκατέρων Θρᾳκίοις ἦσαν Καίσαρι μὲν καὶ Ἀντωνίῳ

and abundant water. At any rate, Antony's daring, even if   450
it arose out of a lack of options, shocked the enemy, given
that he so contemptuously pitched camp beside them immediately after arriving. He raised numerous redoubts
and quickly strengthened his whole position with ditches
and walls and palisades. The enemy also continued to
strengthen any weak points they had left. Noticing the   451
frantic nature of Antony's momentum, Cassius built a defensive wall across the only remaining stretch of land,
from the camp to the marsh, which had been overlooked
because it was so short. The result was that nothing was
left undefended except the cliffs on Brutus' flank, and on
Cassius', the marsh, and beyond it the sea. Everything in
the middle had been cut off by a ditch and palisade and
wall and gates.

108. In this way both sides fortified their position, while   452
at the same time they made trial of each other, although
only with their cavalry and missile exchanges. When they   453
had completed all their plans, and Octavian had arrived—
he was not yet strong enough for battle, and was carried
to the lines in a litter—Octavian's forces immediately deployed for battle, and Brutus arrayed his army in response
on the higher ground, but did not come down: for they had
decided not to precipitate the battle, in the hope that their
supply problems would wear the enemy down. With re-   454
gards to infantry, each side had nineteen legions, those of
Brutus being under strength, those of Octavian actually
over strength. As to cavalry, including the Thracians on
both sides, Octavian and Antony had thirteen thousand,

---

32 ἐπλεόναζον ἑκατέρωθεν codd.; ἑκατέρωθεν del. Bekker

μύριοι καὶ τρισχίλιοι, Βρούτῳ δὲ καὶ Κασσίῳ δισ-
455 μύριοι. ὥστε πλήθει μὲν ἀνδρῶν καὶ θράσει καὶ ἀρετῇ
στρατηγῶν καὶ ὅπλοις καὶ παρασκευῇ λαμπροτάτην
ἑκατέρων παράταξιν ὀφθῆναι, ἄπρακτον δὲ ἐς πολλὰς
ἡμέρας, οὐκ ἐθελόντων συμπλέκεσθαι τῶν ἀμφὶ τὸν
Βροῦτον, ἀλλὰ ταῖς ἀγοραῖς προεκτρύχειν τοὺς πολεμίους, αὐτοὶ μὲν ἔχοντες Ἀσίαν χορηγὸν καὶ ἐξ
ἐγγίονος πάντα διὰ θαλάσσης ποριζόμενοι, τοῖς δὲ
456 πολεμίοις οὐδὲν ὂν δαψιλὲς οὐδὲ οἰκεῖον· οὔτε γάρ τι
δι' ἐμπόρων ἀπ' Αἰγύπτου λαβεῖν εἶχον, ὑπὸ λιμοῦ
τῆς χώρας δεδαπανημένης, οὔτε ἐξ Ἰβηρίας ἢ Λιβύης διὰ Πομπήιον οὔτε ἐκ τῆς Ἰταλίας διὰ Μοῦρκον
καὶ Δομίτιον. οὐκ ἐς πολὺ δ' αὐτοῖς ἔμελλον ἀρκέσειν
Μακεδονία τε καὶ Θεσσαλία, μόναι σφίσιν ἐν τῷ τότε
χορηγοῦσαι.

457   109. Ὧν οἱ μὲν ἀμφὶ τὸν Βροῦτον ἐνθυμούμενοι
μάλιστα διέτριβον· ὁ δὲ Ἀντώνιος αὐτὰ δεδιὼς ἔγνω
βιάσασθαι τοὺς ἄνδρας ἐς μάχην καὶ ἐπενόησεν, εἰ
δύναιτο βάσιμον τὸ ἕλος ἐργάσασθαι λαθών, ἵνα
κατόπιν τῶν ἐχθρῶν ἔτι ἀγνοούντων γενόμενος τὴν
ἀγορὰν σφᾶς ἀφέλοιτο τὴν ἀπὸ τῆς Θάσου κομιζο-
458 μένην. ἐκτάσσων οὖν αὖθις ἑκάστοτε ἐς μάχην τὰ
σημεῖα τοῦ στρατοῦ πάντα, ἵνα ὅλος ἐκτετάχθαι νο-
μίζοιτο, μέρει τινὶ νυκτός τε καὶ ἡμέρας ἔκοπτεν ἐν τῷ
ἕλει δίοδον στενήν, κείρων τε τὸν δόνακα καὶ χῶμα
ἐπιβάλλων καὶ λίθους ἑκατέρωθεν, ἵνα μὴ τὸ χῶμα
διαπίπτοι, τὰ δὲ βαθέα διεσταύρου καὶ ἐγεφύρου μετὰ
σιωπῆς βαθυτάτης. ἀφῄρητο δὲ τὴν ὄψιν τοῦ ἔργου

Brutus and Cassius twenty thousand. The result was that   455
in terms of the number of men, of daring and courageous
generals, of weapons and of equipment, both battle lines
provided a brilliant sight. And yet there was no action for
many days, as Brutus did not want to join battle, but to use
the supply situation to wear the enemy down first: with
Asia as their supply base, they themselves could bring everything by sea from a relatively short distance away, while
the enemy had nothing in abundance and nothing from
their own territory. For it was not possible for them to use   456
merchants to get anything from Egypt, since the country
was exhausted by famine, or from Spain or Africa because
of Pompeius, or from Italy because of Murcus and Domitius. Macedonia and Thessaly, which were the only countries then supplying them, would not be sufficient for very
long.

109. With this situation particularly in mind, Brutus   457
tried to delay, while Antony, fearful for the same reason,
decided to force his opponents into battle. He formed a
plan to see if he could in secret make the marsh passable,
in order to get behind the enemy without their knowledge,
and deprive them of their supply route from Thasos. So   458
while drawing up his forces for battle again, on each occasion he included all the military standards, to create the
belief that his entire army had been marshaled. With one
unit, however, he worked day and night to carve a narrow
path in the marsh, cutting down reeds, building a causeway on top with rocks on either side to prevent the bank
subsiding, driving piles into the deep parts and bridging
them, and all the while keeping the deepest silence. The
reeds, which were still growing around the roadway, pre-

τοὺς πολεμίους ὁ πεφυκὼς ἔτι δόναξ ἀμφὶ τῇ διόδῳ.
459 δέκα δ' ἡμέρας ἐργασάμενος ὧδε ἐσέπεμψε λόχους
ὀρθίους νυκτὸς ἄφνω καὶ τὰ ἐρυμνὰ τῶν ἐντὸς κατ-
460 έλαβε καὶ ἐχαράκωσε φρούρια ὁμοῦ πολλά. ὁ δὲ
Κάσσιος κατεπλάγη μὲν τοῦ ἔργου τὴν ἐπίνοιάν τε
καὶ κλοπήν, ἀντεπινοῶν δὲ ἀποτεμέσθαι τὰ φρούρια
τὸν Ἀντώνιον, διετείχιζε καὶ αὐτὸς ἐπικάρσιον τὸ ἕλος
ἅπαν, ἀρχόμενος[33] ἀπὸ τοῦ στρατοπέδου μέχρι τῆς
θαλάσσης, κόπτων ὁμοίως καὶ γεφυρῶν καὶ τὸν
χάρακα τοῖς στεριφώμασιν ἐπιτιθεὶς καὶ τὴν ὑπὸ
Ἀντωνίου γεγενημένην δίοδον ἀπολαμβάνων, ἵνα
μήτε ἐκδραμεῖν ἐς αὐτὸν οἱ ἔνδον ἔτι δυνηθεῖεν μήτε
ἐκεῖνος αὐτοῖς ἐπιβοηθεῖν.

461 110. Ταῦτα δὲ ὁ Ἀντώνιος ἰδὼν περὶ μεσημβρίαν,
ὡς εἶχεν, αὐτίκα σὺν ὁρμῇ τε καὶ ὀργῇ τὸν στρατὸν
τὸν ἴδιον, ἐπὶ θάτερα τεταγμένον, ἦγεν ἐπιστρέφων
εἰς τὸ διατείχισμα τοῦ Κασσίου, μεταξὺ τοῦ ἕλους
καὶ τοῦ στρατοπέδου, σιδήρια φέρων καὶ κλίμακας,
ὡς ἐξελῶν αὐτὸ καὶ παροδεύσων ἐς τὸ τοῦ Κασσίου
462 στρατόπεδον. γιγνομένου δὲ αὐτῷ τοῦ δρόμου σὺν
τόλμῃ πλαγίου τε καὶ πρὸς ἄναντες, κατ' αὐτὸ δὴ τὸ
μεταίχμιον τῶν στρατιῶν ἑκατέρων, περιήλγησαν οἱ
τοῦ Βρούτου στρατιῶται ἐπὶ τῇ ὕβρει, ὧδε μάλα θρασέως αὐτοὺς ὄντας ἐνόπλους ἐχθρῶν διαθεόντων, καὶ
ἐπέδραμον αὐτοῖς αὐτοκέλευστοι πρό τινος ἐκ τῶν
ἡγεμόνων ἐπιτάγματος καὶ ἔκτεινον οἷα πλαγίους
463 ἀθρόως οὓς καταλάβοιεν. ἀρξάμενοι δ' ἅπαξ ἔργου
καὶ τῷ Καίσαρος στρατῷ τεταγμένῳ μάλιστα κατὰ

vented the enemy from seeing the work. After laboring for   459
ten days in this way he suddenly sent in a column of troops
by night, who seized the strong positions in the interior,
and fortified several posts at the same time. Cassius was   460
amazed at the ingenuity and secrecy of the work, but devised a counterscheme to cut Antony off from his outposts
by also traversing the whole marsh with a wall built at right
angles across it. Starting at his camp and going all the way
to the sea, cutting and bridging the marsh in the same way
as Antony, he erected his palisade on firm foundations and
intercepted the pathway made by Antony, to render it
impossible for those on the other side to escape to him, or
for him to come to their assistance.

110. When Antony saw this about midday, without de-   461
lay he immediately turned his own army, which was drawn
up in the other direction, and led it with urgency and anger against Cassius' cross-wall between his camp and the
marsh. He carried iron tools and ladders intending to destroy it and make his way through to Cassius' camp. His   462
charge was a daring one, uphill and exposing his flank, and
right in the middle between the two armies. Brutus' soldiers were very annoyed at the insolence with which the
enemy were so audaciously running past them, ready under arms as they were, and on their own initiative charged
them before any order was issued by their officers. They
killed en masse those they could overtake, as you would
expect with a flanking attack. Now that they had once   463
started the battle, they also charged Octavian's troops,

---

³³ ἀρχόμενον LBJ; ἀρχόμενος P

σφᾶς ἐπέδραμον καὶ τρέψαντες ἐδίωκον, μέχρι καὶ τὸ
στρατόπεδον ἐξεῖλον, ὃ κοινὸν ἦν Ἀντωνίῳ τε καὶ
Καίσαρι, Καίσαρος αὐτοῦ δι᾽ ἐνύπνιον ἔνδον οὐκ ὄντος, ἀλλὰ φυλαξαμένου τὴν ἡμέραν, ὡς αὐτὸς ἐν τοῖς
ὑπομνήμασιν ἔγραψεν.

464   111. Ὁ δὲ Ἀντώνιος ὁρῶν τὴν μάχην συνερρωγυῖαν
ἥσθη μὲν ὡς ἀναγκάσας (πάνυ γὰρ ἐπὶ ταῖς ἀγοραῖς
ἐδεδίει), ἀναστρέφειν δὲ εἰς τὸ πεδίον οὐκ ἔκρινεν, μὴ
τὴν φάλαγγα ἀνελίσσων ταράξειεν, ὡς ἀρξάμενος δ᾽
εἶχεν ὁρμῆς, ἐχεῖτο δρόμῳ καὶ ἀνέβαινε, βαλλόμενός
τε καὶ χαλεπῶς, μέχρι βιαζόμενος ἐνέκυρσε τῇ
φάλαγγι τῇ Κασσίου, τὴν τάξιν τὴν δεδομένην φυ-
λασσούσῃ καὶ τὸ γιγνόμενον ὡς ἄλογον καταπε-
465   πληγμένῃ. ῥήξας δ᾽ αὐτὴν ὑπὸ τόλμης ἐπὶ τὸ διατείχισμα ὥρμα, τὸ μεταξὺ τοῦ τε ἕλους καὶ τοῦ
στρατοπέδου, τόν τε χάρακα ἀνασπῶν καὶ τὴν τάφρον ἐγχωννὺς καὶ τὸ οἰκοδόμημα ὑπορύσσων καὶ
τοὺς ἐν ταῖς πύλαις καταφονεύων καὶ τὰ ἐπιπίπτοντα
ἐκ τοῦ τείχους ὑπομένων, ἕως αὐτὸς μὲν ἐσήλατο διὰ
τῶν πυλῶν ἔνδον, ἕτεροι δὲ ταῖς ὑπωρυχίαις ἐσῆλθον,
466   οἱ δὲ καὶ τοῖς πεπτωκόσιν ἐπανέβαινον. καὶ πάντα
οὕτως ἐγίγνετο ὀξέως, ὥστε τοῖς τὸ ἕλος ἐργαζομένοις
ἐπιβοηθοῦσιν ὑπήντων ἑλόντες ἤδη τὸ διατείχισμα.
τρεψάμενοι δὲ καὶ τούσδε σὺν ὁρμῇ βιαίῳ καὶ ἐς τὸ
ἕλος κατώσαντες ἐπανήεσαν ἐς αὐτὸ ἤδη τὸ στρατό-

who had been drawn up right opposite them, routed them, and pursued them all the way to the camp which Antony and Octavian shared, and captured it. Octavian himself was not there, because of a dream, but was taking precautions that day, as he himself wrote in his memoirs.[75]

111. When Antony saw that battle had been joined he 464 was delighted that he had forced it, for he had been very anxious about his supplies. He decided not to wheel round back into the plain, for fear that an about-turn would throw his battle line into disorder, but maintaining his original direction of attack, he continued to charge uphill under heavy missile fire until he forced his way to an encounter with Cassius' battle line, which was holding its assigned position in astonishment at the unaccountable turn of events. Daringly breaking this line, he rushed 465 against the wall that ran between the marsh and the camp, pulled down the palisade, filled in the ditch, undermined the structure, and killed the men at the gates, standing firm against the missiles thrown down from the wall. Eventually Antony himself rushed inside through the gates, while others made their way in through breaches in the wall, some even climbing up over the bodies of the fallen. All this happened so quickly that they had already 466 captured the wall when they confronted the men working in the marsh who were coming to give assistance. These too they put to flight with a powerful charge, and after driving them into the marsh, now turned back against Cas-

[75] Plutarch (*Ant.* 22.2) also refers to this dream recorded in Augustus' memoirs. These memoirs were presumably the autobiography (*De vita sua*) in thirteen books mentioned by Suetonius (*Aug.* 85.1).

πεδον τοῦ Κασσίου, μόνοι σὺν τῷ Ἀντωνίῳ, ὅσοι τὸ
διατείχισμα ὑπερῆλθον, τοῦ ἄλλου πλήθους ἑκατέρων
ἐκτὸς ἀλλήλοις μαχομένου.

467   112. Τὸ δὲ στρατόπεδον ὡς ἐρυμνὸν ὀλίγοι πάμπαν
ἐφύλασσον· ὅθεν αὐτῶν εὐμαρῶς ἐκράτησεν ὁ Ἀντώνιος. ἤδη δὲ καὶ ἔξω τοῦ Κασσίου στρατὸς ἡσσᾶτο
καὶ τὴν κατάληψιν ἰδὼν τοῦ στρατοπέδου διεσκίδνατο
468   ἀκόσμως. καὶ τὸ ἔργον ἦν ἐντελὲς ἑκατέροις καὶ
ὅμοιον· Βροῦτός τε γὰρ τὸ λαιὸν τῶν πολεμίων ἐτέ-
τραπτο καὶ τὸ στρατόπεδον ᾑρήκει, Ἀντώνιός τε
Κασσίου κρατῶν σὺν ἀμηχάνῳ τόλμῃ τὸ στρατόπε-
469   δον ἐπόρθει. φόνος τε ἦν ἑκατέρων ποικίλος· ὑπὸ δὲ
μεγέθους πεδίου τε καὶ κονιορτοῦ τὰ ἀλλήλων ἠγνόουν, μέχρι ποτὲ ἐπύθοντο καὶ τοὺς λοιποὺς ἀνεκάλουν.
470   οἱ δὲ ἐπανῇεσαν, ἀχθοφόροις ἐοικότες μᾶλλον ἢ
στρατιώταις· καὶ οὐδὲ τότε ἀλλήλων ᾐσθάνοντο οὐδὲ
καθεώρων, ἐπεὶ ῥίψαντές γε, ὅσα ἔφερον, οἱ ἕτεροι
μέγα ἂν εἰργάσαντο κατὰ τῶν ἑτέρων, ἀσυντάκτως
471   ὧδε ἀχθοφορούντων. τὸν δ' ἀριθμὸν τῶν ἀποθανόν-
των εἰκάζουσι τῶν μὲν ἀμφὶ τὸν Κάσσιον ἐς ὀκτακισ-
χιλίους σὺν τοῖς παρασπίζουσι θεράπουσι γενέσθαι,
τῶν δ' ἀμφὶ τὸν Καίσαρα διπλασίονα.

472   113. Κάσσιος δὲ ἐξ οὗ τῶν διατειχισμάτων ἐξέωστο
καὶ οὐδὲ ἐσελθεῖν ἔτι εἶχεν ἐς τὸ στρατόπεδον, ἀνέ-
δραμεν ἐς τὸν Φιλίππων λόφον καὶ τὰ γιγνόμενα
ἐφεώρα. οὐκ ἀκριβῶς δὲ αὐτὰ διὰ τὸν κονιορτὸν οὐδὲ
πάντα ὁρῶν, ἀλλ' ἢ τὸ στρατόπεδον ἑαυτοῦ μόνον
εἰλημμένον, ἐκέλευσε Πινδάρῳ τῷ ὑπασπιστῇ προσ-

sius' actual camp. Antony had with him only those men who had scaled the wall, the rest of both forces fighting each other on the other side of the wall.

112. As the camp was thought to be in a strong position, only a very few men were guarding it, which is why Antony easily overcame them. Cassius' army on the outside were already being beaten, and when they saw that the camp had been captured, they scattered in disorder. And so the battle came to a similar conclusion on both sides. For Brutus had routed the enemy left wing and captured their camp, while Antony had with his irresistible daring defeated Cassius and sacked his camp. The slaughter on both sides varied, but because of the size of the plain and the clouds of dust they did not know what had happened to each other until they were told and recalled the survivors. Those who returned looked more like porters than soldiers, and even then did not recognize or see each other clearly, or else they would have thrown aside all they were carrying and fought fiercely one against the other, weighed down and in disorder as they were. Estimates of the number killed were, on Cassius' side about eight thousand, including slave batmen, and double that on Octavian's.

113. When Cassius was driven out of his fortifications and could no longer even get into his camp, he hurried to the hill of Philippi and tried to survey what was happening. Because of the dust he could not get an accurate picture of the situation, or see everything, only that his camp had been captured, and he ordered his aide-de-camp, Pinda-

467

468

469

470

471

472

473 πεσεῖν οἳ καὶ διαφθεῖραι. διαμέλλοντος δ' ἔτι τοῦ Πινδάρου προσέθει τις ἀγγελῶν[34] Βροῦτον ἐπὶ θάτερα
νικᾶν καὶ τὸ στρατόπεδον τῶν πολεμίων πορθεῖν. ὁ δὲ
τούτῳ μὲν τοσόνδε ἀπεκρίνατο· "Νικῴης, λέγε αὐτῷ,
παντελῆ νίκην," ἐς δὲ τὸν Πίνδαρον ἐπιστραφείς, "Τί
βραδύνεις;" ἔφη, "Τί τῆς ἐμῆς αἰσχύνης με οὐκ ἀπαλ-
λάσσεις;" Πίνδαρος μὲν δὴ τὸν δεσπότην, ὑπέχοντα
τὴν σφαγήν, διεχρήσατο. καί τισιν οὕτως ἀποθανεῖν

474 δοκεῖ Κάσσιον. ἕτεροι δὲ αὐτὸν οἴονται, προσιόντων
ἐς εὐαγγέλιον ἱππέων Βρούτου, νομίσαντα εἶναι πολεμίους, πέμψαι τὸ ἀκριβὲς εἰσόμενον Τιτίνιον· τὸν δὲ
τῶν ἱππέων ὡς Κασσίου φίλον περισχόντων τε σὺν
ἡδονῇ καὶ ἐπὶ τῷδε καὶ ἀλαλαξάντων μέγα, τὸν Κάσσιον ἡγούμενον ἐς ἐχθροὺς ἐμπεσεῖν Τιτίνιον τοῦτο
φάναι· "Περιμένομεν φίλον ἁρπαζόμενον ἰδεῖν," καὶ
ἔς τινα σκηνὴν ὑποχωρῆσαι μετὰ τοῦ Πινδάρου καὶ
τὸν Πίνδαρον οὐκέτι φανῆναι. διὸ καὶ νομίζουσί τινες

475 οὔπω κεκελευσμένον ἐργάσασθαι. Κασσίῳ μὲν δὴ
τέλος ἦν τοῦ βίου κατὰ τὴν αὐτοῦ Κασσίου γενέθλιον
ἡμέραν, ὧδε τῆς μάχης γενέσθαι συμπεσούσης, καὶ
Τιτίνιος ὡς βραδύνας ἑαυτὸν ἔκτεινε·

476 114. Βροῦτος δὲ Κασσίου τὸν νέκυν περικλαίων,
ἀνεκάλει τελευταῖον ἄνδρα Ῥωμαίων, ὡς οὔ τινος ἔτι
τοιοῦδε ἐς ἀρετὴν ἐσομένου, ταχυεργίας τε αὐτῷ καὶ
προπετείας ἐνεκάλει καὶ ἐμακάριζεν ὁμοῦ φροντίδων
καὶ ἀνίας ἀπηλλαγμένον, αἳ Βροῦτον ἐς ποῖον ἄρα

---

[34] ἀγγέλλων codd.; τις ἀγγελῶν Gaillard-Goukowsky

rus, to set upon and kill him. Pindarus was still hesitating   473
when someone ran up to announce that Brutus had been
victorious on the other wing, and was sacking the enemy's
camp. Cassius' answer to the man was merely this, "Say to
him, 'May your victory be complete.'" Turning to Pindarus, he said, "What are you waiting for? Why won't you
deliver me from my shame?" And when Cassius offered
his throat, Pindarus did away with his master. This is how
some people think Cassius died. Others believe that when   474
some of Brutus' cavalrymen came up to deliver his good
news, Cassius thought they were the enemy, and sent Titinius to get accurate information. The cavalrymen gathered around Titinius knowing he was a companion of Cassius, and also shouted out with pleasure, but Cassius
thought that Titinius had fallen into the hands of the enemy and said, "So we were waiting just to see our companion being taken prisoner." He then retired to a tent with
Pindarus, who was never seen again. For this reason some
people think that he killed Cassius before he got the order
to do so. The death of Cassius actually occurred on his   475
birthday—that is when the battle happened to take
place—and Titinius also took his own life because he had
been too late.

114. Brutus wept over the corpse of Cassius and called   476
him the last of the Romans, because there would never
again be anyone to match his excellence. He reproached
him for haste and impulsiveness, but at the same time
declared him happy to be freed from the cares and anxiety
that would accompany Brutus to who knew what end.

APPIAN

477 τέλος ὁδηγοῦσι. παραδοὺς δὲ τὸ σῶμα τοῖς φίλοις,
ἔνθα λαθραίως θάψειαν, ἵνα μὴ καταδακρύσειε τὸν
στρατὸν ὁρῶντα, αὐτὸς ἄσιτός τε καὶ ἀτημέλητος ἀνὰ
τὴν νύκτα πᾶσαν τὸ Κασσίου στρατόπεδον καθ-
478 ίστατο. ἅμα δ' ἡμέρᾳ τῶν πολεμίων τὸν στρατὸν
παρατασσόντων ἐς μάχην, ἵνα μὴ δοκοῖεν ἡλασσῶ-
σθαι, συνεὶς τοῦ ἐνθυμήματος, "Ὁπλισώμεθα," ἔφη,
"Καὶ ἡμεῖς καὶ ἀνθυποκριθῶμεν ἐλάσσονα παθεῖν."
ὡς δὲ παρέταξεν, οἱ μὲν ἀνεχώρουν, ὁ δὲ Βροῦτος
ἐπιτωθάσας ἔφη τοῖς φίλοις· "Οἱ μὲν δὴ προκαλούμε-
νοι ἡμᾶς ὡς κεκμηκότας οὐδὲ ἀπεπείρασαν."
479 115. Ἦι δὲ ἡμέρᾳ τὴν μάχην ἐν Φιλίπποις συν-
έβαινεν εἶναι, καὶ ἐν τῷ Ἰονίῳ τοιόνδε πάθος ἄλλο
ἐγίγνετο μέγα. Δομίτιος Καλουῖνος ἐπὶ ὁλκάδων ἦγεν
ὁπλιτῶν δύο τέλη Καίσαρι, καὶ τὸ διώνυμον ἦν αὐτῶν,
τὸ Ἄρειον, ὃ ἐπὶ τιμῇ τῆς ἀλκῆς ὠνόμαζον. ἦγε δὲ καὶ
στρατηγίδα σπεῖραν, ἐς δισχιλίους ἄνδρας, ἱππέων
τε ἴλας τέσσαρας καὶ ἕτερον πλῆθος ἐπειλεγμένον
480 καὶ τριήρεις αὐτοὺς παρέπεμπον ὀλίγαι. Μοῦρκος δ'
αὐτοῖς καὶ Ἀηνόβαρβος ἑκατὸν καὶ τριάκοντα μακραῖς ὑπήντων. καὶ αὐτοὺς αἱ ὁλκάδες ἱστίῳ μὲν αἱ
πρῶται διέφυγον ὀλίγαι, αἱ λοιπαὶ δέ, χαλάσαντος
ἄφνω τοῦ πνεύματος, ἐν γαλήνῃ σταθερᾷ κατὰ τὸ
πέλαγος ἡλῶντο, ὑπό του θεῶν ἐκδεδομέναι τοῖς πο-
481 λεμίοις. ἐνέβαλλον γὰρ ἀδεῶς ἑκάστη καὶ ἀνερρή-
γνυον· οὐδὲ αἱ παραπέμπουσαί σφας τριήρεις ἐπικου-
482 ρεῖν ἐδύναντο, διὰ τὴν ὀλιγότητα κυκλούμεναι. ἔργα

He handed over the body to his companions for secret 477
burial, to avoid moving the army to tears at the sight, while
he himself spent the whole night without food and without care for his own person, restoring order in Cassius'
camp. In the morning the enemy drew up their army for 478
battle, to give the impression that they had not been defeated. Brutus understood their intention and said, "Let
us arm too and offer the counterpretense that we have
suffered less." But when he deployed his forces, the enemy withdrew, and Brutus said to his friends mockingly,
"To be sure, they challenged us when they thought we
were exhausted, but they did not even make trial of us."

115. On the same day that the battle at Philippi took 479
place, another disaster as great as this one occurred in the
Ionian gulf. Domitius Calvinus was bringing two legions
of infantry on transport ships to Octavian, one of which
was the famous legion of Mars, a name bestowed on it in
honor of its bravery.[76] He was also bringing a praetorian
cohort of about two thousand men, four squadrons of cavalry, and another body of select troops. A small number of
triremes escorted them. Murcus and Ahenobarbus met 480
them with one hundred and thirty warships. A few of the
transports in front got away under sail, but the wind suddenly failed, and the rest drifted on the sea in a dead calm,
delivered by some god into the hands of their enemies,
who without fear rammed each ship and shattered it; nor 481
could the triremes escorting them help, since they were
surrounded by reason of their small number. The men 482

[76] Gnaeus Domitius Calvinus (tribune 59, praetor 56, consul
53) had commanded Caesar's center at the battle of Pharsalus in
48 (App. *BCiv.* 2.76). He was consul for a second time in 40.

δ' ἦν τῶν κινδυνευόντων πολλὰ καὶ ποικίλα, ὁτὲ μὲν τὰ πλοῖα συναγόντων ἀπὸ κάλω σπουδῇ καὶ κοντοῖς ἁρμοζόντων ἐς ἄλληλα, ἵνα μὴ διεκπλεῖν αὐτὰ ἔχοιεν

483 οἱ πολέμιοι. ὅτε δὲ τούτου κρατήσειαν, ὁ μὲν Μοῦρκος αὐτοῖς ἐπέβαλλε τοξεύματα πυρός, οἱ δὲ τοὺς συνδέσμους ἀνέλυον ὀξέως καὶ ἀπέφευγον ἀλλήλων διὰ τὸ πῦρ αὖθίς τε ἐγίγνοντο ταῖς τριήρεσιν ἐς περίπλουν καὶ ἐμβολὴν ἕτοιμοι.

484   116. Ἀγανακτοῦντες δὲ οἱ ἄνδρες, καὶ μάλιστα αὐτῶν οἱ Ἄρειοι, ὅτι κρείττους ὄντες ἀλκὴν δι' ἀπραξίας ἀπώλλυντο, οἱ μὲν πρὸ τοῦ πυρὸς ἑαυτοὺς ἀνῄρουν, οἱ δὲ ἐς τὰς τριήρεις τῶν πολεμίων ἐναλλό-

485 μενοι τὰ μὲν ἔδρων, τὰ δὲ ἔπασχον. νῆές τε ἡμίφλεκτοι μέχρι πολλοῦ περιέπλεον, ἄνδρας ἔχουσαι τοὺς μὲν ὑπὸ τοῦ πυρός, τοὺς δ' ὑπὸ λιμοῦ καὶ δίψης δαπανωμένους· οἱ δὲ καὶ ἱστῶν ἢ σανίδων ἐχόμενοι ἐς

486 πέτρας ἢ ἀκτὰς ἐξεφέροντο ἐρήμους. καὶ εἰσὶν αὐτῶν, οἳ καὶ περιεσώθησαν ἐκ παραλόγου· τινὲς δὲ καὶ ἐς πέντε διήρκεσαν ἡμέρας, λιχμώμενοι τὴν πίσσαν ἢ ἱστίων ἢ κάλων διαμασώμενοι, μέχρι σφᾶς ὁ κλύδων ἐξήνεγκεν ἐπὶ τὴν γῆν. πολὺ δ' ἦν, ὃ καὶ τοῖς πολεμίοις ἑαυτὸ ἐπέτρεπεν, ὑπὸ τῶν συμφορῶν ἡσσώμε-

487 νον. ἐπέτρεψαν δὲ καὶ τῶν τριήρων ἑπτακαίδεκα. καὶ τοὺς μὲν ἄνδρας οἱ περὶ Μοῦρκον ἐς ἑαυτοὺς μεθώρκουν, ὁ δὲ στρατηγὸς αὐτῶν Καλουῖνος ἐπὶ τῆς ἑαυτοῦ νεὼς ἐπανῆλθεν ἐς τὸ Βρεντέσιον ἡμέρᾳ πέμπτῃ,

488 δόξας ἀπολωλέναι. τοιοῦτο μὲν δὴ πάθος τῆς αὐτῆς ἡμέρας τῇ περὶ Φιλίππους μάχῃ κατὰ τὸν Ἰόνιον ἐπ-

who were exposed to this danger carried out many and varied actions. One moment they hastily brought their ships together with ropes and attached them to each other with spars so that the enemy would not be able to sail through their line. But when they succeeded in doing this, 483 Murcus fired burning arrows at them, and they quickly undid the bindings and moved away from each other on account of the fire, and again became vulnerable to encirclement and ramming by the triremes.

116. The men, and particularly those of the legion of 484 Mars, were indignant that they were being destroyed through inaction when they were superior with regard to military prowess, and some killed themselves before the fire reached them, while others leaped onto the enemy triremes to kill and be killed. Half-burned vessels drifted 485 around for a long time, with men on board being consumed—some by fire, others by hunger and thirst. Others again, clinging to masts or planks, were washed up on deserted rocks or coasts. Among them there were also 486 some who were saved unexpectedly. A few even lasted five days by licking pitch, or chewing sails or ropes, until the tide carried them to the land. A substantial number, overcome by their misfortunes, surrendered to the enemy. They handed over seventeen of their triremes. Murcus 487 swore the men in to his own army, but their general, Calvinus, who was believed to have died, returned to Brundisium on his own ship five days later. Such was the catas- 488 trophe, whether you should call it a shipwreck or a naval battle, that took place in the Ionian gulf on the same day

εγίγνετο, εἴτε ναυάγιον εἴτε ναυμαχίαν ὀνομάσαι
χρή· καὶ ἐξέπλησσε τὸ συγκύρημα τῶν ἔργων ὕστερον ἐπιγνωσθέν.

489   117. Ὁ δὲ Βροῦτος τὸν στρατὸν ἐς ἐκκλησίαν συναγαγὼν ἔλεξεν ὧδε· "Οὐδὲν ἔστιν, ὦ συστρατιῶται,
παρὰ τὸν χθὲς ἀγῶνα, ἐν ᾧ μὴ κρείσσους ἐγένεσθε
490   τῶν πολεμίων. τῆς τε γὰρ μάχης ἤρξατε προθύμως,
εἰ καὶ χωρὶς παραγγέλματος· καὶ τὸ τέταρτον τέλος,
ὃ περιώνυμον αὐτοῖς ὂν ἐπεπίστευτο τὸ κέρας, δι-
εφθείρατε ἅπαν καὶ τοὺς ἐπιτεταγμένους αὐτῷ μέχρι
τοῦ στρατοπέδου· καὶ τὸ στρατόπεδον αὐτὸ εἵλετε
πρότερον καὶ διηρπάσατε· ὡς προύχειν τάδε παρὰ
491   πολὺ τῆς ἐπὶ τοῦ λαιοῦ βλάβης ἡμῶν. δυνηθέντες δ'
ἂν ὅλον ἐργάσασθαι τὸ ἔργον, ἁρπάσαι μᾶλλον εἵ-
λεσθε ἢ κτείνειν τοὺς ἡσσωμένους· οἱ γὰρ πλέονες
ὑμῶν τοὺς πολεμίους παροδεύοντες ἐπὶ τὰ τῶν πο-
492   λεμίων ὥρμων. καὶ ἐν τῷδε αὖ πάλιν οἱ μὲν διήρπα-
σαν δύο τῶν ἡμετέρων στρατοπέδων ὄντων τὸ ἕτερον,
ἡμεῖς δὲ ἐκείνων ἅπαντα ἔχομεν, ὡς καὶ τῷδε τὴν
493   ἐπίκτησιν τῆς βλάβης διπλασίονα εἶναι. καὶ τὰ μὲν
ἐν τῇ μάχῃ πλεονεκτήματα τοσαῦτα· ὅσα δὲ ἕτερα
προύχομεν αὐτῶν, ἔχετε καὶ παρὰ τῶν αἰχμαλώτων
μανθάνειν, περί τε ἀπορίας σίτου καὶ ἐπιτιμήσεως
αὐτοῦ καὶ κομιδῆς κακοπαθοῦς καὶ παρ' ὀλίγου ἤδη
494   σαφοῦς ἐπιλείψεως. οὔτε γὰρ ἐκ Σικελίας ἢ Σαρδόνος
ἢ Λιβύης ἢ Ἰβηρίας ἔστιν αὐτοῖς λαβεῖν διὰ Πομπήιον καὶ Μοῦρκον καὶ Ἀηνόβαρβον, ναυσὶν ἑξήκοντα καὶ διακοσίαις ἀποκλείοντας αὐτοῖς τὸ πέλα-

as the battle near Philippi. The coincidence of the two battles caused amazement when it became known later.

117. Brutus summoned his army to an assembly and addressed it as follows: "My fellow soldiers, there was no part of yesterday's engagement in which you were not superior to the enemy. You began the fighting enthusiastically, although without orders, and their fourth legion, which has such a wide reputation among them and to whom that wing had been entrusted, you completely destroyed along with all its supporting troops right up to their camp; and the camp itself you first took and then sacked. These gains far outweigh the damage we suffered on our left wing. But when it was in your power to complete the whole task, you chose to plunder rather than kill the defeated: for most of you bypassed the enemy and made a rush for their property. Meanwhile they in their turn seized one of our two camps, but we hold everything of theirs, so on this count too they have suffered twice the damage we have. Such are the advantages we won in the battle. As for all the other ways in which we have the better of them, you can learn from our prisoners about their shortage of food, the high price of it, the difficulty of transporting it, and what are now clearly their all but exhausted stocks. They can get nothing from Sicily or Sardinia or Africa or Iberia, because of Pompeius and Murcus and Ahenobarbus, who are shutting off their access to the sea with two hundred and sixty ships. They have already ex-

489

490

491

492

493

494

γος· Μακεδονίαν τε ἐξαναλώκασιν ἤδη καὶ ἐκ μόνης
ἄρτι Θεσσαλίας ἔχουσιν, ἢ ἐς πόσον αὐτοῖς ἔτι ἀρκέσει;

495   118. "Ὅταν οὖν αὐτοὺς ἐπειγομένους εἰς μάχην
μάλιστα ἴδητε, τότε ἡγεῖσθε διωκομένους ὑπὸ λιμοῦ
τὸν ἐν χερσὶ θάνατον αἱρεῖσθαι. ἡμεῖς δ' ἀντιμηχα-
νησώμεθα αὐτοῖς τὸν λιμὸν ἡμῶν προπολεμεῖν, ἵν'
ἀσθενεστέροις καὶ τετρυμένοις ἐντύχοιμεν, ὅτε χρή.

496   μηδ' ἐκφερώμεθα ταῖς προθυμίαις παρὰ καιρόν, μηδὲ
βραδυτῆτά τις ἡγείσθω τὴν ἀπειρίαν,[35] ἐς τὴν ὀπίσω
θάλασσαν ἀφορῶν, ἢ τοσαύτας ἡμῖν ὑπηρεσίας καὶ
τροφὰς ἐπιπέμπουσα δίδωσιν ἀκινδύνου νίκης ἐπιτυ-
χεῖν, ἢν ὑπομένητε καὶ μὴ ἀδοξῆτε, εἰ προσπαίζονταί
τε ἡμῖν καὶ προκαλοῦνται, οὐκ ἀμείνονες ὄντες, ὡς
διέδειξε τὸ ἐχθὲς ἔργον, ἀλλὰ ἕτερον δέος ἰώμενοι.
τὴν δὲ προθυμίαν, ἧς νῦν ὑμᾶς ἀξιῶ κρατεῖν, ἀθρόαν

497   ἀπόδοτε, ὅταν αἰτῶμεν. ἐγὼ δ' ὑμῖν τὰ νικητήρια
ἐντελῆ μέν, ὅταν οἱ θεοὶ κρίνωσι, ἐπὶ ἐντελέσι τοῖς
ἔργοις διαλύσομαι· νῦν δὲ τῆς ἐχθὲς ἀρετῆς ἀνὰ χιλίας ἑκάστῳ στρατιώτῃ δραχμὰς ἐπιδίδωμι καὶ τοῖς

498   ἡγεμόσιν ὑμῶν ἀνὰ λόγον." ὁ μὲν οὕτως εἶπεν καὶ
αὐτίκα διεμέτρει τὴν δωρεὰν κατὰ τέλη· δοκεῖ δέ τισι
καὶ Λακεδαίμονα καὶ Θεσσαλονίκην ἐς διαρπαγὴν
αὐτοῖς δώσειν ὑποσχέσθαι.

499   119. Ὁ δὲ Καῖσαρ καὶ ὁ Ἀντώνιος, εἰδότες οὐ μα-
χούμενον ἑκόντα τὸν Βροῦτον, τοὺς ἰδίους συνῆγον,

hausted Macedonia and recently Thessaly is their only
source of supply. And how much longer will it be enough
for them?

118. "So when you see them particularly eager for
battle, that is when you should bear in mind that they are
being pursued by famine and prefer death in battle. For
our part, let us devise a counterstrategy for hunger to fight
against them on our behalf, so that when we have to fight
we find them weaker and worn out. And we should not be
carried away by our passions before the timing is right. Let
no one look back at the sea behind us and regard moving
slowly as a sign of inexperience. The sea brings us significant reinforcements and supplies, and gives us the chance
to win victory without danger, if you wait patiently and
disregard the enemy when they jeer and challenge us to
fight: as the engagement yesterday demonstrated, they are
no better than us, but merely trying to counteract a different fear. When I ask for it, give full vent to that zeal which
I now require you to suppress. The rewards of total victory
I myself will pay you in full, when the gods grant it. And
now for your bravery yesterday, I grant each soldier an
extra one thousand drachmas and a proportionate amount
to your officers." Such was his speech, and he immediately
distributed the donative legion by legion. Some people
think that he also promised to give them Lacedaemon and
Thessalonica to plunder.

119. Octavian and Antony knew that Brutus would not
willingly fight a battle, and assembled their men. Antony

495

496

497

498

499

---

35 ἐμπειρίαν ἢ ταχυτῆτα codd.; ἢ ταχυτῆτα del. Musgrave;
ἀπειρίαν nos.

καὶ ὁ Ἀντώνιος ἔλεξε· "Τὸ ἐχθὲς ἔργον, ὦ ἄνδρες, τοῖς
μὲν λόγοις οἶδα ὅτι καὶ οἱ πολέμιοι μερίζονται, ὡς
διώξαντές τινας ἡμῶν καὶ τὸ στρατόπεδον διαρπάσαν-
τες, ἔργῳ δὲ ἐπιδείξουσιν ἅπαν ὑμέτερον· ὑπισχνοῦμαι
γὰρ ὑμῖν οὔτε αὔριον οὔτε ταῖς ἐπιούσαις ἑκόντας
500   αὐτοὺς ἐς μάχην ἥξειν. ὁ σαφεστάτη πίστις ἐστὶ τῆς
ἐχθὲς ἥσσης καὶ φόβου, ὅταν ὥσπερ ἐν τοῖς γυμνικοῖς ἀφιστῶνται τοῦ ἀγῶνος οἱ ἐλάττονες· οὐ γὰρ ἐς
τοῦτό γε στρατὸν ἤγειρον τοσόνδε, ἵνα τῶν Θρᾳκῶν
501   ἐρημίαν οἰκῶσι διατειχίσαντες. ἀλλὰ αὐτὴν διετείχισαν μὲν ἔτι προσιόντων ὑμῶν διὰ δέος, ἐλθόντων δὲ
ἐνοικοῦσι διὰ τὴν ἐχθὲς ἧσσαν· ἐφ' ᾗ καὶ τῶν στρατηγῶν ὁ πρεσβύτερός τε καὶ ἐμπειρότερος πάντα
ἀπογνοὺς ἑαυτὸν διεχρήσατο, ὃ καὶ αὐτὸ μεγίστη
502   συμφορῶν ἐστιν ἀπόδειξις. ὅταν οὖν ἡμῶν αὐτοὺς
προκαλουμένων μὴ δέχωνται μηδὲ καταβαίνωσιν ἀπὸ
τῶν ὁρῶν, ἀλλὰ ἀντὶ τῶν χειρῶν πιστεύωσι τοῖς κρη-
μνοῖς, τότε μοι θαρροῦντες ὑμεῖς, ὦ ἄνδρες Ῥωμαῖοι,
συναναγκάσατε αὐτοὺς αὖθις, ὥσπερ ἐχθὲς ἠναγκά-
σατε, αἰσχρὸν ἡγούμενοι δεδιότων ἐλασσοῦσθαι καὶ
ὀκνούντων ἀπέχεσθαι καὶ τειχῶν ἄνδρες ὄντες ἀσθε-
503   νέστεροι γενέσθαι. οὐ γὰρ ἤλθομέν γε καὶ ἡμεῖς ἐν
πεδίῳ βιώσοντες, οὐδ' ἔστι βραδύνουσιν οὐδὲν αὔταρ-
κες. ἀλλὰ δεῖ τοῖς εὖ φρονοῦσι τοὺς μὲν πολέμους
ὀξεῖς, τὴν δὲ εἰρήνην ἐπὶ μήκιστον εἶναι.

504   120. "Τοὺς μὲν οὖν καιροὺς καὶ τὰ ἐς τοῦτον ἔργα
ἐπιμηχανησόμεθα ἡμεῖς, οὐ μεμπτοὶ καὶ τῆς ἐχθὲς
ὁρμῆς τε καὶ μηχανῆς ὑμῖν γενόμενοι· τὴν δ' ἀρετὴν

then addressed them as follows: "Soldiers, I know that in their speeches our enemies too claim a share of yesterday's engagement because they drove some of us before them and plundered our camp, but in practice they will show that it was entirely yours. For I promise you that neither tomorrow nor on any subsequent day will they be willing to come out and fight. This reluctance is the clearest proof   500
of their defeat yesterday and of their fear: it is like when the losers in athletic contests withdraw from the competition. For they did not collect such a large army just to wall off and inhabit the wilds of Thrace. It was, rather, through   501
fear that they fortified Thrace with a wall while you were still approaching; and now that you have arrived they are staying behind it because of yesterday's defeat. On top of the defeat, in complete despair the older and more experienced of their generals also took his own life, an act that is in itself the most telling sign of their misfortunes. So   502
when they decline our challenge and refuse to come down from the high ground, but put their trust in cliffs rather than their own hands, then, men of Rome, have confidence in me and join me in forcing them to fight, just as you forced them to fight yesterday: you should consider it a disgrace to be beaten by a scared enemy, to hold back from confronting waverers, or to let real men like you be weaker than walls. We too did not come here to live our   503
lives on a plain, and those who delay have no control over their fate. Sensible people should have short wars and peace for as long as possible.

120. "As you did not find fault with us for yesterday's   504
plan of attack, we will be the ones to devise the opportunities and battles to achieve this. As for you, repay your

505 ὑμεῖς, ὅταν αἰτῆσθε, ἀποδίδοτε τοῖς στρατηγοῖς. μηδὲ
ἄχθεσθε τῆς ἐχθὲς ἁρπαγῆς μηδ' ἐπ' ὀλίγον· οὐ γὰρ
ἐν οἷς ἔχομέν ἐστι τὸ πλουτεῖν, ἀλλ' ἐν τῷ κρατεῖν
ταῖς δυνάμεσιν, ὃ καὶ τὰ ἐχθὲς ἀφαιρεθέντα, ἔτι ὄντα
παρὰ τοῖς πολεμίοις σῶα, καὶ τὰ πολέμια αὐτὰ ἐπ'
ἐκείνοις κρατοῦσιν ἡμῖν ἀποδώσει. καὶ εἰ ἐπειγόμεθα
506 αὐτὰ λαβεῖν, ἐπειγώμεθα ἐπὶ τὴν μάχην. ἱκανὰ δὲ καὶ
ἐχθὲς ἀντειλήφαμεν αὐτῶν καὶ τῶν ἡμετέρων ἴσως
ἱκανώτερα· οἱ μὲν γὰρ ἐκ τῆς Ἀσίας πάνθ', ὅσα ἐβιά-
σαντο καὶ ἥρπασαν, ἐπήγοντο, ὑμεῖς δ' ὡς ἐκ πατρίδος ἰόντες τὰ μὲν δαψιλέστερα οἴκοι ὑπελίπεσθε, τὰ
δ' ἀναγκαῖα μόνα ἐπήγεσθε. εἰ δέ τι καὶ δαψιλὲς ἦν,
ἡμέτερον ἦν τῶν στρατηγῶν, οἳ πάντα ἐσμὲν ὑπὲρ
507 τῆς ὑμετέρας νίκης ἐπιδιδόναι πρόθυμοι. καὶ τῆς
τοιαύτης δ' ὅμως ζημίας ὑμῖν ἕνεκα ἐπιδώσομεν νικητήρια, δραχμὰς ἑκάστῳ στρατιώτῃ πεντακισχιλίας,
λοχαγῷ δὲ πεντάκις τοσαύτας, χιλιάρχῃ δὲ τὸ διπλάσιον τοῦ λοχαγοῦ."

508 121. Τοιαῦτα εἰπὼν τῆς ἐπιούσης πάλιν ἐξέτασσε·
καὶ οὐ κατιόντων οὐδὲ τότε τῶν πολεμίων ὁ μὲν
Ἀντώνιος ἐβαρυθύμει καὶ ἐξέτασσεν αἰεί, ὁ δὲ Βροῦτος
τοῦ στρατοῦ τὸ μὲν εἶχε συντεταγμένον, μὴ ἀναγκα-
σθείη μάχεσθαι, τῷ δὲ τὰς ὁδοὺς τῆς κομιδῆς τῶν
509 ἀναγκαίων διελάμβανε. λόφος δὲ ἦν ἀγχοτάτω τοῦ
Κασσίου στρατοπέδου, δυσχερὴς μὲν ὑπὸ ἐχθρῶν
καταληφθῆναι, διὰ τὴν ἐγγύτητα ἐστοξεύεσθαι δυ-
ναμένων· ὁ δὲ Κάσσιος αὐτὸν ὅμως ἐφρούρει, μὴ καὶ
510 παρὰ δόξαν ἐπιτολμήσειέ τις. ἐκλειφθέντα δὲ ὑπὸ τοῦ

generals with courage, when you are asked for it. And   505
don't worry even for a moment about what was seized
from you yesterday. For wealth lies not in what we possess,
but in victory and power, which will not only restore to us
as victors what was taken yesterday, and remains safe with
the enemy, but will also yield the enemy's possessions in
addition. And if we are eager to get these things, let us be
eager for battle. Even yesterday we took enough from   506
them to balance our losses, perhaps more than enough.
For they brought with them all that they had violently
plundered from Asia, while you, coming from your native
land, left the greater part of what you own at home, and
brought with you only what was strictly necessary. If there
was any extra, it was the property of us your generals, and
we are keen to give it all to you as a reward for your victory.
However, as compensation for such loss as you suffered   507
we will give you an additional reward for victory: five thousand drachmas for each soldier, five times as much for
each centurion, and twice this amount to each tribune."

121. Such was his speech. Next day, he again arrayed   508
his men for battle, but even then the enemy did not come
down from their position. Antony was disheartened, but
continued to form up for battle every day, while Brutus
kept one part of his army in battle formation in case he
was forced to fight, and with the other set about cutting
the roads by which the enemy's supplies were transported.
There was a hill very near the camp of Cassius, which was   509
difficult for the enemy to occupy, because it was close
enough to be in range of arrow attack. Nevertheless, Cassius had a guard post on it, in case anyone attacked, even
unexpectedly. It had, however, been abandoned by Bru-   510

Βρούτου κατέλαβον οἱ περὶ τὸν Καίσαρα νυκτὸς
τέτρασι τέλεσιν, ἐπαγόμενοι γέρρα πολλὰ καὶ διφθέ-
511 ρας ἐς προβολὴν τοῖς τοξεύμασιν. ὡς δὲ κατέσχον,
ἄλλα τέλη δέκα μετεστρατοπέδευον ὑπὲρ πέντε σταδίους ἀπιοῦσιν ἐπὶ τὴν θάλασσαν καὶ ὑπὲρ ἄλλους
τέσσαρας δύο, ὡς τῷδε τῷ τρόπῳ προελευσόμενοι
μέχρι θαλάσσης καὶ ἢ παρ' αὐτὴν ἄρα τὴν θάλασσαν ἢ διὰ τῶν ἑλῶν ἢ ὅν τινα τρόπον ἄλλον ἐπενόουν,
βιασόμενοι καὶ τὴν ἀγορὰν ἀποκλείσοντες τῶν πολεμίων. καὶ ὁ Βροῦτος αὐτοῖς ἀντεμηχανᾶτο, ἄλλα τε
καὶ φρούρια ἀντικαθιστὰς τοῖς ἐκείνων στρατοπέδοις.

512 122. Τὸ δὲ ἔργον ἤπειγε τοὺς ἀμφὶ τὸν Καίσαρα,
καὶ λιμὸς ἦν ἤδη σαφής, ἔς τε μέγεθος καὶ δέος ἑκάστης ἡμέρας ἐπεγίνετο. οὔτε γὰρ ἐκ Θεσσαλίας
αὐτοῖς ἔτι τὰ ἀρκοῦντα ἐκομίζετο, οὔτε τις ἦν ἐλπὶς
ἐκ θαλάσσης, ναυκρατούντων πανταχῇ τῶν πολεμίων·
513 τῆς τε ἔναγχος περὶ τὸν Ἰόνιον συμφορᾶς ἐξηγγελ-
μένης ἐς ἑκατέρους ἤδη, μᾶλλον ἐδεδοίκεσαν αὐτά τε
καὶ τὸν χειμῶνα προσιόντα ὡς ἐν πεδίῳ πηλώδει
σταθμεύοντες. ὧν ἐνθυμούμενοι τέλος μὲν ὁπλιτῶν ἐς
Ἀχαΐαν ἐξέπεμψαν, ἀγείρειν τὰ ἐντυγχάνοντα πάντα
514 καὶ πέμπειν σφίσι κατὰ σπουδήν. οὐκ ἀνεχόμενοι δὲ
κινδύνου τοσοῦδε προσιόντος οὔτε τῶν ἄλλων ἐπι-
τεχνήσεων οὔτε ἐν τῷ πεδίῳ λοιπὸν ἐκτάσσειν, παρὰ
τὸ τείχισμα τῶν ἐχθρῶν ἀνέβαινον μετὰ βοῆς καὶ τὸν
Βροῦτον ἐκάλουν ἐς μάχην, ἐπισκώπτοντες ἅμα καὶ
λοιδοροῦντες καὶ ἐγνωκότες οὐ πολιορκίας τρόπῳ

tus, and Octavian seized it at night with four legions who had brought up many screens of wickerwork and skin as a defense against arrows. When they had secured the posi- 511 tion, they moved the camp of ten other legions more than five stades closer to the sea, and of two more legions another four stades further. Their intention was to advance as far as the sea in this manner, and by forcing their way along the sea itself, or through the marshes or by some other way, to cut off the enemy's supplies. Brutus devised various countermeasures, among them the placing of guard posts opposite their camps.

122. Battle was becoming an urgent matter for Octa- 512 vian, as hunger was now evident and with respect to its extent fear grew every day. For they were no longer getting sufficient supplies from Thessaly, and there was no hope from the sea, which was under the control of the enemy in all areas. News of the recent disaster in the Io- 513 nian gulf now reached both armies, causing Octavian's forces even more anxiety about the situation and the coming winter, stationed as they were in a marshy plain. With these considerations in mind, they sent a legion of troops off to Achaea to collect all the food they could find and send it to them with speed. Refusing to accept the ap- 514 proach of such great danger and the other schemes being devised against them, and to deploying for battle in the plain, they climbed up to the enemy's fortifications, and shouted their challenge to Brutus to fight, mocking and insulting him, determined to join battle with him even

μᾶλλον ἢ μανιώδει φορᾷ μὴ βουλομένῳ συμπλέκεσθαι.

515   123. Τῷ δὲ αὐτῷ μὲν ἔγνωστο τὰ ἀπ᾽ ἀρχῆς, καὶ μᾶλλον ἔτι πυνθανομένῳ περί τε τοῦ λιμοῦ καὶ περὶ τῆς κατὰ τὸν Ἰόνιον εὐπραξίας καὶ τῶν πολεμίων ὁρῶντι τὴν ἐκ τῆς ἀπορίας ἀπόνοιαν· καὶ ᾑρεῖτο πολιορκίας καὶ ἄλλου παντὸς ἀνέχεσθαι, μᾶλλον ἢ ἐς χεῖρας ἰέναι ἀνδράσιν ἐπειγομένοις ὑπὸ λιμοῦ, καὶ ἀπογινώσκουσιν ἐκ τῶν ἄλλων ἑαυτοὺς καὶ ἐν μόναις

516   ταῖς χερσὶ τὴν ἐλπίδα ἔχουσιν. ὁ δὲ στρατὸς οὐχ ὁμοίως εἶχεν ὑπὸ ἀφροσύνης, ἀλλ᾽ ἐδυσφόρουν γυναικῶν τρόπον ἔνδον μετὰ ἀπραξίας καὶ φόβου κατα-

517   κεκλεισμένοι. ἐδυσχέραινον δὲ καὶ οἱ ἡγεμόνες αὐτῶν, ἐπαινοῦντες μὲν τὸ ἐνθύμημα τοῦ Βρούτου, νομίζοντες δὲ καὶ θᾶσσον ἐπικρατήσειν τῶν πολεμίων μετὰ προ-

518   θύμου στρατοῦ. αἴτιον δὲ τούτων ἦν αὐτὸ τὸ Βροῦτον ἐπιεικῆ καὶ φιλόφρονα ἐς ἅπαντας εἶναι καὶ ἀνόμοιον Κασσίῳ, αὐστηρῷ καὶ ἀρχικῷ περὶ πάντα γεγενημένῳ· ὅθεν ἐκείνῳ μὲν ἐξ ἐπιτάγματος ὑπήκουον, οὐ παραστρατηγοῦντες οὐδὲ τὰς αἰτίας μανθάνοντες οὐδὲ εὐθύνοντες, ὅτε καὶ μάθοιεν, Βρούτῳ δὲ οὐδὲν

519   ἀλλ᾽ ἢ συστρατηγεῖν ἠξίουν διὰ πρᾳύτητα. τέλος δὲ τοῦ στρατοῦ φανερώτερον ἤδη κατὰ ἴλας καὶ κατὰ συστάσεις διαπυνθανομένου· "Τί κατέγνωκεν ἡμῶν ὁ στρατηγός; τί ἔναγχος ἡμάρτομεν οἱ νικήσαντες, οἱ διώξαντες, οἱ τοὺς καθ᾽ ἡμᾶς πολεμίους κατακανόντες, οἱ τὸ στρατόπεδον αὐτῶν ἑλόντες;" Βροῦτος ἑκὼν ἠμέλει. καὶ ἐς ἐκκλησίαν οὐ συνῆγε, μὴ ἀπρεπέστε-

though he did not want to, not by siege but rather by ferocious assault.

123. But Brutus decided to stick to his original plan, 515
even more so when he learned of the famine and the success in the Ionian gulf, and observed the enemy's desperation at their lack of supplies. He preferred to endure
a siege, or anything else rather than join battle with men
driven by hunger, men whose hopes rested solely on fighting because they despaired of all other means. His sol- 516
diers, however, in their folly were not of the same opinion,
but were annoyed at being shut in, doing nothing and
afraid, like women. Their officers, although they approved 517
of Brutus' logic, were also dissatisfied, because they believed that they would defeat the enemy more quickly with
an enthusiastic army. The reason for this situation was the 518
fact that Brutus himself was reasonable and friendly to
everyone, unlike Cassius, who had been severe and authoritative in all matters—which is why men obeyed him
when ordered, did not countermand his orders as general,
and did not ask the reasons for them or criticize them
when they were told. But in the case of Brutus, because
he was so obliging, they required nothing less than to
share the command with him. Eventually, in their platoons 519
and companies the men began to ask more and more
openly, "Why has the general convicted us? What have we
just done wrong in defeating, pursuing and killing the enemy facing us, and in capturing their camp?" Brutus deliberately paid no attention to them, and did not call them
to assembly, for fear that he would be forced rather inap-

ρον ὑπὸ τοῦ πλήθους ἀλογίστως ἐκβιασθείη, καὶ
μάλιστα μισθοφόρων, οἷς ἐστιν αἰεί, καθὰ καὶ τοῖς
εὐχερέσιν οἰκέταις ἐς ἑτέρους δεσπότας, ἐλπὶς ἐς σωτηρίαν ἡ ἐς τὸ ἀντίπαλον μεταβολή.

520   124. Ἐνοχλούντων δὲ αὐτῷ καὶ τῶν ἡγεμόνων καὶ
κελευόντων νῦν μὲν ἀποχρήσασθαι τοῦ στρατοῦ τῇ
προθυμίᾳ, τάχα τι λαμπρὸν ἐργασομένου, ἢν δ' ἀντι-
πίπτῃ τι παρὰ τὴν μάχην, ἐπανιέναι πάλιν ἐς τὰ
τείχη καὶ προβάλλεσθαι τὰ αὐτὰ χαρακώματα, χαλεπήνας ὁ Βροῦτος τοῖσδε μάλιστα ἡγεμόσιν οὖσι καὶ
περιαλγήσας, ὅτι τὸν αὐτόν οἱ κίνδυνον ἐπικείμενοι
συμφέρονται τῷ στρατῷ κούφως, ἀμφίβολον καὶ
ὀξεῖαν τύχην προτιθέντι νίκης ἀκινδύνου, εἶξεν ἐπ'
οἰκείῳ καὶ σφῶν ἐκείνων ὀλέθρῳ, τοσόνδε ἐπιμεμψάμενος αὐτοῖς· "Ἐοίκαμεν ὡς Πομπήιος Μάγνος
πολεμήσειν, οὐ στρατηγοῦντες ἔτι μᾶλλον ἢ στρατη-
521   γούμενοι." καί μοι δοκεῖ τόδε μόνον ἐξειπεῖν, ἐπικρύπτων, ὃ ἐδεδοίκει μάλιστα, μὴ ὁ στρατὸς οἷα τοῦ
πάλαι Καίσαρος γεγονὼς ἀγανακτήσειέ τε καὶ μετα-
βάλοιτο· ὅπερ ἐξ ἀρχῆς αὐτός τε καὶ Κάσσιος ὑφορώμενοι ἐς οὐδὲν ἔργον αὐτοῖς πρόφασιν ἀγανακτήσεως
ἐπὶ σφίσιν ἐνεδίδουν.

522   125. Ὧδε μὲν δὴ καὶ ὁ Βροῦτος ἐξῆγεν ἄκων καὶ
ἐς τάξεις διεκόσμει πρὸ τοῦ τείχους καὶ ἐδίδασκε μὴ
πολὺ προύχειν τοῦ λόφου, ἵνα αὐτοῖς ἥ τε ἀναχώρη-
σις, εἰ δεήσειεν, εὐχερὴς εἴη καὶ τὰ ἐς τοὺς πολεμίους

propriately into irrational action by the rank and file, and especially by the mercenaries, whose hope of safety is always to go over to the other side, like unscrupulous slaves going over to different masters.

124. His officers also badgered him, telling him to 520 make use of the enthusiasm of the soldiers right now, and they would quickly achieve a brilliant result; but if something went wrong in the battle, they could return again to the walls, and use the same palisade as protection. Brutus was annoyed with them, particularly because they were his officers, and he was offended that although they were exposed to the same danger as him, they were thoughtlessly going along with the troops, who placed an uncertain and swift fate ahead of victory without danger. But, to the ruin of himself and them, he gave in, reproaching them with these words, "It seems I am going to wage war like Pompey the Great, no longer in command, but under the command of others."[77] I think that this is all Brutus said be- 521 cause he wanted to conceal his greatest fear, that those of his soldiers who had formerly served under Caesar would become disaffected and desert. Both he and Cassius had suspected this from the beginning, and for that reason had, with regard to all operations, given no excuse for resentment toward themselves.

125. So it was then that Brutus too, but against his will, 522 led out his army and formed them into ranks in front of the wall, ordering them not to advance very far from the hill so that they had an easy line of retreat, if it was needed, and the missiles thrown at the enemy would hit their tar-

[77] Pompey had also allowed himself to be talked into battle against his better judgment, as Appian (*BCiv.* 2.69.286) records.

403

523 ἀφιέμενα ἐπιδέξια. ἦν δὲ ἑκατέρωθεν παρακέλευσίς τε
πάντων ἐς ἀλλήλους καὶ φρόνημα ἐπὶ τῷ ἔργῳ μέγα
καὶ θρασύτης ὑπὲρ λόγον ἀναγκαῖον, τοῖς μὲν ὑπὸ
δέους λιμοῦ, τοῖς δὲ ὑπὸ αἰδοῦς δικαίας, βιασαμένοις
τὸν στρατηγὸν ἀναβαλλόμενον ἔτι, μὴ χείροσιν ὧν
ὑπέσχοντο ὀφθῆναι μηδὲ ἀσθενεστέροις ὧν ἐθρασύ-
νοντο, μηδὲ προπετείας ὑπευθύνοις μᾶλλον ἢ ἀξιεπαί-
524 νοις εὐβουλίας. ἃ καὶ ὁ Βροῦτος αὐτοῖς, ἐπὶ ἵππου
περιθέων, σοβαρῷ τῷ προσώπῳ προενέφαινε καὶ δι᾽
ὀλίγων ὑπεμίμνησκεν, ὅσων ὁ καιρὸς ἐδίδου· "Ὑμεῖς
ἠθελήσατε μάχεσθαι, ὑμεῖς με ἑτέρως ἔχοντα νικᾶν
ἐβιάσασθε· μὴ δὲ ψεύσησθε τῆς ἐλπίδος μήτε ἐμὲ
μήτε αὑτούς. ἔχετε καὶ λόφον σύμμαχον καὶ τὰ κατὰ
νώτου πάντα ἴδια. οἱ πολέμιοι δ᾽ εἰσὶν ἐν ἀμφιβόλῳ·
μεταξὺ γάρ εἰσιν ὑμῶν τε καὶ λιμοῦ."

525 126. Ὁ μὲν τοιαῦτα λέγων διετρόχαζε, καὶ αὐτὸν αἱ
τάξεις ἐπήλπιζον καὶ μετὰ βοῆς παρέπεμπον εὐφή-
μου· ὁ δὲ Καῖσαρ καὶ ὁ Ἀντώνιος τοὺς ἰδίους περιθέοντες τήν τε δεξιὰν ὤρεγον, ἐφ᾽ οὓς παραγένοιντο,
καὶ σοβαρώτερον ἔτι οἵδε ἐπέσπερχον αὐτοὺς καὶ τὸν
λιμὸν οὐκ ἐπέκρυπτον ὡς εὔκαιρον ἐς εὐτολμίαν προ-
526 φέρειν. "Εὕρομεν, ὦ ἄνδρες, τοὺς πολεμίους· ἔχομεν
οὓς ἐζητοῦμεν ἔξω τείχους λαβεῖν. μὴ δή τις ὑμῶν
τὴν ἰδίαν πρόκλησιν καταισχύνῃ μηδὲ τῆς ἀπειλῆς
ἐλάττων γένηται· μηδὲ λιμόν, ὄλεθρον ἀμήχανόν τε
καὶ ἐπώδυνον, ἕληται μᾶλλον ἢ πολεμίων τείχη καὶ
σώματα, ἃ καὶ τόλμαις ἐνδίδωσι καὶ σιδήρῳ καὶ ἀπο-

get. In both armies all the men encouraged each other, 523
and there was great spirit for the battle and a daring beyond the necessary measure. On one side was the fear of
famine, on the other justifiable embarrassment, having
forced the hand of their commanding officer who was still
in favor of delaying, at the prospect of failing to meet their
promises, proving weaker than their boasts, and exposing
themselves to the charge of rashness instead of winning
praise for good counsel. Riding around on his horse, a 524
haughty expression on his face, Brutus made these things
clear to them and reminded them in a few words, such as
the situation allowed: "It is you who wanted to fight, you
who forced me to do so, when I had another plan for victory. So do not prove my hopes or your own false. You have
a hill as your ally, and to your rear everything belongs to
you. The enemy, on the other hand, are in a difficult position, for they are in the middle between you and starvation."

126. With these words he rode among his men at a trot, 525
and the soldiers in the ranks gave him hope and their
cheers of good omen accompanied him on his way. As for
Octavian and Antony, they assiduously did the rounds of
their own men, offering their right hand to those they
encountered, and urging them on even more insistently
than Brutus, making no attempt to hide famine as an op-
portune incitement to bravery. "Men, we have found the 526
enemy. We were trying to get them outside their wall, and
we now have them. Let none of you shame your own challenge or show yourselves not up to meeting the threat.
And let none of you prefer hunger, which is destructive,
unmanageable, and painful, to the walls and bodies of the
enemy, which give way before daring, iron, and despera-

APPIAN

527 νοίᾳ. ἔχει δὲ ἡμῖν ἐπείξεως ὧδε τὰ παρόντα, ὡς μηδὲν
ἐς τὴν ἐπιοῦσαν ἡμέραν ἀνατίθεσθαι, ἀλλὰ σήμερον
περὶ ἁπάντων διακριθῆναι μέχρι νίκης ἐντελοῦς ἢ εὐ-
528 γενοῦς θανάτου. νικῶσι δ' ἔστι λαβεῖν διὰ μιᾶς
ἡμέρας καὶ δι' ἑνὸς ἔργου τροφὰς καὶ χρήματα καὶ
ναῦς καὶ στρατόπεδα καὶ τὰ νικητήρια παρ' ἡμῶν.
529 ἔσται δὲ ταῦτα, ἢν πρῶτον μὲν ἐμβάλλοντες αὐτοῖς
μνημονεύωμεν τῶν ἐπειγόντων, εἶτα παραρρήξαντες
εὐθὺς ἀποκλείωμεν ἀπὸ τῶν πυλῶν, ἐς δὲ τοὺς κρημνοὺς ἢ τὰ πεδία περιωθῶμεν, ἵνα μὴ ὁ πόλεμος
αὖθις ἀναφύοιτο μηδὲ ἐς τὴν ἀργίαν πάλιν οἱ ἐχθροὶ
διαδιδράσκοιεν, οἳ δι' ἀσθένειαν, μόνοι δὴ πολεμίων,
οὐκ ἐν τῷ μάχεσθαι τὰς ἐλπίδας ἔχουσιν, ἀλλ' ἐν τῷ
μὴ μάχεσθαι.''

530 127. Οὕτω μὲν ὁ Καῖσαρ καὶ ὁ Ἀντώνιος παρώτρυ-
νον, ἐφ' οὓς παραγένοιντο. καὶ πᾶσιν ἦν αἰδὼς ἀξίοις
τε φανῆναι τῶν στρατηγῶν καὶ τὴν ἀπορίαν ἐκφυγεῖν, ὑπεραυξηθεῖσαν ἐκ παραλόγου διὰ τὰ ἐν τῷ Ἰονίῳ γενόμενα. ᾑροῦντό τε ἐν ἔργῳ καὶ ἐν ἐλπίσιν, εἰ
δέοι, τι παθεῖν μᾶλλον ἢ ὑπὸ ἀμηχάνου κακοῦ δα-
531 πανώμενοι. ὧδε δὲ ἐχόντων αὐτῶν καὶ πρὸς τὸν ἐγγὺς
αὐτὰ ἐκφέροντος ἑκάστου, ὁ θυμὸς ἀμφοτέρων ηὔξετο
μάλιστα καὶ ἐνεπίμπλαντο τόλμης ἀκαταπλήκτου· οὐδέν τε ἐν τῷ παρόντι ἀλλήλων ὅτι ἦσαν πολῖται οὐδὲ
ἐπεμέμνηντο, ἀλλ' ὡς ἐκ φύσεως καὶ γένους ἐχθροῖς
ἐπηπείλουν. οὕτως ἡ παραυτίκα ὀργὴ τὸν λογισμὸν
αὐτοῖς καὶ τὴν φύσιν ἔσβεσεν. ἐπεμαντεύοντο δὲ

tion. For us, the situation is so pressing that nothing can 527
be put off till tomorrow: everything must be decided today, including total victory or noble death. If you win, a 528
single day and a single battle will enable you to get provisions and money and ships and camps and the rewards of
victory from us. These things will come about if, first of 529
all, we keep in mind when attacking them the pressures
we face; and then, when we break their battle line, if we
immediately cut them off from their gates and push them
toward the cliffs or the plain, and thus prevent the fighting
flaring up again and the enemy taking refuge again in doing nothing—an enemy, who through weakness, are surely
the only ones to place their hopes not in battle, but in
avoiding battle."

127. In this way Octavian and Antony urged on the men 530
they encountered. A sense of honor inspired all of them
to appear worthy of their commanders and to escape their
predicament, which had unexpectedly been made much
worse by what had happened in the Ionian gulf. They
chose to die, if necessary, in action and in hope, rather
than be worn down by an evil against which they could do
nothing. Such was their state of mind, and with each man 531
communicating these thoughts to his neighbor, morale on
both sides prospered substantially and they were filled
with undaunted daring. In the present circumstances it
did not even occur to them that they were fellow citizens,
but they threatened each other as if they were natural
born enemies: to such an extent did their present anger
extinguish their nature and ability to think logically. They

ὁμαλῶς ἑκάτεροι τήνδε τὴν ἡμέραν ἐν τῷδε τῷ ἔργῳ
πάντα τὰ Ῥωμαίων πράγματα κρινεῖν. καὶ ἐκρίθη.

532   128. Ἤδη δὲ τῆς ἡμέρας ἀμφὶ τήνδε τὴν παρασκευὴν ἐς ἐνάτην ὥραν δεδαπανημένης αἰετοὶ δύο ἐς
τὸ μεταίχμιον συμπεσόντες ἀλλήλοις ἐπολέμουν· καὶ
ἦν σιγὴ βαθυτάτη. φυγόντος δὲ τοῦ κατὰ Βροῦτον
βοή τε παρὰ τῶν πολεμίων ὀξεῖα ἠγέρθη καὶ τὰ σημεῖα ἑκατέρωθεν ἐπῆρτο, καὶ ἔφοδος ἦν σοβαρά τε
533   καὶ ἀπηνής. τοξευμάτων μὲν δὴ καὶ λίθων ἢ ἀκον-
τισμάτων ὀλίγον αὐτοῖς ἐδέησε πολέμου νόμῳ, ἐπεὶ
οὐδὲ τῇ ἄλλῃ τέχνῃ καὶ τάξει τῶν ἔργων ἐχρῶντο,
ἀλλὰ γυμνοῖς τοῖς ξίφεσι συμπλεκόμενοι ἔκοπτόν τε
καὶ ἐκόπτοντο καὶ ἀλλήλους ἐξώθουν ἀπὸ τῆς τάξεως,
οἱ μὲν περὶ σωτηρίας μᾶλλον ἢ νίκης, οἱ δὲ περὶ
534   νίκης καὶ παρηγορίας στρατηγοῦ βεβιασμένου. φόνος δὲ ἦν καὶ στόνος πολύς, καὶ τὰ μὲν σώματα
αὐτοῖς ὑπεξεφέρετο, ἕτεροι δὲ ἀντικαθίσταντο ἐκ τῶν
535   ἐπιτεταγμένων. οἱ στρατηγοὶ δὲ σφᾶς, περιθέοντες
καὶ ὁρώμενοι πανταχοῦ, ταῖς τε ὁρμαῖς ἀνέφερον καὶ
παρεκάλουν πονοῦντας ἔτι προσπονῆσαι καὶ τοὺς
κεκμηκότας ἐνήλλασσον, ὥστε ὁ θυμὸς αἰεὶ τοῖς ἐπὶ
536   τοῦ μετώπου καινὸς ἦν. τέλος δὲ οἱ τοῦ Καίσαρος,
εἴτε διὰ δέος τοῦ λιμοῦ, εἴτε δι᾽ αὐτοῦ Καίσαρος εὐτυ-
χίαν (οὐ γὰρ ἐπίμεμπτοί γε ἦσαν οὐδὲ οἱ Βρούτειοι),
τὴν φάλαγγα τῶν ἐχθρῶν ἐκίνουν, ὥσπερ τι μηχά-
537   νημα τῶν βαρυτάτων ἀνατρέποντες. οἱ δ᾽ ἀνεωθοῦντο
μὲν ἐπὶ πόδας ἐς τὸ ὀπίσω βάδην ἔτι καὶ μετὰ φρο-
νήματος· ὡς δὲ αὐτοῖς καὶ ἡ σύνταξις ἤδη παρελέλυτο,

both similarly predicted that this day and this battle would decide the entire fate of Rome. And it was decided.

128. These preparations had already used up the day 532 as far as the ninth hour, when two eagles attacked each other and fought in the space between the battle lines. This took place in the deepest silence, but when the eagle on Brutus' side of the field fled, a sharp cry arose from the enemy, the standards on both sides were raised, and the onslaught was both intense and ferocious. Indeed, they 533 had little need of arrows, stones, or javelins in the usual manner of war, since they employed none of the other arts and tactics of battle, but engaged the enemy with swords drawn, delivering and receiving blows and trying to push each other out of the line. One side fought for deliverance rather than victory, the other for victory and to appease a general who had been forced into battle. There was wide- 534 spread slaughter and groaning as the dead bodies were carried away and others took their place from the reserves. The generals rushed around and were to be seen ev- 535 erywhere, buoying up the men in their attacks, urging those struggling to redouble their efforts and replacing the exhausted, so that there was constantly fresh resolve at the front. Eventually, Octavian's men, whether out of fear of 536 hunger or because of his own good fortune (for the troops of Brutus were certainly not to blame), began to move the enemy phalanx as if they were pushing back a siege engine of the heaviest type. Their opponents were forced back 537 step by step, still gradually and with purpose. But when their ranks had been broken, they began to retreat more

ὀξύτερον ὑπεχώρουν καί, τῶν ἐπιτεταγμένων σφίσι
δευτέρων καὶ τρίτων συνυποχωρούντων, μισγόμενοι
πάντες ἀλλήλοις ἀκόσμως ἐθλίβοντο ὑπὸ σφῶν καὶ
τῶν πολεμίων ἀπαύστως αὐτοῖς ἐπικειμένων, ἕως
538 ἔφευγον ἤδη σαφῶς. καὶ οἱ τοῦ Καίσαρος τότε μάλιστα τοῦ παρηγγελμένου σφίσιν ἐγκρατῶς ἐχόμενοι
τὰς πύλας προελάμβανον σφόδρα ἐπικινδύνως (ἄνω-
θέν τε γὰρ ἐβάλλοντο καὶ ἐκ τοῦ μετώπου), μέχρι
πολλοὺς ἐσδραμεῖν ἐκώλυσαν, οἳ διέφυγον ἐπί τε τὴν
θάλασσαν καὶ ἐς τὰ ὄρη διὰ τοῦ ποταμοῦ τοῦ Ζυ-
γάκτου.

539   129. Γενομένης δὲ τῆς τροπῆς τὸ λοιπὸν ἔργον οἱ
στρατηγοὶ διῃροῦντο, Καῖσαρ μὲν αἱρεῖν τοὺς ἐκ-
πίπτοντας ἐκ τοῦ στρατοπέδου καὶ αὐτὸ φυλάσσειν
τὸ στρατόπεδον· ὁ δὲ Ἀντώνιος πάντα ἦν καὶ πᾶσιν
ἐνέπιπτε, τοῖς τε φεύγουσι καὶ τοῖς ἔτι συνεστῶσι καὶ
τοῖς ἄλλοις στρατοπέδοις αὐτῶν, ὁρμῇ τε ὑπερηφάνῳ
540 πάντα ἐβιάζετο ὁμοῦ. καὶ περὶ τοῖς ἡγεμόσι δείσας,
μὴ αὐτὸν διαφυγόντες αὖθις ἕτερον στρατὸν ἀγείρειαν,
τοὺς ἱππέας ἐξέπεμπεν ἐπὶ τὰς ὁδούς τε καὶ ἐκβολὰς
541 τῆς μάχης, αἱρεῖν τοὺς ἀποδιδράσκοντας· οἳ ⟨μὲν⟩[36]
διελόμενοι τὸ ἔργον ἀνά τε τὸ ὄρος ἐφέροντο σὺν τῷ
Θρᾳκίῳ Ῥάσκῳ, δι᾿ ἐμπειρίαν ὁδῶν συναπεσταλμένῳ,
καὶ τὰ χαρακώματα καὶ κρημνοὺς περιστάντες τοὺς
ἐκφεύγοντας ἐκυνηγέτουν καὶ τοὺς ἐντὸς ἐφρούρουν.
542 οἱ δὲ Βροῦτον αὐτὸν ἐδίωκον· καὶ αὐτοὺς ἀσχέτως
ἔχοντας τοῦ δρόμου Λουκίλιος ἰδὼν ὑπέστη καὶ ὡς
Βροῦτος ὢν ἠξίου πρὸς Ἀντώνιον ἀντὶ τοῦ Καίσαρος

quickly, and with the second and third lines of reserves joining in the retreat, they all mixed with each other chaotically and were crushed by their own men and by the enemy who attacked relentlessly until they now clearly broke into flight. At that moment particularly, Octavian's 538 men held firmly to their orders and took immediate possession of the gates while facing extreme danger (for they were under fire both from above and from the front), thus preventing many from getting in. These escaped to the sea or to the mountains across the river Zygactes.

129. After the rout the generals divided up what re- 539 mained to be done. Octavian was to guard the camp itself and capture any who sallied out. Antony was everywhere and threw himself at everything—at those who were fleeing, those who were still resisting, the enemy's other camps—crushing all alike with splendid vehemence. Fearing that the officers would elude him and again col- 540 lect another army, he sent out the cavalry on the roads and exits from the battlefield, to capture those trying to escape. These divided their work, some hurrying up to high 541 ground with Rhascus the Thracian, who was sent with them because of his knowledge of the routes. They surrounded the palisades and hilltops, hunting down those who escaped from them and guarding the ones inside. Others went after Brutus himself. Seeing them rushing on 542 inexorably, Lucilius stood his ground and, pretending to be Brutus, asked to be taken to Antony instead of Octa-

---

36 μὲν add. Gaillard-Goukowsky

APPIAN

ἀναχθῆναι· ᾧ δὴ καὶ μάλιστα εἶναι Βροῦτος ἐνομί-
543 σθη, τὸν ἀδιάλλακτον ἐχθρὸν ἐκκλίνων. ἀγομένου δὲ
αὐτοῦ πυθόμενος ὁ Ἀντώνιος ἀπήντα σὺν ἐπιστάσει,
τὴν τύχην ὁμοῦ καὶ τὸ ἀξίωμα τἀνδρὸς καὶ ἀρετὴν
544 ἐνθυμούμενος, ὅπως Βροῦτον ὑποδέξαιτο. πλησιά-
σαντι δ' ὁ Λουκίλιος ἐντυχὼν μάλα θρασέως εἶπε·
"Βροῦτος μὲν οὐχ ἑάλωκεν, οὐδὲ ἁλώσεταί ποτε πρὸς
κακίας ἀρετή· ἐγὼ δὲ τούσδε ἀπατήσας ὧδέ σοι πάρ-
545 ειμι." καὶ ὁ Ἀντώνιος τοὺς ἱππέας ἰδὼν αἰδουμένους
παρηγόρει καί, "Οὐ μείονά μοι τήνδε ἄγραν," εἶπεν,
"Ἀλλὰ ἀμείνονα ἧς ἐνομίζετε ἐθηρεύσατε, ὅσῳ κρείτ-
των ἐχθροῦ φίλος." καὶ τὸν Λουκίλιον τότε μέν τινι
τῶν φίλων ἔδωκε θεραπεύειν, ὕστερον δὲ αὐτὸς ἔχων
ἐχρῆτο ὡς πιστῷ.

546   130. Ὁ δὲ Βροῦτος ἀναφεύγει μὲν ἐς τὰ ὄρη σὺν
ἱκανῷ πλήθει, ὡς νυκτὸς ἐς τὸ στρατόπεδον ὑποστρέ-
ψων ἢ καταβησόμενος ἐπὶ τὴν θάλασσαν· ἐπεὶ δὲ
περιείληπτο πάντα φυλακαῖς, διενυκτέρευεν ἔνοπλος
547 μετὰ πάντων. καί φασιν αὐτὸν ἐς τοὺς ἀστέρας ἀνα-
βλέποντα εἰπεῖν·

Ζεῦ, μὴ λάθοι σε τῶνδ' ὃς αἴτιος κακῶν,

ἐνσημαινόμενον ἄρα τὸν Ἀντώνιον. ὁ καὶ αὐτὸν
Ἀντώνιόν φασιν ὕστερον ἐν τοῖς ἰδίοις κινδύνοις
μεταγινώσκοντα εἰπεῖν, ὅτι συνεξετάζεσθαι Κασσίῳ
καὶ Βρούτῳ δυνάμενος ὑπηρέτης γένοιτο Ὀκταουίου.

vian. It was this in particular that gave rise to the belief
that he was Brutus, trying to avoid his implacable enemy.
When Antony heard that he was being brought in, he went 543
to meet him, stopping to consider how he would receive
Brutus, in consideration of the man's fate, his reputation,
and his courage. As he was approaching, Lucilius con- 544
fronted him very daringly and said, "Brutus has not been
captured, and virtue will never be made prisoner by vice.
I deceived these men and so here I am in your presence."
Antony saw that the cavalrymen were embarrassed, and 545
consoled them by saying, "The game you have caught for
me is not worse, but better than you think, as much better
as a friend is than an enemy." For the moment he gave
Lucilius to one of his associates to look after, but later kept
him as one of his personal circle, and treated him as a man
to be trusted.

130. Brutus takes refuge up in the mountains with a 546
considerable force, intending to return to his camp by
night, or to move down to the sea. But since he had been
entirely surrounded by guard posts, he spent the night
under arms with all his men. And they say that, looking up 547
to the stars, he said:

> Do not forget, Zeus, the man responsible for these
> woes,[78]

referring, of course, to Antony. It is said that Antony himself also quoted this verse on a later occasion in the midst
of his own dangers, regretting that he became the servant
of Octavian, when he could have aligned himself with Cas-

---

[78] Euripides, *Med*. 332. Plutarch also records the quotation in
Brut. 51.1.

548 τότε γε μὴν καὶ ὁ Ἀντώνιος ἔνοπλος ἐπὶ τῶν φυλα-
κτηρίων ἀντιδιενυκτέρευε τῷ Βρούτῳ, χάρακα περιθέμενος ἐκ νεκρῶν σωμάτων καὶ λαφύρων συμφορη-
θέντων. ὁ δὲ Καῖσαρ ἐς μέσην νύκτα πονηθεὶς
ἀνεχώρησε διὰ τὴν νόσον, Νωρβανῷ φυλάσσειν
παραδοὺς τὸ στρατόπεδον.

549   131. Βροῦτος δὲ καὶ τῆς ἐπιούσης ὁρῶν τὰς ἐφε-
δρείας τῶν ἐχθρῶν ἐπιμενούσας, ἔχων οὐ πλήρη τέσσαρα τέλη συναναβάντα οἱ, αὐτὸς μὲν ἐπελθεῖν ἐπ'
αὐτοὺς ἐφυλάξατο, τοὺς δὲ ἡγουμένους αὐτῶν, αἰδουμένους τε τὸ ἁμάρτημα καὶ μετανοοῦντας, ἔπεμπεν
ἀποπειράσοντας αὐτῶν, εἰ ἐθελήσουσιν ὤσασθαι διὰ
τῶν ἐφεδρειῶν καὶ ἀναλαβεῖν τὰ ἴδια, ἔτι φυλασσό-
550 μενα ὑπὸ τῶν οἰκείων ὑπολελειμμένων. οἱ δὲ ἀβου-
λότατα μὲν ἐς τὸ ἔργον ὁρμήσαντες, εὐψυχότατοι δὲ
τὸ μέχρι πλείστου γενόμενοι, τότε, βλάπτοντος ἤδη
τοῦ θεοῦ, τῷ στρατηγῷ σφῶν ἀπεκρίναντο ἀναξίως
βουλεύεσθαι περὶ αὑτοῦ· αὐτοὶ γάρ, τῆς τύχης πολλάκις πεπειραμένοι, οὐκ ἀνατρέψειν τὴν ἔτι λοιπὴν
551 διαλλαγῶν ἐλπίδα. καὶ ὁ Βροῦτος ἐς τοὺς φίλους εἰ-
πών· "Οὐδὲν οὖν ἔτι εἰμὶ τῇ πατρίδι χρήσιμος, ὧδε
καὶ τούτων ἐχόντων," ἐκάλει Στράτωνα τὸν Ἠπει-
ρώτην, ὄντα φίλον ἑαυτῷ, καὶ ἐγχειρεῖν ἐκέλευε τῷ
552 σώματι. τούτου δὲ ἔτι βουλεύεσθαι παραινοῦντος
ἐκάλει τινὰ τῶν οἰκετῶν. καὶ ὁ Στράτων, "Οὐκ ἀπορή-
σεις," εἶπεν, "Ὦ Βροῦτε, φίλου μᾶλλον ἢ οἰκετῶν ἐς
τὰ ὕστατα προστάγματα, εἰ ἤδη κέκριται." καὶ εἰπὼν

sius and Brutus. On this occasion, however, Antony also   548
spent the night under arms in his outposts bivouacked
opposite Brutus, having protected himself with an en-
trenchment made of dead bodies and spoils mixed together. Octavian was busy until midnight and then retired
because of his illness, leaving Norbanus to keep guard
over the camp.

131. On the following day Brutus could see that the   549
enemy pickets were still in position. He had four under-
strength legions that had come up into the high ground
with him, but took care not to approach the men himself,
and sent their officers instead, who were ashamed at their
failure, and repentant. They were to test the men and see
if they were willing to force their way through the blockad-
ing pickets and regain their own position, which was still
being held by the men of their own army who had been
left behind. These officers, although they had rushed into   550
battle most unadvisedly, had displayed the greatest courage for a very long time. At this point, however, with the
divinity now deluding them, they shamefully replied to
their own commanding officer that he should look after his
own interests. For their part, having tempted fate on many
occasions, they would not ruin whatever hope still remained of reaching an accommodation. Then Brutus said   551
to his entourage, "I can no longer be of service to my
country, if such is the outlook of even these men," and
calling Strato of Epirus, who was one of his close associates, ordered him to take a sword to his person. But when   552
Strato urged him to think again, Brutus summoned one of
his slaves, and Strato said, "Brutus, you will not lack a
friend, rather than slaves, to carry out you last commands,
if your decision has already been made." And with these

415

ἐνήρεισε ταῖς λαγόσι τοῦ Βρούτου τὸ ξίφος οὔτε ἀπο-
στραφέντος οὔτε ἐνδόντος.

553   132. Ὧδε μὲν δὴ Κάσσιος καὶ Βροῦτο ἐθνῃσκέτην,
ἄνδρε Ῥωμαίων εὐγενεστάτω τε καὶ περιφανεστάτω
καὶ ἐς ἀρετὴν ἀδηρίτω, χωρὶς ἄγους ἑνός, ᾧ γε καὶ
Γάιος Καῖσαρ, ὄντε τῆς Μάγνου Πομπηίου μοίρας, ἐκ
μὲν ἐχθροῖν καὶ πολεμίοιν ἐποιήσατο φίλων, ἐκ δὲ
554   φίλοιν ἦγεν ὡς υἱώ. καὶ ἡ βουλὴ περιποθήτω τε εἶχεν
αἰεὶ καὶ ἀτυχήσαντε ἐλεεινὼ δυοῖν τε τούτοιν ἕνεκα
πᾶσιν ἀμνηστίαν ἐτίθετο καὶ φυγόντοιν αὐτοῖν ἔπεμψεν <ἐς>[37] ἡγεμονίας, ἵνα μὴ φυγάδες εἶεν, οὐκ ἀμε-
λοῦσα μὲν Γαΐου Καίσαρος οὐδὲ ἐφηδομένη τοῖς
γεγονόσιν, ὅπου καὶ ζῶντα τῆς ἀρετῆς καὶ τύχης
ἐθαύμαζε καὶ ἀποθανόντα ἔθαπτε δημοσίᾳ καὶ ἐκύρου
τὰ ἔργα ἀθάνατα εἶναι ἀρχάς τε καὶ ἡγεμονίας ἐς
πολὺ ἐκ τῶν ὑπογραφῶν ἐποίει τῶν Καίσαρος, οὐδὲν
ἡγουμένη κρεῖσσον εὑρήσειν ὧν ἐκεῖνος ἐνόησεν.
555   ἀλλ' ἡ περὶ τῶδε τὼ ἄνδρε σπουδὴ καὶ δέος τὸ ὑπὲρ
αὐτοῖν προήγαγεν αὐτὴν ἐς ὑπεροψίαν διαβολῆς·
556   οὕτως ἅπασιν ἐγενέσθην τιμίω. ἐγενέσθην δὲ καὶ τῶν
φυγόντων τοῖς ἀρίστοις τιμιωτέρω Πομπίου, πλησιάζοντος καὶ οὐκ ἀδιάλλακτον ἔχοντος αἰτίαν, πορρωτέρω τε ὄντε αὐτὼ καὶ ἀδιαλλάκτω.

557   133. Ἐπεί γε μὴν ἔργων ἐδέησε, δυοῖν οὐδὲ ὅλοιν

[37] ἐς add. Gaillard-Goukowsky

words he thrust his sword into the side of Brutus, who neither turned away nor flinched.

132. Such was the death of Cassius and Brutus, two of the most noble and distinguished Romans, and of incomparable virtue, with the exception of a single crime. Although they belonged to the party of Pompey the Great, Gaius Caesar turned them from personal and public enemies into friends, and from being friends he treated them as sons. The senate always held them in high esteem and felt sorry for them in their misfortune. It was for the sake of these two men that they issued an amnesty to everyone, and when they fled, the senate appointed them to provincial commands, so that they would not be exiles. It was not out of disdain for Gaius Caesar that they did this, or because they were pleased at what had happened, for when he was alive they admired his bravery, and when he died they gave him a public funeral, ratified his acts permanently, and for a long time awarded magistracies and governorships in accordance with his written instructions, in the belief that they would devise no better policy than what he had planned. But the senate's enthusiasm and concern for these two men led it into contempt for slanderous accusations, such was the honor in which the two were held by everyone.[79] They were more highly regarded by the nobles in exile than Pompeius, even though he was nearer to Rome and did not face an accusation that allowed for no reconciliation, while they were further away and impossible to reconcile.

133. When it became necessary to fight, in less than

553

554

555

556

557

[79] The accusation being that the senate had been complicit in the assassination of Caesar.

ἐτοῖν στρατιάν τε συνέλεξαν ὑπὲρ εἴκοσιν ὁπλιτῶν
τέλη καὶ ἱππέας ἀμφὶ τοὺς δισμυρίους καὶ ναῦς μα-
κρὰς ὑπὲρ τὰς διακοσίας τήν τε ἄλλην παρασκευὴν
ἀξιόλογον καὶ χρήματα ἄπειρα καὶ παρ᾽ ἑκόντων καὶ
παρὰ ἀκόντων, πολέμους τε ἐπολέμησαν ἔθνεσι καὶ
πόλεσι καὶ τῶν ἀντιστασιωτῶν πολλοῖς καὶ κατώρ-
558   θουν. ἐθνῶν τε ἐκράτησαν ἀπὸ Μακεδονίας μέχρι Εὐ-
φράτου· καὶ ὅσους ἐπολέμησαν, ἐς συμμαχίαν αὐτοῖς
ἔπεισαν καὶ βεβαιοτάτοις ἐχρήσαντο. ἐχρήσαντο δὲ
καὶ βασιλεῦσι καὶ δυνάσταις, καὶ Παρθυαίοις καίπερ
οὖσιν ἐχθροῖς ἐς τὰ βραχύτερα· ἐπὶ δὲ τὸ μεῖζον ἔργον οὐκ ἀνέμειναν ἐρχομένους, ἵνα μὴ βάρβαρον ἢ
559   ἀντίπαλον ἔθνος ἐθίσειαν ἐπὶ Ῥωμαίοις. ὃ δὲ δὴ
μάλιστα πάντων ἀδοκητότατον ἦν, ὁ στρατὸς ὁ
πλείων ὅδε Γαΐου Καίσαρος ἐγεγένητο, καὶ δαιμονίως
αὐτὸν εὐνοίας καὶ σπουδῆς ἔχοντα ἐς ἐκεῖνον μετέπει-
σαν οἱ σφαγεῖς οἵδε τοῦ Καίσαρος, καὶ ἐπὶ τὸν τοῦ
Καίσαρος υἱὸν ἔσποντο αὐτοῖς πιστότερον ἢ Ἀντωνίῳ
τῷ Καίσαρος συναγωνιστῇ τε καὶ συνάρχῳ· οὐ γάρ
τις αὐτῶν Βροῦτον ἢ Κάσσιον οὐδὲ ἡσσωμένους
ἀπέλιπεν, οἱ Ἀντώνιον ἀμφὶ τὸ Βρεντέσιον καὶ πρὸ
560   πείρας ἀπολιπόντες· ἦν τε πρόφασις αὐτοῖς τῶν
πόνων, καὶ ἐπὶ Πομπηίου καὶ νῦν, οὐχ ὑπὲρ σφῶν
αὐτῶν, ἀλλ᾽ ὑπὲρ δημοκρατίας, ὀνόματος εὐειδοῦς
μέν, ἀλυσιτελοῦς δὲ αἰεί. σφῶν τε αὐτῶν, ὅτε μηδὲν
ἐδόκουν ἔτι εἶναι χρήσιμοι τῇ πατρίδι, ἄμφω κατ-
561   εφρόνησαν ὁμοίως. ἐν δὲ ταῖς φροντίσι καὶ πόνοις ὁ
μὲν Κάσσιος ἀμεταστρεπτί, καθάπερ ἐς τὸν ἀγωνι-

two full years Brutus and Cassius recruited an army of more than twenty legions of infantry, about twenty thousand cavalry, over two hundred warships, other impressive equipment, and enormous sums of money collected from both willing and unwilling contributors. They fought and won wars with nations and cities and many of their political opponents. They became masters of the provinces 558 from Macedonia to the Euphrates, and all those they fought against they persuaded to join them as allies, and found them to be most reliable. They also had the services of kings and princes, even, for less important matters, of the Parthians, who were enemies. For the main battle, however, they did not wait for them to come, out of fear that they would allow a barbarous and rival nation to get used to fighting against Rome. Most unexpected of all was 559 the fact that the greater part of this army had served under Gaius Caesar and were extraordinarily enthusiastic and well disposed toward him, and yet Brutus and Cassius, the murderers of Caesar, got the men to change their allegiance so that they followed the two of them against Caesar's son more loyally than they had followed Antony, who had been Caesar's colleague in arms and in office; for not one of them deserted Brutus and Cassius even after their defeat, although some of them had abandoned Antony at Brundisium before the war began. The reason they gave 560 for their efforts, and it was the same for Pompeius at the present time, was the defense not of their own interests, but of democracy—a handsome word, but not one that ever brought profit. Both men, when they thought they could no longer be of service to their country, were equally disdainful of their own lives. In the midst of their cares 561 and labors, Cassius, like gladiators facing their opponent,

419

APPIAN

στὴν οἱ μονομαχοῦντες, ἐς μόνον τὸν πόλεμον ἀφε-
ώρα· ὁ δὲ Βροῦτος, ὅπη γίγνοιτο, καὶ φιλοθεάμων ἦν
καὶ φιλήκοος, ἅτε καὶ φιλοσοφήσας οὐκ ἀγεννῶς.

562   134. Ἀλλὰ καὶ τοιοῖσδε οὖσιν αὐτοῖς ἀντιθετέον[38]
ἐς ἅπαντα ἦν τὸ ἄγος τὸ ἐς Καίσαρα. ὅ γε οὐδὲ
ἁπλοῦν ἄγος ἦν οὐδὲ ἐν ὀλίγῳ· καὶ γὰρ ἐς φίλον
ἐγίγνετο παραλόγως καὶ ἐς εὐεργέτην ἐκ πολέμου
περισώσαντα ἀχαρίστως καὶ ἐς αὐτοκράτορα ἀθεμίστως καὶ ἐν βουλευτηρίῳ καὶ ἐς ἱερέα καὶ ἱερὰν
ἐσθῆτα ἐπικείμενον καὶ δυνάστην μὲν οἷον οὐχ ἕτερον, χρησιμώτατον δὲ ὑπὲρ ἅπαντας τῇ τε πατρίδι
563   καὶ τῇ ἡγεμονίᾳ γενόμενον. ἃ καὶ τὸ δαιμόνιον αὐτοῖς
ἄρα ἐνεμέσησε καὶ προεσήμηνε πολλάκις. Κασσίῳ τε
γὰρ τὸν στρατὸν καθαίροντι ὁ ῥαβδοῦχος ἀνεστραμ-
μένον τὸν στέφανον ἐπέθηκε· καὶ Νίκη, χρύσεον
ἀνάθημα Κασσίου, κατέπεσεν, ὄρνεά τε πολλὰ ὑπὲρ
τὸ στρατόπεδον αὐτοῦ καθιέμενα κλαγγὴν οὐδεμίαν
ἠφίει, καὶ μελισσῶν ἐπεκάθηντο συνεχεῖς ἐσμοί.
564   Βροῦτον δὲ ἐν Σάμῳ γενεθλιάζοντά φασι παρὰ τὸν
πότον, οὐδὲ εὐχερῆ πρὸς τὰ τοιαῦτα ὄντα, ἀλόγως
τόδε τὸ ἔπος ἀναβοῆσαι·

ἀλλά με μοῖρ᾽ ὀλοὴ καὶ Λητοῦς ἔκτανεν υἱός.

565   μέλλοντα δὲ περᾶν ἐκ τῆς Ἀσίας ἐς τὴν Εὐρώπην σὺν
τῷ στρατῷ, νυκτὸς ἐγρηγορότα, μαραινομένου τοῦ
φωτὸς ὄψιν ἰδεῖν ἐφεστῶσάν οἱ παράλογον καὶ πυθέ-

38 ἀντιθετέον Gaillard-Goukowsky; ἀντίθετον codd.

420

was single-minded in his focus on the war alone; while Brutus, no matter where he was, liked to observe and listen, being a man who had practiced philosophy with some distinction.

134. Even for men such as these, there had to be set 562 against everything the crime committed against Caesar. And to be sure, it was no simple or minor crime. For it was committed irrationally against a friend, ungratefully against a benefactor who had brought them safely out of war, and impiously against an Imperator; it was committed in the senate, against a priest wearing sacred dress, against a prince like no other, who had far surpassed everyone in his service to his country and empire. For these reasons 563 the gods were justifiably angry at them, and gave frequent warnings of this. When Cassius was performing a purification of the army, his lictor put the garland on his head upside down; a gold statue of Victory dedicated by Cassius fell over; a large number of birds swooped down over his camp without uttering a sound, and swarms of bees continually colonized it too. While Brutus was celebrating his 564 birthday at Samos, they say that during the drinking party, although not a man given to such behavior, for no reason he shouted out this verse:

But deadly fate and Leto's son have killed me.[80]

When he was about to cross from Asia to Europe with his 565 army, and was lying awake at night with the lamp burning low, he saw a supernatural apparition standing by him, and

[80] These are the last words of Patroclus at Hom. *Il.* 16.849. How Apollo (Leto's son) was responsible for Brutus' death is not clear.

σθαι μὲν εὐθαρσῶς, ὅς τις ἀνθρώπων ἢ θεῶν εἴη, τὸ
δὲ φάσμα εἰπεῖν· "Ὁ σός, ὦ Βροῦτε, δαίμων κακός·
ὀφθήσομαι δέ σοι καὶ ἐν Φιλίπποις." καὶ ⟨αὖθις⟩³⁹

566 ὀφθῆναί φασιν αὐτῷ πρὸ τῆς τελευταίας μάχης. ἐξι-
όντι δὲ τῷ στρατῷ πρὸ τῶν πυλῶν αἰθίοψ ὑπήντησε·
καὶ τόνδε μὲν ὡς οἰώνισμα φαῦλον ὁ στρατὸς αὐτίκα
συνέκοψε, δαιμόνια δ' ἦν αὐτοῖς ἄρα καὶ τάδε, Κάσσιον μὲν ἐν ἀμφηρίστῳ νίκῃ πάντα ἀλόγως ἀπογνῶ-
ναι, Βροῦτον δὲ εὐβούλου βραδυτῆτος ἐκβιασθῆναι
καὶ ἐς χεῖρας ἐλθεῖν ἀνδράσι διωκομένοις ὑπὸ λιμοῦ,
δαψιλῶς αὐτὸν ἔχοντα ἀγορᾶς καὶ ναυκρατοῦντα, καὶ
τόδε παθεῖν ὑπὸ τῶν οἰκείων μᾶλλον ἢ τῶν πολεμίων,

567 καὶ μὴν πολλάκις ἀγώνων μετασχόντες ἐν μὲν ταῖς
μάχαις οὐδὲν ἔπαθον, ἄμφω δ' αὐτῶν ἐγένοντο αὐθέν-
ται καθάπερ ἐγένοντο τοῦ Καίσαρος. Κάσσιος μὲν δὴ
καὶ Βροῦτος τοιάνδε δίκην ἐδεδώκεσαν.

568   135. Καὶ Βροῦτον Ἀντώνιος ἀνευρὼν περιέβαλέ τε
τῇ ἀρίστῃ φοινικίδι εὐθὺς καὶ καύσας τὰ λείψανα τῇ
μητρὶ Σερουιλίᾳ ἔπεμψεν. ὁ δὲ σὺν τῷ Βροῦτῳ στρα-
τός, ὅτε ἐπύθοντο τεθνάναι Βροῦτον, πρέσβεις ἐς Καίσαρα καὶ Ἀντώνιον ἔπεμπον καὶ συγγνώμης ἔτυχον
καὶ ἐς τὰ στρατεύματα αὐτῶν διῃρέθησαν· καὶ ἦσαν

569 ἀμφὶ τοὺς μυρίους καὶ τετρακισχιλίους. παρέδοσαν
δὲ ἐπὶ τοῖς αὐτοῖς ἑαυτοὺς καὶ οἱ κατὰ τὰ φρούρια,
πολλὰ ὄντα. τὰ δὲ φρούρια αὐτὰ καὶ τὸ στρατόπεδον
ἐδόθη τοῖς Καίσαρος καὶ Ἀντωνίου στρατοῖς διαρπά-

570 σαι. τῶν δ' ἀμφὶ τὸν Βροῦτον ἀνδρῶν ἐπιφανῶν οἱ
μὲν ἐν ταῖς μάχαις ἀπέθανον, οἱ δὲ αὐτοὺς ἐξήγαγον

when he boldly asked what man or god he was, the phantom answered, "I am your evil spirit, Brutus. I will appear to you at Philippi too." And they say that it did appear to him before the last battle. On another occasion, when the army were leaving camp, an Ethiopian met them in front of the gates, and the soldiers immediately cut him down as an evil omen. There was also surely some divine influence in the fact that when victory was still in the balance, Cassius for no reason gave up completely; and that Brutus was forced to abandon his policy of sensible inactivity and join battle with men dogged by hunger, while he himself had an abundance of supplies and controlled the sea; and that he suffered this at the hands of his own men rather than the enemy. And again, while they often took part in combat they were never wounded in the fighting, and yet both men took their own lives, just as they had taken Caesar's. Such, then, was the price paid by Cassius and Brutus.

135. On finding Brutus' body, Antony immediately wrapped it in the finest purple, had it cremated and sent the remains to his mother Servilia. When the soldiers on Brutus' side learned of his death, they sent representatives to Octavian and Antony, were pardoned and distributed among their forces: there were about fourteen thousand of them. The men in the forts, a large number, also surrendered on the same terms. The forts themselves and the camp were given to the soldiers of Octavian and Antony to plunder. Of the distinguished men on Brutus' side some died in the battles, others killed themselves as their gener-

566

567

568

569

570

---

39 αὖθις add. Gaillard-Goukowsky

APPIAN

ὁμοίως τοῖς στρατηγοῖς, οἱ δὲ καὶ ἐξεπίτηδες ἐμαχέ-
571 σαντο μέχρι θανάτου· ὧν ἦν Λεύκιός τε Κάσσιος, ὁ
ἀδελφιδοῦς αὐτοῦ Κασσίου, καὶ Κάτων ὁ Κάτωνος,
ἐμπίπτων ὅδε τοῖς πολεμίοις πολλάκις, εἶθ᾽ ὑποχω-
ρούντων ἀναλύσας τὸ κράνος, ἵνα ἢ γνώριμος ἢ εὔ-
572 βλητος ἢ ἀμφότερα εἴη. Λαβεὼν δέ, ἐπὶ σοφίᾳ γνώριμος, ὁ πατὴρ Λαβεῶνος τοῦ κατ᾽ ἐμπειρίαν νόμων ἔτι
νῦν περιωνύμου, βόθρον ἐν τῇ σκηνῇ τὸ μέγεθος
αὐτάρκη σώματι ὀρυξάμενος καὶ τὰ λοιπὰ τοῖς θεράπουσιν ἐντειλάμενος ἐπέσκηψε τῇ γυναικὶ καὶ τοῖς
παισί, περὶ ὧν ἐβούλετο, καὶ τὰ γράμματα φέρειν
ἔδωκε τοῖς οἰκέταις· τοῦ δὲ πιστοτάτου τῆς δεξιᾶς λαβόμενος καὶ περιστρέψας αὐτόν, ὡς ἔθος ἐστὶ Ῥωμαίοις ἐλευθεροῦν, ἐπιστρεφομένῳ ξίφος ἔδωκε καὶ
τὴν σφαγὴν ὑπέσχε. καὶ τῷδε μὲν ἡ σκηνὴ τάφος
ἐγένετο.

573   136. Ῥάσκος δὲ ὁ Θρᾷξ ἐπανήγαγεν ἐκ τῶν ὀρῶν
πολλούς, καὶ γέρας ᾔτησέ τε καὶ ἔλαβε σῴζεσθαι τὸν
ἀδελφὸν ἑαυτοῦ Ῥασκούπολιν· ᾧ καὶ διεδείχθη, ὅτι
οὐδ᾽ ἀπ᾽ ἀρχῆς ἀλλήλοις οἶδε οἱ Θρᾷκες διεφέροντο,
ἀλλὰ δύο στρατοπέδων μεγάλων τε καὶ ἀμφηρίστων
περὶ τὴν ἐκείνων γῆν συμφερομένων τὸ ἄδηλον τῆς
τύχης ἐμερίσαντο, ἵνα ὁ νικῶν περισῴζοι τὸν ἡσσώ-
574 μενον. Πορκία δ᾽, ἡ Βρούτου μὲν γυνή, Κάτωνος δὲ
ἀδελφὴ τοῦ νεωτέρου, ἐπείτε ἀμφοῖν ὧδε ἀποθανόν-
τοιν ἐπύθετο, φυλασσομένη πρὸς τῶν οἰκείων πάνυ

424

als had done, others again fought on intentionally to the
death. Among them were Lucius Cassius, nephew of Cas-   571
sius himself, and Cato, the son of Cato. The latter charged
the enemy many times; then, when they gave way, he took
off his helmet to make himself recognizable, or an easy
target, or both. Labeo, a man renowned for learning, fa-   572
ther of the Labeo who is still celebrated for his knowledge
of the laws, dug a trench in his tent big enough for his
body, gave orders to his assistants concerning things remaining to be done, issued instructions to his wife and
children about his last wishes, and gave the letter to his
servants to deliver.[81] Then, taking his most faithful slave
by the right hand and spinning him in a circle, as is the
Roman custom for freeing a slave, as soon as he turned
round he gave him a sword and presented his throat. And
so his tent became his tomb.

136. Rhascus the Thracian brought many troops down   573
from the mountains, for which he asked and received as
his reward the preservation of his brother Rhascupolis'
life. This showed clearly that even right from the start
these Thracians were not at odds with each other, but with
two mighty and evenly matched armies fighting it out in
their country, and they divided up the risk posed by the
uncertainty of fate, so that the victor might save the vanquished. Porcia, the wife of Brutus and sister of the youn-   574
ger Cato, when she learned that both had died in the
manner described, although very carefully watched by her

---

[81] Pacuvius Antistius Labeo was one of the conspirators
against Caesar. His son, Marcus Antistius Labeo, became one of
the most celebrated Roman jurists, renowned for his indepen-
dent spirit (Tac. *Ann.* 3.75).

APPIAN

ἐγκρατῶς, ἐσχάρας πυρὸς ἐνεχθείσης ἁρπάσασα τῶν
575 ἀνθράκων κατέπιεν. ὅσοι δ᾽ ἄλλοι τῶν ἐπιφανῶν ἐς
Θάσον διέφυγον, οἱ μὲν αὐτῶν ἐξέπλευσαν, οἱ δὲ
ἐπέτρεψαν ἑαυτοὺς ἅμα τῷ λοιπῷ στρατῷ τῶν ὁμοτίμων Μεσσάλᾳ τε Κορουίνῳ καὶ Λευκίῳ Βύβλῳ, ὅ τι
576 βουλεύσοιντο περὶ σφῶν, ποιεῖν περὶ ἁπάντων. οἱ δὲ
συνθέμενοι τοῖς περὶ τὸν Ἀντώνιον, Ἀντωνίῳ διαπλεύ-
σαντι ἐς τὴν Θάσον παρέδοσαν, ὅσα ἦν ἐν Θάσῳ
χρήματά τε καὶ ὅπλα καὶ τροφαὶ δαψιλεῖς καὶ ἄλλη
παρασκευὴ πολλή.

577   137. Οὕτω μὲν δὴ Καίσαρί τε καὶ Ἀντωνίῳ διὰ
τόλμης ἐπισφαλοῦς καὶ δυοῖν πεζομαχίαιν τηλι-
κοῦτον ἔργον ἤνυστο, οἷον οὐχ ἕτερον ἐγένετο πρὸ
ἐκείνου. οὔτε γὰρ στρατὸς τοσοῦτος ἢ τοιοῦτος ἐς
χεῖρας πρότερον ἦλθε Ῥωμαίων ἑκατέρωθεν, οὐχ ὑπὸ
συντάξει πολιτικῇ στρατευσαμένων, ἀλλὰ ἀριστίν-
δην ἐπειλεγμένων οὐδ᾽ ἀπειροπολέμων ἔτι, ἀλλ᾽ ἐκ
πολλοῦ γεγυμνασμένων ἐπί τε σφᾶς καὶ οὐκ ἀλλό-
578 φυλα ἢ βάρβαρα ἔθνη τρεπομένων. ἀλλὰ καὶ γλώσ-
σης μιᾶς ὄντες καὶ τέχνης πολέμων μιᾶς καὶ ἀσκή-
σεως καὶ καρτερίας ὁμοίας, δυσκαταγώνιστοι παρ᾽
αὐτὸ ἦσαν ἀλλήλοις. οὐδὲ ὁρμῇ καὶ τόλμῃ τοσῇδέ
τινες ἐχρήσαντο ἐν πολέμῳ, πολῖταί τε ὄντες ἀλλήλων καὶ οἰκεῖοι καὶ συστρατιῶται γενόμενοι. τεκ-
μήριον δέ, ὅτι τῶν νεκρῶν ὁ ἀριθμός, ἐπανισουμένης
ἑκατέρας μάχης, οὐκ ἐλάσσων ἔδοξεν οὐδὲ παρὰ τοῖς
νικῶσιν εἶναι.

household, grabbed some hot coals off a brazier being brought in, and swallowed them. Of the other nobles who   575 escaped to Thasos, some took ship from there, others entrusted themselves along with the rest of the army to Messalla Corvinus and Lucius Bibulus, men of equal rank, to treat everyone in whatever way they decided to treat themselves. They came to an arrangement with Antony,   576 and when he sailed across to Thasos they handed over to him all the money there, and arms, abundant supplies, and a great quantity of other equipment.

137. In this way, by means of a daring policy that was   577 fraught with danger and of two land battles, Octavian and Antony brought to an end this great conflict, the like of which had never occurred before. For in the past no armies of such size and quality composed of Romans on both sides had fought each other; the men were not enlisted through the citizen levy, but specially picked for their courage; and, no longer inexperienced, but having undergone long training, they were turned against each other, not against foreign or barbarian nations. Because   578 they spoke the same language, used the same military tactics, and had similar training and discipline, for these reasons they were very difficult opponents for each other. No one had employed such vehemence and daring in war, and these were fellow citizens, relatives, and companions in arms. The proof of this is that, taking both battles into the account, the number of the dead appeared to be no less, even among the victors.

579   138. Ὁ δὲ στρατὸς ὁ Ἀντωνίου καὶ Καίσαρος τὸν
τῶν στρατηγῶν λόγον ἐπηλήθευσαν διὰ μιᾶς ἡμέρας
καὶ δι᾽ ἑνὸς ἔργου κίνδυνον ἔσχατον λιμοῦ καὶ δέος
ἀπωλείας ἐς εὐπορίαν δαψιλῆ καὶ σωτηρίαν ἀσφαλῆ
580 καὶ νίκην εὐκλεῆ μεταβαλόντες. ἀπήντησέ γε μὴν
αὐτοῖς καὶ ὃ συνιόντες ἐς τὴν μάχην ἐπεμαντεύσαντο
Ῥωμαίοις· ἐκρίθη γὰρ αὐτῶν ἡ πολιτεία παρ᾽ ἐκεῖνο
τὸ ἔργον μάλιστα καὶ οὐκ ἐπανῆλθεν ἐς δημοκρατίαν
ἔτι, οὐδὲ πόνων αὐτοῖς ἐς ἀλλήλους ἐδέησεν ὁμοίων,
χωρίς γε τῆς μετ᾽ οὐ πολὺ Ἀντωνίου καὶ Καίσαρος
581 στάσεως, ὑστάτης Ῥωμαίοις γενομένης. τὰ δ᾽ ἐν
μέσῳ μετὰ Βροῦτον ὑπό τε Πομπηίου καὶ τῶν δια-
φυγόντων Κασσίου καὶ Βρούτου φίλων, λείψανα
τοσῆσδε παρασκευῆς μεγάλα ἐχόντων, οὔτε ταῖς τόλμαις ὅμοια ἔτι ἐγίγνετο οὔτε ταῖς τῶν ἀνδρῶν ἢ
πόλεων ἢ στρατῶν ἐς τοὺς ἡγεμόνας ὁρμαῖς· οὐ γάρ
τις αὐτοῖς τῶν ἐπιφανῶν ἔτι οὐδ᾽ ἡ βουλὴ οὐδὲ ἡ δόξα
αὕτη, ὡς ἐς Κάσσιόν τε καὶ Βροῦτον, ἀπήντα.

138. The army of Antony and Octavian proved the 579
words of their commanders right, in that on a single day
and by means of a single battle they had exchanged the
extreme danger of starvation and fear of destruction for a
generous abundance of supplies, their safety assured, and
a brilliant victory. And, as a matter of fact, what they pre- 580
dicted for Rome when they joined battle also turned out
to be the case: for it was in particular this battle that decided their constitution, which has still not returned to
democracy. Nor was there any further need of similar
struggles against each other, except for the civil conflict
between Antony and Octavian not long after, which was
the last that Rome experienced.[82] The events that hap- 581
pened between the death of Brutus and that conflict, under Sextus Pompeius and the associates of Cassius and
Brutus who escaped and brought with them the substantial remnants of that huge force, produced no more similar
deeds of daring, nor similar devotion of men or cities or
armies toward their leaders. For neither the senate nor
any of the nobility supported them any longer, as they had
Cassius and Brutus, nor did they enjoy the same reputation.

[82] A strange statement in view of the extensive civil wars of
AD 68 to 69, the "year of the four emperors."